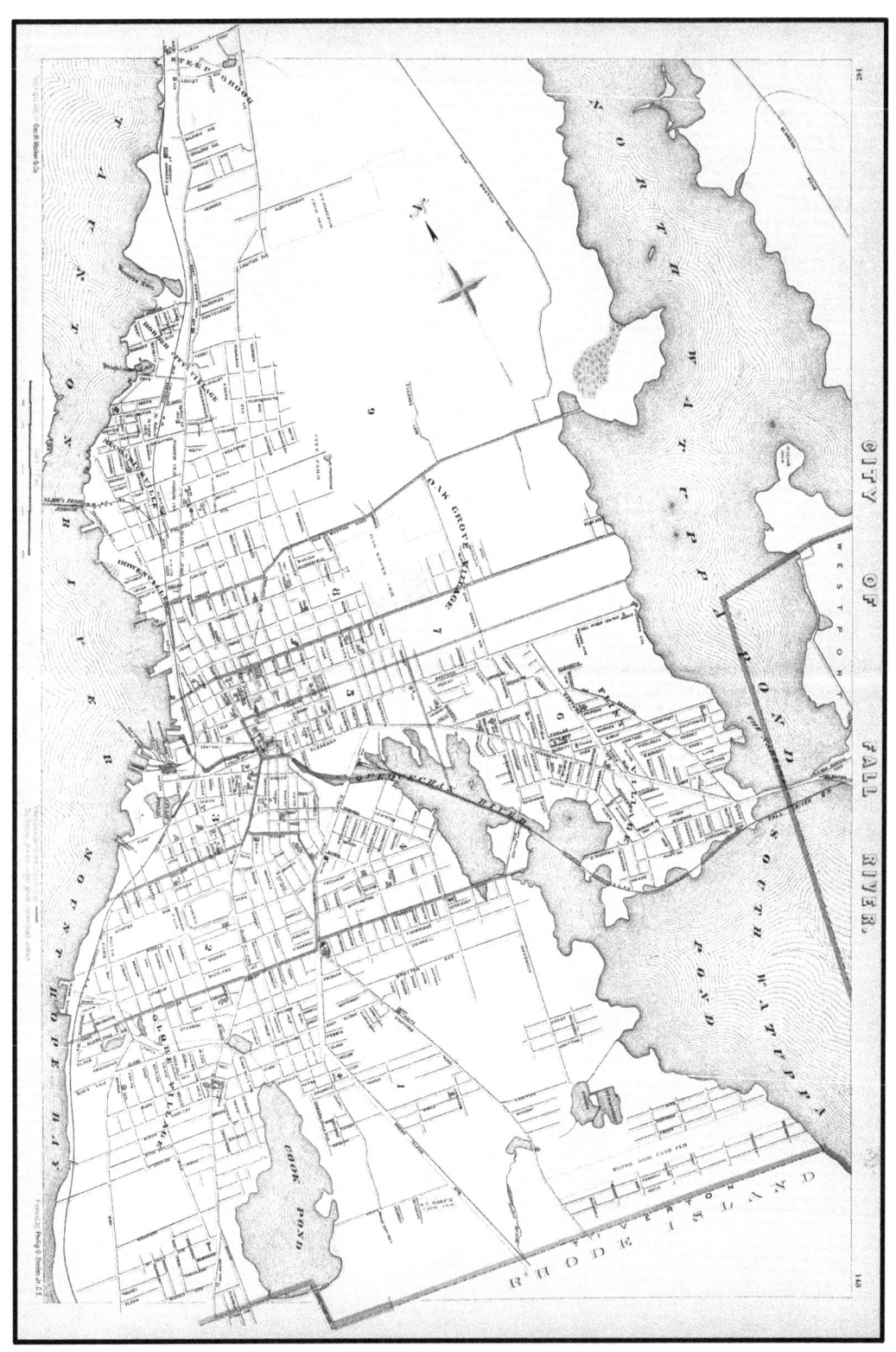

# America's Voices

An oral history of Fall River, Massachusetts,
from 1900 to 1950

**EDITED BY**
**ALFRED J. LIMA**

Fall River, MA

PearTree Press
P.O. Box 9585
Fall River, MA 02720
peartree-press.com

*All rights reserved. No part of this book may be used or reproduced in any manner whatsoever scanned, or distributed in any printed or electronic form without written permission from the publisher, except in the case of brief quotations embodied in critical articles and reviews.*

For information, write us at PearTree Press, P.O. Box 9585, Fall River, MA 02720.

LIBRARY OF CONGRESS CONTROL NUMBER: 2014958608

ISBN-13: 978-0-9908161-0-2

Printed in the United States of America on acid-free paper.

*Book design by Stefani Koorey*

Copyright © 2014 by Alfred J. Lima

Frontis photograph is map of 1891 Fall River, Massachusetts

Printed in the United States of America

# America's Voices

# CONTENTS

| | |
|---|---|
| Introduction | xi |
| | |
| Alvaro, Al | 3 |
| Assad, Faheem J. and Gladys T. (Coury) | 5 |
| Auclair, Fernand Charles E. | 11 |
| Bonner, Howard F. | 19 |
| Borkowski, Cecile | 23 |
| Botelho, Ann (Occhiuti) | 29 |
| Bouchard, Dorothy (Motta) | 37 |
| Bouchard, Louis | 43 |
| Brightman, Priscilla (Getchell) | 51 |
| Brightman, Robert Nilson | 55 |
| Cabral, Isabelle (Cunha) | 57 |
| Cadrin, Lionel and Lorraine | 63 |
| Caron, Helen K. (Mythowicz) | 69 |
| Caron, Louise (Duquette) | 77 |
| Carvalho, Mary (Theresa) | 81 |
| Castro, Everett | 83 |
| Chavenson, Robert | 91 |
| Chebot, William M. | 95 |
| Chouinard, Robert and Gertrude (Francoeur) | 101 |
| Clifton, Dr. Robert | 109 |
| Codega, Vincent | 113 |
| Coelho, Maria Amalia (Zaredo) | 115 |
| Conforti, John | 119 |
| Cooper, Gertrude (Morris) | 123 |
| Correia, Lillian (Souza) | 129 |
| Cottrell, J. Thomas Jr. | 133 |
| Couture, Ronald | 137 |
| Derbyshire, Dr. Bruce | 141 |
| Desmaris, Eva (Tardi) | 145 |

| | |
|---|---|
| Doncaster, Madeline (Lima) | 149 |
| Dufault, Leo and Theresa | 157 |
| Duquette, Gerard | 339 |
| Ehrenhaus, Abraham | 161 |
| Fairhurst, Franklin | 165 |
| Finglas, James | 171 |
| Finglas, Norma (Gifford) | 177 |
| Forcier, Robert E. | 181 |
| French, Lynwood Hathaway | 189 |
| George, Loretta | 5 |
| Giroux, George | 201 |
| Giroux, Rolande (Pelletier) | 207 |
| Griffin, Margaret (Donovan) | 213 |
| Guillemette, Joseph L. and Theresa Claire | 221 |
| Hadley, Frank Bennett "Brud" | 231 |
| Hadley, Lucille (Roussell) | 239 |
| Hall, Mildred (Hayes) | 243 |
| Hicks, Henry F. Jr. | 249 |
| Horvitz, Isidore Philip | 259 |
| Hurley, Dennis C. Jr. | 267 |
| Jean, Joe and Marian | 101 |
| Kerrigan, William James Jr. | 273 |
| Kitchen, Robert | 277 |
| Kostas, Mary (Yankopoulos) | 283 |
| Kuliopulos, Argirios | 287 |
| Kuliopulos, Polixeny | 293 |
| LaFrance, Rita (Fallon) | 295 |
| Lepes, Lillian (Golub) | 299 |
| Lucove, George Joseph | 303 |
| Luddy, James Francis Jr. | 309 |
| Machado, Edmond | 315 |
| Mancini, Yvette (Boucher) | 323 |
| Martel, Hilda (Martin) | 333 |
| Masse, Roland | 339 |
| McDonald, Frederick B. | 345 |
| McIntyre, James | 353 |
| Medeiros, Gilbert Viera | 349 |
| Melker, Mary Margaret (McNeill) | 359 |
| Mello, Dolores Anne (Alves) | 371 |

| | |
|---|---|
| Menard, Leon Jr. | 375 |
| Millerick, Robert | 379 |
| Mitchell, John S. | 387 |
| Moriarty, John | 393 |
| Motta, Diamantina "Diane" | 403 |
| Mullins, James | 409 |
| Nolan, Robert G. | 419 |
| Novo, Mary | 423 |
| Palmer, Valentine Samuel Jr. | 427 |
| Panos, James Stephen | 433 |
| Perry, Aurora (D'Adamo) | 439 |
| Perry, Richard and Julie | 101 |
| Petrucci, August "James" | 443 |
| Petrucci, Theresa (Pretrillo) | 445 |
| Pontes, Frank | 451 |
| Pontes, Lorraine (Fernandes) | 455 |
| Reddy, Daniel | 461 |
| Rocha, Helen (Franco) | 465 |
| Roy, Andy and Jeannette | 101 |
| Sirois, Germaine Francoeur | 101 |
| Stavros, Angelo | 471 |
| Stavros, Cremilde (Torres) | 473 |
| Sullivan, Elizabeth (Turner) | 477 |
| Sunderland, Paul Lawton | 483 |
| Thompson, Elisabeth "Libby" (Hammond) | 491 |
| Thompson, Raymond "Bud" | 493 |
| Thorp, Leo | 499 |
| Valcourt, Paul | 339 |
| Vernon, Robert Eaton | 505 |
| Waring, Sumner James Jr. | 513 |
| Whitty, Genevieve (Haggerty) | 521 |
| Wordell, Mary Ann and William Francis | 527 |
| Wray, James Henry | 535 |
| Zalkind, Anna (Horvitz) | 541 |
| | |
| Afterword | 545 |

AMERICA'S VOICES

# INTRODUCTION

These are the voices of the residents of Fall River, Massachusetts, but they are also America's voices. Small towns, mill towns, and cities across America would yield similar stories from this period in our history.

I began this oral history project in 2004. At that time, I wanted to gather as many memories of growing up in Fall River as I could from city residents in order to record their experiences and get a picture of the city from those who lived here through the first half of the twentieth century.

One way to write about history is by doing research using newspapers, published histories, and unpublished works. Another way is to ask people about their lives, memories, family experiences, and opinions. I believe that sharing real life stories makes history come alive much more vividly for readers.

Standardized techniques were used in conducting these oral histories—asking open-ended questions, avoiding leading questions that may encourage people to say what they think the interviewer wants to hear, and reviewing the completed interview with the subject to allow for editing and clarification.

Oral histories are used by historians, sociologists, journalists, linguists, folklorists, and anthropologists to uncover truths and compile narratives about events, places, and people. Histories of the city of Fall River are plentiful—oral histories are not. It is my hope that this work will add to the rich story that is Fall River and serve as a document that preserves observed events and memories for future generations.

There are many reasons why it is beneficial to conduct oral histories: they help to preserve the past; they connect us with our roots; they are a source of pride; they help us to connect with older members of our family; they help us to see older persons in a new light; they preserve family histories for future generations; and they are great stories!

Speaking of which, the stories you are about to read are the memories of those individuals and are not presented as the only truth of any occurrence or experience. I am sure as you read through these personal accounts of what it was like to grow up in Fall River you will be reminded of your own family's stories of these places and events. Perhaps your memories will be quite different or you will find a "mistake" or two along the way. That is how our own memories work—errors of exactitude are normal. But I have endeavored not only to correctly transcribe these interviews, but to confirm, as well as I could the details of these oral histories.

I hope you enjoy reading them as much as I did hearing them when I met with the folks presented within these pages.

It has been a long time in the making, and many individuals interviewed have since passed way. For those who lived the lives described in these pages, I give my heartfelt thanks for opening up your lives to the readers of these pages and for sharing your family's history of growing up in Fall River.

# Oral Histories

# Al Alvaro

**Memories of a Barber**

Barbers in the old days wore a shirt and tie to the shop. Mugs were kept on the wall for each customer who came in each morning to be shaved. A soap cake was inserted into each mug. When the customer came in, hot water was put in the mug and lather was made with a brush and put on the beard with the brush. The barber used a straight-edged razor to shave the beard. This was the in the days before safety razors.

Why didn't men shave themselves at home? One reason was the danger in using the straight-edged razor. Other reasons probably included the inconvenience of having to shave in the pantry when there were no bathrooms in the cold water flats. Toilet facilities were either outhouses or basic toilets in the basement. Also, light might have been poor in the early mornings in the pantries, cold water had to be heated up, etc.

My grandfather was apprenticed to a barber after his father saw him cutting the hair of a

brother. He started working as an apprentice in the barber shop across the street in the village where he lived in Portugal. He started by sweeping the floor and lathering up customers' beards.

My father's shop was just down from where Columbia Bakery is now, just one store up on Columbia Street from Eagle Street.

Not that long ago, barbers also acted as doctors. Once, when I was roughing it up with a friend near Santo Christo Church, I fell back and cut the back of my head. My father cleaned the wound with an antiseptic that he used in the shop and tied the strands of my hair on either side of the cut. It healed fine. Once, when a customer of mine recently slipped and fell on ice outside the shop and opened a wound on his skull, I did the same and treated the wound with antiseptic and tied his hair to close the cut. He then went to the emergency room, where the doctor exclaimed that whomever did this work knew what he was doing. The doctor said that the wound required no additional stitches or work and sent him home.

During Hurricane Carol in 1956, one of my father's regular customers came in anyway and had his shave. He had just bought a new Nash Rambler, the large model, and the car was in danger of being hit with flying debris. However, he was determined to have his shave. He simply said, "It's insured." He was a salesman at Mason's Furniture.

# Faheem and Gladys T. (Coury) Assad and Loretta George

*Faheem was born on September 26, 1926, died on October 25, 2011*
*Gladys was born on July 4, 1928*
*Loretta was born in September 1928, died on November 30, 2013*

The Lebanese started coming to Fall River in the 1890s. The Lebanese neighborhood in the Flint included the following streets: Quequechan Street, Harrison Street, Flint Street, Jencks Street, Weybosset Street, Wamsutta Street, Lebanon Street (formerly Barnard), and Alden Street.

**Family Background**
Faheem's father came to the United States in 1910, the only one in his family to emigrate. He worked in the textile mills, became a citizen, and sent money home to Lebanon.

Faheem's mother immigrated to the United States in 1912, following her father and two brothers, who had immigrated here earlier. Her father went back to Lebanon but she and her brothers remained. One brother owned a grocery store. Faheem's father and mother, who were cousins, were married in Fall River. In Lebanon, it was not unusual for cousins to marry, and it is still common practice in the Middle East.

Faheem's father worked in the textile mills as a weaver in Fall River and New Bedford for forty-eight years. He was a self-educated man, who taught himself to read and write Arabic and became very proficient. He also taught Faheem to read and write Arabic, and Faheem would read the Epistle in Arabic at the 11:00 am Sunday liturgy, an unusual feat for someone his age.

When Faheem's father was fifty-eight, he tried to get work in Fall River as a weaver but was told that he was too old. So he went to the Wamsutta Mills in New Bedford and got a job there and stayed until he retired at sixty-five.

Gladys' mother and father were both born in Fall River. Her father began working in the textile mills, went to school at night, and became an agent for the Prudential Insurance Company and, later, a district manager for the corporation. Her mother worked in a garment factory. Gladys' father was president of the Lebanese-American Society and received the regional Massabki Medal from the Diocese of St. Maron for his years of service to his parish, the St. Anthony of the Desert Church.

Gladys was for many years the recorded church historian for St. Anthony of the Desert Church and for the Lebanese-American Society Auxiliary, as church historian and secretary. In that capacity, she has been a guest speaker at many church and social commemorative banquets.

Loretta's family owned the popular Empire Bowling Alley near the corner of Pleasant and Third Streets.

When Faheem came home from World War II in 1946, the family still had an icebox and had no telephone or television. Even without a telephone, there was always communication between families and friends because, in this closely-knit neighborhood, many residents saw one another every day through social activities, home visits, and church activities.

*Faheem:* We didn't know we were poor because we were all in the same condition.

*Gladys:* We didn't know we were not affluent because we always had enough to eat, always had food, clothing, shelter, fun activities ,and we all lived the same and were happy and satisfied, although we all aspired to a better life through material gains.

My father, Joseph W. Coury, would set off fireworks on the 4th of July, which is my birthday, in Grandfather's yard on Harrison Street, just across the street from our home, and all of the neighbors would come to see them. I always thought that all of the 4th of July fireworks were for me, until I got older. It was a great adventure.

## Religious Life

*Faheem:* Every Lebanese family attended St. Anthony of the Desert Church at 359 Quequechan Street, at the end of Alden Street.

*Gladys:* The pastor was Chorbishop Joseph Eid, who arrived in Fall River in 1929 and had come from Lebanon to Rome, where he received a Doctorate in Sacred Theology. He was a man of great intellect and compassion and charisma. The Chorbishop Eid high rise apartments on Quequechan Street are named in his honor. It was his wisdom and foresight that led to the purchase of the beautiful area on North Eastern Avenue where our new church is located. His successor was Chorbishop Norman J. Ferris, who was the pastor at St. Anthony's for thirty-three years. The other church still located there is the Calvary United Presbyterian Church, and the congregation is composed of Syrian/Lebanese faithful.

*Faheem:* St. Anthony's is a congregation of Maronites and some Melkites. The Maronite and Melkite churches are under the Pope of Rome but have their own bishops. The mass is said partly in Syriac and Aramaic, the languages spoken by Christ, but most of the mass is in English. Hymns are sung in Arabic, Syriac, and English. The Fall River area has its own diocese and eparchy, headed by Bishop Gregory Mansour.

On Palm Sunday, the blessing of the palms is held, which is followed by the blessing of the children, who hold decorated candles and flowers.

*Loretta:* The church was a central part of their lives: it brought together the spiritual, social, and community aspects of the Lebanese. The parishioners of the church were definitely our extended family. My father helped to establish St. Anthony of the Desert Church. I am proud that forty-five years to the day after my father established the church, I was named to be general chairman of the rebuilding committee for the new church when the old one burned in 1970.

There is also a Presbyterian Lebanese Church in the Flint.

## Work Life

*Faheem:* In the old days, when you turned sixteen, you went to work; few persons went to high school. When I was in grammar school in 1939-40, I would get up before 2:00 am and start delivering milk door to door at 2:00 am. I helped to hitch up the horse and I and the owner brought it and the wagon from Doyle Street to the Fall River Dairy, at the northwest corner of Bedford and Quarry Streets (where the Hood Dairy was later located). The wagon had a kerosene lantern attached to it to light the way in the early hours of the morning. I would bring the glass bottles of milk up three flights of stairs to customers, since the owner was too old to climb three flights of stairs. I continued to deliver milk early in the morning into my high school years.

Later, in high school and in the hot summer months, I and my fellow delivery person would deliver milk in our bathing suits for Sunshine Dairy, which succeeded the Fall River Dairy. In the early 1920s, in the winter snow the horse pulled a sled. Later, a law forbade the delivery of milk before 7:00 am because of the noise involved.

When my father returned from work in the summertime around 6:30 in the morning, I would meet him in Westport and we would go pick blueberries and sell them to bakeries for extra cash. A quart of blueberries brought forty cents. Blueberries were also brought home where my mother, Najeebi, who was a fabulous cook, would make many blueberry pies for the family and friends for their own enjoyment.

I later worked for SB [Salamy Brothers] Cone Company. The wages were six dollars a week.

During World War II, I served in the Seabees, the Naval Construction Battalion in Okinawa. I was there when the atom bombs were dropped on Hiroshima and Nagasaki.

I was a sergeant in the Fall River Police Department. In 1952, during Truman's presidential campaign, when I was a motorcycle policeman, six other motorcycle policemen accompanied Truman from the Narrows to South Park [now Kennedy Park] along Pleasant Street. There were crowds along the route and a great deal of excitement and a lot of applause as the entourage drove by.

*Gladys:* During World War II, when I was still in high school, I worked in the Fall River Knitting Mills, trimming the ends off of Army sweaters. When I graduated from high school, I worked for attorney Milton Epstein for nine years and later for Dr. James Sabra for twenty-five years. For many years, Dr. Sabra was the only Lebanese physician in Fall River.

*Faheem:* I had one brother and three sisters. My brother Roger eventually became the principal of the Brayton Avenue School. My sisters worked in the garment factories. I and his sister Louise graduated from high school. She became a secretary for a local corporation.

When they returned from Lebanon in 1985, my sister and niece moved into our third floor apartment, where they live today.

**School Life**

*Faheem:* All of the Lebanese kids went to the Aldrich School, between Quequechan and Harrison Streets, from first to fifth grades. From there, we went to the Davis School for sixth, seventh, and eighth grades.

*Gladys:* We were all obedient in school. The teacher was the parent away from home. There was no cafeteria at the schools. We went home for lunch from 11:30 am to 1:00 pm and left for the day at 3:15 pm. Both Faheem and I were school monitors. Monitors were students in the upper grades that led lines of kids home in two lines of pairs. It didn't take long for the line to reduce, since most kids lived near the school.

**Neighborhood Experiences**

*Faheem:* The restaurants on Pleasant Street that served Lebanese food were Long's Restaurant, Zekes' Restaurant, on the corner of Wamsutta Street, and Morin's Restaurant. Zeke's served the original Wimpy Burger and Coney Island hot dogs.

There were three Lebanese bakeries in the Flint: Sam's (Yamin) Bakery, Ashook's Bakery, on

Flint Street, and Halitt's Bakery. Pyramid Bakery was on the lower end of Pleasant Street, near Seventeenth Street.

The Lebanese have strong family ties of warmth and friendship. There was a great sense of togetherness among the Lebanese residents of the Flint.

Relatives still live in close proximity. Gladys' aunt still lives next door; her uncle once lived around the corner on County Street; a cousin lives across the street on County Street. The neighbor across the street is Lebanese and her nephew lives in the second floor apartment above them.

*Gladys:* I can go next door to visit my aunt in my housecoat if I wish.

*Faheem:* The Faris family owned a furniture store on Columbia Street for many years. Gladys' uncle Albert Faris and his brothers and sisters owned the furniture and attached dry goods store.

**Courtship and Marriage**

*Faheem:* My first date with Gladys was a trip downtown to the Durfee Theatre and then to go to the Mark You restaurant for a chow mein sandwich. The bus fare cost five cents, the theatre forty cents each, and the chow mein sandwiches ten cents each. The whole date cost less than two dollars.

**Recreation and Entertainment**

*Gladys:* Children played in the streets; there were few cars then. The streets were our playground.

*Faheem:* Sports were kick the can, dodge ball, jump rope, roller skating, hopscotch, glassies (marbles), and other games.

Saturday at the Strand Theatre was popular, with the guys skipping in and the girls paying for their ticket. There were the usual short subjects and a double feature for two or three hours. The Strand usually got the films that were shown at the Durfee Theatre downtown the week before. The Strand was a second-run theatre for the Durfee.

Ball games were played at Lafayette Park and there was skating on the park pond in winter. Winter sledding occurred on the upper part of Bedford Street (above Eastern Avenue) and on the hill on Quarry Street.

Adult women groups played card games in their homes.

Following World War II, the Rough Riders football team was formed. It was an amateur neighborhood team composed of almost all Lebanese young men The team was a part of a city league and played with full equipment, unlike earlier teams that played without equipment.

The neighborhood also sponsored the Lebanese-American Drum and Bugle Corps. I was a bugler and Gladys was a drummer in the Corps. The Corps was invited to play at the 1938 World's Fair in New York City. I was only thirteen years old and Gladys only eleven. The seventy members of the Corps, the largest in Fall River, went to the fair by bus and played at the Lebanese pavilion.

*Gladys:* It a great and thrilling experience.

**Lebanese-American Society**

*Faheem:* Next to the St. Anthony of the Desert Church, the Lebanese-American Society was the center of life for the Lebanese community. Everyone walked to the hall, since no one had cars. The men played cards, backgammon, dominoes, read the Arabic newspapers and books, or just conversed with their friends. The hall wasn't only for first generation Lebanese, because second and third and fourth generation residents visit the hall as well. The hall is still at its original location at 341 Quequechan Street.

*Gladys:* It was and is the center of our lives.

*Faheem:* Located beside to the original site of the St. Anthony of the Desert Church, the hall has been the place for wedding receptions, showers, dances, showing of Arabic movies, plays, New Year's Eve parties, carnivals, and fund-raisers. (Gladys had her shower there and Faheem and Gladys had their wedding reception there). Politicians also came to the hall to speak. The dignitaries who visited the hall included Camille Chamoun, the former president of Lebanon, Dr. Charles Habib Malik, former president of the United Nations General Assembly, and Khalil Gibran, renowned author and poet.

The hall was also used for wakes, given its proximity to the church. Since the deceased was left in the hall overnight, members of the family had to stay with the body all night long, until that practice was changed so that the wakes ended instead at midnight.

Established in 1911, the Fall River Lebanese-American Society is the longest continuously-operating Lebanese-American organization in the United States. Loretta was the president of the Ladies Auxiliary at one time. The Ladies Auxiliary gave the various national flags that fly in the plaza opposite Government Center and they planted trees at Pulaski Park (as it happened, on the same day that Pope John Paul was installed). Loretta was also a leader in realizing the building that houses the Carousel in Fall River.

**Food and Meals**

*Gladys:* The Lebanese are very hospitable. Every time someone entered a home, food would be brought out to welcome them.

The average meal included many non-meat dishes, what I call peasant food. Dishes included fattoush, stuffed eggplant and vegetables, stuffed squash and grape leaves, yogurt, tabouli, hummus, baba ghanoush. Very little meat was added to the meals.

Menish was a favorite. Housewives would prepare a mix of zaatar consisting of thyme, other spices, sesame, and oil and put it in a jar. It would be brought to the Lebanese bakery and the baker would pour it over the uncooked pita dough and bake it in his ovens. He would then charge only for a dozen breads. This is no longer in practice.

Kibbeh is also a favorite, made from lamb and other ingredients, eaten both cooked and raw. Raw kibbeh is a Lebanese favorite, like steak tartar.

**Christmas, Holidays, and Special Occasions**

*Gladys:* At Christmas, everyone went to Midnight Mass, with its crèche and hymns sung in Arabic. Prior to Mass, mom hosted an open house where lots of food was served. She played the piano and we all sang Christmas carols.

Easter was the big religious holiday for Maronite Christians. The greeting at the door in Arabic was, "Christ has risen," and the response was, "Truly, he has." Eggs were dyed different colors and the traditional egg "popping" occurred, where each person has an egg and hits it against another's egg. The person with the unbroken egg wins. Sometimes eggs were boiled in onion skins, which gave the eggs a bronze color.

# Fernand Charles E. Auclair

*Born on September 17, 1918*
*Died on January 14, 2011*

**Family Background**

I was born at 122 Leonard Street in Fall River, in our home above my father's grocery store, located on the corner of Brightman and Leonard Streets. I was delivered by Dr. Blanchette, who had the office later occupied by Dr. Boudreau.

My parents were Francis Xavier and Valida (LeBoeuf) Auclair. My father came from Canada but my mother was born in Fall River.

My father's family lived with his father's brother, who was from Bay St. Paul in Quebec. After my grandfather and his brother had an argument, my grandfather placed his family in a wagon and drove the horse and wagon in the dead of winter to Manchester, New Hampshire. He was told that there was no work there but that work could be found in Fall River, so he brought his family here.

My mother was born in Fall River's North End. My mother-in-law's family was from Lawrence, Massachusetts, and moved to Fall River for the same reason—because there was work here.

**Family Life**

At first, my father worked in the mills, but he hated it. He found a job with a Mr. Gagnon, who owned a grocery store. He helped Mr. Gagnon go from door to door selling meat off of a butcher's cart. My dad would load and unload the meat for Mr. Gagnon and help with the route. After working a year for Mr. Gagnon, my father decided to open his own store at 64 Brightman Street on the northeast corner of Leonard Street.

A Mr. Vernon promised to give financial backing to my father for the store, but he backed out at the last minute. However, my father said, "Oh, no you don't," and convinced Mr. Vernon to follow through on his commitment to back the venture. My father would give second mortgages to persons who wanted to buy a home but couldn't get all of the financing from banks. His own tenements were four dollars a week, which was a good deal.

My father was a hard worker and liked to play cards for recreation. My mom stayed home to raise the kids and loved to tend the yard at the Somerset home. She lived to age ninety-three and my dad lived to age eighty-two.

My father and mother had four boys and three girls. I was third in birth order, following my two older sisters. I was the first boy born in the extended family, following lots of girls, so my birth was an event. That's why I have lots of names.

Before electricity, we had gas jets that provided light. We sold mantles at the store that went around the jet to provide bright light, the same kind of mantles that are now used for camping lights. My grandfather and almost everyone had kerosene lanterns that they used for light, and they smelled!

I remember when electricity came in; I was just a little boy. They put the electric wires through the gas lines and electrified the gas jet fixtures. It took a while for the conversion to electricity to take place. People would come into the store for years exclaiming how wonderful it was switch a button and have the lights come on.

**School Life**

I attended St. Mathieu's School, part of St. Mathieu's parish. My parents then sent me to Montreal to a religious high school there named the *Petit Séminaire de Montreal*, run by the Sulpician Fathers. I took the classical course, which included intensive Latin and Greek. It involved lots of memorization. While there, I played hockey. It was a boarding school and I guess reasonable in price for my parents, but I was very lonesome there.

Two of my sisters also went to Canada for high school and boarded at the schools. We still had relatives in Canada at that time. My school included other kids from New England, from such places as Woonsocket and Lawrence.

**Recreation and Entertainment**

I played pickup baseball a lot, including peggy ball. My dad loved baseball, so we would go to watch baseball games at North Park. Many of the teams that played there were very good and were at semi-pro level. We would go to Boston a lot to see the games. Boston had two professional teams then, the Red Sox and the Braves.

My father had a seven-passenger Studebaker car. He enjoyed amusement parks, so we would go to not only Lincoln Park but also Crescent and Rocky Point Parks. I loved going on the merry-go-rounds as a kid. Every Sunday, we would go for a ride to Colt Farm or to New Bedford then stop at the Eagle Restaurant. The Eagle was the best restaurant in Fall River for any kind of food. It was destroyed by the 1928 fire but rebuilt again. Later, my wife and I would take the North Main Street bus to the Durfee Theatre for a show and then stop at the Eagle. On Saturdays, I would occasionally go to the Royal Theatre for the kid's shows, but Saturday was usually a workday for me.

I had one of the first radios, which was a crystal set. It was a little thing with small earphones like earplugs. One day, my aunt called us kids to "come on up" and when we entered her place we were surprised with a real Atwater Kent radio that she had bought. Her apartment was wired with an antenna, since the signals were weak then.

Before we even had electricity in our house, we had a radio. My father took two wet auto batteries and connected a radio to the batteries, which were placed below the radio. Later, we had a radio with a record player set in one console. I also saw television come in. The first sets had small round screens and the programming was unreliable and was only on a few hours a day.

**Food and Meals**

Lard was commonly used instead of butter for cooking. It made a great crust for pies, although it spoiled within a day if not eaten. My mother made pancakes on Fridays; the lard she used to oil the pan made them taste good.

She made good pea soup, baked beans, fresh pork shoulders, and whatever dad brought home from the store. People brought a lot of molasses at the store. One of the favorite snacks was bread, butter, and molasses.

## Courtship and Marriage

My wife, Jeanne N. Bilodeau, came to Fall River from Lawrence with her family, who came to the city in 1924 to find work.

One Sunday in 1941, when Jeanne and I were dating, we took a ride to a dance in Onset. On the way back, we were listening on the radio when the program was interrupted and President Roosevelt came to say that Pearl Harbor had been attacked. What an awful feeling that was!

When I got home after the war was over in 1945, and was about to get married to Jeanne, my parents got a telegram from the government saying that my brother Robert had been killed in the last days of the war—killed by a kamikaze plane in Okinawa. He was serving duty on the *USS Curtis*, a seaplane tender. We weren't sure if we should continue planning for the marriage but our parish priest, Rev. Monsignor Prévost, suggested that our brother would have wanted us to continue our plans and get married, so we did.

We lived behind the store when we were first married. One day, on the way to visit my parents at their home at 3587 Riverside Avenue in Somerset, my wife asked me if I thought that my parents would be interested in switching houses, since they were alone in their big house and we had seven kids, and my parents agreed to it.

## Auclair's Market

Dad bought the store, Auclair's Market, in 1918, the year I was born. The previous owner stocked what he wanted, but my father catered to what people wanted and did a better business as a result. His meats were from Swift Meat Packing Company, and were the best available.

I began working in the market when I was very young, delivering groceries and doing other chores after school and on Saturdays. When I got to the store after school, the orders would be lined up on the floor for me to deliver on my bicycle. Our store had a pot-bellied stove that is now on display in the Somerset Historical Society.

Many things came in wooden barrels, tubs, or boxes. Sugar, dried peas and beans, and fresh turkeys came in barrels, as did pickles (at five cents each) and lard, which we scooped out of a wooden tub. Tea came from China in wooden boxes, and we mixed it beforehand and sold what we called mixed tea. It included green and pekoe teas. Chewing tobacco also came in wooden boxes and was cut it for sale with a guillotine-like knife, which is also in the Somerset Historical Society. Molasses also came in bulk and was pumped from a wooden barrel, as was vinegar.

Butter came in a wooden tub that was wider at the top than the bottom. To get the butter out, my father would take the top off, tip over the tub, and lift the tub. Cutting the butter in pound pieces occurred by the use of a wire cutter. The cutter was a circle of strong piano-like wire, wide enough to fit over the mound of butter, and it had a wooden handle attached. To cut the butter, he would put the wire over the butter and cut it in layers of a certain thickness. Then these layers were cut in pieces. They were very good at cutting pieces that were close to a pound. Later, butter came prepackaged in pound containers as it is today. The wire butter cutter is now on display at the Somerset Historical Society.

Fresh turkeys also came in barrels. They came without their feathers, but with everything else. They were skinny things and had a blueish tint to them. They came with everything inside, so it was my unpleasant task on Mondays to eviscerate every one of them. I would cut a hole in their rectum large enough to get the intestines, heart, gizzards, and all of the other stuff out of them, and I cut their feet and head off. It was an unpleasant, smelly business, since the turkeys had accumulated a gas inside them. Every time I cleaned the turkeys, the day after I would have a splitting headache; I guess it was from this gas. Fully dressed turkeys didn't start coming from Swifts until the 1930s. Turkeys were a novelty then for Thanksgiving and were also rather expensive. Before turkeys came in common use, people would have chickens, pork or fresh shoulders for Thanksgiving.

We also eviscerated chickens in the store, since they also came with everything but the feathers. They usually came in wire crates.

Whenever business was slow, we would weigh things for the weekend. In addition to cutting butter, we would weigh and put in paper bags bulk items that came in barrels. One of my jobs was to take large burlap bags of potatoes, empty them on the floor, and bag them in peck bags (fifteen pounds) and half-peck bags (seven-and-a-half pounds). We also scooped out sugar and weighed it in two-pound paper bags.

When we weighed requested bulk items for customers as they waited, we had to compute the sales price in our heads, multiplying the price per pound by the fraction of what it weighed. Scales then were just scales; they didn't compute the sales price for you as they do today.

Meat was delivered from Swift Meat Packing or Wilson's in whole sides of an animal, and we had to cut it in salable pieces into such cuts as chops or chuck. Before the war, we cut meat by hand with knives and cleavers, exerting work which was often dangerous. However, after I came out of the service, I bought a power saw to cut meat, which made it so much easier.

We gave credit, and so many people owed my father money. My father was very generous and, during the Depression, people owed him lots of money. If a person lost his job, he couldn't pay. Dad would let him pay what he could. The Portuguese tended to run up high bills but always paid. Farmers would run up bills for the whole year and pay when crops were sold.

We kept tally of accounts by use of the McCaskey system. Each family got a number. Items were written out in a sales slip booklet with a carbon in between the white and yellow pages. The store kept the white page and the customer got the yellow. If the sale was credit, we kept a record and the customer received a copy. When bills were paid, they went on the metal spindle or spike and were tallied at the end of the day. Paydays were usually on Thursdays. We were open on Saturday nights, and it was slow, so we spent the time tallying the slips. One fellow came in with a twenty dollar bill that he had received in his pay envelope and he was so amazed to see a twenty dollar bill, which he used to pay his store bill.

My dad was one of the first groceries to get refrigeration. Before that, the walk-in coolers were chilled by the use of ice that was put on upper shelves. As the ice melted, the water was collected and directed to the basement and to a sink to drain. Buying was tight to prevent spoilage; if someone came in at the end of the day and we didn't have something, they bought something else. If we had a leftover leg of lamb, my father would bring it home for Sunday's dinner. My father was very happy when refrigeration was installed in the store.

I took over the store from my father in the early 1940s, before I entered the service. Auclair's Market is eighty-three years old [in 2005, when the interview was conducted] and is now operated by my son Dennis. The highway took the Brightman Street store and, since much of our business was in Somerset, we opened a new store across County Street from where the new store is now located.

## The North End

There were five large mills in the North End. On North Main Street, there was the Narragansett Mill, the Border City Mill, and the Sagamore Mills. On Davol Street, there was the Weetamoe Mill and the Mechanics Mill. The Weetamoe Mill burnt to the ground [on February 6, 1940]. Most of the people who worked in the mills were weavers and loom fixers.

The looms were belt-driven. The noise in the mills was unbearable; workers would use sign language and many lost their hearing. Many students from nearby schools would pick up lunch pails from homes in wagons and would bring the dinner pails to the workers at the mills. I believe they were paid twenty-five cents per week.

Other grocery stores in the North End included Red Gagnon's Market, located on the corner of Davidson and Brightman (they raised chickens in the back yard; Leo Gagnon made ice cream there and sold it to other stores), Lauzier's Market, on Brightman Street opposite Morton Street, Gaudreau's Market, on Fulton Street near the North End Laundry, the Puritan Store (later the P&M Market, for Perron and Machado), on Brightman Street between our store and Lauzier's Market, Torres Grocery, on the corner of Brightman and Leonard Streets, and the Lindsey Red and White Market, on Lindsey Street at the northeast corner of Cory Street. Capeto Market was located next to the Republican Club on Lindsey Street. The Lima's owned a grocery store at the northeast corner of Oregon and Cory Streets. Another grocery store near the Lima's on Oregon Street was owned by Dan Shalloo. He would deliver his orders with a horse and wagon. He was very well liked. His son became a priest, Father Shalloo, later Monsignor Shalloo.

Other stores on Brightman Street included D'Arruda's Hardware, at the southwest corner of Brightman and Leonard Streets, across the street from our market. A few doors down from them was Benevides Hardware. There were also a few pharmacies, including Vogel's Pharmacy, on the southeast corner of Brightman and Lindsey Streets, and Leo's Pharmacy. Before it became Vogel's Pharmacy, Murray's Store was located there. Marchand's Café was located on the northeast corner of Brightman and Leonard Streets. Walter Marchand owned it and it was always a well-run and clean establishment. Mello's Chourico was located on Brightman Street, on the corner of Garside Street near North Main Street. Michael's Chourico was located then next to the Republican Club on Lindsey Street, between George and Brightman Streets.

Brightman Street had many variety stores and an excellent bakery—Clouet's Bakery. The owner came from France and was probably the best baker in town. On Saturday morning, people from the area would bring their bean pots to either to Clouet's or Gold Medal Bakery and for ten cents they would bake the beans, to be picked up at 4:00 pm. The ovens were shut down but hot enough to cook from the embers. Next door to the bakery was a really good fish market run by a Mr. Ferreira. You never had a foul odor there.

In the same building, on the southeast corner of Lindsey Street, was a good shoe store, owned by a Mr. Patenaude. There were many stores on Lindsey Street. A Mr. Smith owned a clothing store where people found everything they needed. You must remember that autos were scarce and people shopped in their neighborhood.

The first Moy Lee's Chinese Restaurant was located on the north side of Brightman Street, near our market, and Moy Lee lived above it. Moy Lee was the number one chef at the Eagle Restaurant. His son later opened another restaurant across the street and further down on Brightman Street, nearer the Royal Theatre. A chow mein sandwich cost five cents and was wrapped in wax paper, which, amazingly enough, kept the liquid from leaking out. Many Chinese chefs came from the

Eagle Restaurant and started their own restaurants in the city.

On Brightman Street, there were shoe repair shops and they were all busy; people had their shoes fixed in those days. There was a Mr. Bonin on Brightman Street (between Leo's Pharmacy and the furniture store), John Dulash on Lindsey Street, across from Vaillancourt's Barber Shop [at 406 Lindsey Street]. There was an excellent plumber there by the name of Cayer and Sons. They were located next to Guay's Painting Shop. Guay's Painting turned into Phil's Barber Shop. On Leonard Street, between Brightman and George Streets, was a blacksmith shop that shoed horses there run by a Mr. Lapore; it later became a garage.

Morton Street was also very commercial then, although it is almost residential now. One of the businesses on Morton was Dufour Bakery.

Dairies in the North End included Amaral's Dairy on Murray Street next to the railroad tracks and the North End Dairy behind St. Joseph's Church.

The three LeComte brothers were based in the North End. Alphonse LeComte owned LeComte Dairy. Auguste LeComte owned the Gold Medal Bakery in the North End, and now on Bay Street, when it was dislocated by the highway. Welliston owned the Fall River Laundry in the North End and it closed when the highway forced it to relocate or close.

LeComte Dairy is still operating in Somerset. The Gold Medal Bakery on Bay Street bakes bread for private labels such as Cumberland Farms. It is also the regional bakery for Holsum Bread. At one time, Gold Medal gave out things as promotions. My son Dennis married one of the LeComte Dairy girls.

All dairies delivered milk and bread with horse and wagons. In the wintertime, they used horses and sleds. The North End Laundry also delivered its laundry with a horse and wagon and a sled in winter. The driver of the sled would let me sit next to him as he drove. The streets were never plowed, and the switch to sleds when it snowed was better for the horses. Believe it or not, horses did go up and down these hills. The horses were equipped with special horseshoes in the wintertime that had little chisels on them to give the horses footing and traction on the ice. Most of the streets in the North End were dirt until the1920s. Leonard Street was dirt for a while. There was no trolley on Brightman Street, only on North Main Street.

Horse manure remained on the street, but some people picked it up for their vegetable gardens and flowers. Birds ate the seeds that remained in the manure. I believe that the city might also have picked it up. Swill, or wet garbage, was picked up by the city to go to the pig farms.

Some of the other businesses in the city were the Fall River Dairy, at 840 Bedford Street, on the corner of Quarry Street, which later became Hood Dairy, and Rousseau's Bakery, near the corner of South Main Street and East Main Street. Rousseau's was a large bakery that made Skippy Bread.

Before Shell Oil moved to its site, the New England Oil Company operated a refinery there. It was horrible. The smell from the refinery was so bad and the air so thick that we couldn't sleep with our windows open. When Shell Oil came in, they began pumping oil to West Boylston for loading on tanker trucks.

New England Oil sponsored a baseball team. It included such great players as Matt Lajoie, who later played in the major leagues for the Boston Braves. Instead of paying the players, N.E. Oil gave them all jobs at the refinery. It was the best ball team around.

Harry Truman came through the North End, but I only saw him as his car crossed the Brightman Street Bridge and traveled down Davol Street.

**World War II**

I joined the Navy in 1941 and was a radioman, 2nd class. After schooling, I went to Africa, England, and Ireland. I went to many radio schools, but my last stint was in Londonderry, Ireland. I worked at the transmitter station, where we relayed messages from Washington, D.C. to Paris, France, via Londonderry.

One day, while on duty, I saw the message where Hitler surrendered that was being sent to Franklin Roosevelt, our president.

I was in Portland, England, on D-Day—only about twenty-two miles from the Normandy coast. A buddy and I were put in a shack on the beach and we constantly sent fake radio messages, using the call sign of the *USS Ancon* that housed all of the brass, including all of the generals and admirals from all countries. We were a decoy to fool the Germans, but our lives were at stake. We had the same equipment and same power as that on the *Ancon*. There were hundreds of barrage balloons making it difficult for the enemy to bomb us.

One day, while at work, we were visited by a short man standing over me. It was Admiral Stark, Chief of Naval Operations. He was in full uniform, with plenty of gold. He was very nice and told us to keep working. Another time, we were working and saw this impressive convoy with a motorcycle escort coming to us. It was the King of England, but at the time we had no idea who he was. He, too, watched us work. He was not a big man, but he had a nice smile.

I later did radio work in Plymouth, England, which was the major naval seaport for the British Navy. Plymouth was completely bombed and destroyed but it was later rebuilt. When I was there, the battleship *Hood* was there, the ship that sank the *Bismark*. Later still, I was stationed at Londonderry in Ireland at a transmitter station. The transmitter had these huge tubes for the radio transmitter that were water-cooled.

When it was time to leave, we left from Scotland on the *Queen Elizabeth* and sailed to New York. What a beautiful sight it was to see the Statue of Liberty! I was the happiest person in the world. I was coming home to marry my sweetheart. I had been overseas twenty-two months.

**Religious Life**

The North End had three Roman Catholic parishes—St. Joseph's on North Main Street for the Irish, St. Michael's on Essex Street for the Portuguese, and St. Mathieu's Church on St. Mary's Street for the French. When Route 79 came through, it affected St. Mathieu's and displaced hundreds of families. It was a beautiful church, but they tore it down.

St. Mathieu's School was staffed by St. Joseph's nuns, some of them were very good teachers. I was an altar boy at St. Mathieu's. Monsignor Cain, the pastor, would give us a dime for serving a funeral Mass. The church had a powerful pipe organ, made in Canada (Quebec) by the Casavant Brothers. The organist was a Mr. Charles Letendre, who could have been called a prodigy; the church shook when he played.

**The Fall River Line**

A man who lived in our house, named Mr. Cox, would travel on a regular basis on what we called the "New York boat." Once, a local priest wanted to visit his sister in New York City and asked me to drive him. I suggested riding the New York boat instead. I believe it was only five dollars round-trip per person, and another five dollars if you wanted a bed for the night. We slept on the chairs. The food was very good, although we didn't eat on the boat. The ship had an excellent orchestra and dancing. Many newly married couples went on their honeymoons on the boats. People got off of the Boston train and were happy as can be as they got on the boat.

We left on the *Commonwealth* and came back on the *Priscilla*. The interiors of the ships were beautiful and very impressive. My dad would drive us to Common Fence Point [in Portsmouth, Rhode Island] to watch the boats go by. The *Commonwealth* looked beautiful, and on a summer night, with all of its lights on, it looked gorgeous.

At the end, a labor strike was threatened. The owners said that if there were a strike, it would be all over. The boat left for New York, a strike occurred, and the boats never returned.

The *Commonwealth*

The *Priscilla*

# Howard F. Bonner

*Born in 1943*

**Family Background**

I was born in Fall River at Truesdale Hospital. My father was Daniel Bonner, born in Fall River in 1902. My mother was Mabel Gertrude (Parker) Bonner, born in Utah. Dad had fourteen siblings, eleven of which lived. Dad was the middle one.

My father's parents were Charles Bonner (a loom-fixer) and Margaret ("Maggie") Ryan. My mother's parents were Bertrum Levi Parker and Mattie Mada Fritz.

My father's father was born in Scotland. They came from a family of weavers. My grandmother was from Tipperary in Ireland. Her father, William Ryan, was in the Irish independence movement, the Sinn Féin, and was imprisoned and died at the hands of the British. His wife and family were sent to the United States by the Morrison family, who were also Irish independence supporters.

My grandmother on my mother's side had a German accent, even though she was a fourth generation American. She lived in Ohio in an insular German community.

My dad was a military lad. At fifteen, he took his brother's birth certificate and went into the Army. My parents met when my father was in the service. He came out of the service in 1938 to join his brother in the flower business. When World War II came, he went back in the service at the age of forty-one and stayed until 1953, rejoining his brother in the business.

**Family Life**

We kept coming back and forth to Fall River. At one point we lived in France, where my dad was stationed. We came back briefly in 1952, and dad put me in Sacred Heart School. As a young child, I remember coming through Somerset and Swansea via Route 103; I remember the white fire trucks in Swansea.

In 1938, my parents bought a house at 318 Dexter Street, corner of Robeson Street. The house was built in 1900 and was tiny. That house on Dexter Street was their pride and joy. No matter where they lived, it was important to them that they owned a house in Fall River.

My uncle Frankie was a boxer. He tried to keep this fact from his mother by naming himself "Red Barnett." He was a champion boxer in two boxing categories. Uncle Frankie was two years older than my father. He would come home bloodied and try to explain it to his mother. Later, he boxed in the Army. My father also boxed and neither my dad nor Uncle Frankie had cartilage in their noses.

Uncle Bill ran away from home at the age of twelve or fifteen and went to Attleboro, Massachusetts, to work in the jewelry business. Then he was a bellhop at a hotel. During Prohibition, Bill ran booze from Canada to the United States; my dad helped him in this business for a few years.

Bill later became a salesman for Monsanto Chemical. He later opened a cement mixing business in his basement in Dorchester. He would put the mixture in molds and go to restaurants and sell it as a dish-washing detergent. After a while he became the biggest distributor to restaurants in Boston and was doing sixty to seventy million dollars a year in business.

Uncle Alfie worked at the Kresge store in Fall River as a kid. He later worked his way up in the Kresge business by working in various stores throughout the country.

One day, my dad was driving down Bedford Street and said, "There's my cousin." It was an old man, bent over with the shakes. He was injured in the "First War." He was also a West Point graduate. Everyone wondered how could this happen in an immigrant family, where one of their kids would be accepted at West Point. But I researched it and it's true.

I am the last Bonner in Fall River; when I die, there will be no Bonners in the city.

**Bonner's Florist**
The Bonners first lived on Seabury Street, just behind Sacred Heart Church. My grandmother had a candy store in the first floor of the house. Then they moved to Robeson Street. She started to sell flowers for weddings and funerals. My grandfather started growing cut flowers in the yard. He had a hogshead [large barrel that could hold 60 to 140 gallons] and would gather manure from pig and other farms in the area. He grew gladiolas and other flowers. They didn't have a truck or a car, so they delivered the arrangements by carrying them on a trolley.

The Bonner Florist business was started in 1923 by my grandmother, Maggie Ryan Bonner. Uncle John ran florist shops in New York City. He was a real salesman—a hawker. He had gone to Bristol Aggie [in Dighton, Massachusetts] and then to Cornell University, where he remained for a year and a half. My grandmother borrowed from every relative to pay for his college education.

My uncle John would search the newspapers for marriage intentions and then run down and contact them and convince them that Bonner's should supply them with flowers for the wedding. After work, my grandmother would make ribbon arrangements, into which she would place a flower arrangement on top. She was so good at it that she could do it automatically.

Bonner and Buffinton were the two big florists and were rivals. Camilla Pickering of Buffinton and my family were friends. We bought orchids that Buffinton's grew. When she was older, Camilla sold out and went to work for Bonner. They were all older then, and the greenhouse looked like an old folks' home. But they loved it and had a lot of fun together. My uncle John would tell Irish jokes that only he laughed at. He was a character. He made a fortune in Wall Street on stocks. You would never know it, though. He always wore a Stetson hat that he flattened out on top.

Bonner Florist bought an old greenhouse that was from New York. They put it together and installed an old coal furnace. My dad took care of the greenhouse. It burned soft coal and we had to shake the grates in the furnace and keep it going in the winter.

There were a lot of florist suppliers in the area. Olson's Greenhouses in Taunton was one. Joe Koppelman, the founder of Fall River Florist Supply, brought dish gardens from New York City to sell here. There were some fellows in the Reservation and on Wilson Road who grew gladiolas.

We would go to Horseneck Road in Westport to cut laurel along the road. It grew wild and we got it for nothing. We would fill the trunk of the Pontiac or the truck and bring it back to the greenhouse. We used it as an arrangement base. We kids had the task of filling up the baskets or arrangements with the laurel. The branches hurt your hands. We would also go to the officer's beach in Newport to get bittersweet for nothing.

The Kanes and the Bonners lived on Dover Street. When Kane became mayor, we decorated the Armory for his inauguration.

In the flower business, the parishes were important. It was a big deal to know the priests since they would recommend florists. At Easter, we decorated the Central Congregational Church. We had three trucks and one station wagon loaded with flowers and palms in their driveway. There were 300 to 400 plants: Easter lilies, hydrangeas, hyacinths, gardenias, and azaleas. When we brought them in, one of the women in the parish would direct us where to place them to get the right balance of color.

**Work Life**

My mother worked at Sears downtown for twenty-five years; when they moved to Swansea, they laid her off. She was devastated. She was a real company girl; very loyal. She felt betrayed at age sixty-five.

My dad was in the 13th Air Corps in World War II. He never served in the continental United States. They island hopped to get in back of Japan. He ended up on the Treasury Islands, on Sterling Island. There was an explosion and his legs were hurt. A Navy Corpsman [enlisted medical specialist] came to his side. It was Henry Lord, his buddy from the corner. Another Fall River Navy Corpsman was Henry Mello, who worked in the hospital. He later became a captain in the Fall River Police Department. James Tansey was a writer for the *Teamsters* magazine.

James Tansey, the union organizer for whom the school is named, was my uncle Frankie's manager when he was boxing. Bill Grant, later the mayor of Fall River, said that he loved to go to The Casino [50 Morgan Street] to see Frankie box.

I worked at Bristol Knitting and ran the jacquard machines. During the first two weeks of July, we were laid off for vacation and we had to collect unemployment. All the companies did the same thing, so there were long lines at the unemployment office. James Tansey's mother worked at the unemployment office and she would see me and send me to the front of the line.

In the old days, industrial accidents were not reported as such. One of my uncles fell off of a wagon carrying cotton bales and died. I once tried to find a record of his death, but it wasn't reported. Another uncle was killed when struck by a shuttle cock in a mill, but his death was reported as a cardiopulmonary death.

**School Life**

I went to St. Joseph's School and graduated from the eighth grade in 1957. My father wanted me to go to Coyle or to another Catholic high school, but I put my foot down and said that I wanted to go to Durfee. [B.M.C.] Durfee High School was a place of great tradition. However, coming from a Catholic elementary school, I was definitely in the minority, since the kids from Morton or Henry Lord had their cliques already formed before we arrived.

# Cecile Borkowski

*Born on April 21, 1922*
*Died on November 21, 2013*

**Family Background**

I was born at home and have lived at 132 Seventeenth Street (on the second floor) all my life. My father built this house in 1923.

My parents were John (né, Jan) T. (born in Poland) and Wladyslawa [Alice] (Luszcz) Borkowski, born in Fall River.

My father's father was named Leopold Borkowski. My father's stepmother was named Rose (Stupnicki). My father's mother died when he was five years old; a surviving baby sister died soon after. Rose had four daughters with Leopold following their marriage and immigration to the United States. She came over after my grandfather and father came here first. They lived in Westport, Massachusetts, near Lincoln Park, and then moved to Pawtucket, Rhode Island.

My mother's parents were Stanislaw and Maria (Banek) Luszcz. They had six children: Emilia, Jennie, Alice, Joseph, (an unnamed baby died here), and Cecile.

**Family Life**

My father had a shoe store at 1564 Pleasant Street for fifty-nine years [J.T.'s Shoe Store]. His father worked for him in the store. It sold men's and boy's shoes and repaired shoes. Before my mom married, she worked in the mills; after that she stayed at home. In Poland, my father and his father lived in a village and would make shoes and travel from village to village to sell and repair shoes. He was paid not in cash but in vegetables and other food. They lived in Buberka, which is a suburb of Lwów in Poland [now Lviv, Ukraine]. It was on the border with Russia and was constantly changing hands between the Russians and the Germans.

My father was quick-tempered. He didn't join any organizations until later in life, when he joined the Kosciuszko Men's Club. My mother was a kind and generous person. She always had something to give you. She later became president of the Polish Women's Club and Vice President of the Polish National Alliance, Lodge 1887.

I had a very active life when I was young. I took dance lessons and tap dancing. I also took piano lessons and violin lessons; my aunt was a violin teacher. I started singing in the church choir at St. Stanislaus Church and did so for thirty-five years. Once a year, the dance school had a revue and a May festival in a hall. It was called Ney's Dance Studio and was located at the corner of South Main and Columbia Streets, on the second floor.

I joined the Kosciuszko Women's Club and was treasurer there. I belonged to the Polish National Alliance, first in Lodge 767 and then later in Lodge 1887, and was active in regional lodge affairs in the Fall River, New Bedford, Taunton, and Bridgewater area. I was and still am a director of the Polish National Home.

I was also a director in the Red Feather Community Fund and a corresponding secretary for the National Secretary's Association. I joined the Allegro Glee Club and was a member for

Jan T. Borkowski Shoe Repairers, 1564 Pleasant Street

twenty-five years. I was a drummer in the Harcerze Drum Corps for Lodge 1887 and marched in parades. Harcerze means scouts.

I was fluent in Polish, mostly learned from my mom.

We have always lived on the second floor here. George and Alice Biltcliffe lived on the first floor. He worked for the Armour Meat Packing Company and went from city to city for that company. It was a good position. Later, my mother's mother lived on the third floor for many years.

On Sundays, we would go to church and after church have dinner. We would then go to Pawtucket, Rhode Island, to see my grandfather (my father's father). This was a Sunday ritual. My father owned a Studebaker, a Lincoln, two Buicks, a Pontiac, and a deluxe Rambler. Family members in Michigan gave me a 1973 Plymouth Valiant (which I have in running condition and currently use). They gave my mom a refrigerator and my aunt got a trip to Poland. This was for taking care of their two sisters from Michigan who came back here when they became ill.

Mom and dad loved to dance and won prizes for their ballroom dancing. They danced at the Polish Home, the Pulaski (Pulawski) Hall (located at the corner of East Main and Palmer Streets, on the top floor) and at Polish affairs at various locations.

Every village has a different dance in Poland. Additionally, there are different dances, music, and costumes by region. The costumes are beautiful, with cut work and detailing. We would meet on Saturdays and everyone would make a different part of the costume, depending on their ability. One person would cut, another would fit, etc. While sewing the costumes, we would be singing and enjoying ourselves. Performances were two-and-a-half hours long. Every dance had a different costume. We would run off of the stage while the orchestra played a number, and then we were back in three minutes. The orchestra consisted of an accordion, a violin, and a bass viol.

**Food and Meals**

Gołąbki is the correct spelling of the cabbage roll. We ate pierogies and a rice pudding called legumina, which was apples and raisins put in buttered crumb in a dish with an egg on top and a little milk for moisture. It is then baked for an hour. Kapusta is cabbage cooked with kielbasa and beans and boiled like a boiled dinner.

**School Life**

I first went to the Brown School, from grades one to six. It was where the Boys and Girls Club is now on Bedford Street. For grades seven to nine, I went to the Davis School on Quequechan Street. One day a week, we had to go to the Watson School on Eastern Avenue for lessons in cooking and sewing. Then I went to [B.M.C.] Durfee High School, where I graduated in 1940.

After Durfee, I went to the F.G. Allen Secretarial School in Fall River, located at the corner of Central and North Main Streets, on the second floor of the Granite Block.

At the Brown School, my teachers were Miss Kathryn Whalen for the first grade, Elizabeth Remington for the second grade, and Miss White for the third grade. Kathryn Whalen sent me a beautiful handkerchief and card when I graduated from Durfee, and I only saw her once after leaving first grade. Florence G. Mercer was the fourth grade teacher. She vacationed on the Cape and sent me a card every year from there.

**Recreation and Entertainment**

We played tag, hide and seek, hopscotch, strolled dolls in carriages, rode our tricycles, and roller skated. I would cut dolls from newspapers and tape paper as backing and propped them up by folding the paper. I would put them up on the floor and talk to them like a teacher.

In those days, you stayed close to home. When you went out, it was with your parents and only to shop for clothes or food. The people that you met were neighborhood people.

The Biltcliffe's on the first floor of our house knew the doctors at Union Hospital and would have parties for the doctors in their home. Dr. French, Dr. Truesdale, and others came to the parties.

**Work Life**

My first job was at the American Thread Company. I had to type invoices each day at night and put them on the teletype machine to send to the company headquarters in Suncook, New Hampshire. After two years in that job, I went to work for fifteen years at Pacific Oil in Fall River. I was secretary to the president and vice-president. Fall River was the headquarters of the company, and we had offices in New Bedford, Newport, and Taunton. Pacific Oil was located to the rear of Central Lunch on Central Street. Durfee Bowling Alley were next to it. From the corner of North

Main and Central Streets was Schulte Cigar Store, then a taxi stand, then Sullivan's Card Shop, then Singer Sewing Machine Store, then the office of Pacific Oil.

Then I took care of sick relatives for twenty-eight years. I quit work at age thirty-eight to take care of family members, but I am suffering now because I have little Social Security as a result. Dad lived until he was ninety and my mother until she was eighty-four. My mother's family was good to me. An aunt sent me money every month for taking care of family members.

**Neighborhood Experiences**

There was a dry goods store on Columbia Street where you could put it "on the book." A person would pay by the week. One man said to grandma, "You can have anything you want because you pay me a quarter a week." She never failed, even with all those children. Woolworth's sold costume jewelry and some of it was quite good, since they would get lot ends from better stores. Jewish men would come house-to-house selling jewelry.

My friends included Rita Joubert, in the house next door (118 Seventeenth Street), Lorraine Dupont, at the corner house (104 Seventeenth Street), and Eleanore Riley and Marjorie Almeida in the house next door (150 Seventeenth Street). There weren't many boys in the neighborhood.

On the corner of Seventeenth and Merchant Streets, where Victoria's Portuguese Store is now, there was Houle's Grocery Store, later Van's Grocery Store. Magnus Folster Movers was on Pleasant Street, near the corner of Seventeenth Street, next to a vacant lot on the corner. Next to that was a small laundry, to the rear of my property. On Eighteenth Street, close to Pleasant Street, there was the Independent Laundry, owned by a Jewish person. The Fall River Dairy was on Bedford Street, on the corner of Seventeenth Street. The old St. Anthony of Padua Church was on the corner of Bedford and Sixteenth Streets, facing Sixteenth. The neighborhood was served by two bus lines, one on Pleasant Street and one on Bedford Street. George's Poultry Store was next to my father's store.

My father would take me to watch the fireworks at Columbus Park on Columbus Day. I would stand on the fence with my father. Sometimes, it would snow on Columbus Day. We would go for bread at the Italian bakeries on Bedford Street. There were Jewish bakeries in the area of Washington and Union Streets, below South Main Street. They were Gordon's, Lipchitz's, and Bernstein's Bakeries. There was a Portuguese bakery next to Ventura's Drug Store, but it had another name from the present bakery there now.

**Christmas, Holidays, and Special Occasions**

We always had a Christmas supper. There was no meat served. There was always a chair left vacant for a guest who might come along. This was called *Wigilia*. When the first star came out, we had supper then went to Midnight Mass. We sang carols in Polish and had a good time.

After midnight, the Salvation Army would come in a truck and sing carols in the street, accompanied by trumpets. The lady across the street belonged to the Salvation Army and they sang from the back of the truck for her, sometimes as late as 3:00 am.

At Easter, there was the blessing of the food in the home: ham, kielbasa, eggs. Polish colored Easter eggs are called pisanki.

## Downtown

I didn't go downtown often; we didn't have the money. When we did go, we took the electric trolleys. Everyone went downtown shopping on Saturdays. There were so many people on South Main Street that you couldn't walk on the sidewalks.

Trolleys were in the middle of the road and had electric wires. A pass gave you eight rides. I never rode much. I walked to school and to Durfee High School. Sometimes the snow was up to your knees. I walked to the Watson School once a week also, and the wind from the ponds in the wintertime was awful. We had no insulated clothes.

## Health and Illness

When mom was a child and hurt her thumb, a person called a Polish "medicine man" came to the house. All he would say is, "Dear child, come here and let me look at it." He took a large leaf from the yard, wrapped it around her thumb, and it healed. My father would never take medicine. He would take prunes and salted cashew nuts after each meal. He was skinny, about 135 pounds and 5 feet, 5 inches tall. My mother was 5 feet, 3 inches tall and weighed 128 pounds. My father liked to walk and always walked to work, rain or shine, and never took the trolley or bus. He lived until he was ninety and never saw a doctor until he had an accident later in life.

He was about seventy years old when I got a call from Walter's Service Station telling me that my father got hit by a taxi at Thirteenth and Pleasant Streets that night. He was brought to the operating room with a compound fracture. His leg flapped and the doctor said that he would lose control of the leg. However, we took him to a chiropractor and he healed my father's leg that the doctor gave up on, and my father walked normally again. My mother advised a person who was in the furniture business to go to a chiropractor and he bought me a bicycle. I guess the chiropractor worked.

South Main Street, looking north

**The Depression**
During the Depression, families had little wagons that they used to go down Pleasant Street to Troy Street, where they would give you a bag of flour or potatoes. Then they would bring it home. Few people saw meat; that is how they lived then.

The Depression was hard for my dad; he almost lost his business and his house. Thank God, my grandmother had a little savings so he could pay the mortgage.

People went to work or to church; if they lived near to the Polish Home, they went there to play parlor games.

No one had money to be ahead of anyone else. We were all poor and all in the same boat. We made things out of strings, anything. If someone had an organ, we met and sang and danced in the home. We made do and were happy. We had friends; that was important. We didn't have to keep up with the Joneses.

Our family was happy with the Roosevelts. We listened to Roosevelt's fireside chats on the radio. Mrs. Roosevelt came on the radio also. My father always said, "When the Republicans are in, there is always a war." He was always a Democrat.

**The Fall River Line**
During the late 1930s, I sailed to New York on the *Priscilla*. It had beautiful upholstery inside and everything was carpeted. All the furniture was covered in velvet. The woodwork was in the Provincial style. The dining rooms were beautiful with chandeliers and crystal. There was dancing and music. Staterooms had upper and lower bunks. The restaurant had good food.

**Miscellaneous Memories**
During the 1938 hurricane, I was coming home from Durfee High School, walking with friends. The wind was so strong we could hardly walk. One window blew out in the apartment. A few bricks fell into the chimney, which sounded awful. My mom grabbed me, not knowing what to do; should we go out or stay in? We were alone in the house. When the man downstairs came home, he took a scatter rug that he had and nailed it over the open window. Dad didn't know how bad it was until he got out of his shop. We had never heard of a hurricane.

When the Merchant's Mill burned [destroyed by fire on January 29, 1934; one of the largest mill buildings in the city], the trees in the Brown School yard burned. Men from the CCC [Civilian Conservation Corps] camps came to take us out of our homes in case the fire came close. "Take only what you need," they told us. Across from the Merchant's Mill, nearer to us, there was the Cox Paper Box Company that also caught on fire. The ignited cotton and cardboard was flying all over the place. People were spraying the roofs of their houses and the roofs were covered in ice. It was a very windy day. I was in third or fourth grade when it happened and we were all dressed up to go out if we had to.

We loved one another. We were happy. We cared for one another. I'm happy with what I have.

# Ann (Occhiuti) Botelho

*Born on December 3, 1927*

**Family Background**

I was born at home at 62 Johnson Street in Fall River.

My parents were Frank and Adeline (Trombino) Occhiuti. He was born in Acri, Italy, in 1901, and immigrated to Fall River in 1925. I believe he was a welder at Davis Roller Print for years and a craftsman in his field. He did some of the iron railings in the Durfee Theatre. He was artistically inclined and played three musical instruments—guitar, mandolin, and Jewish harp.

My mother was born in Fall River in 1900 and left school to work as a spinner in one of the local mills.

Their marriage was a (mis) match, and ended in 1941, after producing four children—myself, Vincent, Frank, and Joseph.

My mother's parents were Pasquale and Pasqualina (Trombino) Devita. Pasqualina was born on the Albanian border of Italy and traveled as an orphan with a band of gypsies to the southern part of Italy (Cosenza). Pasquale was a widow with eight children when he married Pasqualina, and was a laborer who worked at Beattie's Ledge in Fall River.

My father's parents were Vincenzo and Filomena Occhiuti. Both were born in Acri, Italy. They had nine children and immigrated to the United States, making Fall River their home.

My husband, Frank P. Botelho, died in 1980 at age fifty-nine of a massive heart attack. He was born at home in Gloucester, Massachusetts, in 1920. His parents had four children and came to live in Fall River after they lost their jobs in the Gordon-Pew Fish Factory. Frank quit school, did odd jobs, and then enlisted in the Army in June of 1940. He saw action in Anzio, Italy, France, and Germany. He was discharged in 1946 after receiving many distinguished service medals. Frank worked for thirty-two years with the Massachusetts Department of Public Works.

We have three children, Jean Parenteau, Stephen, and Paul.

**Family Life**

When I was a child, the "old folks" all spoke Italian and although we youngsters understood what they were saying, we responded in English, much to my regret today. I was always proud of my Italian background and still am, although we are a dying breed in Fall River.

My mother made homemade beer and root beer. I helped "cap" the bottles. We had to pull down the shades and draw the curtains when my father made moonshine in the cellar. He bought the various flavorings (Anisette, Strega) at Ventura's Drug Store on Bedford Street.

My mother canned pears from a tree we had in our yard. We also had a bing cherry tree and we had to pick the cherries as soon as they ripened, before the birds got to them. She also canned tomatoes, tomato paste, and pickled peppers. She made Italian sausage, which was hung on poles in an upstairs bedroom or put in crocks with melted lard. None of us ever got salmonella or got sick from food that was not refrigerated.

The Italian neighborhood was a one big family. We all knew one another, went to the same church, played in Columbus Park, followed the older boys to Beattie's Ledge where they "duked" it out after a disagreement.

My brothers and I respected my mother and took care of her until she died at eighty-seven years of age. We got along well. We all valued education and made sure that our children went to college.

I loved going to my non-Italian friends' homes. Their parents never spoke loudly or gestured with their hands. They spoke one language—English. It seemed that my friends were indulged more by their parents than were Italian children. Their parents were never too busy to answer their questions.

For example, one friend asked her mother, during a school-related conversation, if she could change schools and attend a parochial school the following year. The mother quietly responded with, "Your dad and I will discuss it when he comes home tonight." An Italian child's mother, when asked the similar question, would probably respond with, "Be quiet. You're giving me a headache." You never asked an Italian mother a question if you were unemployed. You could almost bet that her response would be, "Go get a job."

In Italian homes, life seemed to revolve around adults rather than children. Italian parents indulged their children, but in a different manner. Fathers "ruled the roost" and most leaned toward being either lenient or strict, silent or vocal. From my experience, some Italian fathers answered their children's questions as best they could; a lot of them understood little English and many had no formal education. Italian children were adept at interpreting their father's pauses and body and facial expressions, particularly if their questions required a yes or no answer. If Papa didn't know the answer, he would say, "Go ask your mother." Mama was always busy putting "patche" on overalls, making chicken or pigeon soup, or worrying about the future. "Who's going to make the tomato sauce and meatballs for the kids, if I drop dead tomorrow?" To successfully participate in a conversation with an Italian family, you had to have a knowledge of Italian customs and manners, basic debating skills, and a good set of lungs.

Italian parents were loyal to their children and steadfastly stood by them, no matter how bad they were. The loyalty made up for the lack of individual attention their children received.

**School Life**

Grades one through six were at the Dubuque School on Oak Grove Avenue. Grades seven and eight were at the Davis School on Quequechan Street, which is now housing for the elderly. I went to [B.M.C.] Durfee High School on Rock Street. They were the best years of my younger life.

I was very active in high school—vice president of my freshman class, homeroom director for four years, girl councilor, on the pin and ring committee, wrote articles for the school newspaper, *The Hilltop*, business manager of the record book, played basketball, and was in the National Honor Society.

I loved Mr. Ambrose Keeley, my English teacher. Mr. John Crowley was my journalism teacher and like a father figure to all of us. Mr. Keeley's classes were unique. He acted the characters in stories. Every class was interesting. Mr. Crowley was a friend and we couldn't wait to go to his class. Marie Shalloo was also a great freshman teacher. I believe she taught English. She was young, pretty, and nice to all of us. Spanish was not a favorite subject. I understood it, but had difficulty with the grammar. Adios!!

"This picture was taken of my husband and me on the wedding day of one of my son's friends. He asked for us to be his parents for the day. What an honor!"

**Recreation and Entertainment**

After I graduated from Durfee in 1945, I began to go dancing at Lincoln Park. The bus would pick up my girlfriends and me at the corner of Pleasant and Quarry Streets. It was wartime, and the hall abounded with servicemen, mostly sailors who were stationed in Newport [Rhode Island]. One time, a group of us volunteered to go on a bus provided by the naval station to Newport for a special dance.

I entertained myself by playing the piano. Still do. I was always drawing (still do) on the street with colored chalk or on any paper I could find. Yes, I caught fireflies in an empty bottle and thought it was great to watch them when it was dark.

Tag, kick the can, leap frog, hide and seek were all games we played in the neighborhood. We walked to the Narrows to swim in the South Watuppa Pond. And also walked to Lafayette Park to cool off under the sprinklers that were turned on when the weather was extremely hot.

The winters were brutal in the 1930s. When snow was plowed from the neighborhood streets, it was dumped into mounds in Columbus Park. The mounds looked like igloos. We dug holes in them or hopped from one to the other.

We would take a piece of cardboard (couldn't afford a sled) and go into the woods, where Hillside Manor is now, and slide down the snow-covered hills.

As a little girl, I frequented the public library often. It was a treat to take out books. It was a place to got to. I am still involved with the library as a member of the Friends of the Library. On the way home from the library, I would stop in the post office and pick the barrels for postage stamps. I had a stamp collection at the time. I would be thrilled to find a special one.

It was long ago, yet I still remember a pleasure many friends and I enjoyed—riding the Bedford-County bus with what adults called the "pass," and we thought was a magical ticket.

The "pass" cost one dollar in 1937, which was a lot of money at a time when workers earned five cents an hour. It was valid for one week, from early Sunday morning through Saturday night. You could ride anywhere in the city and as many times as you wished. If you had to travel to different sections of the city, you would obtain a transfer slip from the bus driver which enabled you to change buses in order to reach your final destination.

At the end of the week, when parents, aunts, uncles, and adult friends no longer needed their passes to go to work, they were given to us kids. We could hardly wait for Saturday night.

With passes in hand, we would ride from one point of town to the other—from downtown to Borden's Wharf, located off Bay Street, or Lannigan's Beach in the north end of the city, a total of approximately six miles—without getting off the bus. Some Saturday nights, we'd take a different route—from downtown we'd hop on the Pleasant Street coach and ride to the Narrows in the east end, get off, and walk to Howard Johnson's for a coffee milk shake. Howard Johnson's was a popular restaurant in the area. Its menu listed a roast lamb dinner, complete with dessert and coffee, for fifty cents, and a full-course dinner of roast rib or beef cost seventy-five cents. Ho Jo's, as we called it, also had a nifty ice cream selection—a waffle cone with two scoops of ice cream was five cents. Milkshakes were ten or fifteen cents, as I recall. Some years later, this restaurant was demolished to make way for Route 195.

One Saturday night, after having a great time bus riding around Fall River with my cousin Eda, I got home at 9:00 pm, later than usual, but who was thinking of time? I opened the door to my house and met my mother head-on. She stood there, all two hundred pounds of her, armed with a floor broom. Before I could answer her question, "Where have you been?" she swung the missile. Because I was young (ten years old), lean, and fast-moving, I was able to elude the upward/downward motion of the broom and run for a safe haven where neither could reach me. Underneath the bed in the closest bedroom was my refuge for the night.

I was grounded for several weeks after that incident. When I resumed my Saturday night jaunts, I would hide the broom before I left the house, just in case.

**Food and Meals**

Most of the vegetables that Italians served at their tables were from their own backyard gardens. Italian immigrants yearned for a return to the soil. In their backyard plots they planted herbs, tomatoes, beans, peppers, and zucchini. The grape arbor provided a pleasant place to perform household tasks and to entertain in the summer.

Italian grandmothers and mothers believed that using store-bought spaghetti sauce from a jar was the third sign of the Apocalypse. Consequently, steaming, simmering pots of tomato sauce made with fresh tomatoes, garlic, fresh basil, olive oil, and Italian sausage were common in every Italian household. Pasta, in every length and form, combined with either lentils, peas, and onions, faggioli, or potatoes, was eaten every night. Ever present on the table was a bottle of wine. Ever present in the medicine cabinet was Brioschi, the Italian Alka-Seltzer.

In contrast to the many herbs and spices Italians used in their cooking, non-Italians cooked with little else than salt and pepper. Their meals, to me, were uncomplicated with meat and potatoes seeming to be what they enjoyed most. Serving tea was a daily ritual for many of my non-Italian friends. My friends had never tasted wine. I was introduced to tapioca pudding for the first time at one of their houses. The creamy, vanilla-flavored dessert was unlike anything I had ever tasted. Besides that, the tapioca beads that the pudding was made from fascinated me. They were shaped like fish eyes. I couldn't wait to go home to tell my mother about that special pudding. It seemed that Italian children favored fresh fruit to pudding desserts, no doubt, because they were not served pudding in Italian households.

**Health and Illness**

For some reason, I had nosebleeds often. The cure was to hold a cold stove poker or hold a cold towel on the back of your neck. I believe I had chicken pox and whooping cough. Our doctor, Bernard Mangione, would come to the house carrying a small, black satchel. His fee? Nothing. My mother would force him to take a dollar.

When inoculations for the above and diphtheria were enforced, we went to a clinic on Second or Third Street (we could see the Quequechan River flowing beside the building from the clinic window). We had to wear a plastic bubble on our arm to protect a crust that would form over the inoculation. The scar could be seen for years.

**Courtship and Marriage**

My husband, Frank Botelho, was the boy next door who owned a Chevy convertible. He was handsome. Once I remarked to my girlfriend when Frank was driving by us in the car, "How would you like to own that car?" The rest is history.

He was wonderful to me. The only person who ever had brought me flowers, opened the car door for me, taught me how to drive when I was nineteen years old, and loaned me the convertible to go on a date with a former classmate who had come home on leave from the Navy.

My wedding was a small one at Holy Rosary Church (Father Pannoni). My cousin, Marguerite Vickers, was my maid of honor and Louis Botelho, Frank's younger brother, was best man. The reception was at the Sons of Italy hall. We drove to Niagara Falls and New York City on our honeymoon.

**Work Life**

Before I went to Saturday morning catechism, I washed stairs for Jewish people on Chavenson Street for twenty-five cents. My brother Frank delivered papers and would find me customers. I did housework for several Italian families to earn money. I also babysat.

During high school, I worked at McWhirr's after school from 2:30 to 5:30 pm and Saturdays from 9:30 am to 9:00 pm. I wrapped bundles to be delivered. I earned a salary of $7.53 a week.

After I graduated, an Italian contractor friend of my mother's got me a job at RCA on Wall

Street in New York City. I passed the physical and written exam and was hired to start work when my mother had me come home because she was afraid that someone was going to kidnap me on the subway. I was seventeen years old and devastated.

I came home and couldn't find an office job. A cousin of mine helped me to be hired at the American Thread Company as a machine operator. Devastation #2. I hated that job. I worked there a year and a half before I received a miracle through a friend of mine whose office manager was looking for a junior clerk with an Italian background.

I was hired at the Division of Employment (State) Security on April 6, 1947, and went up the ranks to head interviewer, retiring after almost forty-one years of service. It was a rewarding job and I assisted hundreds of people find employment.

**Neighborhood Experiences**

Mark You's was a favorite restaurant when we could spare a nickel to buy a chow mein sandwich. Bedford Street Pharmacy gave you a good-sized cone of ice cream for five cents. There was a Howard Johnson's Restaurant at the Narrows that was a favorite spot when you had an extra quarter to spare.

The Columbus Park area consisted of Italian, Irish, Portuguese, and French families. The shopped at Mauretti's Market, Leo's Store, Thistlewaite's Variety, Marum's Variety, Britto's Market, Marzilli's Bakery, Marcucci's Bakery, The Macaroni Shop, Ventura's Pharmacy, and Bedford Pharmacy.

The ragman collected rags and bottles as he pushed his cart along neighborhood streets. Milk was delivered by a horse-drawn wagon, also ice for iceboxes, fish on Fridays, and fruit the same. Peddlers would summon housewives with a horn-type speaker. The women would come onto the street wearing aprons to make their purchases.

Except for going home to lunch, having dinner, and going to sleep, my brothers and I literally lived at Columbus Park during the 1930s and 1940s. It was a safe place close to home where the neighborhood youngsters, most of whom were of Italian descent and Holy Rosary Church parishioners, played baseball, jumped hurdles, engaged in arts and crafts, and just hung out under the long-gone pavilion. It was not unusual to wait what seemed like an eternity for a turn on a swing.

My first childhood gift to my mother was made at the park when I was eight years old. I constructed a bill holder out of two paper plates, one of which was cut in half and attached to the other with colored yarn. An option to its completion, which I chose, was to paste a colored picture of flowers on the front of the holder. My mother proudly hung it on the wall next to the wooden clothes dryer in the kitchen. It probably cost a penny or two to make, but the love and pride it contained was priceless.

Summer nights were spent on the park benches telling ghost stories or seeing who could spit the furthest. The banter was light, the humor pleasant and decent—we were all so innocent.

Columbus Park provided breathing space and relief from our heavily populated neighborhood. The time spent there was educational. As youngsters, we learned how to bond, we learned fair play, we learned how to appreciate art and music. Most of all, it provided me with special memories of my childhood.

## The Depression

I can still remember walking down Bedford Street to the building across the street from the old police station to get food distributions—cabbage, carrots, bread, and margarine (it looked like lard and came with a small package of yellow coloring which you mixed with the grease so that it looked like butter). We received that and also ate the home grown vegetables and fruit from the yard trees, pigs feet and tails, chicken feet, rabbit, and lots of macaroni.

## World War II

My family was on the way to Fairhaven when we heard over the car radio that Pearl Harbor had been bombed. We were stunned by the news.

Meat and sugar was rationed as were nylon stockings. While I was in high school, I was chosen along with other students to register Fall Riverites at the Ruggles School on Pine Street. They were given ration stamps to purchase these items.

During the war, there was an aerial act that came to the city to promote the sale of war bonds. They performed in front of the beautiful city hall. Their names were Betty and Benny Fox. Dorothy Lamour also came to the city to promote the sale of bonds.

## Italians in Fall River

Italians first came to Fall River between 1890 and 1914. Most came from the southern part of Italy. Most arrived with little money and lived as boarders with Italian immigrants who had come before them. They came to make a better living than what they had in what they called "the old country."

They settled in two sections of the city—the Columbus Park area and in the south end of the city in an area known as "the Globe."

Soon, there were approximately 1,500 Italians in the city. Not long afterward, plans were made for the construction of an Italian church, Our Lady of the Holy Rosary.

Few Italians went to work in the cotton mills in Fall River. They preferred construction work and some became stonecutters at the Beattie and Wilcox quarries. Italian laborers worked a ten hour day for $1.50, the cost of an ice cream cone today.

Many Italians opened their own businesses. They opened fruit and grocery stores, bakeries, barber shops, and shoe repair shops. Others went to work in the hat manufacturing shops in the city.

Italians had strong family ties. The husband was the head of the household. The woman provided the family's strength. Italian immigrants worshiped their mothers.

Because they were poor, the food they ate was filling and inexpensive. Soup was considered a full meal. Pasta was standard fare and wine was served at every dinner.

In warm weather, Italians enjoyed picnics with their families and friends. Kratch's Grove in Westport was a favorite spot. Barrels of beer, eating, dancing, and bocce ball playing all made for a day of fun and relaxation.

## Italian Superstitions

Superstitions among Italians in my neighborhood when I was growing up were commonplace. These beliefs, practices, and customs were brought from Italy to America by the old folks, along with their other baggage. The superstitions were exercised and shared with their *paisani*.

The *malocchio*, or evil eye, was one of the most common superstitions. The obvious symptoms of this "curse" were a headache, continual yawning, and an overall feeling of tiredness. There was no mystery to these signs. They were real, believe me. I experienced "it" many times.

Evidence of the evil eye seemed to occur several hours after a person verbally complimented you without saying, "God bless you." One time, I got the *malocchio* after a friend admired my thick, curly hair. My mother always washed my hair with Octagon soap (we couldn't afford shampoo). She then banana curled my hair with strips of clean, white pieces of cloth, a la Shirley Temple, who was popular then. The compliment, minus the blessing, gave me the curse. I was doomed.

The treatment to dispel the *malocchio* was interesting and, best of all, free. When I had "it," my mother would put the pair of socks or undershirt I had worn that day in a brown paper bag and would send me along with the clothing to an elderly Italian lady named Zia Concetta, who lived on the second floor of a six-tenement house next door to our cottage.

As soon as I opened the door, and before I had a chance to answer her question, "Che succedere" (what happened), she would have the clothing out of the bag and aside the basin of water she had prepared and placed on a counter in her pantry. As I stood before her, all four feet tall and still yawning, Zia Concetta would pour a drop of pure olive oil into the basin. If the oil split in two parts and resembled eyes, I was in trouble. It always did and I always was.

Years later, when I thought of that practice, I wondered whether or not the oil actually parted. I was too scared to look.

Then, Zia Concetta would have placed one hand on her apron-covered breast, her other hand was on top of my head. She would mumble a prayer while making the sign of the cross on my forehead with her right thumb. This prayer had to be learned at midnight on Christmas eve. The ritual lasted about ten minutes and whether it was mind over matter, I felt better afterward.

When I got home, my mother would have me wash my face (with both hands in an upward direction) in a basin of cold water and salt. At the time, we believed in this ritual.

Superstitions rapidly disappeared as people became more educated. The traditional forms of beliefs or customs died with the old folks when they passed away. The symptoms thought to be the evil eye are readily cured today by taking an aspirin or Tylenol tablet.

**Final Thoughts**

I would like to be remembered as being kind and trying to do a good deed every day. I believe in God and pray every day. I tell my family to count their blessings and not to ever do things for money, for it truly is the root of all evil. And to remember me as being a good listener. I really am! Also, to never keep a grudge. It's not good for your soul or your arteries.

# Dorothy (Motta) Bouchard

*Born on July 6, 1924*

**Family Background**

My parents were Manuel and Diamentina (Barboza) Motta. My mother's parents were Frank and Theresa (Vincent) Barboza.

My sisters, in order of birth, were: me (Dorothy), Donarta (Doris), Diane (Dime), and Dolores (Curly).

My husband's name is Albert Bouchard. We were married when I was seventeen years old, in 1941. Our children are named Bobby and Allen.

**Family Life**

My father was born on Cherry Street and his family later bought a house in Swansea. My mother was born in Portugal and came here when she was five years old. She went to work in the mills at age eleven.

My uncle Richard was a milkman and had green eyes and bright red hair. He was called "carrot-top" because of his hair. He also had very white skin, like milk. People would kid him by telling him, "Your mother must have a boyfriend who was a milkman."

Milk was delivered in bottles. We had tin containers to hold milk and eggs, but we got our eggs from the farm for nothing. I believe it was Amaral's Dairy that delivered our milk.

We had an iceman and had to put a card in the window if we wanted ice. There were no refrigerators. My mother bought the first refrigerator in the family. I would buy stuff and run across the street and put my food in her refrigerator. After a while, she said, "You buy your own." We would put a pan under the icebox to catch the water.

I would take care of Diane and Curly, and when they were about fourteen, they would go up in the attic and smoke. They would open the window and blow the smoke out. My father once played a drum in parades, he really loved it, and his big old drum was in the attic. My sisters made a hole in the drum and put their cigarette butts in it. They covered for one another. My father and mother were always working, so they didn't know what was going on. Diane and Curly were like two birds of a feather.

My mother worked in the Foster Mills, where the Fall River Florist Supply is now. I and my sisters would sometimes bring her lunch. One day, my mother was sick and came home early. When she came around the corner, she froze. She saw the two birds smoking at the window. "My God," she said. "That can't be my two daughters!" Instead of taking them by surprise, she started screaming as she went up the stairs. It was hell to pay. All the screaming!

My grandmother was wonderful to me. She was a strong woman. My grandfather couldn't speak English; my grandmother could speak a little. When he got mad at the help, he would come out with English words.

My grandmother would go to Portugal every summer. We would bring her to Boston to take the boat and it would take a week to get to Portugal. She loved to go by boat. She went all by herself. She had family, including brothers, in Portugal. I was elected to help her get tickets at a travel agency located on Bay Street. She would be driven from Assonet to George Street, then we would take a bus to downtown, and transfer to the Bay Street bus. I was her translator on the bus and at the travel agency.

We would all go to Boston to see her off. We were crying and hugging her. Two to three cars went up. All of the family. The ship was right at the wharf. We stayed until the big horn blew. We told her, "Get near the rail so we can see you." There were hundreds of people waving on the wharf. My aunts would be crying. "Why are you crying; she's not dying." After her husband died, she didn't go again.

Aunt Virginia, who lived downstairs at 23 George Street, had no kids and would treat us like her children. We would obey her; she was our second mother. Diane was her pet and we all knew it. Diane could do nothing wrong.

**Barboza's Dairy**

We would go to the farm every Sunday—my mother, Diane, Curly, and me. My father wouldn't go. One of my uncles would pick us up and bring us home. It was named Hillview Farm and had a large sign. The farm had no fences and was wide open, like a ranch.

My uncle Bob and Touinette lived on the farm. In fact, his first-born died there of diphtheria at the age of four. He was my grandfather's first grandson and he was his pride and joy. When he died, we thought we were going to lose my grandfather. The boy had blond, curly hair. They didn't know what he had until it was too late. They didn't have medicines like they do today. He was laid out in the house for two days.

It was a big farm. The farm had a dairy with about thirty cows—Barboza's Dairy. The Barboza Dairy distributed in Taunton, Massachusetts. The bottles said "Barboza Dairy" and under that it said "Raw Milk." In the mornings, the cows were brought from the big barn in the back and led by two men along the driveway next to the house to the fields across the street. The men had long sticks to make the cows obey. My grandmother had beautiful flowers in the yard, but the cows never bothered them. The cows would stay in the fields all day and came back later to be milked and stay in the barn all night.

They also grew vegetables like tomatoes and corn. In the summer, the help would load a big truck with vegetables and drive to the farmer's market in Boston the night before (to avoid the traffic) to get a spot at the market for the next day. This was before the highway was built and it took a while to get to Boston. They went up often from the latter part of June through August. After that, they kept the vegetables for home use and canned a lot of them. My grandmother canned everything. I don't know how that woman did it.

They made wine on the farm. The men loved it. They would have it with their dinner.

The pig farm smelled. We were not allowed to go down there. There were flies over everything. A brook ran through the property that the pigs drank from.

Malt and hops were delivered to the farm from a brewery in Newport for the pigs to eat. It must have been good for them because the pigs were fat. The hops came in enormous trucks, with water leaking from the trucks from the wet hops. The trucks would stop by the house and the drivers would chat with my grandmother. My grandfather complained that the smell of the hops would make people say that we were booze hounds.

They killed pigs on the farm. Everyone in the family, including Curly and Diane, would go on a weekend in October from Friday to Sunday. I didn't want to go; I would cry. Three to four large pigs were killed. I hated that month. They would kill the pigs away from the house. We could hear the pigs squealing.

We arrived at the farm on Friday night and the pigs were killed early Saturday morning; many persons killed the pigs. Six to seven men helped, each knowing what they had to do. The ladies waited for the men to bring them the pork to the basement to prepare. It had to be a nice day, not raining.

First, they drained the blood in a pan to make blood pudding, morcella. Morcella had tons of ground onions and spices in it. The smell was awful!

The pork was put in large crock pots and covered with lard. The food never spoiled. The crocks were put in the back basement, which had a dirt floor and was very cold in the winter; you had to put a coat on to go in there. In the summer, it was beautiful, nice and cool.

When I was about eleven years old, I started going to the farm for the summer [most of July and two weeks in August]. I loved it! Curly and Diane didn't want to go. They were too attached to my mother.

I would sleep in the cottages in the summertime with grandmother. It was beautiful on the farm and so quiet compared to the city! But there was always something doing. People were always coming in and out to do business with my grandfather.

There a was hen house on the farm and the rooster would crow at four in the morning—I would curse that rooster—and wake us up. I would go in the hen house about 8:00 in the morning to feed the hens and collect the eggs that were laid during the night—I'd better not break any! The noise in the hen house was loud. There were so many eggs that they sold some.

The help, who were all Portuguese, ate in the basement for dinner [lunch] on long tables [with picnic-like seats]. The family was not allowed to eat with them. They would talk and laugh a lot. My grandmother would cook a hardy meal every day; you name it, they ate it. She did it all herself. I never saw anyone help her. She got up at 3:00 in the morning to do it.

There was no plumbing inside, except for the sink, so we used an outhouse. Before the farmhouse had a bathroom, we washed up in oval galvanized tubs. In summer, when it was hot and when it was dusk, people would wash up outside with a hose. I believe that plumbing came in before grandmother died, since I remember it and I didn't go to the house after she died.

I was a regular teenager and, after about fourteen, I found the farm too quiet and wanted to stay in the city.

**Food and Meals**

We had anything we wanted for breakfast. There was as much as you could eat, including bacon and eggs. We had bacon until it was coming out of our ears. Grandmother also made bread in the morning.

All our meals were hot and there were lots of vegetables. Sometimes, I wouldn't like what she cooked, like a squash soup. She would say, "If the men can eat it, you can eat it."

All the help lived in Taunton. None of them had a car. My uncle would pick them up and bring them home at 4:00 or 4:30 pm. It was nice and quiet after that. By then, we were hungry and we would have dinner and everything was hunky-dory.

My mother made white farmer's cheese. Milk was left out for one or two days to sour and then it was strained through a towel or cheesecloth. She stopped making it when it became available at the stores. The cheese was delivered on Thursdays to the Red and White Market. They still sell white cheese.

When we were young, my father made breakfast for us. We went to the Borden School and couldn't eat lunch there; we had to come home for lunch. For those kids that didn't have breakfast, the school served milk and graham crackers, but you had to pay for it. We could pass if you had breakfast at home. Later, in Morton, we had a cafeteria.

We always got dressed up for church. After Mass, we stopped for warm bread from the North Star Bakery. We always had a big dinner on Sunday, and always a roast. Family and friends would come to visit on Sundays and wouldn't leave until after supper. My mother had to cook for them. My father would go to the Republican Club.

Moy Lees was on Brightman Street, in the North End, near our house. We went there every Friday for meatless chow mein sandwiches.

**Recreation and Entertainment**

We had lots of friends. The boys couldn't come in the yard. My father wouldn't let them. Mrs. Silvia, the wife of the baker, was a devil. No one liked her. They had three or four sons who delivered the bread. In our area, there were three or four streets that were all Portuguese. Once in a while there would be a Frenchman. My father didn't like Frenchmen for some reason.

Leo's Drugstore was owned by a Frenchman. He liked my father because he was always there. My father had an account there. When we would go in for something, they would say, "Put it down for Manny's daughters."

We would go to the Royal Theater for the Saturday matinée. We had to go right home after that.

I loved the circus. It was a treat. The whole family would take the bus to the circus grounds.

**Christmas, Holidays, and Special Occasions**

At Christmas, a band would come to our door to play at 1:00, 2:00, or even 3:00 in the morning. It was a tradition in Portuguese families. The band would include Julie, Aunt Mary, and her husband. They would visit neighbors first then go to family later. The song they sang went something like, "If you give me permission to come in…," then the people inside would answer back and then let them in. They would come anytime they wanted.

My father would tell my mother, "You're not going to let them in, are you?" But, of course, she did and he got up also and let them in. You would have to give them liquor. By the time they arrived at our house, they were drunk. My mother complained to my grandmother that my father didn't like them coming so late, but she would say, "It's Christmas, what does he want?" I don't know how they got home.

When someone died, you put a wreath on the door. That's how you knew someone died. You would go to pay your respects; there were no special visiting hours. My grandparents were laid out in the house in Assonet. The wives would be upstairs and the husbands would be downstairs playing cards. The clock in the house was stopped at the hour of death.

**Neighborhood Experiences**

We got our groceries from Red and White Market on Lindsey Street. Everything was delivered: groceries, the cleaners, even the insurance man came for his payment. We had no car, and my father never drove. We called our orders in on Thursday and it would be delivered on Friday. During the week, the kids would go to the market to pick up items. The kids weren't allowed to carry money. The store kept a running account in a book of what you owed. Then you paid the deliveryman. We never lacked for anything; my mother paid some big grocery bills; we ate very well.

**Health and Illness**

Until later in life, my father never went to the hospital. My mother did, for a hysterectomy and a kidney operation. All doctors made house calls. Dr. Hughes came to the house for Alan [as late as in the 1960s].

My mother had all of her children at home. And, do you know who the midwife was? Her mother! She came from Assonet and stayed in the house until my mother had the baby. In those days, you stayed in bed for a few days after birth. No one I knew went to the hospital for babies then. Grandmother cooked for the kids while my mother was in bed. After the baby was born she went home.

When Bobby was born, we never had Pampers; all diapers were cloth. I washed clothes with a scrub board. It was metal. I have an all-wood washboard that I've had for over thirty-six years. I hung all of my clothes on the line. In the winter when you hung out the clothes, your hands would freeze and the clothes would freeze. Sometimes, you would have to hang the clothes in the cellar.

My husband's father died when he was eleven. His mother was crippled with polio and his sisters were older and married, so he had to learn how to cook.

My father with got sick with ulcers and had to stay in bed when I was fourteen years old and at Morton. My mother had to go see Miss Sullivan, the principal, to say that her husband was sick and asked if I could have a "home permit" so I could stay and take care of my father. Miss Sullivan said no, that I was advanced and should go to high school. Instead, they took Doris out of school for a while, but that didn't work out. She didn't want to do it. So, Dotty had to quit school to take care of Dad. My father stayed two years in bed. Dr. Pettrone was his doctor (his wife was a doctor, too). After that, he got up and went back to work.

We had the measles and mumps, but we never went to the hospital. If we were really bad with a fever, the doctor would come to the house. If we had a sore throat, we were given Smith Brothers cough drops. The doctor didn't agree and said they were candy.

**Work Life**

For twenty-eight years, I ironed in the sweat shops doing piece work. We had a blank piece of paper every morning next to us at the end of the table that the supervisor used to keep track of what we made that day. The boss supervisor was a German, and she was a devil. If we didn't put out enough that day, we were called into the office. There was a reason that they were called sweat shops—there was no air conditioning. The windows were opened sky high and the fans were going constantly. We would sweat like crazy. Our blouses were soaking wet. It wasn't easy. The greenhorns wouldn't complain; they were tough; but the Americans did.

My father's mother brought up Doris. I was brought up by my mother's mother. We stayed with them until we went to school. I lived on the farm until I was six. My father would get Doris from his mother's house on Friday for the weekend and would return her on Sunday night. I was brought from Assonet by a farm person. People worked ten hours in the mills. We had to be taken care of by our grandmothers.

My mother started working the second shift when we started school. My father was a bartender and could choose his hours. At that time, family took care of the children.

My mother went to work early, before the legal age, and they dressed her up in a long cotton dress to make her look older. She worked ten hours a day and walked in the snow to work.

**The Great Depression**

I remember the Depression. I was born in 1924. We wore other's clothes. Everyone went on welfare. All the jobs were gone. We got powered milk, but we used it only for coffee. At that time, my mother didn't have any work and my father was a bartender. The men always found a few pennies for a beer. There was no such thing as package stores then. If you wanted a drink, you went to a bar.

**Hurricane of 1938**

During the 1938 hurricane, I was in Morton School. The worst of it started after lunch and we were home by then. We could see the Brightman Street Bridge from our house. A ship got caught against the bridge. The bridge was closed for three days. The river was rising and we thought that we would have to leave the house. My mother said that we should get ready to leave, just in case.

**World War II**

We heard about Pearl Harbor on Sunday morning when Roosevelt came on the radio and said that the Japanese had attacked. I was married in September and the war started in December. Albert and I lived across the street from my parents. Albert was called up two times to go to Boston and left from the North Main Street train depot. He failed both times. They said he had blood problems. Eight months after the first visit, he was failed again.

The third time he was called up, he was drafted. He told his mother he was going oversees but not me. After thirty days of training in Georgia, he was shipped out. He had a one-week pass before he left. He told his mother not to tell me that he was going over.

He went to Europe on the *Queen Elizabeth* from New York City. He fought in Germany and was a prisoner of war. His own brother liberated him. His brother drove a Sherman tank. Albert didn't know that his brother would be there. The Germans ran away when the Americans arrived.

When he was liberated, Albert was full of lice and bugs. The prisoners were stripped and sprayed and their clothes burned. They were then shipped to England to go to a hospital because they were malnourished. Albert weighed eighty pounds. His brother heard the name Albert Bouchard being read and asked to see him.

# Louis Bouchard

*Born on December 8, 1918*
*Died on September 30, 2011*

**Family Background**

I was born on Plymouth Avenue, two blocks up from Rodman Street. The house is still there. I was delivered by a doctor.

My parents were Ovide and Emma (originally Emmarentinne Bruneau) Bouchard. My father's siblings were named Alfred, David, and Francois. My mother's siblings were named Joseph and Odile. My mother came from a family of seven children. Her father died in Canada and her mother immigrated to Fall River. She didn't have any family here.

My father's parents were Ovide and Marie (Guay) Bouchard. My mother's parents were Napoleon and Olive (Mimeo) Bruneau.

I have had four siblings: Charles, Louis (died at birth), Jeanne, and George.

I have lived on the following streets in Fall River: Plymouth Avenue, Rockland Street (a cottage, since torn down), East Main Street, Barrett Street, Warren Street, Oxford Street, Mott Street, and Niagara Street.

My first wife was named Doreen (Chapman) Bouchard. Marie Bouchard is my second wife. I have four children: Rosalie Lewis, Robyn, Robert Greenslade, and Janice Greenslade Kelly.

**Family life**

My first recollection was being in the carriage and a next-door neighbor was throwing stones at me. My mother came out and there was a scuffle. I remember that. Amazing how I can remember that far back. I also remember family members putting me on the back of a leather couch and letting me slide down to the seat. In those years, we didn't have the fancy things that we do today.

My dad was a teamster for Berkshire Hathaway or another big mill in town. I remember when he pulled up to our house on Rockland Street with a rig of two horses and he put me on one of the horses. What a thrill that was!

After Mass at St. Anne's Church, the men would gather in the basement of my uncle Alfred's house on Hamlet Street and have a few beers. During Prohibition, my uncle made his own brew and his own wine also. He had a cup on the table for collecting five or ten cents for a glass of beer. Once, my dad had my uncle put up a jug of wine to take home to East Main Street. It was early winter. My uncle tells my dad, "Do not go by East Main Street; go by Montaup Street." But my father was stubborn and goes home by East Main Street.

Well, a plainclothes policeman was in Talbot's Drug Store on the corner and sees my father with the jug on his shoulder. The policeman comes out and says, "Hey, stop. What have you got there?" He got a screwdriver from the druggist, opened the jug, and brought my dad down to the police station on Freedom Street and jailed him. My mother wasn't happy and gave my dad a tongue-lashing.

My father's brother, uncle David, was the oddball in the family. He didn't mince words. He hated his brother-in-law. Once, when Uncle David was taking me for a walk, we were at the corner of East Main and Hamlet Streets. Up comes his nemesis Uncle Pete Saucier, driving a team of horses. Uncle Pete was the spitting image of Buffalo Bill, complete with a goatee, etc. My uncle David said to me, "Yell out to him, 'Hey, Buffalo Bill, son of a bitch; give me a ride.'" I did. Uncle Pete pulled the horses up in a flash. I told my parents, "Uncle told me to say it," but I got a licking anyway.

My cousins, Alfred's sons, were cut-ups. It was hellish when they got together. The brothers were in the contracting business. All my uncles were carpenters except my dad. My cousin Albert, Alfred's son, was called "The Pope" because he was infallible; he knew everything. Albert once drove my mother, brother, and me to a farm in Tiverton, Rhode Island, to pick blueberries. The road going into the farm had deep ruts in it. Cousin Albert was a speed king and drove fast down the road as we came out of the farm. The blueberries were flying all over the back of the truck. My mother kept yelling at him to slow down.

Once, Albert was building a house on Palmer Street and the stairs were not yet installed. They were plastering the walls upstairs, and there were huge tubs of plaster with lime in them. I was just a young kid, and he had me go to the second floor to get a hammer. They then took the ladder down and I couldn't get down and started crying. I had to jump off the second floor. They caught me, but just barely, and my hands fell into the plaster and burned me. My mother sailed into them.

Back then, there was a big to-do when a house was hooked up with electricity. When I was little, one of the other children asked me to blow on a light bulb. When I did, they flipped a switch and the light came on. "Oh, my God," I said. That was when electricity was still new.

We placed a card in the window if we wanted ice. The iceman would carry a chunk of ice with a cover pad on his shoulder. He used a pair of tongs. He delivered the ice to the iceboxes that were located in the hallway, not in the house. Each family had their individual icebox in the hallway. No one went into the other's icebox. This was an understanding and this was always respected. The pans under the iceboxes had to be changed regularly. In the wintertime, we didn't have ice delivered—food was put out on a shelf that was hooked on to the windowsill from the outside.

We spoke French at home. When we started going to school, it faded from home use. Both parents applied for and got citizenship. After that, French was spoken only occasionally. When family gathered, a mixture of English and French was spoken.

Before the telephone, we waited until we saw one another to talk. We visited back and forth. There were days when you went out to visit relatives or the relatives lived close to you. Aunt Odile, my mother's sister, lived off of Rodman Street near Brayton Avenue. That area was called "Pig Town" because there were small farmers there that had pigs. We lived on East Main Street at the time. When we walked over to visit, there was a small brook in the woods near Brayton Avenue and Rodman Street that we crossed. When we came out of the woods, my aunt would say, "Here they come. I'll put more potatoes in the pot."

While at St. Anne's School, we came home for lunch. Then my mother got a job at the King Philip Mill working as a spinner. We would go home and my grandmother would have lunch ready to take to my mother. I would take the lunch pail and deliver it to my mother, then I would rush back to have my lunch, and then go back to school.

The spinning room was loud, but not as loud as the weaving room, with the frames that went back and forth. One time, when I left the spinning room, something came across me and I took both hands and ran my fingers along the threads on a spinning machine and broke all the threads. My mother was not happy and put a fright into me. I never did that again!

My mother and father were quiet, my father especially. They were strict but lovable. My mother could be playful. When she was pregnant with her last child, she went out and played skip-rope with the kids.

My first wife and I rented an apartment on Warren Street, then a cottage at 100 Oxford Street. We were friendly with Walter Broughton of Broughton Cleaners, and he had lived there and was moving. He suggested that we buy the place, and we did.

When I was stationed in New Zealand, my wife joined me there. Shortly after, her mother became seriously ill and my wife went back to live with her mother. It was a long ride in a prop plane! We had a child by then who was sixteen months old.

We stayed there for three years, me as a civilian. I worked there first at an auto repair garage and then went to a major retail store servicing their fleet as a mechanic. That company had a subsidiary and they had an opening. The subsidiary was Hobart Berkell; they made food slicing machines and things like that. I stayed with them as a serviceman. I went out in the field and serviced and sold equipment.

When we came back to the United States, and I was rehired at Everett Motors. I worked my butt off by going to school and training at General Motors centers. I was fortunate enough to become service manager at the dealership on South Main Street. In those days, Oliver Street went to St. Anne's School, and Everett Motors was located there. We sold and serviced Cadillacs and Oldsmobiles. I was there for thirty-three years.

I lost my wife after she gave birth to our second child. Prior to my wife's death, we got involved in St. Luke's Episcopal Church. I offered my services as a Sunday School teacher. A few years passed, and I was elected to Senior Warden of the parish, which is second in command of the church. I served in that capacity for twenty-one-and-a-half years.

A few years passed, and then the husband and father of a parishioner died when a storm came up while they were on a fishing trip off of Cuttyhunk. She was left a widow with two children. Time passed, and we were married and remained married for forty years. I lost her in 2000.

**Friends**
Oscar Martel (called "Minnie") was my closest friend. There were ten children in his family. His father was a loom fixer. His father bought a new car and was underneath the car fixing it every weekend. This became a ritual. His wife became frustrated and kept asking, "Why don't we ever use it?" They lived on Vale Street in a three-decker. The Gagnons lived on the first floor, the Martels on the second floor, and the Paquettes on the third floor. A portion of the basement was given over to the boys for a playhouse. It was nice of them.

Mr. Martel made his own brew. Mrs. Paquette made pickles and stored the jars in the basement. One day, the boys began dipping into the pickles. Soon, Mrs. Paquette began noticing that some of her pickles were missing. Mr. Martel also noticed that the flue to the chimney wasn't working as it should. He checked into the flue and found it full of pickle jars.

Roland Gagnon and Ferdinand LeMay were both good friends. I was brought up with them. They were both killed during the Normandy invasion.

**School Life**

I went to St. Anne's School for eight years and graduated from there. Girls were on one side of the school and boys were on the other. We spoke English in the morning and French in the afternoon. One teaching nun was my cousin, my father's brother's daughter. I said hello to her, and she said, "I'm not your cousin here; I'm Sister Bernadette." The brothers were tough; both the nuns and the brothers were strict. We were taught by both nuns and brothers. As penance, the sisters would make us kneel on dry peas spread on the floor. The nuns had clickers that were used as signals. Instead of shouting to the group, they used the clickers.

The brothers could be equally mean. In the rear of St. Anne's School was a retaining wall, with the top sloped to drain water. There was a brother at the school, Brother Albert, who was a snotty little bugger. Once, when a boy was walking on the top of the wall, he whistled to the boy and pointed his finger at him to come down to him. He kept his finger out until the boy got in front of him. He then slapped the boy in the face and gave him a tongue-lashing.

I remember vividly walking to school and then us kids remaining in line with our fingers on our lips so we wouldn't talk. We had to do this only for the early grades. When school let out, everyone formed ranks as to where they lived. Guides marched us from the schoolyard to Osborne Street, all the way up. A leader was chosen from the class. First the nuns and brothers would lead, then a student led us the rest of the way.

Those were happy days there; some were difficult. One time, I was punished for doing a paper poorly and had to do it over a hundred times. To shorten the process, I took two pencils in one hand and wrote two lines at a time. So I had to do it only fifty times.

When I went to Henry Lord Junior High, the boys and girls were mixed together. My God; boys and girls mixed! It took me a while to adjust, but it wore off after a while.

One teacher left quite an impression on me and many others in the city. Her name was Doris Fitton, an English teacher at Henry Lord. She was a wonderful teacher. Miss Fitton was so involved in literature that she tried to get her students to do the same. When she covered *Romeo and Juliet*, for example, she not only read the parts but also had us read them. We thought she was a bit eccentric and a bit of a wacko at first, but we got to love playing the parts and were eager to be the first in line to read. She was a marvelous, exceptional person. Other teachers were great, too, but she really stands out.

At Henry Lord, we had some of our classes in quonset huts that were on either side of the main school building. They were heated with pot-bellied stoves in the entrance, with long flues at each side. Each hut had two separate rooms. It was cold inside. Instead of going out to get in line, we would open the windows and jump out. Those were good memories.

**Recreation and Entertainment**

We played peggy ball in the street, in this case Vale Street. There were no homes there at that time, so we played in the field. In the wintertime we went tobogganing. We tobogganed and sledded down Osborne Street, also on Sprague Street to Bay Street. We used a bow-top toboggan with six people on it. The person in front would steer the toboggan with his right foot. We would slide all the way from Broadway down Sprague Street across Bay Street and plowed into a chain-link fence.

We also went ice-skating on the South Watuppa. We gathered at the Narrows at a shop called Napert's. They had a huge pot-bellied stove. There was a bench there to warm up and chat. There

St. Anne's School, Forest Street, Fall River

was a small pond and the big pond. We were warned not to go on the big pond, but we went anyway. We would open our coats and the wind would push us down to the other end of the pond. It was tough getting back, though, because we were going against the wind. The ice was thick.

In the coldest part of winter, I remember horses pulling a wagon on the ice on Mount Hope Bay and men cutting the ice with hand saws to open up the channel so the ships to go through—the bay was frozen that much!

In the summer, we would go down to Staples Wharf to swim. If you didn't swim, you were pushed off the wharf and had to learn how to swim. No one chased us away. We weren't destructive and, as long as we weren't, no one bothered us.

**Work Life**

The Depression was difficult, but we managed. My father lost his teamster's job and we had to get help for a while. We would go to the corner of Plymouth Avenue and Rodman Street to the main office of the Richard Borden mill. There they distributed food, like potatoes, to the needy. My father later became a painter and decorator.

I attended one year at [B.M.C.] Durfee High School, but had to leave because my dad lost his job. When I was seventeen or eighteen, I worked in the King Philip Mill as a sweeper. Two young men and I went to Bridgeport, Connecticut, to look for work. We got a place for one person and the other two snuck in at night. They were not hired but I was. We continued the sneak-in arrangement, but it was too much. I came back to Fall River and got part-time work. I went to Bradford Durfee Tech for about a year and worked in their machine shop.

I was not happy with my life and condition. A friend of mine mentioned the local union, the ILGWU [International Ladies Garment Workers Union]. She got me interested. I was interviewed by a company representative and got a strike for thirteen weeks. The union was taken by my work and hired me. I worked for the union as an organizer. It was frightening. I had nothing to sell but protection. Every time I went to a door, I had no idea what the reception would be. Parents would say, "Union no good." The threats were frequent and scary. We tried to organize Har-Lee on Pleasant Street at the time. Many of the union officers were threatened and beat up.

My wife was worried. "Chuck it in; life is worth more," she would say. One of the employees of the union had a husband who was starting a business of his own. He took me on, but the work was too much for him and he got out of it. I then went to Diman [Diman Regional Vocational Technical High School] on the GI Bill and did well. When I got back, I found employment at Everett Motors. I went to school to learn about autos. When the service manager became ill, I was approached about replacing him temporarily. However, he passed away and I became the service manager of the dealership. It was a different life, I'll tell you.

**Neighborhood Experiences**

In the winter, ice would accumulate in the recesses around the trolley tracks. People and merchants along the street would pour hot water on the tracks to melt the ice. People helped one another more then than now.

We walked to most places. We walked to Capitol Beach, which was beyond Sandy Beach. It was a wooded area way down the bottom of the last street in the city. Capitol Park had just a beach and a wooded area for picnicking. Sandy Beach was very crowded then. As a young man, I would go to the South Park [now Kennedy Park] pavilion to see the Fall River Line boats go by with all of their lights on. It was very impressive. Horses hauled bales of cotton to one plant to another and to the railroad yards. Delivery of ice was by horse. Farmers came by horse and wagon.

**Downtown**

When we lived on East Main Street, I went with my mother downtown to the People's Market. I remember walking back and carrying parcels home with her. Later, I went downtown with my two youngsters on Saturdays to one of the 5 & 10s, such as Woolworth's. We would have a sundae there and they loved it. It became a ritual with us. We went through the shops, bought them clothing. Easter was a special time, especially for clothes.

Van Dykes coffee shop was special. You could smell the coffee grounds as you crossed the street. The odor of coffee was wonderful. The Nonpareil was very clean and the place to meet friends. Next to Van Dykes was a hat blocker and shoeshine place. I remember as a young man going there to get my first shoeshine. I still have my shoeshine box after all these years.

**Health and Illness**

When I had an earache as a child, my father had his own way of curing it. He smoked a pipe, and to cure my earache, he would take the lit pipe, wrap a cloth around the end of the stem of the pipe, put the end in my ear, and blow into the bowl so that the hot smoke would come into my ear. The hot smoke gave me relief; it worked!

South Park, later renamed Kennedy Park

I didn't get many colds. When I did get sick, my mother would make a concoction of molasses and some other ingredients that tasted awful.

When someone died, they were waked in the house. There would be a bough or wreath on the door to signify that someone had died. It was typical that the females gathered around the body and the men gathered in the other room to drink and talk.

**Hurricane of 1938**

During the hurricane of 1938, I was working in a mill off of Bay Street where the Kuss School is now. They let us out. I walked home up Globe Street to South Main Street, where I had to hang on to a utility pole, the wind was so strong. It was one heck of a disastrous storm.

**World War II**

We were living on Barrett Street when Pearl Harbor was announced. A few months later, I got drafted. We went to Boston on a bus, we raised our hand, and we were in. We didn't come back home to say goodbye. Everyone wanted to call home.

During World War II, I was in the Army for three-and-a-half years and spent three years overseas. After basic training on the West Coast, I went to New Zealand. I rose to the rank of staff sergeant, supply sergeant. I was the meanest SOB in the Army. It was tough to get supplies and I was tough giving them out.

It took twenty-three days to get from San Francisco to New Zealand because we had to zigzag the whole way to avoid enemy submarines. We arrived at New Zealand and boarded a train to go to the training camp. The highlight of the six weeks of training was that we got to go on leave for eight hours. They drove us by truck to Auckland and dropped us off at Queen Street. We went up and down the street looking at shops and people. Well, lo and behold, there was a USO on the street on the second floor. We began to go up the stairs and, halfway up, a Marine was coming down. We may have been Americans, but we were from different outfits. We bumped shoulders, and got our fists ready to have a go at each other. We got ready to hit, and then he says, "Jesus Christ!" It was Philippe Desruseau from my class at St. Anne's School. I had graduated with him. We hugged one another and then went inside, had a few coffees, and gabbed and gabbed.

My last stop was in Saipan, off the coast of Japan. When the war ended, the CO was reassigned to lead a unit into Japan, but I had enough and wanted to get back home. The service makes you realize how wonderful this country is.

I came out of the service a different person. I was freer, more cognizant of others. I was rather disappointed with the people of Fall River, especially its leaders, and in the abilities and knowledge of Fall River compared to where I had been. One night I went to a City Council meeting. There was a dispute between the city and Coca Cola about locating on Davol Street. The lawyers for Coca Cola spoke their piece. After that, one City Councilor said, "Listen, yous guys." I wanted to crawl under my seat.

**Ending Thoughts**

My philosophy is live for today; no one knows what tomorrow will bring. Tomorrow may never come.

South Main Street, looking north

# Priscilla (Getchell) Brightman

*Born on October 5, 1932*

**Family Background**

I was born in Fall River at Union Hospital. We lived at 8 Knox Street and I have lived here all my life. My parents were Daniel Lynwood and Eunice (Terry) Getchell.

My siblings (in birth order, including me) were: Sally Ann (she died at age seven and a half), Choice Elizabeth, Priscilla Catherine, Dawson Macomber, and Hope Christine.

My father's parents were Augustus and Mary G. (Mahoney) Getchell. My mother's parents were William H. and Catherine (Macomber) Terry.

My father's siblings were Eva and John S. Getchell.

My mother's siblings were Choice (Terry) Butler and Preston Terry.

My husband is Robert Nilson Brightman [Robert's interview follows this one in the book] and we have two children: Alan Clifford Brightman and Steven Robert Brightman.

There are a lot of Getchells in Maine. My grandmother on my father's side was in a convent school in Chelsea. My grandfather was on his way down from Maine to work on a potato farm at the end of New Boston Road owned by Sam Hyde. Along the way, my grandmother ran away with him. She was Irish through and through.

**Family Life**

My great-grandfather built this house in 1864. Coal was brought into our house in a canvas bag attached to a person's back. The man would squat and position the bag at the back of the coal truck and someone would open the chute and fill the bag. They would then walk down the cellar stairs and empty the bag in the coal bin. The men were all as black as your hat. You couldn't tell who they were. It was a terrible job. Imagine what they inhaled!

Sometimes, my grandmother would babysit for us and would put our hair up to curl it. She asked for rags and then tore them up in long strips. She would then wet our hair with a solution of sugar and water and roll up the hair with the strips and tie them up. We all looked like Topsy. Our hair was stiff in the morning when we took out the rags.

We were the last house to get modern conveniences, including TV. We had lots of food to eat, and if we were sick, we went to a doctor. We didn't have that many home remedies. If we got sick from a cold, there would be custard in the oven and soup for us.

My Irish grandmother was born on St. Patrick's Day. We would ask her, "When's your birthday, Grandmother?" She would reply, "The 17th of Ireland, lovey." She called all of us "lovey." We would also ask her, "How old are you?" and she would reply, "Twice as old as half." We never knew what half was.

Once, my grandfather Terry got spiffed up to go downtown. My grandmother became worried that he hadn't come home yet. He later walked in and said, "I got myself a jitney." That surprised us, since he was born here and no one called cabs jitneys.

We had electricity here but no gas lines, so, before electricity, we used kerosene lamps for light. I remember that we had an icebox and everyone had to empty the pan. My grandfather solved this problem by putting a drain line through the floor into the basement. The first refrigerator we had was a gas one. We also had a Vulcan hot water heater, which was round and had a door that opened to a gas grate that was lit when needed. Before that, we had to heat our hot water on the stove.

**School Life**

I went to the Academy of the Sacred Hearts Elementary School, then to the Sacred Hearts Academy on Prospect Street. The elementary school was located in the Catholic Women's house, next to the Bishop's house, on Highland Avenue at Lincoln Avenue.

I have lived in Fall River all of my life, except when I was away at school at Fitchburg State and Burbank Hospital Fitchburg. I then went to Union Hospital Nursing School and taught there for ten years.

Each hospital in the city had its own nursing school with its own faculty. The Union's nursing school was located at the hospital, except the science classes, which were taught at Bradford Durfee Tech. The Union Hospital Nursing School faculty had to cover for staff on weekends and during severe snow storms. The three schools ceased and merged into one program when Bristol Community College and UMass Dartmouth started their nursing schools.

**Recreation and Entertainment**

In the summer, we spent a lot of time at Horseneck Beach. Before the 1938 hurricane, we would put a tent on the beach and stay there days on end. All of the beach was privately-owned. The hurricane leveled all of the houses on East Beach to a pile of rubble.

My mother and father were both horse people, so we went to every horse show we could find, including those at North Park. My mother and father would ride all the way to Horseneck Beach on horses because the salt water was good for the horses' feet and legs.

Dr. Atwood's daughter Betty (who was the wife of Rev. Robert Lawrence) was a horse woman. She was one of the prettiest things you could see on a horse. Her horse's name was Golden Dream. We also went to the circus grounds near Bay Street. I remember that they were good circuses. We went to South Park [now Kennedy Park] for fireworks on the 4th of July.

We were happy kids. There was always something to do: hopscotch, jump rope, roller skates with keys to tighten them on your shoe.

Some of my classmates sang on various radio programs on Saturday mornings. Dr. Buck's oldest son had a beautiful voice. His name was Alfred Augustus Buck, or "Buzzy" Buck.

**Work Life**

My father had eleven cows on the Lapre's turkey farm, where Bishop Connolly High School is now. My father also had a dairy on New Boston Road, where Reed Street ends. It was called the Highland Creamery. We had one car. It was a Beach Wagon. Its seats were removable, and my father removed them to deliver milk. On Sundays, my father put the seat back in the Beach Wagon. On Saturdays, my mother would go to collect the milk money and sell eggs we had from chickens on our place. She would pile us into the car if she couldn't find a babysitter.

On Sundays, we went to Lizzie Borden's church, the Central Congregational Church. We would ride down to the church in a limousine with Aunt Mary, who lived next door and was named Mary Ella Young; the chauffeur was Lloyd Dixon. Lizzie Borden's chauffeur, Mr. Ernest Terry, was a cousin of ours. The Terrys were on my mother's side.

My father worked seven days a week. He pasteurized milk for two other farms. During World War II, all the help went into the service, so he ended up selling the dairy to Arthur Guimond. Guimond bought up a lot of dairies during the war. Then, my father became Guimond's manager. He said that he was going to sleep one day a week, and he could do it once he sold the cows.

My grandfather who lived with us was a stickler. He didn't like it if we went on the stone walls. If it rained, we were not to walk on the wet grass because it would make footprints on the grass. Once, he suspected that the boys next door had walked on the wet grass, so, when they visited and took off their boots, my grandfather took the boots and matched them to the footprints on the wet grass. This caused some tension among the families.

My first jobs were babysitting. I was also a waitress at the nurses' home at Union Hospital. Pay was awful for nursing. We got a little more than school teachers, then the teachers got a jump.

**Neighborhood Experiences**

All of the Terrys lived in this area. My great-grandfather lived in the house next door. My family had goats, chickens, and rabbits. When I was young, this area was not developed and was mostly open space. At that time, before Route 24 was built, President Avenue ended at Elsbree Street. The Morin's had a farm at the end of President Avenue at Elsbree Street, on the right.

The house that is now at the corner of Rosedale and Ward Streets was originally at the end of New Boston Road when Route 24 was put through. It was Dr. Murphy's place. They had horses and a riding school there, called Murphy's Riding School, and was operated by Mrs. Murphy.

The area from Ward, Garden Street, and New Boston Road was all orchard, with wetlands and a pond. The pond was close to New Boston Road. There were lots of wetlands here then.

Warburton's Florist and their greenhouses were located on New Boston Road, where Garden Street meets and where the Kimwell Nursing Home is now. The Warburton's had a florist shop downtown on Bedford Street. Their place later became King's Florist, who also had greenhouses on Meridian Street. There was a brook there that came from this area.

There were no homes from Stetson to Ward Streets; it was a field. Pearce Street ended at Stetson. It was all fields and woods here. We would ride horses in the area. People walked through here a lot, including on their way to Holy Name Church. They would stop in for a cup of tea.

My father said that he remembered the totally-blind fish monger who came through the neighborhood in his horse-drawn wagon. If a person asked for a fish, he would take it and fillet the fish on the wagon. My father also said that there was a one-armed paper hanger who lived on Warburton Street. He could cut, paste, and get the paper on the wall easily.

When my mother and father were growing up, the bishop had horses on his property. They could be seen from the bishop's house. My mother and father would go get the bishop's horses and ride them. One day, a nurse came to the bishop's house and she knew my father. The bishop said, "I wonder who those children are who exercise my horses?" Then they could go "exercise" the horses anytime. My father would grin every time my mother told the story.

Both of my parents rode horses in the Newport horse shows for the Vanderbilts and others. They kept the winnings, since the owners only kept the ribbons.

Angus Bailey lived in a house that was located where Tedeschi's [convenience store] is now, on the northwest corner of New Boston Road and Robeson Street. Murray's Drug Store was on the northwest corner of New Boston Road and Madison Street. We would stop at the fountain there on the way home. It's now a beauty parlor.

There was a little market near Charlotte Street on New Boston Road. Abe Packer was the owner. My mother would tell me to go there to pick up something. "He knows what I want," she would say. He would give me calf's liver, sliced very thin. My mother would make it with onions and bacon.

There were a lot of kids around here. My mother had five and took in a cousin for seven years. This was a two-family house then. There were five boys living next door.

**World War II**

During World War II, there was a Victory Garden at the top of President Avenue at Garden Street, on the General Hospital site, where President Village is now. We had our own Victory Garden at the Terry farm on Meridian Street. Our two great aunts (who were Macombers) also lived on Meridian Street.

**Fall River Lore**

On New Boston Road, at the bottom of Garden Street, was the house of Ernest Terry. He was the chauffeur for Lizzie Borden. He is the only one who stayed with Lizzie and Emma. His house was a one-story small house that he lived in with his wife. When he told Lizzie that they were going to have a child, Lizzie said he had to put a second floor on the house. She said that she would pay for it provided she could name the child. The child was a girl and named Grace. Lizzie paid for Grace to attend Simmons College. The couple next had a boy. Lizzie named him Alden, and she put him through medical school. Grace is still alive and living in New Hampshire. We saw Alden every now and then, but he ended up in Kentucky. One day, he was teaching Sunday School and, as he walked out of the building, someone shot him. His widow and children went to New Hampshire to live near Grace.

# Robert Nilson Brightman

*Born on February 6, 1927*

### Family Background

I was born in Fall River at General Hospital on a stormy winter's day. My father was Richard Brightman. He was English and a captain in the Fall River Fire Department and served at the Prospect Street station and the Stanley Street station, among others. My mother was Veda Branzell. Her family was from Sweden. After my mother was born here, she and her parents returned to Sweden, then came back. My father had one brother, Charles Brightman, but my mother was an only child.

I had one sibling, Richard (an older brother, who is now deceased).

My father's parents were Charles and Almy Jane Brightman.

My mother's parents were P. August (1864-1929) and Hilma J. (Nilson) Branzell (1872-1938).

I am married to Priscilla (Getchell) Brightman [Priscilla's interview precedes this one in the book] and we have two sons: Alan C. and Steven R.

My early Swedish relatives came to the Arlington area. They sponsored my maternal grandparents to come here. My grandfather was an iron worker and made lots of gates and fences for the mansions in Newport. We would take Grandmother Hilma Branzell out every Sunday afternoon for a drive.

### Family Life

My family lived at 838 Robeson Street, opposite the Elite Garage, which is now the Highland Restaurant Supply. The garage became a Guimond Farms garage and then the Highland Restaurant Supply. The house was owned by my mother's parents. When my grandfather died, my grandmother moved to another place and we moved from the third floor to the first.

Every Saturday, the supper ritual was hot dogs and beans and brown bread. On Sundays we had roasts.

I had to tend the furnace, which included taking out the ashes and disposing them. The coal came out of the coal truck via a chute from the street. Or the coal was carried in on the back of a person in leather satchels. Later they got sophisticated and shot the coal in through the front cellar window into bins. Ashes from the furnace were used to put on sidewalks when it snowed. It was pretty messy. My other chores included cutting grass, shoveling snow, or raking leaves in our yard. I would also go to the A&P on New Boston Road for daily food needs.

I had a paper route on Sundays. The papers were dropped off at the corner of Hanover Street and New Boston Road and I would distribute them with my wagon. It was my first job. I also worked in Carlton Dubitsky's Highland Drug Store, on the northwest corner of Robeson Street and New Boston Road, and Yates Drug Store, on the northwest corner of New Boston Road and Charlotte Street. During the busy Christmas season, I worked for the post office delivering mail.

We played on Berry's lot, an open lot on Hanover Street. Back then, there was a separate wet garbage pickup by the city. For a Halloween prank, we would take a neighbor's garbage can and hang it on a telephone pole. Telephone poles then had spikes in them to allow telephone and electrical workers to climb them.

On Saturday morning, we would go to the Durfee Theatre. It was five cents for the bus, ten cents to get into the Saturday morning show, and five cents for a candy bar. There was a short feature, previews, cartoons, and the main feature. The main feature was a Tarzan movie or a cowboy picture.

It was a happy time; we never knew there was a Depression, since my father had a pay from working in the Fire Department. Gas was nineteen cents (or less) a gallon and a loaf of bread was ten cents.

**School Life**

I went to the Highland School, Morton Junior High School, and [B.M.C.] Durfee High School, where I graduated in 1945. I have lived in Fall River my whole life, except for my military service. I got my diploma early from Durfee and left at the end of February, 1945, to join the Navy.

**Recreation and Entertainment**

I belonged to a football team named the "Highland Wildcats." We kids also played pick-up football and baseball. We played against other neighborhoods. We also played peggy ball on Madison Street. It's a wonder that we didn't break any windows there. We used the Highland School field to play ball. After Christmas, we would collect Christmas trees and make tepees with them. We would slide all the way down Pearce Street, almost to North Main Street. It was quite a walk back up the hill. For the smaller kids, sledding was on Pearce Street, from Robeson to Stetson. I was also in the Boy Scouts and camped at Camp Noquochoke in Westport. I am still involved with the scouts as the chairman of the board for Troop 24.

**World War II**

I was in the Navy in World War II and in the Korean War. After World War II, I left the Navy in 1946 and entered Brown University on the GI Bill. I graduated from Brown with a degree in mechanical engineering. I then went into the Naval Reserves to supplement my income.

When the Korean War broke out, I was the first in Fall River to be called into active duty. I went to Officer Candidate School in Newport, commissioned an ensign, and then rose to the rank of lieutenant commander.

# Isabelle (Cunha) Cabral

*Born on July 4, 1919*
*Died in 2014*

**Family Background**

My parents were John (born in Portugal) and Mary (Lima) Cunha (born in Fall River). I don't know any aunts or uncles on my father's side, but my mother had three siblings: Manuel, Joe, and Isabelle.

My father's parents remained in Portugal and I don't know their names. My mother's parents were Manuel Curt Lima Sr. and Maria (Miranda) Lima.

Grandfather Lima didn't know his parents. He came over here as a stowaway on a ship. He was thirteen years old at the time. He said that he was brought up by an aunt and uncle. He was leaving them to have a new life in America. When he first came over, he boarded with the Miranda family who lived Down North. He fell in love with the youngest girl, Maria.

There are persons called *miranos* in Portuguese who are part Jewish. I'm sure that Grandfather Lima had Jewish blood in him. Grandfather recalled that Friday evenings were a ritual of prayers with the lighting of candles. He liked beet soup (his name for it), which is the same as borscht. He was an astute businessman and saved his money. When he arrived in the city, he went to work in the Mechanics Mill on Davol Street.

I have one sibling, a sister named Maria ("Mamie").

My husband's name was Gilbert Cabral (his family lived on St. Mary Street). Gilbert died in 1965. We had one child, John.

We have lived on the following streets in Fall River: North High Street (to the rear of St. Joseph's Church), Thompson Street, Oregon Street (when I worked in the store), and Covel Street (we lived on the first floor and Mom and Mamie lived on the second).

**Family Life**

They called my father "professor" because he could hold a conversation quite well. We always had reading material in the house. He had National Geographic history books that were paid by the month. My father spoke English at all times. He was a salesman. My father died when I was ten and Mamie was eighteen.

My father built me a doll's house with intricate pieces of furniture. He would buy small dolls at the 5 & 10, cute little dolls. I would make coverlets and shams for the doll's house.

Grandfather Lima owned one house with six tenements on the northeast corner of Oregon and Cory Streets. The Lima store was on the corner. One entrance was on Cory Street and one on Oregon Street. On the Cory Street entrance, on the second floor, over the store, lived Mrs. Bertha Larchevesque and her son Alfonse and daughter-in-law, Rita Larchevesque. On the third floor lived Mrs. Larchevesque's mother. A third tenement was on the first floor in back of the store. That was where my grandparents lived with Isabelle and Joe. Before the store was there, it was a coal store.

The Oregon Street entrance to the building was just north of the store. This is where Uncle Manuel and Minnie lived when they first got married. That is also where we moved to when we moved from the North High Street house.

My grandfather owned two stores, the market on Oregon Street and a market in Somerset [Massachusetts] on Riverside Avenue that was operated by Uncle Joe. The Somerset store was a small place, with things like vegetables and canned goods. However, Joe was enterprising, and if someone wanted something that he didn't have, he would get it from the main store.

I liked Uncle Joe. He had a different temperament from Uncle Manuel. He had nothing in common with Uncle Manuel. He was more easy-going. Uncle Joe was a bachelor until he got married in his forties. He married a widow with no children named Connie. He wanted a family. They had two children together, James and Joseph. I would sing to them as children.

Isabelle forced Joe out of the Somerset store after he was married. He then got the store on the northeastern corner of Eastern Avenue and County Street. After they were married, Joe and Connie moved to an apartment in a duplex on Hood Street, near General Hospital.

Isabelle was engaged to a man who was killed in World War I. She always kept a picture of him on her bureau. His family had a grocery store in the Flint. She had quite a trousseau, with beautiful things in it, such as beautiful crystal, linens, and gold and sterling silver artifacts.

Uncle Manuel worked as a meat jobber for Armour Provisions in Fall River, on Durfee Street.

My grandfather and I would come early in the morning to open the store and lower the awnings. I did this because my grandfather had heart problems. My grandfather later had a heart attack in front of me and fell over on the counter; he died from that attack.

We had large bread bins at the store for Sunbeam and other breads. There were a few left-over day-old breads on the side. Most of the people who bought the day-old bread had big families and were poor. When children came in, they always received some candy from me or my grandma.

The Torres family lived diagonally across the store at Oregon and Cory Streets, on the southwest corner. They were sponsors for the feasts at St. Michael's Church. Beatrice, me, and the Torres daughters (Lea and Millie) would march in the processions.

Prior to the Hanover Street house, the Manuel Limas lived in the house at the northwest corner of North Main Street and President Avenue. Aunt Minnie sold cloth from a store in the basement of the building. They also owned a two-family cottage to the rear of this building. Behind that was Morton Junior High School. The kids were reared more in this house than the Hanover house.

Aunt Minnie founded the Portuguese American Civic League of Fall River. Mrs. Olivia Perry assisted her in this effort. My sister Mamie helped her when Aunt Minnie had her lawn parties at the Hanover Street house. Mamie wore a frilly apron to serve food.

Beatrice liked the finer things of life. She was the first child and therefore closest to her mother. I had different surroundings that made me more stable. One time, Bea had a small store on South Main Street and I went to see her. The store didn't last long.

Uncle Manuel would go to Boston to Mr. Cohen's to buy bolts of material for the North Main Street store. There were so many seamstresses around then.

One of the bolts of material was my graduation dress gift. Aunt Isabelle made the dress. They don't have that kind of material (called dimity-voile) any more. It was embroidered with flowers in the material. Isabelle made a dress for me and Beatrice from ponge taffeta; Isabelle was a gifted seamstress.

My mother worked in the mills before my sister was born; once Mamie was born, she didn't work any more. When she became a widow, we supported her.

**Food and Meals**

Almost every Saturday we would go to the Central Lunch on Central Street downtown to have lunch. When we walked in, they would say, "Here comes the Lima brood." We would sit in the booth and the owner would come around.

On Sundays, we would go to my grandmother's home and she would always serve me hot Ovaltine. Later, I would help my grandmother make beet soup (borscht) for Grandfather. We would take the beets and cook them and peel them. Then we would cut them up and put them in the small grinder that was in the store. Then she would make the soup from that.

My mother cooked more English-style than Portuguese-style dishes. She had English or Irish friends that she worked with, and they became bonded.

**Recreation and Entertainment**

I loved movies and would go with my two girlfriends. We always stopped at The Nonpareil for an ice cream treat afterwards. We were at the Empire Theatre when Pearl Harbor was bombed and it was announced on the screen. Our money was refunded. All of us were stunned and crying and hugging. I will always remember that Sunday afternoon.

In my teens, I didn't stay at the store all of the time but would be with my girlfriends. I would always think of something for us to participate in. On a rainy Saturday, I would organize and coordinate a drama, mostly skits, that we held in the store basement. I would always take along an assortment of penny candies for the audience. I loved the story of *Little Women* and adapted it for our dramas, along with Nancy Drew mysteries, etc.

**Courtship and Marriage**

Gilbert was in the Navy in World War II. He was a handsome sailor with a flock of hair. He looked like Harry James. His family came from Down North, near St. Mathieu's School, and he was baptized in St. Michael's Church. Before he went into the service, I would see this young guy come to the church with his sister. All of a sudden, I met his sister Dorothy and I spoke with her. "We moved," she said. "Now we live near Dan Shalloo's store on Ballard Street. Where do you work?" I told her that I work at my grandfather's store near where she now lives.

A few days later, Gil's mom, Mary Lucy, came into the store. She spoke English as well as Portuguese. She was a tall woman, very stately. She wore white gloves to church. She liked me right away. She spoke about her son in the service and had me read a letter that Gil wrote to her. This was interesting, given that she had children who could read the letter to her. Gil was her last son. She said, "I hope that my Gil would get together with a girl like you."

She died soon after that. Gil came home from the service to attend his mom's funeral. When he came home, he came to the store to buy gum and cigarettes. "What kind of cigarettes would you like," I asked, and we began to have a conversation. My heart was going *pitter-patter*. When he went back into the service following the funeral, we started corresponding.

Manuel, Gil's oldest brother, liked me. He married a cousin of the Rogers Funeral Home family. It didn't work out, and he moved to California. Gil was the youngest boy in the family; his brothers were Manuel and John.

I worked every Saturday, but Gil and I dated on weekends. We would occasionally go to a dance. Close friends were Bob and May Collins, who we visited for supper on Saturday nights. They were nice people. They lived in the North Main Street area across from Mulvaney's Pharmacy on the corner of President Avenue. We would have a nice supper, play cards, and dance to the Victrola. They had two small boys.

Many a Saturday evening after dinner, we would stroll up President Avenue and, on the way down, stop at a small café at the corner of President Avenue and North Main Street. We chatted and listened to the music on the juke box. We all had a favorite song. Gil taught me about astronomy; as we would walk down President Avenue, he would point out the constellations.

After we were married, we moved into the Purcell Apartments on South Main Street, in Fall River. Mr. Purcell owned the Embassy Theatre on Purchase Street. As a wedding gift, Uncle Joe and Aunt Connie paid for one year's rent on the apartment.

**Work Life**

When we lived on North High Street, I loved staying in the store and being with my grandmother when I was very young, as soon as I could hold a pencil. I was so small that my grandfather provided me with a stool for me to stand on so customers could see me. Customers would call my aunt "Big Isabelle" and me "Little Isabelle" in Portuguese. Sometimes, I wouldn't get a chance to eat at the store and would have to grab a peach or something to eat. My grandmother would remind me to eat. Later, when we moved to my grandfather's house on Oregon Street, I would work in the store after school helping to stock cans and other work until I was declared an employee after I graduated from [B.M.C.] Durfee High School. I worked at the store until I was married; I made twenty-five dollars a week.

One of my jobs in the store was to take potatoes from sacks and put them in paper bags that were half a peck and one-peck bags. I did this every week. The potatoes were full of dirt in those days, not like today where they are washed and clean. I got dirt all over my face. My grandmother would bring a basin of warm water and a facecloth to clean my face. Every week, 100-pound bags of sugar were emptied into bins in the back room. I would take five pound bags and fill them with sugar during the ration days.

Bananas brought to the store were on long stalks and were green, green. The fruit dealer delivery person would take the stalk and hang it from a hook from the ceiling in the back of the store. When we needed to bring bananas out to the store, we would take a big knife and cut bunches off of the stalk. I would arrange them and other fruits in displays in the front windows. I would decorate the windows with displays that were considered the best in the area.

I spoke fluent French. When I babysat for Mrs. Bertha Larchevesque, I asked her to tutor me in French. She was pleased to do so. When they celebrated New Year's Eve, it was always a blast, and I was always a privileged guest.

The Lima's store had a black and white tile floor and white shelves with black borders. It had two monumental show cases. It was a big thing when we renovated the store. Dan Shalloo, father of Monsignor Shalloo, had a store on Ballard Street that was much smaller than ours that had sawdust on the floor.

I had an excellent memory; I could remember the numbers of all of our customers. I would call them without looking up their numbers to take their orders and to mention many new products to them. I would also attend to the duty of packing these orders.

Mrs. Rogers, mother of the Rogers Funeral Home family, was very nice to me when I made deliveries. She made wonderful raisin squares and she always gave me one with a glass of milk. She wanted to fortify me, and she always said that she admired my endurance and energy.

I made leaflets and copied them on heavy-duty white paper. I printed them in black and red. They included the specials of the weekend on them. There was a small printer's shop called Capeto & Sons, at the corner of Bailey and North Main Streets, where the leaflets were printed and delivered and billed to Grandpa. For twenty-five cents, two young boys would deliver them to houses in the area and also up to the Highlands. Older Isabelle would say, "I'll know if you throw them away in the sewers." This promoted new customers from the Highlands area, since the store carried new products for diabetics and healthy foods.

I delivered leaflets to homes. My arm would be sore and red from carrying the stack of leaflets. I never thought of it as a burden. Everyone accepted me and was glad to see me.

Payment to the store was on the honor system. People were expected to pay off the bill every week. If they had other bills that week, if the kids were sick, for example, we would carry over the balance. Some families couldn't give all of what was due every week, so the cumulative bill kept adding up every week. Many people who owed would cross the street rather than walk in front of the store. I had to go to homes that were delinquent in payments. I showed them where they were delinquent and in arrears. My grandfather would not give them credit any longer.

Dr. Ramos was the only Portuguese optometrist in Fall River. He would come into the store to pay his bill and pull on my curls, which were long in the back. He said, "If you had a twin, I would ask her to work in my office." He died early and his wife came later into the store and said to Aunt Isabelle, "A nice young Jewish man has bought my husband's practice. His name is Fradkin." That is how I first heard about Dr. Fradkin.

Frank Lipis was friendly with Dr. Fradkin and would come in and bring us coffee every day. He was the sole selling agent for Americana Terrace, located in Somerset. He owned the building that Dr. Fradkin started his practice in when he bought Dr. Ramos' practice.

**Downtown**

On the [northwest] corner of South Main and Columbia Streets was Virginia Dare. Next to it on South Main was Adaskins Furniture Store and Sears. Before Virginia Dare, that space was occupied by a food market owned by Larry Zais. Morganstein's Shoe Store was where Harry's Lunch is now.

**World War II**

Beatrice was in the USO during the war. They would dance with the servicemen and serve them coffee and food. My life was working in the store; I didn't have any time for much else. Rations were allotted by the size of the family. During that time, Beatrice was also hostess at the Latin Quarter Night Club in Fall River.

I was a "Gray Lady" for the Red Cross. I still have my uniform at home. It is gray and white striped seersucker uniform, with white cuffs, epaulets, a white collar, and the Red Cross insignia. The dress went down to your ankles. There was an initiation period and orientation. Then we went in the Red Cross van to the Brockton Veteran's Hospital and were assigned to a unit. The men there, both young and old, were traumatized by the wars.

We would be brought in and there was a counselor present. The men were sitting around and the counselor would say, "These young ladies are from Fall River," and introduce each of us. After that, we were on our own. Some of the men would look up and smile. I would say, "My name is Isabelle." From then on, you know who will respond, then you have a conversation. I had a few that would look forward to seeing me. They would say, "Here's my Fall River girl! Here's my Fall River girl!" You had to know when to approach them, then try to open them up.

One man had poor vision. He mentioned that he loved to read. I brought him an assortment of books in large print. He also said that he liked the tone of my voice when I would read poems to him. On some occasions, we would talk about different places that we would enjoy visiting. We voiced our choices and discussed them. We called it our fantasy trips.

Every three months, the Red Cross would assemble us in an auditorium and give us awards. I received two chevrons, and I'm very proud of them.

South Main Street, looking south

# Lionel "Leo" and Lorraine (Raymond) Cadrin

*Lionel was born on September 15, 1928*
*Lorraine was born on July 14, 1928, and died on December 12, 2012*

## Family Background

Leo was born at the family home at 192 Thomas Street. Lorraine was born at the family home at 105 Thomas Street.

Leo's parents were Aime (born in Fall River in the Flint on Raymond Street) and Anna (Dumais) Cadrin (born in Cornwall, Ontario, Canada). Leo's parents were older when they were married, waiting until after World War I to marry in 1919. Leo was forty-two when his father died.

Lorraine's parents were Narcise and Florida (Pouliot) Raymond. Her mother was born in Westport, Massachusetts, and her father in Canada. Florida was fifteen when she married Raymond. Narcise was an interior decorator. Florida remained home to care for the twelve children. Florida was an only child and wanted a big family. She lived to age ninety-two and her own mother lived to ninety-four. Narcise died at the age of fifty-two, when Lorraine was fourteen.

Leo's grandfather on his mother's side, Louis Dumais, was a stonecutter who worked at the Fall River quarries and built Fall River textile mills and churches in Fall River and elsewhere. He was one of the builders of Notre Dame de Lourdes Church in the Flint.

The mother of Leo's father died when Aime was seven years of age. Since his father never remarried, Aime and his siblings were raised at St. Joseph's Orphanage. Aime worked at the Berkshire Hathaway textile mills on Grinnell Street and later at the Mt. Hope Finishing Works in North Dighton [Massachusetts]. At Berkshire Hathaway, Aime unloaded bales of cotton into a shed and sorted them for quality.

Aime's wife, Anna Dumais, was a weaver. Leo and Lorraine were married in 1950.

## Family Life

When Lorraine was about thirteen, the family moved from Thomas Street to a larger apartment at 1814 Pleasant Street, on Bogle Hill. Leo also moved from Thomas Street at about thirteen or fourteen.

On his lunch hour from school, Leo would deliver lunch to his father in a gray enamel lunch pail that he has preserved to this day. Lunch always consisted of hot food such as soups, stews, roasts, or fricassees. On Fridays, clam chowder was delivered. On most days, a lunch bag was tied to the handle of the pail that carried bread in it. The cover of the pail was usually tied down so that the swinging of the pail by kids did not spill the contents. Leo would travel to the mill over the Quequechan River bridge at Quequechan Street. Leo would arrive about 11:40 am and Leo's father would put the pail on hot steam pipes that passed through his work area to keep the food hot until the lunch break.

During her grammar school years, Lorraine also brought a lunch pail to her older brother who worked at the Kerr Thread Mill. Lorraine also took care of her grandmother.

On Pleasant Street, one of Lorraine's chores was to bring barrels of heating oil from the basement to the fourth floor where they lived.

Leo's family lived in a tenement that had a bathroom with a tub. Lorraine's family lived without a tub and had to bring in the galvanized oval tub into the center of a room for the family to take a bath. She remembers that all of the kids had to wash in the same water, so everyone wanted to go first to avoid washing in the dirty water after everyone else.

When a baby was born, the kids would be sent to their older married sister's home. "We were told," said Lorraine, "that the Indians were coming to deliver a boy or a girl." In Leo's house, the family on the first floor had ten children, and every time that a child was born, adults told the kids that "the Indians came."

**School Life**

Leo attended Notre Dame School until fifth grade and then attended Prevost High School (before the Prevost annex was opened).

Lorraine attended the Coughlin School until the sixth grade. After school she was very active and took courses in arts and crafts, dancing (tap), ran track, and played basketball and softball. She later attended Diman Vocational School and majored in Home Economics, which she really liked. She had wanted to be a nurse, but her mother refused to allow her to follow that vocation.

Lorraine sometimes misbehaved at school. One day, she was punished in the usual way by having to crouch under the teacher's desk. The teacher was wearing sandals and had painted her toes. Lorraine proceeded to peel off the teacher's nail polish while the teacher kicked in protest.

**Work Life**

Leo's father's first job was delivering laundry and coal by horse and wagon. He carried coal in a long wicker basket on his back up to third floor tenements if there was no storage in the basement. His horse would proceed along the street and always know where to stop at a customer's home. Because of all of the climbing with heavy loads, he became flat-footed and was therefore not drafted into World War I.

Following school, Lorraine went to work in a sewing shop but didn't like it. She then went to work at the Arkwright Finishing Company as a cloth inspector for about nine years. While there, she lost her first baby due to lifting heavy bolts of cloth as they came off of the finishing press. The doctor advised her to quit and she did. She then went to the Kerr Mill retail store for about nine years.

As an older teenager, Lorraine's brother Alban delivered ice full-time. This involved carrying heavy cakes of ice with ice tongs up three flights of stairs to customers. He provided ice for the family for free. In the winter, the ice carriers delivered oil from tanks on the beds of pickup trucks.

As a young teenager of fifteen or sixteen during the war, Leo worked at Oak Grove Pharmacy on Bedford Street, on the corner of Haffards Street at the end of Oak Grove Avenue. He made great frappes there. He would work either 3:00 to 6:00 pm or 6:00 to 10:00 pm. If he worked the late shift to 10:00 pm, the local cop on the beat would walk him home. Later, Leo worked as a stock boy at the McClellan's 5 & 10 and moved up to assistant manager. He was the assistant manager at stores in Bristol, Rhode Island, and elsewhere as part of the company's training program.

Following that, he went to First National Store at 1601 South Main Street in 1951 and remained there for thirty years, when a major layoff occurred.

## Recreation and Entertainment

Local kids played kick the can and tomahawk (where kids jumped on top of one another until they collapsed). The girls played marbles and hopscotch. They also went blueberry picking at the Reservation where Diman Regional Vocational Technical High School is now. "If we got lost in the woods, as sometimes happened," Leo said, "a kid would climb a tree and look for the towers of Notre Dame Church, and we would find our way back."

Leo's mother wouldn't allow her children to go swimming because she experienced an incident in Canada where, as a girl, she was on a boat that overturned on a lake.

In the winter, kids would go skating at the Narrows on South Watuppa Pond, on the small pond between Route 6 and the railroad tracks. Robillard and Napert boat houses were there and provided heat from a stove and compartments to store shoes.

Kids would go to the Strand for ten cents on Saturday matinées for a double feature, serials, and short subjects. "We would make popcorn at home and bring it with us to the Strand and see an Errol Flynn pirate movie," said Leo. Lorraine liked Tyrone Power and westerns.

Friday nights were dish nights at the Strand. Lorraine's older sister collected the whole set and, in later years, distributed the pieces among family members.

Leo's house on Thomas Street was four houses from the corner of Pleasant Street, and his mother would sit by the window and observe the lines of people waiting to get into the Strand.

Later in their marriage, Leo and Lorraine were bowling enthusiasts, Leo in duckpins and Lorraine in ten pins.

Before television, a major source of recreation was to attend the baseball games at Lafayette Park. All of the churches had their own teams and the CYO [Catholic Youth Organization] League. There was also the City League, which was secular. These teams included young men aged about twenty-five to twenty-seven. The CYO games were popular and would attract 300 to 400 spectators.

During the Depression, nothing went to waste. Orange crates made great kid's vehicles. The crate would be turned over and two boards would be fastened to its underside. Roller skates would be disassembled and mounted on the boards on the four corners of the crate. Wooden "railings" would be attached to either side. Leo said that one leg would hang over the side and propel the go-cart; his vehicle could really careen down the sidewalk. The boards attached to the underside of the crate provided two shelves for storing such things as bags of potatoes or other items that Leo was asked to bring home.

## Neighborhood Experiences

Pleasant Street was very busy when they were young. "Pleasant Street was wall-to-wall people on Friday nights and Saturday," said Lorraine. People would be lined up on the sidewalk to get into Kennedy's Butter & Egg Store. Peanut butter at Kennedy's was doled out from a barrel by a clerk.

"On Friday night," said Leo, " I would accompany my mother with a red wagon to Minkin's Meat Market. It was so crowded we had to take a number." The market was on Pleasant Street, between Boutwell and Notre Dame Streets.

On Pleasant Street was Cutlers Fish and Chips, on Bogle Hill. Lussier had two grocery markets on the street. There were several men's clothing stores on Pleasant Street, including Pierre Picard and Brodcur's Men's Shop.

The McClellan 5 & 10 store was on Pleasant Street opposite Mason Street, as was Woolworth's. Pomfret's Bakery was also on Pleasant Street between Quequechan and Rocliffe Streets in the Granite Building. They had the best cream donuts in town. Vanasse Bakery was the best, with an excellent crust and soft interior. It was on Pleasant Street near Barlow Street. There were five to eight barber shops and many bar rooms on the street.

Leo says that Mr. Cote, who owned the Cote Piano Company on Alden Street, lived in the large brick house across from Lafayette Park. At one time, the statue of Lafayette faced inside the park, instead of facing Eastern Avenue, as it now does. Mr. Cote complained to city authorities that he was tired of looking at the statue's behind and got the city to reverse the statue to face toward his house.

## Downtown

"Everyone walked or took the bus downtown. By the time the bus reached Quequechan Street, it was full of people," said Leo. When his sister wanted to go downtown, she would bribe Leo into going by promising him an ice cream sandwich when they arrived. Leo's father would go downtown to buy cookies by the pound, including "washboard" and wine cookies.

## Food and Meals

Leo remembers that he could predict what his mother would serve by the day of the week. Wednesdays she would serve crepes for breakfast and on Friday she would serve pancakes. On Saturday night, beans would be the meal. The beans would be brought to Poirier's Bakery Saturday morning and picked up at 5:00 pm. Lorraine's brother Alban worked at Poirier's Bakery, starting at 5:00 am.

Lorraine's father taught her mother how to cook, since he had been a short-order cook. Among the dishes her mom made were salmon pies. There was always gorton, a ground pork that was also used in meat pies on New Year's.

Lorraine said that an after-school snack frequently consisted of a slice of bread with butter and ketchup spread on it and folded once. Leo would frequently have bread with butter and sugar spread on it and folded.

There was no canned baby food as we know it now. Baby food was breast feeding plus cookies crushed into milk. There were wine cookies that were similar to milk cookies or milk biscuits but thinner.

## The Depression

Lorraine's father worked part-time on Fridays and Saturdays for Zais Meat and Grocery Store, on Pleasant Street. He not only got paid for this work but got food for the family at a discount. Distinguished General Melvin Zais of Fall River was the son of the grocery store owner.

Full-time work was difficult to get during the Depression, and many people took two or more part-time jobs to make ends meet. At one point, Lorraine's family had to go on welfare to keep the family in food; she remembers bringing a wagon down to Alden Street to bring government surplus food and clothing home.

Toilet paper was a luxury during the Depression, and Leo remembers that the tissue paper that oranges were wrapped and shipped in was brought home for that use.

**Christmas, Holidays, and Special Occasions**

In order to have gifts for the kids, Lorraine's older brother delivered French language newspapers as an additional part-time job to raise extra money. Then he would give the money to his mother on Christmas eve. Every Christmas, the gifts would be the same: a brown bag with everyone's name written on it that would include an orange, candy, and a paper doll for Lorraine (one year, it was her favorite, Shirley Temple).

Lorraine had a full Christmas tree, but Leo's family had a table tree. He also received a gift of a lunch bag with his name on it and fruit and candy in it. He also got major gifts like small train sets.

**Hurricane of 1938**

When a baby was born, the mother would stay in bed with the baby for nine days. When the 1938 hurricane hit, Lorraine's mother was in bed with her baby boy of six days. During the hurricane, the window next to the bed broke and her mother quickly covered herself and the baby with a blanket. The bed was covered with glass. Lorraine's father asked Lorraine, when she returned from school, to go out again to purchase candles. Lorraine protested that the weather was too awful, and she only made it to the store across the street.

Their aunt had a cottage on Horseneck Beach, but it blew away during the hurricane.

**World War II**

Four of Lorraine's brothers left on the same day after being drafted. Two were sent to the war and two got rejected for medical reasons. Her brother Al, who went, had ulcers and his mother tried to get him discharged because the ulcers required a special diet that wasn't available in the service, but to do this, she had to prove that he had this condition before he left for the war. She was finally able to do it with a doctor's certificate. It was later learned that all of the soldiers in Al's unit were killed in the Pacific.

At one point, Lorraine's mother was notified by the Red Cross that one of her sons had been knifed in the shoulder during combat and therefore would not be writing home.

Leo's cousin George was rejected by the draft board because he was too short at 4 feet, 11 inches tall. So, with the assistance of friends, he stretched himself on pipes until he reached the 5 feet minimum height. He was accepted and was later killed in Okinawa in April 1945, just four months before the Japanese surrendered.

Women lined up for rationed silk stockings on Pleasant Street at a store near the Strand.

When the war ended, everyone came out on Pleasant Street, including the servicemen. Lorraine said that was when she saw her sister's husband for the first time following the war. Bells were ringing and they walked downtown to join others there.

# Helen K. (Mythowicz) Caron

*Born in 1922*
*Died February 7, 2013*

**Family Background**

I was born at home at 175 Smith Street, as were all ten children in our family.

My father's name was Josef Mythowicz. I don't know why he left Poland. My father was a weaver at the Parker Mill A, off of Jefferson Street.

My mother's name was Katarzyna (Piekarska). She came to America when she was sixteen years old to make money and send it back to the family in Poland. She was sent to an aunt in Warren [Rhode Island] and started working in a mill there. Later, my mother was a spinner at the Shawmut Mill on Jefferson Street in Fall River. My mother lived until she was ninety.

My brothers and sisters, from oldest to youngest, were: Ann, Mary, Victoria, Dora (who passed away at the age of two from diphtheria), Dora, John, Frank, Walter, Helen (me), and Mildred, the youngest.

My husband is Paul J. Caron and we have two children, Susan H. deVillers and Gerald A. Caron.

**Family Life**

What do I remember most? We were so poor, although we didn't realize it at the time; everyone was in the same boat. We walked everywhere; there were no cars.

We moved all the time; I never knew why, but it was always in Maplewood [neighborhood in Fall River]. Before here [188 Baker Street], we lived at the corner of Brayton Avenue and Rodman Street, above Caron's Market, which was owned by my father-in-law. We were there for ten years following our marriage (the market was where Tony's Fish Restaurant is now).

We slept three to a bed. Since I was younger, I had to sleep in the middle. In the summer, it was so hot there. In the winter, the bedroom got so cold that the goldfish bowl had ice in it. The windows were all frosted.

If I went back now, the thing that I would miss most would be heat; central heating. We had a wood stove in the kitchen, but the bedrooms were freezing. My father would get up early in the morning and light the stove. We used wood, coke, and coal.

We didn't get a phone until I was nineteen and on Albert Street. When our older sister moved in with us, we got a phone. To keep in contact, before and after that, we did a lot of visiting, especially on Sunday. You didn't have to call; you would just drop in. We would visit my married sister in Providence.

My younger sister and I changed the beds, swept, did the dishes, and would go to the store every day. Everyone in the neighborhood went to the store every day; all we had was an icebox to keep food in and it didn't keep long.

My sister and I were the last kids in the house, and my mother would leave and say, "Stay in the yard until I get back from work." And we did. I took care of my sister. We obeyed our mother;

we didn't question, we just did it. We never answered her back; never. Whatever she said, you never answered her back.

My father-in-law had a grocery store, a hardware store, and was a carpenter. He was a man of few words but a good, good man. When his wife was going to have a baby, he would get a nun to stay with her. My mother-in-law never worked. Their house was on the corner of Albert and Rodman Streets and was a big white house. After the war, the two girls in the family ran the grocery. Those girls did everything. The youngest carried orders and they cut meat and carried large sides of beef from the refrigerator.

My husband was a carpenter, then he went into the refrigeration business, and then to work in the torpedo factory in Newport during the war.

After marriage, I didn't work. Most of the mothers in this neighborhood didn't work.

**School Life**

I went to the Green School until third grade. I liked it. One teacher at the Green School stayed in my mind, a Miss Kingston. At morning recess, we would get a small glass bottle of milk and two graham crackers each. It was a real treat.

If you wanted to take First Holy Communion, you had to go to the Holy Cross School, which was attached to the Polish Holy Cross parish. The nuns there ruled with an iron hand. We got hit with a rattan if we misbehaved. We were so scared of them. We spoke Polish and English at school. Catechism was in both Polish and English.

Then I went to the Henry Lord School until ninth grade and on to [B.M.C.] Durfee High School. I was the only one in my family to graduate from Durfee. My parents insisted that the others leave school to work.

I walked to Durfee every day. I didn't have the five cents to ride the bus from Plymouth Avenue. If it was raining, I got to school all wet. Once, I got a pair of shoes from one of my sisters and they were too tight, but I didn't want to tell my mother. The shoes would be killing me as I walked all the way to Durfee.

**Recreation and Entertainment**

The circus train would arrive at 5:00 in the morning and unload at the Rodman Street tracks, then go down Rodman Street as a parade to the circus grounds at the Globe. We had no money to go to the circus. My brothers would go, but not the girls.

I never had a bathing suit because my mother wouldn't allow us girls go swimming. The boys could go, and went to the Watuppa Pond to swim.

We made up our own games. One was where we took two tin cans, put two holes in each, put a rope through them, and knotted the rope. Then we walked on the cans like stilts holding the ropes.

We would flip a knife to see how it would stick in the lawn. We played jacks, but we had no money for jacks. I never had a doll. We made up things like picking a flower and digging a hole and put the flower in the hole. Then we would put a piece of broken glass over it then cover it with dirt. Then we would try to find it later.

Whenever I could get a clean piece of paper, I would sketch on it. When my mother got a piece of cardboard with a new shirt, I would get it to draw on.

The Durfee girls would go dancing at Lincoln Park. We couldn't do it. I didn't get to go to

Lincoln Park until I was married and we would bring the kids once a year.

On the radio, we would listen to Bob Hope and Red Skelton, but after I was married. We didn't have a radio when I was young.

When girls and guys got married, they would go to New York on their honeymoons on the New York boat.

**Neighborhood Experiences**

There was a store on every corner in the neighborhood. DeVillers was always there. Plourde's Bakery was across from St. John's Club. The St. John's Club building was a bowling alley. Between Cambridge Street and Brayton Avenue was all fields.

My mother would send me to get milk from Mrs. Kulpa, who had cows. I would bring a glass milk bottle and Mrs. Kulpa would fill it with milk.

The area between Jefferson and Rodman Streets, north of Brayton Avenue, was known as pigtown because of the piggeries there. It was an area of farms.

The Jarabeks lived up the street on Brayton Avenue and had a farm there. The Jarabek geese would chase us up Brayton Avenue on our way to school, so we would walk on the opposite side of the street. They had cows, turkeys, chickens, and geese. Alan Jarabek had a pig farm later in Westport [Massachusetts]. Mr. Machado had a horse and wagon that he used to pick up garbage; I don't know what he did with it. Alan Jarabek would sit on the wagon to help Mr. Machado on his route.

The area near Warren Street, near the intersection of Rodman Street, was all the Quequechan River then and it was very wide there. Where Watuppa Heights is now was a dump. There was a little bridge on Warren Street where the water would go under. Next to the mills was all water.

There was a Polish store on Rodman Street next to Watuppa Heights. Across from the Polish store was a cobbler shop and down the street a barber shop.

Warren Street had four or five bakeries. Riley's Bakery was excellent. Their food was to die for. They had delicious custard and pork pies. Auclair's Bakery was further down toward Plymouth Avenue, on Warren Street.

Stafford Road had a department store on the same block as Duffy's Pharmacy. Bottomley's Ice Cream Shop was also on Stafford Road. They put salted pecans on top of their ice cream. They were across the street from Duffy's, maybe on the corner of Peckham Street. Later, I would wheel the baby carriage up there to get their wonderful ice cream.

A man named Charlie with a horse-drawn wagon would come by during the week to pick up rags. He would give my mother twenty-five cents for a bag of rags. The same man would come by on Friday with fish and whatever was in season. He would deliver ice also. We had a card that we put in the window that signaled whether we wanted a ten cent piece or a twenty cent piece of ice. You rotated the card to show the piece that you wanted.

A bread man would also come by named Pasquale and had a car. A Jewish man with a horse and wagon sold bagels and other things. There was also the ice cream man called Happy Joe's Ice Cream, who came by in a horse and wagon. He served ice cream cones.

There was a place on Warren Street, down from Baker Street, that sold fish. It was in the basement and a man named Ike in a fisherman's cap sat around and ran it. He had all kinds of fish in barrels. He also had pickles for one cent. I was really small then and my mother would send me to get fish every day, sometimes to get a pickled herring. He would take the fish out of the barrel and, with it dripping, put it on a piece of cardboard and wrap it in newspaper. On the way home, the fish would be dripping on me and my clothes.

There was never any rubbish; we saved everything. Bags were used for our lunches, which sometimes embarrassed me.

People moved to and lived around their churches.

**Food and Meals**

We had very little food. What little we had, my mother managed to make into a meal out of nothing. We had lots of soups, stews, and chowders. I didn't like corn chowder.

For breakfast, my mother would make a big pot of coffee and sweetened it with sugar and condensed milk. Then we all had a piece of rye bread with butter. That was our breakfast every morning.

My mother had a little garden with tomatoes and stuff. It was small and the yard had a grapevine. She put up jellies, jams, pickles, and such. We had no sweets like dessert today. As my sisters got older, they baked cakes. All of us sisters sewed and knitted. We made our own clothes.

**Work Life**

I had one hour for lunch at the Polish School. My mother would have the dinner pails ready for me to deliver to my father and sister at the Parker Mill. Food would be in the bottom and coffee in the top. The bottom was bigger. Dinner included stews, potatoes, and meat, and things like that. I had to be careful not to spill coffee into the food if I swung the pails too much.

Mom took the older kids out of school in the fourth grade to tend to the younger children.

I saw my mother work in the mill. I wondered how she could tend all of those spindles. She had to watch to see when a thread broke and tie it up. The noise in the weaving room where my father worked was deafening. They had to yell or use sign language in the weaving room. Many people who worked in the weaving rooms lost their hearing. It was very hot in the mills.

The looms were powered by wide leather straps. If a strap was discarded, my father would bring it home and use it to "tap," or resole, our shoes. He had the equipment to resole the shoes. He put a row of tacks in his mouth while he was working, and I remember wondering how he never swallowed one. He also cut our hair, until Ann became a hairdresser, when she did it.

When my sister Ann was sixteen, a Polish lady told my mom that she was leaving the employment of a Highlands family. My mother told Ann that she was going Monday to work for the family. Mrs. Horton taught Ann about books, the library, and culture in general. She was a nice lady and gave us furniture and clothes.

My sister Ann wanted to be a hairdresser. There was no formal training needed then to be a hairdresser. She worked for a lady that had a beauty shop. Ann later had a beauty shop on Main Street and had five girls working for her. It was called Ann's Beauty Salon. At first, it was in the Academy Building. Then she moved to a place at North Main and Bedford Streets, in the Burke Building. She worked there until she was seventy-five, then she moved her shop to her home in Somerset [Massachusetts].

I wanted to be a telephone operator so badly, but they had a training period that was unpaid and my mother needed the money. Instead, I went to work in a needle shop in the Durfee Mills for ten dollars for forty-eight hours while I was in training. After the training was over, I got fourteen dollars a week. The work there was awful. You didn't dare lift your head or say much.

If you lifted your head, the owner would come by and say, "What's your problem?" You were clocked when you went to the bathroom. When the unions came in 1939, things got better. We paid twenty-five cents in dues. It was awful before the unions.

Every day we had a slip of what you made the day before. I was a pocket setter, who sewed pockets into the slit left in the dress. If we didn't meet the quota, the boss would say, "What's your excuse today?" There was a certain amount that you had to do. If a machine broke, and you had to wait for the mechanic to fix it, it would take all of your time. We made cheap cotton house dresses. Once, when the buttonhole girl made a mistake on a number of dresses and my pockets were off as a result, the boss started yelling at me and I walked out—for good.

I then went to the Shelburne Shirt factory. They asked what I could do and I said that I was a pocket-setter and he said okay and hired me. I figured that men's shirts had only one pocket. I worked there for a few years. He was better to work for.

My mom worked on the family farm in Poland. They worked all summer and had animals and cows. In the winter, they embroidered and sewed. She never went to school in Poland. My father, however, had an education and played the violin. He had beautiful handwriting.

I had just got the job in the sewing shop when the 1938 hurricane struck. Slate was coming off of the roofs of buildings. When I got home, my mother was unfazed; it was just a big wind for her and didn't bother her.

**Courtship and Marriage**

We moved from Smith Street to Albert Street, next to Maplewood Park. My future husband lived next door in a family of eleven children. I had to take the bus at the corner of Brayton Avenue and he would come by in his car, a Ford with a rumble seat, and ask, "Can I give you a ride?" At first I said no, then, when my sister was at General Hospital, I said yes. Then we started dating.

We had "date nights" which were Tuesday, Thursday, and Saturday nights, and Sunday afternoons. On Sunday nights, we would go for rides. If we had fifty cents, we would go to a movie, which was twenty-five cents each. When we went to the movies then, we went all dressed up with a hat. We also ate at home before we left; we didn't go out to eat as they do today. We would do simple things, such as go down to the water for a ride.

At my wedding reception, my mother and aunt cooked a turkey dinner for forty family members. We set up tables in the house. My sister made my dress. That was in 1941.

Polish weddings were something. My cousin had a wedding that lasted for three days. I was a bridesmaid and, when I arrived at the house down on Baker Street, there was a band playing on the sidewalk. We partied for those three days. People would put money into the hole of the bass fiddle for the couple.

**Christmas, Holidays, and Special Occasions**

We never celebrated Christmas except as a religious holiday. Our lives revolved around the church. We had the usual Polish food for Christmas. When my sisters were older and working, they would give us younger kids stockings with candy in them.

One tradition that we had at Christmas was when my Polish uncle would come, knock on the door and, when the door was opened, he would throw shelled nuts in the room. The throwing of nuts was related to the martyrdom stoning of St. Stephen.

Between Christmas and New Year's Day, the priest from Holy Cross would come to bless the house. He would also take a piece of chalk and write the initials of the wise men on the door and the date of the coming year. It would read "KNN & B, 1930."

Easter was the big Polish holiday. My mother made golumkies, pierogies, kielbasa, and hard-boiled eggs. When I was little, we couldn't eat until the priest blessed the food at Easter. My mother would take a potato and make designs in it, like a wood block, including diamonds and other designs. Then she would press the potato on to soft butter to make a design in the butter, as a decoration for Easter.

## The Depression

We were on welfare for a while. My father didn't want anyone to know that we were and would take the back streets to avoid being seen when he went to the welfare office for food. If bananas came in that week, we got loaded with bananas. We had so many beans left over from the Depression that my mother used to give them to us to use in metal bean shooters.

One of my brothers joined the CCC [Civilian Conservation Corps] and was sent to a camp in Danvers [Massachusetts] to clean the woods. The camps were for older teenagers. He came home on weekends with a stipend. Another brother worked for the WPA [Works Progress Administration], building and cleaning streets. Another brother joined the Army and was stationed in Hawaii before Pearl Harbor. There were no jobs, but everyone had something to do.

We loved the Roosevelts; that's when things started to get better. We would listen to the fireside chats. He was a wonderful man.

## World War II

I was on my way to my future mother-in-law's house on Sunday to go out on a date with my future husband when the news came that Pearl Harbor had been attacked. When I arrived, everyone was crying. It was awful.

Blackout shades had to be in the windows. We used black cloth as drapes and closed them at night.

My brother was in Italy in the war and was missing in action. A house was demolished and he was in the basement with a buddy. He got many medals for his service in the war.

When we lived over Caron's Market, we heard all of the family members crying at 6:00 in the morning as the youngest son was going off to the troop train. It was very sad.

Rationing was terrible. Things were in short supply. On Fridays, I helped in the market to bag orders for delivery on Saturday. While we did that, we would put a pork pie on the hot stove to warm up. Everyone in the family was in the store on Fridays filling and setting up orders. People would either come in to give their orders or they would call them in.

Turkeys came in to the store fresh without feathers but with everything else intact. We would have to take out their innards and clean them up.

My mother once bought a chicken killed on a farm on Cook Street. She brought it home, took off the feathers, and cleaned it.

## Health and Illness

There was a Dr. Sullivan on Warren Street. He would come to the home and was wonderful to poor people. When my younger sister and I had to have our tonsils out, he charged my mother a price for two. He removed them from both of us for thirty-five dollars. We had to walk to St. Anne's Hospital for the operation.

Even when I had Gerry and Susan, a pediatrician came to the house.

If I got a bad cold, my mother would heat milk and put a lump of butter in it. Then she would spread Vicks on a rag and wrap it around my neck. It really opened up your passages and worked wonderfully.

My French in-laws used ginger tea for colds. If you scraped your knee, my mother would pick a wide leaf from a plant in the yard and rub it on my knee.

Common illnesses were scarlet fever, mumps, and chicken pox. For scarlet fever, a sign would have to be put up on the door of the house by the Board of Health.

Wakes were held in the house. My mother and father were waked at home. We stayed up all night with the body. A wreath was put on the door and the grandfather clock was stopped at the time that the person died. Wakes lasted for three days.

**Popular Expressions**
"Lay them out in lavender."
"Chewing them out."
"Like a skunk at a picnic."
Mom had a few sayings that rhymed in Polish, for example: "I sent him out for fish and he came back with lobster."

She would call my younger sister, "The bell on Helen's behind," in Polish, which rhymed, because my sister was always following me wherever I would go.

# Louise (Duquette) Caron

*Born on January 11, 1912*

**Family Background**

I was born on Flint Street and the family remained there until I was six months old. Two of my brothers and sisters were also born at home. Then we moved to 103 Canonicus Street at the corner of Jencks Street. Then we moved to 75 Haffards Street, which my father bought. I lived there until I was married.

My parents were Melchoir and Rosanna (Garant) Duquette.

Their children were (in order of birth): Romeo, Wilfred, Blanche (LeValle), Yvone (Wilke), Arthur, me, and Raoul.

My mother's father was Lawrence Garant. They had seven children; my mother's mother died early. He married again, and they had three children of their own. They lived in the Flint. Then he moved to Bay Street about three houses from Sandy Beach. He died there when I was about seven years old.

My father's father was from Canada and lived in Champlain, New York, in one of the first houses this side of the Canadian border. We would go there during Prohibition. We would get the run-runners going through my grandparents' back yard, trying to escape from the cops. It was quite a scene.

My father was a Republican and worked for the party. He was angry when I married a Democrat. When a Republican won, he would come to the house to gloat; I would tell him to get out (in jest). My father belonged to men's clubs, including the Canadian Club on Jenks Street. The Calumet Club at the corner of South Main and Rodman Streets was for families and I would go there for the dances.

I was married to Roland Caron and we were married for sixty-one years. I was married at St. Roch's Church in 1934 and now have sixteen grandchildren and thirty-three great-grandchildren.

My husband's grandfather founded a town in Canada that bears the family name: Levesque. There is a statue of him in the town church. The family home is now a funeral home.

When I was married, we moved to a two-bedroom house on Fifth Street that had no bath. The rent was a dollar and fifty cents a week. Then we moved to Albion Street in the Flint (we moved two times on Albion Street). Then we moved to 1033 Bedford Street, across from Columbus Park, which we later bought. That was a very Italian neighborhood, and we were the only French family in the neighborhood. Later, we bought the 1748 GAR Highway house.

I met my husband through my brother, who had a girlfriend on a farm in Swansea. The brother of his girlfriend became my husband. I met him again in Ocean Grove [Swansea, Massachusetts]. There was no electricity on the farm until we were married in the 1930s.

My husband was first a mechanic and then later worked most of his life in the construction business for the Callan Construction Company.

My husband was in the Seabees for eight months. Then the war ended. He was the first one out because he had three children.

My children's names are Reinette, Joscelyn, Roger, and Philip.

**Family Life**

When we lived on Canonicus Street, I remember the lamplighter. My mother would call us to the window to watch the lamplighter light the gas lights. I was about five years old. He would come by just as it was getting dark.

We were not very poor, because my father always had a job. He was an insurance man for John Hancock. We were the first family on the street to have a telephone when it first came out. Neighbors would come by to use the phone. To this day, I don't like to stay on the phone because I remember my mother telling me to stay off of the phone to allow others to use it.

My mother never went to the store. The bread man delivered bread and butter (when margarine first came out, he wasn't allowed to sell it, but my father was friends with him and he sold it to us). A man would come to take our order for groceries (before we had a phone) and then bring the groceries the next day. Bread was about five cents a loaf. Hamburger was about fifteen cents a pound.

My mother's cooking schedule never varied:
    Sunday: alternating meat or chicken roast;
    Monday: leftovers;
    Tuesday: hamburger (and to the movies to get the dishes);
    Wednesday: stew beef;
    Thursday: alternating steak or pork chops;
    Friday: salmon pies;
    Saturday: beans and meat pies.

On Friday nights, we would bring our beans to Pomfret's Bakery and the next morning we would go to pick them up. The bakeries didn't use their ovens on weekends and no bakeries were open on Sundays.

My mother knitted clothes for us kids. She would make salmon pies and sell them from a little garage/house on Haffards Street. My mother would also sell day-old cakes that my brother brought from the New York boat. He would go down to the pier to get them and sell them at various stores. Later, my brother worked for many years on the first Alaskan pipeline.

At a store on Oak Grove Avenue, you could buy a big bag of sugar cones for five cents a bag.

**Work Life**

When we lived on Haffards Street, when I was ten years old, my brother and I would get paid to bring dinner pails to workers at the Kerr Mill.

My first job at sixteen years old was in the Pepperell Mills as a bobbin cleaner for five dollars a week. A bobbin cleaner took the thread off of the bobbins before they were changed. The mill was hot (there was no air conditioning then) and I worked from 7:00 am to 5:00 pm.

Then I went to work at a curtain factory on Montaup Street for eight dollars a week for forty-eight hours. I made patterns there. The Avon Curtain Company boss asked if I would go to his place for ten dollars a week, and I did, given that it was located in the Flint. I worked until I had my third child, then I quit work.

**Lizzie Borden**

I want you to know that I saw Lizzie Borden. I was about seven or eight. I went with my mother to Steiger's Department Store where she went to buy gloves. Lizzie Borden was there to buy gloves also. The place was very quiet. She was dressed in black and had a veil. I couldn't see her. Steiger's was located at the corner of South Main and Columbia Streets, where the Crystal Palace Restaurant is now located.

Grandfather knew Mr. [Andrew Jackson] Borden. Mr. Borden was very stern. My grandfather had a long beard and supplied wood to Mr. Borden. He sold wood and coal. Just a few days before the murders, my grandfather had been to the house to make a delivery.

**Recreation and Entertainment**

We played in the school lot (the Covel School was to the rear of our house) and in an empty lot next door. We played baseball, jumped rope, and hide and seek. In the wintertime, there was great sliding in a vacant lot on Haffards Street. We also walked to South Park [now Kennedy Park] to go ice skating; I would meet my friend who lived at John Street. We also went ice skating at the Narrows.

I was very athletic; I was on a baseball team that played at Lafayette Park.

We went to Lincoln Park on the trolleys. You could flip the seats depending on which way the trolley was going.

At the big brick building at the corner of Flint and Pleasant Street, occasionally a man would leap from the top of the building into a tub of water. About once a year.

There was another theatre where you had to climb up the stairs every Saturday morning to watch cowboys. It was silent movies with a piano player providing background music. We went to the Strand, the Academy, and the Durfee theatres. I walked a lot to downtown and other places. Maybe that's why I'm in such good shape.

Never went to the circus. My husband would go to Rodman Street and watch the circus unload. When the Firestone fire occurred, a hose broke and the hose went flying into the air.

Sandy Beach wasn't a fancy beach, but it was good for us; we missed it. When my children were born, we went to Island Park [Cashman's Park, Portsmouth, Rhode Island], where we had friends who had a cottage there.

**Neighborhood Experiences**

The Portuguese and other groups stayed to themselves. In those days, you couldn't marry across ethnic cultures. I used to play with some Jewish girls. Where we lived on Haffards Street was mostly Jewish. I was allowed to play with the Jewish girls, including the Kaufmann and Goldstein girls. I got interested in Jewish ceremonies by visiting their homes and they would give me crackers and things like the lighting of the candles interested me. But, that was until I was about fourteen; then I couldn't play with them any more. People then wanted their children to marry their own. We spoke French in our house until my sister married an English man.

My family life was not very happy, so I adopted my best friend's family, which consisted of thirteen kids. I would join them in saying the rosary every night to be a part of their family. Every Sunday at 3:00 pm, I would go to vespers with my best friend, Annette.

The newspapers included the *Fall River Globe* and the French *L'Independent*. Kids would write stories for the paper and, if published, would get a few dollars.

Once when we were coming back from church, we saw a commotion at the quarry. A little boy had drowned. We saw him as he was being taken out and I have never forgotten it. There were lots of drownings at the quarries, and they were finally closed.

## School Life

I went to the Davol School then to the Covel Street when we moved to Haffards Street. Then to the Dubuque School and then to the Davis School, where I graduated. I went to Durfee [B.M.C. Durfee High School] for two years, then to work at sixteen, which was expected at that time.

Mrs. Caylor was one of my teachers and she was strict. In those days, you had to be strict. Her husband died; in those days, you couldn't teach if you were married.

Covel School was only for fourth grade. Kids changed schools a lot back then.

## Hurricane of 1938

We used to go to Sandy and Horseneck Beaches (my husband worked at Horseneck). We had friends who had a summer cottage on Horseneck, but it disappeared in the 1938 hurricane. We were living on Haffards Street when the hurricane hit, and I remember windows breaking along the street. During the 1954 hurricane, everyone in this area (GAR Highway) was evacuated and located to Lee's River Lodge. Traffic was stopped on Route 6 because the flooding prevented drivers from going any further.

## Health and Illness

Consumption was common; patients went to the TB [tuberculosis] hospital.

Aspirin was a common medicine. We also gave kids Father John's Medicine. No one knows why we gave the kids this. It was a cough medicine and for other ills. Because there was a priest's picture on the bottle, we all thought that it had to be good. There were also Vicks pads. My husband would make a medicine of honey and onions and sugar and cook it. We called it "Roland's medicine."

If someone in the house had diphtheria or scarlet fever, a big card would be put on the door from the Board of Health. When a wake occurred in the house, a big black bow would be put in the window. On Bedford Street, when a girl passed away, we could hear the *bang, bang* of the coffin against the wall as the men brought it down the stairs.

# Mary (Theresa) Carvalho

*Born on October 20, 1920*

### Family Life

My earliest memory was from six or seven when I was crowned at Santo Christo Church and marched in a religious parade down Columbia Street. My grandmother lived with us and was like a medicine man. Some women saw my grandmother like they would a doctor or nurse.

My parents were Joseph and Adeline (Cavaco) Carvalho. My siblings are John, Alice, and Beatrice. My father's parents were Manuel and Alexandria Carvalho. My mother's parents were Edwardo and Lucia Cavaco.

My father was a dentist and his office was at 422 Columbia Street. We lived on the two floors above the office. I lived there until I graduated from college in 1943. Later we moved to 491 Hood Street.

My father owned a three-family next door to the Columbia Street address and always rented to doctors—Dr. Rosa, Dr. Lobo (from Africa), and Dr. Coelho. All were on the first floor. Dr. Costa lived near the church on Columbia—everyone liked him. Dr. Lobo would give us children candy; chocolate bars.

We had the most loving parents a person could have. In the evenings on summer nights, my father would sometimes take us to a drugstore and buy us an ice cream cone or an ice cream soda. We would wait until he finished his work so we could go after supper to the drugstore.

During the Depression, my father must have extracted hundreds of teeth for nothing. He was very charitable in his practice. "Oh, those teeth were very loose," he would say.

### School Life

I went to first grade at Dominican Academy. My grandfather would walk me to school. I went to the Robeson School for second grade and Miss Keys was my teacher. I went to McDonough School for fifth to eighth grades, then to Sacred Hearts Academy for high school. I went to New Rochelle College in New York—it was a girl's Catholic college—graduating in 1942.

My brother decided that I should be a dental hygienist and so I went to the Forsythe School for Dental Hygienists, then worked for my brother for a few years. Later, I got a masters of education from Bridgewater [now Bridgewater State College] and became a teacher. I started at James Tansey School teaching pre-primary to third grade for ten years. Then I taught conversational French to grades from four to eight at various schools. Much later, I was asked to take over the Portuguese class at Durfee [B.M.C. Durfee High School] and taught that for four years.

### Downtown

At downtown, the M.J. Doran store, at the corner of South Main and Spring Streets, was very nice. There was McWhirr's, Cherry and Webb, Van Dykes, and the 5 & 10s. There was a nice Chinese restaurant upstairs across from Cherry and Webb. I remember Hilltson's Bakery on

South Main Street near Columbia Street. The Nonpareil was a nice restaurant. I would go there with my mother.

Grant's 5 & 10 sold cookies and candies and they had goldfish downstairs. Grant's had beautiful music in the back of the store. A woman usually had all of the sheet music. She was very popular. She would play the piano and people would buy the sheet music from her.

**Recreation and Entertainment**

When we went to the movies we had to go to the Durfee or the Empire. The Plaza was the "flea theatre"—inexpensive. We would go to the Boys Club for five cents to see the movies on Saturday afternoons—a big crowd of kids.

My father had a home in Tiverton, and we spent the summers there. Relatives and friends who were going to Island Park [Cashman's Park, Portsmouth, Rhode Island] would stop along the way at the Tiverton house.

As a child we played hopscotch, jump rope, tag, and roller skated. I never rode a bike; my mom would never let us children go out on a bike. It was too dangerous on Columbia Street.

I loved sports. I played tennis, golf (for forty-nine years in a group at the New Bedford Country Club), and skied in college. We went skiing for forty years in New Hampshire, until my back told me not to go anymore.

I remember outings to different parks, like Crescent Park, Rocky Point, and Lincoln Park. Cashman's Park [Island Park, Portsmouth, Rhode Island] had a lovely dance floor and had all-night dances going day and night. It was just spectacular. My father would take us. We loved that.

**Neighborhood Experiences**

It was a very friendly neighborhood; mostly Portuguese, but also Irish and Polish. Most people walked in those days. As people walked up and down the streets, you got to know everybody. You would stop and talk to people who you knew in their yards and sometimes they asked you to come in. During hot days, we sat outdoors a lot; everyone would be outside; it was hot there too.

**Hurricane of 1938**

In 1938, my mother and father took me to New Rochelle College. My parents stayed in New York for two days and got the news of the hurricane. They called to say that they were stranded there. All the train rails were under water. They had to stay in New York for a few more days. They saw a grand piano floating in the water. When they got home, they got the bad news that Mrs. Rose Olivera (the wife of the undertaker) was driving in a car that got washed away and she died.

**World War II**

I was at college and the news from Pearl Harbor came over the radio. Girls were yelling "Come listen, come listen." I wanted to go into the Navy as an officer, but my mom wouldn't hear of that. "No young lady would do that," she said.

I had just graduated from college in 1942 when I came to work for my father. I took care of his real estate business and his dental office. My brother John went into the service as a dentist. I remember going on South Main Street to lines at Kennedy's, where they sold eggs and butter. There were big lines to both. During the war, I remember the rationing, gas rationing, and rationing of sugar also.

# Everett Castro

*Born on July 16, 1943*

**Family Background**

I was born July 16, 1943, but I prefer to go by my conception date, which was in October, because that is a more accurate measure of how long you have been alive. I was born at Union Hospital, which is now Charlton. We lived on North Belmont Street in an apartment in the North End, right next to North Park—a four-tenement house, two above and two below.

At home my crib faced east. I remember awakening to the summer sun beaming through my window. It was bright, warm, and wonderful. I believed I had a connection to that sun. That I was created, came from that "sun god" and a celestial being, my mother, had been sent to feed and take care of me. I was sorely disappointed when I eventually discovered that I was just one more, common Homo sapiens child and that my mother had not been divinely sent.

My mother's name was either Angelina Mary Oliveira or Mary Angelina Oliveira. I never really figured that out. She was known to family as both Angie and Mary. My mother loved all children, enjoyed cooking, and also was a great seamstress. She made most of our clothes and bought the cloth for those clothes from Lima's Fabric Remnants Shop on North Main Street near Stewart Street. My mother had two sisters, Eva and Tina.

My father's name was Joseph Castro and he was in the Army Air Corps during World War II. The Army Air Corps later became the Air Force. I was born when he was overseas. I vaguely remember when he came home. I told my mother to throw that man out of the house. My Mom and I we were having a great time together and I didn't want any strangers living with us.

I have a sister, Mary Angela, who is three years older than me.

**Family Life**

My mother and most of her friends didn't work outside the home; they were all busy raising children and most of them had husbands in some branch of the military. My father's Army paycheck was sent back home to my mother.

Although a baby, I distinctly remember my mother arguing with a woman who turned out to be our neighborhood air raid warden. Apparently, fearing a German air attack on the east coast, or a west coast Japanese bombing raid, the United States Office of Defense recruited thousands of volunteers to serve as neighborhood air raid wardens to monitor air raid drills. Their job was to make sure that when the air raid siren sounded, people turned off electric lights and stayed off the street when air raid alarms were issued.

My mother was feeding me at the time of this particular drill and failed to turn off the light in the kitchen. The warden showed up at the door demanding my mother comply or face arrest. By the time they were done arguing with each other, I had been fed and my mother complied and turned off the light. The warden did her job and my mother felt she had done hers too. Fortunately, the Luftwaffe never made it to Fall River while my mother's kitchen light was on!

After he came home from the war, my father was a smash-piecer and a weaver in a cotton textile mill. When the shuttle in the loom is going too fast, the humidity is not correct, or for some other reason the cotton threads break, he would "piece" them back together. He worked in Sagamore Mill #3, but also in other mills owned by the same company.

Occasionally my father would take me fishing down at the Taunton River behind the Sagamore Mills, but most of my father's week was taken up by mill work or by working on weekends as a watchman and boiler attendant at the mill.

Our landlord on Belmont Street had a large vegetable garden and chickens in the back yard. Many others in the neighborhood also had large vegetable gardens, grape arbors, chickens, pigeons, and a few had goats—all this in a highly populated neighborhood of two- and three-decker houses!

Our landlord had some kind of problem in the family, a divorce or something, and we received an eviction notice because they needed the apartment for their family, so my mother said, "Let's get our own house."

We began looking at houses and went to the bank for a loan. The bank asked my father what he had for collateral. Did he have a car? No, he didn't. Although he had learned to drive in the service, we did not have our own car. No car for collateral? No loan!

My parents were born in Fall River, but my grandfather and grandmother Castro were from Oporto, Portugal. My grandfather and grandmother Oliveira were from São Miguel, Azores.

My father was the youngest in his family. He had three brothers, Antonio (Tony), Charles, Ernest, and a sister, Rose. His parents were skilled weavers and originally settled in Biddeford, Maine, to work in the cotton mills there. Labor problems in Biddeford brought them to Fall River in search of a friendlier work environment.

My father was thin and just over 6 feet tall. Everyone back then had nicknames. My father's nickname was Slim. Others in the neighborhood had nicknames such as Shiny, Rabby, Rigor, Lu Lu and La La (who I think were twins), Mac, Beany, Fat Man, etc.

As mentioned, my father's parents came from Portugal and my mother's parents came from the Azores. As a child, I noticed that generally, in my extended family, mainland Portuguese were taller than the Azorean Portuguese. Hoping that I would grow up to be a tall as my father, I was intrigued, and concerned, by the difference in height between my Castro family members and my Oliveira family members.

Having read in school about the Shetland ponies that originated from the Shetland Islands, I figured that, like those ponies, my Azorean ancestors, with a similar limited food supply and land area, adapted to their restricted island environment and stayed small in size. That realization meant it was doubtful I'd reach my father's height and, sure enough, I ended up as an adult closer in height to my Shetland-pony-sized Oliveira grandfather. Grandpa Oliveira, whenever we were together, would always tell me how great America was because in the Azores all he had to eat was grass. In America, he could eat whatever he wanted, whenever he wanted.

My mother loved education for education sake. She loved rounding up all the neighborhood kids, including hers, and playing school. She thought of Fall River as a wonderful city—except for the mills—and was very interested in local history. In the summer she would lead all of us on walks to the public library, historical society, browsing at Adam's Book Store, and out into area woodlands for picnics and nature study. For someone who had to drop out of school and go to work to support her family, she was very well read and loved New England.

As a kid interested in the arts and our natural environment, my mother spent a lot of time at "The People's University," our public library, and roaming about the Watuppa Reservation and Spencer Borden's Interlachen area. A restricted area because it is part of Fall River's municipal water supply lands, we were thrown out of Interlachen by the water department's watershed protection patrol a number of times.

That interest in everything New England and in our environment, taught to me by my mother over the years, means that by the time I was in my twenties I had hiked and camped in all of our New England states. Locally, I've walked almost every natural area in southeastern Massachusetts and neighboring Rhode Island. To this day, I have a fondness for the flora, fauna, and natural cycles of nature. I feel compelled to see, up close, the natural happenings that occur as seasons change, like it might not happen if I am not there to witness it.

**Food and Meals**

Not yet old enough for school, every morning my mother would turn on the radio and we'd listen to "Don McNeil's Breakfast Club" while eating our own breakfast and then follow Don by "marching around the breakfast table."

Various breakfast cereals were great back then because they came with neat trinkets like "secret decoder rings" and other neat stuff any kid would want. I remember choking down some pretty horrible cereal to get my reward, which was always at the very bottom of the box, hidden under the last few pieces of what, with milk added, turned out to be tasteless gruel.

After breakfast with Don McNeil came "The Arthur Godfrey Time." Sometimes, while listening to Arthur Godfrey, we would bake bread or, since various products, like butter, were heavily rationed due to the war, we'd make faux butter. Oleo or oleomargarine was a white mass

Charlton Hospital

South Main Street, looking north, circa 1955

of lard or some type of probably hydrogenated vegetable shortening that was sold as a butter substitute. It came in a plastic bag with a red dot in the middle of the bag that you had to squeeze and move around until the whole thing turned yellow like butter. It didn't taste like butter, but it was all that was available.

**"Uptown"**

When it was time to go shopping, my mom and I would walk to the corner of Weetamoe and North Main Streets, across from St. Joseph's Church, and wait at the bus stop for the bus that would take us "uptown."

Uptown was fantastic. It was more than a place. To a small child—and I think to many adults too—it was magical. When in the crowd, it seemed like there were thousands of people, all with important destinations. The Granite Block, across from present day Government Center, as its name implies, was a monolithic structure built from the very same granite that created Fall River. With professional offices above, and stores and shops below, it bustled with activity. All of South Main Street, in the heart of Fall River, was filled with shops and shoppers. Police walked their beats and others directed traffic at busy downtown intersections. Like everyone else, Mom and would shop at Kresge's, Woolworth's, and J.J. Newberry's 5 & 10 cent stores. Anchoring all this commerce was, of course, McWhirr's Department Store. At Christmas time, I and many other kids could spend hours watching trains in McWhirr's toy department chugging through mountains and around farms and villages.

Cherry and Webb Department Store was a more serious place. My mother could shop there for days at a time—or so it seemed to a little boy. If I behaved I would be rewarded with some pistachio nuts from Van Dykes or with messy powdered donuts from one of the 5 & 10 cent stores—where one could peer through the windows of an automated donut machine and watch the donuts magically being made. Every few seconds the donut dough would pop out of a tube in the shape of a white donut and land in a moat of hot oil. The donuts would float around a sinuous course until browned on one side. A spatula-like device would suddenly appear and flip the doughnut at just the right time to assure the other side would be evenly browned too. A special treat was scoring a strawberry ice cream soda at The Nonpareil on the west side of South Main Street.

**Recreation and Entertainment**

We played in the streets with a broomstick and a little ball, an old rag-stuffed sock for a football, kick the can, and flipped baseball cards off the curb. If you had a leaner, and you knocked it down, you got to keep the cards.

In the summer, fishing at the Taunton River was a fun thing to do. We would start out at low tide so my father could dig the rocky shore for fat seaworms that we would use for bait during high tide. My job was to spot the worms in the sand, mud, and rocks turned over by my father's clam fork, grab them and drop them in our bait pail. I usually became distracted by crabs and other shoreline creatures and my father, with sweat dripping off his nose, would have to do my job too.

In the late 1940s, before the waste-water treatment plant on Bay Street, the Taunton River, at low tide, was little more than a huge sewer. Many mills and other businesses along the river had sewer pipes that dumped directly into the river. Despite those conditions, many years before the 1972 Clean Water Act, we caught dozens of tautog, winter flounder (flatfish), eels, tomcod, cunner, and white perch from the river. On rare occasions, in May and June, we'd also catch striped bass.

One summer morning we caught so many large white perch from near the Shell Oil Tank Farm, now Route 79 where they filled in the river, that we stopped at all the neighborhood bars between the river and home, starting with the Old Trail Café, and gave away all the fish. Although the river is much cleaner today, the fish are not as abundant.

**School Life**

I walked through North Park to attend Borden Elementary School, which was located on the President Avenue side of the Park, just east of Morton Junior High, now Morton Middle School. I had just finished fourth grade when the school burned to the ground.

The school department decided to take the now schoolless Borden kids and bus them to the Westall School or Wiley School. My mother didn't want me bused so I enrolled in St. Michael's School, which was in two buildings, one on Fulton Street and the other Lindsey Street.

St. Michael's School was staffed by nuns from the Holy Union of the Sacred Hearts. I soon learned that they didn't fool around. Unlike public school, the parochial school students were given nightly homework assignments and the nuns in the classroom were fair, but much more serious, than the teachers I had at public school.

A little "corporal punishment"—in both public and parochial—kept most kids in line. In public school corporal punishment was administered via the feared "rattan." The rattan, often incorrectly called the "rat's hand" by scared-out-of-their-wits younger children, was a pliable piece of palm frond that the school principal would administer across the fingers of one's outstretched hand. The sting of the rattan on flesh was usually enough to convince most kids never to want to experience it again. The few it had little or no effect on eventually, we were told, ended up in "reform school" or, as adults, in some correctional facility.

I remember Sister Mary Jeremiah and Sister Jean Regis as being friendly and helpful to the students they were charged with educating. One sister, whose first name was Margaret, was the only one I remember that would tell us stories about her life before she joined the Holy Union Sisters. She was a nun with a history and would freely tell you about it. She was young. She was attractive. She would talk about art and nature—my two favorite interests.

School used to break for an hour and half at noontime and Sister Margaret used to take us down to the river, near the Bridge Diner, by the old Brightman Street Bridge. We would eat our lunches that we brought from home and she would point out shorebirds and crabs and seaweed and we would have a little science lesson.

Sister Margaret once told a story about when she was a girl and how her family would trap muskrats on Chesapeake Bay for their fur. After listening to her story, I thought it would be great to get some muskrats and make belts out of them. Wouldn't that be cool! So I got a number of my fellow students from the neighborhood, bought some rat traps from Benny's Hardware, and we set them down by the river and caught some big, nasty, Norway river rats. At lunch, we removed our catch from the traps and brought them back to school. We were going to skin the rats after school and make our cool belts that we just knew everyone would envy.

On lunch break, we found that we had caught three big river rats, but we couldn't bring them into the school and we had to hide them somewhere until the end of the school day. Back then one could still burn trash, and the school would burn trash in a fifty-five-gallon drum out back. It was a job for an eighth grader, a more mature kid, to burn the daily trash. We had our rats hidden behind the trash barrel for after-school pickup. Well, at afternoon recess, the kid who was the trash burner found the rats and, being a boy, he decided to chase the eighth grade girls with them.

The girls ran to Sister Jane Chantel. A big inquisition was held to find out where these rats came from. Sure enough, someone ratted me out!

Sister called me into her office but, before I reached her door, she yelled, "Stay right there, don't come any closer!" And then she tells me, in graphic detail, all about this big influenza epidemic from 1910 or something where people were dying right and left from diseases they caught from rats. I'm also told about the plague, the Black Death from the Middle Ages. She's so intense and convincing, I'm beginning to believe she was there, in the Middle Ages, and witnessed these terrible happenings.

She told me I had to take off my hat, and jacket, and sweater, since they could possibly be contaminated with rat germs, and put them outside until the end of the school day and sit outside of the office in this broken chair that pinched your bottom. At the close of school, I was told not to return to school unless accompanied by my father. He wasn't pleased since he had to take a day out of work and talk, mostly listen, to Sister Jane Chantel, so I would be allowed back into school. I was forbidden to go and catch another rat, but we did retrieve and stash our catch, since I couldn't bring them home, in Peter Silvestre's father's garage. We did skin them in the garage, when Peter's father wasn't around, and made our belts. Unfortunately, lacking knowledge of fur tanning, our cool belts soon smelled so badly we had to bury them.

**Neighborhood Experiences**

As can be seen, my childhood was spent in a wonderful neighborhood, typical of many in the city. In my neighborhood, the Portuguese went to St. Michael's Church, Irish to St. Joseph's, French Canadians to St. Mathieu's, Jews to Temple Beth-El, and the English to St. James, Union United Methodist, or Park United.

We had a neighborhood "rag man" with horse and wagon that would travel the streets yelling, "Rags, rags!" A similar fish peddler yelled through his horn the types of fish he had for sale on that particular day, usually Thursday, so that all the Catholics could have fish on Fridays. There were also numerous salesmen such as the Fuller Brush Man and weekly deliverymen bringing milk, newspapers, soda, and bread to your door. Neighborhoods were busy places.

Henry's Market was a butcher shop, with sawdust floors and fly paper strips hanging from the ceiling to waylay incoming flies before they landed on the meat being cut or ground and packaged right on the counter in front of the purchasers. Corky was the cobbler and there were variety stores, drug stores, markets, and bars within a five to fifteen minute walk of anyone in the North End.

When I was a kid, North Park was beautiful. I used to walk through it every day on my way to school and then back home. There were flowers planted in the park gardens each spring, there were park laborers who maintained them, and there were park police who patrolled the city parks and yelled at kids if they strayed into flower beds or disturbed another's enjoyment of the park. In the fall, we would collect acorns and sticks, fashion little pipes, and pretend we were smoking. For Thanksgiving, we'd gather pine cones and add pipe cleaner legs and neck and, with some added construction paper heads and tails, turn the pine cones into miniature turkeys.

In the winter, the city park department would add water to the park ponds and skating areas so that ice would freeze evenly and one could ice skate on them. In the spring and summer, kids would wade around with little sailboats on strings. Fall River's neighborhood parks were beautiful.

Apparently, polio and television changed all that. I'm sure there were other reasons too why the city parks were ignored and left to decay. Ponds were drained to halt polio and other "diseases," folks stayed closer to home because, suddenly, tiny black and white televisions, with big magnifying glasses in front of them, appeared and held people hostage. Yes, TV helped kill the city parks.

I was born at the extreme tail end of the Wild West era, less than 100 years after the Civil War. The Battle of the Little Bighorn/Custer's Last Stand was in 1876. Books, movies, and especially TV were all "cowboys and Indians"—Roy Rogers, Dale Evans, Hopalong Cassidy, The Lone Ranger, Cisco Kid, Wyatt Earp, and hundreds more. My sister had a cowgirl outfit; we all had shiny, faux pearl-handled revolvers and lots of rolls of caps. If I close my eyes, I can still smell the gun smoke. If you were a young boy or girl, you would run around like you were on a horse with your hands holding the reins.

That section of the city, in the North End, near Brightman Street and the Brightman Street Bridge, was known as the Village. The Village had its own shops, markets, restaurants, and theater—the Royal. One store I frequented on lunch break from school was Parente's Variety, on the corner of Norfolk and Fulton Streets. Parente's had the most extensive line of penny candy and, amazingly, two-for-a-penny candies than anywhere in the North End. The store was frequented by hordes of kids from both St. Michael's and St. Mathieu's schools. Old and seemingly slow to us kids, Mr. Parente was watching all the time and any horsing around or other unruly behavior could get you banned from the store.

In the early 1950s, kids and dogs roamed freely from dawn until our mothers yelled for us to come home just before dark. Early on we were warned about "strangers," but there were apparently very few roaming around our neighborhood back then. By twelve years old, most of us were hitchhiking, "thumbing rides," to get uptown and back. In my circle of acquaintances I don't remember anyone not surviving that activity.

Of course, all that was about to slowly change over the next decade, but during the 1940s and 1950s, Fall River was a great place to be if you were a child—and I and my friends had some wonderful times during all seasons.

# Robert Chavenson

*Born in 1928*

**Family Background**

I was born in Fall River at Union Hospital. My parents were David and Ida (Levin) Chavenson.

My father's parents were Aaron and Bessie (Yoken) Chavenson. My mother's parents were Samuel and Celia (Sandler) Levin. My mother's parents married in Fall River on June 26 1892.

My mother was born in 1893, at their home on the corner of Hope and Union Streets, and then lived on East Main Street. My mother was the oldest in her family. My mother's brother Isadore went to Harvard in 1919, and graduated in the class of 1923. He became an attorney in Fall River and was one of the oldest attorneys in the city when he ceased practicing at the age of eighty-nine. My mother's father was a butcher before he got into the wholesale grocery business. She said that her father would take her to Somerset to buy meat. She enjoyed crossing the Slade's Ferry Bridge with its rail tracks above. A trip to Somerset was a thrill for my mother.

Cousin Richard Levin became a law partner of my uncle Isadore Levin, his son. They had an office at 57 North Main Street, on the third floor above the Fall River National Bank. My uncle Isadore insisted that his last name be pronounced as if it was spelled as Levine. So, the name of the firm was Levin and Levin (the latter pronounced as if it were Levine). My uncle said that his father was very proud of that name and its unique pronunciation. My uncle was Dick Levin's father; Dick currently has his office on Rock Street.

My mother and father were married in 1914 and went on the New York boat on their honeymoon.

My father grew up in the Orthodox Synagogue on Union Street. My mother's father was president of that synagogue. He wouldn't ride on Jewish holidays. My father's father lived on the second floor of 592 Broadway. He was president of the synagogue on Quarry Street for thirty-five years. He and his son, my father, did not go to the same synagogue. My father preferred the Union Street Synagogue because he could walk to it. My mother and father later became members of Temple Beth El on High Street.

My father had five siblings: Maria (nee Rye), Lottie, Lillian, Hattie, and Marcia (nee Minnie). My mother had seven siblings: Michael, Isadore, Francis, Louis, Mildred, Gertrude, and Bernice Rosalie. My father came from Russia when he was four months old.

I have three siblings: Anita (Gross), born in 1916, Morton, born in 1918, and Robert, born in 1928.

Our family lived in Fall River at 592-594 Broadway.

My wife's name is Ann (Shriberg) Chavenson. We were married in 1952.

**Family Life**

I was born at 298 Third Street, close to the Lizzie Borden house. In 1929, we moved to 592 Broadway.

My sister Anita was pretty and was an actress and an artist. She won the "most versatile" title in the Durfee [B.M.C. Durfee High School] yearbook, class of 1933.

In his later years, my grandfather was blind, but he always knew the time. He would lift up the phone, the operator would come on, and he would say, "This is Mr. Chavenson and I would like to know the time." I guess the operator felt sorry for him and always told him the time. One night, I came home late, tripped over a rope, and made some noise. My grandfather called out and I said, "It's only me, Grandpa." The next day, I told him I came in at 12:30 am. "You're a liar," he said. "You came in at 2:30." I was mystified as to how he knew the real time. Later, my cousin told me that he had been on the phone with the operator and got the time.

My father was a lousy traveler. I'm not sure he ever went on the New York boats more than once. He didn't like to travel. He loved baseball and would listen to it on the radio. When he was asked to go see a Red Sox game in Boston, he replied, "But it's too long to get there." When the Fall River Line went down, their fixtures were sold. My mother bought a fancy towel hamper that she kept for years.

Dr. Sanford Udis and I were partners in buying a hundred dollar share in the production of *Below the Hill*.

Since my father was in the food business, my mother knew the vendors and would go into the markets and squeeze the produce. After my father died, I would take her to the circus grounds market. She would parade in the store and squeeze the tomatoes and other produce. Once, she had a basket of tomatoes and calls over a sales guy. "One of these is too soft," she said, and told the guy to replace it. I was embarrassed and told the guy to forgive her. He replied, "You're Mrs. Chavenson's son? Don't worry. Anything she wants is okay."

My mom liked bankbooks. She liked to see in black and white what she put in the bank. She stayed in line and got in front. "I'm an old lady," she told the other people waiting in line. I said, "I have to apologize for her; she's ninety-eight." It was okay by them.

The Chavenson's didn't build the houses on Chavenson Street. My grandfather, Aaron Chavenson, gave the land to the City of Fall River if it named the street for him.

**Food and Meals**

We ate well. My grandfather and father were both in the wholesale grocery business. If my mother wanted a can of tomato juice, she had to take a whole case. She had no room in the kitchen, so the cellar was full of canned goods. I never had coffee until college.

**School Life**

I went to the Osborn School for first and second grades. From there, I went to the Fowler School on Sprague Street for six years and graduated from there in 1941. I then attended Henry Lord Junior High for one year, class of 1942. From Henry Lord, I went to Durfee High School for my sophomore year. I attended Dean Academy in Franklin, where I played football, basketball, and baseball. From there, I went to Westminster College in New Wilmington, Pennsylvania, for four years and earned my BA.

At Durfee, we had a Latin teacher, Frances Langford, who had been at Durfee in 1912 when my mother graduated from there. She flunked me in Latin II. She caught me using a "trot," or a translation. She told the whole class, "I want you to listen to something," and then she read from my paper and the trot.

**Recreation and Entertainment**

We lived one and one-half blocks from South Park [now Kennedy Park]. All our activities were in South Park. We ice skated and played baseball and football in the park. We loved the park. We were very fortunate to live near a public park.

I lived near the Broadway circus grounds. When the circus came to town, the kids were allowed to be excused from school to go to the matinée performance of the circus. The teacher would say, "All those excused for the circus, raise your hands." Five or six of us would raise our hands and be excused. We walked from the Fowler School to the circus. The school considered it an educational experience.

The circus parade came right up Broadway. The circus animals were discharged, sometimes in the night, from the train at the bottom of Broadway, near Columbia Street. As the parade came up Broadway, I got up in the middle of the night to watch them. Sometimes, they would go through the downtown during the day. They spent two days in the city. The circus included a Wild West Show, with cowboys on horses, shooting guns. There were three rings. The better seats were in the middle of the ring; we sat more to the end. The side-shows had a separate admission. The circus included freaks like ladies with beards and lions and tigers. They were cheaper than the main shows. There were peep shows, also, with ladies showing skin. No kids were allowed.

**Work Life**

Grandfather Chavenson's first wholesale grocery business was at 1030 Pleasant Street, above where County and Quarry Streets meet Pleasant Street (where the U-Haul truck rental business is now) at Stafford Square. It was called Aaron Chavenson and Son; later, when my father bought it, he renamed it the American Wholesale Grocery Company, and that business was located at 29 Anawan Street, near Water Street.

My mother's father, Sam Levin, owned the New England Wholesale Company, located at the corner of Union and Columbia Streets. It was in the lower Spring Street neighborhood, which was then a Jewish ghetto. Both grandfathers were friendly competitors in the wholesale grocery business.

When I got out of the service, I joined my cousin in Ann Dale Products in Fall River. My first cousin on my father's side, David Rubin, started it here in 1943-1944. We made 4-H cookies. We got to know all of the 4-H agents. I became active in 4-H and Bristol Aggie activities. I remained at Ann Dale from 1953 to 1978, when Ann Dale closed in Fall River.

From there, I founded a company called Club Sales, Inc. We are a national cookie and candy distributor and make club cookies for the 4-H clubs. The 4-H is the only organization that I know of that would take a shot at competing with the Girl Scouts. Most of the 4-H clubs were in the mid-Atlantic states.

**Neighborhood Experiences**

I took the trolley to downtown. My father had an auto and my brother drove it. My brother would drive me to Henry Lord Junior High School. We were so geographically-oriented that we hung around with our own South End guys even at Durfee.

Many deliveries were made to the home. Kosher bread was delivered by a local baker, Sammy Burstein. I remember when Sammy put bread in a bag and wrote the amount on a pad that hung at the door. Eggs and blueberries were delivered by a knock at the door.

**World War II**

When Pearl Harbor struck that Sunday, I was playing Glen Miller records at my house. When we got the word, I walked over to our Broadway hangout on the corner of Middle Street and Broadway and met the gang in front of Pete's Spa. We were talking about the invasion. The next day, the President said it was a "Day of Infamy." In December of 1941, Charlie Meretsky said that he was going to join up and, when he turned sixteen a few months later, he went into the Navy.

I was the youngest in the gang and didn't get called into the service. It was not until I was in college in 1945, at eighteen, when my roommate got called; he was three months older than I was. He got called and I didn't. I was that close to being called.

I went to New York City for two years, from 1949 to 1951, to work in the plastic drapery business, then into the military service during the Korean War, where I served in Germany in an Army Band. I played trumpet and English horn. The Germans enjoyed marching music. It was good PR for the Army. We had a specialist who taught us how to make numerals in the field. We played at half-time during soccer games. We were stationed in the bombed-out city of Ulm on the Danube, between Bavaria and Hess. Ulm separated the two states. Einstein was born there. I was in the military from 1951 to 1953.

Ann was allowed to stay with me for six months in Germany. We lived in a hotel and ate and lived well. I had a Class A pass, which allowed me to be on duty only during working hours. In the morning, I would drive to where I had to go on duty. I would practice my music with the band. When I drove in, they would salute me because of my hat; they didn't know my real rank. Three months after that, we rented a room with a German family consisting of a husband, a wife, and an aunt. The husband held a job with the town of Ulm. He was educated and spoke some English. Ann was taking conversational German and he helped her with her German and she helped him with his English. He also educated her on German culture. He made it very clear that he had never been a Nazi, but his wife was an admitted Nazi but repentant. They made it clear that they held no ill feelings for Jews. We remained in contact with them for thirty-one years.

The street conductors in Germany at that time looked like SS officers, with high black boots. The guy I bought a car from there was a committed Nazi. He used a German-English dictionary to talk with me. His wife was the daughter of a banker, and the Nazi military didn't like bankers. At the time they were married, the military gave her father the job of sweeping streets. We remained friends with the couple.

# William M. Chebot

*Born on December 29, 1927*

**Family Background**

My parents were Norman B. and Elizabeth M. (Ostroff) Chebot. I have two siblings, Bernard and Paul.

I lived at 637 Birch Street, in the Globe, from my birth to twelve years old, and at 473 Madison Street, from twelve to the Army and marriage.

My father's parents were Boruch and Pauline (Schraer) Chebot. My mother's parents were Jacob and Ida (Dondis) Ostroff.

My mother's siblings were Benjamin, Bessie, and Sonia.

My wife is Nehoma ("Hummy") Chebot.

**Family Life**

My father owned a furniture store on South Main Street, between Benjamin and Dwelly Streets, called Norman Mills. There weren't many Jewish people in the South End or the Globe. A lot of people called us "those rich Jews." We had a new car every other year and we had a maid. We were comfortable but not wealthy.

My father owned the three-family house that we lived in on Birch Street. He was a lenient landlord. The upstairs family worked in the textile mills. When the mills were idle, he would say to them, "Don't worry about the rent. We'll take care of it." They were all great tenants, who helped out around the house, including the yard.

We had a summer cottage at Common Fence Point [in Portsmouth, Rhode Island] and Bob Chavenson would come over to visit. There was a bellboy [buoy] at the tip of Common Fence Point that had clappers. At night, the sound of the bells was calming and soothing. One day, when Bob was visiting, we went out on the water with our speedboat and Bob said, "I want to go out to the bellboy." He got on the bellboy and started making the bellboy sway and ring. We thought we would play a trick on him and started the boat and sped away. He was upset being stranded on the bellboy, but we came back to get him.

My wife's family lived on Chavenson Street. They lived at 15 Chavenson Street and were one of the first families to buy a house on the street when it was first built. The street was mostly Jewish, except for one or two families. All of the houses on the street (triple-deckers) were the same. My wife had an uncle who was an artist. He didn't drive. He would visit his brother, my father-in-law, occasionally by train from Boston to get away from the city's heat. In those days, no one locked their doors. Once, he came down late in the night and went into the house and into the bedroom where he usually went to go to bed. The son saw him and said, "What are you doing here?" He asked him, "What are *you* doing here?" Finally, he realized that he had gone to the right apartment in the wrong building. They were friends of the family, so there were no repercussions.

My brother Bernard was a concert violinist. He had a masters degree from Julliard. He was quite talented. He played under Leopold Stokowski and Walter Damrosch. He was also a soloist.

When he was at Julliard, Howard Wetherall, a local textile manufacturer, said to him, "I have a friend named Booth Tarkington, an author of many famous books, who would love to hear you play. Could you come to Kennebunkport, Maine, and play for him?" Bernard got a fellow student pianist to accompany him to Fall River, where they met up with Mr. Wetherall and proceeded up to Kennebunkport in Mr. Wetherall's chauffeur-driven Packard limousine. Bernard played for him and Mr. Tarkington was impressed and autographed one of his books for Bernard. Bernard also played for the aluminum industrialist Henry Kaiser.

When Bernard was in the Navy, he was on the cruiser *USS Augusta*, the ship that took President Harry Truman to the Potsdam conference. The ship captain asked Bernard if he would put a program together and perform for the president, and he did. Truman was impressed. The president called him over after and pressed his hand. Truman wrote on the program for Bernard, "From one musician to another, Harry S. Truman." Truman, of course, played the piano.

When Bernard graduated from [B.M.C.] Durfee High School, he applied for a scholarship from the school. However, the scholarship committee said that they didn't give aid to a student who was going to a music school, but they made an exception in his case.

When we lived at 473 Madison Street, we had a paperboy who was dressed in ragged and torn clothes. My mother took pity on him and would invite him in for hot chocolate and sweets. One day, she wanted to give him some decent clothes to wear, but he said, "No, that's all right; I like these old clothes." As it turns out, he lived in the big brick house on the northeast corner of Highland Avenue and Hood Street. Imagine! My mom thought he was poor.

**School Life**

I attended the Harriett T. Healy School for kindergarten, then the Slade School through seventh grade. When we moved to 473 Madison Street, I went to Morton Junior High School and started in the eighth grade. When I entered Morton, I was put into shop class. I wanted to study at a higher level and wanted to study Latin. However, the Latin classes were full, and the principal said, "How would you want to go into a French class?" I did quite well and graduated from Morton.

I then went to [B.M.C.] Durfee High School for three years. I played the oboe and the piano and participated in many activities there, including the orchestra and the drama program.

**Holidays and Special Occasions**

At Rosh Hashanah, on the Jewish New Year, I blow the shofar, which is a Jewish instrument. It is a real horn made from a ram's horn. Except for the four years I was away in college and two years in the Army, I have blown the shofar for sixty years at Temple Beth El. I have blown it every year except when Rosh Hashanah falls on the Sabbath, when you can't do any work, and blowing the shofar is considered work.

My Ostroff grandparents were strictly kosher. Everything had to be just so. Once, when we went to New York, my mom came home, opened the refrigerator and found a ham there. My mother was horrified and asked the live-in maid, "Olga, what is this?" Olga said, "Oh, it's okay; it's wrapped up in a package." My mom replied, "But, it shouldn't be in the house!" She called her parents to ask them what to do. Should she have the refrigerator taken away? What to do? They said, "Take out the shelves, take them out and bury them in the ground and then scald them. Then, scrub the refrigerator thoroughly."

## Recreation and Entertainment

We played baseball and football. We played cowboys, police, and aviators. We made up our stories as we went along. At Halloween there was no trick or treating, at least not in our neighborhood. We would just go out with costumes and walk around on the streets making noise.

I loved the cowboy Tom Mix. I had the official Tom Mix cowboy suit. My grandfather would put up circus posters on his store window and would get free tickets to the circus as a result. I wanted to see Tom Mix. I listened to his show on the radio called the "Ralston Straight Shooters." Ralston was a cereal company and the sponsor.

My grandfather gave us passes and our upstairs neighbor took us. I went wearing my Tom Mix cowboy suit. "Do you want to see Tom Mix?" they asked. We met him backstage. I couldn't contain myself. He shook my hand and patted me on the back. "Glad to meet you," he said. I told him that I listened to him on the radio every day. I didn't know that it was an actor playing him on the radio. I couldn't wait to go to school the next day to tell the kids that I had met Tom Mix. I was about six or seven at the time.

We had a summer place at Island Park [Cashman's Park, Portsmouth, Rhode Island] that the 1938 hurricane took away. We had to hand-pump water at the cottage and go back to Fall River to take a bath. We always had a boat and went fishing in it. We would watch the big boats go by on their way to the Tiverton Yacht Club. The Cherrys from Cherry and Webb had one of these yachts and Rhode Island Governor Metcalf also had one of them. We would wave to them and they would wave back.

## Work Life

When I was in high school, my father owned a furniture store, the New England Furniture Co. In those days, everyone bought on credit. Customers put two or five dollars down and paid twenty-five or fifty cents or a dollar a week. My first job was working for my father going door to door collecting. When I got my license, I started doing it. I knocked on the door and they would give me a quarter or a half-dollar. They had a card and I had a card, and I marked both. I initialed each card next to the amount paid. Stores had carrying charges for credit purchases. Once, a customer said, "No, I have a truck to carry it, so don't charge a carrying charge," and my father had to explain what a carrying charge meant.

## Neighborhood Memories

Before we moved to the house on Madison Street, there was a big parcel of vacant land on Highland Avenue between Weetamoe and Stewart Streets. One day, my father said that he wanted to build a house on part of the land. My father asked the gardener, Phil Landsenorfer, who owned the land. "Dr. Truesdale," he said. This was Dr. Philemon Truesdale of Truesdale Hospital. My father found out who the agent for the land was and bought the lot on the corner of Highland Avenue and Weetamoe Street. He had plans made for an English Tudor house with a master bedroom on the first floor, for when he got old. He put it out to bid and awarded it to a contractor. However, before the work started, the contractor went broke. Since there were no materials during the war, my father decided to wait until after the war and come back to the project. But by then he had bought the Madison Street house. He made extensive renovations to the house. I was twelve at the time and remained there except when I was in college and then into the Army.

Judge Cook was one of our neighbors when we lived at 473 Madison Street and my father knew

Slade School at the turn of the century

the judge quite well. When we got married, we needed something like a waiting period waived so we could get married before I left for Korea. The judge arranged it. Some of our neighbors on Madison Street were the Staffords from Stafford Insurance. Their son, John Stafford, was my brother's age and friends with him. Next door was Joseph Horowitz, who owned Darwood Manufacturing.

**Downtown**
The trolley took my mom and me downtown. My mother took driving lessons from my uncle's chauffeur, but when something got into her eye while she was driving, she decided she no longer wanted to drive. My father took her where she wanted to go.

The downtown was crowded. My middle brother Paul once took his wife shopping at McWhirr's. His wife had come down with cancer and walked with the aid of a walker, and it took her a while to get around. He told her that he would drop her off in front of the store. Paul parked his car in the parking lot in back of the store. When he made it to the front, his wife told him that as she walked to the store entrance people passing by were putting money into the basket on front of her walker.

**Health and Illness**
When we had sore throats, my mother got tincture of benzine. We would go to the bathroom, pour steaming hot water in the wash bowl, on a towel, and put a towel over our heads to breathe the steam vapors to relieve the condition. It was not an unpleasant inhalation.

**World War II**

During World War II, it was hard to get furniture for the store. Only big stores like Mason's, Adaskin's, and Modern Furniture could get an allocation of furniture and only because they had been in operation for a while.

In 1944, my father went to Boston, to the Singer Sewing Machine Company, to get machinery to start a sewing shop. He went to the Singer Company. However, because of the war, you couldn't get machinery. A Mr. Eustice said, "I'll see what I can do." A few days later, they sent my father eight sewing machines. He rented a vacant store next to his furniture store on East Main Street and hired a forelady. Eight girls were hired to start. When my father came in to open the first day, he found that he was being picketed. "Why am I being picketed?" he asked. "Because you're not a union shop," they said. "But, there are more people outside picketing than I have working inside." My father made a deal so that he would get the union in after he got going.

As the business grew, he discontinued the furniture store and made it one big shop at 252 East Main Street. He had a nice crew there. He then moved to 135 Alden Street and named it NBC Garment, for Norman B. Chebot. Later, he decided to form a sportswear company and called it CBS, Chebot Brothers Sportswear. At one time, he had ninety people working for him. He did this until the garment industry went south where there were no unions.

**The Fall River Line**

The first time I went on the Fall River Line, my brother was at the Julliard at the time. My father was going to New York on business, and we kids wanted to go. "I'll take you on the boat, but you have to get off at Newport. Harold [a neighbor] will pick you up there and bring you back." We got on board the ship and arrived at Newport. "We have to get off now," we said. Then he said, "Surprise! We all are going all the way to New York!" I was about seven then and happy to be going to New York. We were on the steamship *Plymouth* of the Fall River Line.

When we had the cottage on Common Fence Point, we would watch the New York boats go by. We watched them all the time. Once, I took the speed boat and tried to ride the wake, but it was too much. The boat almost capsized. I never tried it again!

When the Fall River Line was disbanded, they were selling off all kinds of things. My father bought six life preservers with pockets that had cork in them as flotation devices. We used to tie them together and float on them. I don't know what happened to them.

**Military Career**

I was in the Army stationed at Fort Dix [near Trenton, New Jersey]. Every Friday night, we had Jewish services. Chaplain Max Daina heard me singing and asked me to assist him in conducting the services, which I did. I was scheduled to work for the Quartermaster Corps. "Do you want to do that or be my assistant?" He got ordered to Germany. This was at the time of the Korean War. He asked me if I wanted to go with him, but I would have had to re-up for two more years, and I said no. He said, "Let me see what I can do for you." He called Camp Edwards Air Force Base and spoke with the chaplain there; he knew the post chaplain, Father Stoltz. He told the chaplain, "I'm going to Germany and I have an assistant working for me and he can't since he doesn't have enough time left in the service. Can you use him?" And he said he needed a Jewish assistant.

In the chaplain's office, I conducted services, visited men in hospitals, and brought them kosher food from the Jewish Welfare Board.

Then an edict came down: anyone in our unit who hadn't been overseas will go to Korea. My fiancé was upset. "Let's get married," she said. I was due to be sent over almost immediately. Her sister made the arrangements for the wedding. Rabbi [Samuel] Ruderman was fond of us. He was away for the months and I called him up and said, "We are getting married on August 8th. We don't want to spoil your vacation, however." He said, "Billy, if I were in China, I would come back to marry you." And we got married.

A couple days later, the personnel officer who knew me from attending Jewish services came in and asked, "How would you like to go to Germany rather than Korea?" I went to Germany and was stationed in a God-forsaken town called Sonthofen, where I interviewed incoming soldiers to determine what they could do. We had a chart that showed the openings for things like truck mechanics, cooks, etc.

It was all right, but I was interested in getting back to being a chaplain's assistant. It happened that Chaplain Daina was a chaplain in Nuremberg. He called me and said, "Bill, I was wondering what happened to you. Do you want to come and work for me?" "Sure," I said, and shortly got transfer papers for Nuremberg.

In Nuremberg, my office was in a tremendous building called the Palace of Justice, where the Nazi war crimes trials were held. The courtroom was still set up as they had it during the trials, with the headphones on the desks. The execution area was in the back, where they hung some of the guilty defendants.

In a case of poetic justice, they had knocked down several partitions between the offices of Nazi bigwigs and made a beautiful Jewish chapel there. We had services there every Friday. Before Passover, the Quartermaster Corps got new pots and pans and plates and silverware for our Kosher Passover Seder. All of the European Command were invited to the services. We even got an article in the *Stars and Stripes* paper.

Because my wife wasn't with me the first six months of my tour of duty in Germany, I accumulated a lot of leave. So when she got to Germany, I took forty-five days of leave time and we traveled all over Europe together, to make up for the honeymoon we had stateside on a three-day pass.

I had a picture of my wife on my desk. One day, a Jewish civilian, who had come to our services, came by and asked who it was. I told him and said that I couldn't bring her over because I wasn't going to be in Germany long enough to obtain government quarters. Also, the accommodations were poor because Nuremberg was bombed out. "Why didn't you tell me," he said. "I own an apartment house and one of the renters is a stockholder in a major US corporation and is away and is not due back for a while. If I ask him to sublet, I'm sure he will." When I saw the apartment, I couldn't believe it. It was an eight-room apartment, and it came with a maid. "I can't afford this on a corporal's pay!" The rent was only twenty-five dollars a month, which I could afford. He said, "Don't worry; I want someone in the apartment to keep the lights on."

In those days, few people flew on airplanes, so my wife came over on the *SS America*. She couldn't believe the apartment. I had six months left of my one-year tour in Germany. After he attended the Passover Seder services, Bob Chavenson (from Fall River) came to the apartment to visit. He was also stationed in Germany.

# Robert and Gertrude (Francoeur) Chouinard

*Robert was born on December 29, 1927*

*Present during this interview were:*
- *Robert and Gertrude (Francoeur) Chouinard. Bob was born on the third floor of 430 Eastern Avenue. Gert was born at 192 Thomas Street and lived there until she was married. The house is still occupied by family members.*
- *Richard and Julie Perry. Richard was born on December 14, 1930; Julia was born on June 6, 1936.*
- *Germaine (Francoeur) Sirois, born on May 31, 1924, on Flint Street, across from Chouinard's grocery store.*
- *Andy and Jeannette (Francoeur) Roy. Jeannette was born on January 18, 1927, at 192 Thomas Street and grew up there. Andy was born on April 26, 1926, on Knight Street and was raised there.*
- *Joe and Marian Jean. Joe grew up at 171 McCloskey Street. Marian was raised at 162 Tremont Street. Joseph Jean was born on August 30, 1921, and died on October 31, 2010.*

**Family Life**

*Robert:* The family gathered around the radio. You had to use your imagination when listing to shows like "The Shadow," "Lux Presents Hollywood," "Inner Sanctum," and the "Green Hornet."

*Germaine:* There were eleven children in our family, but one died in childbirth. One of our brothers joined the Society of Brothers at aged thirteen.

*Marion:* If a girl wasn't married by twenty-one, that was a problem. Girls typically got married at eighteen. We got married at 8:00 in the morning and just family came to the breakfast. In the afternoon, we had a reception for friends and served sandwiches and our wedding cake. That was the typical: a breakfast for family and a simple afternoon reception for friends. There was a best man and maid of honor, but the fathers were part of the ceremony.

*Robert:* Many wedding receptions were held at home also. Wakes were also held from the home. Some of us paid for our own weddings when our parents didn't. Gifts were all practical items to start the household.

*Germaine:* Babies were born at home. When mom had a baby, we kids were sent away to stay with relatives. Once, I remember that we were sent to the movies and our oldest sister came and made sure that we stayed through as many movies as it took until it was all right to come home. When we arrived home, we found a new baby brother. We were always told that our new brothers and sisters were "brought by Indians." Of course, we believed them. We were all very innocent then.

*Andy:* When shoes got holes in their soles, a new sole would be glued over the existing sole.

However, when it rained, the sole would come loose and start flapping. Some kids wore cardboard in their shoes when the soles got holes.

*Germaine:* We found out later in life that Dad was once a trapeze artist. When he met and fell in love with Mom, she said it was either she or the circus, since she was not going to have a husband who was traveling with the circus. When the circus came to town, Dad would always bring us kids there. Each time, the circus people would try to get Dad to join the circus again. He would discuss this with Mom, who finally said enough with the talk of going away with the circus. She then took his old trapeze uniform and she made them into short and long pants for the older boys. He never lost his circus ways, however, and was always an antic with the kids.

*Jeannette:* Father's occupation was a paperhanger, and he would go from job to job with his bicycle and a cart that held his paperhanging materials. Later, he bought a station wagon with wood-paneled sides. On a trip to Maine, along the old state highways (beginning with Route 138), we would stop in Mattapan [outside of Boston] and get "mile-long" hot dogs and ice cream. We always looked forward to stopping there. It took forever to get there and we were always asking, "Are we there yet," and Dad would say, "Yes, it's just ahead, I can see it." There were ten kids in that station wagon.

## Christmas, Holidays, and Special Occasions

*Germaine:* The first Christmas tree we got was the year my sister Noella was born. The nurse who came to the house to see after my mother told my mother and father that just a tree with a few lights would make it look more like Christmas. My sister was born on Christmas Day, 1932.

*Gertrude:* When we old enough, we could attend Midnight Mass, then gathered for French meat pies, called *tourtière*. As family members married and had families of their own, all came to Mom and Dad's on Christmas Day for a family meal.

*Jeannette:* Christmas was a great time at our house. We would all go to Mass on Christmas Eve with our friends. After Mass, everyone would come to our house. Mom would have the table set and we would have meat pies and apple pies (Mom would make four or five pies). When Christmas morning arrived, we all had a stack of toys under the tree in the parlor and a stocking filled with an apple, an orange, nuts, and all sorts of candy. Our friends were always welcome.

## Recreation and Entertainment

*Robert:* The streets were our playground. We played kick the can, marbles, peggy ball, or peggy stick. When the streetlights went on, we had to come into the house.

*Julie:* Grandmother would keep an eye on us from the porch; we always had to stay in view. We played in the yard a lot. We girls couldn't go out of the yard. However, we played hide and seek and other games in the yard. Everyone had a fence between their yards. Grandfather played checkers on the front porch and the neighborhood kids came up to play with him. Grandfather was known to cheat. Paper dolls were popular; we would spend hours playing with our paper dolls. A few families would trade comic books.

*Robert:* Lafayette Park was a site of much recreational activity. We played tennis on the courts and used stoops to hit tennis balls to the first, second and third floors of houses.

*Gertrude:* We would put our ice skates on and walk on our skates to Lafayette Park to skate on the outdoors rink.

*Robert:* We played soccer with the brothers and they were excellent players, but tough! They would tie up their cassocks to play. Some of us thought they had metal under their cassocks!

The Strand and the Nickelodeon were the movie theatres on Pleasant Street. Tuesday night was dish night at the Strand, twenty-five cents for adults and ten cents for kids. When we were older, we would go downtown to the Durfee Theatre with its ushers who were all dressed up in their uniforms. We remember head usher John McAvoy in his caped uniform.

*Joe:* On Saturday night, we would ride the buses and pass the ticket to our friends or let them in by the side door. At Talbot's Ice Cream, we would call in orders for ice cream sundaes ten minutes before closing. We would put old floor nails on the train track and the train would flatten it so it looked like a quarter, which we used for the movies. Some kids would pull the rod off the electric wires and the trolley would stop.

*Robert:* There were Friday night dances, with a one-man band (Leon Mello) that played records called "Colorvox" and accompanied the records with various instruments.

*Joe:* When the Fall River Line steamboats would dock, they would sometimes let the kids go on the ships, under the watchful eye of a staff person. I went on the *Plymouth* and the *Commonwealth*. The *Commonwealth* was impressive and had a double sweeping staircase very much like the staircase of the *Titanic*.

*Robert:* We could rent boats for twenty-five cents an hour at Napert boathouse at the Narrows.

*Joe:* We would go ice skating at the Narrows. Once, when a party went skating, my older, twenty-year-old brother went on the ice first and fell through the ice. Under the ice, he couldn't find his way out and drowned. When they brought him up, he had a rosary in his hand.

*Gertrude:* On Lake Noquochoke, across from Lincoln Park, there was "Musical Beach," a favorite spot in the summer. We took a bus up to Lincoln Park, then cut across through woods with a path to Reed Road and Musical Beach.

*Robert:* There was an electric trolley car on Pleasant Street that went all the way to Lincoln Park. It was open and swayed back and forth as it moved.

*Joe:* Dancing at Lincoln Park was popular. Richard and Julie first met there in 1954. Every Wednesday, Friday, and Saturday night the big bands would play there. Band leaders included Buddy Braga, Buddy Reis, Gene Marshall, and Charlie Weygand. Big name singers like Vaughn Monroe and Glen Grey would sing there. My niece sang for Vaughn Monroe. He wanted her to go to Atlantic City with him, but her dad said no, because he knew what it was like being on the road in show business. He was a musician with the NBC Orchestra.

*Robert:* The Carnival Drive-In was a great spot for fried clams, as was McCray's on Route 6.

**School Life**

*Jeannette:* We all went to Notre Dame School. Tuition was fifty cents per month. Half of the day we spoke French. The teachers were the Jesus Mary Sisters. The teachers at Prevost were the Brothers of Christian Instruction. The Sisters of St. Joseph, called the gray nuns, operated the St. Joseph's Orphanage.

*Joe:* Boys stayed at Notre Dame School until the fifth grade and then went to the Prevost Annex. Girls stayed at Notre Dame until the eighth grade and then went to Jesus Mary Academy or Durfee High [B.M.C. Durfee High School]. In addition to French class, religion was taught in French. Some of the brothers who came from Canada spoke only French. Since Prevost was the only Catholic boys high school in the city, kids from all over the city attended there.

*Robert:* Lots of Prevost boys married Jesus Mary girls.

*Jeannette:* When we girls came home for lunch, we had to wear aprons to protect our uniforms. Grandfather, a practical joker, would sometimes untie the aprons and retie them around the back of the chair, so that when we got up, we would fall back into the seat.

*Robert:* One of my first memories is of the 1938 hurricane, when I was eight years old and lived on Bedard Street. A 2x4 came in straight through our window. No one had experienced a hurricane and had no idea what was happening as the winds grew stronger. After the hurricane, everyone came out of their homes and were amazed at the damage.

*Joe:* I went to the Turnpike School, which was at the intersection of Pleasant Street and Eastern Avenue, where the Night Owl is now. I was a little over two years old when I began there. All you needed to attend was a passing knowledge of English and be able to walk. It was a big school. After that, I went to the Eastern Avenue [Watson] School. Once each month, all the classes went to the church for confessions.

*Gertrude:* I was a member of the drill team at Notre Dame. We had no band but we marched and competed with other teams in Massachusetts, Connecticut, and Rhode Island.

*Robert:* There were no dances; the priest didn't believe in it. However, that changed later.

## Neighborhood Experiences

*Joe:* I lived on Pleasant Street on the fourth floor of a building that had businesses on the first floor. Mitchell's Candy Kitchen was on the corner of Pleasant and Choate Streets. It had a marble-topped fountain, ice cream, and candies. Every Sunday we would go for cabinets (frappes or milkshakes) and pistachios, with five cents for the cabinet and five cents for the pistachios. Peter's Candies was also on Pleasant Street. Kennedy's Butter & Egg Store was also on Pleasant Street. Butter was in a big tub and, if you wanted some, the clerk would slice a piece off and wrap it up. When we got home, we put the butter in salt water to keep it fresh.

*Robert:* There were a McClellan's and a Woolworth's on Pleasant Street. Friday night, the stores were open late and the street was a bustle. There was a bowling alley at Pleasant and Raymond Streets. Bshara's Restaurant, on the corner of Pleasant and Notre Dame Streets, was a popular spot. Famous stars appearing at the Highway Casino at the Narrows would come to Bshara's after the shows. There was a hardware store, Amiot's, where you could get anything that you wanted.

*Joe:* All of the iceboxes had drains that went through all three floors and drained into the basement sink. Most iceboxes had a drain pan to catch the melted ice, and it had to be emptied every day. If you wanted ice, you put a card in the window to let the iceman know.

*Robert:* Many things were delivered in those days: milk, bread, pastries, vegetables, groceries, and fish. You could go to a family-owned market and pick up something and pay for the week's purchases at the end of the week. George's Hot Dogs on Pleasant Street was owned by George the Greek. In filling an order, he would line up the hot dogs on his hairy, sweaty arm, and put mustard and other condiments on them like an assembly line, then dole them out. They tasted great.

*Jeannette:* Everything was here. I didn't get to go downtown until I was fifteen, when I had to change buses downtown to go to my housecleaning job.

*Robert:* No one married a non-French person. It was frowned upon. The Portuguese section of the Flint was bounded by Cash Street, Pleasant Street, Eastern Avenue, and Alden Street. The Lebanese section of the Flint was bounded by Cash Street, Pleasant Street, Stafford Square, Quarry Street, and Alden Street. Pleasant Street was the dividing line between the French section of the Flint and the Portuguese and Lebanese sections.

*Gert:* The streets were safe then. We could walk all the way to the Narrows without worry. We walked to the Carnival Drive-In many summer nights for fried clams and french fries.

*Joe:* In the days of the walking police beat, the policeman knew everyone. If kids acted up the cop would whack him on the bottom (not hard, just to scare) and threaten to tell your father. No doors were locked then. We were disciplined. The whole system was disciplined. The Flint was a wonderful place to grow up in.

*Robert:* All of the presidents and candidates came to Fall River, including Roosevelt (Louis Howe, Roosevelt's friend and advisor, was from Fall River), Dewey, and Eisenhower.

Before television, people came out in droves to watch parish teams play baseball. Each parish had a baseball team as part of the CYO [Catholic Youth Organization] league. Individual businesses also supported teams as part of the city league. Since there were no lights, all games were played early. After the games, we would sit in the bleachers and sing in groups.

The championship year was 1941, and Bishop Cassidy came and sat in center field at Lafayette Park to watch the game. Immaculate Conception was the Yankees of the league. The whole field was surrounded with people. The visiting black leagues were very good; they would hit the ball out of the park and over the roofs of homes from Lafayette Park.

**Food and Meals**

*Julie:* Gorton was a favorite, which was ground pork cooked five or six hours. French meat pies and a ragout made from pig ankles were also popular. Pea soup was also frequently served.

*Jeannette:* Mom was always baking something.

*Joe:* My father liked chicken feet which were boiled and the claws pulled out.

*Germaine:* Root beer was made at home. It had to be left in a closet for several days, untouched, to ferment.

*Joe:* My father made home brew.

**Religious Life**

*Robert:* Notre Dame parish had about 8,000 families and eight priests. There were lots of Masses, all said in Latin and French. Sunday masses were at 6:00, 7:00, 8:00, 9:30, 11:00, and 12:00. There were also daily Masses and Masses for the school kids. Masses, vespers, and novenas kept families together. Vespers were held at 3:00 pm on Sunday afternoon and included prayers, the benediction, and lasted about twenty minutes.

We said the rosary around the kitchen table daily. The priest would come to each house for an annual visit and to bless religious objects. Religious societies included the Holy Name Society, St. Jean Baptiste Society, St. Anne's Society, and, later, the Women's Guild.

At Communion breakfasts each month at Notre Dame School about 300 persons would attend. Notre Dame Church sponsored whist parties, outings, and Lenten missions.

*Joe:* At the 8:00 am Sunday Mass, the brothers and nuns would attend. If anyone acted up, a nun would take a "clapper," two pieces of wood that made a loud noise when hit together, and clap it behind the offending kid. On Monday, you would be punished.

**Work Life**

*Jeannette:* My first job was distributing the local French paper, *L'Independent*. It paid for my tuition to Notre Dame School. I cleaned house once a week when I was fifteen for the owner of the Terminal Bakery. Later, I began working at the bakery and earned eighteen dollars for a forty-eight-hour week, six days a week.

*Gremaine:* I worked babysitting from 7:00 to 11:00 pm for a quarter. Later, I worked at Shelburne Shirt for fiftey cents an hour.

*Marian:* I worked at the Union Hospital after school for fifty cents a day. I worked there all day on Saturdays and Sundays and got the same fifty cents a day, for a total of three dollars and fifty cents a week. I delivered food to patients and things like that.

*Joe:* When I was nine years old, I worked at Lajeunesse's Grocery Store on Friday nights and all day Saturdays. I did things like take sugar from large barrels and fill bags for retail sale and deliver groceries. I didn't get any pay; instead the owner gave my family a discount on groceries that we bought there.

*Andy:* In those days, workers were paid with cash in a sealed envelope. I never dared open my pay envelope, but gave it to Mom unopened every week.

*Joe:* At sixteen, I went to work for Modern Plumbing for five dollars a week; after that, I went into the service.

*Richard:* I worked in a bakery decorating cakes and filling donuts for twenty dollars per week, from 6:00 am to 4:00 pm, six days a week.

*Robert:* I have been in the laundry business all my life. At one time, I estimated that I ironed five million shirts. All of our aunts, uncles, and grandparents worked in the mills.

*Andy:* The noise in the weaving rooms was deafening from the loud *clickety-clack* of the looms. When the shuttles of the looms would go back and forth, it would sometimes cause the building to crack. The mill on Quequechan Street had to be repaired because of this reason. In the spinning rooms, workers would come out looking like ghosts because they were covered in cotton dust. You had to have very nimble fingers and work very fast to tie the loose ends of threads.

*Julie:* Inspectors looked for imperfections and if imperfections were found the worker knew about it.

*Andy:* It was stifling hot in the mills and workers would be sweating constantly. Steam vapor from pipes near the ceiling kept spraying steam to the extent that you couldn't see the ceiling for all the steam and spray.

*Germaine:* I brought my father his hot lunch every day in a lunch pail. The lunch pail I remember had a rounded top; the hot container fit right in it and two clips held it in place. The bottom was squared off; the food went in the bottom of the pail; the top came down on the bottom and locked together and a handle on top to carry the pail.

*Germaine and Joe:* Coffee was put in the bottom of the pail and another pail with the food fit into the larger pail, so that the hot coffee kept the food warm. The pail was covered with a lid that had a little knob on it.

## Prohibition

*Joe:* My cousin owned a seaplane and was a bootlegger. Once, when starting the plane (which required cranking the engine by hand on the propeller) part of his clothing got caught and the propeller ripped open his skull. He died seven hours later.

## World War II

*Robert:* Blackouts were common during the war. The top half of car headlights had to be painted black. Mill windows were all painted black. Meat, butter, and nylons were rationed. If you were in uniform and came home, you got extra ration stamps. If you had a son in the service, you put a small banner with a star on it in your window, one for each serviceman. One family had six stars in their window, and they all came home. This was a family of twenty-six kids.

*Joe:* Letters from servicemen were censored and blacked out. I still have a letter that says "Somewhere in Germany," because we couldn't say where we were. Our first clothes were holdovers from World War I. The winter topcoat the Army gave me came down to my ankles and the sleeves were too long. The officers told me to do something about my long coat. When I came home, my sister altered the coat and made it look right for me.

One of the holdovers from World War I Army uniforms was brown belts for formal uniforms in the services. During the early part of World War II, I was with the Army at Hull, Massachusetts, and the Marines were at Hingham Naval Air Station. Once, when the Army and Marine units came together at Nantasket Beach, which had an amusement park at the time, both units got into an altercation where they took off their white belts and began using them on one another. It was quite a scene and, after that incident, we found that Washington immediately decreed that the belts were no longer to be used as part of the uniforms. I was in the service for six years and wore no uniform belts.

I was one of the guinea pigs for tetanus shots and dehydrated foods. The dehydrated food was awful. Once, in England, we were given creamed corn. I was about to eat it when I saw that it was moving. I looked closely and found that the movement was due to maggots.

When I came home from the service, things had already begun to change.

# Dr. Robert Clifton

*Born in 1924*

**Family Background**

My parents were Joseph H. and Amy (Hanson) Clifton. My mother's father was William Hanson Jr.

My father was brought up on Broadway in Fall River. He attended Tufts Medical School and had his dental practice in the Granite Block. Grandfather Hanson owned two three-deckers on New Boston Road.

My wife is Dorothy S. Clifton and we were married at the Ascension Episcopal Church in 1950. We have four children: Judith, Nancy, Andrea, and Betsy.

**School Life**

I went to the Highland School, class of 1936. We would go home for lunch. During recess, we played soccer. The class has had reunions every five years. Tom Cottrell was in the class; Tom is a great friend of mine. Also in the class were Jack Brayton, Frank Andrews, and Arnold Goldstein. Joe Feitelberg and Jack Brayton were instrumental in getting Battleship Cove to Fall River. My mother went to the Highland School and was the valedictorian. She gave the annual "Ivy Speech."

My teachers at the Highland School were Miss Macomber for first grade, Miss Connors for second grade, Miss Borden for third or fourth grade, Miss Connors for fifth grade, Miss Hurley for sixth grade, and Miss Finneran was the principal.

Pop Mann was the beloved janitor at the Highland School. He would sometimes bring a few kids across the street to the Highland Drug Store at recess and buy us a Popsicle. We had a maypole in kindergarten, but my memory of it is vague. We would go around the pole.

From the Highland School, we went to Morton Junior High School.

I went to Dartmouth College for pre-med, class of 1946, and then to Harvard Medical School, class of 1950. I practiced urology in the Merrimack Valley area and lived in Andover. I retired in 1988 and moved to Westport.

**Recreation and Entertainment**

In the winter, we would go to North Park to sled. We would also go to the Fall River Country Club to toboggan down one of their steep hills. We went skating at the bottom of New Boston Road, to the icehouse area. On Saturdays, we would go skating on the Frog Pond and the Duck Pond. We had those double-runner skates that beginners used. We fished on the North Watuppa, but not on the main pond. Even that was not allowed by the game warden, but we got some nice bass and pickerels from the pond.

We went to Lincoln Park [North Dartmouth, Massachusetts] and rode the roller coaster. Before World War II, I saw Glen Miller at the Lincoln Park ballroom.

Our family had an Essex automobile and we would go to Horseneck Beach regularly. People

Highland School on Robeson Street

set up platforms and pitched tents on the beach. There were no houses on Horseneck Beach.

My brother and I flew racing pigeons. Some of the races were up to five hundred miles. You had to clock the pigeons as they came in. Before the race, rubber bands were put on their legs. When the pigeons came in, you had to take the rubber band off, put it in a metal capsule, and crank the handle so that the time was clocked and the band couldn't be taken out until the race was officially recorded. Then, we would take the capsule down to the pigeon club and they would verify the time and clock it in. Sometimes, the reading was down to the third decimal of a mile. Whoever had the pigeon with the fastest time would win the race. The results were shown in the *Fall River Herald News* the next day.

Once, we took ten pigeons to downtown to have the metal and rubber bands put on them. There were about twenty-five competitors in the race. The pigeons were put in big baskets and then on a truck to take them to where the race would originate. They would typically be taken as far as Albany, New York, but the longest race began in Ashtabula, Ohio, which was 525 miles from Fall River. There were about a hundred pigeons in the basket and the race began when the basket was opened and the birds let go.

We would take the pigeons out ten to twelve miles to train them. I don't know how homing pigeons found their way home, although there has been a lot written about it. I remember one day I was pitching a baseball game, and suddenly I remembered that I had to go home to meet the racing pigeons as they returned from a race. We had pigeon coops in the yard at 316 New Boston Road and we built another coop at 420 New Boston Road.

## Neighborhood Experiences

I was born at 316 New Boston Road, two houses down from Stetson Street. When I was twelve, we moved to 420 New Boston Road, on the corner of Meridian Street. Murphy's Riding Academy was the next house on Meridian Street. I remember the fire when the icehouse on Interlachen burned down, leaving only the stone walls.

On the southeast corner of New Boston Road and Stetson Street was a market that my grandfather owned, called Hanson's Market. One of my first memories is going to my grandfather's market and he would give me a penny to buy some candy. The candy was in one of those old curved glass cases. I'd stand there interminably deciding how to spend that penny. Finally, I'd get a licorice cigar or a piece of licorice.

Leemingville extended from Robeson Street east, and from Valentine Street on the north, to about Langley Street on the south. The Leemings were construction people who built modest homes in that area. One of their daughters was a bridesmaid at our wedding.

Harold Lindsey owned a variety store on Robeson Street. Hervey Laundry was located on New Boston Road down from Stetson Street, where the medical office is now. It later became LeComte Laundry and the Ideal Laundry after that. We kids would go in and watch the laundry machinery.

One block in from Robeson Street, on the western corner of Reed Street, was McFarland's

Hanson's Market, southeast corner of New Boston Road and Stetson Street

Bakery. They had a large cone of string above the counter on a rack. They would take a box, take the string, and tie it and knot it. We had a few markets. There was an A&P store on the eastern corner of New Boston Road and Reed Street. Hudner's Market was next to the A&P store. Tom Hudner was in my class at the Highland School and after. He won the Congressional Medal of Honor for his service in the Korean War. One of his fellow airmen was shot down in North Korea and Tom went down to rescue him and brought him back.

Above Hudner's Market was the Issac Robinson family. His daughter, Janet Robinson, later became the CEO of the New York Times Corporation, the owner of the *New York Times*. I wrote a letter to her and asked if she was the Robinson that grew up above Hudner's Market and next to Frank the Barber. She wrote back and said, "Yes, I am." She also sent me a book published by the New York Times Corporation.

**Other Memories**

Dr. Truesdale gained a lot of notoriety by operating on a girl who had a diaphragmatic hernia, called "upside-down stomach." Her name was Mary Jane. She lived with my wife's family for a while.

# Vincent Codega

*Born on September 21, 1938*

**Family Background**

I was born on September 21, 1938, the day of the 1938 hurricane.

My parents were Able, born in Barrington, Rhode Island, and Jeanne Codega, born in Swansea, Massachusetts. My mother's family had a farm in Swansea on Sharp's Lot Road and then moved to Brightman Street. However, every weekend, the family would get in a wagon and stay at the Swansea farm. Then, they headed back to Brightman Street at the end of the weekend.

We lived at 122 Wilson Road, behind my father's gas station, at the corner of Wilson Road and North Main Street, until 1955.

**Food and Meals**

Believe it or not, we ate lobsters twice a week when I was kid and then had scallops every week. Jimmy from Newport would come to visit my father once or twice a week and would bring lobsters that had one claw or were too small. He would bring eight to ten at a time, sometimes twelve. Another friend named Thorngreen was a scalloper and, when he came back in, he would give my father a whole pail of scallops.

I went to my grandmothers because she was an excellent cook. All of the vegetables came out of the garden. There was a salad with every meal. We never had sandwiches. There was always a hot meal: a hot breakfast, a hot lunch, and a hot dinner.

**Recreation and Entertainment**

We spent our summers at Bliffins Beach and Bessie's Beach. We would swim and fish off of the railroad bridge. Every night in the summer, we would sit talking on the porches of the shacks.

**Work Life**

I worked for Charlie Fisher in Somerset. He gave me three dollars a day to pick asparagus. Other farms gave four dollars a day. My mom didn't want me to work on the farms, but at 5:00 am, I and my buddies would sneak out and go to the unemployment office in the city. From there, farm trucks would pick us up and we would jump in. My mother didn't like it at all. I would come home dirty and have to go clean up down cellar.

Every day after school, I went to pick up junk and sold it to the junk yard.

I tried being a caddy. It was not for me. I said, "Why am I carrying around a bag for this fat guy?" I left and never came back. They were angry.

I had a barber shop next to the Lizzie Borden house on Second Street. John McGinn of Leary Press, who owned the murder house, asked me if I wanted to see the inside and I said yes. I saw things like blood stains on the floor and stuff like that, but it wasn't anything much. McGinn rarely let anyone in to see the house.

Both of my barber chairs were used by the production company of *The Great Gatsby* in Newport. They were used to do the makeup in. I would go to Newport twice a week to the set. One of the things they did was to cover over the asphalt roads with sand to make it look like an unpaved road. One of barber chairs ended up in the Belmont Club in Fall River.

**Neighborhood Experiences**

There was a Red and White Market across the street from our house on the corner of North Main Street and Wilson Road. The Green Dragon Inn was in the building on the southwest corner of North Main Street and Wilson Road. People stayed there on the stagecoach ride from Boston to Newport. The old timers said that the train would stop at the Steep Brook Station and people would get off and stay over at the inn.

On the east side of North Main Street, going south from the inn, there was a blacksmith shop and a big watering trough in front of it. Sid Ashley's place, at the corner of Ashley and North Main Streets, was a very old house that was disassembled and each piece marked and reassembled in Vermont.

There were three ponds in the neighborhood: Mill Pond (on Driftwood Road); Aaron's Pond, at what became the industrial park, and Stump Pond, near St. Vincent's Home farm. At the Mill Pond, we would gather wood and build a bonfire in the winter when we kids skated there.

We raced cut-down cars that we hid in the woods.

The Pearson Farm was located at the intersection of Wilson Road and Meridian Street and later became a golf course. Across the street from there, John D. Ferreira bought twenty-eight acres during the Depression for four thousand dollars. He made it back in two years by planting the land with potatoes. He took the potatoes to the Boston market in the fall, but there too many potatoes on the market then. He put the potatoes downstairs in the cellar of the farmhouse and waited until the spring to sell them. It worked. John worked in the Sagamore Mills and his wife worked the farm with his son Jimmy.

In the winter, we would slide down Wilson Road to the river. We would get five gallon buckets of water to pour on Wilson Road and let it freeze. We would slide down the road like a jet. There could be fifty kids sliding on the road, mostly teenagers. We had bobsleds too. Most kids had to be in when the streetlights went on.

Right of Fighting Rock, at the end of Wilson Road, was a school at one time; my father said that he attended that school. The North End includes the Village, which is either side of Brightman Street on the west side of the railroad tracks. I remember Moy Lees on Brightman Street, which had a rack of chow mein and stuff against the wall. The place was really dirty, including the windows. One time, we guys threw a chow mein sandwich up on the ceiling. Moy Lee threw us out and ran out on the street yelling at us.

When the Eagle Restaurant was reopened, my uncle rebuilt all of the stained glass there. There was a flea bag theatre next to Brown's store. The Embassy was on Franklin Street and the Empire on South Main Street.

# Maria Amalia (Zaredo) Coelho

*Born on June 13, 1902*
*Died on November 16, 2007*

**Family Background**

I was born in São Miguel Island, Azores. I came to the United States in 1916. The ship that brought us over was all full of Portuguese and Italians. We landed in Boston.

My parents were Manuel Olivera and Mariz (Martins) Zeredo.

I had seven brothers and three sisters. Their names were Antonio, Joseph, Maria Isabelle, Albert, Amalia, Manuel, Constantina, Albono, Estrella, and Benjamin.

**Family Life**

My father was a shoemaker on São Miguel Island; here he was a cobbler. In São Miguel he make the whole shoe.

I was born at home. My grandmother took care of us. I had my baby at home also. Dr. Milot birthed to my baby on Stafford Road. He was French. The baby died after three days. She had asthma. Today, she might have lived.

My father was very special; a very nice person.

My father had three hothouses where he grew pineapples that he sold to England and Germany to make liquor. When the war [World War I] came, it stopped. It forced him to move to the United States. He was well-off there but poor here. My father died poor. It was his destiny. However, he would give one or two dollars every week so poorer persons could support themselves.

Pineapples were used for liquor. Lagoa [on São Miguel] had plenty of rich people. They went to Germany to learn how to make liquor.

When we arrived from Europe, we lived on Diman Street, then to another place, then to Williams Street. After that, my father bought a single family home at 236 Lawton Street off of Stafford Road. I was eighteen or so when we moved to Lawton Street.

We had electricity in Lagoa, but didn't have electricity here. Rich people lived in Lagoa and set up windmills to generate electricity. Here there were only gas pipes for lighting. We would go out and buy small lanterns for the gas lights that cost forty cents each. There were no toilets here; we ran outside. The mills also had outhouses. When we did have toilets in the house finally, they were small closets in the basement.

There were lots of people here and the bedrooms in houses sometimes had no windows.

My mother had a black stove that burned wood, sometimes coal.

Every corner had a small grocery store, so you didn't have to go too far to shop. The stores were owned by French mostly.

My first church was St. Anne's. Then we went to Santo Christo. When we moved to Maplewood, we went to St. Elizabeth's. I was confirmed at St. Elizabeth's and was married there by Father Mello. Since my marriage, I have been a Christian; I like Billy Graham.

No food was left over, so there wasn't much to preserve or keep. My mother bought food every day and we ate it all. The iceman would come when we put a sign in the window and he would bring the ice in the house.

We were plain people; everyone was good. No one was scared. No doors were locked. If someone knocked, we said, "Come in."

We were very obedient; father was the disciplinarian. Our father wouldn't let us go out. Sometimes, we would go with friends to Broadway to an ice cream store with three girlfriends. If we saw our father coming, we would hide in the store.

My father wanted to go back to the old country, but he never had a chance to do so. He owned the house and garden in Portugal, but his older brother sold it and my father got only a small amount from it.

We always had shoes. When rich people died, my father would make shoes for them. They were like ballerina shoes. He had to go measure them.

I don't remember playing games when I was young. When we were not working, we had to clean all the time. My father was tough on that. My mother was busy taking care of us.

My father promised us that if we washed the floor and polished the stove on Saturday afternoon, we could go to the movies. The shows were very clean and anyone could go to a show. We brothers and sisters would go together. The Plaza and Bijou Theatres were where we went.

My husband came from the old country. We met and liked one another and then he disappeared for about five years. My older sister's husband met him once in South Park [now Kennedy Park] watching a ball game and he asked for me. The next morning, he was waiting for me outside the mill and we started dating.

His name was Antonio Rego Coelho and he worked in the print mills. When the Depression came, we moved to East Providence to live. He worked at McCormick's Tractor and I worked at a woolen mill as a doffer. I worked at a mill in Providence and had to cross the red bridge. We were there for fifteen years, but I was dying to come back to Fall River to be near my family and we did in 1944.

We were in East Providence during the Depression; to survive, some family members took jobs out of town or different jobs.

My husband was in the service in the old country. He could be called if needed. My older brother Antonio stayed in the old country in reserves until after World War I.

My husband and I bought a house at 26 Lisbon Street. We lived there about twenty years. After my husband died, I stayed at home for about four years, then moved to the Milot Apartments near Trinity Church.

**School Life**

I graduated from school in the village of Lagoa in São Miguel. I was twelve years old. This was before World War I started in 1914.

School was fun. We were all greenhorns. We laughed a lot. Teachers would teach us with their hands; they didn't know Portuguese and we didn't know English. To teach us to wash our hands, they would do this [wringing motion of hands]. One time, a teacher didn't do this [wringing of hands] but one guy did this [raised his hands with the palms outwards] and we didn't know what he meant. Sometimes, my brother would do his own interpretations of the teacher's sign language and he would get us all laughing and the teacher would throw him out. We were always full of fun; we loved to laugh and sing.

**Recreation and Entertainment**

My mother's sister had a farm in Swansea [Massachusetts]. Catabias was their name. I would go there once in a while. I once rode through the city in a horse and buggy with my cousin one time. The horse was clearing the air and blew the hair to my blue suit. My cousin's husband laughed. Mr. Catabias, my aunt's husband, would come into the city to go to watch boxing matches at The Casino on Morgan Street on Saturdays.

The circus. I would see the circus parade as it passed the mills on its way from the train station to the parade grounds.

Radio shows. Comedians were best. Bob Hope and Eddy Cantor were good. When we lived in East Providence, the landlady would call me up to listen to Eddy Cantor. She had a pie ready and we would share it after the show. She would knock on the pipe when she wanted me. I was still in touch with her two daughters until recently.

For entertainment, we would sing a lot and joke; we had clean jokes then.

We would go downtown to the show mostly. The sidewalks were full of people all of the time; you couldn't move along them.

**Work Life**

Fall River was all French people then. The Portuguese called Fall River "French Town."

They needed us here; the mills did not have enough workers.

I worked from 6:00 am to 7:00 pm, and Saturday from 6:00 am to 12:00 noon. I was about fourteen when I started working in the mills. I was a spinner, filling up bobbins that would then be taken to the weavers. Old people were usually weavers. Many of us also went to school at night, as I did. I worked at the Fall River Iron Works. When we lived on Stafford Road, we would take the trolley to the top of Columbia Street at Main Street and walk down to the mills. People, mostly older people, wore burlap bags over their shoes so they would not slip and fall on the icy streets.

We would buy sweets for breakfast on the way to the mill. There was a nice bakery on Columbia Street. We had no time to eat until noon, so we went to the water faucet in the mill and ate the sweets with water.

We brought our lunch pails for dinner. We would bring our pails with us, but some people in the mill had theirs brought by brothers or sisters. We brought food such as pork chops, chourico, eggs with chourico, with bread, and things like that. In the bottom of the pail was coffee.

At the mill, we didn't stop until 12:00 noon. Then everyone sat on the floor to eat. Or they would visit a friend in another part of the mill to have dinner together.

We didn't make much, but food was cheap.

We would take the trolleys but we still had to walk a lot to work. No streets were plowed. When we got home, our long skirts and high shoes would be frozen.

There were half French in the mills. All of the bosses were French. They were nice. Sometimes, when we were waiting for the trolley, our French boss would stop and give us a ride home in his car. He lived near Stafford Road. Later the bosses were all Portuguese.

**Christmas, Holidays, and Special Occasions**

For Christmas, relatives would come at Christmas Eve and play and sing at the door, representing Joseph and Mary looking for shelter. We would open the door to let them in and have the table full of massa, nuts, figs, wine, or beer. There were no presents and no tree.

**Health and Illness**

We treated illnesses with tea. Once, I was almost dying and the doctor gave up. My mother went for a chicken and gave me the liver and here I am—the rest are all gone. There were little bottles of peppermint for bellyaches. A drop or two is all we got; it was very good for bellyaches. Herbs were used also and were good. Whiskey (cachaça) was given as a medicine. A stimulant. Ginger brandy was also a good medicine.

Alcohol was made from sweet potatoes. My husband worked where they did that. They would sell the rest for the pigs. Lots of people in our neighborhood made their own wine.

We believed that it was good to wash your feet every day. We put vinegar in the water. In the old country, we would wash my father's feet.

After World War I, we had an epidemic of influenza. People were dying like flies. In one house across the street, the father died in one room and the mother died in the other. And others also. Everyone who was going to have a baby died. My husband's sister died in pregnancy. All pregnant women died from the epidemic.

There was lots of TB [tuberculosis] then. I remember two friends (girls) who died from it. They were young girls.

# John Conforti

*Born in 1942*

**Family Background**

My parents were Orlando and Agnes (Bento) Conforti. My father's parents were Salvatore and Anna (Juliano) Conforti. My mother's parents were Manuel and Alexandirna (Faria) Bento.

I have three siblings: Bill, born in 1943; Joe, born in 1945; and Orlando Jr., born in 1947.

My mother was Portuguese and my father was Italian.

My mother's family came from Povacao in São Miguel Island (Azores). My father's family came from San Pietero, near Reggio, Calabria.

My father was the oldest of nine children. When he was in the eighth grade, he was taken to someone to be an apprentice to a barber. One of my father's duties was to clean the spittoons.

My mom's education ended after two years at [B.M.C.] Durfee High School, when she had to leave to go to work. She worked at clothing stores as a clerk. My mother loved books.

My wife is Jeanne (Levesque) Conforti. She was born in 1947. We have two children, Ann and John Jr.

**Family Life**

We lived in a six-family house at 61 Bowler Street, on the edge of the Italian section of the city, near Bedford Street and Columbus Park. Bowler Street is off of Quarry Street and abuts Stafford Square. It wasn't the most fashionable part of the city. A junkyard (scrap iron) was nearby owned by the Sanft family, who owned our house.

At the end of the street, a Portuguese family had a garden. The garden and its grape arbors were protected by guard dogs. My grandmother tried to get grapes for me by pulling on the vines with her cane.

My grandfather, Salvatore Conforti, lived on 276 Beattie Street. Like all the Italian immigrants, he loved to be outdoors. He had a huge garden behind his house. He had chickens too.

On what is now North Eastern Avenue, there was a collection of lots where locals had gardens. My grandfather grew potatoes there. I remember going up with my father to dig the potatoes. My father built a fire on the lot and he grilled the potatoes over the fire. They were delicious.

My grandfather also had a grape arbor and used these grapes and some California grapes to make wine. I helped him mash and press the grapes. When the wine was ready, between Thanksgiving and Christmas, he would tap the wine.

I had my glass of wine at age five, six, or seven. Wine was not forbidden to kids.

When I as a teenager, and met these guys sneaking beer and getting beer illegally, it didn't make sense to me. We had no problem with liquor in my family. We had it with our meals.

**Friends**

One of my friends was Mike McDonald, who was half Irish and half Polish. He grew up in the South End. Most of his friends were French Canadian, so he joined the Boy Scout Troop at St. Anne's Church to be with his friends. When the roster of kids was being read and Mike's name came up, the priest said, "Hey you, is this your name? Get out!"

**School Life**

I went to the Brown School, which was the twin of the Davis School. The Brown School was built about 1872 or so. It had high windows. All of the teachers there were Irish old maids. In those days, you had to be single to be a teacher in the schools. They were great, caring teachers.

I have fond memories of the school. It was kindergarten to fifth grade. The desks had inkwells and the ink came in a powder. The teacher would mix the ink powder with water to make the ink and it was an honor to be able to fill the inkwells.

When I was in kindergarten—in the winter of 1947, which was one of the snowiest winters—I walked alone to school one day. I approached the school from the back, which had high granite steps. I was in my snowsuit, which limited my movement, and I couldn't get up the steps to get into school. So I went back home. My mother came back with me and helped me up the steps to get me into the school. Having a five-year-old walk to school alone was something you could do in those days.

**Recreation and Entertainment**

My brothers were my best friends. In the summertime, we played ball with other friends in the mill yard of the Stafford Mills. We used a taped-up ball or old balls that people discarded. We made them usable by wrapping them with black electrical tape. In football season, we used shoulder pads and helmets. In one corner of the mill yards, we put up a basketball hoop that drew many people from the area.

When we were younger, we played cowboys and Indians. Roy Rogers and Gene Autry were our heroes. Soon after World War II, there were surplus canteens, insignia, and lots of things that people brought back with them.

We had no TV until 1951. We would go to the house of one of our friends, Bob Potvin, to watch the fifteen-minute kids shows.

We played in the street until dark. A game we played was ball-o-wicket, which was a takeoff on cricket. We had a stick and stacked empty cans in a pyramid. We had to protect the cans while the other team tried to hit the pyramid over. The side that protected the cans was trying to hit the ball and run to the other side.

One of my father's tenets was that you only go to the movies on a rainy day. On Wednesdays, his day off, he would only go to a movie if it was raining. Once a year, my father would take us to a Red Sox game. We went on a Bud Liner and left from the North Main Street station.

My father never learned to drive and never owned a car. Going to the beach meant going to Island Park [Cashman's Park, Portsmouth, Rhode Island]. Once a year, someone would drive us to Island Park, or we would take the bus. We went to South Shore once a year and spend the entire day there.

I remember going to the circus off of Globe Street. There was a huge tent on the circus grounds. Once, when we were entering the grounds, elephants were lined up behind a rope. I was just a little kid then, and my father bought me a bag of popcorn. The next thing I knew, the popcorn was gone. The elephant took my popcorn. One of the workers got it back from the elephant, who was named Johnny. It confused me when the worker said, "Johnny, give the popcorn back."

In the summertime, we had outdoor cookouts at the houses of our grandparents. Our aunts and uncles would gather and have hot dogs and hamburgers. The autumn ritual was to go blueberrying.

The theatres that I remember in the city were the Embassy, the Strand, the Center, and the Capital. On dish night, the kids would take turns going with my mother to get her dishes. Then, you could go to the movies and stay all day. The movies ran continuously.

During the CYO [Catholic Youth Organization] baseball games in South Park [now Kennedy Park], St. Anne's and Santo Christo played against one another. The priest for the St. Anne's team would swear at the Portuguese on the other side.

**Food and Meals**

We ate lots of kaldine [Portuguese kale soup], morcella, and fish on Friday. There was always a war in our house over food; my father didn't like Portuguese food. My mother cooked Italian dishes for him, including veal, meatballs, and spaghetti. Every Sunday, we had pasta. My mother was very predictable in her meals; she made the same meals for each day of the week. We always knew what we were going to get. Sundays were the only day that we had dessert.

My mother didn't have to bake bread because Marzilli's and Marcucci's bakeries were in the neighborhood. You could get the raw dough from them and bring it home to make pizza or bread. The Portuguese bakeries in the area were Moonlight Bakery and Morning Star Bakery on the other side of the street. They made great massas and malasadas.

**Work Life**

My father was a barber and had a shop on Granite Street downtown called the Eagle Barber Shop. Next door was the Eagle Restaurant Annex. We boys would go to the barber shop at the end of the day to clean up. He would then treat us by going to the Eagle Annex for a chow mein sandwich and fried rice.

My father's clientele were businessmen and such. Occasionally, a black man would come in and my father would say, "I don't know how to cut your hair." There was no phone in the barbershop; my father didn't want people to think that he was a bookie. Barbers then had a reputation for being bookies.

**Neighborhood Experiences**

We were poor but not that much. I got an allowance of five cents a week when I was in elementary school. There was a variety store on the corner of Quarry Street and Bowler Street where they sold penny candy. The owner there had the patience of Job as I decided what to buy. There were squirrels, Mary Janes, and dots on paper.

I would walk from home to my father's barbershop. In the winter, gypsies would be in empty storefronts reading palms and telling fortunes. The gypsies camped out sometimes in back of the Stafford Mills.

**Christmas, Holidays, and Special Occasions**

Going to our grandparents' house at Christmas was a big deal. There were special desserts, like cookies pressed into various shapes, with honey and nuts. At Christmastime, Italian men had this custom where the wives stayed at home and remained with company and the men would go to the houses of friends to give them greetings and to have a glass of liquor. Anisette was their favorite.

**Religious Life**

*Mrs. Conforti:* I remember seeing in the St. Anne's annual report the listing of marriages. It listed one hundred weddings and four "mixed" marriages, meaning that these marriages were not with a French person.

*Mr. Conforti*: My father belonged to Holy Rosary and my mother belonged to St. Anthony of Padua. I was baptized at Holy Rosary. However, my mom won the war over the long term. The Church said that children belonged to their mother's church. My father was buried at St. Anthony's.

**Health and Illness**

In the summer, I would get poison ivy. Our home remedy was baking soda mixed with water to make a paste then applied on the affected area. It helped to dry out the skin.

My father was upset that we weren't eating enough. The Macaroni Shop on Bedford Street (where the Boys and Girls Club is now) had an Italian concoction called fernet. It was an awful-tasting concoction of herbs and spices. Each of us got a tablespoon of the stuff before dinner.

*Mrs. Conforti:* Lydia Pinkham was a turn-of-the-century potion for "women's troubles." Its advertising on the bottle said, "A Baby in every bottle." My cousin says she got pregnant from taking it; who knows?

# Gertrude (Morris) Cooper

*Born on August 12, 1916*
*Died on August 28, 2014*

**Family Background**

My parents were Stanley and Maude (Burrows) Morris. My father's parents were John, born in Fall River (ancestry was English), and Esther Morris. My mother's parents were John and Alice Burrows.

My father's brother was the Health Commissioner for Fall River. He left the job when he got a fellowship in Boston. He was a doctor.

My siblings are William (deceased), Ernest (deceased), and Frances.

I have been married three times: Kenneth W. Ashton, Victor Aubry, and Russell Cooper (all deceased). I was married to my last husband for only twelve years before he died, but those were the happiest years of my life. He has a daughter, my step-daughter, and I have one grandchild, three step-grandchildren, and eight great-grandchildren. I have one child, Kenneth W. Ashton Jr., who now lives in California and is married with one child.

**Family Life**

I was born at 80 Hood Street, third floor, at home. I grew up in this home until my father died in 1922. We then moved in with my grandmother in her cottage on Stafford Road for a short while. Then we moved back Down North to 177 Langley Street for three and a half years. Then we moved to 322 Brownell Street, on the first floor, then around the corner to 120 Almy Street, first floor. From there, we moved back to Hood Street, to the second floor of 27 Hood Street, on the other side of North Main from North Park. Then we moved back to Almy Street, to the second floor of 27 Almy. I graduated from high school from there in 1934. From there, we moved to Weetamoe Street, third floor, in back of St. Joseph's Church. From there, my mom, sister, and I moved to the second floor of 110 Cherry Street, downtown, the second house from the corner of Danforth Street. I got married from there.

I was only six when my father died. Mom would get me dressed up so Father could bring me to the fire station so the firemen could see me. He was only thirty-eight years old when he passed away. He worked on the railroad. We didn't have much money when Father died. The oldest child was twelve and the youngest was two. What we had didn't go too far. My father died near Christmas. The wives of the firemen at the station bought doll's cribs for us and dressed them up.

I have a solid cedar chest that was also built at B.M.C. Durfee High School. Inside the chest, they burnt the words "Durfee High School, 1944." My mom bought a chest for me when I was married and one for my brother. It was really heavy; my husband put wheels on it for me.

One year, the *Fall River Herald News* had printed a puzzle. If you matched the animals, you won a free ticket to the circus. My brother and I won a few times and we got to go to the circus. It was quite a walk. We didn't have money for the trolley. We had little money for anything.

My grandmother once gave me a nickel to get two ice cream cones. I couldn't get two cones for a nickel, but that was all she gave me. So, I got one and that was it.

My two brothers got married two weeks apart. One came home one day and said, "I'm getting married," and the other brother said, "So am I."

**School Life**

For first and second grade I went to the school across from the fire station on Brownell Street, where Morton is today. My first grade teacher there was Alice Burns and the second grade teacher was Genevieve McDermott. During recess, we would be out on the veranda. Walker's Market was nearby and had a big pickle barrel. Two teachers loved pickles and would send me to buy a big five-cent pickle. These two teachers knew my parents and would come to the house visiting. After my father died, they took care of me.

After they closed that school, they opened a library there. Then they tore the library down when they built the Morton Junior High School. Then I went to the Borden School that was located in lower North Park near Brownell Street. My brother Ernest was in only the second class to graduate from Morton. I graduated from Durfee in 1934 and my brother graduated from Durfee in 1931, so that meant he graduated from Morton in 1927 or so and that Morton would have opened about 1925.

When we moved to Stafford Road, where we lived with our grandmother following our father's death, I went to Henry Lord School for third grade for six months.

Miss Kelly was my third grade teacher, Miss French (she was a doll) was my fourth grade teacher, and Miss Foster for fifth grade. For the sixth grade, I had Miss Dionne, who I also had for French when she moved to Morton later.

One year, I was out sick for about three-quarters of the year. The principal said that it would be best if I stayed back a grade because if I went to junior high school, I would have to stay back there anyway. I was always a sick child and had trouble with my stomach. I was never too sick to go sledding, but I was too sick to go to school.

**Recreation and Entertainment**

When I was young, I was something of a tomboy. I hung out with the boys. I got along with them. We would toboggan with four or five boys in back of me. We would toboggan all the way down Rock Street, steering the toboggan with a skate, and go across President Avenue and into the park. Police were stationed on President Avenue to stop the traffic when we came by. Going back up Rock Street with the toboggan was tiring, so we hooked on to a car or truck that was going up the hill and got up the hill that way.

I was close to my brother Ernest. I remember going sliding with my brother Ernest at the park. We had a big sled that was made at Durfee High School. We would slide down Snake Road in North Park and go all the way to Hood and North Main Streets. When my brother hit a tree and hurt his foot, that was the end of the sled.

We skated on the pond in the park all the time. I had a friend that lived on Hood Street across from the pond. When we got cold when skating, we would go to her home, *clomp-clomping* up the stairs in our skates, to get warm. Her mother would make us hot chocolate.

In the summertime, we had no car, and I didn't go swimming until I was a teenager. Then we went to Bliffins Beach or Lannigan's Beach. We either walked or took the trolley.

**Food and Meals**

We had oatmeal for breakfast. My mom worked at the cafeteria and she made sure that we ate at the cafeteria. One day, Rose McHale, a shorthand teacher, got up in class to say that she was glad that many people brought their lunch because the food at the cafeteria is not fit to eat. She almost got fired for that. My mom was angry about that and told the story to the Durfee principal, Charlie Carroll. The teacher had to apologize to every class that she taught. All the cooking was done in the cafeteria. My mother even peeled the potatoes. Once lunch was served, she stayed to prepare and get ready for the next day. When I was out of work, I went in to make sandwiches or to do dishes to help out.

For Sunday dinner, we would have something that would go a long way. We would sometimes have a leg of lamb; oh boy, was that good. It would last a couple of meals. My mom was a good cook. You couldn't ask her how to make anything—it was always a pinch of this, a pinch of that. She made the best beef stew. Her gravy was the best. I always asked her, "How do you get it so good?"

**Courtship and Marriage**

I met my first husband, Kenneth Ashton, at Sears, where he worked in the office. I had my son from him. My second husband was a retired carpenter and was fifteen years older than me.

During World War II, I worked at the Fall River Trust Company, and we had to get food stamps. I remember when we got married on May 22, 1943. For our honeymoon, we took the bus to Providence and the train to New York City. We ate at Miss Dutton's Tea Room in Providence before we got on the train.

My third husband graduated in 1933 from Durfee. We knew one another in school. He would come into the bank every day. He worked in the South End. He would say hi and I would say hi, and that's it. He and I were both married to others. When I moved to Borden East, he moved here also. I met his daughter in the elevator one day; she knew me from coming in the bank all of the time. She told her dad, "Do you know who moved into the building? She's very lonesome and needs companionship. Why don't you take her out?" That's how we met again. His first wife died in 1972.

**Work Life**

When my father died, my mother went out washing floors, doing laundry, and housework. She did it for years. Then she got a job in the old Tech High School, now the Kuss Middle School. She worked in the cafeteria for a few weeks before the school burned down about 1920. When the school was rebuilt, she resumed working in the cafeteria until she retired at age sixty-seven. She worked for twenty years there and got no pension when she retired. She wasn't in Social Security long enough to collect anything and there was no civil service then.

Both my brother Ernest and I delivered papers. The two Dr. Fells had paper routes. When they went to college, they gave them up. My mom bought one route of a hundred papers for my brother. You had to buy a paper route in those days. My brother's paper route went from North Main Street from Hood to President Avenue and up the side streets like Belmont Street. My route was about fifty papers and went from Hood Street to where the street ends at the park steps, with some customers on North Underwood Street. I had that route and helped my brother with his route. I delivered papers through high school.

My oldest brother William had to go to work, but the rest of us three graduated from Durfee. When William was eighteen, and employed at the American Print Works, he was using a paper cutter. When he went to take the paper from the cutter, the blade came down and cut his hand off. Only his thumb was left. What a thing to happen at such a young age! He was out of work for a long time. We wanted to get a prosthesis for him but he didn't want it. He wouldn't let anyone do anything for him. He worked at Newport Naval Base afterward until he retired. He moved to Newport during that time.

My brother Ernest graduated from Bradford Durfee Tech and went into textiles. He got a job in the Pilgrim Mill. Then he left the Pilgrim and went to work in the Pepperell Mills working in the office. They made sheets and blankets. When they went out of business here, he was offered a job in their mill in Saco, Maine, and took it. There was nothing here. He worked at that mill until it closed. He was only fifty-eight or fifty-nine then. Then he went to work for the Kennebunk, Maine, Water Department and retired from there. His sons and daughter still live in Kennebunk, Maine.

I worked at the Kerr Mill for two weeks. I had to take two trolleys to get there, one to downtown and one to the mills. There was a special order that came in. I would stick labels on boxes as they came down the line.

When I graduated from Durfee, I couldn't get a job. My mother suggested that I go back to school for another year, which I did. I did housework for people at five dollars a week. Then, Rhode Island Hospital was offering courses in nursery maids. I went to Rhode Island Hospital and took the course and graduated from it.

I then worked for a pediatrician, where I took care of babies when they came home from the hospital. When that baby was secure, I went to another home. I did this for a few years, working for people in Providence and Pawtucket, Rhode Island. I was paid fifteen dollars a week; room and board were considered part of the pay.

After this, I worked for Anderson Little and was offered a job in a bank, the Fall River National Bank. When I became pregnant, I had to leave. I didn't work for a couple of years. However, my husband got laid off from Sears Roebuck, and I had to go back to work again.

That is when I went to work at the Fall River Trust Company, working there twenty-six years.

**Neighborhood Experiences**
Down North was all of the North End, and the Village was that part that was over the railroad tracks, west of the tracks. The railroad ran at that time. We would watch as the circus trains came in. The cinders from the train would fall all over the yard.

There was a branch of the First Baptist Church at Brownell and Almy Streets. We had socials there. My brother Ernest and I would go to St. James Church functions. Now that site is where the Portuguese Club is across the street from the Narragansett Mill. They took the church down to build the club. St. James was Episcopalian. We would go there when they held dances. Ernest had a little orchestra that played mostly at church times.

Father Shalloo's father had a market around Oregon and Cory Streets. We were two houses from the railroad when we lived on Almy Street.

Mulveny's Drug Store was on the southwest corner of President Avenue and North Main Streets. Anne's Restaurant was near President Avenue. South of and abutting Mulveny's was Clark's Bakery. Further south of Clark's and abutting it was the A&P grocery store. It was also called Bill Mahoney's Market. All three were in the same building. There was a Chinese restaurant on the second floor above the A&P.

At the corner of Hood and North Main Streets, there were three stores. On the northwest corner was Micheau's Variety Store. North of Micheau's was Hayes Bakery, an English bakery. My grandmother would send my grandfather to Hayes Bakery for day-old bread. North of Hayes Bakery was a cobbler shop that was owned by a crippled man. On the northeast corner was Maximo's Candy Store. On the southwest corner was an A&P grocery store. On the southeast corner was the Protestant church.

Goodfellow's Drug Store was on the southwest corner of Brownell and North Main Streets. Frank Walker's Market was on North Main Street across the street from the fire station. The Sunnyside Bakery was located on the east side of North Main Street, between Brownell Street and President Avenue. There was a variety store next to it. On the corner of North Main Street and President Avenue was a two- or three-family house. There was a hairdresser in the basement that I went to. In the rear was a two-family house.

I remember Mom sending me to the bakery for tripe. She would say, "Don't forget to tell them that I don't want too much fat on it." The bakery had the tripe in a jar in vinegar on the counter. I would also go to the bakery for blood pudding.

The English blood pudding was not like what you get today. It was full of rice and had a black casing. It had rice and barley and something else. It was good. They were small and round, the size of a big donut, and tied with a piece of string.

There were lamplighters when I was young. I remember seeing Mr. Brad Petty with his ladder lighting the lamps. He was so bow-legged that kids could run through his legs.

**Religious Life**

On Sunday, we went to Sunday School and church. We went to the First Baptist Church downtown, but when we were younger, we went to the Brownell Chapel, which was an offshoot of the First Baptist Church. The chapel was located across from where we lived on 322 Brownell Street. When we were older, we went downtown to go to church.

**Health and Illness**

Scarlet fever, chicken pox, and measles were all common diseases. I had whooping cough when I was thirteen months old. I had the flu during the flu epidemic of 1918, when I was eighteen months old. I almost died. My two brothers went downstairs to stay with my grandmother so they wouldn't get it. My sister was not born yet. My grandmother said, "Give her a shot of whiskey." I had measles and whooping cough at the same time. My sister had scarlet fever.

Vick's VapoRub was rubbed on our chests for colds. There was also Red Sea Balsam, but I don't know what we used it for. Seneca Powder was used to move bowels. Mom made Seneca tea.

When my father died, he was waked in the house. I remember before they put him in the casket, they lay him down on a board in the front parlor. I remember going in. My mother said, "Don't go in there." But it was too late; I saw him. I remember people going out of the house to the funeral. Sis and I stayed with a lady downstairs, since we were too young to go to a funeral. He and Mom are both buried at Oak Grove Cemetery, as are my mother's parents.

## Travel and Transportation

I rode on the trolley cars all the time. Some were open, including the ones that went to Lincoln Park [North Dartmouth, Massachusetts] and to Sandy Beach. The city cars were enclosed.

During my driver's license road test, I had to turn around the car on a hill. Instead of pressing the brake, I pressed the gas pedal and jumped the curb and ran into a fence. The inspector said, "Drive back to the office." Back in the office, he said, "Sign here," but I was shaking too much to sign it. He said, "Okay, take it home and sign it there." I still have it, it's a pink piece of paper.

I remember going to Tiverton to watch the Fall River Line boats go through at night with all of their lights. They looked so nice. Once, my father's cousin and her husband arrived on the boat, and I remember going down to the boat to pick them up.

## Hurricane of 1938

During the 1938 hurricane, I was working in a sewing shop in a mill on Bedford Street. It started getting awful dark and windy. I heard the gravel shifting on the roof next door. The power went off. The Jewish owner said, "Don't worry, the lights will come back on; it's just a storm." There was no way the lights were going to come back on, and I left. I lived on Weetamoe Street, but how was I going to get home? The streetcars weren't working. I went into a gas station on Bedford Street and asked if they would call me a cab. They said, "You're crazy; there were no cabs running." I said, "Try it." I got a cab. Every street we went down had a tree down on it, and we had to go back and forth up and down each street. When I got home, I asked, "Where's Ernie?" My mother replied, "He's down watching the water come up."

## Popular Expressions

"Hot tamale" was a common slang phrase.

Sandy Beach, before the hurricane of 1938

# Lillian (Souza) Correia

*Born on October 17, 1925*

### Family Background

I was born at home, at 1769 North Main Street, and have lived here over eighty years of my life. I was delivered by Doctor Lewis, who had an office on North Main Street near the train station, in the 900 block. The doctor told my father to open the door of the warm oven. He then put me in a basket and placed me on the open door of the oven to keep me warm.

My father was Frank Costa Souza, and was also born in the North End. His family was from the village of São Vicente Ferreira on São Miguel Island in the Azores. His parents and he returned to São Vicente Ferreira when he was around fifteen or sixteen years of age. His mother died while he was there. The family remained there until after World War I. Because his parents didn't take him to the American Consulate in Ponta Delgada, São Miguel, Azores, he was no longer recognized as an American. Around 1940, he became a naturalized citizen, together with my mother.

My mother was two and a half when she emigrated from the village of Santo António Além Capelas (meaning that her village was adjacent to the larger village, Capelas) on São Miguel with her mother and four sisters. She eventually had six sisters and three brothers. She remained at home until she married my father.

My mother's father emigrated first. Once he had established himself, had a job, and an apartment, he sent for his wife and then the four children. My grandfather's name was Joaquim and my grandmother's name was Emilia. The names of the children were Maria, Cora (my mom), Matilda, and Adeline. They arrived at Ellis Island and then went on to Fall River, where Joaquim had an apartment in the Village (on Morton Street, off of Brightman Street). The other three girls (Bella, Gertrude, and Eva) and the three boys (Joseph, Antone, and Manuel) were born in Fall River.

I lost my mother at the age of 103, and my husband died twenty-five days later.

### Family Life

My mother's father built a three-decker at 80 Weetamoe Street, which had all of the modern conveniences of that time. My father's family owned the house at 1769 North Main Street, which was built around 1840 and had gas lights and no electricity. My grandfather had bought the property and then later sold it to my father in the 1920s. My mother told her future husband that she would move in to 1769 only if he put in electricity in the house, which he did. They were subsequently married in 1924.

When my dad returned to the United States, and started working and saving money, he then purchased the house at 1769 North Main Street, with the help of his employer who was the superintendent at the Sagamore Mill. As time went on, he purchased a car from his employer—a Studebaker, I believe. Dad was one of the first residents in the North End to have a car. As a young child of four or five years old, I would climb onto the back of the back seat and lay on the space and look out the window. Of course, that was only when the car was parked in the driveway. My seat when traveling was between dad and mom (there were no seat belts then).

My father was an engineer at the Sagamore Mill across the street. He maintained the machinery that powered the textile machinery. He made thirty-five dollars a week, good wages at that time; however, when the Depression came, his boss said that he would have to cut my father's pay in half. My father said it was better than nothing, and his pay was cut to eighteen dollars a week.

When I was young, I was a child actress. My mother would make all of my clothes and she would play the piano while I performed. When I was nine years old, my father entered me in a Lucky Strike cigarettes contest. I posed with two packs of Lucky Strikes at the pear tree in the back yard. Nothing ever came of it.

I never wanted for anything. My father raised chickens and geese in the back yard, so we always had chicken and eggs on the table.

We had a Kalamazoo stove, which was a coal stove where the coal was put in the top of the stove and the ashes removed daily. The ashes were shaken by a crank and grate and collected in a pan in the bottom of the stove that was emptied daily. The Wilson Coal Yard delivered the coal to us.

**School Life**

Even though we were members of St. Michael's parish, I went to St. Joseph's School. St. Michael's school was just starting at the time. Because St. Michael's was located at Fulton Street, near the Taunton River, and because I had asthma as a child, my father didn't want me to go to school near to the water, which might worsen my asthma. My father needed permission for me to go to school in another parish from Msgr. Ferraz, but the Monsignor would not give it. After my father threatened to desert the parish, the Monsignor relented. Tuition at St. Joseph's was only fifty cents a month.

I remained at St. Joseph's until eighth grade, then went to Morton for ninth grade and then to Durfee [B.M.C. Durfee High School] for three years. I graduated from Durfee in 1944. I had the most memorable and beautiful time at Durfee and was involved in the Dramatic Club, speaker's bureau, and other activities. Elizabeth Leonard was the public speaking teacher and Barbara Wellington was the drama coach. Once, we went to present a play over the radio at WSAR. I played a Russian nurse with a convincing accent.

**Recreation and Entertainment**

As kids, we would walk up to the upper reaches of Langley Street to the "deadwoods," or wetlands, where we would go skating in the winter. We called it the deadwoods because there were so many dead trees standing in the water.

We would also take the bus to the Portsmouth [Rhode Island] roller skating rink on Sundays and rent skates there. I would also go to Lincoln Park [North Dartmouth, Massachusetts], and Mom and Dad would come along.

It was a big deal to go to Providence. My father had a car, so my husband and I and friends would go to Providence to see a movie and to window shop in the downtown.

Once in a while, we would go to Boston. Once, Rabby Raposa's younger brother Victor convinced us to go to the Old Howard [burlesque theatre]. We (Vic's wife Lee and myself) did not expect to see what we saw and, needless to say, we were very embarrassed. While I was married, I was only nineteen and had lived a very sheltered existence. Lee's brother Jim did not want to go to the Old Howard so he purchased a book and sat at the Boston Common until we met him after the show. Later, we would go to New York City to see plays there.

I have been to Bermuda forty-seven times to visit relatives there.

**Neighborhood Experiences**

Next door to our yard, at 1779 North Main Street, was St. Michael's Bakery. Mr. Franco, the baker, would come to the fence, offer me a roll, and say in Portuguese and English, "Want a little bread?" They were hot out of the oven and he would put butter on them. The bakery ovens are still in the basement of 1779 North Main Street. Later, Mr. Franco closed the bakery and opened a gas station. Gas at that time (about 1933-35) was twelve cents a gallon.

**Food and Meals**

My mother would say "no jiggers" to refer to no need to put herbs on a dish. Her spices were salt, pepper, and garlic. Mom would never use a swear word when she was upset or angry. She would say instead, "Sugar the pips."

My mother's kale soup and baked beans were out of this world. Roasts were common. She preserved apples by making applesauce and make applesauce cake with raisins.

She also made apple pies and put up tomatoes and combined peppers and onions together. Chicken and pork roasts were made with a little wine and tomatoes.

My father made wine from grapes grown in the back yard. The same grape vines are still growing in the back yard, but the grapes are not as plentiful as when Dad cared for them. For years, my downstairs tenant, Joao, tended to the vines and used the grapes to make wine down our cellar. He has since died (2004) and the tradition is being carried on by his wife's nephew (also named John) who also tends to the vines and makes his own wine. They supplement our Concord grapes with those purchased from California: white, purple, and one so small they look like raisins.

My father also made chourico, linguica, and morcella (a blood pudding) in the garage that still stands in the back yard (the garage is called the Hide-A-Way because that is our gathering place for summer get-togethers). Mom helped him. She put the casings in salted water and then would fill the casings. At a certain length, she would twist the casing and continue filling. When they had six or eight strands of chourico hung over a pipe, they would bring the pipes to the smoke house, also in the back yard, where special wood was used to smoke the chourico. Then they would let cool. They would then sell the chourico, linguica, and morcella from the back yard.

As neighbors, friends, and relatives bought the chourico and other sausage that was made in the back yard, they asked why not open a store to sell the sausage to the general public. Later, my father opened a store at 1755 North Main Street called Souza's Market. Today, the store is rented to K.E.E. Distributors and Sales.

**The Depression**

My mother's sister Matilda and her husband, Henry, lost their home and had to go on welfare. My mother gave her chickens for her family but her sister insisted that we take the butter and sugar that they got from welfare. Her husband worked for the WPA [Works Progress Administration]. They had one son, Henry Jr., who joined the Navy in the submarine corps during World War II. After the war, Mike (as we called him) went to college, wrote in for a commission in the Air Force, and remained in the service of our country, retiring as a Lt. Colonel.

Fortunately, we never knew what it was to not have food on the table.

My husband's family, the Correias, consisted of Antone, his father, and Anna, his mother. The five boys in the family were Manuel, Joseph (my husband), Antone, Adelino, and Arthur. The five girls were Mary, Lena (who died the same day as my husband, unbeknown to each, Lena at 3:00 am and Joe at 9:30 am), Ida, Alice, and Dorothy. My husband's father would walk up to the Stevens Mill (they made bedspreads) to save the twenty-five cents of trolley fare. His wife would not eat to allow the remainder of the family to eat until her husband and children had their fill.

**Courtship and Marriage**

I was married at St. Michael's Church in 1946 to Joseph Souza Correia. Seven years later, I gave birth to our only child, a son, Paul Francis Correia. He graduated from St. Michael's School, Bishop Connolly High School, and Providence College. He also received a masters degree from Assumption College. He is married to Doris Lotz Correia and has four children: Sarah Jane, Aaron, Saul, and Abram. There is also a family pet, a black lab named Paige. This is my family and the love of my life.

**Work Life**

My husband and I later ran Souza's Market, but the competition from A&P and other new supermarkets led to the store's closure. We emptied the inventory by trading with a store at the corner of Wilson Road and North Main Street. Joe later worked in Taunton making piano keys.

Joe wanted to become a corrections officer, but he worked the second shift and the classes started at 6:00 pm. So I went to class for him, passed my knowledge on to him, and he passed the exam with good marks! He later became a corrections officer at the Bridgewater State Prison.

I started teaching pre-primary at St. Michael's School in 1960. The first class in the morning was fifty children and the second was fifty-one in the afternoon. Within seven years, I was "promoted" to the second grade. In the summer months, I worked at St. Michael's Credit Union. Finally, I left to take care of my mother.

# J. Thomas Cottrell Jr.

*Born on April 12, 1925*

**Family Background**

My parents were James Thomas and Louise (Thompson) Cottrell.

My mother's parents, Richard S. and Edna Louise (Morgan) Thompson, lived in a house he built at 943 Highland Avenue, on the corner of Weetamoe Street. He was one of "The Three Cash Boys" at McWhirr's, later becoming the secretary and treasurer of McWhirr's following the death of Robert Armstrong McWhirr in 1893 at the age of forty-three.

My father's father was in the fishing business and helped his sons, my father and his brother Frank, start the Cottrell Paper Company.

I had one brother, Richard, who is now deceased.

My wife is Margot Cottrell. We were married in 1953.

**Family Life**

In our household, my father worked and mom ran the house. Back then, when they could afford it, the wives took care of the children and did volunteer work.

My father was in the insurance business. He, his brother Frank, and their father Abram started the Cottrell Paper Company in 1926, a company that is still in business. They owned a paper mill in upstate New York but father didn't want to go there to live because he needed to provide for his family, so Grandfather Cottrell provided the capital, Uncle Frank moved his family there to run the business, and my father did the sales from here. This was a job I later had in 1948.

When I was a small boy, my grandfather Thompson would surreptitiously drop a nickel or a dime on the sidewalk and then say, "Let's go for a walk." I was so excited to find it. It was his way of slipping me money.

There was not much awareness in my family of the Depression. I had one set of clothes for school, one outfit to play in, and one set of Sunday clothes. In the winter, a gang of us got together to earn fifty cents for shoveling a whole sidewalk, which divided up to about ten cents each. I didn't get paid to shovel our own walk, as it was my job to do.

The Staffords had money. John Stafford was my age. One Christmas we had went to play with him and he got a log cabin from FAO Schwartz. Our jaws dropped. We got what we wanted from McWhirr's, but this was from FAO!

Father worked for Mass Mutual and had an office in the city. Grandfather Thompson bought a farm in Little Compton [Rhode Island] of ninety acres, and we went there on weekends to play cards with his gang. He hung around with childhood friends, some of them were less fortunate than him. We went there to fish, etc. Grandmother made a big pot of beans.

Aunt Edna had a horse that she kept at Gage Hill, a stable operated by Dinny [Dennis] O'Brien. Murphy's stable, on Meridian Street, had bridle paths around pond which, I think, the CCC [Civilian Conservation Corps] maintained.

**School Life**

When I was in the sixth grade at Highland School, I was part of the safety patrols. We had belts and badges. Policemen patrolled the corner of Stanley and Robeson Streets. We had four safety patrols, two that went north and two that went south, walking the kids home and making sure that they crossed all the streets safely. There were fifteen to twenty kids in a patrol. I was ten years old when I started with the patrols. We went home for lunch every day. I had to walk from Albany Street to Stanley Street, two times up and two times back.

There were big classes at the Highland School, about forty-five to fifty kids in a class. However, we were very disciplined. We had a fifteen-minute recess and played games to stay active. I started kindergarten in 1929 at age four-and-a-half at the Highland School. That was the last year that they had a maypole. The pole had different colored ribbons and we would go around the pole and wrap the ribbon around it. We also had May baskets. We would make a basket and leave it at the front steps of our girlfriend, ring the bell, and run like hell.

**Food and Meals**

My typical breakfast at home was cereal and an egg. On Saturday morning, I had a few boiled eggs. When I came home from school for lunch, I would have a peanut butter and jelly sandwich or a grilled cheese. Lunch was about 11:30 am to 1:00 pm and we got out of school late at 3:30 or 4:00 pm. Some kids had to walk from Leemingville to the Highland School; some of these kids were four years old and had to walk about five miles a day to and from school, including lunch. Once, Miss Hurley sent me to her home to get something she forgot. I lived next door; she lived on the corner of Stanley and Madison Streets.

**Recreation and Entertainment**

Life is a lot easier now; back then, we didn't have much. Penny candy was a big deal. Gum cards, also. We would flip them against the wall, bending the corners. We carried them with us all the time. We played games at school. Our boots had a place to carry a jackknife.

At Halloween, we would put pins in doorbells and run like hell. It was nothing malicious. My brother's gang (he was five years older than me) would make packets of gunpowder and put it on the trolley tracks. When the trolley rode over the packets, they would make a loud *Pow!* They knew the trolley schedules and when to put the packets on the rails.

We would go skiing down Stewart Street. I lost my interest in skiing down the street after receiving a six-inch gash in my leg from the jagged rocks that were the surface of the streets on the hill back then. It was a little safer going sledding at the southern end of North Park. My brother and his buddies made a sled you steered with a wheel. During their first trip down the hill at North Park, they hit a tree and demolished the sled.

There was a swamp between Robeson and Albany Streets, north of Langley and Albany Streets. It would freeze up and we would go skating there between the swamp bushes. We would also go skating at the North Watuppa Pond at the icehouse at Interlachen before the city closed off Interlachen. We also played hockey at the Mill Pond at Swansea [Massachusetts].

Once, we played baseball with the kids at the Children's Home on Robeson Street. Every neighborhood had their teams.

One of our friends lived up at Interlachen—Frank Andrews. Spencer Borden and the Andrews had big houses at Interlachen. As kids, we would go to swim there. Borden's house was a beautiful big home that they tore down. We would walk from Interlachen through the woods to Wilson Road, across the tip of the pond, and then all the way to the Narrows and back again. It would take us all day to do it. Before we left, my mother put a sandwich in my pocket to have for the day. At that time, the CCC was fixing up all the trails in the woods.

**Neighborhood Experiences**

My family lived at 880 Madison Street, near Albany Street, until I was seven years old. John Lindsey's family lived across the street. Bob Mullen lived nearby. John Friar lived next door in the house to the north. The Pecks, the Masons of Mason's Furniture, and the Dondis families all lived nearby [the Dondis family owned the Empire Men's Shop].

When I was seven, we moved to 372 Madison Street, on the first floor of a three-decker, and remained there for forty years. Our house had two bedrooms, two living rooms, a kitchen, and a bath. Every apartment had their own boiler and workshop in the basement. We alternated using the laundry room downstairs, with the first floor using it one day, the second floor the next day, and the third floor the day after.

On the corner of Madison and Stanley Streets lived Miss Hurley, the principal of the Highland School. The Nadiens and the Rubinsteins lived nearby. Bert Stafford lived a block away on Madison Street. Judge Cook lived on the southeastern corner of Madison and Hood Streets. The Frank Arnzen family lived on Madison Street. Ken List, one of the prominent families, lived in the area and later moved to New York City. The Belford's lived on Robeson Street.

Frank Hadley was a little younger than me. He lives at 991 Madison Street, next to the last house at Milton Street. Tom Brown was one of the few colored persons that I knew in the city. I was at Morton with him. He later got involved with Edwin Land at Polaroid and did quite well for himself.

We had a neighborhood here. Every day, about 6:30 or 7:00 pm, a kid would yell out, "Kick the can," and all of the other kids would come out.

The Mitchells lived in Somerset but ran the gas station at Madison and Stanley Streets. The barn on the corner of Hanover and Stanley Streets belonged to Everett Mills, who had a house on Hanover Street. His father was Asa. The Mills took over McWhirr's when Mr. McWhirr died before the turn of the century. Mr. Mills lived on the corner of Hood and Highland Streets and had a beautiful stable on Hanover Street behind our house.

I spent most of my after-school hours in the Florence Street area, where we played pick-up football. Jim Davis was the coach. We practiced across from my grandfather's house on Highland Avenue. The field where we practiced was where Wendell Turner's big house once was. After he died, they tore everything down.

Our team played the Country Day School and beat them in 1937. Dr. Truesdale took movies of the game and filmed Tom Hudner running the whole field for a touchdown. We had our own jerseys and we had to dig deep for them. Mrs. Hudner drove us to the games.

Dr. Truesdale lived in the house on the southern corner of Highland Avenue and Stanley Street, where the nursing home is now. Dr. Barnes owned the Dutch Colonial on the northern corner of those streets. Freddy Barnes and Jack Brayton kept racing pigeons in the Barnes' garage on Hanover Street, in the upper floor.

I've been a collector all of my life. When I was young, I would walk down Pine Street to an antiques shop owned by Hiram Bliss. Bliss strung tennis rackets in his cellar. I bought my first gun at the Bliss shop. Hiram had a .22 revolver in the shop and wanted one dollar for it. He put it away for me and every time I got a dime or a quarter I went down to pay for it. It was my first gun, and it worked.

Ice was delivered to houses from the icehouse. Milk was delivered in horse-drawn wagons. The horses knew the route. The milkman would take a rack of milk to do two or three houses and the horse would follow and know when to stop.

**Work Life**

I have traveled all over the country for my job. My family has had a paper company, the Cottrell Paper Company. We make electrical insulating paper that goes into small electrical motors. Some of the paper is made from denim scraps collected from manufacturers. Our mill is in New York state. We have been in business for eighty-eight years, and it's still going. I worked for fifty-three years in it. Our workers have been there for generations, with fathers, sons, and grandsons working there. A foreign company once tried to buy the company to get a foothold in the business in the United States. However, we knew what would happen if they bought the company. We didn't want that to happen.

**World War II**

I went to college at the University of Pennsylvania. There, I joined the Naval ROTC. My first course was in navigation. It was based on math that I never had—trigonometry. I couldn't do it. I came to school in September and was out by February. I was seventeen. I joined the Army Air Corps and passed the exam to get in at eighteen. Two weeks after I turned eighteen, I got a letter from Uncle Sam. I chose to be a pilot, even though I never flew before. I learned how to fly and was half way through basic training when they reclassified me as gunnery. I earned my second set of wings, was awarded my commission and then sent to bombardier school. Then I went to navigation school, but the war was over by then.

The service gave me an education in people. There was an unbelievable mix of human beings in the armed services, people from all walks of life and parts of the United States. You met guys from the country who worked on the farm all their lives. You met city kids and guys you never would have associated with had you not been in this situation. You learned a great deal about how to get along with everyone. It was quite an experience.

After the war, there was education on a massive scale and some guys cried with joy because they could go to school. Farm boys didn't want to go back home. I went back to college on the GI Bill and got sixty-five dollars a month to support me while I was in school.

# Ronald Couture

**Family Background**

I had two brothers and two sisters. My father never had a car; he took the bus downtown. He died at fifty-seven. He ran the Tap Room at Lincoln Park [North Dartmouth, Massachusetts]. Before that, my father ran a little market on Pleasant Street. His brother ran the frozen custard stand and my aunt ran the roundhouse that sold hot dogs and hamburgers. Her husband ran the penny arcade. Lincoln Park opened just before Easter and weekends and nights. As soon as school let out, it opened full-time.

**Family Life**

I grew up on Harrison Street in the Flint. We then moved to Rocliffe Street, the first house from the corner of Pleasant Street. It was across from Zeke's Restaurant. The Massasoit Café was on the corner. Our yard was their back yard. Mark You's Restaurant was our back yard on Harrison Street. Walter's Drug Store was on the corner.

**Work Life**

I started working at Lincoln Park at the age of fourteen and went home when the labor inspector came around. Mary Frazer ran the clam cake stand next to the frozen custard stand. Many people who worked there were from Fall River and the Flint.

The Tap Room, the penny arcade, and the bowling alley stayed open year-round. The other activities were run by kids in the summer. I worked on the stands that had games.

Some of the entertainers that came there included a few of the stars from *The Lawrence Welk Show*. They had me going down the aisle with popcorn and candy. The Pavilion had clambakes for families or special occasions.

I worked at the McWhirr's lunch counter at the age of sixteen. Mr. Stevenson, who owned Stevenson's Restaurant in Westport [Massachusetts], owned the lunch counter. We worked for him and got paid by him. Walter Stipek ran the counter for Mr. Stevenson. When he retired, then Paul McGovern took over.

When the McWhirr's sales girls arrived in the morning, they all got coffee and a donut before they started working. There were some men, too, those who worked in the shoe department.

When I was at McWhirr's, mothers and their kids would come in every Saturday. I remember one mother and her daughter who came in every Saturday. I would give her a Christmas gift every year. I named my first daughter after her. People still come to McGovern's today and say, "I remember when I would come to the McWhirr's counter."

When I worked at McWhirr's, I also worked for Pleasant Diner on Sunday breakfast. A French pastry chef worked there. He made all their pastry. They made great pancakes. At McWhirr's, we had all kinds of sandwiches, baked stuffed cod, and chowder on Saturdays. All meals were fifty, sixty, and seventy cents, including chow mein and American chop suey.

I worked at White's Spa part-time after McWhirr's. I would go there after I left McWhirr's and work there from 5:00 to 9:00 pm. I worked at their catering business that fronted on Jencks Street.

I gave my mother my whole pay, but I kept my part-time pay for gas and my car.

I worked at Lapre's Turkey Farm for four years. They would cook a whole turkey for you.

On Sundays, I worked at the Night Owl Diner. I worked from 4:00 pm to midnight, then cleaned it immaculately from midnight to 2:00 am. Friday and Saturday they were open until 2:00 am. I would leave at 4:00 am and then go to Al Mac's Diner to work breakfast from 5:00 am to noon. They took out fifty cents or a dollar for your meals. Once, Millie, who did the pays and hiring, told me, "I took out your meals, but then I put it back in for you."

My sister Stella Desrosiers worked for St. Vincent's Home as a chef.

I worked at the Night Owl Diner when it was on Second Street, on the corner of Morgan Street, near McGrevey's Package Store. It was owned by the Oulettes, who owned the oil company. I didn't like their cheese sandwiches. People would go there after shows.

I worked at the Copicut Lodge before it was owned by the Kings. Then the Shakers took it over. I remember coming home from there on a foggy night. It was scary.

I ran Frates in Somerset for five years. Ice cream cones were fifteen cents each, two for twenty-five cents. Sundaes were thirty-five cents and banana splits were fifty cents. We had three takeout windows and had five kids working for us. We had a good food business, including fish and chips and fried clams. Frank Boulay owned it before us; we bought it from him. He had it easier because he had his whole family working for him, including his wife and kids.

I was at McGovern's for forty-three years. I started in Tiverton, when the first McGovern's was in back of Buddy's Restaurant. It was there for two years. That place had four booths, a counter, and a kitchen. Then we moved to the South Main Street site on the corner of Last Street, near the Tiverton line, where the bus turned around. We were there for ten years. Then we went to the current location where there were all rocks and boulders.

**Neighborhood Experiences**

Pomfret's Bakery was in the brick building on Pleasant Street, between Rocliffe and Quequechan Streets, next to George's Hot Dogs. Their name is still there on the building. We would smell the bread baking from our house. When we smelled the bread, we knew they were ready. We would bring our baked beans to Pomfret's in a pot on Saturday and pick them up on Sunday after Mass at Notre Dame Church.

The Blue Bird Café was at Stafford Square [on the southwest corner] operated by one of the Shaker brothers. People would go there for clamboils. Zeke's Restaurant was across the street from the Massasoit Café. They had nice homemade meals there. The other Shaker brother opened Shay's, which later became Shaker's.

The Pleasant Diner was where Kentucky Fried Chicken is now, on the [northwest] corner of Pleasant Street and Robeson. It was owned by the Schwartz brothers: Sam, the oldest, Sid, and Arthur. Sam bought it first, then the brothers joined him. Sam had worked at the Star Lunch downtown. There were two big counters at the Pleasant Diner, left and right, as you entered the door. One counter was just for putting up orders to go. The shops in the mills kept them busy. One person was in charge only of to-go orders. I worked there. When the shops died, it died. One of the Schwartz boys was married to my aunt's family.

Sam Schwartz built Earnshaw's Diner. There was an Earnshaw's near to the Pleasant Diner on Pleasant Street. Sam also built Sambo's Diner on Pleasant Street, near where Dunkin' Donuts is now.

Next to Walter's Drug Store and the Mark You Restaurant was Gerard's Cobbler Shop; a Mrs. Gerard fixed shoes there.

Nora's Restaurant was located on South Main Street and moved to Bank Street behind the banks. It had excellent homemade food. Behind City Hall was another diner.

Most of the 5 & 10s had stand-up counters. One of the 5 & 10s, it may have been Kresge's, had a place to the left as you entered the main door—the main counter was further down. They had hamburgers there that were covered in a juice with onions. They were served on a hamburger bun. They were wonderful.

The Square Diner was at the [northwest] corner of Pleasant and Quarry Streets, where Glazer Glass is now. Leo Bissonette owned it. Later, they opened up the Bus Diner in the former mill office building that was part of the Stafford Mills. It was mostly sit-down. Most diners opened up at 6:00 or 7:00 am. Some diners opened all night, but most did not.

McWhirr's had a cobbler shop downstairs. At Christmas, they had a Santa Claus; they were the first in the area to have a Santa. At Christmastime, McWhirr's was beautiful. McWhirr's would deliver anything. They would deliver a spool of thread. The front doors were rotating and they had five floors. Furniture was on the fifth, the offices were on the fourth. At night, we would put our money in a bag and take it to the office. McWhirr's got fifteen cents on the dollar for the counter. All of the money we collected first went to McWhirr's, and then they distributed Stevenson's their share. Stevenson had to pay his own electric and gas.

The stove was downstairs and we had to bring up food from the basement by the stairs. There was an elevator to the basement, but it was on the other side of the building. Cooking was downstairs and the grill was upstairs. Soups, ham salad, and hot food were made downstairs. We made our own coffee and chocolate syrup there. I still make my own coffee syrup at McGovern's. It's delicious. It's the best around. We make three gallons of it every week. Some people take home a quart of it. It has no preservatives.

In the summertime, there was no air conditioning. It was hot. There were all kinds of fans in the store. We had our own fans at the counter. I had a towel on my shoulder to wipe my forehead.

# Dr. Bruce Derbyshire

*Born on July 17, 1928*

**Family Background**

My parents were Arthur Ralph and Annie Elizabeth (Wardle) Derbyshire. Everyone called her "Liz." (Wardle is a town in England where everyone is called Wardle. It is a corruption of Wordell). My mother founded the first well-baby clinic in Fall River. She also started the first Girl Scout troop in the city.

My father parents were Ralph and Ellen Derbyshire. My mother's parents were Edward and Mary Ann (Greenwood) Wardle.

I have one sibling, named Mary Faith. My wife's name is Elizabeth.

**Family Life**

When I was born, the family lived at 304 Cory Street, just west of North Main Street. It was my grandfather's property. In front was a two-family house (since torn down for a parking lot) and a three-decker to the rear. My aunt and uncle lived on the first floor. My mother and father bought a house in Somerset during the Depression, far out by a school, and moved in. We were there until 1939. My folks built a house at 432 Florence Street in Fall River. We were not there long, until 1941. It was a spec home. There were four homes on Florence Street built by Bill Grant, who built houses on spec. It wasn't substantial.

Also on Florence Street, on the northwest corner of Woodlawn Street, a house was built specifically for Harvey Ashton, son of the undertakers. Fall River in those days had a big English population. There was the Order of the Odd Fellows (and Odd Ladies); my grandmother was the chairman of the Odd Ladies. Aunt Beatrice also got involved. They had a junior thing; I marched in a Fall River parade in an Odd Fellows uniform when I was nine years old. Harvey Ashton was the best man at my parent's wedding.

My grandfather was a member of the Knights of Pythias. When he died, someone came to the house with his regalia. It made a wonderful costume for Halloween. There were many English orders. It was a big community, but everyone knew everyone.

My father's father came the United States when he was about twelve with his mother and brother. His mother died shortly after. Both brothers were brought up in Westport as orphans. Later, they lived in the Flint. My father's mother came over as a young girl of seven or eight and lived in the Flint.

My mother's mother must have been born here, since my great-grandfather was here and my mother's father and mother had a bakery in Border City. They would pack hot lunches to put in the dinner pails of the workers. My grandfather died quite young.

My father's father was a "second hand" in the mill. He was quite a person. One time, he took off for England and bicycled across England and Scotland with two other men. Later, he went to California and bought a farm there. He came back by stagecoach by the southern route. Along the way, they were attacked by robbers, who killed the drivers and the other passengers. My grandfather pleaded with them not to kill him, since he had a wife and children back home, and they spared his life. He walked to the nearest town, and the people in the town raised enough money to send him back east.

My grandfather Derbyshire lived on Barnaby Street, three houses from the southern end of the road. He had a workshop in the house. At one time, there was a policeman in a box in the middle of street in front of City Hall, directing traffic under an umbrella with signs that he held up that said "STOP" and "GO." I could always find my grandfather talking to the policeman in the middle of the road. My grandfather died about 1940 or so.

My father was born John James Derbyshire. However, when he was eight, a John James shot his wife, and my grandmother decided to change his name to Arthur Ralph Derbyshire. Everyone in town knew him because he was on many boards and worked for the Fall River National Bank. He had an eighth grade education. His first job was at the Beef House operated by Anthony and Swift, who had a company here. Anthony and Swift found a way to bypass the middlemen and ship beef direct. It later became Swift and Armour. Swift is an old Cape Cod name. Anthony lived in Swansea [Massachusetts] at the end of Gardners Neck Road and would take the train every day to Boston. When the weather was bad, he would have to go to Swansea Village. He had a bridge built over Lee's River, and his descendants had the new bridge named for him.

Grandmother Wardle would make an English pancake or crepe only on Shrove Tuesday. Shrove Tuesday was the Tuesday before Lent.

My mother wasn't a fantastic cook, but it was good, wholesome food. We were fussy eaters. All groceries were delivered to the house by my mother's cousin, who owned a market on Beacon Street, just beyond South Park [now Kennedy Park], near Globe Corners and the circus grounds. All of our food was from "Uncle John's Store." It was owned by John Hodkinson.

We celebrated St. Patrick's Day because it was my grandmother's birthday. We always had a big party for Grandmother.

My grandfather never wanted to give to the Salvation Army because they wouldn't help strikers. On the other hand, my father was out in front of McWhirr's every Christmas ringing his bell and holding a pail for the Salvation Army.

My father's uncle worked in the mills and later started a ministry. He took a bound book with blank pages and wrote the history of the family, as he knew it. On his birthday each year, he would write on one page what was going on in his family, Fall River, and the world. His first preaching job was at a church in North Westport [Massachusetts]. They passed around a pouch for donations, which he used to buy a pair of shoes. They invited him back for the fiftieth anniversary of the church. He later went to churches at Watch Hill, Newport, and Agawam. I stayed with his son. He became a minister of a church in Little Compton [Rhode Island] and then left to become a Unitarian minister. He was also a drama critic for the *New York Times* and wrote stories for magazines.

## School Life

I first went to the Wiley School. Mr. Redford drove his red-headed daughter Ann (how I loved her!) and my cousin Robert Ashton to school. One day, my cousin came home and my mom asked, "Where's Bruce?" I was "bad" in school and the teacher put me in a closet. I fell asleep, and she forgot me.

I went to Wiley for one-half a day because it had a primary school. Then I went to the Borden School at North Park and then to the Westall School. I would go to my grandmother's house on Barnaby Street for lunch. When we moved to 432 Florence Street, I went to the Highland School and to Morton Junior High. I was president of Morton's Class of 1943, second term.

Freddy Kozak was one of the best football players at [B.M.C.] Durfee High School. At one practice session, he and I had to go to work at 3:00 pm. "Excuse me, Mr. Urban," I said. "I have to go to work now." Urban blew up and said, "I don't want to see you again, ever; not in the corridor, not anywhere. If I see you, get out of the way." That was the extent of my football experience at Durfee. I played squash with Freddy Kozak (his son was a city councilor). Freddy could run like a deer. He went to Brown and was an All-East. He was going to leave Brown, but he was advised to stay. I went to Yale and saw him at the Brown-Yale games.

Dick Fitton and I shared the Sunday paper route. There were better tips on Sundays. I also delivered morning papers; I didn't want to deliver the afternoon papers because I wouldn't be able to play games if I did. Bob Peloquin would do one month of the daily paper route and I would do the other. We would take our money to Mrs. Boland at the *Fall River News*.

My father was called in to Durfee once because I was involved in a fracas. The principal told my father, "Have you ever thought of sending your son away to school?" My father got me into Moses Brown, but they had no accommodations; their dorms were full. They said that they could take me if I was willing to share a room. The fellow that I ended sharing the room with was Dick Fitton, who was 6 feet, 4 inches tall. It was a small room and we were jammed into it. I was on the football team and had lots of friends there.

I graduated in February and applied only to Yale. Why only Yale? My father worked in the Fall River National Bank, and his friend, Richard Hawes, was a graduate of Yale. Hawes was an overseer of the Westminster School and this was the era of the old boy network. Dick Hawes thought the world of my father. Whenever anyone had to be fired in the city my father would go and do the firing. My father did the hiring and firing at the bank. He was the cashier and vice president there. He was also the face of the Fall River National Bank. He could be seen in newspaper photos at openings of businesses, accompanied by Mary Fonseca.

I got into Yale. I always wanted to be a doctor. My sister was born with a deformed spine. It was recognized early. Doctors were heroes to us.

## Recreation and Entertainment

I would go to the Durfee Theatre with Donald Ashton and to the Royal Theatre on Saturdays, where the movie was free but where they got you on the candy.

We would play kick the can in the street; there wasn't much traffic on Florence Street.

Westall School on Maple Street

At the Stone Bridge Inn, the floor was sloped down to the southeast corner. At the end of the dance, you would end up in the southeast corner of the ballroom. The Port West Theatre was in the Stone Bridge Inn. My son Peter built all of the sets for the theatre. Peter went on to Ithaca College and worked on Broadway sets. He also worked on sets for WGBH and PBS. He started designing apartments in Boston and met his wife Stephanie Von Trapp. They have been married for twenty years and live in Adamsville [Rhode Island]. My wife was very active in the Little Theatre and was a former president. She negotiated with the city to get the old fire barn given to the Little Theatre for their rehearsals and performances.

**Work Life**
My father began work at the Burke and Davis clothing shop. Then he worked for the Metacomet Bank as a teller. In the 1928 fire, the Metacomet Bank burned down, and it was absorbed by the B.M.C. Durfee Trust Company.

My mother worked in the mills for a short time and didn't go to high school. Aunt Beatrice went to high school. My mother went to a secretarial school in the Hudner Building called the Thibodeau Business College. She met my father there.

I worked at Waring Jewelers while at Durfee, which was located next to the Durfee Theatre. I delivered things for them and had a bus pass. I also swept the sidewalk and received taunts from my friends for it.

In the summer of 1946, I went to the Cape to work at a hotel. I stopped at one hotel to ask for a job and got four jobs. I was a dishwasher and baker's assistant. There were a hundred waiters and twenty girls. It was crazy. We would go to Jake's in Chatham; we hiked there and got a ride back.

Next summer, I worked at Globe Manufacturing and worked on my golf game. If you were a student, you could join the Fall River Country Club for twenty-five dollars and play unlimited golf. This was when it was a nine-hole course. Ruth Woodard played at the FRCC and was an international champion.

I picked peas at the Simmons farm in Assonet and went to Boston to sell them off of the truck. This was about 1940 or 1941.

**Neighborhood Experiences**
Tom Rogers invented Spandex in his mother's kitchen. We had a small cottage and sold it before the 1938 hurricane. Down the street were the Rogers. The son was a plebe at Annapolis about 1936. I had a toy football and went in swimming with it. Teddy was home with a few classmates. They came in and took the ball and began kicking it around and broke the ball. I was upset. At Christmas, Teddy Rogers came by and gave me a football jersey from the US Naval Academy. A jersey like that was very unusual at that time. I loved it and used it as pajamas.

**Health and Illness**
In the fall of 1943, I was bitten in my left ear by a spider. The resulting infection led to my getting meningitis and becoming very ill. I was treated with a new drug called penicillin. At that time, all trials for penicillin were being conducted by a doctor out of Boston University. I recovered.

# Eva (Tardi) Desmaris

*Born on July 17, 1911*

### Family Background

My parents were Alphonse and Amanda (LeMontaigne) Tardi. Both my parents came from Canada. We lived on Benjamin Street in the South End. My father was a machinist in the mill.

I was one of ten children—seven sisters and two brothers. One brother died in World War II, the other of an aneurysm. We were, in birth order: Aura, Blanch, Marion, Alfonse "Pete" (died in World War II), Adrian, Lucy, Alice, Eva, and Irene.

My husband's name was Wilfred Desmaris and he died in 1984. We have two children, Ernest and Nancy.

### Family Life

When my mother died at the age of forty-two, I was going on eight and my younger sister was four. When my mother died she was laid out in the house. I and the two dogs sat by her coffin. My father never remarried. He said that he didn't want a stepmother for his kids. All the family took responsibility after my mother died. My father was sixty-five when he died and was also buried from the house. My mother's brother bought a big family lot in Notre Dame Cemetery and my mother and father are with them.

With such a large family, as one of us got married or went to work, the next oldest child took over care of the family. I had to leave school at fourteen. I had to do the cooking for my father. Once I burn the potatoes because I went out to play instead.

One day stays with me. We had two Collie dogs and, after my mother died, my father got rid of them, sold them. However, one day my dog Dixie came back and began scratching on the door. I opened the door and said, "Dixie, come under the bed." But the man that my father sold the dog to complained. I pleaded with my father, "Let him stay," but my father said that he had a good home on a farm. I was able to keep him for two days.

After my sister Olivette was married in 1942, at the age of thirty-two, I went to live with her when I was eighteen and remained there for ten years. I went from the city to the country. I lived with my sister on Wilson Road. I hated the city, and my sister had said, "When I get married, you can live with me."

When I was married, our house started from a little shack at 1064 Wilson Road, a few houses up from Meridian Street. My husband's mother lived next door at 1088 Wilson Road. My husband had a little sawmill in the back yard. I took care of the chickens, ducks, goats, a cow named Bessie, and sheep.

I helped at the sawmill by taking away the slags and doing other work for him. My husband and, later, our daughter, Nancy, milked the cow every morning and pastured it. At 3:30 pm, the cow would come right into the barn. I remember a rooster chasing Nancy in the field; I chased it back with a broom. My sister made apple and grape jelly. I would put vegetables up and my husband killed the pigs. All our relatives came to Wilson Road to visit. We always had a full house of people, aunts, and cousins.

We bought the old milk house that was on my mother-in-law's property and my husband moved it to our land. It was very small, with the three kids sleeping in one bedroom. In 1951, we remodeled and expanded it and the kids then had their own bedrooms.

On hot days, I would cook in the morning and then warm the meal up at dinnertime.

My wood stove was a Glenwood range. It was porcelain and colored beige and green. It was made in Taunton. My husband would make toast on top of the stove. I would make baked beans on Saturdays. People would walk in and say, "What a great smell!" I made four fruitcakes a year in that stove. Fruitcakes need an even temperature, and I got the wood stove to provide it. Once, a city person came in and asked where I put the wood in the stove, in the oven? No, I said, in here, and I pointed to the firebox.

I would wash the small clothes and Ideal Laundry would come and pick up the big stuff, like sheets. I did everything by hand. The dairy came and delivered milk, and the ragman came by with his horse and wagon. He would yell, "Rags! Rags!" Nancy was scared of him.

In 1962, we bought forty-two acres of land in the Copicut area and built ourselves a log cabin. Other members of the family later built houses near us. My husband moved his sawmill there. Two grandsons of Nancy now run the Brightman sawmill here and her daughter runs the office. Her husband has a land clearing operation now.

**School Life**

I went to St. Anne's School, then to public school on Cambridge Street. I graduated from the Susan Wixon School. I had to quit school and go to work.

**Recreation and Entertainment**

We kids played across the street in a farm on Benjamin Street. The hay was piled in mounds and we would go jumping in the hay. We played peggy ball. We played marbles when we were older. We would put a clothespin on a window and walk away with a string. When we pulled the string, the clothespin would bang against the window, scaring the person inside. Sometimes we would put a basket of manure on a door step and ring the door bell. We also had bonfires and cooked potatoes and apples in the fire.

We also went to Lincoln Park [North Dartmouth, Massachusetts], although early on they had only dobby horses there. My sisters would go to Island Park [Cashman's Park, Portsmouth, Rhode Island] two or three times a week; I would go only for special occasions. I had a boyfriend at Island Park. We went to the dance hall and the bowling alley. One day, I was supposed to go to the novena, but instead I went to Island Park.

The circus came every year. We would walk around with the girls and look at the animals; we never went inside to see the shows. The circus parade would go from Rodman Street up to the circus grounds.

**Courtship and Marriage**

I gave up on the boyfriend I was going with; I didn't like the city. When I came to live with my sister Olivette, my future husband lived a few houses up on Wilson Road with his mother in a big house. He would come over and do chores for Olivette, such as mowing the lawn, emptying the rubbish, or helping with the garden. Olivette would make cream pies and other desserts and give him some. My husband loved the woods and the outdoors.

We were married in 1932. Mary Ann Wordell's father, Clyde, was our best man. Our daughter, Nancy, was born on Wilson Road. Ernest was born in 1934 and Nancy was born the week after the 1938 hurricane, on September 27, 1938.

**Work Life**

When I quit school, I worked in the rayon textile mills on Pleasant Street in the Durfee Mills. I walked to work. I lived on Kellogg Street then and walked to the mills through side streets.

My husband worked for the Wordells on their farm and for Shell Oil at the tank terminal. However, he wanted the freedom to go home when he wanted to and so began to haul cedar posts. He would go in and cut the posts and carry them out to where the horses were, and they hauled them out to the trailer. He would then load them and deliver them. He had a lump on his shoulder from hauling out so many posts. My husband would then go in to check for logs to cut for the next day. One time, a load was too heavy and a hired hand was hitting the horse to make him pull the load. He told the guy, "I'll hit you with this stick; the load is too big." The horse was laboring and they had to take some of the poles off. He never hired that guy again.

The cedar posts were used for clothes line poles. Nancy used to pull the bark from the cedar posts and got five cents for peeling them. She used a curved knife to do it.

When someone came to pick up their order, I would charge ten cents more than my husband charged. Then I called my sister and said, "Let's go shopping."

My husband's brother Andre was head of the Watuppa Reservation headquarters on Blossom Road. My husband had a contract with the city to take out ten to twelve pine logs a day to bring back to the mill. Nancy and her brother would cut them up and finish about 2 o'clock. It was a day's work. He sold the lumber to Bolduc's Lumber in the South End. Later, he had the cedar post business.

My son, Ernest, went to college and studied forestry in Alaska. Nancy's husband bought the place on South Main Street in Assonet in 1978 and began the business here in 1984. They do planning, finishing, milling, and have kilns. Nancy's grandchildren run the lumber business, and her husband has a land clearing business. A big load of chips now goes to Maine. Everything on the site gets used or recycled.

**Neighborhood Experiences**

My husband believed that the best protection during lightening storms was to get in the car, with its rubber tires, so, during a storm, everyone had to sit in the car to avoid lightening. We had a big crabapple in the yard and one day, during a storm when we were all in the car, a big branch came down on the car.

In the 1940s, our grandmother (our "French Ma," my husband's mother), lived on Wilson Road. The Reeds lived on Meridian Street. King's Florist was also on Meridian Street, near the corner of Wilson Road and Meridian Street, one house in from Wilson Road. Pearson's Dairy Farm was further down on Meridian Street. The Bragas had one cow and sold raw milk.

There was a CCC [Civilian Conservation Corps] camp was near the school on Meridian Street.

**Christmas, Holidays, and Special Occasions**

For Christmas, I got a little cellophane doll in my stocking, which was not the doll that I ordered. We got candy and nuts in our stocking. I don't remember getting anything when I was younger.

# Madeline (Lima) Doncaster

*Born on June 20, 1927*

**Family Background**

When I was born, I was given the name Mary Madeline Lima (Maria Madelana in Portuguese). My parents were Manuel Curt Lima Jr. and Herminia (Souza) Lima.

My father's parents were Manuel Curt Lima Sr. and Maria (Miranda) Lima. I never knew my mother's parents because they died early. My mother's father had a store in the Azores and, when he came here, opened a store in Bristol. My mother and father met when my father visited the store on business.

My father's siblings were named Isabelle, Mary, and Joseph, and my mother's siblings were named Rose, Mary, Sadie, Manuel, and Joe. Manuel's wife was named Gert and she was my godmother.

There were a number of addresses where we lived in Fall River: 1101 North Main Street, at President Avenue (northeast corner, where the gas station is now next to Morton Middle School), 659 Hanover Street, 330 Lincoln Avenue, Rock Street, 63 Chavenson Street, and 374 June Street (my parents moved there after I was married).

My brothers and sisters were named Beatrice, Alfred, Evelyn, Manuel Curt III ("Buddy"), Virginia, and Elizabeth ("Betty").

I was married from 63 Chavenson Street to Robert Allan Doncaster of Newport, Rhode Island. Our children are named Karen, Barbara, Robert, and James.

**Family Life**

The rounded bay in front of the Hanover Street house was where the parlor was; the second floor on that side of the house was my mother's bedroom. There was a trellis in the rear yard, where my mother had her garden parties for the Emblem Club and other organizations. An orchestra would play during the parties. We have news clippings of the parties. My mother wanted to string Chinese lanterns from our house to the Smith house, and they let us do it.

In a corner of the house was a big forsythia bush, with hanging branches. Virginia and I would go under it to play house with our tea set. Buddy would put coins in between the door jambs in his bedroom. My bedroom didn't have a closet, only a small place for hanging clothes.

While the Holy Name Church was being built, Buddy climbed up the scaffolding and carved his initials in the church's tower. Once, when we had kittens, Buddy decided to throw them one by one out the third story window of the Hanover house. I caught some but not all.

During WPA [Works Progress Administration] days, when it was hot, I would take water out to the guys who were working on the street. Mr. Cabeceiras took care of our lawn; I went to school with his son, John Cabeceiras.

We sold the Hanover Street house when I was twelve or thirteen in order to keep the two-tenement houses on North Main Street and President Avenue that my father owned. A man who owned the Taunton Dog Track was supposed to help my father save the house, but he was suddenly killed in a plane crash. I thought the world caved in when we lost Hanover Street.

My father was a meat jobber and delivered meat from the meat packers to the local stores. However, the local stores didn't pay their bills when my father delivered the meat. Instead of going bankrupt, he took his own money and paid the wholesalers like Armour. When my father didn't get the money, another man said that he would help out, but he didn't. My father's father didn't help him out. He felt that my father was living beyond his means by living in the Highlands. We then moved to 330 Lincoln Avenue.

My mother was a great pincher. When Virginia would come in late, I would get pinched all the time while Virginia would rush by and not get pinched.

My sister Betty had Down Syndrome, and I remember my parents taking her to a place in Bristol [Rhode Island] where she stayed. It cost fifty dollars a week—a lot back then. Betty always sang "Silent Night," and I always cry when I hear that now.

Alfred played the violin and later went to Mount St. Charles Academy in Woonsocket, Rhode Island, and stayed there. Beatrice played the piano and went to Sacred Heart Academy. Beatrice, Buddy, and Evelyn graduated from [B.M.C.] Durfee High School.

Buddy was a tormentor. I would get a doll for Christmas and he would open it up and take the "*ma ma*" out. The abbreviation for Madeline was Maude. Buddy always called me "Mud." I've always had an inferiority complex, and that didn't help.

Sacred Heart Academy

My grandparents Lima owned the houses and store on the northeast corner of Corey and Oregon Streets and a house next door on Oregon Street. My grandfather was a penny-pincher and was considered one of the richest men Down North. But he wouldn't help my father save the Hanover house. When my grandfather left the store, my grandmother would put penny candy in a brown bag, twist the bag, and give it to us to take home.

On Sundays, my parents would take us visiting to my mother's family. We visited with Aunt Sadie in Bristol. On other Sundays, we would go to the vegetable farm in Norton owned by my mother's sister Mary. You had to pump water there. Aunt Mary and Uncle Joe would give us corn and other vegetables to take home. Their daughter Gladys made cakes to sell at their vegetable stand. Gladys also painted paintings and sold them there.

My mother started the Portuguese-American Civic League and the Portuguese-American Loyalty Association. My parents were on the committee to create the Prince Henry statue on Eastern Avenue. Their names are in the base of the statue.

My father was a life-long member of the Elks. He loved to bowl and bowled until he died at eighty-seven. Late in life, my father worked for the city's Board of Health. My parents also had a drop cloth business.

Joe Martin, who was speaker of the United States House of Representatives, was a good friend of my father and mother. My father would call him up and he would say, "Okay, Manny, who wants to come over now?" He called my mother "Minnie." After my wedding, I got a nice letter from Joe Martin saying that business in Washington prevented him from coming to my wedding and that he wished me well. My parents also knew Governor Curley and Governor Saltonstall.

Buddy and Laura met in the drugstore on the northeast corner of Robeson Street and New Boston Road (where the laundromat is now). Buddy worked as a soda-jerk there. Laura was seventy-nine and Buddy was eighteen when they met. I have the letter that Laura sent to my father asking his permission to marry Buddy. It was a sensation! The Associated Press called my parents to get a quote, but they were away and I didn't say anything to them. After the marriage, Buddy and Laura went out west for their honeymoon. Laura bought him seven Cadillacs.

**Friends**

My father would take us to St. Michael's School; when he couldn't, he sent a cab for us. I'm glad I went to that school because that's where I met the five Flores sisters: Mary Ann, Vivian, Lorraine, Helen, and Theresa. Their brother was killed at Normandy Beach on his second wedding anniversary. He left a son, an only child. We were all at a Portuguese fiesta when the word came in; we all quickly left to go home.

George Mendonca from Bristol was a friend of my husband Bob and was called "George, the Kissing Sailor. " He was the sailor who was kissing the nurse while celebrating the end of the war in Times Square, the picture that was on the cover of *LIFE* magazine. His girlfriend is standing in back of him. It was proven that he was the sailor in the picture.

**Food and Meals**

For breakfast we had malasadas or cereal such as Rice Krispies, which I loved, or Corn Flakes. Meals were Portuguese soup with mint, carne, or chicken with rice. In the cellar, my mother made ketchup, chourico, root beer, and pimenta muida. Mamie would babysit for us and raid the refrigerator.

**School Life**

The principal of St. Michael's was Sister Gertrude Theresa and I was scared of her. There was also Sister Mary Bilbanna, who was old, short, and in her sixties. She was hard. Sister Helen Marie was sweet and pretty. A woman came in to the school to teach us Portuguese. My mother wanted us to learn the Portuguese language. They kept me back for penmanship one year. I only went to the eighth grade and quit at sixteen. I wish I had gotten an education through high school. I later got my GED in Newport.

Father Cabral came in to give us catechism lessons. He was large in stature. When he moved, or pounded the desk, the room shook. He would ask, "Who's doing that?" and we would say, "You are, Father." Once, I had a missing page from my catechism and couldn't answer a question that he asked, and he slapped me in the face.

We were well-to-do, but it didn't bother me. I wasn't a snob. The school was so poor that the sisters asked us to bring in our Christmas cards so we could write on the inside of them. Christmas cards then were printed on one side and folded. They gave us orange or grapefruit juice in small cups in the morning. We stood in line to get our vaccinations.

Every day of the week, my mother paid Mrs. Malone to give us lunches. She lived on Fulton Street. She had two sons. On Fridays, we would go for chow mein sandwiches. I would ask them to strain it. My father picked us up or we were picked up by a cab.

**Recreation and Entertainment**

Beatrice would have her friends over and Buddy would put on a play for them. The play was called, "The Cursed Piano." Buddy would play the piano; I was dressed as the maid who brought in something. Virginia was also in it. At one point, Buddy would take a drink at the piano and fall over and "die" from it. Hilda Olivera and other of Beatrice's friends would come to see the plays.

We played dodge ball, red rover, tag, and hide and seek. I went to the library a lot and read constantly. I loved Nancy Drew and The Bobbsey Twins. We went ice skating on South Watuppa Pond with the Flores girls. I put on so many layers of clothes that I couldn't move to skate. We never threw snow balls.

After we went roller skating, we would stop at Nick's Hot Dogs, where he would line up the hot dogs up his arm.

During the summertime, we would go to Mayor Harry Monk's place. He would tell my father, "Manny, you bring the chourico and I'll have the watermelon." My father would duck me in the water over my head; I never go near the water now. Freddy once got bitten by a Portuguese man o' war and his hand swelled up and looked like Jell-O.

I played in the yard and in the street. I broke rocks on the sidewalk with Virginia and arranged the pieces in different colored layers in jars. Evelyn read a lot. Evelyn loved to go to the library and the movies. She loved movie stars. She loved Judy Garland and so did I.

I would go to the Roseland Ballroom at Lincoln Park [North Dartmouth, Massachusetts] with the Flores girls. You put lipstick above your lips and tanned your legs below your dress. The things we did to look good!

**Courtship and Marriage**

I met Bob at Bill Medieros and Eleanor's wedding. Bob was part of Bill's group of buddies. Bob asked me for my phone number; I gave it to him and told him, "Don't lose it." I was turning twenty the next day. He didn't call me. I went to a fair across from St. Anne's Church and came home to a birthday party. Then he called me and asked me out. I sat on the couch and started crying. My mother asked, "Why are you crying?" I said, "He asked me out."

We went to the Seekonk Race Track for our first date. On our second date, we were going someplace for dinner and stopped in Marion [Massachusetts], or near there, and walked along the beach. Bob wrote in the sand, "I love you." We later bought lobster, but I couldn't eat it; I was too upset.

Bob and I went to Pre-Cana sessions with the priest. The priest insisted that we meet at 6:00 pm, even though that meant that Bob had to rush from work, clean up, and go from Newport to Fall River and arrive in time. It was difficult for him, but he did it. We asked the priest if he could do it later, but he insisted that he had an important commitment and that was the only time he could do it. However, we found out later that the important reason was that he wanted to get back to the rectory to see the "Mr. Peepers" show on TV. We thought it was for some better reason.

The day before the wedding, the priest called up to say that he had a funeral the next day and couldn't do our wedding. I said, "Can't the body wait? We are ready for tomorrow and the guests will be here for a wedding." He arranged for a priest from Taunton to officiate at the wedding.

The wedding was not in the main church because Bob wasn't Catholic. Bill Medeiros was our best man and Eleanor was the maid of honor. It rained that day and Bill was late. My veil flew up and landed on the car. The hem of my gown fell in the gutter. The reception was at 63 Chavenson Street. The Taunton priest put my name down in the wedding document as Mary W., not Mary M. and Bob joked later that he wasn't married to me but to a Mary W. Lima.

My honeymoon was a whole month. We went to New York City and stayed at the Algonquin Hotel on the first night. Then we drove to New Orleans to the Mardi Gras. I always wanted to go to the Mardi Gras; February was a terrible time to get married, but at least I was able to go to the Mardi Gras. We stayed in a private home there owned by a French lady. Then we went to Miami for two weeks. We returned to the same place at Miami Beach every year and there was always the same man there at the same time as we were sunning himself by the pool. Every year. As it turns out, we found out later that he was a priest. Bob bought a coconut to bring home and claimed he climbed a coconut tree to get it.

While on our honeymoon, I found a little gold pin with a horn of plenty. I also found a cherub angel and a penny. I still have these wrapped up in the handkerchief that I carried when I walked down the aisle at my wedding.

Bob helped to pay for the down payment on our house with the nickels that he saved up in school. At first, we lived with my in-laws. The Doncaster lineage goes back to one of the kings of England.

**Work Life**

When I quit school, I went to work first in a dress shop. A middle-aged woman came in to the shop and tried on a dress. I said, "That print doesn't look right for you." The manager heard me and fired me.

Then I went to work at Firestone on the 8:00 am to 4:30 pm shift, working on Dalehousing bags. I wore black rubber gloves to above my elbows. Then I put nose caps on gas masks for a while. It was hot in there! Then I put lens on gas masks. One time, Army generals came to inspect the plant, and either Douglas MacArthur or Eisenhower stood behind me to observe us.

Then I went to work for Parker Candies. The owners were brothers and named Clarence, Homer, Milton, Henry, and Oscar Parker. They were French. Once, Oscar took us to Common Fence Point [Portsmouth, Rhode Island] and took us for a ride in his plane. It was my first plane ride. He tipped it and really frightened me.

Oscar worked with me bagging candy. He would get close to me, and I would tell him, "If you get any closer, we will be like two pages out of *Forever Amber.*" I loved pistachios and, when I was bagging them, the brothers would say, "There'll be no work done today; Madeline's on the pistachios."

However, my nerves got shot. One day, I didn't go in but, instead, went to a movie and sat for two shows. When I got back, they said, "How are you?" and I said, "Okay," and that was it. I quit Parker's when my mother opened a remnant store in Warren [Rhode Island] and I went there to run it until I got married.

When Mr. Forrest sold his store to my father about 1955, I went there on Saturdays to help out. The store continued to be called Forrest Market and was on the southeast corner of Durfee and Cherry Streets. My father had the most wonderful Polish hams in the store. The undertaker Faria would come in every Saturday and tell my father, "Manny, two pounds; shave it."

**Neighborhood Experiences**

When we first moved to 659 Hanover Street, Holy Name Church (which is now just north of the house) had not been built yet. The property was owned by the Bordens; they had big trees and gardens in the yard where the church is now.

Across the street from us was the Charles Hodgate family, at 664 Hanover Street. Every 4th of July, Mr. Hodgate would shoot fireworks in the street in front of our house. We stayed on our porch; we were not allowed to leave the house because of the fireworks. My mother would only give us sparklers to light.

Also across the street, at 650 Hanover Street, lived Mrs. Gray on the second floor and her daughter, Mrs. Walsh, who lived on the first floor. Mrs. Walsh's son was Cleveland Walsh, who traveled with a swing band. Her husband was named Franklin. Mrs. Gray introduced us kids to bingo, and we played that with the other kids. Sometimes, she would pay us to wash down the hallway stairs with Pine Sol. On Monday nights, Mrs. Walsh would invite us over to have cold roast beef and scalloped potatoes. I fell in love with scalloped potatoes; it was my favorite meal. She would give me some to take home and I would sometimes hide it away for safekeeping. Once, my mother found a dish of scalloped potatoes under my bed, molded.

Another neighbor across the street was Mrs. Conroy. She lived next door to the Walshes and Grays at 664 Pearce Street, on the corner of Hanover and Pearce Streets. Mrs. Conroy would ask me to do errands for her, like going to the store.

Next door to us, on the [northeast] corner of Hanover and Pearce Streets, lived Lidia Smith. Across from them [on the southeast corner of Hanover and Pearce Streets] lived the Dalbec family. Mr. Dalbec played the organ at the Durfee Theatre.

The Rileys lived in the house one down from the Conroys on Pearce Street, next to 664 Pearce Street. The Rileys were two sisters who were not married. Across from them, on the southern side of Pearce Street, was all woods; no houses had been built there yet.

When the snow came we would slide down Pearce Street, on the slight hill that went from Robeson Street to Read Street. We would use cardboard to slide on.

The family that lived in the Japanese house on Highland Avenue were named Ring. They had two children who were younger than me, John and Ruthie Ring, and I played with them. They had a big black dog.

When my mother came back from Aunt Mary's farm in Norton, she would go to Mrs. Gray and other neighbors and bring them corn, potatoes, or tomatoes.

## Christmas, Holidays, and Special Occasions

Our Christmas tree on Hanover Street was in the front bow window. Beatrice had her gifts on the bench with the gifts for Freddy and Evelyn. We younger kids had our gifts under the tree. We didn't have a lot of gifts. Dinner was at home, then friends of Beatrice would visit.

Harry Forrest would bring us dolls every Christmas. My father would give the nuns from Second Street rides from the church to the convent, and they would give us little gifts for Christmas such as a toy washing machine for me and football things for Buddy.

## Downtown

When we went downtown, we would go to Newbury's. They had all kinds of peanuts. Their cashews were fantastic. We would go to buy a coloring book. The three 5 & 10 cent stores downtown were Newbury's, Kresge's, and Woolworth's. At Easter, we would go to Morgan's Shoe Store and buy patent leather shoes that had two straps. Father also bought us a pair of sandals, which were our summer shoes.

My father knew the people at the Durfee Theatre and, when we went there, I was therefore a little girl for a very long time. Virginia and I had twenty-five cents between us, so we would get in at the kid's rate of ten cents each and spend five cents for a big Mr. Goodbar candy bar for the both of us.

During the intermission at Durfee, Lou Dalbec would play the organ. As he played, words would go up on the screen so we could sing songs such as "Daisy, Daisy, Give Me Your Answer Do," and other songs like that. We got our news at the movies. There were the Flash Gordon and Buck Rogers serials and one or two cartoons, such as Betty Boop, Mickey Mouse, or Popeye the Sailor Man.

## Religious Life

During church festivals, my father would bid on pigs. Then, when he won the bid, he would say, "Bid it over again." Our house hosted the crown. Beatrice carried the crown during the processions and Evelyn carried the bird. I played a lesser role. The Lima's have two stained glass windows in St. Michael's Church.

## Health and Illness

My mother lost three children in eighteen months: Beatrice, Freddy, and Betty. When Beatrice was dying, my mother and father came home from the hospital. Between the time they left the hospital and the time they arrived home, the hospital called home to say that Beatrice was dying. As they approached the house, I waved to them from the window, "Go back; go back."

Because of Beatrice and Freddy having tuberculosis, I had to go for a TB [tuberculosis] test. The test results didn't come for awhile; my mother called them and said, "Madeline has lost five pounds because she is worrying over the test results not coming."

When I came home to tell my mother and father about Buddy's death, she broke down. Virginia was the only one who knew why Buddy went into the hospital. I said, "He's gone," and my father said, "Where did he go?" I never forgot that.

When my mother was in the hospital, it was clear that she was not going to come out of it and could be in a coma for a long time. My father cried that he didn't want her to be a vegetable and that he couldn't take care of her if she was in that condition; what should he do? He didn't want to see her live like that. I told the doctors that he would sign the "do not resuscitate" papers. After he signed the papers, I saw the nurse tipping the bed and right after that there was a "Code Blue." Everyone came rushing into the room.

When my father died, they couldn't bury him because it was New Years Day.

I was there when Virginia died at home in bed. I took leave from WalMart so I could be with her. I stayed with her for about a month. Virginia died in March, and her husband, Job, had died the month before, in February. After the funeral, the ashes of both Virginia and Job were taken out to sea, accompanied by many of his friends in their boats. As they dropped the ashes into the ocean, they also dropped flowers and then raised their glasses in a toast to Virginia and Job.

**World War II**
My brother Freddy went to sign up to join the Marines, but he had a punctured eardrum and he was denied.

During the war, we had sugar stamps. Saccharine was a substitute. We saved tin foil from gum wrappers. We never lacked for meat. At Christmas, Swifts, Armour, and Cudahy gave baskets of cheese to the family. My father loved Limburger cheese, but did it ever stink!

When the war ended, we went downtown to celebrate, and it was wild. Everyone was there: teenagers, old people, everyone came downtown to celebrate. Guys were pinching girls. At one point, someone stuck a pin in me. At that time, I thought that if you got stuck with a pin, you had a baby. So, I went to a policeman and told him that I got stuck with a pin and that I could have a baby. I was sixteen at the time. He just smiled.

**Popular Expressions**
"Tell it to the Marines." Some of the superstitions were not going under a ladder, bad luck if a black cat walked in front of you, if one person dies, two are to follow.

# Leo and Theresa Dufault

*Leo was born on December 18, 1926*
*Theresa was born on February 13, 1929*

**Family Life**

*Leo:* I was one of ten children. We slept three to a bed. The tenements were cold. The floors were covered in oilcloth. The cold would curl the edges of the oilcloth and cause cracks in it. Only the living room had heat; there was none in the bedrooms. We had a few scattered rugs. We dressed up quickly because of the cold. Our first stove was coal, then kerosene, then gas. There was a fifty-gallon drum of kerosene in the basement and we brought it up in three-gallon cans to put in its cradle in the rear of the stove. The only light in the rooms was a pull-chain ceiling light; there were no wall outlets, maybe one in the living room for a radio.

Our laundry was sent out in bags and brought back wet. We could have had it dried and folded, but we had it only washed. In the winter, the wet laundry was hung all over the house. We had no hot water. We had to get washed in a tub with no change of water. Hot water was added between kids.

The seven boys in our family wore one another's clothes. All of our socks were in one drawer. If the socks got holes in them, they were mended by putting the sock over a light bulb.

On Sundays, no one worked. We dressed in our best suits with a tie. We had soup and cake for dinner, sometimes cold cuts. My sister Germaine, who was fourteen when my mother died, took over the house and cooked. She had a tutor who came in to teach her. She took care of my father until his death. He had lost one leg from hardening of the arteries.

The church owned quite a bit of property in that area, with its schools and convents. Brothers and nuns came down from Canada to teach or to take care of the orphans. My mother died when I was five years old and left ten children. Most of the children went to the larger extended family, but three went to the orphanage, including me.

When my mother died, me and two of my sisters had to go into St. Joseph's Orphanage. During the summer months, we would get to go home. In my fifth year at the orphanage, I refused to go back in the fall. I hid under a bed and held onto the springs. They couldn't get me out. When they did, I refused to walk and they had to call a cab. When the cab got to the orphanage, I wouldn't walk and they had to carry me up the stairs into the orphanage.

**School Life**

*Leo:* I attended kindergarten and grades one, two, and three at the orphanage. Then I went to Notre Dame School for fourth and fifth grades. I went to sixth to eighth grade at [Monsignor] Prevost [on Eastern Avenue] and then to continuation school at Durfee Tech until I was sixteen.

**Recreation and Entertainment**

*Theresa:* My sister bought a pass on the bus for one dollar that allowed you to use the bus without limit for a week. So we would borrow it and me, my sister, and a girl friend would ride the bus all day long. We would also go roller skating in our short skirts on weekends at Lincoln Park [North Dartmouth, Massachusetts]; we would take the bus on Pleasant Street and ride all the way to the park.

*Leo:* We would also listen to the radio for hours on one station. There were mystery series on the radio and on Friday nights we listened to boxing. Every week, Joe Lewis would take on all contenders anytime, unlike now, when the champions rarely box. At noon, there was the news. Soap operas were on during the afternoon and Kate Smith would have her program every day. Every day, she sang "God Bless America."

*Theresa:* Some of the mystery radio shows we listened to were "The Shadow Knows" and "Inner-Sanctum." We came home from school at 11:30 am and Kate Smith was on. Then the soap operas came on at noon. At the movies, we collected the dish sets that were given out. Then we collected the silverware set.

**Chores and Work**

*Leo:* My father sometimes had two full-time jobs at one time in two different mills. My father was a third hand in the mill, fixing machinery that had broken down. Out of seven boys, at least five worked in the Chase Mill on Rodman Street. They worked in different shifts, either the first, second, or third shift. Our door was never locked.

*Theresa:* My father worked in the mills and, during the Depression, was an insurance man. Both my father and mother worked in the Pepperell Mills. My father was a loom-fixer, and my mother was a spinner.

*Leo:* I worked in the mill, but it was shut down in 1949. I started as a sweeper in the spinning room. People always started as sweepers. There was lots of dust in the spinning room and I had to go back and forth two or three times a day. Doffers would change the bobbins when they became full of thread. They would pull off a full spool and replace it with an empty spool. This was the only job of the doffer. Then, he would go home when he had replaced the spools. There were sixty-four frames from one end of the building to the other and sixty-four on the other side. Each frame was forty feet long.

From there, I went to build the Westport Drive-In [Westport, Massachusetts]. I put up the telegraph poles and the anchors for the screen. Once the pole was in, the anchor would swell up and prevent it from moving. Then I went to Notre Dame Cemetery digging graves by hand with a shovel. In the winter, the deceased went into a special building. From there, I went to Notre Dame School, painting the interior and doing various jobs, such as putting up fire escapes. My barber referred me to a person that he knew at Art Craft on Alden Street. They made electrical fixtures from scratch.

*Theresa:* I went to Notre Dame School and then to Diman [Diman Regional Vocational Technical High School ]until I was sixteen, then I went to work sewing. My first job was at Elbe File on Alden Street, where I stayed for four years. Then I worked at Har-Lee on Pleasant Street. A floor lady said to go to Stella-Ann on Alden Street, where I stayed for twenty-seven years.

**Neighborhood Experiences**

*Leo:* No one had cars. We walked to work, school, and church, rain or shine. If the weather was bad, we took the bus.

On South Pond, they would cut ice in sheets that were eight inches thick by four feet by four

Notre Dame de Lourdes Church, destroyed by fire in May 1982

feet and place them in the icehouses. They were insulated with hay and were stacked from floor to ceiling. The ice would be loaded onto freight train cars and taken elsewhere. Everyone had iceboxes. A drip pan collected the drip water, and sometimes we would forget and the water kept overflowing, so we ran a drip pipe down to the cellar.

Our wet garbage would be picked up by special haulers. We had special pails with heavy covers and foot pedals to prevent animals from getting into them.

There was a Howard Johnson's at the Narrows and a Napert's Boat House. Napert's rented boats to go fishing and sold fishing poles and bait. If you rented a boat, you had to leave your shoes behind or some other kind of license or ID. Theresa's father owned a cottage on the South Watuppa Pond and they didn't own a car. They had to bring everything that they needed on a boat from the Narrows.

In the winter, there could be four feet of snow. Only then, we didn't go to school if there was too much snow. There were no plows and cars had chains. However, even with chains, cars got stuck. There were deep ruts in the street that would last until April or May.

Most of the dead-end streets off of County Street were blocked off to traffic to allow sledding to occur. My brother once made a large twelve-person wooden toboggan that had pedals for each person to push. He took it down California Street and it plowed into the woods at the end of the street. No one was experienced in working it. It was so heavy, it was left in the woods. Luckily, no one was hurt.

**Christmas, Holidays, and Special Occasions**

*Theresa:* Christmas was plain for us. We got one gift, usually from our godparents. We had one stocking (a regular stocking) and got fruit in it. We had no tree. It was a simple day. There was a good dinner for all our family. My mom made French meat pie, a French casserole, and homemade pastry. My mom was a good cook; we never had much, but we ate well.

**The Great Depression**

*Leo:* During the Depression we had no cash. If you were on welfare, you had to go get dry goods from their office and haul it back in wagons. Our local store on Horton Street would take credit and we could pay the bill on payday. Often, you paid only what you could afford. Everything was on credit.

Shoes were repaired until they couldn't be repaired any more. My father, like most homes, had his own shoe repair kit. He would put steel "clickers" on the heels to make them last longer. My father would bring pieces of leather belts from the mill to repair our shoes. The belting system in the mills ran the looms from the main power shaft. When my father had to work on a loom, he would move the belt to the idle position, then back again to start the frame.

**World War II**

*Leo:* Out of seven boys in the family, six were drafted. I didn't go in until 1944-1945 and served in the Occupation Forces in the Philippines.

During the war, we recycled everything. A ragman would come by with his horse and buggy and would take any rags, paper, and metal.

# Abraham Ehrenhaus

*Born in 1924*

**Family Background**

My father was born in Austria and my mother was born in Russia. They were both brought up in New York City. My father and mother moved to Fall River in 1923. I grew up in Leemingville [a cluster of one-family homes east of upper Robeson Street, Fall River].

**Family Life**

My first memory was of the great fire of 1928, when I was about four years old. My father had a business downtown—American Wallpaper, located on the corner of Pleasant and Third Streets. A few years after that, I remember the long lines of people going around the block waiting to get food (vegetables and things like that) at the City Hall Annex (next to where the ILGWU [International Ladies Garment Workers Union] was located) during the Depression. The Welfare Board was in the Annex.

We had no television, but we were busy all of the time reading, working in the garden, and things like that. When I was a child, everyone in the area was into music. My sister was a concertmaster at Durfee [B.M.C. Durfee High School]. She was a violinist. I took piano and flute.

My father was highly disciplined and well-ordered. In the summertime, it was common for my family to host my grandmother and two cousins to spend the summer months in the "country," as they called Fall River, at our home. To assure that we were sufficiently occupied, my father made a chart with our names on one edge and the hours of the day on the other edge. He then filled in each slot with what we were to do with each hour, including practicing the piano or flute, cultivating the garden, reading, or other occupations. My father bought the Harvard Classics and we all had a time slot for reading. We had to account for our time. At dinner, we had to say what we had learned that day. We were busy kids; we were brought up in a culture that valued learning and the mastering of skills.

My mother worked in my father's store but also did a lot of home-cooking. She did a lot of needle-work, knitting, and crocheting.

I remember that my father had a few gallon jugs that he put alcohol in with some berries and sugar to make a liquor. When company came, he would give out shots of it.

In retail you are open six days a week. The store closed early on Saturday, and at 5:00 pm we boarded a Fall River Line steamboat. On Sunday morning, we got off at Pier 14 in New York City. We got on the subway and went to visit our family in New York and New Jersey and have dinner with them. We enjoyed discussing ideas with them after dinner. Then we got back on the boat on Sunday evening and headed back to Fall River and arrived back here on Monday morning to start work and school.

I remember traveling on the *Commonwealth*; it was very beautiful and had wonderful food.

The boats included a game with six horses with dice, and people bet on them. I remember getting seasick after leaving Newport.

**School Life**

I attended the Highland School, from kindergarten to sixth grade. At that time there was one custodian who took care of the whole school. There was one teacher per class, and we had large classes: up to thirty-five kids in a class. There was Little Miss Connors and Big Miss Connors. Little Miss Connors taught second grade and was short in stature; Big Miss Connors taught fifth grade and was tall. That was how we referred to them. There was no discipline problem in any class. Sons and daughters of city leaders were in our class, including Mrs. Brigham's daughter. We had maypole exercises and parents who were not working would come with their kids.

My education in the Jewish tradition consisted of going to Hebrew School a few times a week until my senior year in high school. I continued in the school until I learned Hebrew. Most kids left the school after their Bar Mitzvahs at age thirteen. I stayed on to learn more. I was proficient in translating Biblical Hebrew and won a couple of prizes for this.

I went to Brown University in 1941.

After the war, I went back to Brown where I continued my education in economics. The Brown tuition then was two hundred and fifty dollars for a half-year semester, twenty-three dollars for fees, and one hundred dollars for room. The room fee included a spacious room with three windows looking out on the Brown campus and daily maid service, where a person came in to make our beds.

When I completed my degree, I considered going into academia, but I had been away from home for so long, I just wanted to go home and stay put. By the age of twenty-one, I had already completed my college education and three years of service. That was a lot to do in that number of years. I enjoyed home, and entered into the family business.

**Recreation and Entertainment**

I learned to swim in the Taunton River at Bliffins Beach. The Gladding family taught me to swim. We would bicycle a lot, up and down the hill. We would ride in the Reservation along Blossom Road. We roller skated.

Parents in the neighborhood helped to form the Leemingville Boys Club. The Club would get together at homes of different families on an afternoon or evening each week. Parents would provide refreshments and some kind of treat. We would perform plays that were held in garages. The proceeds of one show we gave to the Red Cross. We were recognized in the newspaper for this. Donald Cole helped kids collect stamps from envelopes. Miss Dolan at Morton formed a stamp club after school; that's something you wouldn't see today.

It was rare to eat out in those days. There were no fast food places. Blake's Market was located in the building where New Boston Bakery is now.

My father had a car, and on Sundays we would go to the beach or fish at South Watuppa Pond. We would go to Napert's or Robillard's on South Watuppa to rent a boat. You had to leave your shoes as a deposit to assure that they got their boats back. We could get a shoebox full of bait shrimp for ten cents. It was clean, clear water with lots of fish. We enjoyed the outdoors more then than today. We enjoyed the fresh air and walking.

The Gage Hill Stables in the northern part of the city were operated by Dinny [Dennis]

O'Brien. He had horses there that belonged to wealthy people in the area, like the Haffenreffer family, who owned Enterprise Brewery. Dinny allowed me to ride the horses along the paths in the Reservation, since someone had to take the horses out and ride them.

**Courtship and Marriage**

While at Brown, I met my wife, Marilyn. We were married in 1949, when she completed her education at Pembroke. It was the custom for people of the Jewish faith that someone would know girls in the area who you could contact. Names were given by friends of the family and by others.

Marilyn and I met at a dance group at school. We have three daughters, eight grandchildren, and three great-grandchildren.

**Work Life**

As a child, I worked in my father's store part-time. There were very few pre-packaged goods in the 1930s. Many goods came in barrels. Barrels of wallpaper paste powder had to be measured out and bagged. The same for lime, used for whitewashing, and calsomine, which was used for ceilings and other dry items. Linseed oil, turpentine, denatured alcohol all came in drums. The drums had to be tapped and the contents put in containers and corked. It took twelve hours every day to package these items. We had to do a lot to manage the barrels.

**Neighborhood Experiences**

Leemingville can be defined as bounded by Harvard Street on the south, Valentine Street on the north, Robeson Street on the west, and the woods (that existed then) on the east.

We had a father and son softball team in this neighborhood. Leemingville also had its own fireworks on the 4th of July. People of different ethnic backgrounds got along here. I don't remember any difficult times with the neighbors.

**Downtown**

I am very familiar with the lower Pleasant Street area. It was the secondary shopping street in Fall River. I have good memories of the Santos Hardware and the Gardiner's Store, managed by Mr. Lanbrodiere. He always wore a straw hat—a flat straw hat with a band around it—and a cloak. They sold farm supplies, seed, and pet supplies, things like that.

There was quite a bit of discrimination then against Jewish people; employers wouldn't hire them, so they started their own businesses instead. There were many businesses in the area owned by Jewish people, including Alpert's Cigar Store, Capitol Furniture, The Hub Clothing Company, S. Gourse and Sons, Goralkik Hats, and Minkin Auto Supplies.

Our building at the corner of Pleasant and Third Streets [the Waterman Building], which came down when the highway was built, had a variety of stores in it. It had a shoe store, Boston Jewelry and Loan, John F. Stafford Insurance Company, the Loom Fixers Union, R.E. Smith and Co., Novelty Braiding (rugs), Bowen's Coal Co., Staples Coal Co., and Smith Printing (which included bookbinding). The Mayflower Restaurant was downtown and the Ideal Restaurant was behind the Post Office.

## Health and Illness

The Jewish cure for ailments is chicken soup. One of the superstitions in the area is that, even though people will have birds in the house, they don't want images of birds on the wall. It is said to bring bad luck and death. We once ordered many rolls of a wallpaper pattern with birds on them and ended up having to eat them.

## World War II

On October 12, 1942, while at Brown, I enlisted in the United States Army. I took a competitive exam and qualified for the Army Specialized Training Program. Out of millions of recruits, only thirty thousand were selected. The purpose of the training program was to conduct specialized studies that the United States wanted done for the war effort. I was sent to Rutgers University to study engineering. I studied chemistry, physics, math, calculus, and other disciplines. I completed the coursework at Rutgers in April of 1944. After that, they closed the program and sent us as replacements for the infantry. From there, we went into the 104th Division of the 413th Infantry and landed at Cherbourg, France, sixty days after the Normandy Invasion. There was a book written about our unit called *Scholars in Foxholes* [*Scholars in Foxholes: The Story of the Army Specialized Training Program in World War II*, by Louis Keefer, 1988]. We remained with the unit for nine months and then were transferred to the 355th Engineering Division.

In April of 1945, our unit accomplished the remarkable feat of constructing a railroad bridge across the Rhine River in only ten days and eight hours. The area was bombed first, then gliders came in. The total length of the bridge was 2,216 feet. Over twelve hundred men were involved in building the bridge. I was with the communications unit and operated a telephone switchboard and delivered instructions on what to do to the men on the construction site. We lost twenty-four men while building the bridge. I sometimes delivered messages while crawling on beams high above the river.

In my three years in the service, I made fifty-four dollars a month at my best pay. With my fifty-four dollars, I was able to buy insurance for six dollars and twenty-five cents a month and saved six dollars and twenty-five cents. In three months, that amounted to eighteen dollars and seventy-five cents. Over three years, I bought twelve, twenty-five dollar Treasury Bonds and after ten years yielded the huge sum of three hundred dollars.

## Popular Expressions

"Fair to middling." A saying used in response to "How are you feeling?" or "How are things going?" This phrase originated in the cotton textile industry. The cotton brokers would take a piece of cotton and stretch the fibers out. If the fibers stretched out a distance, the cotton was of high quality; if the fibers were short, not so. Fair to middling would represent a middle degree of quality.

"That's a corker." That's really funny or that's really unique.

Some of the nicknames of people that we knew or saw downtown were: "Rubber Boots" (he always had rubber boots on year-round); "Mahatma Gandhi" (a guy with Gandhi-like glasses who rode a bike); "Lightning" (a paperhanger who was very fast); and "Sixteen" (a nervous barber in the Siska barber shop, which was above Minkin's on the corner of Pleasant and Fourth Streets).

# Franklin E. Fairhurst

*Born on August 3, 1922*
*Died July 9, 2010*

**Family Background**

I was born in my grandparents (mother's family) house on Walnut Street in Assonet, Massachusetts.

My parents were William A. and Margaret Louise (Wing) Fairhurst. They were divorced and my mother later remarried when I was in high school.

My mother's parents were Charles H. Wing Sr. and Mary (Farohawk) Wing. My father's parents were James and Mary Fairhurst, who lived on Baldwin Street, just off North Main Street, in Fall River.

My father was a fixer at the Foster Spinning Mill. The fixer changed the gears on the spinning frames. He later became a dock builder when the mills closed. My mother worked at the Sagamore cloth room.

My grandfathers never swore (I never swore until I came to Fall River) and they never drank liquor. Grandfather Wing once got sick as a dog and never did it again. Grandfather Fairhurst smoked a pipe and occasionally a cigar and was short. Grandfather Wing was six feet tall.

My uncle Sam Fairhurst was the supervisor at the Foster Mill and was affectionately known by the workers there as "Mr. Sam." They loved him because he saw to it that during the Depression everyone in the mill stayed working, even if only half a day or some other hours. The old guys who swept the floors would be allowed to fill in for absent persons in other higher positions. If someone was out sick, he would come on the floor and yell out, "I need someone to work in this or that position," and a sweeper would take over the job. They loved him. When he left, the sweepers were let go and eventually the younger workers brought in a union.

I remember when my uncle James Fairhurst Jr. would row back across the Taunton River after seeing his girlfriend in Somerset.

My uncle George Wing was the station agent at the Assonet station, across from where the Freetown Historical Society is now. Bullock's cranberry house was where the Historical Society building is now. Women would stand at moving belts and pick leaves and twigs out of the cranberries.

Rev. Gifford, the first pastor of the Assonet South Church (where St. Bernard's is now), was a relative of mine. My great-grandfather was a Hathaway.

I met my wife Jean M. (Chrisler) Fairhurst at Cecil Field in Jacksonville, Florida, when I was in dive bomber school and Jean was stationed there as in the WAVES ["Women Accepted for Volunteer Emergency Service;" official name, U.S. Naval Reserve (Women's Reserve)]. We were married in 1944. Jean is from Wausaw, New York.

**Family Life**

I left Assonet in 1930, when I was eight years old. We moved to 2480 North Main Street, then to 3062-64 North Main Street on the second floor, which is diagonally across and north of 3044 North Main Street. In 1939, 3044 was built when my parents divorced and my mother, stepfather, and I moved in. Mr. Bliffin owned the house and two others south of 3044.

I was lucky growing up, with a lot of good people around me. Mr. Bliffin treated me like a son and Grandfather Fairhurst always spoke kindly to me. He would tell me, "Don't smoke like your father; it will kill you."

For vacation, we would go down the river in the catboat to Potters Cove for up to three days. It took one day to get there and one day to get back. We slept on the boat. I would say, "I don't care if I never go down the river again." I would have preferred to be with my friends; they were swimming and I was going clamming.

**Neighborhood Experiences**

On Steep Brook, below North Main Street, there was a large tank that collected water that was brought to feed the steam boilers of the three Border City and three Sagamore Mills. When the mills were built in the 1870s, the city had not yet brought water service down to the Border City area.

North of Bliffins Beach, there were "ship lots," where ships were once built.

Joe Borges, who owned the gas station in Assonet just off the Four Corners, ran a bus that went from Wilson Road to Assonet Four Corners.

At the northeast corner of North Main Street and Wilson Road was Codega's Variety Store. Blake's Market was a grocery store on the northwest corner of Wilson Road and North Main Street. Ma Lindsey's was a variety store across from the Wiley School on North Main Street. Mrs. O'Neil and later Charlie Wallace had a grocery store attached to his home diagonally across from 3044 North Main Street. Border City had more stores, usually on the first floor of tenement buildings.

The North Main trolley would come to Wilson Road and turn around there. The driver would park on a side track, take his crank from one end of the trolley, and bring it to the other end to go in the other direction. He would also move the rod to the wire so that it switched to the other end of the trolley. The driver always kept an eye out for Kenny Layland, who would come down Wilson Road, hide himself behind a house and, just as the driver was about to take off, would disconnect the rod from the wire. Ironically, Kenny later worked for the trolley company.

The trolleys ran every ten minutes. All of the trolleys converged downtown in front of City Hall. I remember coming out of the Durfee Theatre one Saturday night, and there was a tremendous crowd trying to get on the trolleys. It took us twenty minutes to get from the Durfee to the Granite Block, a half-block away.

**School Life**

My father attended Steep Brook School, which was opposite Ashley Street on the west side of North Main Street. It was a two-story building and had grades one to four. In Assonet, I attended the Village School (still next to Town Hall) and the Bleacher School (on South Main Street opposite the Bleacher Pond, where the bleachery once was). My teacher was Mrs. Cudworth. Mr. Cudworth was the Town Clerk. Mrs. Cudworth also was my mother's teacher. The Cudworth's daughter married a Wing, my second cousin. In those days, there were tables, not desks, in the room with the first and second grades.

Borges ran a bus called "The Stagecoach," because it had a front and rear door, that would pick up the colored kids whose families worked the cranberry bogs, to bring them to the Assonet schools.

When I came to Fall River, I attended the Wiley School. At Wiley, there was a kid named Ray Dewsnap, who got up every day at 4:30 am to milk by hand the cows at the Wordell Farm. In the morning, he would put his head on his desk and fall asleep and the teacher would let him sleep. After recess, though, the teacher made him stay awake.

I attended [B.M.C.] Durfee High School, where I was a member of the Durfee Flying Squadron and the Electrical Club. I then entered the Bradford Durfee Textile School, where I graduated in 1942, majoring in Engineering. I later received a BS in Business Management in 1970.

**Work Life**

In the summer, when I was ten or eleven, I would swim a lot at Bliffins Beach. At twelve, I started working in the lower key house at Bliffins Beach. My job was to hand out keys to swimmers who used the 311 bathhouses, which were small cubicles about four feet by four feet. At fourteen or fifteen, I started working in the top building, which paid more money. I worked there until I graduated from college in 1942. I also worked for Mr. Bliffin cutting lawns (by hand mower) and fixing his houses. He was a great guy and treated me like a son. He paid me twenty-five cents an hour for this.

I worked at the Lincoln Press in high school and, after the war, went back there. I went to Baker Rubber, a small outfit in the Globe Mills. I then took a position at the Shell Terminal here on North Main Street, where I stayed for thirty-two years until I retired.

The Sagamore and Border City Mills supported a hospital on Cove Street, on the right, or north, side of the street before the abutment.

**Recreation and Entertainment**

We played baseball on the Border City lot (where the old water tank was located on Steep Brook) and on a vacant lot below and opposite Herman Street, behind a billboard (which served as one of the bases). We also played ball at St. Vincent's Home, on the north or boys side. On Saturdays, we would play ball until 4:00 pm, when the Catholic kids would head to St. Joseph's to church for confession, the Portuguese kids going in the direction of St. Michael's Church, and the French kids headed towards St. Mathieu's.

We also played football in a field at the top of Sidney Street, where the highway is now. These were pickup teams from the neighborhood. I would fold the ball in my sweater and hold on to the belt of a guy in front of me and run down the field. This upset my mother because the sweater she knitted got out of shape by doing this.

We also skated at Aaron's Pond (which is now a depression in the Industrial Park), at Stump Pond (which was destroyed when Route 24 was built through it), and at Mill Pond, south of Drift Street below Highland Avenue. Mill Pond was the site of a gristmill way back. Ice was cut on the Mill Pond. Grandma Shaw, Fred Shaw's mother, would bake cookies and bring them out to us skaters. She would sit on her porch in a fur coat and watch us skate. She was a grand old lady.

We played peggy ball, where a ball was placed on a board (about four by eight inches) with a depression in it on one side to hold the ball. The board was placed on a fulcrum and a kid would jump on the end of the board opposite to the ball. The ball would jump in the air and when it landed, the player would count the steps from the takeoff to where the ball landed. This was repeated and the steps added to the score.

The game of peggy stick involved taking a broom handle and using it as a bat to hit the ball as it was projected from the board or "plate."

We had no bats and created our own balls. Dad would bring home spools of thread that we wound into balls, and then taped with tape that we bought by cashing in bottles for two cents each. That's how we got our baseballs.

The game of weights involved one team of kids bending over behind one another and holding on to one another (with the first kid against a tree or wall) and kids from the other team would run and jump on the first team. Other kids would pile on to the first team until they crumbled, or until the first team shook off someone from the second team. We could get pretty bruised playing this game.

Kick the can involved making a circle and putting a can in the middle. Two guys would run for it and try to kick it out of the circle. The team of the first guy that got the can out of the circle would run and the other team would have to come find them.

We also played basketball at St. Vincent's gym (only socks and sneakers allowed) and watched church league teams play there.

We also played handball, and Josie Rogers and I were partners. He was left and I played right. Boy, could he whack a ball!

We would go to the Royal Theater next to the railroad tracks on Brightman Street for ten cents a show. If we had an extra five cents, we would go down to Brightman to Moy Lee's and get a chow mein sandwich. We would pay for the movie by collecting soda bottles and redeeming them for two cents each at Ma Lindsey's Variety Store. Ma Lindsey was English and spoke with an English brogue. The store had penny candy, where we could get bubble gum for a penny.

Every summer, the North Christian Church in Steep Brook would have their annual outing to Lincoln Park, and we spent all day there. It was great riding the open trolley to the park along the median on Route 6.

**The Depression**

My grandfather had over three acres of land on Walnut Street in Assonet and grew all kinds of vegetables there, including potatoes, turnips, cabbage, pole beans, rhubarb, and asparagus, among other things. He also had an apple orchard. So we never lacked for food.

My grandfather had a boat in Fall River and we would go to the area around Prudence Island to get quahogs and clams. We ate some and sold the others for gas to go down river again. We ate well.

**The Hurricane of 1938**

We watched the water rise to over the road that goes under the railroad tracks. My grandfather put out another anchor on a longer line to provide enough room and allow the boat to ride out the storm, and we didn't lose it. The oil tanker that broke loose from the Shell Oil terminal almost came ashore here. Instead, the ship landed in Charlie Marvel's yard in Somerset [Massachusetts].

Charlie Marvel would row out to the buoy in the river and my grandfather would row out from the Fall River side and they sit there and chew the fat.

## St. Vincent's Orphanage

Father Donovan was the head of the orphanage and the whole neighborhood loved him. St. Vincent's had a beautiful chapel. The neighbors would go to St. Vincent's for Mass, instead of going to St. Joseph's, St. Michael's, or St. Mathieu's churches, which required them to take a trolley to these churches. The chapel at St. Vincent's would be overflowing because it was more convenient. The priests at the three parishes complained, but it didn't do any good.

St. Vincent's was strict but good to the kids. Sister Kevin was the "ruling queen" there. She would call me "Willie" and I would say that was not my name, that my father was called Willie, but she would just say, "OK, come on, Willie." Sometimes, the nuns would play field games with us and tie their habits to their waists and join in, with their rosaries swaying as they played. As we left the grounds, Sister Kevin checked us all out to see that she didn't lose any orphanage kids.

St. Vincent's had their farm on Highland Avenue that the kids worked at and that was run by a man with two sons. The farm provided the orphanage with milk and vegetables.

Father Donovan would invite the ladies of the neighborhood to have games of whist or bridge on the lawn in front of the orphanage. The grounds were kept in immaculate condition. Father Donovan, who attended school with Bishop Cassidy, eventually left the orphanage and was replaced by Father Harrington, who had more of a businessman's personality. When Father Donovan left, the whole neighborhood turned out to see him off. The kids were crying and everyone was crying around his car as he left.

## World War II

I enlisted in the Naval Air Force on October 9, 1942. We went to flight training school at Middlebury College in Vermont for thirteen weeks, then to other sites to continue the training. On March 17, 1944, I got my wings.

I then went to Cecil Field in Jacksonville, Florida, for dive-bomber training. From there, I went to the West Coast for more training. In San Diego, during a torpedo drop from my plane, the torpedo "porpoised," that is, it bobbed up and down on the surface of the water. It proceeded

Oil tanker run aground in Somerset, Massachusetts, during the hurricane of 1938

past the fantail of a destroyer and almost hit it. The captain of the destroyer told my commanding officer, "Get that son of a bitch out of my sight." I never dropped a torpedo from then on.

When I left for overseas, I had 343 hours of flight training. We went on to the Pacific and took off from Pearl Harbor on a two-day trip to the aircraft carrier. We were to fly from aircraft carriers to spot submarines. We had no Thanksgiving that year, since we crossed the International Date Line and lost a day. We ate sandwiches during the two-day trip. Our destination was the *USS Hoggatt Bay* aircraft carrier. My Thanksgiving meal when I arrived was a quinine pill and a bowl of chili beans.

We flew TBF planes, later upgraded to TBM's. In addition to the pilot, there were two crew members: a gunner and a radio operator. We had to stay at least 800 feet above sea level to avoid enemy fire from ships. Six planes flew in formation, with two in front, two on the sides, and two in the rear. We flew the perimeter of where the ships were concentrated to intercept any subs. We were motivated: if a ship was sunk, we would have nowhere to go when we got back. We also covered for Marines landing on the islands by bombing and strafing the enemy. We took out the targets that were given to us.

The Navy fliers wore brown shoes and the ship personnel wore black shoes. Jean's brother was a destroyer man and commanded three different destroyers.

Jake was my radio gunner and he saved my life. He was from Texas and was very short. He was about seventeen and probably lied about his age when he enlisted. I would ask him, "Shorty, when are you going to call me Frank," and he would reply, "Well, I'll think about that, Mr. Fairhurst."

We got shot up during the Luzon campaign in the Philippines. Our hydraulic line was cut and we couldn't get our wheels down and therefore couldn't land on the ship. I brought the plane down in the sea about eighty miles from Manila. We hit two waves and bounced off of them and plowed into the third. We got the raft out and Jake got out. However, I got my Mae West (life jacket) tangled up. Jake held me up until I got it inflated. Even though I was a damn good swimmer, if he had not been there to hold me up, I would have drowned.

Our squadron, VC-88, and others continued our sub patrols, bombing and strafing and spotting enemy ship fire at Iwo Jima. We landed at Iwo Jima and took Marines back to the ship. From the Admiralty Islands, we went to New Guinea and to Okinawa and left there on May 1, 1945. We were due to land on the Japanese mainland, but thank God and Truman for the atom bomb.

Some of us were not so lucky. When Lt. Colonel Eugene Webb returned from a bombing strike over Luzon, south of Manila, a bomb was loose in the bomb bay located under the plane. The pin of the bomb was somehow activated, and when he landed, the bomb went off blowing a hole in the deck, destroying the plane, and killing Lt. Col. Webb and his crew. One of the crew members ran from the plane, but when he reached the grasp of the ship's crew at the edge of the platform, he collapsed and died.

During the day, the hand on deck would direct us on landing by the use of a paddle in each hand. At night, however, there were only two slits of light on the deck to guide us and a guy dressed in a fluorescent jumpsuit.

I now have arthritis in my vertebrae from the violent snapping motion every time the plane landed on the aircraft carrier and was caught and stopped.

It seems so long ago. Looking back now, it seems strange that I did all this when I was only twenty-three and twenty-four. I don't know how I did it.

# James Finglas

*Born on March 4, 1928*

**Family Background**

I was born at 105 Emmett Street by a doctor (I believe). My parents were John William (born in Ireland), and Lena May (Schlemmer) Finglas (born in Fall River).

My aunts and uncles were a big part of my life. The Finglas family included, in order of birth: Lilly (lived in Rhode Island), John (my father), Molly, Kathleen, Evelyn, Patrick, and Joseph (he was born in the United States; all others born in Ireland). Joe Finglas was a harbor pilot in Fall River, and he gave his brothers and sisters the money to get here.

My brothers and sisters were Mary, Patricia (born on St. Patrick's Day), and Margaret.

My wife is Norma (Gifford) Finglas [Norma's interview follows this one in the book] and our children are named Michael William and James Patrick.

The only two houses I have lived in are both on Emmet Street, 105 and 156.

**Family Life**

The Finglas family comes from St. Peter's Parish in Dublin, named Finglas. It is the toughest part of Dublin. They say in Dublin, "You don't want to go there at night." My father was born in Dronghda, north of Dublin. The Finglas family has ranged from horsemen to bishops.

My father was about six when he came over from Ireland. It took about two weeks to make the trip by boat and all of Finglas family got sick coming over and had fevers. The family that owns McGovern's Restaurant came over on the same boat with them. Members of the Finglas and McGowan families met on the ship and two got married later. Members of both families have been friends since.

I was born at the top of the street at 105 Emmett Street. There were only three houses on Emmett at that time. That house was built by my grandfather. The family lost the house to the bank during the Depression. Fred Dekker, a real estate agent, assured them that they could buy it back. My father's salary was only twelve dollars a week and my mom wasn't working. However, she was a proficient crocheter. For three dollars and fifty cents she would crochet pieces for couch backs and arms and put them in-between wax paper. I don't ever remember her not crocheting.

My father bought the house back. He had to pay three dollars and fifty cents a week to pay on the house. The Fall River Municipal Credit Union financed the house. At that time, they had an office at 10 Purchase Street. It was a swell offer. Every week, my father would go down to Purchase Street to make the payment on 105 Emmett Street. A Mr. Murphy put the money in a cardboard box and logged in the payment in a registry. Mr. Murphy was a custodian at the Letourneau School.

A Glenwood Coal Stove was our central heating. In the winter, we closed off the parlor so we wouldn't waste heat. My three sisters got the second bedroom and I got to sleep in the parlor by putting two chairs together. We had to bank the coal stove at night; if we didn't, there was a danger of freeze-ups occurring. Coal was nine dollars and fifty cents a ton. Our coal bin took up one-quarter of the cellar. The coal was dumped in from a cellar window. While I was in the Navy, they converted to an oil heater. It was a giant step. They put a big grate in the first level floor where the Glenwood was; the burner was suspended in the first floor below in the cellar.

We put the ashes from the coal where the plants were. When it rained, un-burnt coal was revealed and we picked it out and burned it.

Clothes lines had two lines, one a pulley and one a stationary line. When the rope came off of the pulley, I shimmied up the pole to put it back on.

Then there was the famous icebox. We put a card in the window that said "10," "15," "25," and "30" on it. Whatever side was up, that's what you got. The iceman would slice off a piece for the kids. It was my job to empty the icebox drip pan. I would watch the ice water come to the top of the rim of the pan and tempted fate until it spilled. Do you know what a "window box" is? It was kept outside the window in the wintertime to keep food cold. We didn't need ice in the wintertime.

We had no washing machine, only a scrub board. Our kitchen sink had one faucet and our indoor bathroom had a pull chain on the toilet. That's where the saying "pull the chain" comes from. Everyone had a cesspool; there was no city sewage system serving the area.

Everyone had a garden then. There were lots of grape vines. Everyone was still neighborly. I knew a bit about electricity and plumbing, so I've helped my neighbors when they needed my help.

We had no telephones. The only way to communicate in a family was to write a note and have the kids deliver them. My aunt lived at 2 Porter Street near Kerr Thread; the house is now gone because of the highway. I would go over the old Quequechan River bridge up to the end of Quequechan Street to Eastern Avenue and to McGowan Street. We were told not to walk the railroad tracks. However, this time I went as far as the railroad tracks and to Kerr Thread and up to my aunt's house. She put in the note that I walked the railroad tracks and gave it to me to give to my father. When I got back, my father asked, "Did you walk the railroad tracks?" "Yes," I said, "one time," and I never did it again.

I'll tell you why I don't smoke. My father rolled his own cigarettes in Zig-Zag cigarette paper. He smoked Navy tobacco that came in blue packages. At that time, this area was all woods. I went across the street and took corn silk, wrapped it in my father's Zig-Zag paper, and smoked it. After that, I got sick. I had a 103 to 104 fever. My parents called the doctor and he came in. He took his hand and put it on my chest and slapped it on my chest. I thought it was going to bring up smoke rings because I thought that the smoking had made me sick. But it turned out to be the measles, not the smoke.

All of my sisters and I went to the Letourneau School. Where the Harbor Mall is now was a big swamp. I would go to the swamp to pick jack-in-the-pulpits and lady's slippers to bring to class so we could draw them.

We would go to the Tucker Street dump and scour the dump for hours for bottles. We could get two cents for small bottles and five cents for large bottles. When the wind was right, the dump burned virtually every day. It was a full-time job for the Maplewood fire station to go to the dump.

My father shoveled one and one-half tons of coal a night. He wasn't a big man, but he had arms of steel. My mom was quiet. She played the piano by ear and could play any song by ear. When the family got together, we would sing Irish songs. We had fun together.

This was called Rush's Hill. They would put up barricades at the bottom of Chicago Street so we could slide down the hill. The other side of the water tank was an empty lot. We played ball there.

My uncle Pat drove the bus for the Eastern Mass bus line. He started when street cars were in the city, when I was kid. Pat lost a cottage in Assonet on the Taunton River during the hurricane of 1938. They didn't have any kids yet.

On two occasions, we took the bus to Dighton, walked across the Berkley Bridge, and walked five miles to the cottage. We then walked all the way back to get the bus. It was an all-day walk. It was interesting stuff for a kid; there were cows and things like that. Later, I wired the whole cottage for him. The service gave me a good background in electricity and for being an electrician.

My father worked nights and slept during the day when I was growing up. My aunts and uncles filled a big void. They lived on Manchester Street, near Warren Street. It was the second three-decker in from the corner of Warren Street. They lived on the second floor.

**School Life**

In pre-primary at the Letourneau School, I had a Miss Simmons in kindergarten. One day, a kid named Gaudette who sat next to me took a pin and jabbed my arm. I returned the favor and got punished for it. "Sit under my desk," the teacher said. Within five minutes, I found a paper bag and ate the sandwich that was in it. It was her lunch. She never said a word. She lived to be 102 years old.

A second grade teacher commanded great respect from every kid. She was Miss Skeldeson. Her house was on Stafford Road within Notre Dame Cemetery. The kids thought that her name was Miss Skeleton. I must say that I never had a bad teacher.

**Recreation and Entertainment**

We played peggy ball. You took a flat board and, on one end, made a point. On the other end, you made an indentation to hold the ball. You put the flat stick on a round stick on the ground [acting like a fulcrum], put the ball in the indentation, and whack the pointed end of the board. When the board was whacked with a stick, the ball would take off; you had three swings of a stick. The person who whacked the board was the person who got to swing at the ball as it came down. Whoever hit the ball farthest was the winner. They gave me five cents to shag the balls all day.

Every 4th of July, we had a big bonfire in the neighborhood. Two policemen in the area were in charge of it, a Mr. Howland and a Mr. Dean. They would start it. All of the neighborhood residents would bring bundles of stuff to the bonfire site the day before. They always put a chair on top; I don't know why. Then, they lit the bonfire. Sometimes, the fire would burn for days.

When I was a kid, I fished in the Bleachery Pond. We had to ask Mr. Whitehead. He lived in a house by the pond that was owned by the Bleachery. He worked for the Bleachery and, even after the Bleachery closed, we still had to ask him. He would usually say yes. The cove was fed by a great fresh water stream; it was great fishing. When LeBerge took over the property, he filled in part of it and wiped out half of the cove.

There were three floors in the Bleachery Mill. There was a ramp where they slid the bales of cotton down. It was a board with two metal runners on it. We would go in with a piece of cardboard and slide down the ramp. But we had to ask Mr. Whitehead first. He would let us slide down the ramp.

**Work Life**

My dad walked to and from the mill and fired the boiler all night. He worked at the Flint, Stafford, Parker, and Howard Arthur Mills.

I carried my father's dinner pail to him on my bike when I was in high school. Coffee was on the bottom, meat and potatoes on the top. He would put the pail on the water pump to keep it hot. The pump was very hot. One day, I got to the corner of Quequechan Street and Alden Streets and I fell off my bike. I didn't lose the coffee but the food fell out. I put the food back in the pail and, when I got to the mill, I put the pail on the water pump and ran out.

That evening, my father says to my mother, "What the hell did he do to my lunch?" I thought he was going to lower the boom on me, but he never said a God-damned word. I thought that, at any minute, the ax would fall, but it didn't. However, I got the message.

One night, when my father was working at the Howard Arthur Mill, the other fireman didn't come in and I went to help my father out. When I got there, my father told me what to do. I opened the furnace door and this flame shot out. My father said, "Just put the shovel in; put the coal dust in." But I couldn't do it. It was too heavy. I was shaking holding the shovel. Finally, my father said, "Just take the shovel and throw the coal in and hold on to the shovel handle." However, I couldn't throw it very far and the coal fell from the shovel near to the door, making a pile of coal in front. I then took a rake and moved the pile in back. The rake came out red-hot. I never wanted to be a fireman after that. I came home at 6:00 am and stopped on the way at a Portuguese bakery to pick up a loaf of bread. I went to bed that night and slept until 6:00 that night. I didn't remember anything!

I worked for Corey's Dairy Farm in Tiverton. I would come home with green beans and corn. I had no license, but I could drive on the farm. We would bring full milk cans to Hood Dairy. Farmers would put milk on the sidewalk for us to pick up. It was raw milk. I worked on the farm after school when I was in the fourth and fifth grades. After that, I worked at Capitol Fruit Store in the Flint. The store was two stores down from Mason Street. On the corner was a market. I was twelve or thirteen years old at the time. You couldn't work until you were eligible for a school card at the age of fourteen.

Jack would go to the auctions and buy produce right off of the railroad cars. You had to buy big lots. I packed all the potatoes in the wall in back and put them in fifteen-pound bags. I waited on customers soon thereafter. After I got my license, I slept in the front room and we would leave at 4:30 am to go to the food market at the railroad station in Providence. We loaded up and came back. Then I would go off to school. I was sixteen years old.

Once, when Jack was stuck for a driver, I drove the truck to Providence. When the driver didn't show up for the big trucks, I drove to the Boston Food Market. That was when Fanuel Hall was the food market. We would stop in Mattapan [outside of Boston] for breakfast in the Jewish district. In those days, before Route 24 was built, the way to get to Boston was via Route 138. It took two hours to get up there.

He had stores in the Flint, downtown, and the Globe (where the post office is now). I got stopped once on Plymouth Avenue. The cop handed my license back to me and said, "Whoa, how old are you?" You had to be eighteen to drive a truck of that size and I was sixteen.

A typical lunch pail for workers in the mills
*Photo courtesy of the Fall River Historical Society*

**Neighborhood Experiences**

This land was part of the Kennedy farm. The big house on the corner of Grattan Street and Stafford Road was the farm house. The farm extended from Stafford Road to the pond. One house was the Chesler's, a Polish family. She had a cow that was brought to where the east side of my lot is now to the garage. When my mother would cut the green tops off of carrots, I would put them in a bag and bring them down to feed the cows. There was a dirt floor in the basement. The Mulrooney family lived at 1800 Rodman Street. Those were the only other two houses in the area. The rest was all open space. We could see to the other side of the pond, to the Kerr Thread Mills. The wind was strong here, so we had to put our kite strings on rollers; the kites went as far as Kerr Thread.

Where my house is now at 156 Emmett Street was once a gravel pit for the Kennedy farm. The city used the gravel. The Kennedy farm stopped operating about the turn of the century, 1900 or so.

There was a big fire at the Henry Lord School. There was little water pressure to fight the fire so, following that, the city built the water tank next door.

When I went to the Letourneau School, this was the last street for the school. Chicago Street kids went to the Brayton Avenue School. The French kids went to the St. Jean Baptiste School.

When I grew up, everyone was going in the service. They all hung out on the corner on Stafford Road waiting to get in the service. Fortunately, every guy who went in came back; no one was lost.

There were stores on Stafford Road on the corner of Chicago Street, Stafford Road and America Street, and Tucker Road and Stafford Road, which was Dansereau Market. Goyette's

Market was next to where the credit union is now. Next to Goyette's was a package store. Across the street from Goyette's was Demaris Hardware. On the southeast corner of Brayton Avenue and Stafford Road was the A&P Market, which was later Krupa's Hardware and now a cell phone company.

When I grew up, Maplewood Park had a grove where the two ball fields are now.

The first Stop and Shop in the area was in the basement of the mills at Broadway and South Main Street. I would go there with my wagon and get two pecks of potatoes.

There was a family that moved up to Sucker Brook. My father asked me, "Is he colored?" "I don't know; I'll ask him," I said. He never asked me again.

**Military Career**

I went into the Navy when I was seventeen, in 1945. I was a junior in high school when I quit. I was scared to tell my father. My father was in the Navy in World War I. He went as far as the fourth grade. My mom completed the eighth grade. I got out of the Navy in 1949 and went to work in electronics. I became a master technician in radio. When the Korean War broke out, I was called in from 1950 to 1952.

When I was eighteen, I was on the light cruiser *USS Astoria*. The put me in charge of the electrical desk and generators. If anything happened to the generators, the ship would go nowhere. Once, we lost power in one part of the ship. Everyone ran to the electrical desk to see what I could do. The officers on deck said, "He's in charge down there. He's a first-class electrician. He'll get it back on line." I got it back on line. At eighteen, you don't think; you just do it. You learn to accept responsibility very quickly there. You do things there that you never thought in your life you could do.

We had an ensign who just got out of Annapolis as an electrical officer. During our first conversation, he told me that he didn't know a damn thing about electricity and let me explain the electrical workings of the ship. He was a smart and nice guy. He let you do your job and he stayed out of the way.

When we were in Long Beach, California, on the *Astoria*, the Chief of Electricity would go ashore and come back half-smashed. He was in the Navy for thirty-two years. He brought two bottles back with him and the Officer of the Deck saw it. He said, "I won't say anything to the Chief if you walk over to the rail; when you do, I want to hear two splashes." There were two splashes all right. He took off his shoes and threw them overboard. The liquor was worth thirty dollars, but the shoes were worth only five dollars.

The nicest trip we ever took was to Juneau, Alaska, to the Inland Waterway. The scenery there is spectacular. We walked on the Mendenhall Glacier.

# Norma (Gifford) Finglas

*Born on July 30, 1928*

## Family Background

I was born in Fall River at Union Hospital. My parents were Norman and Alice Roseanna Longworth Roosevelt (Anderson) Gifford. She was born the day that Teddy Roosevelt's daughter, Alice Longworth Roosevelt, was born in the White House.

My brothers and sisters, in order of birth, are: Alice, Norman (he died when he was thirteen months old), James Harvey (died in his fifties), me, Virginia Belle, Joan Patricia, John Andrew Anderson Gifford (died at fifty-one), and Carol Lou.

My father's parents were James Harvey and Rose (Vardney) Gifford. My mother's parents were John Andrew (from Norway) and Rose Kate (Harrington) Anderson.

My husband is James Finglas [Jim's interview precedes this one in the book] and we have two children: Michael William and James Patrick.

Growing up, the streets that we lived on include: Nashua Street, Buffinton Street, Boyden Street, Nelson Street, and Pleasant Street. I now live on Emmet Street.

My father's father, James Harvey Gifford, had a shoe store on Pleasant Street called Gifford and Pomfret. It was on lower Pleasant Street, where the old Army and Navy store was, close to Second Street, the second store up from Second Street. He carried expensive women's shoes.

My father's mother was half full-blooded Indian. She was a little woman, about 4 foot, 8 inches tall. Her sister wasn't much taller. This grandmother owned a restaurant on Bedford Street and was a very good cook. My grandmother always put a handful of sugar in her french fries; they were very tasty.

My mother's mother came over from Ireland during the potato famine and sent money back to Ireland. My grandmother was fifteen when she came over and her sister was sixteen. When someone left Ireland, they would have a wake that would last for three days because they were "dying." It was a big time. My grandmother lived in the Highlands as a cook. She salted away her money. She loved working for people and work. It was an easy life for her. Then she and my grandfather bought a boarding house and she didn't have to work for anyone else any more.

## Family Life

When I was little, I loved to read. I would find a quiet place in the house and read there. I liked to cook and helped my mother with the smaller kids. When my mother went back to work, I had a lot of responsibility to take care of the kids. The youngest girl was six and I was twelve. My oldest sister got married at fifteen. My mother worked the second shift and got home after midnight.

My brother and I were very close. I helped him build model planes. We would frame the plane, then put tissue paper over the frame. When we were done, we hung them from the ceiling with tacks.

We lived in Seekonk for a while and I started school there. When he was first married, my father worked at Borden Remington. Then he worked for the National Portland Cement Company. My grandfather had a hand in getting him the job. My father was very bright. At one time, he sold cement for the company in all of Rhode Island. When Route 6 was being constructed of concrete, my father supervised the construction.

I babysat for everyone in the neighborhood. I would do it for nothing, if they had no money, or for ten or twenty-five cents. When I was thirteen years old, I took care of my sister (seven years old), a friend (seven years old), a little girl (fifteen months old), and a new baby (three weeks old), all at the same time!

When we lived at 1839 Pleasant Street, we lived on the third floor. It was next to the fire station, and our bedroom was across from the fire station's sleeping quarters. In hot summer days, me and my sisters would be in our underwear. Joe Janis called out from the fire station, "Good Morning!" and we girls would all fall to the floor not to be seen. My mother said, "Put some clothes on," but it was hot up there. That house was later torn down for a high-rise.

My mother separated from my father. The neighbors would leave produce on our doorstep. There was no acknowledgment; they just left it.

When the seven of us lived on Nelson Street, there was a grapevine. Joe Janis would trim my mom's vine and tie it to the supports. It produced beautiful grapes. He would use the leaves to make Lebanese dishes. We would go to Hood's Market for empty baskets and bring back the baskets full of grapes. We got two dollars a basket. It helped pay for our clothes.

**School Life**

My first memory of school in Seekonk is when I went to get on the bus. The winters were tough, with a lot of sand and silt. My lunch pail fell under the bus and I started to cry. My mother started to come down and gave me a quarter to buy lunch. When I got on the bus, the kids said, "Don't cry." I was six years old. I didn't finish school in Seekonk. We lived in Providence for a while, and we moved three times when I was in first grade. When we moved to Fall River, I started at the William S. Greene School. When I was in the third grade, I went to the Cornell School, then to the Brayton Avenue School for fourth and fifth grade. From the seventh to the ninth grades, I went to the Henry Lord School.

**Recreation and Entertainment**

In our teens, we would go to Lincoln Park [North Dartmouth, Massachusetts], not for dancing but to socialize and go on the rides. On the day of the prom from Henry Lord, we went to Lincoln Park and had a good time. However, we missed the last bus back. When we got to the Narrows, it was 6:00 am. We took our shoes off and caught the Pleasant Street bus that turned around at the Narrows. Jim's white bucks were red from his bleeding feet.

**Courtship and Marriage**

I first met Jim at Maplewood Park in junior high school. They would show movies in the park, like Fred Waring, that were fifteen-minutes long. Jim knew my older brother who was three years older than me and wouldn't let boys near me. My mother loved Jimmy; my mother would make clamboils for Jimmy.

The Narrows

## Work Life

My first job was at the Candy Mart in the Academy Building. It was on the corner of the building at Pleasant and South Main Streets. It also had a soda fountain. My brother worked there. I went in one day and asked Sue Bellerand if she needed help. She said, "I just had a girl walk out on me. When can you start?" "Now," I said. I worked in the basement making baskets. I could hear the rats moving around down there; the other girls saw them.

We could eat as much candy as we wished but not the ice cream. We couldn't touch it. I never got sick from the candy. There was no air conditioning then; we opened the door when it got too hot inside. One day we said, "Let's have some ice cream." So, we took a half-gallon and cut it up. We had no cups, so we ate it with ice cream scoops. Half way through, the manager, Sue Bellerand, came in. I was near the cellar stairs and she couldn't see me. I ran down the stairs with the ice cream and tried to flush it down the toilet, but it wouldn't go down. I kept flushing the toilet. It was hard ice cream. The other girls heard me flushing the toilet and said that I was sick and vomiting. Sue said, "I'm so sorry that you're sick; why don't you go home." And I did.

During the war, we wrapped candy to send to the servicemen overseas. Before sending the box out, I would kiss each box and say, "Be safe." My brother was in the service. We had a special way of wrapping them for the Post Office, with Christmas paper with brown paper over it. They went into a special Post Office box. People would come in and want us to prepare a box that included the favorite candy of their relative who was in the service. Customers came in later and said that the candy was delivered promptly and that it was good.

Greene School on Cambridge Street

Then I went to work at Woolworth's. I prepared an application; half the girls there knew me. I was hired right away and worked at the hardware counter. One day, a man came in with a plug. He said, "I'm looking for a female plug for my male plug." I thought he was talking dirty, and I hid under the counter. He called out, "Miss, miss; did you find it?" The other counter girl came over and he told her the same story. She told me, "Give him the plug." I did and, after he left, I told her that I thought he was talking dirty to me. She said, "You foolish girl. Here's what he meant," and she showed me how the plugs worked. I was so embarrassed.

Then I went to work in the Woolworth's office for four years. It was in the upper part of the store in the back even with the fluorescent lights. It was like a rotisserie. It was hot up there. Seven girls and the boss worked up there. We sat on high stools. In the beginning, I counted money.

A lot of money came in the store, especially at Christmas. We would take bags of cash to the bank and no one tried to steal the bags. We didn't think anything of it. The Woolworth's janitor would take the money to B.M.C. Durfee Trust Co. in a bag that looked like a black doctor's bag. There would be up to fifty thousand dollars in the bag.

Young people were not told when someone was pregnant. One of the girls was getting bigger and bigger. One Saturday night, we were all counting money and she was sitting next to me. All of a sudden, she poked at me. "You gave me a big poke," I said. They all laughed. "You felt my baby," she said. From then on, I helped her when she had to lean over to get something.

### Christmas, Holidays, and Special Occasions

At Christmas, we would take gray berries from plants in the swamp. We would put them in a packet and run the iron over it. The berries waxed the iron and let it slide over the clothes more easily.

# Robert E. Forcier

*Born on March 8, 1925*

**Family Background**

My parents were Edmond and Alice (Gagnon) Forcier. My brothers and sisters are Lorraine, Maurice, and Roger.

My wife is Doris C. (Paquette) Forcier, and we have three children: Janet Scanlon, Michelle Cummings, and Julia Grace.

**Family Life**

I was born and grew up at 87 Newhall Street. A doctor delivered me at home. This area was all wooded or farmland then. Vegetables, strawberries, turnips; all were grown here.

I played in the woods. There were many kids here; we had big families in the neighborhood. I became good friends with everyone. When it was time to work in the garden, all helped out. We would pull potatoes and helped one another harvest the crops.

Our grandparents lived with us for a while; I was seven years old when my grandfather passed away. My grandmother passed away when she was eighty-two. My grandfather was a stonecutter by trade. He was very busy. He chiseled all of the information on headstones, not by power but by hand. I remember my grandmother giving me my grandfather's lunch in a dinner pail to bring to him. Newhall Street [which abuts Notre Dame Cemetery] was a dirt road then and our farmhouse was up on Newhall near Stafford Road; it is gone now. I was just a young thing and a little nervous about going all that way. "I'll watch to see if you're okay," she said. "You can't get lost, Bob." I didn't get lost; I went right to him. When he had his lunch, I brought the pail back. I did it every day.

My grandmother could cook anything at all. She would do her own pastries; she was a fantastic person and raised a big family. She got up bright and early in the morning and raised five boys and two girls. She had her hands full. There were a few cows here when my grandparents first settled at 87 Newhall. She would make her own cream and butter, and she raised hens for eggs. She preserved lots of vegetables.

We had lots of uncles and aunts and cousins. They visited the farm very often. My mother and grandmother did a lot of the cooking. The food was shared with everyone. We played horseshoes and games for kids and the young ladies. Girls played with their dolls and carriages. We shared everything with our cousins. The girls liked to play hopscotch and jump rope.

We would go blueberrying nearby, and they were preserved. We had apple, pear, and peach trees. Preserving fruits and vegetables was hard work, but they loved what they did and took much pride in it. You would open up a jar of fruits or vegetables and they tasted so fresh you would swear they just picked them off the tree. My grandfather made some cider, but not much.

As we got older, my father worked at the Newport Torpedo Station, and he remained there for about forty years. He was a section manager. He got a car and would take us down to the south shore of Rhode Island or to Horseneck Beach. We would bring our cousins with us, and everyone had a grand time.

My grandfather was a great racing man. He loved horse racing. He raised three horses (that I know of) and would go and race them Down North at the sulky racing track. He competed with quite a few. In the winter, when the ice was thick enough, he would race on the South Watuppa Pond. The horse races on the pond were amazing, and my grandfather won prizes in the pond races. They had to be a certain type of horse. The hair on the horses would shine and glisten. They were well taken of.

He eventually sold them to a guy in New Jersey, who had heard about my grandfather's horses. The guy wanted all three, but my grandfather said, "Nothing doing." The guy kept trying and it took a number of visits and tries by the guy to bring the price down. My grandfather said, "No, I'm staying with my price." The horses were raised right here on Newhall Street.

Robert Forcier

Newhall Street was then a dirt road that went down to South Watuppa Pond. He raced horses on the dirt road. Some people on Norman Street had horses. There were about six to eight horses in the area. A Mr. Foster, who owned a stone cutting place on Pleasant Street, was one of the people that my grandfather raced. Sometimes, they would take the horses to Boston to race. They would leave on a Saturday and get back on Sunday evening. Sometimes the races were good and sometimes not. Down North, they had the sulky races; on Newhall Street, they raced saddle horses.

**School Life**

I went to the parish school of St. Jean Baptiste, where the Sisters of St. Joseph taught. I started from pre-primary and up. From there, I went to Henry Lord Junior High School, then to Durfee [B.M.C. Durfee High School]. I was a good student and got good marks—the whole family did. We had dedicated parents who wanted to make sure we had a good education. They made sure that we did our homework. When we didn't understand something, they arranged for us to have tutoring, if required.

**Food and Meals**

Sunday dinners were special at home. We had a nice piece of beef and a nice piece of pork with browned potatoes. Dinner included fresh vegetables, like string beans, carrots, and tomatoes. My mother always made her own gravy and pastries. The table always looked like the best you could get out of a garden. We all had great appetites.

Every now and then, aunts and uncles and cousins would have lunch with us. I was always near the table taking small cuts of meat or cherries from the dessert. My mother would say, "Leave some for the guests, Bob." Everything was so good.

What I didn't like too much was when the relatives left with their laughter and games; it was like a loss of happiness. We have beautiful memories of the times we had.

**The Depression**

During the Depression, things were tough. My mom was a great seamstress and was always altering something to see if it could be made into something new. She was always looking for ways to improve old clothing to make it look as new as she possibly could.

New shoes were not a commodity. My dad took our shoes and put them on an anvil and looked for leather to put on the soles and heels. He would put the anvil between his knees and slide the shoe over it and bang away at it. He made old shoes look like a brand new pair. He shined it up and said, "It looks like new, but it isn't." Anything to save a penny. It took a long time for the economy to turn around.

At Christmastime, times were tough. If I got one toy, I was doing good. One stocking was hung up on the radiator or fireplace, if you had one. They put an orange, apple, banana, or grapes, if you were lucky. Sometimes walnuts. Christmas was less about toys and gifts than today. It was hard for a family to afford toys for children.

Food was expensive then. I thank my mom and dad for all of the food that they grew and preserved. The cellar shelves were stocked with food.

Our family loved the Roosevelts. I don't remember all of their comments, but they were all good. He initiated the NRA [National Recovery Act], the CCC [Civilian Conservation Corps] camps, the WPA [Works Progress Administration], all of which started to boost the economy.

**World War II**

I went to Durfee for two or two and a half years, then World War II started. I had to start making money to help my family. I saw myself going into the service. I worked for two years, then Uncle Sam sent me a beautiful letter. I went to register for the draft, and the final result was, "You have been accepted." I reported to Camp Devens in June of 1943 for one month, then they shipped us down to Camp Wheeler in Georgia for initial training.

It was tough. We were up at 4:00 am, shaved and showered and at the cafeteria by 5:00 am. Then we would report back to barracks, where we got ready for field training. We never got back before 7:00 pm. It was a long day. We ate in the field and ate what they gave you. There were many items that I didn't like, but I ate it and shut up. You did what you were supposed to do.

After training, they shipped us to the Boston Shipyard for embarkation to go overseas. We left the United States on Christmas Eve. Guys cried. It was really cold that evening. The Red Cross was there with donuts that were like cement. Even the coffee couldn't soften them. I laugh about it now, but we didn't laugh about it then.

They loaded the GIs and track and half-track vehicles on the ships. We left about 4:00 am; it was cold. We shipped away with two destroyer escorts headed for North Africa. It took us a week. We had to do zig-zag maneuvers, so it took a long time to get there. German subs were active in the area. Fortunately, there were no encounters with the subs.

We landed in North Africa and had a mission with Rommel. He was a smart man. He wanted North Africa in the worst way. The German soldiers that we encountered there were good fighters. They gave us as good a fight as we gave them. I wasn't wounded there.

North Africa was hot; unbelievably hot, but it wasn't excruciating heat. When we first arrived in North Africa, we couldn't understand how people lived there. They lived in close quarters, with poor sanitary conditions, and different food that was cooked differently. But they were pleasant to talk to and humble in their own ways. If they could do anything to help out, they would do so.

They were always willing to do more than their share. We couldn't get over it.

The loss of men there was horrendous. There was no winner because of the tragic incidents that happened. When we saw that we were gaining, they decided to split us up. One group went to England and one group remained until Rommel got out of there.

We left for England and trained there. When we first arrived in England, we had the hardest time understanding the "King's English." We would order the fish and chips but couldn't make out what they tried to tell us. To avoid any more confusion, we always had the right change. It caused such a problem that our base commander had to get in touch with the English commandant and explain to him, "So many GIs are having trouble understanding your language." So, officials had a meeting of the minds and begged for understanding. "Bear with them," they said. In about a month, things started to make sense.

The English people had a lot of fortitude. They don't give up easily. The damage from German bombing in England was unbelievable. I don't know has those people got through it. Churchill was an amazing man. "Never give up," he said. "Never." I couldn't believe the damage to the shipping areas of Liverpool. The Germans wanted to totally decimate the ports. There was bombardment after bombardment, but the English wouldn't give in.

We knew there was something big coming. Heavy equipment kept coming in. We didn't know about the D-Day invasion; everything was hush-hush. We trained very heavily there, much more than previously. We trained with new equipment and then with green troops. They were not used to military equipment; we had to make sure that what we said penetrated.

Then the big day came. We gathered in the southern part of England and left by night. There were so many troop ships in the English Channel that you wouldn't believe. There were airplanes of all types, including light bombers and heavy bombers. It was massive. We knew what we were headed for; they told us before. We knew it was not going to be a picnic.

The Germans had no idea where we were going to land in France. German intelligence put two and two together with the information they had. The Germans had spent years building fortifications along the French coast to stop the movement of heavy duty tanks. They had time to do this; thousands of Frenchmen were used in forced labor to build it.

It was a nightmare like no one had ever seen. LSTs [Landing Ship, Tank] and LCMs [Landing Craft Mechanized] were loaded with GIs. It was June, but the water was like ice. Our backs were full of equipment and our rifle. It wasn't easy when you stepped in the water and tried to move. It was six feet deep where the LST dropped us off. I went from the platform and went under. A fellow grabbed me when I dropped off. When we got on the ground, we tried to get ground cover on our stomach. Many LSDs and LSMs loaded with GIs never made it to the shore. Some were let off in thirty feet of water.

It took so long to move from the water's edge to the next objective that you wondered, "What is wrong?" We would move a foot. We couldn't get up, we were so exhausted. The only thing that you wanted to do is sit there.

All lieutenants and military personnel began to group in their platoons, and you had to make sure that you were where you were supposed to be. The toughest thing was when you see the arm or leg of a buddy come flying off. You become like a mad man and go after the Germans while trying to keep a level head. War is hell, believe me; it doesn't get any better, it only gets worse.

When GIs get back from active duty, you can't forget what you've seen because it's embedded in your mind. In the military, you form many buddies. You watch for the guy in front of you and the guy in back looks out for you. No matter how much your buddy gets hit, you stay with him and wait until a medic comes by to help. There are many heartaches when a buddy or a good friend is lost. It's like that all the way through. You lose so many of them. For every one that you lose, you make up with another buddy. The feeling, the bond, among GIs is very strong.

When you get wounded, they have what's called field hospitals, and they move up with soldiers that are on the front. The care that you get in these field hospitals is out of this world. They have the best doctors and nurses. They handle all kinds of wounds and loss of limbs, and they do this around the clock, with no stopping. They do whatever they can not to lose a soldier or a limb. These doctors and nurses are under constant pressure; some break down in surgery. They see so much that they can't take it any more.

I didn't get hit on the beach, although I got wounded three weeks later in a German ambush on a Sunday afternoon. I was on top of a knoll and had just gotten through eating C-rations. I said, "This is Sunday afternoon," and my mind went back to the Sunday dinners folks were having now at home, the roast beef and pork and the other food that went with it. There had been shelling forty-five minutes before then. We lost five GIs in that shelling. Out of nowhere, a signal came in. Fourteen men were sitting various distances away. Another shelling started, worse than the previous one. It was so bad that the concussion took the pack on my back and cut it right off. I went flying into a fork of a tree and got wedged there. I was wounded. The fellas that didn't get hit were helping those who got wounded. I kept yelling, "Over here! Over here!" but they couldn't find me. Finally, a corporal saw me. I was bleeding badly. It took two groups to get me out of the tree.

They got me to an area where there was a jeep that had been modified to carry litters, one litter on the right side, one on the left side, and one in the back. It had a capacity of five. Once I was on the stretcher, I didn't remember anything after that. At the field hospital, the nurse said that it looked bad. They tried to stop the bleeding and two orderlies took me to an operating room. I finally blacked out from the intense pain.

I had gotten hit in the back. I had a collapsed lung and fractured ribs on the right and left side of my body. The heel of my right foot was mashed. They did a good job of putting me back together. Through the injuries, I lost a lot of my strength, and I've never been able to get it back. The doctor said, "When you have nerve damage, it affects all of the body. We don't know why the body acts that way; it's the way it is."

I remember coming to and there was a Red Cross nurse at the front of the litter and another nurse or surgery attendant who asked, "How are you doing?" "I'm doing as good as I can be," I replied. "We'll have to notify your parents," she said. "Don't tell them everything; it will break their hearts," I said. She wrote down what she would tell them. She said it will take thirty-six hours to get to the United States and another six hours more to get to the destination. I was in the field hospital for two weeks. The GI in the litter next to me lost his leg and arm and was badly wounded.

They flew us back to England to another field hospital there. It was a big building with many wings. Some lost legs, some lost arms, some had parts of their faces blown off. They took good care of us there. You had the feeling that you can't give up. You see the effort that is being given to all of the group that are there. Anyhow, with all of the effort that we got, that same year, about seventy-five percent of us headed back to the states.

When we left England, there were a total of 275 wounded GIs put on the hospital ship to come to the United States. The name of the ship was the *USS Dogwood*. It took two days to put the GIs on the ship, and we left England by the southern route, by the coast of France and Spain, to the United States.

However, on the way over, we had an encounter with a German sub. The sub wired to the captain of our ship to stop so they could check for weapons. The rule was that a hospital ship could not carry weapons. The Germans detained us for an hour while they searched the ship. Four Germans came on board and went on every floor of the ship to make sure that there were no military armaments on it. When they were through and made their report, they went back on the sub. We never heard anything more. The captain said, "We're not moving now; we'll wait for an hour." We were all sweating it out. When the time came to move, and the signal came to move, what a beautiful sound that was!

When the United States coastline just came into view, the captain said, "Look to the right, you can see the coastline of the United States. For those on the other side of the ship, I will turn the ship around so you can also see it." What a sound came up from the GIs! They were elated just to see the coast of home.

It took two days to unload us. They took such good care of us. The food was terrific. I hadn't tasted food like that in a while. I stayed there for a month. Twelve of us were going back to Camp Devens. There was a big hospital there. We left by military train, and I was in a wheelchair. Others were in litters or on crutches. It took almost two days for the trip to Devens. People who saw the train pass were ecstatic. Military trains had priority.

Devens had a foot of snow; how they managed to get all of us out, I don't know. The Devens hospital ward had so many amputees, it made me sick. It was like a bad dream.

They took care of us for three weeks, and then they came and said, "If you want, we can give you guys a pass for twelve hours if you want to see your folks." We said, "Twelve hours was not enough. Could we have an extension?" The request had to go to the adjutant general. We got the pass. Before leaving, the doctor told us, "I'm going to give you a set of crutches." "No," I said, "my parents will be upset if they see that I'm on crutches. Can you give me two canes instead?" He said, "You're taking a chance."

When the cab came up to the house, I came out with the two canes, and I thought my mother would pass out. My dad was shaking like a leaf. It was a nice occasion but very sad at the same time. I caught pneumonia while at home and was treated by Dr. Morganstein. He told me to take a medication every two hours. Don't stop it. Dr. Morganstein asked who was the responsible doctor at Devens. He called right from there and told them at Devens that I had come down with pneumonia and that I couldn't go back. The doctor at Devens said, "If he needs to stay, so be it." The medicine was a wonder and took care of it.

I was at Devens for three months. Then came the day when they said, "You don't need meds anymore." The doctor signed the report, and then I got released.

I've met all kinds of people in the service; there were some smart, caring individuals in the service. When traveling, I met different people and saw how they live and get along with one another.

[*Editor's Note: In 2008, Mr. Forcier was awarded a medal of honor from the French Government in a ceremony held in Paris and Normandy during the 65th anniversary of the Normandy invasion.*]

**Work Life**

Returning from the war, the first thing I did was to find employment. It was hard. I managed to latch on to a very good job. I had to do something with my education. I worked for Pratt and Whitney in East Hartford, Connecticut, building jet engines. The pay was good, and the overtime was great.

My former boss, before Pratt and Whitney, had said, "Your job, Bob, is here if you want it." Before I left Pratt and Whitney, I had a good talk with my supervisor. I told him, "Listen, I got a good offer to go back to my old job. I'm a newcomer here at Pratt and Whitney and have to start at the bottom." He said, "I'll put it in the record; you will be welcome back anytime." I had more of a comfortable feeling leaving Pratt and Whitney then.

I then went to Standard Coil, located in North Dighton [Massachusetts]. They made TV tubes for all TVs. They were from Chicago and were a big firm. One day, they called all of us in to a meeting. The management said, "I have received bad news from the mother plant; they want to pull out of North Dighton and go back there. Any of you who want to go to Chicago can come." I would have lived nicely if I decided to go, but I decided to stay here.

While this wasn't good news, it allowed me to improve on my education. Later in life, I could put it to good use. I went back to school in Providence at Providence Radio Technical Institute under the GI Bill. I loved it, every aspect of it, and graduated from there.

**Courtship and Marriage**

I decided that it was time to look for a mate. I met a nice young lady who later became my wife. My cousin Eugene married my wife's cousin. He told me, "Bob, I want you to meet a nice young lady; you went to school together." I had been away for a while and didn't know who she was. He had a get-together of some kind and I got there at 7:00 pm. Everyone had a big grin on their faces. I felt that something was wrong. I felt that I was being sucked into something. I came in the door and spotted the young lady. She was one of my school sweethearts. It was Doris Paquette. "Bob," he said, "I don't have to introduce you, do I?" I told her, "I thought you would be married and have a lot of children by now." "No, I'm not married," she said.

After school, I tried to get myself a job with a studio, but I had no luck there. One door closed; would another door open? The Grand Central Market was looking for a head cashier. I saw an ad and went for an interview. I said, "I understand that you are looking for someone of this caliber, and I want to apply for the job." They asked about experience, and I said that I could perform the job without any problem. In a few days, they replied and said, "You're hired." I worked there while I was dating my sweetheart. Now was a good time to get married, and we were married in St. Jean Baptiste Church.

When we were dating, I was living at home, and we would meet over lunch, go to the movies, or go dancing at Lincoln Park [North Dartmouth, Massachusetts] or Roseland in Raynham. We also went on excursions to Atlantic City, Washington, and Canada.

We have three beautiful children, and all are smart. One girl lives away, but the other two are nearby. They are great kids, and we have beautiful grandchildren.

I consider myself a very fortunate man, in so many ways.

# Lynwood Hathaway French

*Born on September 27, 1915*
*Died on February 28, 2010*

**Family Background**

I was born in Fall River when our family home was on Driftwood Street. My wife's name is Virginia Lucy Mycock, and we were married on July 5, 1940.

My mother was Ethel Sisson Cole French. She grew up in Warren, Rhode Island, with her twin sister and other siblings. I only remember one grandmother, my father's mother, and her name was Harriet Hathaway French. My father was Alvah French and he had two sisters, Harriet Ethelyn Owen and Clytie Madera Coombs.

My mother died on Christmas Day in 1918, when I was three. We moved from The Lane up to the top of the street to live with my grandmother and Uncle Benjamin and Aunt Clytie Coombs. It was the house at the corner of The Lane and South Main Street. My father worked in Providence at the time and used to come home some weekends.

I had two older sisters. The oldest was Doris Cole French McCauley, who lived her adult life also at The Lane. The other sister was Edythe Valentine French Terry. She lived just down the street from me on Pleasant Street.

In the summer of 1921, my father married a woman named Harriet. We then moved to the outskirts of Bridgewater [Massachusetts].

**Family Life**

The first thing I remember is living in Assonet [just north of Fall River] on The Lane, which at the time was South Water Street, and playing in the sand in the street. I remember playing with pots and pans and clothespins. There was a kerosene street light in front of the house. Someone used to come and light it. It is now 5 The Lane.

We moved to Assonet because my father worked at Davis Warner during World War I. They made mostly stuff for the military. Davis sold his remaining interest in the factory in 1919, and it closed in that year. At the gun factory, they paid ten cents an hour. The gun shop was just across the river and I remember standing in the yard waiting for the whistle to blow. It was called the Davis Warner at that time.

When the Armistice was signed on November 11, 1918, I remember standing outdoors with all the bells and whistles blowing at once. I was three years old and I thought that was just fine. The more noise the better.

The Kirkers lived across the street where Mary and Richard Brown now live. The Kirkers had chickens, horses, and cows. We had no electricity, just kerosene lights. As a child, I was given a kerosene light when I went to bed. We went to the Kirkers for milk. I would go with my sister Edythe. Electricity was installed while I lived there when I was five years old. Aunt Clytie would send me to Winslow's store for a loaf of bread.

I started school at the Bridgewater Normal School in 1921. The next year we moved to Berkley

Lynwood French with the pony cart
*Left to right*: Janette Bentley, Annah Kirker, James Kirker, and Lynwood French

[Massachusetts]. Neither of these houses had electricity. We were very poor. I went to the Skunk Hill School in Berkley in 1922. The teacher came to school on horseback.

In 1923, we moved to Providence and lived on Cypress Street. Then we moved to Cranston [Rhode Island] in 1924 or 1925. We were poor, dirt poor. I mean we had nothing. In Cranston, I slept on the third floor with no heat and no lights. No one had heat or lights. They used to think that a heated bedroom would kill you. When a person had TB [tuberculosis] and went to a hospital, they made them sleep out of doors on the porch.

While living in Providence and in Cranston I often visited in Assonet when there was school vacation. They would give me the carfare. I would go all alone, get a street car to downtown Providence, walk to the depot, get the train to Fall River, and then get a street car to Steep Brook. I would then get Borges Bus to Assonet. I was eight years old. Borges never charged me to ride on the bus.

My father died in April, 1925. The stepmother did not want the kids so we came to Assonet to live with Grandmother and Uncle Ben and Aunt Clytie. I grew up at the Four Corners, and children nearby would sit on the bread box at the corners. Not my kids, though.

**School Life**

I went to the Village School. From there I went to the South School. From there I went to Morton [Junior High School] in Fall River. We had to take a test and if we didn't pass we had to go to Taunton. I went to Morton and then to Durfee [B.M.C. Durfee High School]. I went to high school with Jimmy Kirker, Norman Henderson, Myron Chace, Donald Copeland, and Anna May Jones.

I played in the band at Durfee. We would have parades down Main Street with the NRA [National Recovery Act] people.

Cranberry pickers' children from the Bullock Bog went to the Forge School. The school was at corner of Forge and Howland Roads, converted to a house in the early 1950s. Some kids didn't get out of third grade by the time they were sixteen.

Edith Cudworth, who taught at the Village School for many years, had one daughter, Alice. She lived most of her life on the farm that is now part of Historical Society grounds on Slab Bridge Road. Edith hated cats. Her husband, Walter Cudworth, lived to be ninety. Every day, he had a breakfast of eggs, fried potatoes, and bacon. If he had his way, he would have lived on Oreo cookies and chocolate cake.

*Mrs. French:* We both graduated in the Durfee Theatre. I lived on School Street. Until age seven, we lived in a house that was on the site of the current Hathaway Town Park on the Assonet River. The house belonged to Welcome Hathaway, who had three sons. The house was rented out by the Hathaways and later donated to the town to be used as a park, now known as Hathaway Park.

Durfee graduation, 1934

**Food and Meals**

*Mr. French:* My father's mother cooked. She made johnnycakes out of corn meal. We had a full breakfast every day. She used salt pork to supply the grease to fry the eggs or something. We ate mostly meat and potatoes and gravy. We had ground corned beef. If we ate meat, only enough was cooked for that meal. You couldn't keep food beyond one meal. In Charlie Marbles' family, they cooked the bacon in the morning, saved the grease, and then poured the grease over the potatoes for the evening meal.

Some people would get a pig's head for fifty cents. They would boil it up to make head cheese. The Fall River English came from poverty. They ate lots of organ meat, and lots of liver, kidneys, tripe, and things like that. Good meats were for rich people. They would make kidney pie and sausages that were smoked and would keep for a while.

We had lots of bread and butter. For breakfast, bread and jam was cheap. Many meals were bread and milk or milk crackers and milk. Supper could be corn and bread. Lots of nights, pancakes were served for supper. We never had pancakes for breakfast. We had lots of eggs. Chicken pie would go a long way. On Saturday night, we always had baked beans.

Fish and meat were preserved with salt; some used pepper. Salt was cheap. Some stuff was pickled. The Swedes pickled fish in lye. Corn kernels were put in a lye solution that took the skin off the kernel of corn. Hominy, it was called. Everyone canned a lot. People who came from different parts of the world brought their own recipes and foods with them, including how to preserve them. Salted codfish was eaten by all nationalities. Each nationality in the area brought their own customs. Salt pork was used a lot in New England and by the French Canadians. They would eat it out of the barrel. The Portuguese immigrants would not throw away a jar or bottle. They were scarce where they came from, but here they were everywhere. We couldn't use all of them.

Hens would lay good in the summertime but not in the wintertime. We would put eggs in a crock with water glass [sodium silicate]. A clear jell went over the eggs and kept the air out of them. We used the eggs for months. We put the eggs in a cool place in the basement and they stayed for several months. Food was stored in the cellars with dirt floors. Root vegetables were put in the cellar. Turnips could be kept for one year; beets and carrots too.

People hunted for food then. Shotguns became popular and were made at the factory. The old-timers would eat wood ducks and squirrels. The wife of George Allen on High Street made squirrel sandwiches with squirrel hamburger.

Local people would take a fifteen-foot pole and go down to the river to catch eels. Eels and johnnycakes were a big meal in New England. It didn't make a big difference where you came from. You caught them with a round net and would walk around in a big circle. A man born in 1849 would tell stories about that.

You could buy a hind quarter of beef from Fall River. The ice kept meat for a few days; it got green after that. If it did, they just wiped it off. You couldn't keep stuff on ice for very long. People cooked meat longer than they do today. If the meat got rotten, they sold it for dog food.

They tried to make corned beef pretty much every week. A lot of this meat was what you couldn't sell anyway. They would wrap it up in ten- to fifteen-pound pieces. They would put it down on Wednesday and sell it by Saturday.

They came out with a little oil burner that could go into a range. A gallon of fuel cost five cents, delivered. It was a lot easier than cutting wood. You could shut off or turn down the range in the summer since you didn't have to have it going all the time. These were Glenwood ranges. The oil was put in a small barrel with a spigot on it and inverted on a stand that drew down the oil as needed. We had to fill it every day. It burned three gallons a day.

**Assonet Village History**

There were a lot of horses around the Village in the 1920s. Freelove Weathers, who lived in the Four Corners, had a team of horses in back of the house. Lou Collins had horses as did Jim Haskins. Charles Terry's horse was named Dexter. We would get Ben Evans' horse for sleigh rides and hay rides.

The Post Office was in the front room of the present library on North Main Street. Mail came by train to the depot. George Allen delivered the mail in the 1930s. He lived in the first house on the left on High Street. He had a wheelbarrow and came to the train in the morning and evening. He had a few bags on the wheelbarrow and would go and pick up a few more bags. In the wintertime, he would deliver the mail by horse and sleigh.

There were lots of stores around the Village. James Winslow had a store that later became Dean and Herberts. Charles Terry had a store. He sold groceries. Everything but meat. He had two three-pound-blocks of ice back of the store, with a hole in the floor to drain the ice. The Terry

Store later became the Village Store when owned by James McCauley in the late 40s. The Store was built by John Peabody in Civil War days. He went into the patent medicine business and dreamed up all kinds of concoctions. There were no government restrictions on what you could sell people. These concoctions usually had alcohol or opium in them. You ended up either drunk or drugged, but you usually felt better after it. His son took over the business.

Before refrigeration, the iceman came only in the summer. Otherwise, you put food in a box outside or in the well.

My uncle, Ben Coombs, owned the first car in Assonet. He had the garage where Borges is now in the Four Corners.

We bought this property in 1951. Eugene Hathaway lived in a small house on the site in 1915. In 1951, he was in a nursing home. We paid sixty dollars for him to sign off nine-tenths of an acre. The last tax payment was made in 1918. I bought the acre on the north side for three hundred dollars. It is part of the 23rd lot of Freeman's Purchase. John Tisdale was the first owner, and his son Joshua the first settler. They were ancestors. John Tisdale came from Duxbury. He had settled in Taunton where he was a selectman and was killed by Indians in 1675, in King Philip's War.

The Cudworths owned from the stone wall here on the south boundary of my property down to the river, about a quarter mile. Luther Cudworth lived in the house on the right in the 1830s. The Thresher family owned it. I don't think that the Captain Cudworth of King Philip's War fame was in the same family. However, Benjamin Church was one of my ancestors.

Luther Cudworth sailed boats out of here, to the Darien and Brunswick, Georgia, area. He would go up river to small plantations to bring products and to get products to export to Europe. A man who inherited a plantation from his uncle got friendly with one of the captains from Assonet. He came up here and bought a house in Assonet next to the Historical Society. A slave family came up with him in the summertime to work for him. He died in 1858 and is buried there. When the town cemetery was founded on the old Muster Grounds, he was moved there. I can remember the oldest slaves that still lived there. I went to South School and to church with them.

The people from Assonet spent the winters in Georgia, logging for thirteen to fourteen dollars a month. These coastal schooners would bring food down to Georgia and bring back firewood to other parts, including Providence and Newport.

Firewood was a big item then. Coal stoves only began to come into general use during Civil War times. They would burn wood in the summertime and coal in the winter in kitchen ranges. They used wood so it would go out and could start it again. There was no refrigeration. Beef and fish were salted to preserve them. Fresh fish was local cold water fish. This was in the early 1900s. There were special catalogs that sold food and shipped it for free.

The mills burnt thousands of tons of coal a week. There was smoke, outhouses, and garbage. When it was hot, it was a real problem.

We would have band concerts in the Village every Monday night. I played the alto horn. The group practiced in the Boy Scouts' hall.

I went in the Boy Scouts in 1927. We had a Boy Scout band in Assonet around 1932. Leo Vazina came from Fall River to give us lessons. He taught all the wind instruments for a dollar per week, and if you didn't have an instrument he would furnish the instrument.

I was a Boy Scout troop leader. The group included ten to twelve people including Mr. Gifford, Job Terry, and me. We used the chairs from the hall for the concerts. We built the first bandstand

Lynwood French in front of the family home at the corner of
Water and North Main Streets, Assonet, 1927

on Charlie Terry's land, in back of Terry's Store, for one year. He agreed to let us put it in there and furnish us with electricity. He sold the ice cream and did more business on Monday night than he did the rest of the week.

There was an old tavern there that was falling down on the property that is now the town park, where the present bandstand is located. The group of people from five or six families that owned it agreed to deed their shares. All but one. Ann Nichols wanted money for it but the others gave it. She was Gilbert Nichols' widow. So, we went around town and got the one hundred and fifty dollars and paid it off. It was then deeded to the town. The town wouldn't accept the land until we filled in the foundation hole, so every Sunday for one year we worked to fill in the tavern foundation hole. Charles Evans had a truck and we obtained sand and gravel from the Nichols' pit. We sold the tavern lumber. Once the hole was filled in, the town accepted the property.

The women sold french fries during the concerts and the store sold ice cream. This was before Prohibition ended. Norman and Ida Henderson lived on the east side of Ralph Francis' house on Elm Street. He used to run the garage at the Four Corners and, when he died, she started baking things like pastries, which she sold Monday nights. She made french fries for ten cents a bag. She made money at it and I think maybe a living at it.

Then we moved the bandstand over and the WPA [Works Progress Administration] fixed it for us. It didn't have any roof on it when it was moved over. WPA made it nice. It was at first a platform.

The Beagle Club in Berkley paid the band to come over and play there. They had bottled home brew available. At the end of every song, all would blow their car horns. Vazina was paid four dollars a night. They took up a collection.

There were many dams on little brooks that supported manufacturing of various kinds. On Bleachery Pond there was a forge that made threshing machines. The owner joined the Gold Rush to California in 1849 and sold the place to John Thwaites, who turned the place into a bleachery.

In 1882, it became Crystal Springs Bleachery and Dying. Another bleachery, Daley's Bleachery, ran until after World War I.

Henry Winslow built the first dam on Locust Street, off Mill Street, on the Assonet River. These were carding mills that cleaned cotton and sold it to spinning mills.

David Terry built a mill on Mill Street that cleaned wool. When the textile mills were running in Fall River, they created waste thread piles. Little places sprung up in Assonet to reclaim this material and to sell it as cotton waste to machine shops and others.

The Fall River Granite Company was in Assonet. A railroad siding went up there and joined the main tracks were Brightman Lumber is now. You can still see where the tracks were. Oxen brought the cars up the hill and gravity brought the cars down again. These cars were controlled with brakes. This was in the late 1800s. There was quite a patch of land used for quarrying up there.

You could get a cord of wood per acre per year, or a thousand cords of wood, from that holding. When the market for cord wood was declining, selling the land to the state looked good. Some of the forest acreage the state didn't pay for. They took it to clear the title. Some people wouldn't sell. They were mad over it. However, most owners were willing to sell.

At one time, there were a lot of stores in the Village. There wasn't much overhead. The Tavern was where the bandstand is now. On the southwest corner of the Four Corners was a market when I was a kid. A fellow from Berkley ran it. Across the street was the Red and White Store. Charlie Evans started a store above the bridge on South Main Street. There was a store near the Bleachery.

The old gas pumps didn't have a way to measure gas. They pumped the gas into a glass bottle or container of five or six gallons. They would show this to the person, then put the hose in the car, and it would run in. Cars were started with hand cranks. There was only one grade of gas.

The Boston Store was where Gramps gas station is now. There was a livery there also. Another building was Pierce's Hall. There was also a millinery store on South Main Street, where Lucy Evans made hats. It was a simple way of doing business. They bought at wholesale and sold by the dozen. All the grocer had to do was to divide the price of a dozen by ten, which provided a twenty percent markup.

In the mid-20s, I went to school with Joe Barboza. It was called the Tripp Farm before it became the Barboza Farm. I remember walking with my father up there when I was six years old, about 1921 or so, and the farm was empty in those days. I liked the farm next door, which was the Town Farm. I remember that someone made scarecrows in the field. It was the home of Lot Strange. He was there when it was the Town Farm too. The town made money on it.

We kids played in the sand in the street. Horses would bring wood down the street. We had kerosene streetlights. I remember going across the street with my sisters when the bells rang and the whistles blew. We got electricity in the Village sometime around 1920. The first road tarred in the area was County Road in East Freetown, around the time when they got electricity.

People had gasoline engines in their basements that powered water pumps that fed water tanks in their attics. In the evening, they ran the engine to bring the water up to the attic tank. They would put the exhaust in a keg of rocks to kill the noise. Windmills with hydraulic systems also brought water up. We also used hand water pumps. We would sit on the floor and pump back and forth.

Jimmy and Edith Chew and their daughters Evelyn and Sylvia lived on North Main Street where the Boy's Club camp is now. The old Quaker meeting house, which was located near what is now Troy Condominiums in Fall River, was moved to the Boys Club and served as a dining hall for many years. Levi Dean owed the house of the Chews. Horace Dean lived in the house where Dr. Schroeder now lives. Levi and Horace bought it at auction in 1783. Tories owned the farm during the Revolution, and the new government seized the land. Dean bought it and gave it to his two sons.

The Miller family lived there for decades. Mrs. French organized the sale of the property to Dr. Schroeder.

James Winslow had the general store in Assonet Four Corners. Dean and Herbert ran it when James Winslow couldn't any longer. Eleanor Winslow still owned it. When the automobile came in, along with electric refrigeration, the stores got bigger. The goods were cheaper and the new stores had more selection, so they couldn't keep the general store open.

The roads were never plowed in town until there was four inches of snow. The roads were never sanded until the end of World War II. Lots of people got killed in accidents. They put sand in flat-bottomed trucks and would sand corners only by shovel. Sand on the streets put an end to sleighing.

We would borrow a horse and go for a sleigh ride. We usually borrowed Ben Evans' horse. He was a selectman for many years. He was also an assessor. When he retired from that, I succeeded him in 1964 and continued for nine years. We were paid about six hundred dollars a year.

There were icehouses on Forge Pond that were operated by Arctic Ice from Fall River. It was originally owned by Anthony and Swift. The icehouses were operated as part of their slaughterhouses. Swift later became a national company. The second slaughterhouse owned by Swift was in Assonet. Anthony brought in cows from the west and slaughtered them here. The lack of refrigeration meant that cows had to be slaughtered near the place where the meat was to be consumed.

Some ice companies had their own icehouses on a pond. Some cranberry growers had icehouses of their own. One ice company in New Bedford owned an icehouse in a cranberry bog in East Freetown. All were made of wood and all burnt down. The walls of the icehouses used long poles with planks nailed to either side of the poles. Sawdust was then poured in between the walls as insulation.

The telephone came into the Village in 1902. It hung on the wall and had to be cranked. The telephone office was in someone's home with a switchboard. It was a toll call to Fall River. Dr. Briggs was number 1. Our number at home was 48. They were all low numbers.

In 1930, there were about 100 telephones in this part of town. About then, the telephone company came out with dial phones. They put it in a small community like Assonet very early to test it and play with it for a while, until it was workable and profitable. Fall River had it earlier, but it didn't work well. They used a new version in Assonet. The equipment was placed in a small building across from Town Hall.

**Work Life**

After high school, I worked some at the Rezendes Sawmill. I was paid twenty-five cents per hour. Then I went to work for Charlie Evans delivering groceries. Then I went to work at Abrasive Machine and Tool in East Providence. Business was slow and I got laid off in the fall of 1938.

I was on the fire department from 1937 to 1950. I was a hose man in 1937. I worked nights and usually I was the only one around the Village to drive the fire engine in the daytime. Frank McCreery was usually with me and he was along in years so sometimes we had to call for help. We had no radios or communication. On a Sunday in May of 1944, we had a call that there was a fire in the State Forest off of Copicut Road, which turned out to be the biggest fire we ever had in town.

Then I got a job at Scott and Williams in New Hampshire for the winter in 1938 and went back to Abrasive Machine and Tool in East Providence the next year. I left there in 1942 and went to Fall River to work at Precision Machine making British torpedoes. The company didn't last long and I left in 1943 and went to work at General Electric in Taunton. I had many different jobs there, mostly in engineering estimating, and I ran the tool room.

**Prohibition**

The Barboza Farm had a still. The feds were after the taxes on the alcohol. There were lots of stills around during Prohibition. John Mendoza had one. Moonshine was a clear liquid. A lot of it was made out of garbage. It didn't matter where it came from. They would use silage too. They would collect the corn juice that came to the bottom of the silo and pump it out. Joe at one time put small stills in the cornfields to elude the feds and ran them at night. You could have a half-dozen stills in the cornfields and no one would know it.

I woke up one morning when shots were being fired at Assonet corners. The feds had stopped a truck that was transporting alcoholic beverage.

During Prohibition people made wine, beer, and other stuff, for sale and home use. After that time, there wasn't much profit in making it. Tom Soares on North Main Street had only good stuff. It was Canadian liquor that came in from Westport Harbor. He lived at what is now 33 North Main Street in Assonet. At that time, there were no address markers on the houses. Addresses didn't get put on houses until the 1970s. Before then, everyone knew where everyone lived.

City politicians had nightclubs in the Hixville area during Prohibition. There were nightclubs that ran all day during Prohibition. There were many places in town to buy it. Most people who wanted to drink found it pretty easily.

The cider factory made barrels and barrels of cider that they put in barn cellars. They had formulas for the best hard cider. When it was ten degrees below zero, they drained out that part that didn't freeze. Vinegar was a big item back then. It covered the taste of bad food. They used it for pickling and preserving food. When white vinegar came out, they demonstrated its preserving power by preserving a banana for weeks.

They drank a lot of hard cider back then, always on the q.t. in the Village. Hard liquors were all the same. There were men at the gun factory, some who had little boats with engines, who would go down the river for miles to hang out for the weekend at Prudence Island. They spent the night there and came back the next day. I swear that they took hard cider with them and could get away from their families.

They bottled hard cider and made wine. They could make alcohol out of everything. Leaves and everything went into making cider. If anyone had apples, they took them to the sawmills and they would gin the cider out of hogshead barrels [large barrels that could hold 60 to 140 gallons]. Cider out of barrels would go into one-half of the hogshead and a rubber hose put in the barrels. The old timers said that building stone walls took two gallons of hard cider per foot or yard of wall.

During the 1840s and 1850s, there was a time that you couldn't buy alcohol. You could only purchase it through the city or town and only for medicinal purposes. One of the whaling captains, Captain Job Terry, had the biggest medicine chest of any of the whalers. Officials kept records of who bought alcohol. Brandy was the favorite medicinal liquor with lots of people. Rum also. They could bring in rum from the West Indies and land with sugar. One man bought a half bottle of brandy for a "sick horse."

**The Depression**
During the Depression, if you worked twelve to fifteen hours a week, you were doing well. There was lots of work for two hours for a quarter. I got paid twenty-five cents an hour at the sawmill, nailing boxes. The sawmill made them for nine cents from lumber furnished by local farmers. The mill was at the corner of Elm and Mill Streets. Joe Rezendes owned it. John B. Wilson owned it before him.

**Hurricane of 1938**
During the 1938 hurricane, I was working in East Providence in a wooden building on a hill overlooking the river. The wind blew some of the windows out on the roof. Then some pine trees came down and went through the roof of the building. We had overhead cranes that stopped the trees from hitting the floor. I left the plant and started for home. On Route 6, shingles were blowing around and at the Palmer River Bridge the water was on the road. There were cars stuck in the water and I tried to go through but the water was too deep. A truck pushed me out and up the road. There was another car behind me and he gave me a ride. It was early afternoon but it was dark by the time we got to Fall River.

We stopped at Gardners Neck Road [Swansea, Massachusetts]. It was flooded down to the Venus de Milo [restaurant]. The police officers came and told us we could get over the Brightman Street Bridge by going through Swansea Village. We couldn't go on Route 138; it was covered with water. We had to cross over to Riverside Avenue [Somerset, Massachusetts] and that is where the ship had washed ashore.

We got over the Brightman Street Bridge and the man wasn't going my way. He let me out and I walked to Assonet in the dark with trees and wires down. It was real late when I arrived home.

The next day someone took me back for my car. We had to go through Dighton and, in several places, we had to go in people's yards to get by the trees. My car was on the side of the road and it was a miracle that it started. It was an old Chevy.

The Four Corners was flooded and the A&P store between Merrills and the Post Office floated out in the Four Corners. The two stores, Terry's Store and Dean and Herbert's Store, lost everything that got wet; canned goods and all the food. In those days, Dr. Briggs was the head of the health department and he was the one who determined what to do. He told the people who had glass jars of food in their cellar to throw them away. There was no electricity for several days.

All of Water Street was flooded. The river went into the wells. I worked on a fire engine for four or five days after pumping the wells out and putting lime down.

Then the next one with flooding was in 1954. That hurricane was Carol. There is a picture at the Historical Society that shows the water. I took two pictures and put them together. The water came up about fourteen feet above high water.

## Marriage and Courtship

Ginny and I were married in 1940. We had a home wedding in Ginny's family home on School Street. We went to New Hampshire on our honeymoon. I lived with Aunt Clytie and Uncle Ben in the Four Corners. We made an apartment upstairs. I was working in Providence at the time. We were living there after our children, Barry and Dianne, were born. So we decided we needed a bigger place to live and finally purchased Frank Barrow's old home on Mill Street. There was very little available at that time. It needed an awful lot of work and we worked on it steady.

The war was on and everything was rationed and it was hard to get anything to work with. The house had no electricity or plumbing and the well had to be cleaned, as it hadn't been used in twenty-five years. Frank Barrows had lived in it since 1852. He was ninety-three at the time. He told me he was sick every day of his life and was never able to work. We lived there until 1950, when I was transferred to Pittsfield. We sold the house to George and Vera Wyatt and we bought one in Lee.

When I was transferred back to the Taunton General Electric plant, we had land on Walnut Street and we were going to build there. My sister Edythe and brother-in-law, Lawrence, wanted us to move to Pleasant Street so we purchased land in 1951 and built a home at 12 Pleasant Street. And we are still living in the same place.

We were the sixth house on the street. Now there are twenty-one homes. The land was wooded and we cut the trees down. We did a lot of work ourselves as to building the house. We purchased some sheep to cut the underbrush, poison ivy, and bull briers. We had a sheep shed and at one time had six sheep. We had rhubarb growing in front of the shed. One day I asked Barry to clean the sheep shed. When I went out, he had shoveled it out the window four feet deep, and I said, "Barry, now how do you think the rhubarb will come up through that?" It did, the tallest ever.

## Closing Thoughts

I have lots of hobbies. I have made four steeple clocks, a grandmother clock, tables, chests, and bookcases. I do photography and made lots of pictures for the Historical Society. I like to putter around in the cellar with tools and, of course, I have my gardening.

I would like to end saying we have three wonderful children, five grandchildren, and five great-grandchildren. We have been married for almost seventy years and I don't think I could have made it this far without Ginny.

Lynwood and Virginia French, Parade Marshals, July 4, 2008

# George Giroux

*Born in 1929*

**Family Background**

I was born at 91 East Main Street, our home in Fall River, and was delivered by Doctor Menard. I lived at this address until I went into the service at age seventeen.

My parents were Aldei and Alice (Potvin) Giroux.

My mother's parents came from the Quebec province of Canada. My grandmother could read and write English, an accomplishment for that time, although her sister never learned English.

My father was an orphan: both his mother and father died when he was about three years old. His parents died within one and a half years of one another in their mid-twenties of tuberculosis. They are buried in Notre Dame Cemetery. Genealogical research conducted by my wife and I shows that they were married in 1895 in St. Mathieu's Church. Grandmother Virginia was born in 1873 and died on July 11, 1898. My grandfather died in 1901.

My wife is Rolande Giroux [Rolande's interview follows this one in the book].

**Family Life**

Both my father and his brother were placed at St. Joseph's Orphanage. He never complained about it, although his brother did sometimes. Since they were not "paying customers," they were treated like domestics and had to work at the orphanage by doing such chores as serving meals and other tasks. At age twelve, being old enough to work in the mills, they were put out on the street.

Their aunt then took in both brothers. They were treated well there, but they had to work to help pay for their board and room. Their aunt lived in the Steep Brook area, across the street from St. Vincent's Home. They went to St. Joseph's Orphanage probably because it was French, whereas St. Vincent's was for the Irish and others.

My father was a weaver and he hated it. The windows to the mill were never opened, regardless of how hot it was outside. It was very hot and humid inside the mill. My mother was a spinner, so the windows could at least be opened.

My father wanted to leave the mill and always wanted to be self-employed, so he later opened a variety store on the corner of East Main and Slade Streets. He would give credit and kept a little book to keep accounts of money owed. However, he was too good and let credit get too extended. One fellow returned three or four years later and gave my father twenty-five dollars that he owed him. It was the wrong time (the Depression) and the wrong kid (I ate too much of the candy) for him to have a store. Later, since he was a World War I veteran, he got a job with the Navy in Newport.

At one point, when he worked in Somerset he would skate back and forth across the river to work in winter.

I had two sisters and one brother, who was three years older than me. Our older brother was killed by an automobile in front of our house when he was six years of age. Grandmother had asked him to go out to tell the iceman to leave two blocks of ice instead of the usual one. She thought that the iceman was on our side of the street but he was going in the other direction, which required that my brother cross the street. He was waked in our home, which was the custom at the time. I was about three at the time and, noticing that my brother had a mole on the side of his face, I asked my mother if the mole was the reason he died.

My grandfather had chickens in the back yard. I also kept chickens, and the roosters would crow in the morning just below my sister's bedroom. She had to keep her window closed and she certainly complained about it.

When my youngest sister was born, I was about nine years old and didn't know that my mother was pregnant; I had no idea where babies came from. Before we went to see the baby in the hospital, my father bought me a pocket watch—we called them "potatoes" then—and when we went in to see my mother, I was surprised and thought, *where did this kid come from?*

On Sundays, I would put on my suit and attend Mass at St. Ann's Church, although later I sometimes skipped church to go camping.

I had all the freedom I wanted, which was unusual then. I could come in as late as I wanted, although Mom would wait up for me. I never did anything wrong, though, so my parents trusted me. If I did do something wrong, I would get punished.

During the Depression, we were all in the same boat. When my brother was killed, my parents received a settlement of $2,000. My mother helped us to survive the Depression by taking out ten dollars each week for us to live on.

My father had a car and put it up on blocks in the wintertime. He took off the tires and wrapped them in newspaper. Why he did this, I don't know; it didn't seem to make any difference in preserving the tires. He then emptied the radiator, since there was no anti-freeze then, only water. He took out the spark plugs and pumped oil in the cylinder walls. There was no point in having a car on the road in the winter when you couldn't use it because the roads weren't plowed.

**School Life**

I started school at St. Ann's School, and then transferred to the Susan H. Wixon School. From there, I attended Diman Vocational School [now Diman Regional Vocational Technical High School] when it was located on Third Street, in the building where Lizzie's Restaurant was once located. Before that, the school had been located at what is now the parking lot opposite the entrance to the state armory. After Third Street, Diman moved to the Hartwell Street location, then to where it is now. I took the machine shop course and had to learn a lot of math as part of the course.

**Recreation and Entertainment**

The neighborhood had its own local jargon. For example, the Park Theatre (where Dunkin' Donuts is now at the corner of South Main and Globe Streets) was always called the "Park Show." The shows were ten cents and part of the show was sitting up front and watching the rats run across the stage into the seats to feed on the popcorn that was dropped on the floor. No one seemed to see them. They didn't bother me; I was an animal lover. Like other theatres in the city, the Park had a dish night during the week.

Beginning about thirteen years of age, I would go camping in the Freetown-Fall River State

Forest with friends. We would take the bus out to the end of the line and walk from there to the Assonet Ledge and other sites in the forest. We would go camping in the winter, when there were no bugs. One year, we went camping there from Sunday to Thursday after eighteen inches of snow had fallen.

I would also go camping with the Boy Scout troop at Camp Noquochoke on Pine Hill Road in Westport.

At Christmas, we got small presents. When I turned twelve, I got a bike. I wore that bike out. I loved it. I was still riding it at sixteen. I went everywhere on that bike.

In the summer, we took the bus to Bliffins Beach or Lannigan's Beach, which was near St. Vincent's Home. We also rode our bikes to Stafford Pond to swim. At other times, we took the bus to Island Park [Cashman's Park, Portsmouth, Rhode Island] to swim there.

To pass the time, we would throw rocks in the Taunton River. Or we would sit by the stormwater/sewage outflow at the bottom of South Park [now Kennedy Park] and watch the sewage go by. Under the railroad bridge at the bottom of South Park, we would wait for a train to approach. We would get under the bridge and press ourselves against the walls as the train passed. The engineer saw us and would give us a blast of steam as he passed us. Nothing much, just for fun. We would also jump on train cars when they were decoupled in the switchyard.

For sports, I played soccer, baseball in the CYO [Catholic Youth Organization] league, and basketball. We kids had a loose league of touch football and played at South Park. We even played a team from Island Park.

When I was younger, we played hide and seek, kick the can, and other games. If we found a can, we would stomp it with our heel and it would wrap around our shoe, and we would then walk with it making a noise on the sidewalk. This lasted for about ten minutes. I also roller-skated around the whole city with my metal roller skates.

I made a "scooter" by taking an orange crate, attached 2x4s to the bottom of it, took a pair of skates apart, and attached them to the 2x4s so that I had four wheels on it. It was handy because I could put stuff in it. We propelled the scooter by pushing it along with one leg while the other leg was in the orange crate. Sometimes, two of us would propel it along, the person on the right using his right leg and the person on the left using his left leg. We could really make it go with two kids propelling it. Once we went down Townsend Hill and hit a bump. Some kids painted their scooters. They were all over the city; orange crates were in short supply because they were in such demand since everyone was making scooters.

In my teens, the guys would converge at Lambert's Drug Store to plan what we would do that evening or day. We would than go to a teen dance or some other destination. Lambert's Drug Store was located at Middle and South Main Streets.

The Circus would arrive by train and unload at the bottom of Columbia Street, to the rear of where the used car lot is now. Next, the circus would proceed up Broadway to the circus grounds as a "circus parade." Horses would pull cages with lions and tigers. A calliope on a horse-drawn wagon would provide music. We would sit on an embankment where St. Stanislaus Church is now or where Schwartz Lumber was once located on Broadway opposite Sprague Street.

We older kids would go to help set up the circus in exchange for free tickets. We would go early in the morning to set up chairs in the tent. We set up a chain of kids and passed the chairs from kid to kid. We would help out all morning in other ways also. Our reward (free tickets) got us seats in the bleachers, the worst seats in the house.

Elephants and horses set up the tents. Harnesses that looked like old fire hose were placed around the elephants and they pulled on the ropes that raised the tents. Once the tents were raised, side flaps were hung on them. There were three rings in the tent. The best seats were in the middle where the best entertainment was held. Girls stood on horseback and elephants stood with their front legs on the backs of elephant in front of them and marched along.

**Neighborhood Experiences**

The East Main Street neighborhood was a mix of French, Polish, some English, and Jewish, who were mostly merchants. It was quite a mixed neighborhood. The ethnic churches influenced where people lived. The Irish lived on that part of the East Main Street closest to St. Patrick's Church. The French were concentrated around that part of the street nearest St. Ann's Church.

Everyone had Victory Gardens during the war.

Dr. Prial's home was a brick house near the beginning of East Main and that was considered the nicer part of the street.

The ragman would come down the street with his horse and wagon and call out, "Rags! Rags!" He would take both rags and bottles. He would weigh the rags and pay you based on the weight. Some persons suspected him of lifting up the weight cradle to shave off some pounds.

Our milkman had a horse-drawn wagon, and the horse would know right where to stop for the milk deliveryman to make his deliveries. The horse knew the whole route. When the man came down from making a delivery, he would organize his empties in the wagon and, meanwhile, the horse would move along and stop at the next right address. At the end of the run, the horse would take the wagon back to the horse barn on Peckham Street all by himself. He even stopped at intersections to allow cars to pass. The milkman came from the Hood Dairy. Milk was bottled there and a big barn was located next to it for the horses. The Charest Dairy also served the neighborhood. The milk came from dairies in the towns surrounding Fall River. The Guimond Farm dairy was located on Bulgermarsh Road in Tiverton [Rhode Island].

I remember walking down Kilburn Street next to the King Philip Mill buildings. Every building was one huge roar. You wonder why the buildings didn't fall apart. Then, at noon, it was as if someone pulled a switch and everything went quiet. I think the mill noise is why many people in Fall River talk so loud.

Only one road was plowed, and that was for the trolley and later the bus route. The city didn't own plows then. The Eastern Mass Street Railway Company owned Walter's plowing company, which cleared all of the trolley and bus routes. Eastern Mass later offered the plows to the city, but they didn't take them up on the offer.

You could get a bus pass that allowed you to ride all week. Sometimes, on Friday nights, riders who only used the pass to get to work during the week would give it to others who used it during the weekend. There were always ways to get around the system, as when a person would get on with a pass, go to the back of the bus, and hand the pass to another person who would use the pass to get on the same bus.

There was one fellow who had a job but his sister did not. Since Cash Street was the point where the fare went from five cents to ten cents, his sister would get off at Cash Street to get the bus as her brother got off.

There was a Krupa's Hardware Store and a Krupa's Furniture Store next to one another on East Main Street for the longest time. There was a Polish enclave in the neighborhood.

At the northwest corner of Globe and East Main Streets, there was a Bernards Dry Goods, which also sold clothing. Malinowski's Market was the first supermarket in Fall River and included pushcarts. They didn't last because the Stop and Shop chain opened a store under the Globe Mill on Globe Street.

There were many mom and pop variety stores on East Main Street and a number of barrooms also. Plourdes was a bakery shop on East Main Street.

At the corner of East Main and Hamlet Streets was the home of Skippy Bread. It was a popular bread and unique in that the store gave out coupons. You could save the coupons and buy gifts with them. Gifts included things like an American Flyer wagon, although we usually cashed them in early and got composition books instead. They made the bread there at the site. The Rousseaus owned it. It was located where East Main Street begins, where the aluminum place is now.

Nearby, on South Main Street, Hartley's Meat Pies was a favorite place, with people lined up to get in.

The placing of the Prince Henry statue at the intersection of Pleasant Street and Eastern Avenue was not well-received in the French community. The statue was called "Prince Baba" (for some unknown reason) by French residents. Toilet paper was wrapped around the statue to bring attention to the way Prince Henry was sitting. In retaliation, the Portuguese kids would put horse manure below the horse of Lafayette at Lafayette Park.

In spite of this, both the French and the Portuguese kids liked each other. I remember that in the summer, when it was very hot, the city would open the showers at Lafayette Park. Kids loved it, and we would run back and forth under them, whether or not we had bathing suits on.

The Lebanese also spoke French, which may be why they were drawn to the Flint. The Lebanese were called Syrians in those days. The Portuguese were concentrated in the Alden Street area near the Espirito Santo Church and school.

I remember the Firestone fire. It just took off. We were sitting on a wall quite a distance away, but we could still feel the heat.

I vaguely remember when my father took me to South Park to see Franklin Roosevelt when he came to the city, but I was too young to remember it.

I remember the first night that the trolley was replaced by buses on East Main Street. I couldn't sleep and looked out the windows every time I heard a bus. Buses were not a common sight in the city at that time. I wanted to watch every bus go by. Airplanes were a new thing, and every time a plane went overhead we stopped what we were doing and came outside to watch.

It was a nice neighborhood; everyone got along.

**Work Life**

My first job was working as a paperboy for the French newspaper *L'Independent*. I had a good section of the Globe that included many French residents. Later, during the war, I was a paperboy for the *Herald News*. The weekly charge for the paper was twenty-four cents, and no one let me keep the penny as a tip. People were still feeling the Depression, I guess.

My first real job at age fourteen was working as an usher in the brand new Center Theatre. Me and a group of six to eight friends were the first ushers there. We received twenty-five cents an hour, which was the minimum wage. I needed a school card to work, which was obtained from the School Department.

**Military Service**

I joined the service at seventeen in 1946. However, I wanted to stay home for the Christmas holidays, so I didn't go in until January, 1947. Because active duty benefits ended in December, 1946, I lost out on a lot of GI benefits by delaying joining until January of 1947.

In the service, I was stationed with the Military Police in the District of Columbia. My outfit guarded the area around the Capital. Once, when I was guarding the entrance to the White House, I was in charge of dropping the chain when persons arrived, including the President, and had to salute. When the President's limousine traveled down Pennsylvania Avenue, it would be going seventy miles an hour. When it approached the White House, it would be going forty-five miles an hour. Once, when President Truman abruptly arrived at the gate, I fumbled with the chain release and the chain dropped just in time. As the President's limo passed me, I saluted and at the same time bent over to take a look at the president (I was about six feet tall) and made a swooping motion as I did, following the car as it passed.

# Rolande (Pelletier) Giroux

*Born on June 16, 1931*

### Family Background

I was born at 103 Earle Street. We were all delivered at home by Dr. Archambault, who made house calls and delivered babies at home. When my youngest sister Anita was born, my mother was very sick, and the doctor wanted my mother to go to the hospital, but she refused. She was afraid that there would be a baby mix-up. A woman came to our house to help with the housework and care for us children. She had a child in tow with a big beautiful top that I wish I could play with. Her son guarded it with his life, so I never did get to touch it.

My mother was Laura (Gendreau) Pelletier. She came from Canada at the age of seven and lived at 103 Earle Street until she moved to 47 St. Joseph Street. Her father owned 103 Earle Street and many of the family members were born there. My mother was very hard-working and very family-oriented. Family was very important to her; the family could do no wrong. My mother had a lovely singing voice, and everyone knew it, as she sang songs all day while working around the house. Consequently, I have a large repertoire of French songs but, unfortunately, I did not inherit her voice.

My father was Dominique Pelletier and he came from northern Maine, just below the Canadian border. He met my mom when he was a soldier at Fort Devens during World War I. He was a cabinet maker and worked for the Puritan Stores, a small chain of grocery stores. He would make wooden walk-in coolers and various shelving and display furnishings for produce, etc.

When he lived in northern Maine, my father was a logger. My father once told us that the camp for the loggers would move as the logs moved down the river. In the evening, the loggers would break up and spread bales of hay and take a long woolen blanket and unroll it over the hay. That would be the bed for the loggers, who slept in a row under the blanket. In the morning, they would roll the blanket up and put it back in the wagon.

My father had considerable artistic skills. At one point he had carved a series of miniature circus figures. He teamed up with a partner, who had a gift of gab, and hit the fairs showing the figurines for an entrance fee. One season, at the Brockton Fair, his partner fled with their money and my father was stranded in this area.

This all happened before he met my mother. He then worked as a carpenter and it was my uncle, with whom he worked, who introduced him to my mom. My parents married late in life, after seven years of courtship: my dad was forty and my mom thirty-three. My grandmother was sickly, and my mother took care of her until she died, then they were married.

His later artistic work included carvings and paintings. His carvings and paintings were in the French Canadian style and included scenes from his logging days, horses, and other subjects. My daughter has a degree in art and she has most of my father's remaining art work.

My mom and dad had three boys and three girls. I was fourth in the family. My older sister had to fight for her rights to shave her legs, wear deodorant, wear makeup, and date, and I benefited from her victories, as did my younger sister, who was given more freedom than I had. I remember my father was always on the front porch stretching when we dated and came home in a car. No lingering in cars was allowed.

My father owned the first Pontiac in Fall River, which he lost in the Depression.

My husband is George Giroux [George's interview precedes this one in the book]. We were married on May 30, 1952.

**Family Life**

When I was two years old, my family moved from 103 Earle Street to 47 St. Joseph Street, across from St. Joseph's Orphanage. After I married my husband, George, at Notre Dame Church, we lived on St. Joseph Street and my son was born there.

I remember hearing that my grandfather had cows on Earle Street and some off of County Street. The cows would be milked and the milk put in big milk cans and sent off in horse-drawn wagons to a local dairy.

My grandmother died before I was born. I well remember my grandfather who died at age ninety-three. He always told interesting stories and always had Canadian peppermints in his pocket, which he shared. He smoked a pipe, so the peppermints were covered with tobacco most of the time. We readily brushed it off and didn't mind. My grandfather limped a lot from an injury in the forest, and walked with a cane. In his later years, he lived in Hartford, Connecticut, with my aunt and uncle. He would come to spend weeks at a time to our house and then moved on to other cousin's houses.

When I was eleven years old, my mother went back to work in the Shawmut Mill. Every Thursday, she would take orders for Friday's lunch from Mark You Restaurant. She would give me the list and I would go to Mark You's to get the order before noon on Friday with my brother and we would carry the large order in his wagon to the mill. We traveled down Quequechan Street to the mill and the guard would wave us in to the mill yard. The mill was so noisy; then, at 12:00 o'clock, a big boom would occur and everything became quiet. We did this every Friday for a year.

Everyone came to our house; that's the way it was done in those days. We had cousins who lived in Westport [Massachusetts] who were dropped off early in the morning by their father before he went to work so the kids could go to Notre Dame School, and my mother would feed them breakfast.

My chores included assisting with the cooking, such as peeling potatoes. Everybody helped, including my brothers, who washed the floors. All the children had jobs outside the home, such as running errands for the neighbors, babysitting, or anything that people were willing to pay us to do. Going to parochial school was expensive, and I remember that when my sister and I were at Jesus Mary Academy, my brother Ed worked for the nuns to help pay for out tuition.

My brothers kept chickens at 47 St. Joseph Street in a yard that we shared with the residents next door. The roosters crowed every morning. My brothers also kept pigeons in the yard.

My father's birthday was on the 14th and mine was the 16th of June. When I was very young, I told my father that I wished we were born on the same day of the year, instead of two days apart. When I mentioned this, he told me a story of how on June 14, 1931, a little black baby was delivered, but on the 16th, happily I arrived.

Our cousins in Connecticut had a sick mother and their father brought the children to Fall River and placed the boy in St. Joseph's Orphanage. The girls went to Jesus Mary Academy as boarders and were treated very well. Their brother didn't fare well there. My mother would invite them to our house for Christmas, holidays, and Sundays.

We didn't have a refrigerator until I was thirteen. We had an icebox that was filled on a regular basis, with a card put in the window (the card said "yes") to let the iceman know if we wanted ice that day. The iceman came down the street every day. When the iceman went upstairs to deliver the ice, the local kids would chip away at the ice in the wagon.

We had no phone for a long time, and we would give our neighbor's phone numbers to guys that we met and wanted to call us. When the neighbors were called, they would knock on our door and say, "You're wanted on the phone." It was embarrassing. When we got a phone, I was about fifteen and it was a four-party phone. You had to wait your turn to get to talk, but it was worth it. Such a luxury!

Our family had a dog named Clipper that liked to chase cars and persons dressed in black. Men in black seemed to be a favorite target of Clipper. My brothers would get the dog going by yelling out a magic word and the dog would dash to the window and start barking. Sometimes, my brothers would open the door and the dog would go flying out and chase the man, who would back up the street facing the dog.

**Food and Meals**

My mother always made a big breakfast for us. We never left home without eating. She often made a large pan of what seemed like a coffee cake.

There were no sweets in the house. A sweet snack consisted of a piece of bread with milk and sugar on it. We walked around eating the bread (there wasn't too much milk on the bread). Sometimes, evaporated milk was used. One drink that my mother made was a mixture of milk, eggs, and cocoa.

Gorton [French-Canadian pork spread] was cooked slowly all night long on top of the stove.

**School Life**

I went to Jesus Mary Academy for the first two years and then to Notre Dame for third to eighth grades. In my time, Jesus Mary had grammar grades. I was advanced to second grade at the age of six. My brothers and sisters taught me how to read before I went to school. In the first grade, boys and girls were together; then the remaining grades were girls only. Dr. Anctil was in my first grade class. There was a fence between JM and the Prevost School yard and we were expected to stay away from the fence.

The children in the first grade and kindergarten were mixed together at JMA. Unlike today, if you could follow the instruction, regardless of age, you were promoted. Consequently, at age six I was in the second grade, and at age sixteen in the twelfth grade. We wore uniforms both at JMA and Notre Dame. In grammar school, the uniforms consisted of black dresses with detachable white collars and cuffs for laundering. Rubber collars and cuffs were also available. In high school, we wore navy blue jumpers with JMA insignia on the upper left side. We wore white blouses. The proper length was required and cleanliness important.

I graduated from Jesus Mary in 1948. Our graduating class was only thirty-two persons.

Some of the nuns switched from Jesus Mary and Notre Dame Schools. JM had boarders and they were usually treated especially well. Aunt Mere Marie Eymard, my mother's sister, was a JMA nun. She was the local artist, taught classes, and had her own studio on the premises. It smelled of paint and oil and I loved to go there. When my daughters were old enough, I would bring them there on Saturday mornings for lessons. My daughter Gayle acquired her love for painting there and now has a degree in it.

I was a member of the Notre Dame School drill team. We practiced drill routines, had uniforms with capes with gold on one side, and marched in parades.

**Recreation and Entertainment**

The whole neighborhood played stick ball, free-the-can, giant steps, aggies (goo-goo's and pickers), and bunny hole, played by girls. Bunny hole consisted of digging a hole about four inches deep and throwing a marble toward it from a certain line in the ground. You then took turns to roll your marble toward the hole (similar to golfing) but with your bent index finger. The first one to get their marble in the hole won.

We played in the road because there were hardly any cars. It didn't matter if you were a big or small kid, everyone played together. We jumped rope in the schoolyard until the bell rang. I also played "secrets," where we would bury things in the yard and put a piece of glass over them, then cover them over.

We ice skated at the pond at the Narrows between Route 6 and the railroad tracks at the Robillard and Napert's Boat Houses. We checked our shoes in the cabinets. Winters were much colder then, and ice would stay on the pond all winter.

The Strand was a favorite place to go; we paid ten cents a show. Dish days were every week and families collected the full set.

We would also go to Lincoln Park and Horseneck Beach; we would always find a way of getting there.

**Neighborhood Experiences**

Everyone spoke French on Pleasant Street. There was a major Jewish commercial presence on Pleasant Street.

Bshara's Restaurant, located on the northwest corner of Pleasant and Notre Dame Streets, was a popular place. The owner of the restaurant was an avid pilot and enjoyed flying over the Flint and "buzzing" Pleasant Street. Rumor had it that one day he flew with his wings vertical between the steeples of Notre Dame Church, and he lost his license because of it.

Lafayette Pharmacy was located at the southeast corner of Pleasant and Cash Streets. Former Mayor Talbot owned it (which later may have become Talbot's Pharmacy). Lafayette Pharmacy was a gathering place for all the locals. There was a soda fountain there and a popular drink was a Coffee Cab (a milk shake with ice cream in it). If you had a little health problem, they made suggestions for a relief or a cure.

Parker's Candy Store was located near the Strand Theatre and Kennedy's Butter & Egg Store. Cute guys worked there, and I would always eager to tell my mother, "Mom, I'll go get the coffee for you." It always smelled nice inside Kennedy's. I remember that sawdust was spread on the floors of other stores that carried food.

There was also a cookie store on Pleasant Street and my mom would buy two pounds of broken cookies at a discount price. Having various cookies to choose from was nice because we could get anything in the selection.

Margaret's Bakery on Pleasant Street made excellent salmon and meat pies. On paydays, we would stop there and order a slice from various pies and bring them home in a box. Most bakeries baked beans for housewives and kids would bring the beans to the bakery in their wagons.

We would also get chicks at the pet store at Easter; the store was located near Bshara's.

I remember trolley tracks on Pleasant Street, although I don't remember the trolleys.

**Christmas, Holidays, and Special Occasions**

Christmas was not the commercial event that it is today. The emphasis was on the birth of Christ. That was more important than gifts. All of the kids would have stockings filled with an orange or a tangerine, some nuts, and candy canes. Oranges and tangerines were not everyday things in the house. We would receive one gift, and we were very pleased.

Attending Midnight Mass was a big thing in our house. I recall that Eddie Bouchard was a wonderful singer and would start singing "Minuit Chretien" (which in English is "O Holy Night") at the stroke of midnight, and you could hear a pin drop. He would begin very low, so you could barely hear him, then he would graduate to such a powerful pitch that it gave you goosebumps.

After Midnight Mass, my mother would have a Réveillon, or time of celebration or awakening. She would serve tourtière, or a large French meat pie. Everyone would come over to our house and everyone, even the kids, would have a little wine.

One Christmas, my twelve-year-old brother developed a ruptured appendix and had to be rushed to General Hospital to prevent blood poisoning, where he was hospitalized for a long time. We were all so happy to see him come home and, when he did, someone had given him a couple of very large oranges. Large oranges were not an ordinary thing around our house, and my mouth was watering for one of them. We all understood that he needed these to get better, and that's what we wanted.

**Work Life**

At the age of sixteen, virtually all of my cousins had to quit school and went to work. I was lucky, and my parents encouraged us to finish high school, which was uncommon at the time in our circles.

My brothers, as was typical at that time, gave their pay envelopes unopened to my mother, and she gave back five dollars for the week for spending money. This happened until you reached twenty-one, then we paid board. I never got to pay board, as I was married shortly before I turned twenty-one.

While I was young, I babysat and prepared people's hair; I always helped. I was also a good seamstress and made my own wedding gown.

I first worked at Firestone and at Anderson Little. I then worked at Charlton Memorial Hospital and remained there for over thirty years as a ward secretary and later as a unit coordinator. I started at Truesdale Hospital, but later we merged with Union Hospital and became Charlton Memorial Hospital.

**The Depression**

Everyone was in the same boat; it was a good life. Our family was never on relief; my parents were too proud to do that. My father was lucky to occasionally have a job, mostly, during the Depression. I envied the kids who were on relief because they had neat clothes, something like a military uniform. They were not stigmatized for wearing those clothes because so many persons wore them. Sometimes, kids would wear coats that would be down to their ankles, since "they would grow into them."

My father was not always employed during the Depression. When there was no work, we scrimped and made do. Neighbors and family always helped one another and shared what they had. Hand-me-downs were the mode of the day, and it was always an adventure to get new used clothes. We all had Victory Gardens planted in any little spot of dirt available.

Neighbors would get blocks of cheese and peanut butter from the relief agency and they would share it with us.

The feed for our chickens would come in cotton bags that had attractive patterns printed on them. We would wash them and make them into pillowcases or make them into dresses.

We had no telephone or car and we never traveled. Providence seemed very far away.

All of the people in our parent's generation, in our circles, thought that FDR [Franklin Delano Roosevelt] was the savior of man. He found innovative ways to put people to work, and things started to get better.

## Hurricane of 1938

We remember the steeples of Notre Dame Church wobbling and swaying in the intense winds. Later, the weakened tops of the steeples had to be shortened. I remember chimneys falling, windows blowing out and electricity failing.

## World War II

I remember that there were ration tokens given out to families, depending on the family's size and their needs. Red tokens were for meat, that I remember. There was one for gas and, if you had a job working for defense, you would be allotted accordingly. I remember that you couldn't buy nylon stockings, but the black market was rampant and, if you knew the right people and had the money, you could get these things. People also tried horse meat, and we had that experience, unknowingly. A friend of my father's came over with what he said was a beef treat and, although the meat was tough, we didn't mind it. He later told us what it was, and we were all upset over it.

# Margaret (Donovan) Griffin

*Born on April 3, 1920*

## Family Background

I was born at 101 Fenner Street, a four-tenement house with two bedrooms in each tenement. We lived on the first floor.

My father was Timothy Louis Donovan. He died at ninety-two in 1978. My mother was Margaret Mary (Murphy) Donovan. She died in 1945.

My father's brothers were James, William, John, Patrick ("Parky"), and Michael Culkin (my father's half-brother, when his mother remarried).

My father's father was a Donovan and passed away when my father was young. After her husband died, my father's mother married Michael Culkin, and they had a son also named Michael Culkin, my father's step-brother. My father's mother was an O'Leary.

My grandfather Murphy helped build St. Patrick's Church. He and Grandmother Murphy lived upstairs over us on the second floor at 101 Fenner Street. He was a weaver in the King Philip Mill. Grandmother Murphy was seventy-five percent Scottish and came over in the steerage of a ship with the cattle. She used to say, "When the cattle were fed, we were fed."

My siblings were Catherine ("Kitty"), born in 1917, Margaret ("Peggy"), and Louis.

My husband's name was John Griffin.

We had ten children and they are named Angela, Timothy, John, Veronica, Joan, Paul, Danny, Margaret (Margie), Joyce, and Michael (born ten years after Joyce, when I was forty-two).

## Family Life

We were poor, but we didn't know it; we always had a clean, warm house. We always had fruit in season, and all our clothes came from Cherry and Webb. Lots of other children worked in the mill. My mom always watched her pennies, though. The five of us were clothed for one-hundred-and-four dollars a year. I know that because my mom would give me two dollars a week to pay the Cherry and Webb cashier for our clothes.

My mom did all of our washing by hand and on a washboard. She was a wonderful cook and made delicious meals every day. Breakfast was usually eggs with bread, butter, and tea. Sometimes oatmeal, but never with lumps. My grandmother's oatmeal always had lumps.

My mother was brought up in the Globe, in the Slade Street area. Globe Village extended to the Tiverton, Rhode Island, line.

In our house, there was a main room when you came in the door that was the dining room, the living room, and the kitchen—all in one room. My father and mother had one bedroom and me and my sister Catherine had the other bedroom. My brother, Louis, slept on the living room couch. We heated with coal and later oil. We paid two dollars and fifty cents a week for rent.

Grandmother and Grandfather Murphy, my mother's parents, lived upstairs. The Palmer's (my mother's sister Catherine and her husband) moved in with our grandparents on the second

St. Patrick's Church on South Main Street

floor. Since the second bedroom was used by my grandfather because my grandmother was sick, my aunt and uncle slept in one of the unheated attic rooms. In the wintertime, they had to bring up a hot water bottle or a heated brick wrapped in a towel to take off some of the chill.

When we needed coal, my father would go into the cellar and shovel the coal into a hod and put it into the stove. We were cold, but my grandparents were always warm because the heat rose to their apartment. They could walk around in their stocking feet.

My father was a homebody and never smoked. He had a daily shot of brandy at home.

My uncle, Jimmy Murphy, was a painter of houses. When Aunt Catherine and her husband were going to move in with my grandparents on the second floor, Uncle Jimmy painted the attic bedroom walls pink for their sleeping room. There was no bathroom in the attic, so they had to use a commode that they kept out in the hallway. Since the hallway was all open up to the attic, someone asked if my cousin Barbara (who was nine or ten years old) wouldn't feel exposed when going to the bathroom, but she said no; you need to do what you need to do. There was just a toilet in the house, not a bath. On Saturday evenings, we all took turns taking a bath in the main room in a galvanized tub.

Catherine worked in the King Philip Mill. She smoked and loved to come down to see my mother iron. She would stay for two hours, chatting. My mother never smoked. My mother ironed everything. On Mondays, she washed and dried clothes and ironed them that night and put them away.

The wife of my mother's brother John Murphy died while undergoing an operation. They had a son, Francis, and my uncle John and cousin Francis came to live with my grandparents, where they had meals in my grandparents' house and slept in the attic rooms. One Halloween night, Francis and his friend (who were both sixteen) brought a rowboat in the back yard. He was in his last year in Durfee [B.M.C. Durfee High School]. He was really smart. At the age of ten he put on plays and at the age of fourteen had set up a printing press in the attic. He was good at it and sold leaflets to various customers.

The rowboat had pontoons on it and he reassured my mother that the boat couldn't sink. It was a bitter cold Halloween night. Later that night, his friend's parents came to the house and called up to my uncle, "Mr. Murphy, is Francis home? We're worried about our son." I remember having a strange feeling when I heard that. Both boys disappeared and were never heard from again.

A year later, my aunt Catherine got a call to come over and identify a boy that was found in the river, to see if it was her nephew. She couldn't identify the face because it was unrecognizable. However, Francis had worn two pairs of pants that night, and the boy had two pairs of pants on. The ice had kept them under water until the spring. At the burial site, my aunt went out cold.

My father's half-brother from his mother's second marriage was Mike Culkin (he was the son from my grandmother's marriage to her second husband). He was a blacksmith and lived on Fenner Street. He was in World War I and worked for General "Blackjack" Pershing. Mike shoed Pershing's horses during the war. When my parents married, Mike gave them a horseshoe for good luck. I gave it to my son Michael, who had it over his door. It is an Irish legend that you have to turn the horseshoe upside down when you hang it; otherwise the luck will run out of it.

When I was in the ninth grade, we had a strange incident. My father had a thermometer hanging on a cup hook on the wall. One day, out of a clear blue sky, it fell. My father said, "How did that fall? It was on a cup hook." This was about 6:00 pm. The next day, Mike Culkin, who lived on Palmer Street, said that my father's brother Jack had passed away at 6:00 pm the previous day, about when the thermometer fell. Jack worked for the *Fall River Herald News*. My uncle Bill Donovan was the advertising manager. My father couldn't get along with his stepfather and went to live with his older brother Bill and his wife for a while.

My uncle Patrick, or "Parky," was called Dapper Dan, The Kid Glove Kid, or the Count of No Account. He wore spats. He taught me how to tie my shoe laces in the unique way that he was taught in the Army. He visited us twice a day and would talk to us for a while. He lived on the fifth floor of an apartment house at 1020 South Main Street. At 6:30 pm, or so, he would come again. He had lost his fingers in a mill accident. They were stubs. He devoted his life to taking care of his mother. When he lost his fingers, he and Granny went on welfare. Their apartment had kerosene lamps and no electricity. It was all that they could afford. They had a coal stove that made the kitchen awfully hot in the summertime. Parky smoked and rolled his own cigarettes.

My mother ironed all of the altar linens for the convent and for St. Patrick's Church. She didn't wear white at her wedding. My mom was highly religious and went to bed on her wedding night fully clothed, shoes and all. It probably took my father a while to persuade her.

**Food and Meals**

When I was five years old, I went to St. Patrick's School. We would go home for lunch. We had all the milk we wanted. Mom didn't use tea bags; only loose tea.

My father came home for supper. We had such meals as pork chops, steak; mom always asked for the best pork chops and steak. For dessert, we would have pies or puddings. Every Sunday, we would have a ham or beef brisket. My father made tapioca pudding or Jell-O with sliced bananas with whipped cream. It took some planning to vary the meals and make them delicious.

My mother was not much of a baker. My father would ask my husband to make an apple pie. They were great. He made chicken patties also. He would take bread, put it in water, squeeze out the excess water, and put it in baking cups and in the oven to crisp up. Then, he took chicken and made a cream sauce with peas and filled up the bread cups. They were wonderful.

Mom would get brown bread sometimes. When it had raisins in it, she called it "fruited." Scones weren't called that back then; they were called "sea foam biscuits." We had hot cross buns during Lent, but there were no crosses on them in frosting, as there is today. Bread was ten cents and a quart of milk was ten cents. In-between we would have jam, peanut butter, fruit, and milk. There were no leftovers. Every day, my mom would go food shopping.

When we were young, we never had a turkey for Thanksgiving; we had chicken. Later, when we had turkey, my father would stuff it.

Dinner was what we call lunch today and supper was what we call dinner.

**Recreation and Entertainment**

When we were kids, Aunt Catherine Murphy Palmer (from the Palmers from Steep Brook) would slide down the street with us. We thought that it was great that a married woman would slide with us. Uncle John Palmer was a Fuller Brush Man and later a driver for the Eastern Mass Street Railway buses.

We sat on the wall on Cook Pond a lot; my shoes were scuffed in the back from hitting them against the wall on Dwelly Street.

**Work Life**

My father worked for Hudner's Market and then for the Marshall Hat Factory. After that, he worked for the Globe Mill, where he met my mother. She was a spooler there. My father went to the Herrick's Institute on Franklin Street nights to take the civil service exam. When they were first married, my mother made more money than my father because he wanted to take the civil service exam to be able to work at the Torpedo Station. He passed it, and went to work as a machinist at the Torpedo Station in Newport [Rhode Island].

My father made twenty-six dollars and thirty-two cents a week at the Torpedo Station. My father never opened his envelope but gave it to my mother. For extra money, he would go to Hartley's Pork Pies once a week and buy pies to bring to the torpedo works. He was known as "Pork Pie Tim." He sold the pies for two for twenty-five cents. He made five cents for every two pies, or thirty cents a dozen. This was his spending money for the week. He paid someone two dollars a week to bring him to Newport. He tied the stack of boxes with sailor's rope and brought them to work that way. They allowed him to sell the pies at work. We never got any pork pies ourselves. People thought that he brought all kinds of donuts home to his kids when they saw him with the stacks of bakery boxes.

There were thirteen in my husband's family and they were poor. He worked in Landry's Market delivering groceries one or two days a week. Then he worked for Western Union delivering telegrams. He also worked on those large coke trucks at dad's company at the Gas Company. Then he went into the Army. My uncle was on the Governor's Council and got him a job with the state.

**Neighborhood Experiences**

Fenner Street was a melting pot. It was mostly Irish, a few English, a few French, a few Polish, and maybe one or two Portuguese. We all got along very well. Fenner Street at that time wasn't paved. We would roller skate and play jacks and tiddlywinks on the entranceway linoleum. Dodgeball was a favorite game to play on the dirt street; there were not many cars that came down Fenner Street.

I met my husband going to band concerts at South Park [now Kennedy Park]. The Park Theatre was not named that; it was called The Park Show. My mother would go get dishes there; she had the complete set. It cost ten cents to go on Saturday afternoon. Near the Park Show was a place we called "The Ice Cream Parlor" [The Nonpareil]. It was run by Dr. Bounakes' family, Greek people. A fellow would come into the Park Show and sell his candy; you can't do that now. There was a Lebanese candy store at Globe Five Corners (not Globe Four Corners!).

A man came by Fenner Street once a year and played the bagpipes. My grandmother from Scotland would go running out and give him some money. She had a picture of Bobby Burns on the wall. She had a thick Scottish brogue.

Townley Dairy delivered milk to us and, when snow was on the ground, would come with a horse and sleigh. We got two quarts of milk a day at home and some at school in the morning and afternoon.

There was a Mr. Bor, a red-headed Jewish man, who came around with carpets and other things for sale.

My mom went to a small First National [grocers], and there was a small A&P down the Globe on South Main Street, between Dwelly and Globe Streets. It was a good-sized A&P. There was an L&B Market on South Main Street; the French speaking went to that. There was Leddy's Bakery, Lomas' Bakery, and Ogden Bakery. Leddy's would save me the edges of the squares and put them in a bag for me. I loved hermits. I grew up with John and Ruth Leddy. We went to St. Patrick's School together.

On East Main Street was Charlie Michaud's Meat Market, where the French usually went. We would then go to Malinowski's Market on East Main, which had wonderful Polish ham. Mom liked that store because they would treat children the same as a grownup.

At the Flatiron Building at South Main Street and Broadway was Sunderland's Furniture Store. My parents bought their furniture there when they married.

I don't remember the lamplighter coming around; I only remember electric street lights. But, on Fenner Street, there was an old gas street light that was still there when I was growing up.

The Parkers across the street always kept chickens. Gabe, Dick, Edmond, and Cyril Parker had a music group that played at the Moose Hall. One of the Parker sisters was snatched off a roof of a cottage in the 1938 hurricane.

**Christmas, Holidays, and Special Occasions**

At Thanksgiving, the Park Show sponsored a turkey raffle. My father won the first turkey, and everyone applauded as he went up on the stage to get it. Then he won the second turkey and, when he went up to get it, everyone booed. There was a meat butcher next to the Park Show, and the meat cutter took care of preparing the turkey. One Thanksgiving, at the height of the Depression, Bishop Cassidy brought in a big turkey for the kids at St. Patrick's School. I remember the bishop saying, "All right; dig in."

At Christmas, we always had a real tree, never an artificial one. A few weeks before Christmas, my father would go get a tree, about five feet tall, and put it in a pail with rocks. We would go out into the street and get rocks. He wrapped the pail in Christmas paper to hide the pail. We had boxes of ornaments and each year we would have a new box. Our thrill would be to throw tinsel on the tree. People passing by on Fenner Street going to work at the King Philip mills would admire our tree and its lights.

My mother made her own cranberry sauce and my father stuffed the turkey for Christmas day. For dessert, we had plum pudding with hard sauce, and was it good. My father's boss' wife, Mrs. Handy, from Common Fence Point [Portsmouth, Rhode Island], made it.

**Downtown**

Saturday, we would go downtown and go in and out of the 5 & 10s. We walked there and all the way home. We would stop on the benches to rest. We would always go to Leddy's Bakery to get whipped cream cake, with real whipped cream, not the awful stuff you get today from some places.

**Religious Life**

We were in church a lot; my mother was devout. There was the benediction at night in the churches and the stations of the cross at Lent. I was in the choir for a few years.

One day, when he was living with me, John came in and said that his finger was itching. He kept rubbing it against the door, but it wouldn't stop itching. He said that he might be getting a wart. All I could see was three red dots. He asked me to look at it closely and I took a magnifying glass to see if there was something in it. I told him to hold his finger under the lamp so I could see. When I looked into the glass, my heart stopped. There was Jesus with his chest opened and his heart showing. His heart was pumping. I couldn't believe my eyes. Jesus gestured to me with outstretched hands. I looked at John and back into the glass. I said, "I don't feel worthy to see what I'm seeing." Then I saw God the Father. John later said, "No one saw God the Father but Moses." When I looked again, Jesus was wearing the crown of thorns.

I looked at John and he said, "What's wrong, Mom; you look white as a sheet." "John, you won't believe what I just saw," I said. I told him what I just seen, and he went into his bedroom with the magnifying glass and stayed in there for a while. When he came out, he confirmed what I had seen; he saw it too. He saw the Sacred Heart of Jesus holding his robe open. Then it changed to the Holy Family. Joseph was standing there. Mary was pulling aside a blanket very, very slowly. Then, a tiny head looked up at John. It was the face of Jesus.

I stood right over there and said, "John, don't tell many people; they will put us away somewhere. They won't believe it." A few days after that, Danny came in and said, "John, do you realize what a privilege that was?" John later said, "If God didn't want you to see it, he wouldn't have shown you." The first person that John told was a nun, Sister Mello. She said, "John, if that happened to me, I'd be walking around in a trance." He said, "How do you think my mother and I feel?" John was devout. He prayed the fifteen-deck rosaries, not the five.

The Purification of Mary came from when women were considered unclean after childbirth and went to a priest for purification. Once, after having one of the babies, I went to our priest and asked to be purified. He said, "We don't do that anymore," but I wanted to and he said, "Come to the altar rail," and he said some prayers over me.

**Health and Illness**

At the torpedo factory, my father was called "Dr. Donovan." He had all kinds of remedies. For poison ivy, my father once made a mild solution of lye and spread it over the poison ivy. "Let me know when it stops itching," my father said. He soon washed it off and there was no more itching.

At the torpedo factory, people would say, "You go ahead [to the doctors], I'm going to see the old man in the tool crib."

My father always said that he didn't want to interfere with the doctors, but if the doctor gave up on someone, he would help. There was one case where the doctor gave up on one of the McQuinney boys. He had stepped on some broken glass and the wound got infected. Mrs. McQuinney sent for my father and he heated a knife and put a "drawing salve" on it. He put a big hunk of salve on the boy's foot. A few days later, a boy came to the door and my father asked, "How's your brother?" "No, It's me," he said. "My mother wanted me to come to thank you for what you did for me."

Any friends who had injuries, my father would take care of it. He made a salve called "Donovan's Dynamite Liniment," made from some kind of plant.

We were always being given laxatives. One was a piece of sulfur put in the mouth. Another was senna leaves and a mix of figs. Stewed prunes and other nature's remedies were meant to keep you regular. Feen-A-Mint laxatives were another product. They were horrible brown pills.

**Popular Expressions**

Some of the sayings we used were "high mucky-mucks" and "hoity-toity."

# Joseph A. and Theresa Claire Guillemette

*Joseph was born on November 15, 1921, and died on May 24, 2014*
*Theresa was born on January 18, 1926*

**Family Background**

Joseph's father was Joseph Guilmette. He was born in Canada. Joseph's mother was Maria Goupil. She was born in Canada and was a squaw in the Iroquois Indian Nation.

Joseph has no siblings (except for a younger sister who died as a baby), and was born on Beden Street in Westport, Massachusetts, which is located behind Lincoln Park.

Theresa's father was Hermengilde Bellefeuille. When in the service, he changed his name to Henry. He was born in Three Rivers, Canada. Theresa's mother was Diana (Caron) Bellefeuille. She was born in the United States.

Theresa had one sister, Henrietta B. Dowling.

Theresa's mother named her Claire Theresa, since she liked the name Claire, and that is the name that she was always known by. However, she didn't know that her real name was Theresa Claire until she went to work. She was born at 169 Horton Street and was married from there.

As a child, Joseph lived in one of the upper floors on the northwest corner of Pleasant Street and Notre Dame Street.

Joseph and Theresa were married on July 20, 1946. They have two children: Ronald and Alfred.

**Family Life**

*Joseph*: One day, when I was about twelve years old, I accompanied my mother on a shopping trip to Woolworth's, next to the Strand Theatre. I really wanted a set of roller skates, and I saw a set of skates on display next to me for eighty-nine cents a pair. My mother said that we couldn't afford them. However, her package had room for skates and I put them in her bag.

One day, I put on the skates and met another boy who had just got his skates. I asked him how to use them and he said just let yourself go down the street. All of a sudden, the door to our house opened and my mother said, "Hey, come here. I didn't buy you any skates." She told me to take them off and said, "Come with me." We went to the store. However, the clerk spoke only English and she spoke only French. He took the skates and thought they were the store's. "What should we do about this?" he asked. My mom said, "Punish him." As he put the skates away, he said, "This is stealing. I'm going to have you come to the store to work." I worked there for a week. Customers would come in and ask me, "What are you doing here?" I would say, "I'm helping out."

The store person said, "I could have called the police. Don't ever do this again." I was so thankful. I told him, "Anytime you need me, I will help you." He said, "I told your mother that I would do something to you that you would remember for the rest of your life." Did I ever remember it! I never took anything again. And I never did get the skates.

*Theresa*: I had only one doll when I was young, and every November the doll would disappear. Then every Christmas, the doll would come back with a new outfit. My mother made new outfits for the dolls of me and my sisters. One year, she made Eskimo outfits from cotton rolls. I still have the dolls. She would get dolls from the Salvation Army that had lost an eye or a leg, fix them up, and make new clothes for them to give to us.

*Joseph*: One year, I took my father and mother to Canada to visit my father's sister that he hadn't seen in ten to twelve years. When we got there, they greeted us on the porch and everyone was speaking in French and they said let's go into the house. Everyone was sitting down and the younger persons were talking about the trip and other things. Finally we realized, after about an hour or an hour and a half, that my father and his sister were just sitting there and weren't talking at all. "Why aren't you talking? You haven't seen one another in twelve years." They said that they enjoyed just looking at one another and enjoying one another's company, and that was enough.

When I was a baby, I spent the night in jail. When I was just a baby, my parents went back to visit relatives in Canada. However, no one told them that they needed papers to get back into the United States. They had to stay over in Canada so, as a baby, I spent the night in jail. The next day, they got help with the papers and crossed back over.

My father worked for Clement, who built homes, and did various contracting work. Sometimes, Clement would tell my father, "I'm going to take the gang to Newport [Rhode Island]; do you want to come?" My father asked me if I wanted to go and I said yes. We kids rode in the back of his truck with open gates. We left at 5:30 or 6:00 in the afternoon and, as it was getting darker, my father and Clement would say, "Won't the kids get scared?"

However, we played games to amuse ourselves. Sometimes, it was so dark that the driver couldn't see the edge of the road. The lights on the truck were not that bright and we would go about fifteen miles per hour. It took about three hours to get to Newport. The kids in the truck sometimes had to look back and guide the driver so he would stay on the road.

*Theresa*: I lived at 169 Horton Street. Across the street from us lived the LaFrance family, the family that now owns White's Restaurant. We had chickens in the yard. My grandmother (my mother's mother) lived with us. When she talked, you listened. We were brought up very strict. My aunt, her daughter, was a cripple and the whole neighborhood loved her and would take her out to visit. She took care of the kids one day a week.

When I was five, my mother became ill and me and my sister had to go to St. Joseph's Orphanage. We were there for five years until my mother got well. We would come home when she felt good enough. My mother recovered and died when she was ninety-three or ninety-four.

The orphanage was a good place. We had our chores to do to help the nuns. I placed the plates on the table for meals. I remember the oatmeal being very thick (I can't stand oatmeal to this day), but it was thinned out with milk. Some nuns were nice and some were rough. One of my fingers is now crooked because once I complained to a nun that this finger was sore. They ignored me until it became infected. When my mother visited on Sunday, she spotted the finger and complained to the Mother Superior, who asked me, "Why didn't you show me this before?" I said, "Sister didn't want me to." From then on, they listened to me because they knew that my mother would be there. Other kids weren't so lucky.

My father's first car was a new Chevy that cost nine hundred dollars. They talked about it for three months before they bought it. It was black. I wanted a two-tone colored car, not a black one, but my mother said, "We'll go with black; we might have to use it to go to a funeral." I was about twelve years old when we got the car. We were considered to be rich because we had a car.

I met Joe at a Halloween party at the Howard Johnson's at the Narrows. I was fifteen. Joe and his friends were hosting the party and Joe was the master of ceremonies. I won first prize, which was two framed metallic cupids, which I still have. I made a date with another boy at that party and wrote his name on the back of one of the frames, and the name is still there.

We couldn't go on a date alone but had to double-date. On one date, my cousin dated Joe and I dated someone else. After that, I started going with Joe.

*Joseph*: When they lived in Canada, my parents lived on a farm with others. They were very poor. They worked all day and then it was time for supper. In those days, the women had only two dresses and they didn't want the dresses to get dirty. In the summer, when my mom and her friend on the farm walked the lunch out to their husbands, they put on only an apron. When they approached their husbands, they wore the apron in the back (so people in the house couldn't see their backsides) and when they came back, they switched their aprons to the front.

*Theresa*: We always thought that the story was made up, but she always insisted that it was definitely true.

We went to Canada one time to visit relatives who lived way in the woods. They were so far in the woods that they had few visitors. Joe's mother was smart and put toilet paper in the trunk of the car. The bathroom was outside in an outhouse. We kept walking and finally reached the outhouse, which was quite a distance from the house. It seemed that the outhouse wasn't used much, since there was a mound of dirt in front of the door. We had difficulty opening the door, but finally we were able to open it enough to get Joe's mother in the door. However, Joe's mother was little stocky, and when she opened to door to come out, the door wouldn't open enough and she couldn't get out. I couldn't open the door and ran back and began yelling for Joe and his father to come. It took a while for them to come and to move the mound of dirt, but we finally got her out.

After that, we went to the toilet in the open, which I didn't like at all. Joe would keep watch. Once, a cow mooed nearby and I couldn't go to the bathroom after that. I was sick from it.

Brodeur's Red and White Market was further up on Horton Street. My mother would send me to get things from the market. I loved hot dogs and would steal a hot dog from our package on my way home. My mother complained to the store owner, "You're short-changing me on hot dogs." He replied, "It's not me; check for holes in the hot dog package."

*Joseph*: My father made beer during Prohibition. We lived above Gaudreau Pharmacy on the northwest corner of Pleasant and Notre Dame Streets. He sold beer from our home. He had lots of friends. A mug cost twenty-five cents. One day, Mr. Gaudreau came upstairs and said to my father, "Hey, Joe, you have a leak in your vat and it's coming through the ceiling downstairs. If Jack Borden (the policeman on the beat, who lived on Mason Street) sees the mark, you will be going to a place that you don't want to go." It was a good thing that they told him.

My father used Blue Ribbon malt to make the beer, which could be bought anyplace.

At the Notre Dame School, there were parties where kids made arrangements. Parents came to see them. The nuns made wonderful things. At one of these events, a kid rigged a stool with a rope on it and when his father went to sit down, the kid pulled the rope and moved the stool as his father was about to sit down. His father fell on his fanny.

When I got home, I decided to do the same. When my father was bottling his beer, he used the same kind of stool. So, I rigged the stool and pulled it out from under him. My father fell and broke two bottles of beer. He was very upset and chased me around the house. I hid under the bed. He tried to fish me out with a broom, but I escaped.

One day, I stayed home with a cold. I said to my mom, "I want to go out." A policeman was parking his car and told me to watch his car as he went to Gaudreau's to eat. I got into the car and released the break. The car began moving down Notre Dame Street toward Pleasant, crossing Notre Dame Street as it moved toward Horvitz Furniture. I put the break on and the car stopped. I was scared. The cop came out and said, "What happened to my car?" I said, "I saw the car moving and was afraid that it was going to hit the another car, so I got in and pulled the break." The cop then said, "Thank you. You did a wonderful thing for me!" I was about twelve at the time.

During Prohibition, moonshine was made locally, including in the Maplewood area. The place was on Stafford Road, near where the fire barn is located. The moonshine was brought to the Flint by boats on the South Watuppa Pond. The person in the Maplewood area who made the moonshine found out that my father made beer (my father would go there to buy food) and asked him if he could store some of the moonshine on his property between two sheds. He could make a few hundred dollars by doing so, a lot of money then. My father was afraid that the police would find out about it. There was enough space to store fifty large bottles of moonshine between the sheds. During the week, they would pack the space four containers high. No one knew about it.

If someone came to the door and wanted a bottle, my father would give them the key and they would take out what they needed.

*Theresa*: My mother was very active in feeding soldiers that came to town. Every Sunday, my sister and I would bring them to the house for dinner. They were always very respectful. Once, when she was running out of coupons for sugar and other staples, she said that she would have to stop hosting the soldiers. However, when she told Dr. Canuel, he got her extra coupons so that she could continue to welcome the soldiers for dinner.

Dr. Canuel, whose home and office was a few houses up Second Street from the Lizzie Borden house, did lots of good deeds. My cousin was trying to undo a knot in her shoe lace with a fork and the fork slipped and went into her eye. She was disfigured and blinded in that eye. The doctor saw her and said that she shouldn't have to live her teen years with a deformed eye, but she was resigned to having the deformed eye for the rest of her life. He personally paid to have her sent to Boston to a specialist to have the eye checked and fixed (which he paid for). He did lots of good deeds like that. His wife was a piano teacher.

**Food and Meals**

*Theresa*: On Sunday, we had a roast or anything that might be on sale. For the next three days, we had leftovers from the roast.

*Joseph*: We had the same as all French Canadians. I liked beans and we had eggs and toast for breakfast. Everyone had shelves in the cellar for canned goods. My mother canned every kind of vegetable that she could get cheap. Pickles, tomatoes, anything that the garden would grow, she canned. We would go to my uncle's farm in Westport and they canned a lot there. There was no floor in the storage cellar.

*Theresa*: On Fridays, we bought big pots of beans to Poirier's Bakery to be cooked overnight for our Saturday meal. It cost fifteen cents. Kennedy's Butter Store had all kinds of different butters in barrels. When they cut a piece of butter, the weight was always what you asked for. There was a Minkin's Meat Store on Pleasant Street. Hamburger cost either fifteen, eighteen, or twenty-one cents a pound, depending on the grade. Once my mom said to get the eighteen cents grade and I got the fifteen cents and she wasn't happy.

## School Life

*Joseph*: Mother Superior was a tiny person and she had a clapper. It was about two to three inches wide and each clapper was about one-half inch thick and make of hard wood. One clap was to get in line and the other was to be quiet. A third clap meant that someone was in trouble. You put your hand out and she would hit it. They really didn't know they could hurt you with it. My hand is now deformed because of being hit with the clapper [the knuckle bone on the index finger of his left hand is severely deformed]. If you got punished at school, you had better not bring it home. The teachers were always right.

*Theresa*: Some nuns were nice and others were mean. One teaching nun at Notre Dame School saw that I was having problems with algebra, no matter how much I tried. She saw that I was trying but couldn't get it. She then asked me if I wanted to stay after school and she would help me to try to learn it. And it worked; I began to learn it.

## Recreation and Entertainment

*Joseph*: Friends of the family would come to play cards every night. I would have to go on my bed to do my homework. We had no money to do much else.

*Theresa*: We listened to the radio and crocheted or knitted. We would go to Lincoln Park. We would walk to save a dime. If we missed the bus, which came by about every hour, we would walk all the way to Lincoln Park. It was different walking then; there were no cars like today. When we were small, Lincoln Park was just a picnic grounds when it first opened. A big outing was to pack a lunch on Sunday and go to Lincoln Park. There were just a few amusements at first.

My sister worked as a checker at the Lincoln Park Ballroom. Me and my girlfriends would go to the LP rink to roller skate. There was a Mr. Gamache there who measured girls skirts to make sure that they were not too short. The hems were not supposed to be more than six inches above your knee. When he measured us, we bent forward to lower the hems. My mother made me a velvet outfit to go roller-skating in at Lincoln Park.

*Joseph*: My uncle worked at Lincoln Park. We didn't need tickets to get in; he would just say, "I'll take care of it." Every day, my uncle was in charge of walking the roller coaster to check for dangerous situations.

*Theresa*: For entertainment, we kids would play ball or kick the can. When the street lights went on, however, you had to come in the house. That was the signal to come in, and we had to. We had a mean neighbor. If a ball went into his yard, he would keep it. We would take cans, put holes in them, and thread long strings through the holes and walk on the cans, like stilts, holding the strings. It would make quite a racket. The neighbors would call the cops on us, and then we would run and hide under the big bushes on the edge of the LaFrance property. When the cops left, we came out. Meanwhile, while we were at it, we went into the neighbor's yard and got our balls.

We girls would roller skate down Horton Street together, with two or three girls holding hands as we skated down the street. There weren't any cars on the street then; we had the street all to ourselves.

We learned songs from music sheets that we bought at the 5 & 10. Each of our girlfriends would buy a single music sheet one week and another girl would buy another sheet the next week. They were part of a songbook. The sheets were ten cents each and had two or three songs on each sheet. Then, we would learn the songs from one another. We would also learn songs from the radio. Sometimes we would write different lyrics to songs. One of our favorites was "Always in My Heart." We listened to Perry Como, Bing Crosby, and Frank Sinatra, among others.

There were lines to get into the Strand Theatre. They showed two full-sized movies, with a Flash Gordon serial, a cartoon, and the news, all for ten cents. That was how our parents got rid of us on Saturday afternoon.

*Joseph*: We would go up in the balcony of the Strand with balloons and go to the men's room to fill them with water. Then we would aim and throw them over the balcony below. We would hear people below yelling, "Oh, my God; what happened?" When the ushers came, we would say, "It couldn't be us."

*Theresa*: At the Durfee Theatre, our group of girls would wait until the scariest part of the movie (we had seen the movie before) and then pop the bags that we had blown up. People would scream. We did this three or four times. When the ushers came, they threw the guys out, not us.

Across the street from Gendreau's furniture store (and Cash Street) was the Star Theatre. It was on the second floor above a bowling alley, with access from Cash Street. It cost us five cents and we sat on boxes.

People drank a lot then; played cards and drank beer.

The destruction of the Durfee Theatre was a real loss. Great names appeared there, including Liberace and Frank Sinatra. We would go to the Durfee and then to the Eagle Restaurant for a chow mein sandwich.

We five girls went to the wrestling matches at The Casino on Morgan Street every week. We screamed so much that we lost our voices. The matches were very popular. Wrestlers came in from Boston and were big names and later appeared on national television.

*Joseph*: My father's brother had a farm in Westport, and from Fall River the rail track went into Westport, not far from Division Road. One day, our uncle Alfonse said, "Let's go to a nice place." Ten of us followed the railroad tracks into Westport to the Highway Casino on Route 6. As we went along, Alfonse did what he had done many times and knocked over the outhouses that were next to the rail line. He would say, "This is what we used to do, but don't you do it," as he knocked over another outhouse. He knocked over a total of four outhouses on the way to The Casino.

When we got to The Casino, my uncle divided us up into younger and older boys. The older boys approached The Casino windows in the rear, where the shades were not pulled all the way down. The boys looked in to see the showgirls changing clothes. Some of the boys were shocked and said, "Oh, my God, what would my mother say?"

*Theresa*: In the winter, there were few cars, and we would get four or five sleds together to slide down the streets. Once, we went over an ice bank and I cut my head and was bleeding. My mother was sick in bed and my father was working (and therefore not reachable). I was brought to St. Anne's Hospital. The doctor instructed the nuns to cut my hair. As the nun pulled up my hair to cut it, I screamed (we had full heads of hair that we pulled up then). The doctor said that the cutting need not be done, and I was given seven stitches in my head.

**Work Life**

*Joseph*: My father worked at the Westport Factory, where the stream comes out of Lake Noquochoke. His brother worked there before him and lived in the house next to the mill (later Bishop's Package Store).

One day, a Mr. Goyette came in our house to have a beer with a friend. Mr. Goyette refinished floors, and he told my father, "I think that you are the man I am looking for." The next day, he picked up my father and they went to Newport to work on some floors. As soon as my father was shown how to sand the floors, he got an idea of how to do it faster. However, he didn't want to seem like a know-it-all after being one day on the job. But my father did mention something to him and Mr. Goyette replied, "Well, if it's better, let's try it." My father got the machines ready in a test area. It worked out well for my father's technique. Goyette came back and said, "You know, you are the first one that I've hired that knows more than I do. I'll keep you for a long time."

My father continued to work with Mr. Goyette, who had a place on Stafford Road and two to three trucks. He and Goyette got very friendly. He decided that he didn't want to make beer any longer and started working for Mr. Goyette. He stayed to show others what to do when the crews went out.

One day, he was at Notre Dame Cemetery and found that they needed a grave digger. He talked to the priest at Notre Dame and the priest said, "Tell them you're interested." He started at Notre Dame and retired from there.

There was an old guy who worked for Amiot Hardware on Pleasant Street who came to work at the cemetery for a few hours a week. My father said, "We got this guy who we tell what to do and he does it for us." Often, when digging a grave, the side of a previously-buried coffin would break open. In that case, the coffin had to be dug out and the body taken out of the coffin so the coffin could be repaired and reburied. They got this guy to take the bodies out of the coffins, since no one else wanted to do it. Mr. Amiot found about it and told the guy, "Don't go there." But the guy replied, "I like it. I'm helping those people who died."

Digging graves in those days was done by hand shovel. Sometimes, when my father was digging a grave, the walls of the grave would collapse in on him and he would have to dig himself out. He didn't want to quit grave digging, even when he reached seventy-eight years old, but he was forced to quit because of his age. He said, "I don't want to go, especially now that the job is getting easier [because of the use of back-hoes] and the pay is better."

*Theresa*: My first job was working at Kerr Thread for thirteen dollars a week for a forty-hour week. After getting my envelope on payday, I stopped on the way home to get a chocolate cake for the family to celebrate my first pay. It cost fifty cents. My mother was very upset that I opened my envelop and spent part of my pay. My father fixed it up with her. It helped that the cake was for the family, not just for me.

I hated it at the Kerr Mill. My mother worked there and she taught me how to do swift spooling. She taught me how to do a swift spool knot; if done right, the knot would go through the eye of a needle. After six months, I was laid off. I said good; I'm not coming back.

From there, I went to work at the Shelburne Shirt. I trimmed cuffs. My hands would swell from the motion of cutting the cuffs to the point where I couldn't put my hands in the scissors. It was piece work, and if you didn't meet the goals, you would get called on the carpet in front of the others. When I couldn't meet my quotas, the girls would chip in and help me meet them.

My girlfriend worked at the Cape Cod Shirt Company (on the top floor of the Wampanoag Mill). She and I would go to lunch. I wanted to leave Shelburne Shirt and asked the supervisor at Cape Cod if I could work there. He asked me to start practicing on the sewing machines during my lunch hour to see how good I could become. They later hired me, and I stayed at Cape Cod Shirt.

I was a button sewer on shirts. When the buttons fell on the floor, the supervisor would say, "Pick up the buttons." I had long hair then, and once when I bent under the machine to pick up the buttons, my hair got caught in the rotating shaft under the machine. These shafts were supposed to be covered, but they weren't. My hair wrapped around the shaft and all of my hair along the top of my head was pulled out. Only the hair along the side of my head was left.

I was brought to the hospital and didn't want anyone to see me, including my son. I was in a four-person room, which made matters worse. My face was so swollen and black and blue that my mother didn't recognize me. I was out of work for three months; my hair didn't grow back for three months. I had to get psychiatric help to get over it.

**Neighborhood Experiences**
*Joseph*: When I was very young, we lived on Harrison Street, two houses from the public school. Next door to us, on the corner of Notre Dame and Pleasant Streets, was Bshara's Restaurant (which had been Gaudreau Pharmacy before). The Simon family had a variety store nearby. We went to Letendre & Boule for groceries. Across the street (near the Paradis Funeral Home) was Minkin's Meat Market. At that time, there were separate stores for meat, vegetables, butter, and other items.

Where White Rose Bakery is now on Pleasant Street, when I was about fourteen or fifteen years old, there once lived an Indian chief on the second floor. Below him was a barber shop. In the big window in the apartment, the chief would hang various Indian decorations. People would stop to take pictures of the decorations. He was very friendly and would bring people upstairs and show them how the decorations were used in ceremonies. He was very nice. He later bought a house in Tiverton off of Stafford Road, just over the Rhode Island border.

Horvitz Furniture was on the northeastern corner of Pleasant and Notre Dame Streets and Gaudreau Pharmacy (later Bshara's Restaurant) was on the northwestern corner. We lived above Gaudreau's.

*Theresa*: People wondered why Notre Dame Church faced away from Eastern Avenue. However, my mother said that when the church was built, Eastern Avenue didn't exist [like it does today] in that area; it was all woods, so the original wooden church was built facing the center of town. Most of the labor was done by members of the parish.

**Christmas, Holidays, and Special Occasions**
*Theresa*: When we were young, New Years was bigger for the French than Christmas. It was a big thing. Everyone had their own special way of making food. Families gathered in a house or rented a hall. It was also a good excuse for liquor and getting drunk and having fun. Joe never had a Christmas tree until we were married.

**Courtship and Marriage**
*Joseph*: Our dates were roller skating or ice skating. Once, when we visited my cousin who lived in Maplewood, we thought that we had lots of time so decided to walk back home. Since we had our skates, we said, "Let's skate across the pond," which we did. Near Kerr Thread, I knew that there was an outlet of hot water, so we skated further into the pond to avoid it. However, the ice began to crack as we skated along it and we had this sensation that we were going to not make it. But we made it to the Narrows.

*Theresa*: We did lots of walking on our dates. We also went dancing. Usually we would go to the movies or go bowling. We dated in groups. On Sunday afternoons, we would stay at home and play the roller piano and sing. Then Mom would cook dinner.

**Downtown**

*Theresa*: Saturday morning, we would go downtown. It was the big trip of the week. We would meet everyone on the bus. We would go up South Main Street and make stops along the way. One place we would stop at to have a cup of coffee. My uncle Alec (Alfonse Bellefeuille) owned a variety store on Spring Street. We would stop there and he would give us candies and I would read comic books in the back of the store. Everyone went to McWhirr's and Cherry and Webb. Back then, there were no credit cards and every store gave credit. You would pay one or two dollars a week on your account. They trusted you, and there were no problems.

**Health and Illness**

*Theresa*: When someone was sick, he or she was taken care of at home by the family. The doctor gave us the medication from the meds that he had in his bag. We had no drug stores.

Whenever the patient died, the funeral director would come take the body to be embalmed then return it home in a coffin for viewing, which would last three days and nights. We would stay with the body, to pay our respects, day and night; we had twenty-four-hour vigils. After this time, the funeral would be held in whatever church you belonged to.

South Main Street, looking north

## The Depression

*Theresa*: All of my family worked in the Kerr Thread Mill. My mother worked two to three days a week. It kept us away from welfare. The mills cut hours for everyone so everyone could stay employed.

My aunt was not so lucky. Her family had to go on welfare. She got three dollars and fifty cents for rent and the rest was provided in food. Everyone would help others. My mother would say, "Take this food to your aunt." My aunt would make three meals on what my mother gave her.

When Joe and I married, we made twenty-five dollars a week but ended up with ten cents for spending money.

## World War II

*Theresa*: When Joe went into the service in 1941, he wanted to get engaged. However, I knew that if I got engaged, my mother wouldn't let me step foot out of the house. I told Joe, "I know that you will be dating other girls and I want the chance to date other boys."

My sister and I belonged to the USO downtown. On Sunday mornings, we would go there and fix breakfast for the servicemen. We couldn't date any servicemen. We danced and would go on buses to the USOs in either Newport or to the Cape at Camp Edwards. We would get there in the bus, go in the hall, and then get on the bus again to go home. We couldn't go out of the hall, otherwise we would be out of the USO. We had good meals there that we couldn't get at home because of the rationing.

During World War II, we were given horse meat to replace beef. It was very lean. Joe's mom said that she would never eat horse meat. However, I used to buy horse meat and hide it from her. She used to brag to other women that she had steaks and hamburger at home. Finally, she asked me, "How come this meat is wrapped in this paper and this other meat is wrapped in this other colored paper?" Finally, she found out.

*Joseph*: We were in a movie in Providence and, when we came out, we heard that Pearl Harbor was bombed by the Japanese. I joined up with my friends Ernest and Nap. All three of us came back. I was an artillery radio man in charge of communications. I served in France, Belgium, and Germany. I received a citation from the people of France for my service there and corresponded with people in France years later. In France, Bing Crosby came to visit us in the service. I went into the service in 1941, right after Pearl Harbor.

## Popular Expressions

*Theresa*: There was a barn and a garage on our property. We kept chickens in the yard. You know the expression "running around like a chicken with his head cut off," well that's true. My grandmother killed chickens in the yard by cutting their heads off. The chickens would then frantically run all over the place with their heads off until they dropped.

# Frank Bennett "Brud" Hadley

*Born on July 18, 1932*

**Family Background**

My parents were Robert Clyde (born May 4, 1890) and Mildred (Miner) Hadley (born July 14, 1900).

The family residence was on Linden Street, the home of my father's parents, James Frank (born February 19, 1856) and Emma (Fruin) Hadley.

My mother's parents were Dwight Maxwell (born January 30, 1864) and Ida S. (Russell) Miner (born April 8, 1866).

My great-grandfather, J. Gillis Hadley, came from Manchester, New Hampshire, and became treasurer of the Durfee Mills. This was a complex of ten or fifteen mill buildings located on the corner of Bedford Street and Plymouth Avenue. He made a hundred dollars a week. I have a pay check issued to him on March 13, 1876, for one hundred dollars, when a six day pay check to a factory worker was five to six dollars. The mill treasurers ran the mills and approved all expenditures.

My mother's family was from Nantucket, but she was brought up in Taunton [Massachusetts]. My grandfather, Dwight Miner, was a graduate of Williams College and was a science teacher in Taunton. My grandfather was bright and picked up thirteen languages he could speak. Because he was so fluent in so many languages, he was hired by the Air Division and carried on correspondence with France concerning the Air Division's business with France during World War I. When he graduated from college, he went to Germany to learn science. There, he would "trade" languages with others. He traded English for German, French for German, etc.

One of my dad's aunts, who's name is now lost, lived a block south of the family homestead and visited 237 Linden Street regularly. The family story goes that she was quite the busy body and even checked Grandma Hadley's garbage to make sure she wasn't throwing away food that could have been used.

On one of her visits, she came across some of the boys in the middle of a project of moving the outhouse in the back yard. You could not use the pit indefinitely. You have to dig a new hole, move the outhouse over onto the new hole, and fill the old hole with dirt.

The boys had completed the task and were tamping down the old hole with their shovel when the aunt in question happened upon them and strongly suggested that they should do a better job of tamping by jumping on the covered earth. She then proceeded to demonstrate the proper method of tamping by hiking up her long skirts and jumping with both feet onto the newly filled hole. Of course, she went right through the dirt to the treasure below, thus immortalizing herself in the Hadley family legend.

My father's siblings, in order of birth, were Charles McClellen (born 1876), Frank Bennett (born 1877), George (born 1879), Josiah (born 1886), Plummer (born 1888), and Mary (born 1892).

My mother's only sibling was Harold Sheldon Miner. He had a very commanding voice. When Uncle Harold spoke, there was no contradicting him.

When Harold was going to law school in Washington, he was secretary to Franklin Delano Roosevelt when Roosevelt was Secretary of the Navy. When Roosevelt left that position, he wanted to make sure that his secretary got a good job. So, Roosevelt got him a job at Manufacturer's Trust Company in New York City, where Harold became vice president. This is the bank that held in its vault the $64,000 for the television program, "The $64,000 Question."

When Uncle Harold graduated from law school in 1915, he was president of his class. The speaker was William Jennings Bryant. After dinner, Harold had the honor of introducing Bryant. Harold later became the first treasurer of CARE, Inc. As part of his work for CARE, he traveled around Europe and met people like Konrad Adenauer and Nikita Khrushchev of the USSR. He was a pretty influential guy.

There are stories of witches in both the Hadley and Parsons families. Susanna (North) Martin, a widow of about seventy years of age, was hanged as a witch in Salem in 1692. Her only child married a Hadley. From that child, the Hadley clan evolved. Jane Martin's daughter was in her thirties when her mother was hanged, yet she continued to live in Salem. Imagine living in a town that hanged your mother?

My parents had three children: Harold "Buck" Miner Hadley (born July 11, 1920), Marylin "Mac" Roberta Hadley (born April 18, 1924), and me, Frank "Brud" Bennett Hadley.

I have lived on the following streets in Fall River: Valentine Street, Weetamoe Street, Florence Street, Langley Street, and Madison Street.

My wife is Virginia Ann (Parsons) Hadley, and we were married in 1954. We have four children: Robert, Karen, Christopher, and Patricia.

**Family Life**

I was born at 578 Valentine Street in the front bedroom. Except for college and my time in the Air Force, I have lived all my life within a mile of my childhood home.

My first recollection was when I was six and I went downtown with my friend of seven. I couldn't read all of the words on the front of the bus and whether the bus read Robeson or Rodman. He taught me how to distinguish between "Rod" vs. "Rob" in the bus title. My mother gave me twenty-five cents, five cents for the bus downtown, five cents for candy, ten cents for the movie, and five cents for the bus to get back home. Sometimes, I spent the second nickel on a candy bar and walked home. Today, who would allow a six year old child to go downtown alone?

My dad was a really great cook. My mom didn't like cooking. Aunt Mary and her mother were great cooks. My mom didn't want to compete with them. Dad cooked on Sundays, Easter, Thanksgiving, and the big meals.

My mom loved doing homework assignments with us; she loved doing papers with us. Once, Miss Williston had us do a notebook on South America. My mother loved the project. She helped us with the cutouts and in putting together the history of a particular country. A friend (Dick Mann) had a bandsaw and cut wood for the front of the notebook. We cut out an outline of South America and glued it to the cover and put holes in the book. We put a leather thong through the holes for a binding and burnished "South America" on the wooden cover. This project got an A.

For May Day, we kids would make May baskets. The baskets were decorated with flowers and pastel colors of blue, yellow, etc. We filled the baskets with candy and cupcakes and anything

Buck, Mac, and Brud Hadley

that you liked. You then left the basket on the door of someone you liked and rang the doorbell. When the person came to the door, they would pretend that they didn't know who left the basket and would say, "Who left this?" and would then go looking for the hiding children. In the fourth grade, I gave my basket (with the rest of the fourth grade kids) to our teacher, Miss Borden, who was a cousin to Lizzie.

The first vehicle that Dad learned to drive was a horse and wagon. He was in his teens when the first "horseless carriage" appeared in Fall River. He vividly remembered running along beside those new contraptions and yelling, "Get a horse!"

After Dad's father died in 1898, all the boys had to work as they could to keep food on the table. Dad carried hot lunches to the men in the mills. Plummer, his next older brother, had a gas light route. Every night, he would carry a ladder and stick matches around his route and light his prescribed gas lamps along the streets.

One night, Plummer could not take care of his route and asked my dad to handle it for him. My dad says he was quite proud to have been given the responsibility. Unfortunately, it rained buckets that night, and as Dad was in the middle of the route, his matches became soggy and useless. He was so upset that he was letting his older brother down that he began crying. Just then, an elderly man came along and showed him a trick he had learned doing the same job. He pulled Dad's billed cap down hard, took some dry stick matches out of his pocket, and shoved them up under the cap band and into Dad's hair, where they would stay dry long enough to finish the route.

My uncle Frank proposed that Dad move our family to his house at 540 Weetamoe Street, assume a share of the mortgage, and own the house jointly. On the surface of things, it looked like a good idea. Uncle Frank was recently a widower and had no family, and Dad didn't have a home to call his own. So Dad, age forty-nine, gets a house, and Uncle Frank, age sixty, gets a family.

This instant family had three kids, ages nineteen, fifteen, and seven. Oh, and an Irish Setter. I don't think Uncle Frank knew what he was in store for. My father's attitude toward the friends of his children was, "This door is never locked to friends of this family. Do not knock, just walk in. This is your house too and you are always welcome here." So it was not long before Buck's friends, Mac's friends, and my friends were slamming in and out of the revolving door at an alarming rate. With a club house on the third floor, the radio on the second floor, and fifty decibels of whoever was on the first floor, my uncle Frank must have thought twice about whether or not this was a good idea!

To his eternal credit, Uncle Frank never once complained openly about his quiet home being turned into a three-ring circus.

**School Life**

I loved Morton. I went to the Highland School, but we came home for lunch; at Morton, we had lunch there and stayed all day at the school. Going to Morton was a different experience. Instead of staying in one room, we now had to go from class to class, which was quite a change of school environment. It was the first time that we had a class schedule to follow. But mostly, I liked the people there. It was also the time of life when you begin to notice girls.

I walked to Morton down the hill. Was it cold in the winter! We would run down Hood Street and get behind a garage to protect us from the cold wind; we would run again and get behind a house. When we got to the park, there was no respite; we had to run all the way to the school.

Morton School was the first time that we had organized sports, including basketball and baseball. Fred Dagata was the coach of both. Fred was on the Providence Steamrollers football team. Morton was the first school that we had that was sports-proud. We had school colors. I played basketball and baseball. There was no football in the middle grades. At that time, Henry Lord and Morton were the only junior high schools in town, but we did play against the ninth grade at Durfee.

I played the bass viol at Morton. Miss Mary Rose Sullivan was my teacher. She was a terrific teacher. The reason that I took up the bass viol is that my friend, Dave Swindells, took it up before me. They were building a city string orchestra that was practicing at the Durfee High School Tech auditorium. Dave and I carried our bass viols up the hill to the Tech auditorium. We met John Moriarty there. He was so helpful to us. He was a sophomore at Durfee [B.M.C. Durfee High School], and we were in the eighth grade. The orchestra leader, Miss Bennett, was tough, but John was nice and made it easier for us.

My teachers have included: Miss Welsh (kindergarten), Miss Wild (first grade), Miss Connors (second grade), Miss Lake (third grade), Miss Borden (fourth grade), Miss Connors (fifth grade), and Miss Hurley (sixth grade).

**Friends**

At Durfee High School, football players were my heroes. My assessment of the value of any man was based on the courage he displayed to me on the football field. I met Dave Swindells when I was four, Ron Larmane when I was five, and Gerry McNally when I was six. They are still my dearest friends. But I can tell you quite honestly there still lingers in my understanding of who they are an admiration of their football courage and determination. After a football game organized when we were in the ninth grade, I would have to include Steve Goldberg in my circle of guys to be admired. I developed great respect for Steve as he held on for a tackle after being knocked over on his back, and we were best friends right through high school.

**Recreation and Entertainment**

We played basketball in the summer and skied in North Park in the winter. The streets were not plowed when it snowed. The *Fall River Herald News* would publish the streets that the city cordoned off for sledding. The only people who could drive on these streets were delivery people. Weetamoe Street was one street that was cordoned off. A friend of mine, Alan Morse, lived on the corner of Adams and Weetamoe Streets. He skied down Weetamoe Street with his feet in the skis. He skied straight down and had no control at all. "What courage," I thought—and still do.

Our family had a cottage on Devol Pond in Westport [Massachusetts]. The day we got out

*Back row, left to right*: Brud Hadley, Herby Rosenthal, Pete Dunlap, Seymour Ellison, Goosey Santos, Murray Lovett, Dean Crook. *Front Row*: David Swindells, Phil Hudner, Saint Cummings, Buzzer Smith. *Background*: Donnelly's store, the Village Spa, taken just before the country day game.

of school, a moving van would come to Valentine Street. We had only one car, and dad drove to work, so we stayed at the cottage for the whole summer.

Some of my earliest and most delightful memories are from my Davol Pond childhood. We lived at "The Shack" on the east side of the pond every summer for the first five years of my life. There was a natural spring flowing out of the pond embankment next to "The Shack" in which we kept our perishables cool. We used kerosene lamps for light and the kids got to sleep in the loft. It was like an attic and you had to climb a ladder up into the ceiling to get to it. That was so much fun, I didn't even mind going to bed.

**Courtship and Marriage**

In the second semester of my sophomore year at UMass Amherst as a business administration major, I had to take economics as a core requirement. The instructor was a Mr. Rivers, whom we naturally named "Muddy." He was a good instructor, but the best part of Economics 101 was the good looking girl with a terrific figure who sat in the front of the class.

I made it my business to speak to Miss Virginia Parsons, only to discover that she was "pinned" to a fellow. I suffered the slings and arrows of outrageous fortune for a whole semester until one lucky day in May. A couple of fraternity brothers and I went to Greene Pond for an early spring swim and the sun break from studying for finals.

Anyone who has been in Amherst in the spring understands that one of the requirements is that you must fall in love. Miss Parsons was at Greene Pond on the blanket next to mine and we were formally introduced. We (Ginny and I) were commissioned to get some take out food for the group, which I strongly endorsed. As we were getting into my car, a 1936 Plymouth with on the floor stick shift and canvas roof, she reminded me that she was pinned. I told her that I was pinned too, which I was (to a girl named Betsy Goss), and Ginny said, "Good, we can be platonic together." I said, "Sure," but I lied. I had no more intention of being platonic with that girl than I had of joining the French Foreign Legion.

We thought it would be a good idea to study for our economics final together so we went to Mikes in North Amherst. We sat down at a table but decided to have a dance before we started studying. We put a quarter in the juke box. I was so bedazzled after that dance, I can't imagine how I ever passed that economics exam.

The course of true love, by tradition, did not run smoothly, but by the following February, 1953, as I left Fall River for pre-flight training at Lackland Air Force Base in Texas, Virginia Ann Parsons was engaged to be married to Frank Bennett Hadley II.

## Work Life

My first job was a paperboy for the *Fall River Herald News*. The cost was twenty-four cents for the paper and delivery. I made four cents from each person for one week of delivery. One person made me give him back the one cent change from the nickel every week.

My first part-time job as an adult was working for the Fall River Gas Company when I was a junior in high school. It was hand shovel work. They would begin the work with a front-end loader and then we would go in and finish it. Then, when the pipe work was done, we would go in and fill and tamp the trench with a hand tamper. We dug for mains and services. There was more hand work for residential work because we couldn't use machines on lawns.

My second part-time job was doing yard work for Shell Oil. They had us swinging the "idiot stick." This involved cutting the grass between the tanks to keep grass on the mounds down. When the foreman was not looking, we played baseball with the idiot stick and flat stones. Flat stones, if thrown, will simulate a baseball curve.

My first paycheck was thirty-one dollars from the Gas Company and fifty-two dollars from Shell for forty hours of work. Dad let me keep the money, and I put most of it in the bank. When I became engaged and going into the service, I bought my wife's engagement ring with this money.

My dad was an insurance agent. He started the agency with his brother in 1912.

When I came back from the service in 1957, I went into the business with my brother in the same agency. My dad died in 1954, and my brother was in the business when my father died. My two sons now own it. So, two brothers are still running it.

## Religious Life

There is one policy of the Congregational Church that has remained constant since the Pilgrims landed in Massachusetts, until about ten years ago. The way it was, you had to belong to the society in order to have a vote in the church. The church and the society were separate. The society ran the church, in that they invested the church's funds and directed the other functions required in the running of the church. The church, on the other hand, was the good works like the Sunday School, visiting parishioners in hospitals, and things of that nature.

That structure developed a group of people who took care of the "secular" part of the church but had little interest in the "church" part of the congregation.

When I was young, the leader of the society for the First Congregational Church was John S. Brayton. He was the CEO of the Durfee Trust Company. He ran the church from the secular side but never went to church.

The minister at the time, Lex King Souter, was a former wrestler and a professional boxer. He said to John S. Brayton, who was also an amateur boxer, "If I give you a black eye in the ring, will you come to church?" Brayton replied, "You will never give me a black eye." Well, didn't Lex King Souter give him a black eye. So, John S. Brayton went to church—one time.

The older generation was old-fashioned, and that included my dad. There was no card-playing or movies on Sundays; they were considered evil. The religious people didn't do it. On Sundays you went to church and then visited relatives and things of that nature. That was true when I was a kid, but by adolescence no so much.

"Uncle Lex" [Lex King Souter] lived a half-block away from us on Greenlawn Street; we lived at 540 Weetamoe Street at the time. He went into the service in 1942, not as a minister but as an intelligence officer in the South Pacific. When I came back from the service, I joined the veteran's group where he was the chief cook and bottle washer. He died in 1957.

He and my dad were close. My dad was superintendent of the Sunday School at the First Congregational Church and then I became superintendent of the Sunday School. Then my son succeeded me as superintendent of the Sunday School.

**Military Experience**

At the end of my sophomore year in college, I was going to be drafted. In order to avoid being drafted between my sophomore and junior year, I joined the ROTC. I could join either the Air Force or the Tank Corps. I joined the Tank Corps because it had a smaller line at registration time, and I hated lines. When I got back to school, I didn't go to the ROTC classes. Major Willoughby of the ROTC reported me to the local draft board, and he told me he did it. I signed in at the Air Force Cadets in Springfield and got accepted in my junior year.

I was sent to San Antonio for training. Then I got a notice that I was drafted. If you were in the top twenty-five percent of your class, you were protected from the draft; otherwise, you were not protected. I joined the Air Force Cadets in February of 1953, and the Korean War ended in March of 1953. Since I was already in when the war was over, I am legally a Korean War veteran for the sake of benefits, although I don't use them.

**Fall River Lore**

My mother told the story of Grandmother Miner's first cousin, Alice Russell, who was called "Lizzie's Turncoat Friend." She lived next to Lizzie and went next door to see what had happened after the murders. Lizzie was busy burning a red-stained dress. Alice asked what she was doing, and Lizzie replied, "It's a paint stain." Alice testified at the trial that Lizzie was guilty. Whenever Alice and Grandmother [Ida Russell] Miner discussed it, they told my mother to leave the room.

I ran across an envelope that had "Lizzie's Turncoat Friend" written on it. Inside was a picture of Alice Russell when she was a resident of the Adams House. The person taking the picture was reflected in the mirror. It was my grandfather Miner. I took it to the Fall River Historical Society. They loved it.

Fall River is not a melting pot. The Flint was French, the North End was Portuguese, the South End was Polish, and Bedford Street was Italian. In the Highlands, there were Jewish, Wasp, and Irish. Most of my friends were Jewish. I never mixed with the other kids until high school. We were not segregated in the high school teams.

Mrs. Brigham's father was known as Judge Benjamin "thirty-day" Cook. He got that name because he gave everyone thirty days. It was almost automatic. He said it was to give defendants time to "cool off."

**Popular Expressions**

My dad remembered that some of the nicknames for people that he knew included "Piggy" White. He didn't know why he was called that. He saw him again after twenty-five years and was embarrassed that he didn't know his real name.

My dad had a lot of sayings and good messages for living properly. When he would be driving his car he would say, "When you see children, bring your horse to a walk."

He would often say these as well: "If you are going to do a job, do it right," "Don't pick up a lazy man's load" (don't pick up too much stuff at once because it may drop, take an extra trip, it is not that much effort and in the long haul you will save yourself some grief), "Never back around a back hand" (a tennis reference that means when a shot presents itself, don't back around the ball and hit a forehand shot), "If you are going to say 'the chicken crossed the road,' then say 'the chicken crossed the road'" (in other words, don't apologize for what you have to say), "It doesn't cost any more to ride on the top half of the tank" (be prepared), and "If you do something that should be done, then someone else won't have to do it."

# Lucille (Roussell) Hadley

*Born on April 6, 1919*
*Died on May 9, 2014*

**Family Background**

My parents were Thomas and Juliette Germaine (Duchemin) Roussell. My father's parents were Thomas and Bella Roussell.

I was born on Palm Sunday in a cottage at 586 Second Street, my grandmother's house. Dr. Fecteau delivered me. My father and grandfather went to church, and when they came home, I was born.

My mother was very beautiful. My father was from Canada. He was fifteen years older than my mother. My mother was born in the same house that I was born in. After World War I, there was a housing shortage, so my mother and father went to live with my mother's parents and my mother's six brothers. It was a two-story house with one unit.

Following World War I, the Influenza epidemic broke out. My mother said that people died like flies. She remembered wagons of people being carted away. I remember her telling me that a man next door went to work one day in the morning and never came back.

My grandmother was a very large fat woman with a bun on the top of her head tied in a knot. She had been very well-educated in Canada in a convent. She came from a happy family and they did extremely well. She left Canada because the mills in Lowell [Massachusetts] and Pawtucket [Rhode Island] were looking for workers. Her father owned asbestos mines and was very rich. She married a man who never spoke or wrote English; he always spoke French.

My grandfather was a wood turner at the Cook Borden Company, located at the bottom of Durfee Street. He made many of the turned stairways [balusters] in the Highlands. He had no education whatsoever and couldn't read or write. He was an orphan in Canada and homeless. He was brought up in spurts by the Indians.

My father's parents died when I was young. I remember going to my grandmother's house; my grandmother always wore a black dress. I liked going there because she had peppermint candies in her apron pocket to give to us.

I have lived on the following streets in Fall River: Second Street, North Main Street, and Linden Street.

My husband is Plummer Hadley, and was oldest of his siblings, which included Earle, Graham, and Ruth. Earle's wife, Edith, inherited the Assonet Inn following the death of her parents.

**Family Life**

After World War II, we bought my husband's grandmother's house at 221 Linden Street. I lived there for over sixty years. My husband was thirty years old when he was drafted; we already had our first baby. He was on a LST [Landing Ship, Tank] in the Pacific. He had twenty-six hits on his LST. When he was away, the battleship *Mississippi* went down. There were five thousand men on it. The five Sullivan brothers from the Boston area went down with the ship.

We had a big coal stove, a Glenwood. My grandfather would go out to chop wood. We would burn coke if we had the money. My grandfather would go into the woods for wood, since we had no money for coal.

My father had a good job, working for a man who had a lot of property, but he lost everything in the Depression. We had to go on welfare. All we could afford for a family of five was a pint of milk from the milkman. I remember my father coming home with a pillowcase on his back. He had to go to Bedford Street to get welfare food. He was ashamed of it. It was so demeaning. We ate a lot of beans, I'll tell you. Then he worked in Newport [Rhode Island] building barracks for servicemen.

I never went on a New York boat—only rich people did—but we would go to South Park [now Kennedy Park] to see the boats going to Newport. On the lower part of the park was a big cliff, and we would go there with our mother to have a picnic. We would go there every night to watch the boats. Some people took the New York boat to Newport, then came back by streetcar.

The gypsies were sometimes in storefronts on lower Bedford Street, near downtown, where they would tell fortunes. In Ocean Grove [Swansea, Massachusetts], my mother would love to go to the gypsies in the storefronts there. My mother didn't go in to see the gypsies; she sat outside in the car with my father to see the characters coming in and out. The gypsies would come into the area every spring. We were always taught to button everything down to protect against the gypsies. They were also in Somerset on a dirt road near the back of what is now the Venus de Milo [restaurant].

**School Life**

I started school at the old Davenport School in Corky Row. When we moved to Ocean Grove, I went to the Gardner School there. We walked a cow path to school. I was six years old when we moved there and ten years old when we moved back to Fall River, where we moved to 506 North Main Street.

Morton Junior High School was wonderful. It was a new school, and everything was shiny and beautiful. Some of the best teachers I remember were George Hoar, who taught math, and Rosemary Sullivan, who was our music teacher. I took piano lessons, but there were 142 persons who were pianists in the school. Everyone played the piano in those days. I played for the chorus.

While at Morton, I won the school spelling bee.

I went to Durfee [B.M.C. Durfee High School] from my sophomore to my senior year, from 1933 to 1936.

**Recreation and Entertainment**

For entertainment, I read a lot, more reading than the family wanted. You know why? Because you would have to get glasses. At night, we would play ["Little Old Man" in French] or Parcheesi on the kitchen table covered with the oilcloth tablecloth.

When we moved back to Fall River from Swansea in the 1930s, I never could go out much, only to the library to get a book. I wouldn't go out without someone with me. Sometimes I lied and said I was going to the library.

## Courting and Marriage

As for dating, in the 1930s, you didn't go out much. My father had to know where you were. We couldn't go out after dark. When I did start to date, I had to be home by 10:00 pm. My father had to know the history of the guy I was dating. If he didn't approve of the person's family or the family had a bad reputation, he would say, "Don't bother with that family."

When I lived on Linden Street and in high school, I was about fifteen. Plum Hadley lived across the street. His aunt took him in when his parents died when he was fourteen. He told his aunt, "See that girl over there, I'm going to marry her." In those days, you didn't talk to a boy.

I was a Catholic, and Plummer was a Protestant. My grandmother was mortified that I would marry a Protestant. But he took her everywhere and was very good to her. She finally decided that he was a good boy.

My husband was a very English person. When he told his family that he was going to marry me, they said, "Plum's going to marry a French girl, but she's nice." I was so glad that they approved [she said, slightly sarcastically].

My first child was born the night of the day that my husband left California to go to the Pacific. He was on an island on the southern tip of Japan when they declared that the war was over.

My first daughter was born at Union Hospital. The City of Fall River paid the bill because my husband was in the service. I never got a bill. He didn't see her until she was two years old. When he came back from the service and we went to meet him at the Providence Railroad Station, she put her arms out and went right to him. He was in his Navy uniform. There was some kind of attachment there.

## Work Life

In 1936, I graduated from Durfee High School. Months before, my shorthand teacher, Miss O'Connor, wanted me to stay after class. I won the shorthand and typing contest at the school. There were no jobs then. A company in Fall River needed a stenographer and would pay eight dollars a week. I went to an interview on Friday with other girls and started work there on Monday. They wanted me to come in after school. I worked there, at US Luggage on Broadway, from 1936 until 1944, when I had my first baby. It was a wonderful experience for me because I learned how to work hard.

I went to work at the Accounting Center at SMU [Southeastern Massachusetts University, now UMass Dartmouth] for two weeks to fill an emergency—and I stayed for fifteen years.

Hadley Insurance began at 237 Linden Street. The Hadleys had been lamplighters.

## Christmas, Holidays, and Special Occasions

At Christmas, everyone we knew was poor. I got one good gift and one cheap gift. We had a tree that was chopped down by my grandfather. We were the first family that we knew to get lights for our Christmas tree. My mother told me stories of people in her day who actually burned candles on the trees.

At Thanksgiving, my grandfather bought the live turkey first, then he would kill it and my grandmother dressed it. My grandmother would stay up all night with the turkey. While it was cooking, my grandmother had to keep putting wood in the stove. We took turns watching the turkey and basting it.

**Health and Illness**

For chest colds, my grandmother would make syrup with sugar and water and a vanilla flavoring. She would warm up a piece of cloth, put the syrup on the cloth, fold it over, heat it up and we would go to bed with that on your chest.

If we went to the beach and got a cut, my grandfather would put chewing tobacco on the cut and then cover it up with a cloth until it fell off. I don't know how he survived.

**Food and Meals**

Gorton was made with ground pork, onions, whole cloves, and other seasonings. Then it was simmered for a while and put into dishes. The fat would rise to the top.

**Prohibition**

I remember Prohibition. I was about ten years old. My grandfather liked his drink. He made his own beer in the basement of his house. When he came home, he would go downstairs for a beer and give me a little bit of it. He would let me tap the bottles for the beer. My grandmother would complain, "Don't let a little girl handle beer."

Rhode Island was wet and Massachusetts was dry. During Prohibition, my grandfather would dress me up every Saturday and we would go to Ocean Grove and to Warren [Rhode Island] for the afternoon. In Warren, he would get his booze for the week from the gypsies.

**Hurricane of 1938**

I was working during the 1938 hurricane. Our boss let us out early. The sky was a strange color of pink and green. Umbrellas were going into the air. When I got to the Granite Block, the wind almost blew me down. My husband's sister was a young widow and lived in Riverside, Rhode Island. He tried every bridge to get to Riverside, but couldn't get through.

**World War II**

World War II was terrible for me. I was married four years and trying to have a baby. My husband came home one day after I had gone to the doctors and I said, "I'm pregnant!" and he said, "That's nice; I just got my draft papers today." And off he went. He got his draft notice the day I found out I was pregnant. He went out to sea. It was terrible for me. I lived in an apartment on Pearce Street. My boss at US Luggage said, "You can work as long as you want to; I'll cut a hole in the desk to accommodate you."

**Popular Expressions**

Everything is swell.

# Mildred (Hayes) Hall

*Born on September 27, 1919*
*Died on June 24, 2010*

### Family Background

I was born at our home at 14 Grinnell Street, but I remember my childhood when living on the second floor of 274 Cambridge Street.

My parents were Daniel Louis and Parmelia (Forest) Hayes. Both were born in Fall River.

My mother's parents were Fabian and Marie Forest, who lived at 83 Prevost Street. My father's parents were Michael and Bridget (Mullen) Hayes.

My father was a supervisor for the city's Department of Public Works and my mother worked at the Arkwright Mills during the Depression. She was a spinner. My mother never spoke of conditions in the mills.

I had one brother and two sisters. My brother was the oldest, five years older than our eldest sister. One sister was older and one younger than me. My bother was Daniel F. Hayes (1912-1953); my older sister is M. Rita Hayes (born 1917), whose married name is Rogers; and my younger sister was Margaret Hayes (1923-2003), whose married name was O'Connor.

### Family Life

For a few years, I was a member of the Girl Scouts and we met at the Deaconess Home at the top of Second Street. The Deaconess Home was a home for wayward girls and orphans, and I believe that they went home in the afternoon.

My mother was a great cook. She could make something out of nothing. Her meals were fantastic. Sundays she would make a pork or beef roast. On Saturdays, we would bring my mother's pot of beans to the local bakery at 798 Plymouth Avenue (where Modern Printing is now) and they would bake the beans all day. At the end of the day, we went to pick up the beans and brought them home for dinner.

When I was ten or eleven, we moved from Cambridge Street to 807 Plymouth Avenue; next door was a tailor (now a pet shop). The house was a cottage on a large lot. There was no central heat, only a coal stove, and it was very cold on the second floor. We heated up bricks and brought them to bed with us. In the morning, the windows would be frosted. Every night, we kids would have to make knots out of newspaper. We did this by rolling up sheets of newspaper and tying them into a knot. My father would use the knots to start the wood in the morning that would in turn start the coal burning. First thing in the morning, we would run down the stairs and warm ourselves by the fire, then get ready for school.

My brother would pole vault and also kept passenger pigeons in the back yard. He would take his pigeons to Connecticut with his old Chevy. There, he would let them go and they would find their way back. My older sister (M. Rita) would stay home on Sunday afternoons and clock and band them when they returned. In return, my brother gave my sister rides in his car during the week to wherever she wanted to go.

I would go shopping with my mother to the Grand Central Market, at the northwest corner of Columbia and South Main Streets, where the Crystal Palace Restaurant is now. My mother liked the meats at that grocery store. We had to carry big bags of groceries up the hill to Plymouth Avenue. All of the bags were paper; there were no plastic bags then.

One of our neighbors and friends of my mothers who lived on the first floor of Cambridge Street (we lived on the second floor) moved to Tiverton [Rhode Island] and bought a bungalow, just over the line. We would go to visit there often, and they would allow us to go up into the upper attic to watch the Fall River Line steamers go by at night. They were a beautiful sight. If our mother wanted to go, we would say, "No, no, we want to stay to see the boat." This neighbor's name was Mrs. Omerod, a little English lady, who worked at McWhirr's and who had a corner there known as "Flying Fingers," where she taught knitting.

My maternal grandmother crocheted and would make curtains that never matched. Her pieces were always off. When she died, none of her crocheted matching pieces matched.

My brother started a paper route for the *Herald News*, then my older sister took it up two years later. Then I took it up. My route covered quite an area: From Plymouth Avenue down to Blackstone Street, to Dover Street, to Tecumseh Street, Rodman Street to Brayton Avenue and Stafford Road. When it was raining or snowing, my father would come with me and hold an umbrella. In tenements, people would share the paper. I did this all year long for two years; I was the last one in my family to deliver newspapers.

We had no telephone on Cambridge Street. I would go visiting with my mom. That's how we learned what was going on.

Under our dresses we wore long underwear in the winter. Our stockings were worn over the underwear, and we rolled up the stockings above the knees. Everyone wore long coats; no one had jackets until much later.

During the 1938 hurricane, I was visiting friends on Locust Street. It was very windy, but I loved the long walk back home down Robeson Street and up Plymouth Avenue.

**School Life**

I attended Sts. Peter and Paul Elementary School and later attended the Dominican Academy for high school. I graduated from Southeastern Massachusetts University (now UMass Dartmouth) in 1976 and attended one year at the University of New Hampshire.

I came home for lunch, which was made by my father during the Depression, since my mother was the only one working. Either my brother or older sister brought my mother lunch in the dinner pail. School hours were from 8:00 to 11:30 am and 1:00 to 3:30 or 4:00 pm.

**Recreation and Entertainment**

We walked everywhere. No one had cars, so that's how we got around. Walking was nothing to us. We walked half way around the city on a Sunday and think nothing of it. A typical Sunday walk went from Cambridge Street, down Plymouth Avenue, up Robeson Street all the way to Wilson Road, and back again on North Main Street.

When I was eleven or thirteen years old, I minded my godmother's children on Linden Street, off of Robeson Street. I would walk all the way to Linden Street from Cambridge Street, and walk back to the Plaza Theatre at the corner of South Main and Morgan Streets. The kids loved the cowboys and Indians movies at the Plaza, where we could stay for hours on Saturdays. I would then walk the children back to Robeson Street, then walk back home to Cambridge Street. Sometimes we would go to the Capitol, the Empire, the Durfee, or the Academy theatres also.

Sundays were special days. When I was about ten to twelve years old, after church and dinner, my mother, my sister, and I would walk down Warren Street to Quequechan Street. From there, we would get on the railroad tracks and continue to Prevost Street to my grandmother's house where we would spend the afternoon. My two aunts were very fashionable and up to date and had many boyfriends. Our aunts would let my sister and me try on their furs and high heels. We loved it. Sometimes, when a boyfriend came by, they would put us in the rumble seat of their car and drive us to Westport [Massachusetts].

My grandmother had a big coal stove, and one of our treats was when she made toast on the stove by putting slices of bread directly on the stove. The bread would be black as coal from the coal blacking but, with butter on it, we loved it. It was a great treat.

When it was 9:00 or 10:00 pm, we would head back home and walk up Prevost Street to Pleasant Street and get on the open electric trolley cars that traveled on tracks. It was freezing half the time, but we loved to see the stores all lit up on Pleasant Street; it was magical.

On Saturdays, Flint stores on Pleasant Street stayed open until 9:00 pm at that time (about 1929).

Between the ages of five to ten years old, our favorite pastimes were jacks, pickers (glassies), two-rope jump-rope (swinging the ropes in opposite directions), kick the can, roller skating in the streets, and (when it rained) cards (Old Maid) and paper dolls. Between eleven to fifteen years, we would use a slingshot to knock empty cans over. We were tomboys and would do everything.

An owner of a house on the large corner of Cambridge and Cogshall Streets had a picket fence around the property that had a flat continuous piece finishing off the top. We would get on top of the fence and walk along it, keeping our balance. We also hung from the fence from the backs of our knees and then swing a leg around and get on to the ground. No one fell off. The owner of the house didn't mind and never got upset at us.

We also did lots of handsprings, like in gymnastics. A few of us could walk on our hands.

Pickers was played by drawing a ring in the dirt, placing a group of glassies in the middle (like a game of pool), and shooting a glassie into the ring with the objective of getting as many glassies out of the ring. Whoever got the most glassies out of the ring won the game. Kick the can was played like soccer, with two sides and one can.

Some of the radio shows that I liked were "The Shadow Knows," a mystery, and the Amos and Andy comedy show, and all of the comedians, such as Abbott and Costello and Jack Benny.

My older brother had a bike first, then he passed it on to me when I was about fourteen or fifteen.

In the summertime, we would go to the beach or play tennis. We went to Bliffins or Lannigan's Beach, Sandy Beach in the South End, Horseneck Beach, or to Dartmouth once in a while to see Colonel Green's yacht. It was a beautiful, big boat, and we loved to look at it. His beach is now the Dartmouth Town Beach. He was a generous person and a wonderful man. We heard so much about how stingy and cruel his mother (Hetty Green) was. When she died, he inherited a vast amount of money. He shared his wealth and his property with the poor people.

We would also go to Rocky Point Park, where they had clambakes and where there was a beach. I didn't know it as well as Lincoln Park.

My aunt had a cottage at Island Park [Cashman's Park, Portsmouth, Rhode Island]. They still had outhouses there.

I would go to the Wixon School to play basketball inside at night. It was dark coming home and the three or four of us would be singing our heads off on Cambridge Street. One of our songs was "My Sweetheart's the Man in the Moon."

The lyrics to the song are:

> My sweetheart's the man in the moon
> I'm going to marry him soon
> It would fill me with bliss
> Just to give him one kiss
> But I know that a dozen
> I never would miss
> I'll go up in a great big balloon
> To see my sweetheart in the moon
> Then behind a dark cloud
> Where there is no one allowed
> I'll make love to the man in the moon.

We would also sing the Ink Spots "Paper Doll" from the top of our lungs. Other songs that we sang were "Indian Love Call," "My Gal, Sue," "Dinah" (I've Been Working on the Railroad), and "Sweet Sue."

Later, when we were of working age, my younger sister, her friend from New Bedford, and I would tent out at Horseneck every weekend during the summer. In the winter, we would go skating on the frog pond at South Park [now Kennedy Park].

To allow for winter sledding, Plymouth Avenue, Lowell, Lonsdale, and Blackstone Streets were cordoned off. People would come from all over to sled and tobaggon down the hills. I didn't go down many times because it was a good hike to walk back up the hill again.

My childhood was a happy time. Everyone enjoyed the same thing. There were no problems with neighbors. We had nothing, but had lots of fun. We were busy, busy all of the time. I have good memories of that time.

**Neighborhood Experiences**

After visiting Grandmother on Sundays, we would get off the Pleasant Street trolley at Plymouth Avenue, where the farmers gathered for selling fruits, vegetables, etc., on Monday morning. At the intersection of Pleasant Street and Plymouth Avenue, there was a large water trough for horses. The farmers would hitch their horses to steel rings that were set into the pavement; the harnesses were tied to the rings, allowing the horses to move, but not much. The wagons would be facing out to Plymouth Avenue. The farmers would stay all night, sleeping in their wagons until Monday morning. It was quite a sight.

There was a Harrington's Market on Coggshall Street, which is now a house. We would call the market to deliver our groceries. This was true for neighborhood markets, not the downtown markets. We would put a sign in the window for ice.

Coal was delivered by truck, usually twice a year. There was a special section of the cellar which was designed to hold coal. The coal truck would have a special attachment on the truck that was placed in the cellar window and the coal would pour in.

When we moved to Plymouth Avenue, one of our neighbors and friends was Catherine (Fournier) Walsh, who was a soprano. She had a radio program where she sang on WSAR [radio] every Saturday morning for fifteen minutes for one year.

The City Barn was located on Second Street, where O'Brien Apartments senior housing is now. The city's horses were kept there.

**The Depression**
During the Depression, there was no money for rent and groceries. Everyone was in the same boat. Mr. Shapiro was our landlord and was the nicest man. He would always say, "Don't worry, don't worry."

**World War II**
During the long term of President Roosevelt, we never knew that he was a cripple. Louis McHenry Howe was a close confidant to Roosevelt and a native of Fall River. When he died, President Roosevelt came to his funeral here. Mrs. Howe later became postmaster for Fall River.

Rationing wasn't all that hard on us; all neighbors were going through the same. If someone was short of sugar and needed some, people would share with one another.

**Friends**
Mr. and Mrs. George Murphy had three children: Virginia, Rosemarie, and a son Richard. They lived at 815 Plymouth Avenue. Virginia was my friend. She was a pianist and arranger for the Fred Waring Band. Virginia later worked at Dartmouth College as an arranger and played classical music there. Rosemarie was married to Thomas Brown, who was the Chief of Police on Martha's Vineyard when Ted Kennedy's Chappaquiddick mishap occurred. Following the incident, he had Kennedy's car impounded in his garage. Richard was an accomplished pianist but worked for the United States Government in Germany.

For forty years, my friend Pauline Sullivan took four of us girls shopping every week, including myself, my younger sister Marge, Mary Proc, and Gertrude Lemoi. None of us was ever allowed to pay for gas. Every Saturday, she would take us shopping to various places in Providence, Warwick, Taunton, and New Bedford. The past few years, we would go to Woonsocket [Rhode Island]. Three of the group have passed on: Mary Proc, Gertrude Lemoi, and Margaret O'Connor. It is just us two now who make the trips.

**Additional Thoughts**
On hot summer days, the firemen at the corner of Plymouth Avenue and Warren Street would turn the hose on to the street and we kids would jump around in the spray.

Washing machines were in the cellar. There were no driers then and all clothes were hung outside on a line. In the winter, the clothes would freeze and were hard to take off the line. The clothes would be stiff as cardboard. Winter would be tough on the hands.

The Hi-Roof was located on the corner of Plymouth Avenue and Snell Street (at 826 Plymouth Avenue, where the Beira Alta Restaurant is now). This was a barroom, and on hot summer nights, about 12:00 midnight, the patrons would be put out. There was singing and laughing, and we kids always looked forward to late Saturday night. It was fun to hear the singing and laughter.

**Popular Expressions**

My mother always greeted us with, "Give us a kiss till payday."

My young co-workers at Bristol Elder Services always got a kick when I was leaving the building and I'd say, "I'm off to the races."

My sister Margaret, when she was leaving, always said, "Love ya and leave ya."

When you didn't quite believe what someone was saying, you would say, "You're full of malarkey," or, "Tell it to the Marines," or, "You're full of baloney," or, "Oh yeah, says who." When someone surprises you, "Well I'll be a monkey's uncle."

# Henry F. Hicks Jr.

*Born in 1929*

**Family Background**

My parents were Henry Hicks Sr. and Vera (Anthony) Hicks. I have no brothers or sisters. My mother was Methodist Episcopalian. My father was of mixed English/Irish heritage.

My mother could trace her ancestry to the Leonards of Taunton, Massachusetts, who came over as iron workers from England. In the Old Colony Historical Society in Taunton there is a wanted poster from England that showed my ancestors who were wanted for plotting to overthrow James II. My father's father, Thomas Hicks, married a beautiful Irish girl named McGee. To the family, it was a scandal that he had married a Roman Catholic.

My mother's parents were John Anthony and May Leonard.

For fifty years, the family lived at 452 Division Street.

My father was the oldest of the three boys in his family. His two siblings are Roland and Eugene. My mother was also the oldest of the children in her family. Her siblings were John, Rowena (Fitzgerald), and Charles.

My wife is Amy (Brown) Hicks and we have two children: Wesley Gordon Hicks and Ruth May Hicks.

**Family Life**

My father was an amateur baseball player and was a pitcher in the AA division in North Carolina. The job was not viable financially. When he quit that job, he still played in the BB division as a pitcher. He played on the Fall River Line team into late in the 1930s, until the line ceased. The Fall River Line team was composed of members of crews from the various boats in the Line who were free during the day.

My father would often bring home pitchers from the other teams. We once had supper with Sachel Page, who then played in the black league. The black leagues competed with the local white teams outside of the South. He also played against a Jewish team called the Sons of David. I remember them all being dressed as if they were Orthodox Jews. At that time, Jews were excluded from the major leagues. They wouldn't play on the Sabbath. Hank Greenberg was the first identifiable Jew in the major leagues.

My father also played baseball for the Sts. Peter and Paul Church baseball team. The AA leagues that my father played in included feeder teams for the Scranton team and the Red Sox. On those teams, there were two classes of men: one class going up and one class going down in their careers. My father was a pitcher in the Piedmont League, but it didn't pay much money and he left.

Since he worked for the railroad, my father could ride free on any railroad. He would take me on the railroad and we would find as many different ways to get to a destination on different rail lines. We found many unique ways to get to Buffalo and other places.

My father was a life-long temperance man because he knew that alcohol was a problem in his family. He became a member of the Irish-American Temperance Society. The Temperance Society building on South Main Street just before South Park [now Kennedy Park] had a basketball court in it. The Society sponsored athletic activities and things like that. The brick building has an inscription on it. My father never lectured me except on the issue of alcohol.

Every drugstore had a soda bar. Every druggist in the city knew my father because he always came in for a coffee soda. A coffee soda was made with coffee syrup, a little bit of milk, and mostly soda water. A "coffee cabinet" is the Rhode Island name for what we now call a frappe.

One day, my mother was visited by the ladies from the Daughters of the American Revolution. They wanted her to join the DAR. My father was in the library listening to the conversation. They asked my mother, "You must have had ancestors in the American Revolution." "Yes," she replied. Expecting her to say that her ancestors were rebels, she had to admit that her ancestors were on the other side, that they were Royalists. That is not what the ladies wanted to hear. Daniel Leonard was the leader of the Royalists in Taunton and, during the Revolution, became the governor of Nova Scotia, then later of Bermuda.

## Food and Meals

While other kids wanted an ice cream sundae, I always wanted a Fall River melted cheese sandwich. I loved hot cheese sandwiches. I knew every drug store in the city that served a coffee soda. A date for me was taking a girl for a chow mein sandwich. Every Sunday, before church, I was sent to Duke's [Variety Store] to get some hot rolls. One was always missing when I came back.

## School Life

I had bronchial asthma as a child. The principal at the Doran School was very kind. She was one of the first Portuguese administrators in the Fall River School System. I missed so much school because of my asthma that the teachers at Doran prepared lesson plans and my mother would pick them up and bring them home to me.

I got a good education at Durfee [B.M.C. Durfee High School]. I had learned to read and write at an early age. I have to take my hat off to the Fall River Public Library. There was a lady in the Children's Room who got tired of having to go upstairs to get me books in the adult area. So she got me an adult library card. My teachers recommended books from their own libraries for me to read.

Fall River was divided by its junior high schools: Morton on the north and Henry Lord on the south. A good portion of the public schools were on the junior high school model. The rest of the city was on the elementary school model. I got a good public school education; it was old-fashioned (lots of memorization) but it was good.

I was accepted at Brown, but we couldn't afford it. Instead, I attended Bridgewater State College [now Bridgewater State University] and studied teaching there. I did my student teaching at Durfee for eight weeks. I was under the direction of Mrs. Sullivan at Durfee; boy, could she teach! Miss Carroll was the head of the English Department. I majored in History but minored in English.

Sullivan and Carroll let me teach. I detested tariffs, but Carroll made me teach it. I taught the sonnets of Shakespeare to the commercial class. At the end of the student teaching period, the classes took up a collection for me, and each class bought me a book.

I was never supervised by someone from Bridgewater while I was at Durfee. The Bridgewater supervisor came once on the last day of teaching. I was almost witness to a homicide. The supervisor, Miss Davis, met with Sullivan and Carroll and they went at it with her. It sounded like a cat-fight. The student teaching grades were posted at Bridgewater, and one of the professors told me to take a look at them. Most were C's but mine was an A-.

One of the tragedies of Fall River is the low educational attainment of its residents. When I graduated from the McDonough School, there were 122 in my class. Of those 122, only eleven graduated from high school.

**Recreation and Entertainment**

I can't emphasize enough the role of the two major Olmsted parks, South Park and North Park, on the youth of the city. As youngsters, we all went to South Park. We didn't have a back yard to play in. We shined our corduroy knickers from sliding down the rock outcroppings on the hill at South Park. The provision of these open spaces were to the credit of the nineteenth century city fathers.

In winter, we sledded down Division Street. I volunteered to be a street guard. The older kids had eight-passenger toboggans. We started at the head of Division Street at South Main and would shoot down Division and flip-flop over Broadway and down to the railroad tracks.

Fall River Public Library, The People's University, North Main Street

Kids would throw snow on Broadway to allow the toboggan to pass over the street. The kids who served as road guards could get a ride on the toboggan.

The Ringling Brothers Circus came to Fall River in five trains with a hundred cars. The circus trains arrived at the freight yard at Broadway. The Cole Brothers Circus also came to the city. Father Edward Sullivan was the chaplain of the circuses. There was a blessing of the trains in Sarasota, Florida, by priests. Every circus had its chaplain. Sarasota was the winter home of the circuses.

Fall River was a great circus town, with all its mill workers. The circus played at two locations in the city. There was a huge lot in the back of Globe Mills that went all the way back to Bay Street. The other site was at the Narrows, where White's Restaurant is now. The circus would come into Fall River from two locations. The big circuses, like the Ringling Brothers Circus, had to split up because they were so big. One yard couldn't handle them. There would be four trains with a hundred cars each. The trains with the tents and supplies and performers would come into the Ferry Street yard. The livestock—elephants and such—came into the city through New Bedford to the Rodman Street yard. Some trains would continue to Newport to the Navy Yard, where the circus would set up.

My father was a big circus fan. He took good care of the circus trains. He got good tickets in the front section. My mother said that we "sat in front of the mayor."

My father would invite circus performers to come to our home for supper. My father was friendly with many of them. One was Felix Adler, one of the circus clowns who had trained pigs and dogs. He wore white makeup and was a great performer. He was a number one clown in many ways. Clowns were always good for a free meal. He wasn't funny without makeup, but he was kind. My mother loved the circus too.

Once, when the Clyde Beatty Circus came to town, my mother and father were met at the entranceway by a clown pretending to be a ticket-taker. His name was Otto Griebling, and his character was a tramp; he was the main competition to Emmett Kelly. He took my mother and father into the lion's cage in the center of the tent and put them on the stand in the tiger stand. The tiger was not in the cage! They were clean, competent shows. My wife and I still go to the circus. Going to the circus was always an experience. I didn't have to go to school on circus day. I got "sick." My wife and I have also been circus fans all of our lives. We have been members of the Circus Historical Society, and I have been president of several circus organizations.

Each neighborhood had its own movie theatre. Socially and ethnically, each neighborhood was different. I went to the Plaza Theatre. The Capitol Theatre had more recent movies.

Fall River had one of the best Vaudeville theatres in the country, the Empire Theatre. It was part of the Keith Circuit. There were always the best plays at the Keith. If you goofed, you were off of the Keith Theatre circuit. The Empire had at least three balconies. A number of the city's theatres downtown on Bedford Street near the old Police Station were destroyed in the 1928 fire.

**Work Life**
During our grammar school years, my friend, Donald Medeiros, and I would make money in the spring by emptying out the ash barrels of our "clients" in the neighborhood. The ash barrels were in the basement where the coal furnaces were located. We took the ash out of the furnaces and put it in the barrels, then brought the barrels up and put them on the street for the city to pick up. We were paid in cash. On the way home, I would stop by Smith's Book Store on North Main

Street (next to the Fall River Five Cents Savings Bank) and spent my money on a book. We had regular ash customers.

During one summer, I worked for McWhirr's as a summer clerk. I polished furniture in the Furniture Department that was about to be delivered. We made sure that there were no marks on the furniture when delivered.

When I got out of college, I started teaching in Dighton, Massachusetts, in sixth, seventh, and eighth grades. From there, I started teaching in Needham and retired as head of the Needham High School History Department.

**Neighborhood Experiences**

I lived in a Portuguese neighborhood. They looked after not only their own children but also after you. I have memories of friendly people in the neighborhood. There was a Syrian family up the street; they introduced me to Middle Eastern bread. I went to St. Louis School, the Irish parish, for St. Patrick's Day. That was positive.

**Downtown**

I would go to the 5 & 10s to look at the toys. Before World War II, the stores still had the heavy lead toys. Kresge's had a fast food bar inside the door with hamburgers there. The hamburgers were ninety-nine percent filler. Hudner's Market had islands of sausages, beef, and poultry in the center island. The Borden Street Bakery produced hard rolls. They had an electric bread cutter; as kids, we would look inside the store to see the bread being cut by the cutter.

Next to Grants was The Nonpareil restaurant. If you really had money in your pocket in High School, you went to The Nonpareil to impress your date.

**Religious Life**

Primitive Methodism was founded in England by an American named Lorenzo Dow about 1807. He had come to Ireland to convert the Irish to Methodism. It was strictly Methodism but had no official affiliation with Methodist Conservatism. He had been an open-air camp meeting preacher where no tent was used. The first meetings in England of Primitive Methodism were held in the open air in Mowcap, the English pottery district. The Wesleyan Methodists wouldn't accept anyone not converted in a church. The denomination was called Primitive because it was early or original or back to the old times.

Primitive Methodism was the church of the lower working class people, especially the coal miners, the tin miners, and the poor agrarian farmers. It was the church of the working poor. It spread in England to a significant part of the population. It originally had the pejorative term of "Ranters" and took on this name. The PMs sent missionaries to America, but it didn't amount to anything.

The PMs were among the forces agitating for a trade movement in England. This was true for agricultural workers also. They were looking for fair labor. Agitators in the textile, coal, and agricultural regions were mostly PMs. This movement led to the formation of the Christian Socialists.

The PMs were different from the Methodist Episcopal Church, which had bishops who appointed ministers to the churches. There were three mainline Methodist Church denominations in Fall River; they eventually merged into the Union United Methodist Church.

Following the Civil War in the 1870s, immigration from England increased and the "Prims" came with their roots. The textile workers in England's Yorkshire and Lancashire provinces were strong adherents to PM. These immigrants were skilled textile machine operators and moved here as families. They sought out and created the Primitive Methodist tradition they were used to in their home country. The PMs proved attractive to the textile mill owners because the PM's were not only skilled but also abstainers and therefore active in the temperance movement.

The PM movement occurred wherever the Lancashire people settled, including the textile centers of Lawrence, Lowell, Methuen, Fall River, North Tiverton, New Bedford, Providence, Pasgog, Centerdale, Allentown, among others. All of the Primitive Methodist churches in these towns were a stone's throw from a textile factory.

When the Lancashire workers first came to Fall River, they settled in the Globe Village. The Globe seems to have attracted the PMs because, at that time, this part of the city was in Rhode Island. When the mills on Rodman Street were built, the PMs settled in that area, where the first and second PM churches were built. The "first church" was at 1871 Plymouth Avenue (the Dover Street church); the "second church" was built on South Main Street (the Dwelly Street church). A third group from Yorkshire settled in the Flint and built a church there. All of the PMs in Fall River were from Lancashire, except for the Yorkshire PMs, who settled in the Flint. A fourth church was built on Brightman Street in the North End, just over the railroad tracks. However, it lasted only twelve years. It could have been where the Royal Theatre later was located and could have been converted from a church to the Pastime Theatre. Another PM church was located just across the Tiverton, Rhode Island, line.

The Yankee English were either Congregationalists or Baptists. The French Huguenots also immigrated here and had two churches in Fall River. A French Huguenot church once existed where the old Embassy Theatre was located downtown. The church was torn down to build the theatre. There was also a French Congregational church on Bogle Street in the Flint.

The PM church on Plymouth Avenue was built on land donated by the owners of the mill that later became the home of Mason's Furniture. The Dwelly Street Church on South Main Street served the Globe. That church was also built on land donated by mill owners.

The Lancashire workers became the labor organizers, and the labor leadership came from them. The fact that the Primitive Methodists provided opportunities for members to talk and speak was a factor in their union organizing. In the PM churches, a person is certified to preach after training. In the PM churches, the ministers are locally-elected—with Bishops elected in the main Methodist churches. Sunday School leaders in the PM churches and other roles provided lots of opportunities to play leadership roles. In many instances, the union organizers were the PM preachers. Many PM preachers were blacklisted by the textile mill owners.

Another unique factor among the PMs was that they allowed women to go into the pulpit as licensed preachers. This was a factor in women becoming active in leadership roles in the union movement. My mother was 4 feet, 8 inches tall and was a union organizer at Firestone.

I remember Mary Mills, who was totally deaf but could read lips. She learned to read lips in England, where she worked in the textile mills. Girls learned to read lips in the textile mills to allow them to communicate above the din of the machines. As a teen, Mary Mills was expelled from a PM church because she danced around a maypole at Bliffins Beach.

David Sykes was the first Primitive Methodist minister in Fall River. The plans of the Plymouth Avenue church were saved and used to build the New Bedford church in the North End. The first church on Plymouth Avenue was a large wooden building that later became a clubhouse and then torn down. It was near the Niagara Fire Station.

L. Dow introduced camp meetings to Ireland and England. The regular Wesleyan Methodists wouldn't accept them because they weren't converted in a church. The Primitive Methodists were a working class church of the poor and for the poor. The Wesleyan church also wouldn't let members belong to unions because it was against the law.

Women were treated the same as men in the Primitive Methodist Church. They were good speakers, since they were used to standing on their feet. Three of the Primitive Methodist Church preachers of the Dover and Dwelly Street churches were blacklisted for union activities.

In Massachusetts, the PMCs were most numerous in the textile manufacturing centers. In Pennsylvania, they were concentrated in the coal mining towns and in the iron manufacturing cities. Primitive Methodists were also successful among agricultural workers. They were highly sectionalized. It was a church of the poor and for the poor and continued that way.

The governance of the PMC is through an annual conference. The local churches elect their ministers. The voting at the conference has to be an equal vote of the laity and the clergy. There are no bishops. The conference controls the church.

The Yorkshire English joined the Flint PM church. The Yorkshire and Lancashire English were always in conflict. In one Primitive Methodist church, there were two stained glass windows commemorating those church members who joined British regiments in World War I. On one side, a stained glass window was dedicated to Yorkshire soldiers who joined Yorkshire regiments, and, on the other side, the window commemorated Lancashire soldiers who joined Lancashire regiments.

The PMs had six acres in Westport from 1900 to 1910 that the Fall River and New Bedford churches used for outdoor camp meetings. It was called Beulah. There is still a Beulah Road there today. There was no tent or building; it was used only for open-air preaching.

During my years at [B.M.C.] Durfee High School, I started tutoring other Durfee students. One student, Thomas Higson, had an extraordinary father who was a World War I vet and a Sunday School teacher at the Plymouth Avenue Primitive Methodist Church. At the outbreak of the war, he went to England to join the English Army. He would hold up six fingers, signifying that he won six medals in the war. He was in the Battle of Gallipoli.

I joined the church and started my ministry serving as minister in the PM church on Block Island during the summertime.

The ethnic parishes fought among themselves, not just between Protestants and Catholics. The Roman Catholic Polish churches fought with the Polish National churches.

I was a local or lay preacher at the Plymouth Primitive Methodist Church. I was not a minister who had to be licensed. I served in five Methodist Episcopal Churches. I served at the Central Congregational Church when they were looking for a new minister. They liked me. They used this period to test people. I came back for three months. They finally found a permanent minister.

My father ceased to be a Roman Catholic at the age of twelve; then he walked away from it. He had a favorite Irish uncle, Father McGee, a priest. My grandfather, my father's father, had deserted his wife and four children, and this uncle had been very kind to my father. Father McGee was assigned to Notre Dame Church and, the day he reported to the parish, the nuns lined up outside the church and threw stones at him. The bishop was angry and had all of the nuns shipped back to Quebec.

My father became a member of the Irish-American Temperance Union. Their four-story brick building still stands on South Main Street, just north of South Park. They had a baseball team and an exercise room and other such facilities in the building.

Hartley's Pork Pies belonged to a Primitive Methodist member who went to the Dwelly Street Church. They made English pork pies.

There was an Italian Methodist Episcopal church on Quarry Street. The minister was a former Roman Catholic priest. There was also a Black African Methodist Episcopal Church in the city; the minister's last name was Hicks.

The most Anglican/Catholic Episcopal Church in the city was St. Stephen's on South Main Street, near the North Tiverton border. It was very high Episcopal. You could smell the incense from the street. The Pope would feel friendly there. It is now an Episcopal Baptist Church.

**Health and Illness**

In the 1930s, the local pharmacist was the major source of medical advice. We were indebted to them. They could prescribe codeine for a bad cold. At our drugstore, on South Main Street, there was a French Canadian pharmacist who was a major source of medical information. He carried leeches in the store. As a kid, I once had a boil on my neck, and he put a leech on it. It worked! The local pharmacist was skilled; this was probably true throughout the city's neighborhoods.

**The Depression and Prohibition**

During the Depression, the WPA [Works Progress Administration] had cultural programs in Fall River for children. The WPA took over the old wooden Doran School next to the "new" brick building. The activities for kids there included theatre, artwork, paper mache, and such activities. It was a chance for children to have something to do.

During Prohibition, there was a big still at "Big Berry" [former granite quarry]. Sometimes, tramps killed themselves drinking sterno or cooking alcohol.

**The Fall River Line**

My mother worked at Firestone during the war making gas masks. She was the treasurer of the local union. From 1921 on to the end, my father was the cotton clerk for the freight boat business of the Fall River Line. After the Fall River Steamship Line closed, my father became a yard clerk at the railroad and worked out of the Fall River freight house. When the Firestone fire started, the family was concerned about him. He had to remain in the yard to bring in the freight cars. In 1936, my mother and I were guests of the commodore of the *Commonwealth* to see the Newport yacht races. The Fall River Line steamships left at "a quarter of eight," never "7:45."

Sometimes, my father would have to go down to New York, so my mother would have to keep a suitcase packed for him. I still hear him yelling, "All ashore that's coming ashore." The freight boats for the Fall River Line included the *City of Fall River*, the *City of Taunton*, and the *City of Brockton*. The freight business was an important part of the Fall River Line operations. After the 1938 hurricane, the *City of Taunton* ended up on the Somerset shoreline. The remains of the boat can still be viewed there. The whole right side of the Fall River Line Pier was reserved for the Fall River Line freight boats. They brought raw cotton up from New York.

I suspect that cotton was smuggled up from the south in the early 1860s. Fall River mills were making uniforms, so the cotton had to come up from the south. There was some stockpiling that

went on before the war, but it wasn't enough. Before 1863, there had to be some other supply of cotton. The North also controlled the cotton grown on the islands off of the coast of Georgia.

*The Fall River Line Journal* was the oldest commercial journal of its kind. It became the model for commercial magazines sponsored by the railroads and airlines.

Had the Fall River Line survived into World War II, it would have been too dangerous to go to New York on Long Island Sound. Oil tankers were being sunk within sight of Point Judith. Two boats in a convoy were sunk in 1942 on a trip from Boston to England.

**World War II**
During World War II, there was no gas for cars, so we occupied ourselves at home or in the area. My father was an airplane spotter at the flatiron building on Plymouth Avenue. We sold war bonds during the war.

**Significant Events**
The Firestone fire of 1939 was overwhelming. One of the objections that I have is that Fall River and New Bedford only get in the national news when there is a disaster. I grew up in the 1940s, still smelling the latex and seeing the latex washed up with the tide. The Doran School had to be closed for a time because of the acrid debris from the fire. Half of the country was supplied with latex from the Firestone site. Boats would come in from Liberia to deliver the latex. The factory played an important role in World War II, supplying gas masks for the war effort.

**Fall River Lore**
Once, my father, mother, and I were having lunch in a diner in Salt Lake City. My father ordered a hamburger and fries with vinegar. "Vinegar?" asked the waitress, surprised. Nearby was a big, portly, Jackie Gleason-like character, dressed in a uniform and carrying two guns at his sides. He comes over to my father, looks directly at him, and says, "All right, Fall River or New Bedford?" He had served in the Navy Shore Patrol in Fall River and New Bedford during World War II and remembered how the locals used malt vinegar on their chips. He said that he was treated well in Fall River and told the waitress, "This is on the house."

Lafayette was a third degree Mason. The Lafayette statue at Lafayette Park has a Masonic medal on the chest of the statue. Roman Catholic bishops didn't like the Masons, and church members were forbidden to join. When the Prince Henry statue was dedicated on Plymouth Avenue, a contingent of English Sons of St. George were there with the St. George's flag. The prince's mother was English; she was the daughter of John of Gaunt, the Duke of Lancaster.

**Miscellaneous Memories**
Fall River was known as the city of "Hills, mills, stills, and pork pies."

The inaugural issue of *American Heritage* magazine featured an article on the Fall River Line. Rudyard Kipling wrote a poem about the Fall River Line.

During the Cold War, I was stationed for a year at Swarthmore College, at the Mary Lyons Finishing School, as part of a secret operation during the Korean War.

Uncle John, my mother's brother, was at Pearl Harbor when it was attacked by the Japanese. He had a ticket on a Yankee Clipper plane to come home for his mother's funeral, but it was never used.

During World War II, the heavy train engines couldn't go over the Newport railroad bridge. My father would break up the trains at the Ferry Street yard before they proceeded further.

Portuguese bands were a part of my life. My interest in brass bands came out of the Azorean brass bands from the Columbia Street religious processions.

The WPA had a theatre at the old wooden building at the Doran School site. My mother belonged to the "English Order of Odd Fellows and Odd Ladies, Manchester Unity." Their building still stands on Bedford Street. It is still an English institution after several generations.

# Isidore "Issy" Philip Horvitz

*Born on July 4, 1916*
*Died on June 9, 2011*

**Family Background**

I was born in Fall River at home.

My parents were Solomon and Clara (Katz) Horvitz. Both came from Russia (my father in 1900) but met in the United States. My mother lived in a little town north of Moscow and her sister was expecting in Fall River, so she came over to be with her and never went back. My mother could only speak Russian.

My father's parents were Ephriam and Tillie Horvitz and both immigrated to the United States; my grandmother died in 1914 and my grandfather died in 1918.

My mother's parents were Issar and Luba Katz. Neither of my maternal grandparents left Russia.

I have two siblings: Anna, born in 1908, and Louis, born in 1911.

My wife's name is Lillian and we have three children: Stephen, Sharon, and Cathy.

**Family Life**

My earliest remembrances (about two years old) was about going to Detroit to visit relatives and being served ice cream from a brick. I wouldn't eat it. I was only familiar with cones. Also, my aunt had a blackbird that was let loose and flew about the kitchen all the time. Those are the only two things that I remember until I went to school.

My mother and father were family-oriented and self-sacrificing. They were caring and unselfish. Two things my father told me when we were growing up: "Keep your head cool and your feet warm."

One of my chores was to crank the hand-powered sewing machine as my mother sewed. I also cranked the gadget to make butter.

In the morning, we had hot cereal, oatmeal or whatever. For the main meal, we would have fish, meat, or lamb chops. I was a fussy eater and ate mostly bread and butter and milk.

**School Life**

I went to the Davol School, the Davis School, and then to Durfee [B.M.C. Durfee High School]. I remember the seating arrangement and the singing sessions. Once a month, the music teacher traveled to the schools. Ruth Haywood was in my class in high school. I had a crush on her. She became a teacher later at Durfee.

I went to Harvard and majored in Anthropology. I thought that I might want to go to medical school. All you needed to take at Harvard at that time was six courses for your major; the other courses were required, such as sciences, math, etc.

## Recreation and Entertainment

For recreation, we played baseball and football (we called it rugby) and ran races. Nothing was organized. We also played hide and go seek, marbles, and ice skated in Lafayette Park. There was a field in back of Chavenson Street that was a ball field at one time. There was a frog pond at the end of the street. Where Durfee High School is now and beyond was all woods at that time.

## Courtship and Marriage

After the war, I went to a party in New Bedford. My wife, who is originally from New York City, came to visit her brother in New Bedford and I met here there. On our second meeting, I proposed to her. We met in March and got married in August, on August 11, 1946, while I was on three months terminal leave.

## Work Life

My father opened the Modern Furniture Store in 1911, and it is the oldest in the city still in operation. I was ten years old when we had an open house for the new store. I ran the elevator.

When I was thirteen, I started going to the store to open crates. At fourteen, I started delivering furniture, after school and on Saturdays. Sometimes, we would have to deliver furniture up to the third floor of a tenement. Refrigerators were a real challenge.

I have had only one job, one wife, one house, and one kind of car (blue Chryslers are the only cars I have owned).

## Neighborhood Experiences

Most extended families lived in the same neighborhood. Most of us didn't have cars. On Sundays, we would congregate in the same relative's house. Everyone was family-oriented. Our friends were our family members. My father didn't go golfing or bicycle riding. There was more separation between the generations then. Kids were more respectful and careful.

Downtown was very busy. On a Saturday afternoon, you couldn't walk on the sidewalk on South Main Street between Pleasant and Columbia Streets. You would have to step off of the curb to get by. All the stores were there—Sears, the three 5 & 10s (Kresge, Woolworth's, and Charlton's), clothing stores, McWhirr's, and Cherry and Webb. Everything was there.

Some of my friends were Red Bogus (Boguslavski), who was a cousin of mine (my mother's sister's son), Melvin Zais, who went on to become a four-star general and served in World War II, Korea, and Vietnam (he lived on McGowan Street), Harry Kradif was killed in Europe in World War II, and Philip Feldman. They are all gone now. I never knew anyone outside the neighborhood; we never went outside the neighborhood.

I was in the Boy Scouts, and we met in the Deaconess Home on Second Street. I walked from Chesworth Street to the Home, which is a long way for a kid to walk. The Boy Scouts had a camp at Lake Noquochoke, and I went there a few times. We decorated soldiers' graves on Memorial Day.

When I was seven or eight, about 1924, the street lights were still gas. I don't remember how they lit them.

About 1924 or 1925, the city took a piece of land between our house and our neighbor's land to create Talbot Street. They then proceeded to construct Talbot Street. They didn't use any heavy equipment but used men with picks and shovels. They dug trenches for the water and sewer pipes.

They used dynamite to loosen the ledge. It was so different from today. In those days, there was no equipment at all. There was a massive number of men, all working one next to another.

In those days, ice, fruit, and coal were all delivered by horse and wagon. People would yell out their window if they wanted something; each wagon carried its own scales. People did go to markets, but many items were delivered. Every neighborhood had a market, a drug store, clothing stores, doctors, and dentists. Everything you needed was within walking distance.

**Religious Life**
The Passover and Seder were based around the meal, and the holiday celebrated the release from slavery and the Exodus from Egypt. It was a good meal where families gathered together. There was wine and the singing of old traditional songs. The Last Supper was a Seder, according to tradition.

**The Depression**
My mother and father were generous to family and other people. People would come to the door asking for a handout and my father would give them a quarter or more, which was a lot during the Depression. Before the Depression, my mother would send me to buy milk for ten cents a quart and bread for six cents.

**World War II**
I volunteered for the Navy when the Germans broke through the lowlands into France. I realized it was going to be a long one. An opportunity came up for persons with college degrees to go to school to become officers in the Navy and become an ensign. I spent a month as an apprentice seaman, then went to midshipman's school for three months. I was assigned to the *USS North Carolina*. It was the first battleship built since World War I. I spent a year on her. The second ship that I was on was a British Corvette. When the United States went to war, we didn't have enough escorts and destroyers. Britain gave us nine Flower class Corvettes. I spent two years on a Corvette escorting convoys and eventually took command of the ship.

I was then transferred to the destroyer *USS Earle V. Johnson* and was made its executive officer. I spent two years escorting convoys in the Mediterranean, Caribbean, the Pacific, New Guinea, Philippines, and Okinawa. I never had a day's shore duty.

We were off Formosa, escorting an Army division from Okinawa to the Philippines, when we picked up a Japanese submarine that resulted in a three-and-a-half hour fight with the sub. One torpedo came at us and went right under the ship. We dropped depth charges on her and she fired her torpedoes. Three manned torpedoes were launched at us. One went under our ship, then turned around and came back at us again and missed again. This was on August 25th, 1945. We fought until 3:30 in the morning.

I had six years of active duty, sent home before the Korean War, and stayed in the active reserves for twenty-six years.

I traveled the American Expeditionary Force and went over in a troop convoy to England, where I was assigned temporarily to the Royal Signal Barracks in Portsmouth, England, to learn about British radar. When I first went into the service, the United States radar was rudimentary, and the British radar was much more advanced than ours. I was in a convoy once where we were the only ship that had radar. Radar was used for surface targets and sonar for submerged subs.

Isadore Horvitz

We escorted a convoy from Whitehall, England (Naval headquarters). We stopped at Newfoundland. At Boston, they modernized the ship, including the installation of showers, refrigeration equipment, compartments to store food, and new gas ranges. They also changed the guns from British guns to American guns. Then the convoy went into the Caribbean.

We were sending the Russians equipment and food. In early 1942, the Mediterranean was not secured and was controlled by the Italians and the Germans. The merchant ships had to go around the Cape of Good Hope to the southern ports of Africa. Two years later, we could use the Mediterranean and the Suez Canal. We sent needed ships to Cuba, then another group would escort the ships to Aruba and the Persian Gulf. Our group had the run from New York City to Guantanamo. Since there was no danger from subs off the coast in the South Atlantic, the convoys could go independently across the Atlantic. The subs would be too far from their bases to be a threat there. Once the Mediterranean was secured from sub attacks later in the war, the convoys went to the Suez Canal and went independently on to the Persian Gulf and to Russia. I went on eighty-five convoy trips in the Atlantic, the Mediterranean, and the Pacific.

There were usually five escorts in a group to protect the convoy. The convoys were typically forty ships, with eight columns and five rows, with a thousand yards between the rows and five hundred yards between the ships astern in line. The five escorts sailed a few miles in front and to the side and maneuvered in a zig-zag fashion as they proceeded forward. The zig-zag movement was to put a sonar screen around the convoy to screen for submarines. Of all the convoys we escorted, only one ship was torpedoed; that's a good record.

One of the major incidents during our convoy trips involved an English ship in the convoy that was carrying liquor and wives of servicemen stationed in South Africa. One woman was flirting with a crew member and the crew broke into the liquor hold. They started getting too familiar with the women and fights broke out. The captain signaled to us for help. My executive officer boarded the ship with a boarding force (I didn't, since I was the captain and had to remain with my ship) and they quieted down.

One of my convoys ran from the United States to Bizerte, Tunisia. Then, escorts took over and went with the transports through the Suez Canal. However, one time, the bubonic plague was rampant in the area of Tunisia around Bizerte. We therefore couldn't get off the ship, spent the night there, and then sailed to Palermo in Sicily and waited for a convoy to come back and take over for us. Then we returned to the States to pick up another group of ships.

Once, we rode out a typhoon off of Okinawa. In heavy seas, we would sometimes roll over fifty degrees. Although the ship was designed to heel over much more (and come back), everything had to be well-secured or be severely tossed about—personnel as well as equipment.

About the first of August, 1945, when we were riding out a typhoon after leaving Okinawa—and a sleepless night during kamikaze attacks—it was reported that "something was rattling" in the hedgehog ammunition ready locker. The hedgehog was a fifty-pound weapon with twenty-four spigots, each with a projectile that fit on top of the spigot. When fired, the twenty-four projectiles would go off in an elliptical pattern. If one of the projectiles touched the submarine, it would explode. When it hit the water, the propeller of the hedgehog started turning and the bomb would be set to go off. If anything like this happens on a ship, it was the duty of the gunnery officer to assume whatever risks might be involved in investigating and resolving the problem.

Naturally, the seas were extremely rough and it was dangerous to proceed on the main deck, especially in the forward part of the ship. I secured a "life line" about the waist of our gunnery officer, Sam Bushman, and tended it several paces behind as he proceeded to the hedgehog stowage locker. Upon opening the hatch, he discovered that, indeed, one of the depth bombs had broken loose, was tossing about the deck, and had to begun to arm itself. The propeller on a hedgehog was already turning, which meant that it was set to go off. Sam lifted it, made his way to the starboard side and heaved it overboard. A few more turns on the arming vanes and it would have set the whole ammo locker off and the ship and crew would have been lost. We would have been blown up.

In the Pacific, we were steaming down the straits of New Guinea (between New Guinea and the islands), taking a convoy to a port in New Guinea. We suddenly saw a port that wasn't supposed to be there. Radar and maps checked it out (dead reckoning) and so did the contour of the land seen on the radar scope; we were on course. However, unknown to us, there was a two-knot current in back of us and pushing us forward. This meant that, in ten hours, we were twenty miles closer to where we were supposed to be. We pulled up and saw that there was a Japanese flag flying in the Japanese-occupied port. As soon as we saw the flag, we signaled the convoy to go back. The contour of the land was exactly the same as the contour of the land approaching the port that was our actual destination.

Being a commanding officer is difficult. You have to make many decisions and are never relaxed; you're always under pressure and are responsible for two hundred lives. I enjoyed being an executive officer more than being a captain. The executive officer is in charge of personnel and, in a destroyer, is also the navigator. Sometimes, we went for two or three days without seeing the stars. There are only a few stars you can shoot. You have to see at least three stars and the horizon. Therefore, shooting the stars has to occur twenty minutes after sunset and twenty minutes before sunrise, when you can see both the horizon and the stars. The best star to shoot from is the Polaris. The light has to be such that you can see both the horizon and the stars. The angle that the North Star makes with the horizon is your latitude. The North Star is over the North Pole.

The tale of two fruitcakes. This is significant to me since similar events occurred in the beginning of hostilities and at the end of hostilities. When we initially went to war, the United States didn't have the ships to escort convoys and therefore we had to rely on British Corvettes.

Isadore Horvitz, center with cap

The British gave us nine Corvettes for this purpose. On the British transports, we got friendly with the Army people, including Army doctors and dentists, and Red Cross girls and Army nurses. Every evening, after dinner, we would go between the ship smokestacks and sing songs, like "Sweet Adeline" and "Let Me Call You Sweetheart" and harmonize. We would sing, talk, and got friendly.

On the last night, one of the girls brought out a fruitcake her grandmother had made several years before. We had it and enjoyed it.

Four years later, a friend of my mother's sent me a fruitcake that took months to reach me in Okinawa. Emma Dondis made the cake; her husband ran the Empire Men's Shop downtown. One night, a kamikaze air raid was going after the destroyers, and we were at our battle stations all night long. I took out the fruitcake and shared it with the men at the battle station. This was just before the end of the war. So that's my tale of the two fruitcakes, one at the beginning and one at the end of the war.

On August 15, 1945, word came from the radio shack that the Japanese had made an offer to surrender. Before we could ponder over the credibility, everything let loose. As normally, the huge anchorage area at Leyte was loaded with ships. A good part of the 7th Fleet and some of the 3rd and 5th Fleet destroyers were there. Almost at once, it seems, every ship, almost on signal, started firing off their pyrotechnics and sounding off their whistles and sirens. At the same time, fire and tug boats, equipped with firefighting hoses, began shooting streams of water into the air. No imaginable fireworks display can ever come close to this awesome sight. Men were not necessarily celebrating a victory, but reacting to the feeling of the burden of uncertainty of remaining alive being lifted and removed.

Upon first realization, I wanted to be alone with my thoughts. I found a quiet spot on my ship, sat down, and "cried it out," allowing myself to sink into deep euphoria, saying to myself, "I'm going to live. I'm going to live." Then, "I'm going back to the 'make believe' where everything is great, where you can sleep all night without interruption or danger, where you have only friends and family."

Four years at war, almost constantly in one war zone or another, living day to day, at an early stage in life, gave me what now seems a strange perspective. Developed early, because in the early stage of the war, Germany controlled practically all of Europe and the Japanese controlled a good part of Asia and the Pacific Islands. I could visualize the war extending beyond my lifetime.

Isadore Horvitz, on right with the sextant

Living day to day, the real world was present; the only real world. The world that I had left in peacetime seemed in the unfathomable past—an imaginary world, a bed of roses, but not the real world. A world that of course I knew I had experienced, but at the same time was not real, and yet at the same time how wonderful to return to. Sixty years have gone by, but I still recall my perspective. The two worlds never mixed.

# Dennis C. Hurley Jr.

*Born on December 17, 1922*
*Died on May 23, 2013*

**Family Background**

I was born in Bridgeport, Connecticut.

My parents were Dennis C. and Mary (Desmond) Hurley. Both my parents were born in Fall River and were married in Sacred Heart Church. My father came from the Corky Row neighborhood and my mother came from the Pine Street neighborhood. My wife's family home is here at 90 Winter Street.

My father's father was Jeremiah Hurley. He died about 1926-27 when I was about four or five years old. The family has an eighteen-grave lot at St. Patrick's Cemetery.

I have one two sisters: Ruth Elizabeth, born in 1919, and Mary, born in 1924.

My wife was Mary Elizabeth "Bette" (O'Brien) Hurley (born January 1, 1923, died April 26, 1993).

**Family Life**

Our family moved to Bridgeport, Connecticut, after the Fall River fire of 1916, before World War I (it was before 1919, since my sister Ruth was born in Bridgeport). That fire destroyed everything on the west side of South Main Street, from the northwest corner of South Main and Spring Streets, across Columbia to South Main and Morgan Streets. The fire destroyed Steiger's Store, which was later rebuilt. My father was managing Murphy's Diner that was located on South Main Street, near Morgan Street. Murphy was wiped out by the fire. When my father's brother Bill in Bridgeport heard about the fire and my father being out of a job, Uncle Bill called and said, "Get on a train in Providence tomorrow and come to Bridgeport," and he would find him a job.

The morning after the fire, my father was on the train to Bridgeport. Uncle Bill had a job lined up elsewhere and wanted his brother to take his existing job. The way he did it is that he told my father to go in to his brother's job the next morning and simply take his place. The Hurley's were big men, ranging from 5 feet, 10 inches to 6 feet, 3 inches tall. My father was a small man, about 5 feet, 7 inches. When the foreman called out, "Where's Hurley?" the next morning, my father answered, "I am." The boss looked at him and said, "You're not the Hurley who was here yesterday." My father replied "No, but I'm the one that's here today." The boss turned on his heels and left. I guess he was only concerned that someone was there and the job was covered. My father stayed on the job. My father later worked for Remington Firearms. In those days, if you got a job someplace, you took the job.

Uncle Bill ended up in Springfield, Massachusetts, working for Gilbarco, the first company to make recording gas pumps for gas stations. Before that, there was no way to measure how much gas was being dispensed into a vehicle from a gas pump.

While we were in Bridgeport, my mother died in childbirth when delivering my younger sister Mary. My father couldn't take care of us, so we three kids came back to Fall River to live with my father's family. We returned on June 1, 1924. My father's family consisted of Grandfather Jeremiah, Uncle Joe, Aunt Mary, and Aunt Margaret at their home at 626 Second Street. I lived there until I got married in 1953. Uncle Joe married and moved when I was about three or four years old. Aunt Mary and Aunt Margaret took care of us. They never married.

Before they lived at 73 Cottage Street, my father's family lived at 626 Second Street, one house south of Branch Street.

Aunt Catherine, Uncle Bill's first wife and the mother of my cousin Janice, also died in childbirth at about that time, and Janice came to live with us as a sister at 73 Cottage Street. Uncle Bill was living in Springfield at the time. She later became a dietitian at St. Anne's Hospital and died early, at the age of forty-four.

My father continued to work in Bridgeport and visited us on holidays. He couldn't come to visit every weekend, since money was too tight then to afford that.

Aunt Margaret worked at McWhirr's and Aunt Mary stayed at home and took care of us. Through the Depression, we never went to bed hungry. At Christmas, we would get a new pair of pants. We would also get a little toy or gift.

Mary did the cooking and washed the clothes. Margaret was more stern. She worked hard selling fabric at McWhirr's. She had to move big rolls of fabric and handle it and cut off cloth. Next to her was the pattern area. Everyone made their own clothes then. My future wife's mother was friendly with Aunt Margaret because that is where she bought her material and sewing needs.

**School Life**

I went to St. Mary's School for the eight years of elementary school. The nuns, the Sisters of Mercy, could be tough but they were good. The Sisters of Mercy also taught at Sts. Peter and Paul School and at St. Louis School. They lived at Mount St. Mary's Convent, on the corner of Second and Middle Streets. Every morning, they would walk down Second Street, from the convent to St. Mary's School. St. Mary's was our parish church.

**Work Life**

After graduation from high school, I worked at McWhirr's for a year. I started as a "cash boy." The cash boy went around and picked up the stuff to be delivered. In those days, most people bought stuff and had it delivered to their home. We picked up the items, put a label on them, and then sent it down a chute to the basement to the delivery trucks that came in the back of the building. Green's Moving had the contract to deliver McWhirr's deliveries. McWhirr's didn't have its own trucks. At Christmas, I did gift wrapping.

In the morning, I picked up the mail when the mailman brought it in big sacks. I gave it to Margaret O'Day, the executive secretary at McWhirr's. I did it again in the afternoon also, because in those days, mail was delivered twice a day. Margaret O'Day distributed the mail to persons within McWhirr's. Her husband, John O'Day, was a buyer for McWhirr's.

Every day at noon, McWhirr's had a radio program. Eddy (I can't remember his last name) was the first DJ in the country. He was a floor walker at McWhirr's and would do the program every noontime. He would play the music and, in-between, tell the listeners the specials that McWhirr's was having that day.

After the Navy machinist job didn't come through after the war, I then knew that I wanted to be a CPA, but I couldn't start until September of 1946 at Bentley University. I knew what I was going to do. I then met William Cyr, who set up all of the parish credit unions in the area, including New Bedford. He helped set up the *Fall River Herald News* and the Corky Row Credit Unions. He owned the Thibodeau Business School that was located in the Hudner Building. The Greater Fall River/New Bedford Credit Union Association is named after him. I spoke with him and he said, "I can get you on at a job until September at Davis Screen," located at the end of Lawrence Street in the Chace Mill. I worked in the office at Davis from April to September. Bentley was located in Boston in those days.

After I finished Bentley, I became a CPA and got a chance to work at Kenneth Gammons in New Bedford, from 1948 to 1958. Then I went to Fall River to Soboloff's. Then we formed the firm of Movouck, Mitchell, and Hurley. We eventually merged with Meyer, Regan, and Wilner.

**Neighborhood Experiences**

The Davenport School was located where the Jimmy Griffin Park is now. When it burned down before the war, I watched while the fire department put it out. My friend Jimmy Harrington lived across the street and we watched the fire from his second floor. The city didn't have the money to rebuild the school. Jimmy Griffin was the first guy from the neighborhood killed in World War II. I knew him vaguely.

Three years ago, the park was a mess. The Corky Row Club got the city to clean it up, got a new stone that listed all of the names of local residents killed in World War II, and rededicated it.

Corky Row was mostly Irish and mostly from County Cork. However, at the top of the hill, between Branch and Lyons, was a group that came from County Claire. They insist that this part of the neighborhood is Corky Row and that the rest of the neighborhood was not. As far as the rest of the neighborhood was concerned, all of the area was Corky Row.

The guy you need to speak with is Frank DePauli, who is Italian. His family lived on the northwest corner of Branch and Third Streets. The Corky Row Club is on the southeast corner of Third and Branch Streets. Frank's older brothers started the Corky Row Club. They were one of the few families in the area that were not Irish. There were a few Portuguese but no French.

My best friend was Jimmy Tierney and his brother Bobby, who lived at 36 Forest Street. Jimmy was a tail gunner in the Air Force out of England. He did at least thirty to thirty-five missions. I was his best man when he married in St. Patrick's when we were in the service. I got there too late for rehearsal, and showed up the next morning for the wedding. I was also the godfather for his daughter. Jim went to work for the Ford Foundation in England. His twin daughters were born in England.

His brother, Bobby Tierney, built the Braga Bridge. He went to Notre Dame and was the district engineer for the Massachusetts DPW [Department of Public Works], out of Taunton. Bobby supervised the construction of the Braga Bridge. He went on to become Commissioner of Public Works for the Mass DPW and lived in Belmont.

Bobby Delaney lived further up on Forest Street on the same side, between Cottage and Park Streets. He was a captain in the Navy and later taught at the Naval War College. Jimmy Robinson lived on Park Street, across from the Dominican Academy. He worked all his life for the post office.

Three of them—Bobby Tierney, Bob Delaney, and Jim Robinson—went to Coyle High School. Freshmen and Sophomores had elocution and competitions. The winner spoke before the whole school. Juniors and senior wrote essays. The two Bobbies were brains. Jimmy managed a team in the Maplewood League. The three of them took the whole honors in the sophomore year. They walked off with all the awards.

In those days, Plymouth Avenue was closed off on one side to let us slide there in the winter. A few other boulevards were also closed off for sliding.

The stores in our neighborhood included Bottomley's (a grocery store), which was located across the street from where O'Rourke's Funeral Home used to be. On the northeast corner of Grant and Second Streets was a Chinese laundry. He was the nicest man. Since I was called Junior, he called me "Junie." One day, he joked that he was going to make chow mein out of Junie. I was five years old and took it literally. I wouldn't go near the place after that. If I had to go to the grocery store, to avoid him, I would walk up the street to Lyons, to Third, to Wade, and to Second Street, and up the hill to get what I was sent for. Then, I reversed it. People asked me why I didn't just cross the street. I said that I wasn't supposed to cross the street alone.

**Recreation and Entertainment**

We played a lot of ball at South Park [now Kennedy Park] and we played in the streets. There were not many cars then. We also played baseball and football in the street. We often made too much noise for the Quinns, who lived two houses up from us. They would politely tell us, "Why don't you boys go down to the park? It is only two blocks from here." Sometimes, when we got too loud, they would call the beat cop.

Someone in the neighborhood had a toboggan. In those days, there was an iron fence with peaks surrounding South Park, all along the driveway of the park from Broadway to Middle Street on South Main Street. Someone took out a section about three feet wide, just enough to get a toboggan through. We would slide down Park Street with guys at Forest and South Main Streets to look out for traffic. Sometimes, we had no one looking out for traffic. If you timed it right, you would head down Park Street through South Main Street and through the hole in the fence at South Park. Then, we started all over again. Then we alternated guys on the toboggan and those looking out for the traffic. You had to time it with the traffic.

I was a member of the Sacred Heart Senior and the St. Mary's Seniors. We would go on field and overnight trips. One trip was to Gavin's in the Catskills.

Noel Henry's Irish Show Band played here in Fall River and in the Catskills. His brother Tommy now has the band. Tommy is a drummer and a singer. I got friendly with them when they came to Fall River. Hank Harrington was very active in the Holy Name parish. He brought Henry's Irish Show Band down a couple of times to play for them. I met them here.

The first time Ken Ledger was asked, "Why don't you sing 'Danny Boy'?" he said, "No, let Dennis sing." Ken led the Clover Club Choir. I took over as choir director for a number of years. I ended up meeting Tommy a few years later and sang with him when St. Patrick's had a celebration at the Venus [restaurant in Swansea, Massachusetts]. Tommy sat up with us and said "You're going to sing a few numbers for us, aren't you?" I said, "If you say so, Tommy."

I also sang at Gavin's. On one side of the mountains is the Borscht Belt, full of Jewish hotels. They are all gone. The New York Jews would go up there for the Jewish holidays to places like Grossingers, which became the top spot in the area.

Brickman's was also big. It was founded by a tailor from Russia. He didn't like being a tailor and bought some land in the mountains. People thought he was crazy. After he died, his wife and two sons built up quite a resort. I spoke with one of the brothers. He said, "One of the biggest mistakes I ever made was to turn the skinny guy down. I thought he would never make it." Do you know who the skinny guy was? It was Frank Sinatra.

**World War II**

Before and during the war, there were novenas held at St. Mary's every day, one at 4:00 pm and one at 8:00 pm. The place was always jammed.

Before I started working at McWhirr's, I took the exam to become an apprentice at the torpedo station in Newport. Then I became an apprentice machinist for about one and one-half years before entering the Navy. I went to the Naval Air Station in Memphis, Tennessee, to the Naval Air Technical Training Command. There, I became an Aviation Machinist Mate, 3rd Class. Later, I became a 2nd Class and 1st Class Machinist Mate.

I flew a double-wing biplane, a two-seater, with one seat in the front and one in the back. The wings were made of a frame covered with fabric.

I spent the summer in the most humid place in the world in Tennessee. You couldn't give me a million dollars to stay down there. I had two wearings of shirts, the humidity ate through the fabric. We read the Sunday papers in bed in our shorts. The sweat would just run off you. You would take a shower and the water would run off you again. There was no escaping it. There were cockroaches everywhere. The slightest bit of moisture would draw them, even in you clothes.

Then we went down by Route 1 to the Green Cove Springs, Florida, and to Naval Air Station in Jacksonville. There were four auxiliaries there. Green Cove was for fighter planes. The other three were for dive bombers and torpedo bombers. There were the Bob Cat (F-4 planes) and the Hell Cat (F-6 planes).

Then I was transferred to the Special Projects Unit Cast, called SPUCast, and worked on Project Cadillac. It was the only project that has priority over the Manhattan Project. It was a radar project. I was a plane captain. I always flew on the right-hand seat. If the plane crashed, I would have gone down with it. It was a very secret mission and they told me, "If you don't bring the plane back, don't you come back." They had a whole section of different type planes: fighters, bombers, the B-24 Liberator. The Navy version was called the Privateer. Not so much a bomber as a fighter.

Theoretically, we were at Squantum Naval Air Station. We were supposed to spend the night there, but we were really in Boston. "I'll pick you up in the morning," the skipper said. Make sure that the Sergeant-in-Arms doesn't see you. Take this crew to the Fargo Building in South Boston. The Fargo was where you went to get processed to get out of the Navy. But we had to go by the Weymouth (Squantum) Naval Air Station where our records were. Our names were called every morning and the response was "absent." We were not in Weymouth and no one knew where we were.

Out comes the commander. He calls out our names. "You Hurley?" he asks. "Yeah," I said. "Is there a problem, sir?" "Yes," he says. "The whole bunch of you are AWOL." "No, sir," I said. "Here's a letter from the Pentagon saying that we are honorably discharged." I knew the guys were getting restless and didn't want to tangle with Shore Patrol. I said, "I'll give you the number to call at the Pentagon to see that it's okay." He decided that the best thing to do with these guys was to send them to the Fargo Building and he let us go. It was too much of a problem. We got our jackets and we were off to Boston and the Fargo Building.

They processed at all hours of the night at the Fargo Building. I got discharged at 3:00 am.

They debriefed you and asked all kinds of questions. We took an oath to get out as well as get into the service. "Now you're a civilian," they said. The problem was how to get to Fall River at three in the morning. There were no buses running. Finally, we got a ride to the bus station. I got out of the Navy in December, 1945. The only part of my Navy uniform that I have left is my folding hat.

The Navy decided that they weren't going to build torpedoes at Newport and moved the operation to the Midwest. They had moved all of the machinery out. The law said that you had to take back servicemen for a year if they were employed with you before going into the service. I went back to the Navy and there was no apprentice school. I got a tour of the Goat Island torpedo facility (at that time, you needed a ferry to get there). In Middletown, they built a new facility and were still testing torpedoes there. I ended up testing the after-body of torpedoes and putting them back together again. They shot it up the river and if it worked three times, it was okay. I did this from January to April, 1946.

There was no manufacturing and they had to give the apprentices something to do. We couldn't complete our apprentices because the school had closed. They couldn't fire us; we were permanent appointments. However, they said, you have the right to bump someone with less seniority. They gave us three choices: Pearl Harbor, Guam, or Treasure Island in California. They offered us this to get off the hook; no one took them up on the offer. There were no jobs for machinist apprentices at that time. Brown and Sharp had its own school, but they couldn't place their own apprentices from their school.

**Miscellaneous Memories**

When I was working for Kenneth Gammons in New Bedford, one noontime I was standing in front of the building and saw a group of men about two blocks away. The next time I looked, they were a block away. The group included attorney Joe Hannify, Ed Berube, and Ernie Paquette (he was then the state representative from the South End). They had this tall, gangling guy with them, who looked like a scarecrow from the *Wizard of Oz*. He was informally dressed.

When they got up to me, Ed Berube says to me, "Dennis, I want you to meet a guy who is going up against Henry Cabot Lodge Jr. for senator. His name is Jack Kennedy."

When he became president, and was vacationing at Hammersmith Farm, and could get the Secret Service to let him out of their sight, Jack would come to Fall River to hang out with the group at Slade's Laundry on Slade Street. "Whitey" Paquette and Bernie Paquette owned the building and laundry. They would meet there every morning. Russ Berube, Ed's brother, and Ed were also in the group, as were Bill Murray and Jimmy Harrington.

Kennedy never had a dime in his pocket. He loved Plourde's chocolate éclairs, and whenever he would go into the bakery, they would have some ready for him. He would walk out without paying, and one of the group would pay the tab the next day. He was one of the richest men in the world, and yet he never had a dime on him.

# William James Kerrigan Jr.

*Born in 1936*

**Family Background**

I was born in Fall River when my parents lived at the southwest corner of North Main Street and Wilson Road, in the building that once was the Green Dragon Inn.

My parents were William and Mildred (Morgan) Kerrigan. My father came from the Cory Street area of the North End and was employed by the employment office. My mother was a nurse until I was born; then became a homemaker. My mother's family moved to Fall River from Lynn, Massachusetts, when my mother was a little girl.

When I was six months old, my parents moved from the Green Dragon Inn house to a home that they bought at 3533 North Main Street.

My father's father came from Taunton, where he worked on area farms. When he moved to Fall River, he worked in the textile mills.

My father's mother died when he was seven years old.

My father's father and his brother married sisters who lived on Hanover Street. My grandfather's brother was a doctor and he lived on Hanover Street with his three sisters. They took my father in to live with them when his mother died.

One of my grandfather's sisters, Sadie Kerrigan, was a third grade teacher at the Ruggles School who taught Cardinal Medeiros when he first came to America. She helped him out when he couldn't speak English. She took him to Boston to visit a college, I believe.

My mother's father died in 1934, when he was a merchant seaman on a ship from the Shell Oil Co. terminal in Fall River. The ship blew up and sank off of Newport, Rhode Island.

My mother's mother died when I was just a little kid.

I married my wife Claire Wing in 1961, and we have three children, seven grandchildren and one great-granddaughter.

**Neighborhood Experiences**

The Steep Brook School was a one-room schoolhouse opposite Ashley Street on North Main Street, on the old Border City lot at Steep Brook.

Steep Brook was very quiet then. I remember when North Main Street was a narrow road. Only once in a while a car would go by. Kids would go out to play in the road, and there was no chance that they would get hurt because there was so little traffic. A neighbor's dog slept all day in the middle of North Main Street. The few cars that came by never went that fast, and they drove around the dog.

One of our neighbors was an old woman named Simmons whose husband was an old sea captain. She lived at 3519 North Main Street. Mr. Campbell moved into the house when Mrs. Simmons died.

There is a Durfee family cemetery near the Ship's Walk apartment building. When the building was built, the stones were removed to Oak Grove Cemetery but the bodies are still in the Durfee cemetery. The stones there date from 1786.

The Thurston family cemetery is also located near the Ship's Walk apartments and near to the Durfee cemetery. It is bigger than the Durfee cemetery and has a wall around it and an iron gate. The Thurston gravestones date from 1782.

Noverca's Sawmill, at the bottom of North Main Street, was in Steep Brook for many years. One of the Noverca sons lost his leg when he slipped and his leg went into the saw.

There was an old stone mill building on Steep Brook on the eastern side of North Main Street. My wife's family lived in an apartment on the top floor of this building.

Stump Pond was located at the eastern end of Driftwood Street, which was then a dirt lane. Joe Ouellette cut ice in Stump Pond for sale, and he had a wooden icehouse there. He had a route where he sold ice to residences in the area. The icehouse had double walls, with sawdust used as insulation between the walls. When the icehouse burned down, he quit. Route 24 now runs through there.

Aaron's Pond was about one-half mile northeast of the intersection of where Route 24 crosses Wilson Road, south of Wilson Road where Driftwood Street once merged into Wilson Road. It was millpond and there was once a mill there and a dam. We would ice skate on that pond. Under the ice, we could see cranberries growing. Pits and piles of clay near the pond were still visible where Clark Shaw once mined clay.

I remember when local farmers went about with horses and wagons and would go around the neighborhood to plow the many gardens in Steep Brook. One of these farmers was old man Heyworth, whose sons were Roger, George, Bob, and Ray. His farm was at the end of Ort Street (just south of Shaw's Plaza), where the industrial park is now and abutting the Reservation. He worked the farm with only horses and would take the team of horses out to plow gardens in Steep Brook. His son George later had a little farm with small animals where the small plaza is now, north of Shaw's.

Lester Allen kept cows and had an orchard on his farm in Steep Brook. Lester Allen's farm was on the west side of North Main Street, where Rolling Green, Waterview, and Castle Court apartment developments are now located. There was a rifle range in the area of the airport.

Dinny [Dennis] O'Brien had a horse stable near Ort Street, east of North Main Street. He had a riding stable there and we rented horses and rode into the Reservation, which was a nice ride. That was before the highway (Route 24) was put through. The highway came when I was about sixteen years old.

Cote also had a stable just west of the North Main Street rotary and had a stone barn in the back of the property. A wooden bridge connected the Cote property with the golf course through an old right-of-way that ran from North Main Street to the golf course.

Dick Wordell's father had his cow farm, where Dick Wordell and his two sisters grew up. They were older than me, but we all rode in the school bus together. Next to the Wordell Farm was the McMurray Farm, which had Ayreshire cows, with their big horns. His son, Chuck McMurray, was a tender later on the Brightman Street Bridge.

**Recreation and Entertainment**
Everyone had a Red Ryder BB gun. I remember getting my Red Ryder BB gun for Christmas when I was ten or twelve years old. I started hunting with a pellet gun when I was fifteen. When

I was sixteen, I got my first .22 rifle and a 12-gauge shotgun for hunting. Back then, people could walk down the road or ride a bus with a gun as long as it wasn't loaded.

Every family in Steep Brook had a boat on the Taunton River. When I was twelve years old, I would go rowing or use the five horse power motor. We fished a lot on the river for perch, eels, and bass. We had a catboat, which had a mast in front of the boat and a sail like that on a ketch. My father and Frank Fairhurst's father would go down to Prudence Island in the boat and fish and dig for clams and quahogs. Bill Fairhurst had the catboat and my father had a lobster boat, which he never used to catch lobsters.

On Sunday, we kids would go hiking in the woods. When I turned sixteen, I went hunting. I would go out with my .22 and target shoot in the woods. From our back yard, we could go right into the woods and reach the Reservation. At sixteen, I got a car and could go hunting in other areas.

In the summer, I swam at Bessie's Beach on the river. It was private land owned by Dave Millard. While you had to pay at Bliffins Beach, Bessie's was free. Bessie's Beach had twelve-foot skiffs on the beach owned by neighborhood residents, who used the skiffs to reach their larger boats on the river. There was even a little boat railway to get the boats out of the water in the fall. We swam and fished in the river all summer long.

In the winter, we would go eeling, or fishing for eels through the ice up the Taunton River. Merrill Gagnon, whose wife was a nurse, told my brother and me that if we brought some eels to his wife, she would cook up a meal of eels and johnnycakes. She cut the eels in pieces and fried them, with johnnycakes on the side. The johnnycakes were nice and golden brown. We really enjoyed those meals. I believe that Fred and Ann's restaurant in Westport still makes johnnycakes and eels.

We sledded a lot in the winter. We sledded down Highland Avenue below the Catholic Memorial Home. There wasn't much traffic on Highland Avenue then. In those days, the City never salted the roads. The plowing that was done never went down to the pavement and so the snow packed down. Everyone with a car had skid chains put on for the winter. We also sledded a lot on the golf course.

One year, Arthur Hancock (who now builds winches on the river) built a big bobsled. One night, about six neighborhood guys brought the bobsled to the top of Weetamoe Street and took off down the hill. Freddy Olivera was in front driving the sled and had goggles on. We were flying so fast that his goggles flew off! We finally came to a stop by smashing into a snow bank in back of St. Joseph's Church.

On some Saturdays, I would go downtown to the movies, especially to the Academy Building theater. I never went to the Royal Theater in the North End.

**School Life**

I attended Wiley School from the first to the sixth grade, and then went to Morton for three more years, until ninth grade. I then went to Bristol Aggie, starting as a freshman, and graduated there in 1956. I loved it. I majored in market gardening and worked in the Aggie vegetable fields and apple orchards. I pruned the apple trees each spring.

While at Aggie, during hunting season, we would go hunting in the morning before school and in the afternoon after school. We would keep our shotguns in the rear seat of my car in the school parking lot. No one thought anything of it. I doubt if you could do that today.

**Work Life**

I worked as a fisherman out of New Bedford for forty years, starting in 1960. I never liked it, but it was good money. I stayed on one boat (of about 105 feet) for sixteen years. We would go out scalloping with eleven men and would be able to bring in 11,000 pounds of scallops in a trip. Trips were usually for ten days, eight days fishing and one day to go and one to return. If we went to Long Island, we fished for nine days. Sometimes we would go fishing off Cape Hatteras, which would take forty hours to go and forty hours to come back. Now, they stay out a lot longer and go with fewer men.

We went dragging for fish also. We dragged mostly for ground fish, such as cod or yellowtail flounder. The nets were held up with yellow eight-inch cans attached to the top of the net to suspend the net and a "door" that held the net open. The net would travel through the water in a V-shape. If we wanted to catch fish that swam higher in the ocean, such as haddock, we put on more cans to raise the net. The net stayed on the bottom of the ocean floor while the cans raised the top of the net.

We towed the net for one and one-half to two and one-half hours and it would take about twenty minutes to get the net back to the boat, haul it in, empty it, and set it out again. When we brought the fish in, we separated them, put them in the hold, and packed them with ice. The ice kept the fresh fish unfrozen but didn't freeze them.

We went out year-round. Winter was pretty rough since there were lots of storms in that season.

Fishing is exhausting because you only get a chance to sleep for short periods. When dragging, we would work eight hours on and only four hours off. Sometimes, we worked for nine hours, with only three hours off. For scalloping, we would work six hours on and six hours off. It's a good job, but you can never get enough sleep. I was always tired and bored.

People from all over the world came to fish in New Bedford. They came for the better paying union jobs. Lots of Maine guys came, since Maine boats didn't pay that well, but there were also fishermen from New Jersey, Mississippi, Newfoundland, Nova Scotia, England, France, Norway, Sweden, Portugal, Spain, Denmark, Italy, and Mexico.

To take a break from fishing, during cranberry season, I worked at Ocean Spray. I worked in the warehouse on separators that dry-picked cranberries. The separators divided the berries into grades. The berries that bounced were the good ones, and these went into packing for direct retail sales. The lesser grades, which didn't bounce, were used for juice. The worst berries, and waste such as vines, were thrown out. The wet-pick berries, where the bogs are flooded and the berries harvested from the water, were used for juice and cranberry sauce.

The machines for dry-separating the berries are made of wood and date from the 1920s and 1930s because they have found that these machines work the best. The company tried other technology but found that nothing works as well as the old machines. A big blower blows the weeds out. These machines were powered by belts and electric motors.

# Robert Kitchen

*Born on July 9, 1937*

**Family Background**

I was born in Fall River in the old Truesdale Hospital. With the exception of my service years, I have always resided here.

My parents were William ("Bill") and Victoria (LePage) Kitchen. My father's parents were Robert and Mary (Wilson) Kitchen. My mother's parents were John and Marie (Madore) LePage. They came from Canada. I had one brother, William Edward Kitchen, now deceased. Our family residences were at 205 Albion Street and 101 Plain Street.

My wife's name is Catherine (Howard) Kitchen. We have three children: Vicky, Rob, and Jon. We have four grandchildren: Nick, Zack, Spencer, and Charlotte.

**Family Life**

I grew up in the Flint, on Albion Street. My mother-in-law, who grew up in the South End, never went to the Flint; she thought of it as a foreign land. She finally went there when she married and her husband took a job in the Flint.

There was something called a "wet wash." The dirty laundry was put out Sunday night and delivery men would pick it up after midnight. Delivery people couldn't deliver on Sundays until after midnight, although they sometimes pushed the time. The clothes were brought to the laundry and washed and spun dry. The wash was returned on Monday and my mother would hang the washed clothes on the clothesline; when they were dry, she would iron them. My mother spent a couple of days of every week ironing.

When medicine shows came to the city, they sometimes offered free tooth extractions; my dad told me that the city offered extractions at City Hall. My dad jokingly said that he thought the guy who pulled the teeth at City Hall was a plumber.

**School Life**

My father went to Sacred Heart School. You had to wear shoes to school. In order to get kicked out of school, my dad and his brother would hide their shoes in a rock crevice on their way to school. They would put their feet out so the nun would see that they didn't have shoes, but the nun would hit their feet with a stick. When they got home, they got hit again.

**Recreation and Entertainment**

My uncle Harry Kitchen owned Kitchen's Market on Pine Street. It was originally Sullivan's Market. My other uncle Joe Kitchen owned Delia's Kitchen on Second Street, across from the Holmes Apartments and above Morgan Street. There was a rooming house on Second Street where the players for the Fall River Indians stayed, and they ate at Delia's. The rooming house was owned by the owner of the Fall River Indians, Joe Madowski. The Indians were part of the Class

B Division of the New England League. It included the Nashua Dodgers and the Lynn Red Sox. The Brooklyn Dodgers' Don Newcomb played for the Nashua Dodgers. The games in Fall River were played at the Fall River Stadium at what is now Britland Park.

There were also midget car races at the stadium; I could hear the noise of the cars from my house on Albion Street. They also had rodeos at the stadium. During the sesquicentennial in 1953, there were several nights of pageants, with people dressed up as Indians and things like that.

Bowl-a-wicket was a takeoff on cricket. We played it on the street. The wicket was made up of three cans, two on the bottom and one sitting on top. A circle was drawn on the street in chalk and that was where you would rest one end of your bat (a broom handle in this case). There was a similar setup thirty-five yards away. The opposing player would then roll the ball along the ground, and the batsman tried to hit the ball. If he did, then the runners would see how many trips back and forth they could make. If the ball knocked the cans over and the batter did not have his bat resting on the circle, that would be an out.

Peggy ball was later played with small wooden balls that you could buy at variety stores. Sunday morning, after Mass, the big guys would play peggy ball for quarters at Lafayette Park. In those days, the parks were full of kids. Today, they are empty.

I would go with my mother to the movies on Tuesdays, which was dish day. Every now and then we would be startled by a dish that would crash to the floor in the theatre, I guess because someone forgot that they had a dish on their lap.

## Neighborhood Experiences

Older guys hung out on corners when I was young. Usually they hung out outside the corner variety store. The owners didn't mind; at least they weren't inside and they usually bought something. They weren't afraid of the kids then. If you did something, the store owner would call your mother. There were certain guys on certain corners.

In my father's day, the guys would hang out on corners and sing popular songs. They went to amateur shows, taking the trolley to theatres in Warren [Rhode Island] or New Bedford to sing.

One of the first TVs on Albion Street was owned by Eli Fortin. We kids would sit on the porch and watch his TV. He would open the window on the porch and about ten of us looked inside his parlor window to watch. He always seemed like a rough guy, but he was nice enough to let us kids watch his TV.

Some of the early TVs were so small they had magnifying glasses mounted in front to enlarge the picture. The first color TVs were just plastic overlays in three colors that stuck to the screen.

During the war, about 1943-44, I remember a man with no legs being dropped off on our street. He would be placed on a small dolly, and he would put his hands in straps on either side of the dolly. He would then go down the street, put his hat in front of him, and sing. He had a wonderful voice. My mother didn't want to go down but sent me down with a quarter to throw in his hat.

There was also a guy with a pony that went around the neighborhood taking pictures of kids on the pony. Once, I had my picture taken with short pants and dirty knees. There was also a two-wheeled Pony Boy Ice Cream donkey cart-like wagon that went through the neighborhood and was pulled by a real pony. Dry ice kept the ice cream cold. We also had a Waffle Man go through the neighborhood. He came in a green truck and made waffles in the truck. He would break them up into four pieces and put powdered sugar on them. They sold for five cents.

**Work Life**

When he was young, my dad would work in the mill until 6:00 pm as a sweeper. He would then go to the bowling alley and set pins for a penny a string. He might make a nickel for setting five strings. When he got the nickel he said he would hold it in his hand and try to decide should he go to the Nickelodeon and see a movie or go to the bakery and buy a piece of pastry. They evidently would use the leftover pastries and make some sort of concoction by breaking up the old cakes and things and molding them into something that they sold cheaply.

My father worked in the mills. He was always a big union man. He helped to organize in the Kerr Mills. In those days, if you went to organize in the mills, they would send the cops after you. He had to hide out and not go home for a few days to avoid the cops.

When my father was very young, the workers went to the mill owners for a two-cents-an-hour raise. In response, the owners closed all of the mills. To survive, the family went to an uncle's small cabin in Ocean Grove [Swansea, Massachusetts]. My grandfather fished there and traded the fish for produce from local farmers. That is how they survived. The mill owners were on top. One of the groups active in the union movement were the Primitive Methodists from Lancashire. They were also active in unionizing in England. There was a British Club in the city.

My great-grandfather was from Lancashire. My other great-grandfather was from Canada.

My father boxed to make money at The Casino on Morgan Street. There were also amateur singing nights at theatres. You could win five dollars. He and another guy would do the amateur nights, going to various casinos and theatres in different cities. They couldn't appear every week at amateur hours, so they had to tour various theatres in various cities to make what little money they could. In addition to boxing in the casinos, my father also sang in theatres in these amateur shows.

My father actually saw Harry Houdini in Fall River. My father said that on one occasion, a performer who imitated Harry Houdini asked people in the audience to come on the stage and tie him up. This time, a few sailors came up and tied him with marine knots, and he couldn't get out.

My father worked for the Eastern Mass[achusetts] Street Railway as a general helper, changing tires and jobs of that nature. When the company went on strike, he lost his job. During the strike, he painted houses, painted fishing boats, and picked apples. Then he worked for the Strand Theatre on Pleasant Street in the Flint. He worked every morning cleaning the theatre, even on his day off. He would go home, clean up, and return to collect tickets. He then worked at the General Hospital and retired from there. After he retired, he worked for Charlton Hospital in the kitchen cleaning pots and pans. He was then in his seventies then, and the doctor told him to stop after he had a fainting spell during work.

**Downtown**

I worked at Kennedy's Butter and Eggs store in the Flint beginning in 1954, and then I moved to the downtown store in my senior year at Durfee [B.M.C. Durfee High School] in 1955 and 1956. I then went into the service. I got out of the service in 1958, and the next day I went back to work at Kennedy's downtown.

Kennedy's sold in bulk. Butter came in forty-pound cardboard boxes wrapped in paper. We cut the butter with a wire instrument through the long blocks. We cut the blocks in several directions to arrive at a pound of butter. It was good butter, with a high fat content. Then, we also had other grades of butter. In those days, people bought butter every week, which they used

Truesdale Hospital, on Highland Avenue, now condominiums

for cooking and to butter their bread. Kennedy's Butter had a high cream content, and it was the richest butter of anyone. If someone wanted butter only for cooking or for a cheaper price, we sold the second grade.

We also sold bulk tea, bulk coffee, and eggs. There were three grades of coffee. We would weigh out a pound of coffee beans in an old-fashioned metal scale and grind it for you. The tea we put up in packages for you. The eggs came un-candled; we had to candle them ourselves. We also sold cookies and ice cream.

Kennedy's had no lunch counter. It had a cold cuts counter. I originally worked in the dairy side; when I came back from the service, I worked on the chicken and deli side.

Some people you could joke with, some not. One time, we had a sale on fowl, which is really stewing chicken. A man came in and said, "Hey, the chicken you sold me last time was tough as hell." We replied, "We thought you were smarter than that." He was obviously someone you could joke with.

A little old lady came in and bought four hot dogs for the week. She bought the regular hot dogs. Unlike skinless dogs, natural casing hot dogs at one end of the string are fatter than hot dogs at the other end. Not all are of equal size. On a regular hot dog, this is the way it is. I told her the story of the irregular filling in the intestines and why that occurs. The dogs were a dollar and twenty cents last week and a dollar and forty cents this week because they were fatter. The lady looked at me and said, "Oh, come on, young man," looking in disbelief. For the most part, we sold high quality items.

Kennedy's was based out of Cambridge. We had store competitions. There were different categories of stores. The store in the Flint, for example, didn't have a deli counter or sell chicken. The Kennedy store downtown, however, did sell fresh chicken. We would bone breasts for customers. Our prices were higher that the supermarkets, but we did extra. We would cut up a whole chicken if requested to do so. The distributor would bring in whole chickens, cut up chicken breasts or legs.

Kennedy's also sold bulk peanut butter. People loved it. We would scoop it out. It was a big seller. We would put it in cardboard containers that looked like ice cream containers.

In the downtown Kennedy's, the chicken and deli were on the right. The rest was all bulk coffee and cheese of all kinds. The butter cases were in back. We cut the butter to order, although we sometimes cut it ahead so customers wouldn't wait too long. There was an office above on a balcony that looked down on the store. There was always the smell of coffee grinding.

On Saturdays, the downtown store had seven employees, which was a lot for a small store with only a few items. Some people came only for the butter.

Kennedy's had no credit and didn't make home deliveries. Deliveries to the store by distributors were made at night from the front door; there was no back door for deliveries. The night before the delivery, we put a canvas tent up toward the front of the store. The driver had a key to the front door and came into the store and left his deliveries there. The canvas tent prevented the driver from going into the main store.

The old metal registers had keys for one, two, five, and ten. Twenty-dollar bills we put under the drawer. The registers didn't tally; we did that on a brown paper bag before the items were put in the bag. One kid wrote very large on the bags, and the manager said, "Not too big." Then we put the total in the register. We pressed the keys with all at once with both hands, for the dollars and cents. The registers were all manual, not electrified, as they were later. If anyone bought more than a certain amount, we would have to ring it twice, like more than twenty dollars. You would have to press twenty, then ten plus two, to make thirty-two. The keys were limited. We had to do this for large drug store sales.

In the Flint, the drugstores had counters that served coffee and coffee cabinets. Lafayette Drug Store would buy its coffee from the Kennedy store. The Night Owl Diner bought its cheese for its hot cheese sandwiches from us. They used our medium strong cheddar, which melted well. They served the hot cheese sandwiches with a bun, onion, and relish. I remember the Night Owl Diner when it was downtown near City Hall. It was on wheels and very small. It consisted of a grill for cooking and stools in a small space.

My aunt also worked downtown at Van Dykes, across the street from Kennedy's. She worked at the lunch counter there. Van Dykes had more expensive stuff than Kennedy's. The counter at Van Dykes was popular; you had to line up to get a seat there. Kennedy's was a chain and had 100 stores in New England, but Van Dykes was a local place; it was the only one. My mother and sister would go downtown to Van Dykes. It was famous for its sandwiches. Van Dykes had only the counter, and there was always someone waiting.

I liked the lunch counter at McWhirr's. The counter was run by Paul McGovern; Paul later opened McGovern's Restaurant. Ronnie worked on the counter there as the counter man. He still works at McGovern's on weekends. He was very affable. I liked McWhirr's counter because they served more than sandwiches. They served hot lunches like American chop suey. Some of the 5 & 10s also had lunch counters.

Paul Woltman was a fancy men's store. My wife bought a sweater there for me as a Christmas gift the first year we dated.

Bessie Russell was a downtown men's and boys' store. They had a method of making change that was like a basket on a chain system. It consisted of a can on a pulley. When the handle was squeezed, it would shoot the can up the wire to the balcony, where the cashier was located.

## Health and Illness

There was something made in Fall River called "Red Sea Balsam." My father still used it for anything. If you didn't feel well, you could drink it. If you had sore muscles, you could put it on your skin. It had a lot of alcohol in it. Father John's Medicine was also widely used.

One day, I went to visit my dad. When I walked into the house, there were pieces of black carbon in the air. My stepmother had a bad head cold and her sister said she should use an old French Canadian remedy called the flannel. You took a piece of flannel cloth and soaked it in warm kerosene then put it on your chest. My stepmother heated the kerosene too much and it caught on fire. That's how the pieces of carbon got in the air.

## The Depression and Prohibition

My father's family was too poor to afford butter, so my father had a lot of lard sandwiches. Their big meal was beans and bread. My grandmother had a total of eight kids. Three died young. During the birth of her last child, my grandmother died in childbirth. My grandfather (my mother's father) worked at the Cote Piano Factory.

Before Social Security, you relied on a large family for income and because at least one of your children would stay with you or take you in when you were old.

"Carrying the bag," meant going downtown to the city's Welfare Office to get a bag of food. The sack was marked and identifiable as coming from the Welfare Office. It discouraged people from going there. In those days, people wouldn't take anything.

My father said that, in his day, if you wanted milk, you went to the grocery store and it was ladled out of a tin can. Flies were drowning in the milk. You brought a bottle to the store and they filled it for you, after moving the flies out of the way. His mother would mix the milk with the center part of a loaf of bread and give it to the kids. My father said that, "If you survived that, you survived anything."

The mills closed for a week for vacation. There was no pay for that week. My grandmother would go down to Sandy Beach for a "vacation" if they had saved enough money that year. There was an amusement park there in those days.

## The Fall River Line and Transportation

Sometimes, when couples didn't have enough money for a honeymoon to New York City on the Fall River Line, they would get off in Newport and stay there. They would then get back on the boat to Fall River when their stay was over.

When I was transcribing letters at the Historical Society, there was a letter dated about 1849, where a brother is telling his sister from Baltimore that, if she wanted to go to Fall River, she should take train to New York, then take the boat to Providence. She should stay on the boat and go to Bristol. He would then pick her up by land there. The route overland, he said, was too long and too dirty.

To get to Providence from Fall River, a person had to take the trolley over the Slade's Ferry Bridge (the trolley passed along the top level of the two-level bridge) to Warren [Rhode Island]. In 1910 (before my time), there was a trolley to Providence every half-hour from Fall River. The trolley took forty-eight minutes to cover the 19.4 miles between Fall River and Providence. There were twenty-seven stops along the route.

# Mary (Yankopoulos) Kostas

*Born on May 14, 1929*

**Family Background**

I was born in a house on Union Street, near Hope Street, where we lived until I was twelve. I lived at 163 Grove Street until age twenty-seven, when I married.

My parents were Leonidas ("Leo") Yankopoulos, who immigrated to the United States from Macedonia, and Helen (Kravatas) Yankopoulos, who came to Fall River from Lowell. Her parents were born in an area of Greece known as Sparta.

My father's parents were Argyrios and Mary (Demos) Yankopoulos. They remained in Greece, although I wrote, in Greek, to my grandmother regularly.

My mother's parents were Costas and Paraskeve (Paraskevopoulos) Kravatas. They emigrated from Greece about 1903 or 1904 and settled in Lowell and worked in the mills there. They came here separately and met here.

My father had two brothers and four sisters. Two sisters lived in Boston and the other two lived in Greece. My mother had two brothers and one sister. They grew up in New Bedford.

I have two brothers, Dean and George.

My father owned a hat cleaning and shoe shining parlor at 200 South Main Street, across from McWhirr's. It was called the Fall River Hat Cleaning and Shoe Shine Parlor. My father dyed shoes for weddings for bridesmaids and dress balls.

My husband is Stratis Kostas and we have two daughters, Ann and Elene.

**Family Life**

I did my homework, read, took my piano lessons, and went to Greek School. In the summer, I would spend a lot of time with my mother's parents in New Bedford. We were always in church. My father and mother were heavily involved with church.

My husband's parents were married in a house that was on the property that Lizzie Borden owned on Durfee Street that was later torn down to build the Animal Rescue League. When it was torn down, they set up residence in New Bedford, where his dad had a partnership in a candy-making business.

My cousins were all on my father's side. Theologos "Teddy" Yanakopoulos had two sons and a daughter. One of the sons was Gus and the daughter was Yolanda. Alexander Yanakopoulos had a restaurant downtown, the Nira Restaurant. It was right next to the Fall River National Bank on North Main Street.

**Food and Meals**

My mother cooked the usual Greek dishes; she loved to make pastries. She made wonderful preserved fruits. They were candied fruits in syrup, including grapefruit and orange skins. Shredded quince was a favorite. When you visited anyone, you got a tiny piece of this fruit with

Yankopoulos family

Mary Yankopoulos

a tiny glass of cognac or brandy and a small cup of Greek coffee. In the summer for refreshment, you were served a concoction of a spoonful of vanilla stirred in a glass of water.

**School Life**

We kids went to Greek Sunday School on Saturday. We had religious education on Saturday because the priest was the teacher. On Monday, Wednesday, and Friday, we went to Greek School. Our mothers would take us and they would hang out in the library while we were in school. When we were old enough, we walked to school.

I graduated from Durfee [B.M.C. Durfee High School] in 1947. I played bass fiddle in the Durfee orchestra and was in the chorus. My favorite teacher was Mr. Williston, who taught chemistry. He opened my eyes to the universe. I went to Bridgewater [now Bridgewater State University] and graduated in 1951.

**Courtship and Marriage**

My husband and I had known one another since childhood through Greek Church youth activities (we have a photograph of the two of us, where I was eight and he was twelve). Stratis' first cousin lived in Fall River and was a friend of mine. We later met again at a relative's christening. Stratis' aunt was the godmother.

**Work Life**

After I graduated from Bridgewater, I taught at the Davol School. While I was there, professors from Bridgewater, who had come to supervise a student teacher, were surprised to see

Leo Yankopolous, at age 76, from 1973, Fall River Hat Cleaning and Shoe Shine Parlor, 200 South Main Street

me there (my education was for advanced sciences classes in the higher grades) and notified the superintendent. I was then assigned to Henry Lord for one-and-a-half years and was then asked to go to Durfee High School to teach there, where I taught in the Math Department.

**Neighborhood Experiences**

The Greeks were involved in all kinds of food establishments, including diners, candy-making, and ice cream. There was a hat cleaning and shoe shining parlor in the Academy Building owned by a Kazantis. The dad of Peter Collias, George Collias, had a shoe shine parlor in the Granite Block. Theologos Yanakopoulos had a grocery store on Pleasant Street. John Jamoulis had a grocery store on Bedford Street.

**Religious Life**

A big feast is the Greek Feast of the Annunciation on March 25th, when the Greek Language School pupils recited poems. We also celebrated the end of the year at Greek School with a program of songs, poems, etc.

Name Day is huge in the Greek community. That is the day of your named saint. We had Name Day parties, where we had open house and relatives and friends came. There were huge amounts of food. We had music, dancing, singing, and lots of camaraderie. The usual stuff that you do at parties. We would also have a big bash on St. Demetrios Day, August 15. He is the patron saint of our community.

In the 1920s and 1930s, the Greeks stayed together. Some of the Greek associations were Ahepa, Sons of Pericles, Daughters of Penelope, and the Greek-American Progressive Association.

I wrote the history of St. Demetrios Church for the church's fiftieth anniversary and my husband and I co-authored the history for the seventy-fifth anniversary of the church. At Greek School, they taught us about Greek culture and history. All boys had to be altar boys at some point.

Father Stephanopoulos was pastor at St. Demetrios from 1959 to 1966. At least three of the Stephanopoulos children were born here during that time. My mother baby-sat for George Stephanopoulos.

**Health and Illness**

Some of the traditional home remedies included putting a piece of cotton in the bottom of a glass, attached to the glass by wax. The cotton was then ignited and the glass inverted on the skin where the pain was located. The suction from the combustion in the glass would draw out the pain. Another remedy was to put some cinnamon on a headband and wrap it around your head. This cured headaches. Midwives were commonly used at births.

Some of the common illnesses at that time were scarlet fever and diphtheria. If there was a case of scarlet fever in the house, the Board of Health put up a quarantine sign on the front door.

**Popular Expressions**

Some slang sayings were "Hot Ticket" and "Bust Your Buttons," a saying in Greek that meant go faster; it was also used to say "scram."

# Argirios Kuliopulos

*Born in 1940*

**Family Background**

My mother's name was Polixeny [Polixeny's interview follows this one in the book]. I have one brother, Theophilos.

In Greece, during the civil war with Turkey, the Turkish Army was killing everyone. Everyone was told to escape my father's village. They were told that the Greek Army was going to be at Siatista, so everyone walked there. The men were in the military. My father was five years old at the time and carried his young cousin. When they got to Siatista, there was no Greek Army there. An old man remembered that there was an antique cannon at the bottom of the cliff. They spent the whole night bringing the cannon up the cliff and fixing the cannon and loading it.

At sunrise, the Turkish Army arrived at the base of the cliff. They gave the signal to kill everyone. The Turks had killed everyone in many towns in Northern Greece. When the Turks charged, the townspeople fired the cannon, and it worked! It was filled with stones and debris. The Turks left. Both my parents were there, but they didn't know one another at the time.

My mother's father came to the United States when he was young. He read that the streets were paved with gold, so he got on a boat and arrived in New York. However, he found that the streets were not paved with gold. In fact, the streets were not paved. If they were paved, the immigrants were expected to do the paving. He was not interested in that. He heard someone say, "Go West, young man," so he got a job building the trans-continental railroad. They lived on the train as it moved with the construction of the railroad; it was like a city. He was there when the west coast and east coast railroad construction teams met and nailed in the golden spike.

With that job done, he read that there is gold in Alaska, so he went to Alaska and got a job with a mining company in a company town. He got paid seven dollars a week and was charged eight dollars a week for room and board. The crew walked up the mountain with high-pressure hoses and washed down the soil that ran in sluices that washed out and captured the gold. When he wanted to leave, he sent a letter to his father requesting money for his fare back to Greece and to pay off the company. When he returned to Greece, he was considered a world traveler, and they elected him mayor of his town.

My father came here with a nickel in his pocket. He initially went to New Bedford and got an ice cream truck working for the New Bedford Ice Cream Co. He went to high school for a year (he was educated in Greece) and from there went to Wentworth Institute to study electrical engineering. He came from a town with twelve homes. There were no jobs in Greece.

He saved ten thousand dollars selling ice cream and went back to Greece. He bought a percent of an estate that was owned by a Turkish pasha in northern Greece, Macedonia, where he was from. The forty-acre estate included a dam and a flour mill. He tried to get a license to build a hydro-electric plant on the dam, but the government preferred that the area not have electricity rather than give the license to someone they didn't know or to whom they were not related.

My mother's dowry included a pasha's estate within the city that included a four-story house with running water and toilet facilities.

My father had to borrow money to come back to the United States. The first time, he had a nickel; the second time he was in debt.

He went to Fall River and worked at Samitas Restaurant. When he was young, Theofanis Samitas had worked for Thomas Edison in New Jersey and worked on developing the phonograph, among other things. He was very intelligent.

Then, my father bought the Liberty Lunch at 208 Bedford Street. There was a hotel at 212 Bedford Street. That was prior to Prohibition. When Prohibition was repealed, he got a liquor license when they first came out. With the liquor license, it became the Liberty Café.

**Family Life**

I was home-delivered in a cold-water flat on Wrightington Place. We had no central heat and no hot water. I was delivered by Dr. Hatfield from Bank Street. We moved to 24 Oak Street when I was five.

We didn't get a telephone until 1953. We had a four-party line. At that time, it cost thirteen dollars a minute to call Greece. Now it is thirteen cents a minute.

My brother Theophilos worked at Bell Labs. He developed the filter that screened out the annoying static that always accompanied long-distance calls. Theophilos made a big map of the area around Oak Street when he was young. He took apart watches, but I don't know if he put them back together.

We spent a lot of time in church. The Greeks were named after patron saints. On or about the first Sunday around the saint's anniversary date, a person would have their patron saint's day. On that Sunday, the family would have an open house. You didn't invite anyone; people just showed up. About fifty people came to our patron saint's day. No one brought anything with them; the host provided everything.

Every Sunday, we would go somewhere to visit relatives and friends. We would go to New York City, to Hartford, New Bedford, Hyannis, Manchester, New Hampshire, Cambridge, Newport, and Brockton. We drove there and stayed for supper. We stayed from about 5:00 pm to 1:00 am. In those days, people drank a lot and smoked a lot. The kids would play spin the bottle and strip poker.

When there was a wedding or a baptism, the whole family was invited. Children were included in everything. My parents were both psychic. They telecommunicated. One year, my father told my mother to cook twice as much food for a patron saint's day gathering. So, she cooked for a hundred people instead of the usual fifty. "What are we going to do with all the food?" she asked. "Don't worry," he said. After church, fifty people came; at 5:00 pm, another fifty people came and cleaned us out. Typically, the people who came at noon were the casuals; those who came in the evening were regulars. My father's telecommunication powers saved the day.

He would tell me that someone had died in Greece. He didn't know who. Several days later, we would get a letter with a black border. It's like radio signals. I have a little of that. I'm afraid to develop it.

We had an icebox. My mother would put a card in the window when we needed a block of ice. The iceman delivered the ice in a horse-drawn wagon. In the summer, he would chop the ice so the children would get slivers of ice.

Before we got a refrigerator—pre-1951—we made ice cream in winter with snow as the coolant instead of ice. We put in the cream, salt a capsule, and put it on the roof in the snow. After we got the refrigerator, we never made ice cream again.

Mr. Mooney and his brother built a house at 1597 Robeson Street. In 1950, my parents happened to buy that house. After our family moved in, my father invited the whole Mooney clan over to the house for a party just for them. While they were there, word came that Mr. Mooney had just died while catching a marlin off of Florida. My father wouldn't let anyone leave. They all got drunk together.

**Recreation and Entertainment**

My typical summer day in the mid-1940s, when I was five or six, was that I would go off to the Central Police Station on Bedford Street to get a drink of water. Then, I'd walk into the main fire station to look at the fire engines. Then, I'd walk to the Quequechan River and throw rocks at the foot-long water rats. I'd then walk to Main Street to go to the four 5 & 10s. There were three in a row. Then, I would walk through Cherry and Webb. It was a women's clothing store with three floors. Then, I'd go through McWhirr's Department Store to visit people that I knew who were secretaries. I knew the McWhirr's secretaries because they were Greek and sometimes neighbors. Helen Karakostos lived on O'Grady Street. Another was Mary Samitas, daughter of Theofanis Samitas.

Then, I'd walk to the waterfront along the railroad tracks where there were naval vessels along the dock. I would poke them and get them moving and kept them moving with sticks until they got to the end of the rope. Then I would go home for supper.

I often walked with the postman for hours as he delivered the mail.

I walked up to the Watuppa Pond one day, and a dog started following me. I had a can of beans with me. I went up to the old icehouse and made a fire in the icehouse. The dog stayed with me until we got back to where he lived on O'Grady Street. I never had a thought of any danger to kids.

On Saturdays, I'd get a quarter from my parents and go to the Strand Theatre on Pleasant Street. They would start with a half-hour of cartoons, then show two movies, one a Tarzan or a Superman movie. In-between, they would have acts like crack-shots, where one person would hold a cookie and another person would shoot at it from the other end of the stage. The person holding the cookie would crush it as it was "hit" by the bullet. They also had contests of eating ice cream. I won one once. Then I'd go home for lunch, get a quarter, and go down Bedford Street for a frappe. The place I went to made home-made ice cream. One store was near Ruggles Park. When I went there, I would climb the stone wall at the park.

On Columbus Day, the whole family would go to Columbus Park for the fireworks and then go to Marzilli's and get two loaves of bread and a square pizza—they were square then. They had a wood-fired oven. We would also go to Horseneck Beach by bus before 1947 and, after that, when my father bought a Packard, we would go by car to Gooseberry Island and play all day unsupervised. We would "borrow" people's boats that were on the beach and take them out rowing to go fishing. I didn't know how to swim. We would always go on Wednesdays, since that's when my relatives had a half-day off.

At Gooseberry, we broke into the military lookout towers at the end of the causeway. German U-Boats were along the coast in World War I, and there were torpedoes in the area. At the end of the war, the buildings remained unused. On the hill, there was a building with refrigeration inside for the military. The tower had a base for a machine gun or a telescope. We were the first to break into the buildings and explore.

On Halloween, sometimes we'd go out with hundreds of kids and line up in a single file at someone's house and ring the doorbell. All night, we would be out on Halloween.

We made gunpowder and cannons and rockets.

One of the benefits of Fall River was that it had a lot of activities that I engaged in. There were ships in the water, the railroad, water rats, different stores, forests. The high school was large and had many activities. The church had a lot of activities. I was an altar boy. Young people read in front of the church; we became comfortable being a presenter to an audience.

In the summer, my brother and I volunteered to be brush firefighters. We would follow the trucks to the fire. They would strap a tank to your back and we would walk into the woods to put out the fire. Tree fires are dangerous because they can spread rapidly. Brush fires move along like a wave.

When I was growing up, the buses ran every fifteen minutes. We would go to Horseneck Beach and everywhere on the bus before 1947. The bus company plowed the streets back then. Basically, there were no cars.

I had a wonderful upbringing, with a stable home. In the summer, we would go to a Greek picnic every Sunday in various locations throughout New England. Every Greek Church had an annual picnic, with Greek dancing. These were held in New Bedford, Newport, Brockton, Manchester, and other cities. The picnics were in the woods and were all-day events. If there was no picnic, we went to Horseneck Beach. When I was growing up, every Sunday was a major holiday with friends and relatives. I was involved with many activities with the church; there was no time to get into trouble.

**School Life**

When my father walked me to my first day at kindergarten, he left me in Miss Quirk's room. After my father left, I didn't realize that I had to stay, and I left. No one told me that I had to stay. So, I left to go play on the trains—the big trains. On parent's night, we all wrote our names on the blackboard. I wrote Argirios Kuliopulos. After I wrote my name on the blackboard, Miss Quirk asked my father, "What do you think of that?" He said, "I think it's wrong." When my father came through Ellis Island, they shortened his name. She had used the original way to spell our name. My mother saw Miss Quirk five years ago in a bank and she asked, "How is Argirios?" She's still alive and she remembered me after all this time.

I went to the Leontine Lincoln School, then to the James Madison Morton Junior High School, then to Durfee [B.M.C. Durfee High School]. One time at Durfee, I found a key that opened the bell tower door. I climbed the bell tower with a hammer and, when the bell rang twelve times, I rang it a thirteenth time. It was noticed. I did this only once.

Durfee was excellent. We had seven hundred students in my graduating class. In high school, I was part of the Hilltop Serenaders, an *a cappella* group. I was also in a senior mixed chorus and in the boy's chorus. I was also president of the Chess Club and the Science Club.

I took courses in accounting and math at night. I couldn't take enough courses at Durfee. I had a full load at college, but I wanted to take more. They wouldn't let me.

One of my fellow students at Durfee was Michelle Kauffman. She was very intelligent. She

Lincoln School, 439 Pine Street

taught Latin 5 as a student. She also taught some classes in physics. She became one of the world's top radio astronomers. She had an assigned time on the Hubble Telescope, which was worth thousands of dollars. Her husband was one of the top mathematicians in the world.

We were not overloaded with homework until the ninth grade. My parents never told me to do homework—it was presumed that I would do it. The only thing that my parents commented on were my grades, when my father asked me why I didn't get an A in English because I was born here.

I applied and was admitted to Brown University and Bridgewater [now Bridgewater State University]. I went to Bridgewater because I could triple major in math, chemistry, and physics.

My Greek heritage gave me a sense of belonging in the world. It gave me roots. I came from somewhere. Knowing Greek fluently helped me in school. Many of the words in biology have Greek roots. When I took my entrance exam for my doctorate at Boston University, I'd say that twenty percent of the questions had Greek roots, twenty percent had Latin roots, and forty percent were math-related. It was a two-hour exam—I blasted through it in one-half hour. On the analogies section, there was only one question where I didn't know the words.

**Religious Life**

I went to Greek School Mondays, Wednesdays, and Fridays for twelve years. On Saturday, we went to catechism. On Sunday, we went to church. I was always involved in choral groups in the church. The church had operas and operettas, also, and the youth were involved in those.

After the war, my grandfather in Greece sent my mother a letter. However, on the envelope, he put only her name and after that "USA." There was no address. The letter was brought over with the first ship after the war. One day, the priest in church, Fr. Comninos, announced that he had an envelope for Mrs. Kuliopulos. It seems that the letter had traveled through the various Greek churches in America and finally arrived at its destination.

My mother took care of George Stephanopoulos and changed his diapers, so she knows him intimately. His father, Fr. Stephanopoulos, was very smart.

**Health and Illness**

My mother was like a doctor. She wanted to become a doctor, but this was unheard of in Greece. One of her home remedies was a cure for diarrhea. You would take dried pomegranate shells and boil them in red wine. Then you drank it. The next day, you were fine. Other persons would buy pills to take for it and it would take several days to cure. Chicken soup was also one of her home remedies.

# Polixeny Kuliopulos

*Born in 1912*

*Polixeny's son, Argirios Kuliopulos, whose interview precedes this one in the book, was present at the interview and occasionally added commentary to assist his frail mother of 102 years.*

## Family Background

My father and my husband's father were partners in Greece. They made flour in a mill. He was looking for a girl to marry. My brother said, "Don't go anywhere until you see my sister." My brother got a photo of me upstairs to show him. He took my photo to show his sister and said, "Maybe I marry this girl."

After we were married, my husband came to the United States to stay just two years. You would lose your papers after two years. If he stayed in Greece more than two years, he would lose his papers. He left his wife and mother. He had a first cousin in New York, and the cousin said to him, "Nick, Why are you here? There are no jobs here. Go back to Greece." It was in the middle of the Depression. Before he lost his papers, he had to come back, and he took the boat to come. He had come here alone.

It was very hard to bring me here. The United States said, "You can't bring your wife." "But, she's my wife," he said. He said that he had a job at a Greek restaurant, Mr. Samitas restaurant. Mr. Samitas helped him come here and to bring me here. He gave my husband a job and an apartment for us to live in.

When I came here, the first night I was walking on the street while my husband was working in the restaurant. Someone started talking to me in English on Bedford Street, and I didn't know what he was saying. I thought he was going to kill me.

My husband had first cousins in New York, so we would go there on the New York boats. We would leave at night and stay on the boat all night, then I would go shopping the next day and then come back the same day.

In Greece, people who supported the king were Royalists. When the king was overthrown, they were going to kill him and his family. The king went out to see my grandfather and my grandfather dressed the king and his family in peasant clothing and brought them to my grandfather's mother's house in a village in the mountains (my great-grandmother). My grandfather arranged for transport by ship of the king and his family and gave them the money to get out of Greece. The king went to my father because he was a Royalist.

*Argirios Kuliopulos:* My mom has correspondence with the royal family since then. A photo of the king and his family was sent by the king every year. In 1953, we were visiting Greece, and the king drove through the town we were in. My mother presented him with flowers. The king drove; he didn't trust anyone but himself to drive. The king's sister Sophia married the king of Spain.

*Polixeny Kuliopulos:* The downtown [of Fall River] had a beautiful City Hall and the Granite Block. All of the stores there and the restaurants were beautiful. I went shopping there every Wednesday with girlfriends. I was good friends with the wife of my husband's cousin. Every Wednesday we would go downtown to go to the 5 & 10s. We would eat at the McWhirr's counter and then go to the movies. The kids would come home for lunch.

*Argirios Kuliopulos:* Some families had twelve to seventeen children. My mother was the first woman bartender in Fall River after my father had his bar. She became a bartender after my father died. She ran the bar. She memorized the Constitution before she became a citizen. She would go to the library to learn English. She drove until about three years ago [at the age of ninety-nine].

*Polixeny Kuliopulos:* I was president of Philoptous for two years; it was a women's group at church. One time, we went to Greece. I told the president to prepare the papers in Greek. About thirty to forty people from the church belonged to the group.

*Argirios Kuliopulos:* Turkish women in harems showed my mother how to make cosmetics during the occupation. First, the southern part of Greece got free, then the northern part. My mother was born the day the *Titanic* was launched.

*Polixeny Kuliopulos:* The first Christmas here was wonderful; I had never seen anything like that. I was twenty-five when I came to the United States. After I moved, we found a store to buy and bought a house. I never moved after that. The barroom opened at 1:00 pm on Sundays, after church. I made a big mistake in not going to school. Back then, women didn't go to school.

*Argirios Kuliopulos:* After World War II, there was a program that repackaged food and clothing for citizens of Greece. My parents had a factory in the house where they would get extra clothing from factories and mail them to Greece. It was like a second full-time job. People were very generous. Greece was destroyed, first by the Germans and then by the Communists in the massive civil war.

# Rita (Fallon) LaFrance

*Born in 1923*

**Family Background**

My parents were James Patrick and Mary Louise (Crowell) Fallon.

I have five sisters: Kathleen, Mary ("May"), Jean and Joan (twins), and Patricia.

I have lived at the following addresses in Fall River: 44 Thompson Street, 105 Ballard Street, 33 North Court Street (married from there), 110 Horton Street (lived with in-laws), 170 Horton Street (first house we bought).

My husband is Amie LaFrance. We have one child, Richard.

My father was a mill worker. My mother brought up six children. Before that, she worked in the mill. They were both born in Fall River. My grandparents were all brought up in Fall River. My father came from 16 Colfax Street, near Ruggles Park.

**Family Life**

Every Sunday, we would march up to Aunt Mamie's. "You have to go visit your aunt." Aunt Mamie was the oldest of my father's sisters and the oldest in the family. Aunt Mamie had an old coal stove, and everyone met around the stove in that warm room. She was good to us kids. All the kids came over. Aunt Aggie lived next door. All the aunts and uncles would go there. We walked all the way from Down North to Colfax Street. We had good walking legs in those days.

My father worked at the Border City Mill when he wanted to work. He always said that he had rheumatism.

There were railroad tracks in back of us and, when a train went by, our mom would say, "You girls go pick up the coal and bring it back." It was free coal.

My mother made all my sister's clothes. I couldn't afford a new wedding dress, so I got married in a borrowed wedding gown. My sisters borrowed the dresses for the maids of honor.

When I went to Durfee [B.M.C. Durfee High School], after school I went to a recreation program that taught us how to sew. I dressed all my sisters up. Patty, Joan, and Jean. When I was at Morton, there was a recreation program for kids. I went eight years to St. Joseph's, one year to Morton, and three years to Durfee. I graduated from Durfee in 1940 at seventeen.

All the sisters were born in the house. Dr. Lewis was our doctor. He had an old-time doctor's office Down North. When my mother was giving birth to the fourth baby, I never forgot what Dr. Lewis said. "Hold it, May," he said, "there's another one coming." She was having twins. My father passed out. I was thirteen at the time. We were allowed to stay in the house when my mother was giving birth.

There was a fire in the Ballard Street house and we lost a lot of our clothes. On Sunday, after the fire, Kay and I would meet in the tunnel under the tracks between masses to change coats because we had only one coat. On her way back from Mass, I would take the coat and go to the next Mass.

My grandmother, my mother's mother, was named Katherine. We lived near Grandmother Crowell. She looked after us during the week and was good to us. I never knew Grandmother Fallon.

My father owned a candy store on North Court Street, but it didn't last very long.

## Christmas, Holidays, and Special Occasions

Every Christmas, our grandmother brought us something, either a doll or something else. In those days, there was not enough money for gifts. We never went to see Santa Claus. We didn't have a telephone; I don't remember when we got a phone. If we wanted to get a message to someone, we had to walk. My mother would say to my sister Kay, "Go get that for grandmother." My grandmother lived on the third floor on Oregon Street across from Dan Shalloo's store. My grandmother would tell my sister, "Kathleen, go get some milk." Kay would say, "Grandmother, I can't." "But, you've got to go." So, Kay would go for the milk and come back and put the milk on the sidewalk and say, "Come down and get it." "Blast you, Kathleen." My grandmother would always say. That Kay was a bugger.

Birthdays were very simple; my mother would bake a cake. My mom made honey rolls and would say, "These rolls are for Amie when he comes to see Rita."

## School Life

When I was in St. Joseph's School, Father Lyons would come in at Christmas and give everyone an orange and an apple. If you were caught chewing gum by the nuns, you would be warned once. If you didn't take the gum out of your mouth after the first warning, the nun would take it out and put it in your hair. The nuns lived in the nearby convent. I remember Sister Mary Virginia.

## Recreation and Entertainment

We didn't have the money for sleds, so we would go to Dan Shalloo's corner store and ask, "Mr. Dan, can we have some cardboard to slide on?" Then, we would go to Weetamoe Street to slide. Weetamoe was our main sliding street.

We would go ice-skating at North Park. We couldn't afford skates for all of us, so we borrowed one another's skates. "It's my turn," we would say. We roller-skated in the streets; we jumped rope. We didn't have bicycles; we couldn't afford them. Few people had them. There were no pools or sprinklers for kids then.

## Courtship and Marriage

I met my husband through my sister. She was going out with a friend of my husband. He told my sister that I was cute: "Maybe she'll go out with me." I thought he was too old. He wore a soft hat and looked too old. My sister never married the guy she was going with. My husband, Amie LaFrance, was a great man. He started in the Maplewood section but his family moved to the Flint, where he lived when we were married.

We were married when Amie was in the service. We went to see Father Lyons about getting married. We were going together around two years, and he was out on furlough. At first, Father Lyons said, "Rita, wait until the war is over." "But," I said, "we have been going out for two years." "Alright, wait anyway until the war is over. When you wait until after the war, marry your own kind." Amie was right there in the room when he said that!

Father Shalloo married us. He wouldn't let the wedding party come in the front door, though. We had to go in the side door at St. Joseph's.

**Work Life and the Creation of White's Family Restaurant**

While I was sixteen and going to high school, I got a job working twice a week at Woolworth's 5 & 10 in the hardware department. I had to walk to the store from school. The only time that we got money to ride the bus was when it was pouring rain.

One of my early jobs was working as a waitress at Al Mac's Diner. My mother said, "Your younger sister is working at Al Mac's Diner; you can make good money there." My uncle John was a policeman and walked me home. His wife was my mother's sister. He had a walking beat in the neighborhood and his family lived nearby. I worked at Al Mac's until Amie came home from the service. I also worked at Nora's on Bank Street downtown. My sister Mary got me all the jobs. She later married Chip Marchand. Mary was a classic good waitress, a very good waitress. She later ran the Somerset Lodge with Chip. Her husband's parents opened the Lodge and Mary and Chip later worked it. Chips father owned Marchand's Café in Somerset.

After I graduated from Durfee, I worked at Hoffman and Lyons making jump ropes. My older sister made dish mops there. They were located in the Border City Mill area. We sisters turned over our pay to our mother. I worked there until I got married.

Amie worked in the Pleasant Street A&P from the time he was seventeen, then he went into the service as a volunteer. When the war broke out in 1941, he joined the Air Force. On the first day, a major came in and said, "Anyone here know how to cut meat?" My husband had cut meat for the A&P. He got interested in cooking in the service. By the time he got out, it was in his blood by then. That is how he ended up in the restaurant business; he loved to cook.

After the service, he went back to the A&P. We had to find housing, and we went to live with my mother-in-law in the Flint on Horton Street. One day, a small place at 1436 Pleasant Street owned by two sisters came up for sale. It was a white building and called White's Spa. It had a soda fountain and a soda counter. He bought it, and both my husband and I worked there.

Our catering business started when someone from the Dover Club nearby came in one day and said, "Could you cater us a little meal?" We didn't know how to do catering; we had a four-burner stove. We took on the job, though, and from there we entered the catering business.

Mr. Yamins owned the building and told my husband, "Mr. LaFrance, I want to give you more space and build you a kitchen." He was the one that really got us started in the catering business. From that beginning, the White Spa Caterers was born. We wanted to keep the same name. From that point, we began to grow. Our first big banquet was for 1,000 people at Lincoln Park [North Dartmouth, Massachusetts]. It was for Mayor Kane.

The regulars at White's Spa worked in the stores and shops in the Flint. We did a lot of business with the shops and the stores in the Flint. They came from the mills like Shelburne Shirt. Stop and Shop was across the street. On Fridays, they would be out the door in line waiting for our fish and chips for fifty-five cents. We closed about 5:00 pm or so and were open for breakfast and lunch. Friday night we stayed open because the stores stayed open that night. Breakfast was a big thing for us.

White's Spa had a soda fountain. I ran the counter and he would do the cooking and catering. We had nine stools and four booths. I was the waitress. The grill was in back. When we got going in the catering business and the kitchen was enlarged out back, I ran all of the Spa. When Richard came out of school, I would bring him to the Spa. When Anna LaFrance got out of work at the Royal Store, she took him home with her.

My husband took in his two brothers in as partners. When he bought White's here, one of the brothers, Roger, took over the catering business and he and his son took over White's Spa.

This place was a restaurant ("Ruth's Restaurant") and a nightclub ("The Lamplighter"). We bought it in 1954, and it opened as White's Family Restaurant on Easter Sunday in 1955. We had family-style service in White's. We would go to all the halls and cater to them. Later, the name was changed by Richard to White's of Westport.

My husband was the cook on the Mamie [Battleship *Massachusetts*] when it was brought up from the south.

Everything was always paid in cash, including pay. Here at White's also.

*Richard LaFrance*: Chains dominate the restaurant scene now. People's eating habits have come full-circle. "Comfort food" has come back. Before, lunch was the big thing for us and men were the main patrons; now women come for lunch. Families today come out more for dinner. We did a big mill business here for lunch. We served a lot of Manhattans then.

**Health and Illness**

I had diphtheria in the fourth grade and was in the hospital for a while. My grandmother lived with Aunt Ann and Uncle John and I got ten cents each from my grandmother and Aunt Ann for each day I was in the hospital for a few weeks. They saved it for me all the time I was in the hospital and gave it to me when I came home. That was nice of them. Diphtheria was a big thing in those days; many people died from it. That was the only real illness that I had.

If you had a cough, my mother gave us cough drops. When we had a fever, she gave us stale ginger ale from a bottle that had the fizz out of it. "This will cure you," she said. We got cod liver oil also.

**The Depression**

During the Depression, people got shoes at the welfare office. Mothers were not allowed in the store with their kids. However, my mother would stand outside the window and in sign language say, "Don't take that pair." They tried to give my sister boy's boots.

There was a place on George Street where they would give you food from the Welfare Office. You could get beans and bread there. My mother would tell my father, "Johnny, you've got to get work. The kids need the money."

**Popular Expressions and Nicknames**

"Go pound tar." "Shug a lug."

# Lillian (Golub) Lepes

*Born on August 14, 1918*

**Family Background**

I was born in Fall River at Union Hospital.
My husband is Hyman Lepes.

**Family Life**

My parents came from Russia. They came here only for their honeymoon to visit Anna's mother Clara Horvitz, who was giving birth to Anna [Horvitz Zalkind]. My mother was going to help them with the baby.

My grandfather had money. Cossacks would come into my grandfather's house with horses and daggers and kill everyone in sight. They took everything you had, especially if you were Jewish. My grandfather, my mother's father, was a grain merchant. My father worked for my grandfather. My father married the boss' daughter. When my mother married my father, my grandfather had money. My parents were supposed to go back to Russia, but then World War I broke out, and then they kept extending the stay.

In Russia, any person of stature had a samovar to make tea. My mother had seven fur coats when she came over. She later used the coats to provide fur trim for coats that she made. She made beautiful clothes. She made me the most gorgeous clothes that I ever had.

I was raised at 27 Chavenson Street on the second floor. It is the third house in on the right from Bedford Street. My family bought it. Before that, we lived and rented at 55 Chavenson Street, next to 63 Chavenson Street. There was no road at that time. We had to walk on planks to get into our houses.

**School Life**

I went to the Dubuque School. A fellow would punch me every time he went down the aisle to see the teacher. I wanted to scream. He was my boyfriend!

After Dubuque, I went to the Davis School on Quequechan Street for seventh and eighth grades. It was a horrible place. The teachers were not very good. After Davis, I went to Durfee [B.M.C. Durfee High School]; we walked there.

**Recreation and Entertainment**

We played in the middle of the street. We played hide and seek; a fellow kissed me when we were playing hide and seek. I was just as rough and tough as my three brothers. I played baseball and football like them. We played in the street, since there was no traffic. It was later paved.

Beyond 63 Chavenson Street was a big frog pond. The frogs croaked day and night; we heard them up to my house. Lots of Indian relics liked arrowheads were still around the pond then.

Everyone went ice skating; there was nothing else to do. We went to Island Park [Cashman's

Park, Portsmouth, Rhode Island] or to Sandy Beach. All of Fall River went to Sandy Beach. It had all kinds of amusements, including a roller coaster and dodge-em cars; everything.

**Courtship and Marriage**

Hy worked his way through college in New York City. We met on a blind date. His father wanted him to come back to work for him in the building business. A friend fixed us up.

**Neighborhood Experiences**

The first drive-in ice cream stand in the area was in Touisset [Warren, Rhode Island]. My family would take us there as kids. It was just a stand. They made their own ice cream. It was one hundred percent butter fat and very good.

Mary Mitchell was a neighbor. The Mitchell's lived in a very old house on Bark Street off of Eastern Avenue, when there were just a few houses on it. Mary and I would go to Lafayette Park to play tennis. We would walk along the Reservation to the Narrows all the time. We would take a lunch with us, have a picnic, and then come home.

The Strand Theatre on Pleasant Street was five cents, which was a lot of money in those days. Mary and I would go to the Mark You Restaurant with five cents and couldn't decide what to get, a chow mein sandwich or an order of french fries.

Columbus Park had the best fireworks on Columbus Day. My first boyfriend was Italian.

When the houses on Chavenson Street were first built, they had coal furnaces. Mr. Chavenson built and owned all the houses on the street. A guy named Joe worked for Mr. Chavenson and Joe went from house to house stoking the furnaces. Mr. Chavenson built a total of fourteen houses; he later sold them to individual owners.

Every day, merchants with their horse and buggies would deliver ice, fish, fruits, and vegetables. All the housewives would come down with pots and fill them up.

People came here from New York because they couldn't make a living there. They were poor as church mice. They went to the factories and rented a few rooms. They manufactured pants and various things. They had nothing when they came. To get people to work in the factories, the boat from the Azores would come in. Whole families would get on the boat and get off right in Fall River. Manufacturers from New York would go down to the dock and pick up whole families. Within a few weeks, the whole family would have an apartment, a car. No visas were needed. Whole families worked; they pooled their money and saved.

When we lived on Chavenson Street, I remember going to Lapre's Turkey Farm. President Avenue came to an end at the turkey farm. An old homestead and horse farm was there. On weekends, they rented their horses to people who wanted to go horseback riding for a dollar.

We moved to a house on Bark Street where the rents were lower. We would go sledding down Bedford Street where the Water Works is located. The hill was about one-half mile.

**Downtown**

Pleasant Street was a great downtown. It had everything you could think of. It was a very busy area. Predominately French and Portuguese were spoken there. When my father arrived in Fall River, he had to learn three languages at once: English, French, and Portuguese. The Italians were concentrated around Columbus Park, which wasn't far from where we lived.

We walked everywhere. My friend walked from County Street a mile every day to deliver a dinner pail to her father in the mill. She was only five or six years old at the time. Every noon, a factory whistle blew.

There was Drake's fish market on Second Street. It had fresh fish at twenty-five cents a pound.

**Health and Illness**

Honey was given for coughs. My mother brought remedies from Russia. One was an egg beaten with milk and honey. We got better immediately. That remedy is coming back in style. It's called "Goggle-Nogle."

**The Fall River Line**

The Fall River Line was very luxurious thing in those days. Actors and actresses and well-to-do people would come to Fall River just to take the ships to New York. You could get a stateroom if you wanted and meals. People would come in from New York just to take the boat. When I was sixteen, three or four girls from Durfee took the boat to New York, where we stayed for a few days. We saw a play.

**World War II**

On December 7, 1941, I was at an engagement party for my brother.

During World War II, Hy was drafted, even though he was thirty-two and married with a child. The service wouldn't allow him to go to officers' training school, even though he had a college degree; he was too old! I was a bookkeeper at my father's business in New Bedford. That was my first job. I got sixty dollars a month to live on from the government. I had a nine-month old baby and a mortgage. My parents moved in with me so my father could assume paying the mortgage. My mom took care of the baby while I worked in New Bedford. I didn't see Hy for a year.

I had three brothers and they were all in the service. Albert, my youngest brother, went into the Navy. He was on an English ship; we didn't have enough of ours. It was a dirty English ship. He went to Africa through Palermo. He had gone to Massachusetts College of Optometry in Boston after Durfee for a few months before he was drafted and for that they made him a doctor on an LST [Landing Ship, Tank]. He had no training in medicine at all. Someone on the ship had an appendectomy attack and he had to operate. He had someone looking at a book instructing him what to do. The person survived! Another day, during a battle, he had to amputate a leg of a serviceman by candlelight. My brother was about eighteen at the time. The amputee lived!

Later, he went to the Pacific side where they got caught up in a typhoon. The whole ship was lost, and my parents got a notice that he was lost at sea. No one knew what happened to them. Since he was the "doctor" of the ship, he was responsible for the men eating and surviving. When he came back from the war, he wouldn't look at a fish. All they had to eat on the island was fish.

My brother Harry was on a destroyer escort that brought fuel for the troops. He was constantly being kamakized. Robert, my third oldest brother, was in London during the Blitzkrieg all the time the city was being bombed. He worked in a hospital. He was in the medical corps and was sent to England to do inspections of medical facilities. Hy was in the Philippines.

**Miscellaneous Memories**

My husband owned a good part of the land north of the Fall River Country Club at one time, when it was still an orchard. The land was owned by the Allen family and was called the Allen Orchard. The Allen family was given the land from the King of England in the 1600s. The land was one mile long and one-half mile wide and was on the water. While we owned for years, we didn't do anything with it. Once, two policemen came to our house to see me. They said that marijuana was being grown on the property. The property was in my name. At that time, the city was flooded with marijuana.

The police decided to go across the river with binoculars and look at the farm. While they were looking, a boat would come down the river and get off at the Allen's Farm. The people in the boats brought big water buckets to collect the marijuana, which was being grown between the trees. I had to go to court and deal with the situation.

When we bought the Allen land in the 1950s, the trees were full of apples. Allen didn't want them and we didn't know what to do with them. My husband called Bishop Cassidy and said, "This is Hy Lepes and I own an apple orchard full of apples and other fruit. You can have all of the fruit for your orphanages if you have someone come and pick them." The bishop replied, "Thank you very much, Mr. Lepes. If you will pick them, we will eat them." My husband let the fruit rot on the trees. We never took a piece of fruit from the orchard.

Douglas Richardson was the trustee of everything. He was the head of the Fall River Five Bank and on so many boards, including chairman of the Rotary board and everything in the city that was charitable. He was also the head of the UMass Dartmouth board when the university was formed. He was good friends with Hy. Hy was on the Fall River Five board and they hung out together. Doug was also the leader of the Baptist Temple downtown when they were looking for a site to build a new church. Hy and a partner owned land on North Eastern Avenue, and Hy donated it to the Baptist Temple.

Once Mrs. Auchincloss, Jacki Kennedy's mother, called. She had heard about him and wanted his advice. Hy called Doug Richardson and said, "I'm going to see Mrs. Auchincloss; want to come?" Mrs. Auchincloss told Hy, "Why don't you bring your wife down to see where the Kennedy's lived?" I never went; I was too busy playing golf.

Mrs. Auchincloss came to greet him. Her husband is in an iron lung. He could stay out of the iron lung for one hour, and he wanted to be in on the conversation. She didn't know what to do. She couldn't afford the estate and heard that Hy was a genius in finance. "What should I do?" she asked.

She did exactly what he suggested. There was a good-sized manager's house on the estate and she moved into it. She donated the estate to the Newport Preservation Society to avoid paying taxes. The Auchincloss son still lives in that house.

My husband was a developer in Tiverton and Portsmouth. He developed the Vanderbilt estate in Portsmouth, now called Sandy Point Farms.

# George Joseph Lucove

*Born on May 7, 1916*
*Died on February 17, 2013*

**Family Background**

I was born in Fall River on Davis Street. I lived in the Flint until I was twenty-two years old.

My parents were Moses ("Morris") and Bessie (Bassovsky) Lucove. My mother's parents were Jacob and "Minnie." My father's parents remained in Russia.

I have five brothers and sisters, (in birth order, including me): Faye, Sarah (both Faye and Sarah were born in Russia), Irving, myself, Bertha, and Mildred.

My father and mother came here from Russia during the pogroms of Czar Nicholas I. My mother said that the Cossacks would come through the villages killing people. She once had to hide in a chicken coop to escape. They came from a village near Kiev in the Ukraine.

My mother's parents came here first. My grandparents came here before my parents. They had a house on Flint Street. Everyone that came after them lived in the six-tenement house. Three or four in the family came first, then the others later. My grandfather owned a rag-picking business. He would pick up junk and bring it to the junkyard. He made enough money to buy a big six-tenement house on Flint Street, right next to the Davol School. The house has since been taken down.

My wife is May (Altman) Lucove.

I have lived in the following residences in Fall River: Davis Street; Canonicus Street; Quequechan Street; 30 Rocliffe Street (age five to twenty-two); 303 High Street (across from Durfee High School; demolished for funeral home parking); 587 June Street; and 39 Belmont Street.

**Family Life**

My growing up was different from Christians. Living in the Flint as a Jewish kid was difficult. I remember being sworn at because I killed Christ. "How do you know I killed Christ?" I asked. They said, "It's here in the Catechism: Jesus was killed by the Jews." Sure enough, it was in the Catechism. How could I have killed him? I didn't even know who he was. I got into a lot of fights over that. Jews had a tough time in the Flint. Ninety percent of the Flint was French at that time.

I always had my own views about religion; I was more of an atheist. I find that religion is a tremendous reward for anyone who wants to stay religious.

The house that my father built on Rocliffe Street had no central heat. We had a big parlor stove in the kitchen. My mother baked bread in a big Dutch oven on top of the stove. It would be set there to rise and then to bake. We would all wait around the stove for the bread to be baked and then we would eat it nice and hot.

My grandmother was fond of her grandchildren. During recess at the Davol School, my grandmother would put an apple and a piece of pastry in a paper bag and throw it down to me in the school yard, since their house abutted the yard. It was terrific. It provided a great snack.

## Friends

I entered Durfee [B.M.C. Durfee High School] in 1929 and was in the main building for the first year. The next three years, I was in the Durfee Tech building. The first year was wonderful. My two chums were Tommy Moore and Billy August. We three skipped classes the whole first term. Tommy Moore would get into movies without paying. His father was a purser on one of the New York boats. We would go on the boats and roam around. I got away with it because I was a favorite of my mother's. When the school called, she covered for me and said I was sick. It finally came to an end. Tommy Moore went from a below grade the first term to above A the second term. He became the city's fire chief and was the youngest fire chief that the city ever had.

"Red Bogus" owned Ideal Furniture Store on Pleasant Street. It was originally a furniture store built by N.P. Tessier and called the N.P. Tessier Furniture Store. He built the house on Highland Avenue with the red tile roof that was later owned by Leviton, the owner of Great Scott Supermarkets. There was a Great Scott Supermarket at the old bus terminal on Stafford Road.

I went to school with "Red Bogus," Isadore Boguslavski. His older married brother had a son who was a teacher at Durfee. I bought all my furniture from Red at Ideal Furniture. In those days, you got a credit book and paid by the week. They would mark your payment in the book. I paid eighty-nine dollars for a solid mahogany bedroom set, thirty-nine dollars for a kitchen set—five hundred dollars to furnish the whole house. I paid five dollars a week on credit.

Izzy had bright red hair. He was very sharp. He was a lawyer but never practiced. He had one son. I was bigger than Izzy when young. He was a little guy, but tough.

## School Life

About 1920 or so, I went to kindergarten at a school that was located at the intersection of Pleasant Street and Eastern Avenue. Then I went to the Davol School for grades one to four and to the Davis School for grades five to eight. Then to Durfee. I graduated from Durfee in 1933 and went to college in that year at Providence College. However, after the crash of 1929, there was no money and I left PC.

## Recreation and Entertainment

I spent the whole summer at South Watuppa fishing and playing. It was wonderful. At that time, there were two ponds at South Watuppa, one of which was the small pond formed between Route 6 and the railroad tracks. My father built a boat in our yard on Rocliffe Street. He had the propeller cast in a brass foundry in Fall River and put a one-cylinder engine with a flywheel on the boat. My father was a big fisherman. I still have the anchor and oars from my father's old row boat.

The Watuppa Boat Club is shown in a postcard. Toilets went right into the pond from the boathouses. The Watuppa Boat Club had mostly English and French members. Each member had a locker. My father was the only Jewish member. The only reason he got in was because he had friends in the club. They wouldn't allow any other Jewish members. That's the way it was in the Flint.

There was a chow mein place, a Chinese restaurant, at the corner of Rock and Bedford Streets. I would go in and get a chow mein sandwich for five or ten cents. I would then go down near the Fall River Line Pier and bait the fishing hooks with the chow mein. I caught small fish with it.

We kids would fish on the Quequechan River off of Quequechan Street. There would be three or four of us fishing. We caught "Paddy Roaches," or sunfish. There were lots of them. We walked along the river on the railroad tracks. Trains were still running on the tracks then.

For games, we played hide and seek and peggy ball. We would go to the field at the end of Rocliffe Street on the other side of County; Rocliffe Street didn't extend beyond County then. There was a big field there. To play peggy ball, you placed a stick on the ground, another stick on top of it at right angles, and used a cue stick to hit the ball. The ball was wooden and this size [about the size of a small plum]. You took your cue stick and hit the other stick to make the ball fly up. Then you hit the ball.

Red Light was played by a kid counting to ten while hiding his face. When he was done counting, he turned around and, if you were moving, you were it. You couldn't be moving; you had to be rigid. There was also Buck, Buck, where kids leaned over against a wall and other kids would jump on them. The last person would yell out, "Buck, Buck, how many fingers do I have up?" If you guessed it, you reversed positions. In the summertime, we would go to South [Watuppa] Pond to swim.

Throughout high school, we would go camping at Cranberry Neck in Westport on the South Pond. It was about one mile from the bridge on Route 6. It is now the Rod and Gun Club. We would pitch a tent and stay there three to four weeks in the summer and not come home. We would catch fish and eat them. The pond was so clean that we would get a pitcher and go to the pond to get water to drink. The water was clean and clear.

Once in a while, one of us would go back and buy supplies. We would troll the pond at night to get fish. No one bothered us. It was absolutely like utopia. I had free reign as a boy; I had to answer to nobody.

Even though the American Thread put out some awful stuff in the pond, it was clean where we were. American Thread had two water systems, one from North Watuppa for drinking, and one from South Watuppa for flushing toilets.

I got into trouble once. I fooled around with a cowboy's lasso rope made from a clothesline. A neighborhood kid named Johnny White was riding his bicycle on Rocliffe Street. He said, "I bet you can't rope me while I ride my bike down the street." I said, "Yes, I can." "Once you feel the rope, you better stop the bike, because the rope will close up." So, he came down Rocliffe Street and the lasso went around his neck. He tried to shake his head to get rid of the rope and got knocked off the bike and hit his head. He got blue in the face. I was so scared that I ran in the woods near the water works and I stayed there the whole night, I was so petrified. They found he was okay. My father gave me a beating (not so much). I was petrified.

**Courtship and Marriage**

For fun, we guys from Fall River would go to New Bedford. There were four girls in my wife's family. One time, we went and the girls weren't home but were visiting another house. We went to that house and May was there. We started dating.

We would go to the movies or go swimming at Colonel Green's. His mother was the richest woman in the world. Colonel Green was a cripple. There was something wrong with his leg, but his mother wouldn't take care of it because she wouldn't pay for it. The story is in [the book] *The Day They Shook the Plum Tree* [by Arthur H. Lewis]. The house was huge, like a castle. He had an airplane on the estate and an electric car. He had a tremendous garage that MIT used for some secret war effort. He sent a lot of kids to college. He owned his own railroad.

The beach was private, but he allowed anyone go there to swim. On the shore was the *Charles W. Morgan*. We would go on the *Morgan* from top to bottom. Now it is at the Mystic Seaport. The place was called Round Hill.

**Work Life**

My father was a painter and wallpaper hanger. Once or twice I helped him, but then stopped.

I sold the *Fall River Herald* and the *Fall River Globe*. I paid one and one-half cents for the *Herald* and sold it for two cents. The *Globe* cost one cent. My spot for selling the papers was in front of the Public Library. When the boat trains came in, I would sell papers to people getting off the train. Sometimes I got a nickel for a paper from the big shots. The boat left the pier for New York at twenty minutes to 8:00 pm.

I also had a paper route for the *Fall River Herald News*. They would put an ad in the paper looking for paper boys for various sections of the city. They would drop off the bound papers at various corners along the route. We got fifteen cents a week.

I would go to Earnshaw's Diner on Pleasant Street, where the new police station is now, and have a coffee and piece of pie for fifteen cents. Earnshaw's had two diners, one on Pleasant Street and one on Pocasset Street.

Before I started my own business, I worked at Har-Lee in the shipping room, which was located in the small building at the Durfee Mills. I worked for thirteen dollars a week. Roosevelt passed the NRA [National Recovery Act] that said you couldn't pay a worker less than thirteen dollars a week. I didn't give my mother much of the thirteen dollars, so I was able to buy a car. It was a 1932 black and white Chevy Roadster. All the time I worked at Har-Lee, I would look out the window at the car. The Roadster had a canvas roof and no windows. You put down the roof and there was a rumble seat in back, with two seats. I couldn't wait until five o'clock to get out of work and go to New Bedford.

A week or two after the 1938 hurricane, I decided to go into business for myself. When I got to New York, and they saw my license plate, people would say, "You're from Massachusetts?" as if I survived a disaster. I went to the East Side with my mother and two hundred dollars and got a carload of stuff, mostly clothes. I took them home and began going door-to-door selling. I would knock on doors and people would say, "Come in." You can't do that now.

I was called in once to the Highland Avenue house of one of the Cherrys of Cherry and Webb. It was a gorgeous house. I went there because they wanted curtains or something. They had good stuff, but the rugs and draperies were worn out. Rich people love to travel; they want to spend their money that way and don't much care about replacing stuff when it wears out.

I once called to E.P. Charlton's mansion on Westport Harbor. They wanted me to reline the draperies. They were gorgeous draperies on the windows, but they looked like they were there for one thousand years. They said they would like to reline them. I told them that I couldn't or they would fall apart. The sun had been beating on them for years. The house had a big elevator in it and a big greenhouse on the property.

**Neighborhood Experiences**

There was a nice bakery on Pleasant Street called Pomfret's. It was in a building located between Rocliffe and Quequechan Streets. They made all kinds of wonderful stuff. We would go in and buy stuff that didn't quite come out well, like malformed bread, for five and six cents. There was a place on Jencks Street owned by a Syrian fellow down by the end of the street that made ice cream cones. They sold whole bags of broken cones for five cents a bag. It had no name and was on the bottom of a tenement house.

Some of the Jewish kids were delivered by the same doctor, Dr. Schwartz—Izzy Horvitz, Isadore "Red" Bogus (Boguslavski). I was born May 7th and delivered the same day from Dr. Schwartz as was Melvin Zais, the general from Fall River. I was delivered at our home on Davis Street. When the doctor came, he would deliver the baby and put the name and date on a piece of paper and put it in his pocket to bring to City Hall later. Sometimes, the slips got mixed up. In City Hall, they put my middle name down as Josef.

On Rocliffe Street, there was a family next door who had a son that got gassed during World War I. He would go on screaming tirades once in a while. You could hear him all over the street. Then, he would quiet down. When I bought this house, there were only two cars on the street. Mr. Sears was an old-time Yankee. His father built the house. From what I understand, he was quite a pianist. He had a big baby grand in his house. His father didn't think that a pianist was much of an occupation. From what I heard, his son was frustrated all his life because he wanted to be a pianist. The third floor of the Sears house had a beautiful pool table.

Chesworth and Chavenson Streets were nice Jewish areas. Lots of business people.

Years ago, an old school teacher lived in the house on Belmont Street—north of mine. Her father was Beattie, the owner of the [granite quarry] ledge on Quarry Street. I went swimming at the ledge one year. It was big and a dangerous place.

*Mr. Lucove's son*: I remember going to the Strand Theatre. My grandfather gave me twenty-five cents for a Saturday double feature. In between the two shows, we put our ticket stubs in a barrel and they drew the tickets for prizes. The Strand gave out dishes and carnival glass also.

*Mr. Lucove*: Some stores gave you a different gardening book for twenty-six weeks. I saved all of the books and put them together.

**Downtown**

Downtown had Newbury's, Grant's, Kresge's, and Woolworth's 5 & 10 cent stores. Grant's quality was the best. They sold yard goods. Yamins Dry Goods store was at the top of Columbia Street, near South Main Street. He was a wholesaler. He had a daughter that lived on Dougherty Street and married a guy named Green. I remember one time when I went into the store and old man Yamins was looking at the stock market section of the newspaper. There was no one in the store. I said to him, "It's kind of quiet here today," and he replied (referring to the stock market), "Oh, that's all right. I've already made my money today."

The Hub [clothing store] was on the northeast corner of Pleasant and Troy Streets. It had quality stuff. I bought my graduation jacket and clothes there. They would give you a birthday gift. They gave you individual attention, not like today.

**Health and Illness**

If you got sick with the measles, they put up a red card on the house that said "Measles." A green card was for scarlet fever. There was a lot of scarlet fever going around at that time. Whooping cough was also a problem. Doctors offices were on the first floor of tenement houses then. One doctor was on Quequechan Street and we would run over to his office when we were sick and he would fix us up.

When we got seriously banged up playing, we went to Union Hospital. Every Friday, Union Hospital was free for anyone who wanted to come in. You would sit and wait and they would come out to take you in. They had cracker-jack doctors.

### The Depression

During the Depression, my mother sewed at home. She taught everyone in the family how to sew. That is how I made a living. I remember going out to get coke from the train. The trains used coal for steam and, at some of the stations, they would empty out the ashes from the train and dump them on the side of the tracks. I would pick out the coke from the ashes, which were still warm, and bring the coke home to heat the house.

The Depression was terrible. People jumped out of buildings in New York, selling apples for five cents on Broadway. The brothers were nice to us at PC [Providence College]. I had only two hundred dollars saved up and they were willing to have me continue my sophomore year if we wanted to, but I had to get a job.

### The Fall River Line

I was on the Fall River Line more than once. When my mother and father had an argument, my mother would take us kids and go to her sister's house in New York. Mom would take two or three kids and get a stateroom for two or three dollars. We walked around the boat. We went on the *Commonwealth*, *Priscilla*, and the *Providence*. We all got sick when the boats rounded Point Judith, since that area has rough waters. At other times, I would go down to the Fall River Line pier and fish off the pier.

The Fall River Line had its own silverware and coffee pots with the names of the ships on them. Some of the ships had paddle wheels and some had propellers. They were beautiful inside, all carpeted. There were prostitutes who worked the boats. One of the books on Fall River recounts this. The book is *February Hill* [by Fall River native Victoria Lincoln].

The train was convenient for me when I lived on June Street. I would walk down the hill to the station on North Main Street and take the train to Boston. The train left at 7:40 am and arrived at South Station at 9:00 am. It was just a short walk to Kneeland Street and the cloth stores.

### Hurricane of 1938

During the 1938 hurricane, some slates started falling from the roofs of the police and fire station on Pleasant Street. I walked down to the river and saw whole houses floating down the Taunton River. Island Park [Cashman's Park, Portsmouth, Rhode Island] was wiped out. Atwater Coal and other coal yards on the wharf were wiped out. Later, I remember seeing big boats on the lawn of Fairhaven High School and on the Fairhaven Bridge. There was a terrible wind blowing. The coal buildings were swept off the wharf.

### World War II

During World War II, I was 4-F because of my eyesight. During the war, the government chose certain people that had certain qualities that they needed at the time. Other times, they took you even though there was a lot wrong with you. Izzy Bogus, for example, had the worst eyes, but they took him.

# James Francis Luddy Jr.

*Born on January 15, 1926*
*Died on August 4, 2012*

**Family Background**

I don't know if I was born at home, but I presume that I was, since my brother was born at home and he was born eleven years after I was. My mother died when I was eleven, a few months after my brother was born.

My mother's father came from England with eight of his nine children. He came first, then his wife. My mom's parents lived on King Philip Street; we would visit them on Sundays. My uncle Ed (my mother's uncle; he was married to the sister of my mother's mother) was a barber (who cut my hair) and later worked the elevators at McWhirr's. We would go downtown on Saturdays to McWhirr's, where Uncle Ed would let me go up and down in the elevator.

The Irish part of the family, my father's family, came to America in the 1850s during the Great Famine.

My father had two brothers, John and Dan, and a sister, Elizabeth. My father was the only one who married. Both of my grandfathers were married twice. My father came from the second marriage. He was the only child from the second marriage.

Edward St. John was a cousin of my father's and the publisher of the *Fall River Herald News*. He was from the first marriage of my grandfather. He and his sister, Helen, ended up at St. Vincent's Home. We would visit them sometimes on Sundays. The place was terrible; it was big and dark and full of kids. St. Vincent's was run by the Sisters of Mercy and they did it credit.

Grandmother Anne (Timlin) Costello died early and left four daughters: Grace Costello, Evelyn, Ruth, and Gladys. Near the entrance to St. Patrick's Cemetery there is a family monument, an obelisk with a ball on the top. I don't know how people of such modest means could afford such grand monuments.

My aunt Lizzie was a professional cook and took care of us kids when my mother died. She was a cook at Wellesley College and came home when her parents died. She was a wonderful cook and always had bread in the oven or a soup on the stove. Aunt Lizzie was truly a saint; I can't say enough about her. She could cook and manage a home with six persons with variable lifestyles.

My wife is Evelyn (Smith) Luddy and we have five children: James F. Luddy III, Elizabeth H. Cordega, Maureen E. Britland, Kevin M. Luddy, and Alison E. Makuch.

**Family Life**

My childhood was magical. My mother struggled. She worked at Schneierson and Sons making high-end women's underwear. She died of tuberculosis. I saw her being brought out in a stretcher from our home. The last time I saw her was at the city's General Hospital. At my mother's funeral, the nun brought our school class to the Mass. On our way out, she gave me a smile as if to say, "Everything is going to be all right." I never forgot that.

My uncle (my father's half-brother) John worked in the post office, so we had a pay check every week during the Depression. Uncle John helped us out and, when my mother died, we moved to the second floor (60 Palmer Street) to live with him and his sister Elizabeth. John was a disabled vet from World War I—he got shot in the leg—and walked with a limp. He worked the shift at the post office from 1:30 pm to 10:30 pm. He would get out of bed at 10:30 in the morning and take his time shaving and getting ready.

He would pay us kids a quarter a night plus bus fare to bring him his supper of a mason jar of coffee and a sandwich. My sister and I took turns delivering his supper. I would walk to the post office and save the five cents bus fare.

Uncle John was very generous and kept us in good clothing. He paid for my sister Anne to go to Dominican Academy; we never lacked for anything. When I graduated from high school, he brought me to New York City and we stayed a week. He paid for it. I had heard that New Yorkers didn't like two dollar bills, so I brought a stack with me to hand out.

For a few years after my mother died, my sister and I would stay all summer with my mother's sister in South Hadley, Massachusetts. As we had no car, my uncle paid Queeney to drive us there. I recall one time that it was Friday and Aunt Lizzie asked John, who had gone along for the ride, what they had for dinner, and Uncle John said steak, and Aunt Lizzie almost died.

**Religious Life**

Religion and the church were big things in your life in those days. In our neighborhood, people either went to St. Patrick's Church or St. Anne's Church. My father's cousins were White Sisters in Vermont. The second wife of my grandfather had a sister who was a Maryknoll nun in China.

Sometime around Easter, every church would have a "Coffee Supper." They served ham and beans at these suppers. A week before, they would have a minstrel show. Two guys would do banter back and forth; one was called Mr. Bones. It was a big thing. The tickets were twenty-five cents or so.

Every week, the women of the church would have bridge or whist parties. They had score cards to punch and we altar boys would have to run around the tables and punch the cards. Every Christmas, St. Patrick's Church held parties for the kids. They would give us bags of fruit and one toy. Even today, the smell and taste of tangerines brings me back to those Christmas bags.

**Downtown**

We lived next door to a school teacher and the assistant finance director for the city. The father, John Connolly, was the brother of the future Bishop Connolly. John was an Elk. On flag day, they would go down to a big flagpole in South Park [now Kennedy Park], in front of St. Anne's Church. The flagpole was huge and was constantly being struck by lightening.

Every day, Pineau's Market on East Main Street sent their son Butch to the house in the morning to get the order for the day, and then he returned at 4:00 pm with the groceries.

Everything was delivered by horse and wagon, including ice and milk. The milk wagons had iron wheels that made a racket early in the morning going over the cobblestone streets. People complained that they couldn't sleep, and so Hood Milk covered the wheels with rubber. We rode the trolleys and would put a penny on the rails to squish them and flatten them out.

Street vendors would cheat people when they could. At 64 Palmer Street there lived the city's Sealer of Weights and Measures, George Fletcher. Because the vendors had to answer to the

Sealer, we always got a fair measure from the vendors. Fletcher's brother was in the Maryknoll order and his sister was a Sister of Mercy.

**Neighborhood Experiences**

George Howe lived next door and was one of my best friends. He was a nephew of Bishop Connolly. He became a merchant seaman. George Fletcher, another good friend, became a Linotype operator at the *Fall River Herald News*. Later in life, he got Parkinson's Disease and died at the Vets Home in Bristol. He lived at 64 Palmer Street, next to Queeney's Variety.

The Queeney family lived on the second floor above their variety store, and John Connolly and his wife lived on the first floor. Queeney was a character and a real nickel-grabber. Every time there was a parade or an event, he would set up a makeshift hot dog stand and sell hot dogs. We local kids would help him out and get a free hot dog. Later, he worked for the Taunton Dog Track in Dighton [Massachusetts] and he would give us his pass so we didn't have to pay the two dollar entrance fee. He was like that; always had an angle.

In the back of the variety store, Queeney hung a large canvas curtain. Behind the curtain was an endless poker game going on in back. Once, the Tom Mix Circus was in town and Queeney asked me if I wanted to meet Tom Mix. I said yes, and he brought me in back. He said to this guy, "Show the kid your gun," and this guy pulls out this long gun from under his jacket. I never knew if it was really Tom Mix or a local cop.

Queeney would post magazine pages and newspaper headlines in his window. Once, my uncle John made up a newspaper headline and page that said, "John Luddy loses the last hair on his head," and Queeney put it up in the window. Everyone crossed the street to find out what it was all about. Queeney had two daughters, Margaret and Dorothy.

We had four houses in our yard, and we lived in one of the back houses (50 and 60 Palmer Street were in back). Every afternoon, the mothers would go out in the yard and sit and talk as they watched over the kids. Originally, my parents lived at 50 Palmer, then moved to 60 Palmer when the first floor apartment became available. At 60 Palmer, we lived on the first floor, my father's brother and sister (John and Lizzie) lived on the second floor, and my father's uncle Frank and his wife Margaret lived on the third floor.

Margaret was a real Irishwoman, with a thick brogue. One Sunday morning at Mass, one of Queeney's daughters fainted and fell, allowing her slip to show. That happened a lot, when you had to fast to get communion. Margaret told Aunt Lizzie, "You would have been proud of her; her slip was as clean as snow." She didn't care if she was okay, as long as her slip was clean.

**Courtship and Marriage**

I met my wife on a blind date. My friend's girlfriend lived in New Jersey and moved to Providence to live in the YWCA. Evelyn (my future wife) worked at the Hillsgrove Airport, now Green Airport. There was also an airport across from the Seekonk Speedway on Route 6 that was called the Providence Airport. She also moved to the YWCA to save on travel time. When she walked out of the elevator, I said to myself, "She is too beautiful; she'll never have anything to do with me." She was gorgeous. She turned my proposals for marriage down three times.

Evelyn and I were married on April 30, 1949. She was from Burrellville, Rhode Island, and said that she wasn't moving to Fall River. So we got a duplex in Swansea. It was on the water and was a dump. Our only heat was from a kerosene heater. On Palmer Street, we heated with coal

In front of Queeney's Store on Palmer Street, 1940s; Margaret Queeney on left, Dorothy Queeney on right, George Fletcher in back; *Front row*: Bill Howe, Midge Blahey, Ed Kolakowski

and I had to bring it up three flights of stairs. Kerosene was great; all I needed to do was go in the yard to the tank and fill a bottle.

The father of the guy who owned the house was a dean at Kalamazoo College and then went to Brown. He later worked at Dow Chemical and invented Saran Wrap. The place was great in the sense that when I came home from work in the summertime, I would go in one door, peel off my clothes and go out the other door into the river swimming. We had more clams and quahogs than we could eat. The neighbors would always be out in the river filling up burlap bags of clams and quahogs that they would bring to Harry's Seafoods in Swansea. They wanted us to join them in harvesting, but we said no thanks.

At our fiftieth wedding anniversary, I asked her why she turned me down, and she said, "I was waiting for you to grow up. I'm still waiting for you to grow up." We have raised five super kids.

**Recreation and Entertainment**

There were lots of theaters in Fall River at one time. The Plaza downtown was a real fleabag. My mom and my aunt would go to the Plaza, buy a ticket, pick up a dish, and give the ticket away.

Next to Queeney's Variety was a concrete wall that we used to bounce balls from to see how far they would go, a form of baseball. Depending on how far the ball went, it would be a single, double, triple, or a home run. Sometimes the ball would land up on the top of the variety store, which had a flat roof. One time, I got on top of the roof to get the ball and got my pants stuck in the fence on the way down. I fell and hit my head badly. I still have the scar. My sister complained about it many years later, because she was older and was expected to look out after me. Later, I fell in a skating accident at South Park and opened a wound in the same place. The doctor told me that I had better not get another cut there because he was out of skin to pull it together.

The circus was amazing; they put up a whole city in a day, including tents and mess halls. I remember six or eight guys with sledge hammers standing in a circle around a stake. They would go around the circle taking turns hitting the stake, one at a time, until it was in the ground. Then they brought in the elephants to pull the ropes to raise the tents up. At night, when the circus was over, everything came down just as fast. The next morning, you would never know they were there except for the trash from popcorn boxes and stuff.

Except for the big stars, everyone wore many hats in a circus. They had multiple jobs; after they did their performance, they went out to sell programs or popcorn.

When they came into town and when they left, they had a big parade in the streets back to the train station. People said that they put on the parades to get people out of their houses so the roust-abouts could go in their homes and steal from them. The mothers always hung onto their children because everyone was convinced that the circus people stole kids.

Aunt Lizzie told me one story about me and the circus. I was a youngster in St. John's Day Nursery, which was located across the street from St. Patrick's School. One day, my uncle Dan, my father's step-brother, and brother to John and Lizzie, came to pick me up. I must have been four or five. The nun, careful because the circus was in town, asked me if I knew the man who was picking me up. I said "no" and she wouldn't let my uncle take me home. I imagine that my mother had to come get me after she finished work.

I remember going to amusements parks free, courtesy of local labor unions. We would go the state pier, get on a boat, and sail across the bay to Rocky Point Park. Money was not needed; apparently, the union would rent the park for a day and everything was free, meals and all. Aunt Lizzie would accompany us kids. It was a fabulous day: rides, food, boat ride. I also recall going one day with my good friend George Fletcher. Same thing. A union treat. We went to a park up toward Boston. Can't remember the name. One thing that they gave us was a lobster. Well, George and I had never even seen lobster, let alone have eaten one. We were perplexed, so we decided to watch the people in the next table and follow their lead. Worked pretty good. I remember going on the trolley with my mother to Lincoln Park [North Dartmouth, Massachusetts].

**World War II**

When I graduated from Durfee [B.M.C. Durfee High School] in 1943, I was seventeen and I wanted to enlist. My parents said no, you are too young. Then, the service started drafting at age eighteen. I convinced my father to sign papers for me to go into the Navy. I signed up and the Navy said to go have something to eat and be at the rail station at a certain time. They sent us to upstate New York but de-toured us via Pennsylvania. We traveled up the Leigh Valley coal country in the Leigh Valley Railroad. It was filthy, with coal dust on the seats and window sills.

I spent two years in the Navy. During World War II, I was on the destroyer #DD 733, the *Mannert L. Abele*. Abele was a captain of a submarine that was sunk with him in it in early World War II. A year ago January, the *Reader's Digest* had a story on the finding of the submarine. Abele was a summer resident of Tiverton. The *Mannert L. Abele* was sunk in the South China Sea, with eighty-four men lost.

I went to the Samson, New York, training station and stayed there a month. I then went to Boston Navy Yard and the Fargo Building, where I stayed and awaited orders. While I was there, the Navy did extensive dental work on me. Then I went to Norfolk on a destroyer. It had been in the Atlantic where it was painted black and gray and had to be repainted with Pacific colors, which were blue and gray. One of the great experiences of my life was sailing through the lock system of the Panama Canal. We were not allowed to take pictures or keep diaries, in case the enemy got them, but the enemy could as well have read *National Geographic* and got the same information. We sailed to San Diego and then on to Pearl Harbor, where we went back and forth to various islands like Guam and others.

I spent Christmas of 1944 at Pearl Harbor. It was strange, with everything green and everyone in shorts. I celebrated New Year's Eve at the Royal Hawaiian Hotel that the Navy took over for R&R. Then I got shipped out to Iwo Jima.

James Brady wrote a book [*Flag of Our Fathers*] about the six guys that were photographed planting the flag on Iwo Jima. Three of those guys never came off of the island. His father was one of the flag bearers. In his book, Brady says that the Navy abandoned the Marines at Iwo Jima, which was not true; the Navy never abandoned the Marines. Brady came to the dedication of the

James Luddy Jr.

Iwo Jima statue at Bicentennial Park land told me that he included that in the book to needle the Navy admirals. I brought his book to the dedication and it had already been signed by him. After speaking to me, he took the book and signed it again, saying, "To Jim, who was at Iwo Jima with my father."

After Iwo Jima, we took part in the invasion of Okinawa, which was a much bigger invasion than D-Day in Normandy. Twelve days after the April 1st invasion, our ship got hit by a kamikaze pilot. A Japanese plane dropped a manned, five-thousand-pound bomb that sunk us. The pilot steered the bomb to its target and it finished us off. There were about three hundred sailors on the ship and eighty-four died when the ship was hit. Two of my best friends on the ship were in the ship's radar room and took a direct hit from the bomb. The survivors of the ship had annual reunions, but there are only about ten of us left.

After the invasion, I was shipped back to the States and sent to a hospital in the mountains of Idaho. All the while I was in the Navy, I had this continuing sore throat, which turned out to be a growth, and they sent me to Idaho to remove it. When I arrived, I was told to meet with a Doctor Hooker. When I went into the office, I asked the corpsman, "Where is this bastard?" As it turns out, he was standing right in back of me. I could have been in real trouble. Dr. Hooker was a small guy, balding with a halo of hair below his bald head. He was stern but very capable and really loved by the hospital staff; word got around about what I said and no one liked it. He was the doctor who ended up operating on me.

I was stationed there two months and got to know Doctor Hooker really well. I was part of a small group of guys who he invited in to have sandwiches and drinks. He asked me where I came from and I said Fall River and he lit up. "Oh, Fall River! When I was in Boston in med school, I would take the Fall River Line all the time and got laid a lot in those boats. It was like a floating whore house." When I was about to leave, Dr. Hooker told me to fill our forms for a disability. I told him I didn't have one, but he insisted that I left the Navy different from when I entered it and therefore qualified for a disability. I applied for it and got it. He was very smart, because the disability was important in getting a job after the military service.

**Work Life**

I've been very lucky. I came back from the Navy, while eighty-four of my buddies, including two of my best buddies, were lost when the ship went down. I got to go to college and the VA paid for all of it. The job prospects in the 1950s were pretty grim, but my uncle said to take the post office exam and I had a good position in the post office for twenty-seven years.

# Edmond Machado

*Born on September 1, 1932*

**Family Background**

I was born in Fall River, at home on Grinnell Street. My parents were Louis (Luiz) and Maria Nascment (Correia) Machado. I did not know my grandparents names and occupations.

I have lived at the following residences in Fall River: 1354 Rodman Street, on the second floor, across the street from St. John's Athletic Club (from birth to marriage); 304 Cambridge Street, first floor (when married in 1964), with my mother living on the second floor from 1964 to 1977; and 2097 Highland Avenue.

My father was a loom fixer and then the night superintendent at the Kerr Mill. My mother was a homemaker.

There were seven kids in our family and I was the youngest: Mamie, Louis, James, Alice (who had a twin who died), Arthur, Gilbert, and me.

My wife is Claire (Martin) Machado, and we have three children: Matthew, Peter, and Julie.

**Family Life**

When we lived on the second floor of a three-family tenement at 1354 Rodman Street, the people downstairs were French. Their name was Ruby. The Lima's lived on the third floor. The Ruby's lost their restaurant and after that worked for the Limas at their restaurant in Newport [Rhode Island]. We couldn't wear shoes on the second floor because it would wake up the Rubys, who had restaurant hours.

My mother learned to make pies and pastries from the person who owned Caron's Bakery on Warren Street, on the corner of Baker Street.

No one knew they were poor. My father had a shoe last that he used to repair our shoes. He carved the leather according to our shoe size and repaired them. Sometimes, if there was no time to repair the shoes, we put cardboard in them. In the summer, we went barefoot.

During the winter, when my mother put the clothes out on the line, they came in stiff. We had two space heaters, one in the kitchen and one in the parlor (which we never went in, except on holidays). There was this thing on the wall with wooden tongs on it and she would put the laundry on it. I always wondered, why not put the laundry on the tongs in the first place and hang them inside?

In the winter in my bedroom, I could scratch the frost off my walls—off the walls, not the window. My father made storm windows, since the landlords didn't give you storm windows.

On Saturdays, I washed the back stairs with Pine Sol, which had a horrible smell. I would leave the door open to listen to "Let's Pretend." It opened up with a string quartet. I went to the Brayton Avenue School. The principal was Miss Crush. She walked around with a rubber-tipped pointer and either hit you with the pointer or grabbed you by the ears.

We didn't want to be Portuguese; we spoke Portuguese only at home. My father wanted to

Edmond Machado's brother Jimmy's wedding to Hilda Pacheco; Edmond is kneeling. Mrs. Lima is on far right, who lived on the 3rd floor of 1354 Rodman Street. Picture taken in the back yard of that address.

learn English and put up a new word every day on the mirror when he shaved in the morning. When he went to Boston, he didn't want to sound illiterate.

My father was a bright man. He bought a car and proceeded to take it apart and put it back together again. He taught machinery at Durfee Tech [Bradford Durfee College of Technology]. He and mom were both from São Miguel Island, Azores. My father was also an officer at the St. John's Club.

My father was very knowledgeable. When asked a question, he liked to ramble on about what it was. My mother knew how to read in Portuguese and learned to read and speak English by herself. She read the newspaper and spoke broken English. She never wanted to hear the family embarrassed. She never went out by herself, but always had one of the kids with her. She developed a liking for Chinese food; there was a Chinese restaurant at the Flatiron Building on Second Street.

My mom was fifteen when she got married. My father was a trumpet player in a band at a church. She was gorgeous. Her family was going back to the Azores and she stayed with relatives. They "kept company." My mother listened to "Aunt Jenny" soaps on the radio at noontime when I came home for lunch.

## Food and Meals

My father would make beer, wine, and booze, called cashasa (ca-sha'-sa) or moonshine. After the cashasa was made, they flavored it to make liquor. During Prohibition, it was illegal to make it. It needed a lot of sugar to make it, so we had to buy the sugar in small quantities to avoid being found out. We made it in the apartment, not in the cellar.

The annual killing of the pig meant that we went to our uncle's place, my father's brother-in-law (he was a Machado too), at his farm in Westport. They would take the pig and pull it up on a pulley. They would next cut its throat open so the blood would flow out. I had to stir the blood to prevent it from coagulating. It didn't bother me; I liked to help. They burn the pig to take the hair off before cutting it up. They then butchered it. They would then take the casings (the ta-ri'-pish) and use a funnel to put the meat into it. These pigs were massive, over 300 pounds.

The meat and sausage would then be put into big beautiful vats made of shiny porcelain and they would fill the vat with lard. When you took the sausage or meat out of the vat, a wonderful smell came out. The killing of the pig was always a feast; whole families got together to do it.

We would put a sign out for ice. The sign just said "Ice." The iceman would put it in the icebox. Sometimes, the iceman would take the shavings and give it to us kids.

Sundays were visiting days or people would visit us. Sundays were a big deal. Mom roasted chicken and roast together, and the potatoes were always orange from the chourico. There was always food available. Mom would make Sunday dinner, which was the only day of the week when we had a big meal at noon. Every other day, our big meal was in the evening. Lunch was called dinner and the evening meal was called supper.

Breakfast was usually toast. I wanted my mother to get Wheaties because inside there was a secret puzzle that had a code that could be solved from clues given on the radio. You used your imagination a lot in those days.

We never had hamburger in the house; my mother didn't trust it. She also never bought "sweet" fish from fresh water; we only ate salt water fish. Later, she was getting to be more "American" and had a salad of lettuce, tomatoes, and vinegar. My mom couldn't stand mayonnaise. None of my aunts ate mayonnaise. We also couldn't eat milk products with a clamboil or fish.

My mom made her own pimenta muida. Her hands would turn red and burn like hell so that she almost cried. However, she never bought it; she had to make it.

I took my father's lunch pail to where he worked at the Shawmut Mills. I had to run to make sure it stayed warm. He always left me something in the pail to eat. I would say, "Let me see; let me see." We had an hour for lunch.

## Neighborhood Experiences

I remember sitting on the porch and going to the drugstore to buy some maple walnut ice cream. I gave them Monopoly money for it and they took it. However, it didn't work when I tried it the second time.

The kids would generally go to the variety store for small items. Mom and dad would go on Fridays to shop for groceries and, if the money was good that week, they would bring back a big bag of potato chips and two bottles of soda.

During the 4th of July, people would run in the middle of Brayton Avenue and Rodman Street, where DeVillars is, and pile up a lot of stuff and light it up in a big bonfire.

Groups would go to Luke Urban's place off of Stafford Road in Tiverton [Rhode Island].

There was a pond there and buildings. Several shemeritas groups in the city would go there, busloads of people. The groups would dance and sing in Portuguese.

My mom's cousin had a market around the Letourneau School. They had a horse and wagon and delivered groceries that way in the enclosed wagon. Fish mongers also came in their horse and wagons and yelled, "Pesch!" The fish monger never held the reins of the horse; the horse just followed along and knew where to stop. The Jewish merchants who sold clothes door to door could speak fluent Portuguese and French. Another guy came in a truck and sharpened knives. We would fool with him and he would pretend that he would kill us.

We had two grocery stores in our neighborhood. One was Freitas and Perreira, owned by Louie Perreira's father, and the other was Mello's Market, next to it on the right. They were on the left side of Rodman Street, facing Cambridge Street. At Freitas and Perreira, they had a file on clips for each family. Sometimes a family couldn't pay the bill all the time. My father had to run up some credit but finally paid the bill, which was up to one hundred dollars.

There was a café on the corner of Rodman Street and Brayton Avenue where a mostly young crowd hung out. Next to it was a barber shop owned by a Tache, who was related to Roger Tache. We wouldn't recognize alcoholism in those days; we had "happy" drinking.

There was a trolley from Rodman Street to Main Street. In the wintertime, a special trolley came down with a plow in front. They were electric trolleys and had bells that went *jing-jing*. The streets were never plowed. You had to put chains on the back wheels of cars or trucks.

Right next to the Protestant church at the top of Cambridge and Rodman Streets was a store where you could buy cigarettes for a penny each. Kids could buy them; there were no restrictions on who could buy cigarettes. Old Gold cigarettes had redemption stamps on them. Raleigh cigarettes also had coupons that provided prizes.

**Recreation and Entertainment**

My father took us to the Durfee Theatre to see Blackstone the Magician. He made an elephant disappear from the Durfee stage. He was big back then.

In the summertime, we would go to Depression Beach, otherwise known as Bareass Beach, which was at the bottom of Brayton Avenue, before it was cut through. We would follow the railroad tracks to the beach to the South Watuppa Pond. Sometimes we would go in without clothes.

Warren Street was a hill for sledding. We had someone on Rodman Street waiting and yelling go when it was free to go. We made our own scooters made from fruit boxes. They were in two sections. My father made the handlebars of wood with a piece of wood on the bottom. One pair of skates provided the wheels. One foot was on the board and one foot pedaled while we stood up. Then I got a real scooter with a brake on the back. When we got bikes, that was real freedom; then we went beyond Rodman Street.

For games, we played kick the can, hide and seek, peggy ball, may I, Simon says, red rover, and king of the hill (where we pushed off kids from a mound and the last one was the king of the hill). Sometimes we made up new rules; we just made them up. We played in the meadows. Next to the St. John's Club, there was a field with cows. When we ran through the field to school, we would step in the cow flap. Behind St. John's, there was a big block of granite, and we would smash up all kinds of bottles so that they would be like powder.

To the rear of St. John's was the ladies entrance. Ladies never went in the bar. They would go to the back of the place to eat with a gentleman. St. John's was a small place then. St. John's showed movies outside. They were usually sponsored by a tobacco company, like Lucky Strikes or Camels. There were cartoons, Laurel and Hardy; I can't remember if it had sound.

**School Life**

When I was in college at Boston University, some freshman kids were invited to the president's house. My father was dying at the time. My father was thrilled that I was going to college. He said go. When I came back, he wanted to know what it was like. He said all of the things that I wanted to hear as a child. My father died when I had two years to go in college. My mother gave me food to take back with me. She gave me food she should have kept for herself. She went without. She was a very good lady. Very strict in some ways but lovable in others. She died of Alzheimer's at the age of eighty-eight, in 1998. She was born on Christmas and died on the Feast of the Ascension. She was very religious and walked to church every day.

**Courtship and Marriage**

We met when Claire had an hour and a quarter for lunch when she worked for John Cummings' father and wanted to take violin lessons during lunch. Mitch was the violin teacher. We were married on October 10, 1964.

My mom didn't want to know when Claire was pregnant. "Don't tell me," she said. When we told her that Claire had gone to the hospital, she said "I don't want to know about it." Subjects of this nature were never discussed with mom. The hospitals say that there is something called Portuguese Mass Hysteria (PMH) or Acute Portuguese Hysteria (APH), when whole families come to visit a patient and get excited over the fate of a relative.

**Friends**

Some of my friends were "Duke" Cabral, who lived on the corner of Rodman and Grinnell Streets. Louis Perreira lived on Brayton Avenue. Joe Perry lived on Rodman Street. Our universe was from Brayton Avenue to the end of the church lot, or about four blocks, maybe. Very rarely did we leave that area. Maybe we would go as far as Stafford Road. When the street lights came on, it was time to go home. If we did anything bad, we would hear it from the adults. "I know you; I will tell your father!"

I went to school with Alan Jarabek; he worked for my uncle. My uncle had one son, who ran away from home and became a jockey. He died when he fell from his horse and the horse stepped on his head. My two brothers knew where he was but didn't tell.

My friend Tommy died when he was seven years old. His mother gave my mother his clothes. It didn't bother me. I remember praying for him a lot. His father had a brand new Studebaker. I never knew any rich kids. The exception was Justin Morganstein, who lived in the white house on Brayton Avenue, near where The Pub is now. He was Dr. Morganstein's son. They had a maid.

**Christmas, Holidays, and Special Occasions**

Christmas were happy times. It would start after supper on Christmas Eve. My father played the trumpet and a friend of my father's played the concertina. There was also a violinist. They would start with four or five people and end up with thirty or forty by the time they were finished. Drinks and food were provided at each house.

At the door, the visitors would sing:

> We don't want your riches;
> We want your blessings,
> Of Jesus the baby (baby Jesus).
> We are here to see you Mr. _____
> We know that you are very generous.

People would laugh and make up lyrics, like, "The massa was not fresh, but okay," and things like that, poking good fun at them. They would joke on the way out.

The table was always set up with food. There was always a room full of mangers.

## Downtown

We went downtown for clothes. During the holidays, you couldn't move downtown. You had to walk in the streets. The police were in boxes in the center of intersections directing traffic. In the summertime, they had an umbrella to protect them from the heat. They used whistles to direct traffic.

## Hurricane of 1938

I was six or seven when the 1938 hurricane happened. My father came home when he saw that the telephone poles were bending. The window in the hallway broke and it risked taking off the roof. The damage was incredible. Island Park [Cashman's Park, Portsmouth, Rhode Island] was awful.

## Religious Life

During the feast of the Holy Ghost, someone stood in front of Our Lady of Health Church and someone stood at the corner of Rodman and another corner of Rodman and Cambridge Streets. Both had white flags. At the consecration of the host and the ringing of the six bells, the flagman at the front of the church signaled the flagman at Rodman Street and he in turn signaled to the person operating the cannon at St. John's field. Every time the bells rang, the cannon would fire. When a feast was held, it was held on the church grounds, not on St. John's Club grounds. St. John's Club was careful to keep religion separate from it. Carnivals were held in the St. John's field.

## Health and Illness

The typical diseases were measles, chicken pox, and scarlet fever. If you had TB [tuberculosis], you went to the contagious hospital. My godmother's son died of TB. The lady next door had infantile paralysis [polio]. Often it reappeared in adulthood as post-polio syndrome. We were given warm wine for colds and fevers. Father John's medicine was common. Whole raw eggs were drunk in anything. We had cod liver oil every morning.

*Claire*: My mom put camphor bags around our necks to prevent colds. The whole classroom smelled of camphor. For toothaches, my father smoked a pipe and he would take some tobacco and munched it up and put it on our gums. It worked; it numbed it.

*Ed*: Wakes were held in the home. Somebody had to stay up all night with the body. They took shifts. People brought food and drink and stayed for hours and hours. When people first got there they were sober, but when the men started drinking, there was more levity. They would start laughing when they talked about when the deceased did this or that.

**World War II**

When Pearl Harbor struck on Sunday, December 7th, I was really ticked because I couldn't listen to "The Shadow." That was a turning point in our lives. My brothers went into the service. We would look at the windows with gold stars, where families had lost a son. I still have a ration book, some for gas and some for meat and sugar. We would wait in line at Kennedy's for butter.

I remember during World War II when Dorothy Lamour came down Main Street selling war bonds in an open car.

**Popular Expressions**

*Ed*: "See you later alligator."

*Claire*: The girls wore slips then. If a slip showed below your dress, we would say, "It's snowing down south."

Photograph of Island Park (Cashman's Park) in Portsmouth, Rhode Island, showing the destruction from the hurricane of 1938

# Yvette (Boucher) Mancini

*Born on May 31, 1917*

**Family Background**

I was born at home at 659 Eastern Avenue, where the Notre Dame Credit Union is now.

My parents were Edgar (born in Canada in 1893) and Marie Rose (Durand) Boucher (born in Fall River in 1887).

My father's parents were Theophile (born in 1848) and Celina (Cote) Boucher (born in 1866). My mother's parents were Phillipe and Lumina Bergeron Durand.

My sister's names are (in order of birth, including me): Yevette, Lorraine (Carter), Annette (Miller), and Jeannine (Warburton).

I was married to Joseph Ray Mancini on Thanksgiving Day, 1939. We had two children, Richard Robert and Raymond Francis.

**Family Life**

My father came to the United States at the age of nine. He was born on the Saint Lawrence River at Sandy Bay. In the winter, his father was a boss on a lumberjack group; in the summer, he was a captain on a vessel on the Saint Lawrence River. My father said that every time his father came home, he had a new baby and made a new baby. He had twenty-two children.

Peerless Laundry was located in back of 659 Eastern Avenue and it released steam into our yard. My father had to tell them not to do that since his kids could get burnt.

Our house was a cottage, but my father made it into a two-story house. When the Depression came, we lost the house. It broke his heart. The sheriff put a red flag on the buildings that were up for auction.

In the median of Eastern Avenue (toward Kerr Mill) off of Pleasant Street was a horse trough for watering horses. When I was a kid, there were more horses than cars.

We then moved to New Bedford to live with an uncle and his family for three years. My uncle was a supervisor for New Bedford Gas and wasn't affected by the Depression. Then we came back to Fall River and went on welfare so that we would have something to eat. There were no cash payments from welfare then, only bulk food.

We had neighbors whose whole family worked in the Kerr Mills (the only mill that never closed during the Depression). The neighbors would give us leftovers from their Thursday meal to eat. However, the meal was usually meat and we couldn't eat meat on Fridays. So my father asked the priest if we could get an exception. The priest said, yes, you have to feed your family.

We wore the same shoes, which had big holes in them. Every day, we would put fresh cardboard in the shoe.

There were four girls in the family, and I was the oldest. My mother would dress us up so-so. We were little princesses. We had no brothers so never learned to skate or ride a bike.

On Sunday morning, following Mass, we girls would stay dressed and I would take my three sisters down Eastern Avenue to where it ended at Bedford Street. At the end of Eastern Avenue, there was a big sign that looked like a book facing the avenue. It was open and turned back and had the history of the city written on it. I remember reading about Massasoit and how the city developed. This was about 1929. No one that I know has ever seen it or heard about it.

When I was seventeen years old, I went to do housework for a lady. I did all kinds of work for her, including ironing, washing the stairs, and taking care of her two children, all for fifty cents a day. It was good. I gave all of my money to my parents. My father was too proud to let people know that he couldn't afford fifteen cents for his church seat (thirty cents for both him and my mother) and he used my money for that and other needs.

Before the Depression, we had toys for Christmas and a tree. My mother made our dresses. Before the Depression, I had a fur coat. We also had Mary Janes patent leather shoes. They were noisy when new, and we would grease them so they wouldn't make noise. I got my first heels when I was twelve years old. They were low "Cuban heels." I thought that I was a big girl. My cousin and I decided to go walking with our shoes on Pleasant Street. Two sailors started whistling at us, and we ran across the street. Sailors didn't have a good reputation then. Our older cousin did the Charleston. We also had "overshoes" that had buckles to secure them.

When my father arrived in the United States at the age of nine, he went to work in the mills right away as a sweeper. He couldn't read and didn't speak English until he married my mother and she taught him. He became perfect in English, as good as anyone.

My father was a weaver at the Pilgrim Mill. He would wear his Sunday best to the mill and change into his work clothes when he got there. He was so well-dressed that people thought he was a boss and would come to the house asking for a job. Later, he was loom fixer at the Pepperell Mill and worked until he was seventy-five years old, when he was forced to retire because of his age.

My grandfather lived across the street from the Shove Mills on Shove Street and worked there until he was ninety-two, oiling the looms. Finally, his daughter told the supervisor that he was too old to be there and that, "you have to fire him, otherwise he'll keep on working." But the supervisor said, "He won't give up."

My father always walked and never had a car. Until he died at ninety-seven, he walked a mile around the grounds of Catholic Memorial grounds. He was very vital. All of his brothers and sisters died in their nineties.

When we were able to get electricity, the wires were installed in the gas fixtures. I did not have a telephone until 1940. When I was about age fourteen, I was babysitting for a family that did have a phone. It rang and I was too afraid to answer it; I didn't know what to do. As it turns out, it was the parents of the children calling to see how things were. Before the telephone, people communicated by visiting.

My husband's stepfather helped demolish the Fall River Line steamers. He obtained a dozen Fall River Line silverware from the *Priscilla* and gave them to us. We used them for a while but didn't keep them.

My husband and I lived in Florida for twenty years, where I taught water aerobics, clogging, and participated in theatre groups. We had a recreational trailer, an Avion, and traveled all over the country. When in Florida, I was a tour escort for a travel bureau. I have been a contestant for the Ms. Senior Sweetheart Pageant and competed by hula dancing. I'm now on the Miss Senior Sweethearts committee now, and we have weekly meetings. I do yoga and walk a lot.

## Prohibition

My father made beer during Prohibition. He had a big copper boiler, something that you needed to make good beer. Malt, yeast, and hops were required to make the beer. He would start by making a batch of hot water and then add the ingredients. He checked it and put a cloth over the open batch of beer for a week. During the second week, he would bottle the beer and the third week he tasted it. This was a Thursday night event. Since I had no brothers and I was the oldest sister, I had to help. My mother would complain, "You will make a drunk out of her." My mother made root beer. We would buy caps and bottles and cap the root beer.

## Food and Meals

For breakfast, we always had cooked oatmeal. There were no fancy cereals then. Maybe we had toast sometimes. I never drank milk; I drank only tea. My sisters drank milk, however.

Our meals were usually meat and potatoes, with a pot roast on Sundays. The roast included carrots and one day a week we had a stew with carrots and cabbage. Those were the only vegetables we had. We never had things like salads. Once, later in life, my mother came back from visiting her sister in Worcester and was impressed with a salad that her sister served and said, "Let's make a salad."

During the Depression, it cost only ten cents for a peck of potatoes. So, my mother cut them up into french fries and fried them in fat renderings that we kept on the stove. That was our only meal for that day.

The welfare food distribution place was on Alden Street, where you had to wait in line to get butter and other staples. My father was so proud, too proud to wait in line. I was fourteen years old at the time and so waited in line for him. In 1938, things were still bad.

If you wanted the iceman to stop, you put a sign in the window. If the sign was placed on one side, that meant that you wanted a big piece of ice; if it was placed on the other side, it meant that you wanted a small piece. The ice was delivered by horse and wagon.

On Fridays, a guy with a horse and wagon would come by to sell fish. All of the ladies in the neighborhood would come out to buy his fish. A rag man also came by, yelling, "Rags, rags!" He bought clothes and paper. There was also a knife sharpener with a horse and wagon. The sharpener was powered by a foot pedal.

My mother had a Glenwood stove that she shined every week with Carbox shine. The stove had an oven that we opened when we came in from the cold and wanted to warm our hands. Every tenement had its own coal bin downstairs. Each bin had its own window that the coal truck used to slide the coal into the bin.

Sunday meal was a roast with potatoes and carrots. Monday was a hash with the leftover roast. Tuesday was fried pork chops and mashed potatoes. Wednesday was a beef stew, with some carrots. Thursday was steak. Friday was a fish or chowder. Saturday was hot dogs or smoked ham.

Beans were soaked overnight on Friday night and the beans prepared with salt pork on Saturday. They were delivered to Porier's Bakery on Saturday and picked up on Sunday after Mass. Beans were Sunday breakfast. We would fast before Mass.

Gorton [French-Canadian pork spread] was a favorite. It was made from ground pork cooked with onions rendered in lard. When it was cooked, it was put in a dish and white lard would float to the top. It was put in a cool place and spread on bread. The French people ate lots of pork. Chicken was very expensive when I was young.

Some of the things my mother preserved included piccalilli, made from green tomatoes. Mom's finest preserve was a marmalade made from apricots and pineapples. It was excellent.

**School Life**

I went to kindergarten at the Turnpike School, where the Nite Owl Diner is now at Pleasant Street and Eastern Avenue. Then I went to the Notre Dame School. Notre Dame School was free. We had two cherry trees in our back yard and, during recess at the Turnpike School, my mother would collect the cherries from the trees and give them to me to give to the other kids. I was very popular. The only teacher I remember from the school was a Miss Grace.

At first grade, I could read. The teachers would call on me to read to the kids in the third grade to shame them into reading better. Teachers did that then. I skipped second grade.

I loved school, but at age fourteen I had to quit school to help support the family. In those days, you could get permission to quit school at that age, but you had to go to Continuation School that was located on Morgan Street. We had to go one morning a week until we were sixteen. Later, I got my GED and my LPN.

**Recreation and Entertainment**

When she was young, my mother was involved in a Sunday excursion boat accident on the Taunton River with four or five of her sisters. There was a fire and explosion on the boat. She was pulled out of the water by her hair. One man was killed in the accident. The next day, my grandmother was in the market. She overheard another woman say that it was good enough for the Durand sisters who were on the boat, since they should have been in church, but instead went out with boys. My grandmother was angry and spoke up and said that the girls were chaperoned by their older married sister and that the boat trip was proper.

As a girl, my favorite game was hopscotch, and we also played hide and go seek and tag. We had a big wooden swing in our yard, with seats on either side. We also had a regular rope swing. My mother was a champion skater but was afraid to let us girls go skating. We really missed out from not having a brother.

In the summer, we would go to Steep Brook for two weeks. Our parents belonged to a club that paid so much each week. Each family got a cottage for two weeks. When we became teenagers, we went to Ocean Grove [Swansea, Massachusetts]. We had no car, but a friend did have one, and as teenagers we took day trips with them to Ocean Grove.

When we went in the water at the beach as a child, we wore sailor's uniforms with collars as bathing suits. We also wore black stockings and white sneakers. We also had a bonnet on our heads. Everyone dressed to go to the beach. We were cold when we got out of the water.

In winter and when there was snow, there was always someone who had a toboggan. The toboggans would hold six or seven persons, with the boy in front steering and the boy in back braking. We would start at the top of Eastern Avenue near the Notre Dame rectory and slide down the avenue. Someone stood at Pleasant Street to watch out for occasional cars, just in case a car had to be stopped. Sometimes, if we got a good push, we could slide all the way to the Watson School.

A few times, we went down to Jefferson Street early in the morning to watch elephants and other animals get off of the circus train.

In 1935, I belonged to the YMCA. The pool was reserved for men except for Wednesdays, when it was reserved only for ladies. I was a member until 1944. In those days, the men swam nude in the pool, but the women had to stay covered because the lifeguard was a man. Swimsuits then were made of wool, but wool clogged the pool's drains. Therefore, the women had to wear cotton swimsuits that were made at home.

When I first joined the Y, I was sixteen years old. It was considered a Christian organization but the priest said that I was forbidden to join it. I joined it just the same. My mother didn't talk to me for two weeks. I was a real rebel. Years later, when I was visiting my sisters in Myrtle Beach, South Carolina, one of my sisters introduced me to one of her friends by saying "This is my sister, the rebel."

Before the Depression, we would go to the theatre for five cents on Saturdays to watch Tom Mix and the Perils of Pauline. Every week, Pauline would be on the railroad tracks or some other situation at the end of the serial. This was at the Star Theater that was on the second floor and faced Cash Street. The seats in the theatre were soapboxes.

I was a member of the Drill Team at Notre Dame Church. We won five cups and eighteen medals throughout New England. I was the captain who yelled out commands. When we traveled, we were escorted by a matron and our instructor. The Drill Team escorted me on my wedding day, as it did at weddings for other members of the team. Our uniforms were very military and were paid for by a French society, the Union of St. Jean Baptiste. They raised money through whist parties and other events. The members of the drill team also ran dances to make money for our competition trips all over New England.

On Sunday nights, our friends would meet in one of the girl's house and sing by the piano. A boy would play the piano using music sheets.

We went dancing at the Lincoln Park [North Dartmouth, Massachusetts] Ballroom. We would walk to the Narrows and take the trolley there. During intermission, we would go ride the dobby horses for five cents a ride. Dobby horses are now called the carousel.

At other times, we would go dancing at Frontenac Hall, located on the second floor of a building at the corner of East Main and Peckham Streets. We danced to a live band and would dance one set of American dances and one set of French quadrilles. Four boys and four girls were in a quadrille group. In a circle, the boys twirled the girls and, as they twirled, the girls lifted their legs in the air. At intermission, the boys who belonged to the club went downstairs for a beer and a girl could accompany him if he was a club member. We walked all the way home, unless someone had a car. We made sure that at least one friend was in the car with a girl and a guy, so that the last girl left off wasn't alone in the car with a guy.

At home, we would turn over the oilcloth table cover, and played Parcheesi on it on the markings on the reverse of the oilcloth. We had fun and never locked our doors.

We would go to the vaudeville shows at the local theatres. While waiting for a bus at the corner of Pleasant and South Main Streets one night, I saw Rose Marie pass by me. I remember that she was crying. She was staying at the Mellon Hotel and was performing at the Empire Theatre.

From 1935 to 1938, I had my own radio program on WSAR. During and after that, I still sang with a quartet on the Franco-American Radio Hour. I was also a soloist at Notre Dame Church. I took training and voice lessons and was a mezzo-soprano. My friend, who was a coloratura soprano, had a chance to go to New York to sing in the chorus at the Metropolitan Opera, and was very angry that I wouldn't go with her. I got married instead.

My husband was a musician and was in the musician's union. He had his own four-piece band when he was young at the time we were married. He could play any instrument. His father was a music teacher. He had a big Italian band, and my husband played the trumpet in the band. The members were from around Columbus Park. My husband was eleven years old when his father passed away. His father and mother had four boys, and all played the piano by ear. His father taught every instrument you could think of, except the piano. He said that he couldn't get the hand coordination. My husband played in a union band at South Park [now Kennedy Park] pavilion every Sunday in the summer during the 1940s and 1950s.

Island Park [Cashman's Park, Portsmouth, Rhode Island] was the place to go on Sundays. Service boys from Newport [Rhode Island] would go there. My sisters met two boys who were both on a PT [Patrol Torpedo] boat together. One was from Illinois and one was from South Carolina. My sisters married these two friends and then moved to Illinois and South Carolina.

Earlier, my sister had a boyfriend in the service, but suddenly he stopped writing to her. She thought that it was because he didn't want her anymore. Much later, a letter came to the house from him saying that he was a prisoner of war. In the meantime, my sister had married and my mother and I didn't have the heart to tell her the story. We told her later.

**Courtship and Marriage**

My mother and father met at Island Park, where my mother and some of her friends rented a cottage and some boys next door had also rented a cottage.

I first met my husband at St. Anthony's School in New Bedford. He teased me terribly. He had also lived in Fall River at one time, but his family moved to New Bedford to live with his grandmother after his father died. After we moved back to Fall River, his family also moved back to the city—to a house on Lafayette Street, right across the street from our family. His mother was French and his father Italian.

I was married on Thanksgiving Day in 1938. It was also the date of my parents twenty-fifth wedding anniversary. It snowed that day. The Drill Team met us at the car (a 1936 Chevy) and escorted us inside Notre Dame Church. Horvitz Furniture usually supplied a white carpet up the walk to the church but, because of the snow, we didn't have it. I was a member of the Solidarity of Mary, which was a church society for unmarried ladies. It allowed you to marry inside the communion rail. Because it was a holiday, and because I was a member of the choir, the whole choir and a soloist performed at my wedding.

Everything in our wedding was free. Our limo was owned by one of my husband's band members. The wedding breakfast for family (aunts and uncles) was at my parent's house. Our reception was at the American Legion Hall, which we got at no charge because the commander was the instructor of our Drill Team. My husband's band provided the music and I sang. My husband played in the band and he played and I sang "I Love You Truly." "Mexicali Rose" was one of our favorite songs. The Drill Team also put on a performance. All that we paid for was our clothes and our pictures.

In those days, friends and family would follow you as you left on the way to your honeymoon. We circled the city and finally lost them. We then went back to the tenement next to my parents that we rented and stayed the night. The next day, we left for the Mohawk Trail. We had intended to go to New York City on the Fall River Line, but the Line closed in 1938.

**Work Life**

My first job as a child was to remove the rust from the table knives. Every Saturday, I would take the knives out in the yard and run them in and out of the ground to remove the rust.

I became a licensed practical nurse. In the early 1950s, I worked at St. Anne's Hospital as a nurse's aide. I became very proficient and, with a few hours of medical training and the grandfather clause, I was allowed to take the two-day test in Boston at and received my license.

My husband tested torpedoes at Newport and therefore didn't go into the service. He started working in textiles and then at Raytheon, Sylvania, and Honeywell. He had heart attacks and then went to New England Tech. He repaired television sets at Kaplan's Furniture Store. He lived until he was age eighty-one.

**Neighborhood Experiences**

I remember the lamplighter coming around the neighborhood to light the gas street lamps. He had a ladder (about eight feet) over his shoulder that he laid against the lamp. He would take the top of the light fixture off, light the lamp with a match, put the top back on, and go to the next lamp. In the early morning, he would shut the light out. There was a gas lamp at the corner of Eastern Avenue and Raymond Street. When electricity came into the homes, they used the same gas fixtures and pipe for the electricity.

I remember that a man would come by the neighborhood with a pony and a camera, and you could have your picture taken on the pony.

New Year's was a big thing for French people. They went around waking people up. It was called *Le Réveillon de Noël*, or The Awakening. During the night people would drop in at midnight to one or two in the morning and you had to serve them something. My mother made meat pies for New Years.

**Downtown**

We got our music sheets from Kresge's, which was the high-toned 5 & 10. There was a woman in the basement who sold sheet music and played the piano as she sang the songs on the sheet music. If you liked the song, you bought the music sheet.

I always remember going to Cherry and Webb to get my favorite perfume. As soon as you opened the door, you got a strong scent of the perfume that they wanted to sell that week.

**Religious Life**

On Sunday, we paid fifteen cents a seat at Notre Dame Church. If you gave a quarter, you got a dime back from the ushers. Then, the priest came by with a second collection basket, but no one had any money during the Depression to put in.

**Health and Illness**

When you died, you were waked in the home. A black crepe ribbon was hung on the door. All of the men wore a black band on their sleeves when family members died. Everyone dressed in black. If a parent or sibling died, you wore black for six months and purple for the next six months.

A wake could last all night and turn into a party. When my grandfather was waked, there were two old maids who came to the wake and protested that people were making a party out of the wake. Someone stood up all night with the deceased. Breakfast was served to those who were there. The deceased stayed in the house until they left for the church and the cemetery. I don't know if they were embalmed in the home. They would put the person on a plank before the coffin came in.

When a friend or relative died, my mother would go to wash them from head to toe before the undertaker came. There was one person who was so heavy that my mother couldn't turn her around, and my mother said, "Come on, Mary, help me out," to the deceased.

My sister had scarlet fever. We had to put a quarantine sign on the door. My mother was the only one who could take care of her. My sister used special dishes. She was only twelve years old and was so delirious that she once fell out of bed. I had German measles five times, but not anything else. My sisters had whooping cough, diphtheria, chicken pox.

I had an uncle that got "barber's itch" [a deep infection of hair follicles] which was gotten from barbers. He passed on to his daughter, our cousin, and two of my sisters got it when they were babysitting there. I didn't get it. It was also known as the "seven year itch."

Two of my sisters had earaches and, as a cure, my mother would take flax seeds and make an oil from them and put it in their ears. When girls menstruated, they were given Lydia Pinkham compound to build up their system. Scott's Emulsion was also given to build up the system and to ward off TB [tuberculosis]. No one had TB in my family.

After he was married, my father had his tonsils out in his house. They laid him on the dining room table and took them out right there. Back then, tonsils were blamed for everything.

In the wintertime, we kids wore a medallion of camphor around our necks all winter long. This was thought to ward off colds. Everyone smelled of camphor in school. In the spring, we were given a dose of sulfur and molasses to "clean you out."

To keep warm, girls and boys wore "union suits" that opened in the back. The girls wore black stockings over them. We also wore high-buttoned shoes.

## The Depression

When we were in New Bedford during the Depression, my father worked part-time in a furniture store. They had round glass things that they gave away, and that was my only gift that Christmas.

My mother was a good seamstress and, when we were in New Bedford, she was approached by someone who sold little cotton dresses door-to-door. He convinced my mother to work for him for one dollar a week. He would bring in all of the cut pieces and she would sew them together for pennies each.

There were always collectors at the door. Once, my mother answered the door and this old man was selling pencils. My mother said no and closed the door. She then heard him crying in the hall. She felt so bad.

Everyone listened to Roosevelt's fireside chats. They were wonderful. My husband was in the Civilian Conservation Corps in Irving, Massachusetts. My brother was in the WPA [Works Progress Administration]. Only one person per family was allowed to work for the WPA. My husband's brother was in the CCC [Civilian Conservation Corps] for thirteen months in 1933 and liked it so much that he signed up for a second stint using his brother's name. After we were married, we would go to the Mohawk Trail and stop at the CCC camp so he could remember the good times there.

## Travel and Transportation

I remember as a child leaving the North Main train station to go to Worcester to visit my mother's sister. We went over the Slade's Ferry Bridge. I remember going to the bathroom on the train, which was just a hole going down to the tracks. I didn't use it because I was afraid that I would fall through the hole and onto the tracks.

We would ride the trolley to New Bedford. It was an open trolley, with everyone seated facing front. On one side was a rail and the other was a running board. The conductor would come along the running board collecting fares. At night, at the Narrows, night "fish flies" would come swarming into the open trolley.

The uncle that we stayed with in New Bedford had a big sedan called a Reo during the 1920s. There were no heaters in the early cars. Our first car after being married didn't have a heater either. You always had to have a blanket in the car.

## Hurricane of 1938

During the 1938 hurricane, the spires of Notre Dame Church were moving. My two sisters were working in sweat shops at the time and came home and said that the wind was awful. I and my future husband went out to look and had to hold onto a tree. The police had put yellow rope around Pleasant Street and all the way to Eastern Avenue in case the spires fell.

St. Anne's Church and Hospital, South Main Street at South Park (now Kennedy Park)

**World War II**

During the war, my mother took in service boys for Sunday meals who were stationed in Middletown [Rhode Island]. My mother-in-law did also. One day, my mother-in-law got a call from a serviceman named Mancini who said that every time he was stationed in a new town, he would look up the name Mancini in the phone book and call them to invite himself over. She invited him over. Everyone was good in those days.

During World War II, we had to put black cloth over our windows to keep out all light. If any light showed, the warden would let you know. We also put hoods over our car lights. Volunteer wardens walked the street all night to make sure our enemies could not see a light.

My sisters wanted to go in the WAVES ["Women Accepted for Volunteer Emergency Service;" official name, U.S. Naval Reserve (Women's Reserve)] or the WACs [Woman's Army Corps], but my mother said no. If I wasn't married, I would have gone into the service anyway. I was very independent.

**Popular Expressions**

Jiminy Cricket.

Slade's Ferry Bridge

# Hilda (Martin) Martel

*Born on February 1, 1924*
*Died on June 28, 2013*

### Family Background

I was born in Fall River when we lived at 99 Pitman Street.

My parents were Antone and Clara (Nunes) Martin.

My father went into the service in World War I. If you enlisted in those days, you got citizenship. When he was discharged, his discharge papers had the name of Antone Martin, altered from the original spelling Martins.

My mother's mother was Margarida Farias Nunes. My father's parents were Francisco Couto and Francisca Martins.

I was the first born of three sisters. Their names are Olive (Machado) and Margaret (Medeiros).

My husband is Raymond Joseph Martel and we have two children, Arlene Rita Martel, and Ronald Paul Martel.

### Family Life

My mom didn't speak English. My father made her speak English. I would speak to him in English and to her in Portuguese.

I did whatever my mother wanted me to do. I washed the stairs religiously. We used bleach water to make the stairs look good. Mom said that if you go up the stairs, you know what was inside the home. We also washed down the sidewalks.

My father came here when he was very young with his family. The family left and left my father here alone. They said, "You've got to earn your keep." He worked for a grocery store and delivered orders.

My father worked in the Kerr Mill in the spinning room. I worked there myself for four or five years. I would bring my father his dinner pail during my lunch hour, which was only three-quarters of an hour. I would have to go to the Kerr Mill, climb the stairs, and get there on time, since my father didn't want the pail to be left there and subject to bugs. On Friday, because we couldn't eat meat, I brought him fruit cocktail. Then I would go back home to have my lunch and back to school. During the Depression, my father always had a job at the Kerr Mills, but his hours went down to two days a week.

We were poor, but we didn't know that we were poor because everyone else was poor. However, our bellies were always full. We had good parents. We always had something to eat. We had nothing to give, but we gave what we had. St. Vincent de Paul Society gave us boots and big bags of food. The Society really helped out. They gave to the poor. They are a good organization.

### Food and Meals

My mom cooked lots of fried food. I didn't like fried food. It's too fatty. But, if you didn't like what my mother cooked, you left it there and got nothing else. On Sundays, it was obligatory to go to grandmother's house; no questions asked. If *Vavo* made kale soup, everyone had to show up. It was a command performance.

When Portuguese soup was first made, you put a shoulder in it. Then you watered it down every time you served it. Day-old bread was added to the soup to bulk it up.

Tea and coffee were served in bowls, not cups. The bowls were narrow and deep. A common breakfast in Portuguese homes was milk crackers broken up and softened in milk.

My father got gassed by the Germans in the war [World War I] and had trouble with his stomach. He couldn't eat much. It was mustard gas. It burned his esophagus and stomach. He had to be fussy about what he could eat.

We made wine in the cellar every year in the fall. Moonshine was also made in the cellar. It was made differently from wine, since it was distilled spirits, and had to be set up with a still. They flavored it to make liquor. You can tell if its moonshine if, when lit, it burns with a blue flame. Storage areas were in the basement for wine and canned food.

**School Life**

I went to Espirito Santo School in the Flint, one of the oldest Catholic schools in the country. The nuns at the school spoke English and French. When they didn't want us to know what they were saying, they would speak in French. I would tell them, "This is a Portuguese school. You're not speaking Portuguese." I was feisty for a little kid. However, I got put in my place by the nuns.

**Recreation and Entertainment**

My father raised racing pigeons. He would go up to Gifford Road (Beulah Road) in Westport, release them, and come home to see them return. The pigeons had tags on their legs. When they came home to the coop, they went through a box and it recorded the time of their arrival.

Women were not allowed in social clubs in those days. Sometimes I had to go to St. Michael's Club to get my father and my brother-in-law Joseph Machado, who played professional-level soccer from the club. Fall River had the oldest soccer league in the country. My sister's husband played soccer in Cuba and elsewhere. He played at Bigberry Stadium.

Women had to be ladylike in those days. We were not allowed to play sports. We came to Westport to visit relatives. In the summer, we stayed over. I would bum a ride with the milkman, who was a relative, to the Medeiros farm on Sodom Road in Westport. It is still a functioning farm called High View. We did nothing in the wintertime; Portuguese girls didn't go out.

My husband and I went dancing all the time at Lincoln Park for twenty years. They had good big bands and it had a beautiful floor. We didn't jitterbug but just ballroom dancing. We went there until it closed.

My cousin Lou Martin was a boxer and owned the Martinique Night Club at the Narrows.

**Courtship and Marriage**

I met my husband at Lincoln Park. We took the bus to Lincoln Park from Webster Street for five cents. His family lived on Barrett Street in Fall River, then moved to Old County Road, Westport. We dated for five years; it took a long time for him to propose. We married at Espirito Santo Church, with Fathers John Medeiros and Rev. Manuel Travassos officiating.

There was just family in the church. The reception was at the Fall River Bowling Green Club, where Lepage's Seafood & Grill is today on Route 6. We were married on September 16, 1950. For our two-week honeymoon, we went on a tour by car of the New England states, including stops at the Polar Caves, and sites throughout the White Mountains: Franconia Notch State Park (New Hampshire), Mt. Washington, and the Flume Gorge.

**Work Life**

My husband worked as a machinist and foreman at the Naval Torpedo Station, Newport, Rhode Island (Naval Underwater Weapons Station) for thirty-eight years.

I went to Thibodeau Business College, which was on South Main Street across from Cherry and Webb. From there, in the late 1940s, I was a bookkeeper at MacKenzie and Winslow, Inc., on Rodman Street.

My husband's family were chicken farmers where their house is here. My father-in-law would pick up the eggs, sort them in a sorter weighing machine, put them in crates, and delivered the eggs to Fall River to sell from the back of his car. People at work were his customers. I helped out but didn't like to carry the big crates of eggs in to the customers. So I wore high heels and a skirt to discourage people from asking me to bring in the crates. Wholesalers came to the farm to get most of the eggs.

**Neighborhood Experiences**

The Flint was the only world that we knew. We knew all of the people there. We only bought from people that spoke our language. I didn't know lots of English words when I went to school and didn't learn many words until later. Once, when I wanted to tell the teacher that I had a headache, I said, "I'm crazy in my head."

Raymond and Hilda Martel on their wedding day

On Pitman Street, there was Olivera's Grocery Store. On Alden Street, a Jewish man had a store and he spoke Portuguese very fluently. You couldn't fool him. His store was next to Mary Fonseca's mother's house. We paid a dollar down and a dollar a week. The whole world then relied on a dollar down and a dollar a week.

A fellow from New Bedford had a truck that came to the neighborhood to sell fresh fish. If you wanted fish that day, you went down to get it from the fish man. That was all the fish you got all week; there was no fresh fish in the local stores.

Whole families lived in tenement houses. They depended on one another. The same language drew us together. My mother would mind the husband of a neighbor when the neighbor was out. He had asthma.

The interior stairwells of the tenement houses were all open. We could walk into anyone's house, since we were mostly family. Cooking smells came from every door. You could tell who was cooking what. We would go on our porches to watch parades, talk to neighbors. Sometimes, kids slept out there on hot nights.

**Christmas, Holidays, and Special Occasions**

The biggest event of the year was the Holy Ghost Feast. It was based on the feast of the Epiphany. It has a connection to the queen of Portugal. One view says that the queen came out and gave food to the poor in a time of need. The parade was the big event. It was like a homecoming. If you couldn't make it home for Thanksgiving or Christmas, you came for the feast. It's also where you met the boys.

The Holy Ghost Crown passed from home to home, and people gathered at the home to say the rosary. You submitted your name to be a host.

When you hosted the Holy Ghost Crown, it was a reason to fix up the house and get new clothes, because everyone would be coming to the house. Wine and liqueur were served as well as sweetbread.

When the procession came by, you put your best bedspreads out the window as a sign of respect. My dad would decorate the streets with colored sawdust; in the old country they use flower petals. They also put mint on the ground, so that when you stepped on it, it smelled.

For Christmas, you got the best that you got. We received hand-made gifts made by my mother. On Christmas Eve, relatives would go door to door singing, "Open the door; let me in."

My uncle, John Morris, was a well-known fado singer. He would go from place to place to sing and vary songs for the occasion.

**Health and Illness**

Our family was lucky as far as illness goes. You did anything in your power to stay out of the hospital. We did anything to avoid it.

Hilda (Martin) Martel

If you went into the hospital, you went to die. If you did go into the hospital, everyone had to go visit. You were not only obligated to visit but to stay and sit by the bedside.

Tuberculosis was prevalent.

Portuguese culture requires that a widow dress all in black for at least a year, as a sign of respect, when her husband dies. Most widows wore black the rest of their lives.

When I had a sore throat, my mother would warm up some chicken fat and put it on my throat. The sore throat was gone the next day. Garlic was put in a packet on a string and hung around your neck to ward off colds.

Wine and whiskey were taken for health. My father had a shot of brandy every night.

Santa Claus and unidentified child from
Hilda (Martin) Martel's photo collection

# Roland Masse, Paul Valcourt, Gerard Duquette

―――※―――

*Present at the interview were the following: Roland Masse, Paul Valcourt (born February 6, 1941), and Gerard Duquette (born February 1, 1928; died March 9, 2011).*

**School Life**

All three of us attended Notre Dame School. After fifth grade, there was no mixing of boys and girls. After that we went to Prevost or the Prevost Annex. The nuns weren't called sisters as elsewhere but Mothers. Morning classes were all in French and afternoon classes were in English.

We had an hour and a half for lunch at Notre Dame School, from 11:30 am to 1:00 pm, and everyone went home for a hot lunch. Some of us lived not far from the school, but others had to run as far away as Quarry Street and back. Prevost had only a half-hour for lunch, but they had a cafeteria. On Fridays at Prevost, we ordered out and Coffee Sam's delivered forty-five orders of baked blue fish in their panel truck. That was the favorite and only dish on Fridays.

If we were bad at home, we were threatened with being sent to the orphanage (where Stafford Place is now). The orphanage was run by the Sisters of Charity of Quebec, known as the gray nuns because of their gray habits. They were scary. "My father once drove me to the orphanage when I was misbehaving," said Roland, "and stopped in front and said 'are you going to be bad or good?'"

The gray nuns were also in charge of making the hosts. On the Thursday before the First Friday Devotion, we would go to the rear door and buy small bags of the remainders of the hosts for ten cents a bag. They were pretty insubstantial.

The Jesus Marie nuns would make and sell taffy lollipops; on Valentine Day, they would make the taffy red.

**Recreation and Entertainment**

Recreation after school depended on the season. In winter, we slid down the dead-end streets in the area, including Keeley, Reney, Lafayette, Barnes, and California Streets. We either used our Flyer sleds or steered toboggans with an ice skating shoe. Many an ankle was broken.

We went skating at the small pond between Route 6 and the railroad causeway at the Narrows, which we called the "little pond" or the "Little South Watuppa." Robillard's rented skates there and put lights on the pond and provided an oil tank with a stovepipe as a place to warm up.

In the summer we would play street games. At other times, we would tell our mothers that we were "going to the woods." Street games included: 1, 2, 3, red-light; buck, buck, buck, how many fingers do I have up; may I; hopscotch; hide and seek; 3-cans hit or ball; pink ball; and peggy ball. There would be annual trips to Lincoln Park and to the movie drive-ins.

We biked and skated a lot. Everyone had a bike then. Skates were metal skates that strapped to your shoes and expanded by sliding open to fit your shoe size. The metal wheels made a racket on the sidewalks, much to the annoyance of some neighbors. "When the street lights came on," Roland said, "that was the signal to come home, otherwise there were consequences."

Robillard's sold rods and reels for fishing and also rented boats. We would catch crayfish in the "canal," the interceptor ditch that runs along North Watuppa Pond, and go fishing in the small pond at South Watuppa or, even better, at North Watuppa, but always on the lookout for the Reservation guards.

For fun, we little kids would break open bobbins from the mills to get the three metal rings at the bottom. At variety stores, we would ask for bottle caps that were left in the receptacle below the bottle opener on soda machines and we would compare caps. We then made "roads" on the pavement by lining up the caps and drove our cars and tanks along the roads.

Going to "the woods" then meant going to the end of the street where the woods began. Before Route 24 was constructed, there were continuous woods between where houses ended and North Watuppa Pond. This was way before Diman [Diman Regional Vocational Technical High School] and the Talbot schools were constructed and before new homes were built between Eastern Avenue and North Watuppa. Eastern Avenue ended at Locust Street on the north and McGowan Street on the south, near the Kerr Mills. Martine Street continued from Eastern Avenue to the Narrows.

"In the early 1940s," said Gerard Duquette, "Troupe 15 of the Boy Scouts, based at Notre Dame Church, on Saturdays would take a hike around North Watuppa Pond. Ross Vandal, the city's only motorcycle cop, was our scout leader. We would walk by the Narrows, past the Lamplighter (now White's Restaurant) and Sampson's potato farm and on to Blossom Road. We would take sandwiches and our canteen and stop and run up and down the hills and play cowboys and Indians. The hike would take the whole day."

Kids would go camping on the South Watuppa Pond where the Rod and Gun Club is now. In the early 1940s, Gerard Duquette, while camping on the South Watuppa, where the Rod and Gun Club is now, caught the largest fish in the lake at that time. Said Gerard Duquette, "I was fourteen years old and the large fish had a smaller fish in its mouth to prove to the 'doubting Thomases' how large the fish was. After dressing it, it made an excellent fish chowder."

Paul Valcourt's playground was the field in front of the Kerr Mills. It was only busy when the mill shifts changed. "I admired my uncle Leo, who had a crutch and glasses, and I wanted to be just like him. He also lived on McGowan Street on the corner of Knight Street. So my uncle made me a crutch (I already had glasses). One day, my mom looked out the window and saw me on the sidewalk panhandling with my glasses, a tin cup, and a crutch as the workers from the Kerr Mill were walking by on their way home. She came tearing out of the house and brought me home. I collected quite a bit." At times, he would go along the mill and pick up the unwanted spools of thread that were thrown out the window and bring them home to his mother.

The quarry at the end of Eastern Avenue at Martine Street was inactive when we were kids and was filled in when I-195 was constructed. The water in the quarry hole was green and very deep and contained various debris. Kids would walk along the quarry and smoke. "I would hide my cigarettes in an opening in the quarry wall," Paul remembers.

On Saturdays, we went to the Strand Theatre on Pleasant Street for a matinée movie for twenty-five cents.

For those of us who were altar boys, we received five cents for assisting at the 6:30 am Mass. However, if we didn't attend Vespers on Sunday afternoon, we wouldn't get our twenty-five cents.

Where Cottell Heights is now, on the corner of Pleasant and Raymond Streets, there was a bowling alley where Gerard Duquette set pins at five cents a setup. "This was before the days of automatic pin-setters. You often took your life in your hands when the pins flew. After that work, we would go to Duffy's Pharmacy at the corner of Pleasant and Barlow Streets for an ice cream sundae." Roland's father was a pin boy there also, and even ran the place for a while.

There was also a roller skating rink on Pleasant Street where St. Vincent de Paul's is now. Roland's father was in charge of that also for a while.

Paul said, "Our family would summer in Portsmouth [Rhode Island], and the only time that I had my shoes on the whole summer was to go to church."

Television came into the neighborhood between 1948 and 1951. The early televisions had very small screen, about six inches across. At first, there weren't many programs on the TV. John Cameron Swayze came on every weeknight with fifteen minutes of news. Bishop Sheen was very popular in the neighborhood and "was the law." On weekdays, from noon to 1:00 pm, Brother Bob Emory had his show from Boston for kids. Roland remembers that, on every show, Bob would lead the kids in offering a milk toast and the pledge of allegiance to President Eisenhower's picture on the wall. "If I watched the entire show," Roland said, " I would be late for the afternoon school session. I often was!"

**Work Life**

The Woolworth's and McCrory's on Pleasant Street hired only girls from Jesus-Marie Academy for their part-time jobs.

Roland Masse said, "I worked for the nuns doing landscape work for twenty cents an hour, increasing five cents a year until I reached forty-five cents an hour."

"My first job," said Gerard Duquette, "was at Ross Couture's Paint Shop on County Street. I was designated to sand, by hand, the rusted spots on a car before getting it painted. He didn't pay very much and, needless to say, I left that job within a month."

Roland's father drove the bus and preferred the Bedford-County run that covered the northern end of the Flint. Roland's father came home for lunch but worked through dinnertime. Roland would wait at the corner of County Street with his father's usual supper, a fried egg sandwich made by mom. His father would pick Roland up, drive to the end of the run at the end of Keeley Street, eat his sandwich, and drop off Roland at the corner where he picked him up. "Sometimes, I would go to the wrong route stop and then have to chase him down."

Before he operated the Duke's Tavern, Gerry's father was a boss loom fixer at the Kruger Mills in New Bedford. Paul's mother was a paymaster at the King Philip Mill. Roland's mother was a floor lady at Korber Hats manufacturing, then she became an at-home mom.

Roland's grandfather owned an icehouse that sold ice wholesale. All of the icehouses were dug into the ground; there was more icehouse below ground than above. Straw was layered between the ice blocks. At the end of the summer, the ice had melted away from the walls. His grandfather sold the icehouse about 1925.

**Neighborhood Experiences**

In the 1950s, few families had cars. The garage on Roland's property was originally a horse barn. Residents could be fairly isolated in the Flint because everything that a person needed was available here. Flint residents went downtown to shop for Easter clothes and for Christmas;

otherwise, Pleasant Street had everything that you needed, whether it was grocery stores, drug stores, clothing stores, doctors offices, and a movie theater. We even had our own Woolworth's. Places like McWhirr's in the downtown had specialty things like official Boy Scouts uniforms and equipment. "I got my first knickers and great coat there," said Gerard Duquette. Roland's mother went downtown for her Easter hat.

There were the Vanasse and Poirier bakeries, where housewives brought their bean pots filled with beans prepared at home. The bakers would then bake the beans in the bakery oven and we would pick them up, with brown bread on the side, to bring home for Saturday supper or Sunday breakfast. Barrett Donuts had great donuts, including its unique twister donut.

At the corner of Pleasant and Cash Streets was a Chinese Restaurant on the second floor called Mien Farlow. Roland's father worked there as a bus boy. Bus boys could get one meal and Roland's father asked for pork chops. The owner said, "No, no, chow mein, chow mein!" Roland's father was born in 1903, so this was probably about 1913. The Mark You restaurant and the Grace Wong were also on Pleasant Street, with Mark You still there.

Gerry's father owned Duke's Tavern at 913 County Street (where the O'Gil Restaurant is now; the license for Duke's is still on the restaurant wall). There were only five taverns in Fall River. Women were not allowed in taverns, only in cafés. You could rent rooms in the taverns and have limited food. Taverns would sponsor outings and competitions with other taverns, such as pitch tournaments. The taverns sold bar food like pickled eggs and pickled pigs feet. "I remember cooking dozens of eggs to bring to the tavern on Saturdays."

The Flint north of Pleasant Street was almost all French. Roland could remember only one Portuguese family on Arizona Street and they moved away. Only when he went to Prevost high school, did he meet another Portuguese student.

The French were not happy when the statue of Prince Henry the Navigator was erected at the corner of Pleasant Street and Eastern Avenue, and the statue endured its share of graffiti. Roland gave his father a statue of Prince Henry one year, "and he almost died."

"In May, the Commonwealth of Massachusetts celebrates Lafayette Day," said Roland. "Often the present Baron of Lafayette is an honored guest. He was often invited to come to Fall River by local French groups such as the Franco-American Civic League, the Association-Canado-Américaine, the Francophone Club, or the Richelieu Club. Part of his visit would include a wreath laying ceremony at the Lafayette statue on Eastern Avenue.

**Food and Meals**

French households cooked lots of pork. One favorite was ground fresh pork called gorton [French-Canadian pork spread]. Paul's wife still makes it for him for breakfast. She is Portuguese but learned how to make it from Paul's mother. "When my wife makes gorton for breakfast, I'm in heaven."

Paul's father had a store on Brightman Street and his mother made gorton for sale there. She would sell the gorton in porcelain bowls and the bowls would be returned to the store.

Breakfast usually included eggs. Gerry's family raised chickens on their lot, like many families in the Flint. There was also a ragout of pig's hocks and pork meatballs that required the browning of flour to make a gravy. It was a specialty on New Year's Day.

French style blood pudding, called boudin, is smoother than the Portuguese blood pudding and gray in color due to the natural casings.

When Roland's mom cooked pork chops, Roland's father insisted on having sausage and blood pudding with it.

Roland remembers whole fully-cooked chickens in a can. When people visited, Mom would take out the canned chicken and make a dish. She would make a white sauce and potatoes with it.

Says Roland, "On Saturday nights, my mother would make a big platter of french fries and we would eat them in front of the TV. That was it; just french fries and ketchup."

Smoked and fresh shoulders were also popular. French homes cooked only French food.

Paul said that he ate at the home of his Portuguese friends whenever he had the chance.

The first soft ice cream introduced in the Flint in the 1950s was a sensation. The shop was on Eastern Avenue where the real estate office is now.

**Religious Life**

Weddings were held in Notre Dame Church during the regular early morning masses at 6:30 or 7:00 am. There was no best man or maid of honor; instead the fathers of the bride and groom were the witnesses, or brothers if the fathers were deceased. For baptisms, mothers stayed at home; only fathers attended baptisms.

Funerals at Notre Dame were first, second, and third class. First class funerals had a high Mass with three priests and all of the lights lit. Second class funerals had one priest and the lights lit. Third class funerals had a priest and a Mass.

For the really first class funerals, a "catafalque" was erected. The catafalque was a three-tiered structure that had a hollow casket on the second and third tiers and the real casket on the first tier. It was black with gold highlights. It took two or three men all day to assemble it. Its use was discontinued in the 1950s. In addition to the catafalque, purple banners were put up around all of the statues.

There were lots of funerals then, about nine or ten a week at Notre Dame.

# Frederick B. McDonald

*Born in 1931*

**Family Background**

I was born at Union Hospital.

My parents were Thomas J. and Charlotte E. (Barker) McDonald. My father died in 1941, when I was in the seventh grade. There were three of us in elementary and high school when my father died. My mother had to go to work.

I am the youngest of five children, named: Thomas J., Vincent P., Joseph W., and Charlotte G.

We lived at two addresses in Fall River: 582 Walnut Street (corner of Grove) for seventeen years, and 162 Hanover Street.

My mother's father was Joseph Baker and his wife's maiden name was Ward.

**Family Life**

On Sundays, we would take the bus to Tiverton [Rhode Island] to see my grandmother, my mother's mother. We took the Eastern Mass Street Railway bus to the Fall River line, then took a Massey's Bus from there into Tiverton. My grandmother was blind and spent many years in bed, cared for by her daughters. Later, we rode in my aunt's car. My oldest brother drove it. It was a '37 Chevy, which cost eight hundred dollars new. We would pack lunches and also go to Benson's Wild Animal Farm in New Hampshire. On Sundays, gasoline was on special: seven gallons for one dollar.

My father was a salesman for a few companies in the Midwest who manufactured order forms for companies. He had his regular customers.

**School Life**

Our parish was Sacred Heart Church and I went to Sacred Heart School. Each grade had two classes. There were forty-two kids in a class. There was a half-day for kindergarten. All the classes were taught by nuns; the only lay people there were the custodians. The whole family, all of my brothers and my sister, went to Sacred Heart School. Everyone came home for lunch. Grades K through six came home for lunch at 11:30 am, went back to school at 1:30 pm and were released at 3:30 pm. The seventh and eighth grades came back at 1:00 pm and got out at 3:00 pm. There was no fooling around: you towed the mark or you got a ruler across the hand.

I went to [Bishop] Coyle in Taunton for high school. Four buses went from Fall River to Coyle. If I missed the bus, I had to take the 8:00 am bus to Taunton. Coyle had more students from Fall River than from Taunton. All four of my brothers also went to Coyle.

I worked for a few years between high school and college. After Coyle, I went to Bradford Durfee Tech in textile engineering and graduated in 1955. Tuition was a hundred dollars a year. Then, it went to one-hundred-and-fifty dollars. I got a few scholarships. It was an excellent education.

**Recreation and Entertainment**

In the winter, we ice skated at Ruggles Park. We also sledded on the walks in the park, starting at the corner near Robeson and Locust Streets and ending at the corner of Pine and Seabury Streets. We were careful of pedestrians. There was a little changing station across Pine Street.

We would make our own cars out of wooden crates we got from Peloquin's Market. We would attach roller skates to them and push them with one foot. Fireworks were legal and were five cents a package. Kids used sparklers.

We would go dancing at Lincoln Park [North Dartmouth, Massachusetts] and the Fall River Casino. The Casino also had boxing on Thursday nights. Some world champs and big names fought there.

Buses were five cents and ten cents. Bus passes were one dollar a week. My father used the bus to visit clients, and I got his pass on Saturday. We would ride the bus on Sundays and see all parts of the city. At rush hour at 5:00 or 5:30 pm there was standing room only.

The CYO [Catholic Youth Organization] playoff games were played at Ruggles Park at the end of the season. The teams from Fall River would play the teams from New Bedford and Taunton. There would be five thousand people there. From 1945 to 1947, I did the collections there to support the teams. The Fall River Indians played at the Bigberry Stadium.

**Work Life**

My first job was a paper route for the *Fall River Herald News*. My brother had it before me, but I took it over when he finished high school. I had 105 papers to distribute every day. Everyone got a paper in those days; there were many third floor stairs to climb. On Thursdays there were inserts in the paper and I had to have two bags, one on each shoulder, to carry them. Sometimes, I got another kid to help me. The charge for the paper was twenty cents a week for six days. When customers gave you a quarter and said, "Keep the change," you thought you were in heaven. Only one customer gave me that extra five cents. At Christmastime, I did well with tips. I thought I died and went to heaven when I got those Christmas tips.

From 1947 to 1948, I worked at Fitzgerald's Drug Store, which was located at the corner of Locust and Linden Streets. Fitzgerald's Drug Store opened around 7:00 or 8:00 am and closed at 10:00 pm. On Saturdays, it stayed open until 10:30 pm because the nearby Eagle's Hall had dancing on Saturday nights and, at intermission, people at the dance came down to have frappes and other fountain drinks. We got sixty cents an hour at the drug store, which was good pay then. They took out Social Security.

We made the best frappes. Ice cream cones were five cents. "Cabinets" were twenty cents. The best-selling item at the fountain was hot coffee. We also sold coffee milk. Milk came to the store in half-pint containers. We sold Speedwell Farms Ice Cream, made in the south end of the city. Wilson's Variety Store sold Hood and Sons Ice Cream. Fitzgerald's had two little tables to sit down at. The tops were see-through glass where cosmetics and other things like that were displayed. They were display and sales tables. There were no stools at the counter, standing only. Men mostly stood at the counter.

From 1948 to 1951, after I left high school and before I entered college, I worked at Small Brothers Manufacturing, who were rope manufacturers. It was a long building that faced on Hillside Street. Hoffman Lion Mill was in the same building. My mother worked there in the printing shop. They made the twine for venetian blinds, shoe laces, and jump ropes, among other things. At Small Brothers, I delivered yarn to the departments on spools to the grading areas.

I worked at the Sagamore Mills for a while, working through each department. But I saw the handwriting on the wall. Sagamore worked in cotton and Pepperell worked in synthetics. After that, I worked for Duro Finishing.

After the service, I worked at Pepperell Manufacturing for a year. My brother worked there but got transferred to New York. Someone said to me, "The city has a shortage of teachers; you should look into it." I had no training in teaching, so I went to Bridgewater [now Bridgewater State University] to get my certification and masters degree.

I started in the Fall River School Department in 1959 and began teaching sixth grade for six to seven years at the John Doran School. My first principal position was at the Harriet Healy School on Hicks Street for five years. Then, I went to the Ralph M. Small School and was principal there for twenty-two years. There were 360 kids in the Small School. It was bi-lingual and a site for handicapped kids, since the school was all on one floor. The service area of the school included Hillside Manor public housing development. Even so, I can count on one hand the kids who got into any serious trouble.

**Neighborhood Experiences**

Every Saturday, we went to Hudner's Market downtown for fresh vegetables. While we were there, I would watch as they were corning the beef in the back. The beef was floating in brine. The downtown A&P was where Smith's Office Supplies was located.

Sacred Heart Church

Connors and Peloquin's Markets were the larger and more expensive stores in our neighborhood. Hudner's Market on New Boston Road was also. Connors was more higher-end than all of them. Connors Market was located at the corner of Walnut and Linden Streets. Chauffeurs would park their cars in front of Connors Market. I was fascinated by them and would go up to see them.

At the northwest corner of Locust and Linden Streets, where Knight's Service Station is now, was a vacant lot where the Victory Gardens were located during World War II. After the war, we kids would go there to play ball after school.

There were trolley tracks that came up from Bank Street to Linden and onto Prospect Street to Union Hospital. They took a right onto Winter Street and onto Hanover Street, and east on Stanley Street to the General Hospital. The tracks remained in these streets for quite a while.

## Downtown

My aunt worked in Woolworth's in the office for a number of years. My mother made Easter baskets for Woolworth's for years and years when she worked there. I'm sure that Woolworth's was the first store in Fall River that had an escalator.

The Nite Owl Diner was downtown, between City Hall and the bank. The truck was connected to a cab that drove it there and then disconnected at night. The cab came back to take the diner away during the day.

## World War II and Service Life

We kids sold the special editions of the *Fall River Herald News* downtown. I remember being downtown selling the special edition of the Pearl Harbor attack and VJ Day.

Rationing was by rationing stubs. The blue stubs were for canned goods (I guess to ration the metal in the cans) and the red stubs were for meat. Our names were on the front of the ration book. The stubs had to last.

I registered for the draft before going into college, but I never got a call to go in. In the fall of 1955, however, I was notified by the Draft Board that I had to serve Uncle Sam for two years. The Navy needed 10,000 men a month. I wanted the Navy and got it in September of 1955.

On December 8th, I went in and was sent to boot camp in Bambridge, Maryland, for nine weeks. When I finished boot camp, I got orders to go to the Naval Air Station in Pensacola, Florida, as a special services officer. The special services unit organized all of the entertainment and events on the base. It was a big base. Any officer that wanted to be a pilot went to Pensacola. We would get big bands to play there; there were three movie theatres on the base.

If you did one year of base duty, you had to do one year of sea duty. Our duty was on the *USS Tarawa*. However, it was in dry dock in Boston getting a complete overhaul. My Fall River friend had a car, and we would leave the city at 4:30 or 5:00 am to be aboard the ship at 7:00 am two or three times a week for five or six months. Route 24 was only partially finished then. We had a shakedown cruise in the waters off of Cuba; however, I got out [of the Navy] before our ship left for the Mediterranean. I was an education officer aboard the ship.

# Gilbert Viera "Duke" Medeiros

*Born on November 6, 1925*
*Died on November 2, 2010*

**Family Background**

I was born in Fall River when we lived on the first floor of 103 Division Street, one house above Bay Street. I was delivered there by a midwife.

My father was Manuel Medeiros. He was born in Fenais Da Luz, São Miguel Island, Azores. My mother was Maria (Viera) Medeiros. She was born in Relva, São Miguel Island, Azores.

My father's parents were Julio Vieira Medeiros and Margarida (DeJesus) Rego. My mother's parents were John and Maria (doCarmo) Oliveira.

I am the youngest of six children. Their names are Mary, Sarah, Laura, Emily, Ruth (Ruthie), and Edward (Eddy).

I was married twice. My children's names are Wayne, Dana, Gregory, Kevin, Marc, and Stephanie.

**Family Life**

My father owned a poolroom with four tables, located in the basement of the house. It cost five cents to play pool. Ex-cops came there, mostly. Everything was put on the book. There was no cash. The poolroom took the whole cellar.

A boy's mother died and my mother took him in. He was Freddy Furtado. He slept with me and my brother in our bed. I was in the middle. Fred was a peach of a guy, a nice guy.

My father raised racing pigeons in the back yard. My father had three pigeon coops for racing. Lots of Portuguese people raised and raced pigeons. It was a big thing for the men years ago. There were all kinds of pigeon clubs in the city.

My father married five daughters but never went to one wedding, even though the wedding receptions were in the house. My mom never got mad. The pigeons were his whole world. He would be in back tending to them with his overalls with holes in them.

My father made moonshine and his own beer too. As soon as you opened the basement door, you could smell the beer.

The only room that had heat in our house was the kitchen; there was no heat in the rest of the house.

I once went out with a Polish girl from Hall Street. My parents didn't like it. My mother thought that she had put a spell on me, since I didn't want to leave the girl. My mother though that her family had given me a potion to drink that affected me. My mother went to see a "fietsada," or witch, to see what to do. So, she went to the house of the girl and spread salt and herbs on the hall stairs of their house to make the spell go away and remove the curse. I was embarrassed.

I remember walking through the park to the houses of family and friends to let them know every time one of my older married sisters had a baby, even in the wintertime. I was the messenger boy, because we had no phone.

My father was called Old Man July. He was always serious and very quiet. My father never got paid all that was owed him; he would say, "They'll pay when they have it."

My mother was a very loving and caring person; she was always feeding the neighbors because we had a little more than they had. If you were bad, our parents would say that the rag man was going to take you or you were going to St. Vincent's Home. When the street lights came on, you had to come in, otherwise you got whacked.

When I came home from school, all my shoes and clothes came off. We had school clothes, play clothes, and church clothes.

The iceman came with his horse and wagon. We kids would take ice from the ice wagon, until he caught us at it. It was a big treat for us.

I got the name of "Duke" because I wouldn't wear bib overalls or knickers. I hated knickers. I got lickings for it. I had five sisters and one brother, and I was the youngest and spoiled, so I got away with wearing slacks. My friends would say, "Who do you think you are, a duke?" and the name stuck. I wore a zoot suit with big long chains down to my knee caps. I was a slick dresser.

"Duke" Medeiros and parents

I had a cranberry convertible. Once, my friend and I wanted to pick up a few girls and wanted the car to look shiny. So, we polished it with oil. We drove to Newport and, by the time we got there, the dust from the road had stuck to the car. It looked terrible. It was a '36 Ford and I was seventeen or so. This was in 1942 or 1943. My first car didn't have a floor. You could see to the ground. It was a junk. I would drive around Bay Street when the cops weren't around.

Wakes were held in the parlor. My father, mother, and one sister were waked in the house. The wakes were three days and held around the clock. Friends and family would bring food and offer it up for the person's soul.

**Food and Meals**

My family made chourico and blood pudding. We ate a lot of Portuguese soup (called soupish), bananas, beans, bread with lard and sugar on it.

**Recreation and Entertainment**

I played a lot of baseball, soccer, horseshoes, flew kites, and climbed trees. I loved to watch the Fall River Line ships come in and out of city. Also, I went to hear the bands when they played at South Park [now Kennedy Park].

I was always in the park, up in the trees. Once, I broke my arm when I fell from the tree and a local lady, Tia Cuta (Aunt Cuta) took care of it. She broke eggs and mixed them with flour, then put it on my arm and wrapped rags around it to form a cast. It worked. She was noted for that. People came from all over to have her take care of them.

My brother has only one eye from playing jackknife. To play the game, you formed a circle. Each person threw the knife up and did tricks so the knife stuck in the ground. My brother threw the knife and looked up and the knife came into his eye. Even with one eye, my brother got drafted. He was stationed at Atlantic City to protect against the Japanese from coming into the States.

I was really spoiled. I got a like-new 1935 Ford with a rumble seat. I would go to Lincoln Park to dance and take a few girls from the neighborhood with me. I told them, "I'll take you, but if I get a date there, you're on your own getting back." If I got a date, they took the trolley back.

Every Friday night, we would wait at the trolley car terminal at about 4 or 5 o'clock. People would give away their weekly passes. We would then ride the trolleys all over the city on Saturday on our free passes.

**Work Life**

I had a shoe shine box that I made myself. I would go to Schneierson's and shine the shoes of people who came out. I sold ice cream, too, like Fudgsicles and Popsicles. I kept the ice cream in a little box that I kept next to me. I would make between a dollar-and-a-half and two dollars; I was a rich man. Schneierson's was at the bottom of Griffin and Globe Streets. My sister and other relatives worked there.

My first job was at US Luggage, located at Globe Corners. Then I became a cutter in the sweat shops. I started as a floor boy and learned how to cut dresses. I did piece work at Har-Lee and other places. When I learned how to cut, I started on dresses. Then I progressed to plaid work, which is tough because you have to match the pattern. I got New York pay because we did work for New York, which was unionized. I worked at Kay Windsor, then went to Boston to work part-time, then full-time. I liked the work; it was good money at the time.

**Neighborhood Experiences**

Old Man Ferry would come by with his horse and wagon and shovel in coal into the basement. He later came with a '31 Ford. My mother would come out and give him a glass of beer. We would pick up coal on the railroad tracks. The sheriff walked the tracks so you had to be careful. We would go on the coal trains and pick coal from them. Someone would yell out, "The sheriff is coming; get out of here," and we would pick up our bags of coal and run for it.

August 14, 1939, building house on Powell Street

The train turntable was at the bottom of Division Street below Bay Street. We would go and watch the trains being turned around.

Places in the neighborhood were Nobrega's, on Columbia Street, Hope Bakery, on Hope Street, Talbot's Drug Store, on Columbia Street, and Campos Market, at the bottom of Division Street at Howard Street. There was a barbershop and a store next to one another. The barber was so short that he had to stand on a box to cut hair. Markey's Market was a variety store. Tony's Spa on Almond Street was one of four stores on that corner; the others were Mello's, Jimmy Morris,' and a cleaners. Duke's Variety was on Columbia Street near Santo Christo Church. Ritchie the Barber was at the corner of Division and Bay Streets, next to my father's pool hall.

**Religious Life**

We had Domingas in our house, which is the hosting of the Holy Ghost. The crown was brought home and an open house was held for three weeks. My mom made sure that she got the last pick, so she could keep the crown the longest. Food was put out and rosaries would be said. People would come from New Bedford to the Domingas. That's how boys and girls met. It was expensive, but all my sisters handed in their pays to support the family.

**The Depression**

My family was on welfare for a while during the Depression. My brother Eddy would walk from Division Street to downtown to get food or rations from welfare and pull the team home. We got no meat but other stuff. We ate lots of bananas that year.

My mother would feel sorry for those who had less than us and go leave milk or bread for those who couldn't afford it. My five sisters provided us with a good income. My father would share his garden produce with people; I would deliver it.

L to R: "Boots," "Duke," Ted, and Bill (last names not indicated)

# James McIntyre

*Born in 1930*

**Family Background**

My parents were John and Mary (Reardon) McIntyre. My father died in 1945, when I was fifteen years old.

I was the youngest of seven children in the household, whose names are Timmy, James McIntyre (my father's brother's son, adopted upon the death of his father), Mary, John, Joseph, and Thomas.

Our family residence was a cottage at 30 Division Street, Fall River, and I lived there from birth to when I left for the service at the age of twenty.

All five of my brothers were in World War II, and all are now deceased. One brother was in the Army; the others were in the Navy. Two of my brothers served on the same ship, the *USS Newman K. Perry*.

I have been married twice; both wives are deceased. I was married to Elizabeth Nolan for twenty-three years and Joan (Harper) Rego for nineteen years. Harper is her name from her first marriage. Rego was her maiden name. I have an adopted daughter from my first marriage and two step-sons from my second to Joan.

**Family Life**

My father was a stone mason. He worked for Beattie and Cornell [granite quarry]. Many sidewalks in the city have the brass plates that identify Beattie and Cornell as the builders of the sidewalks. My father would tell me of the times when someone wanted granite, he would go to the Beattie quarry with his horse and team and brothers, who were all stone masons, and move a big piece of granite.

My father worked in building the Mt. Hope Bridge. He said that one man is still encased in the bridge. When they were pouring the cement for the supports, an individual fell in and he is still there as far as we know.

When the building trades slowed down in the Depression, my father went to work for American Thread Company at the Kerr Mill.

My father came indirectly from Ireland. My brother was twelve years older than I was. When my father first came to the city, he lived up on Eastern Avenue, near Notre Dame Church. When he married my mother, they moved to 30 Division Street.

My father did all the grocery shopping. My mother never went downtown. My mother was always doing something, from the moment she got up to the moment she went to bed. My father rode the bus up Columbia Street and told me that he was taking the 2:00 pm bus back home. I would be waiting at the corner for him with my team. He would unload the groceries from the bus and we would bring them home. We had a working horse when we lived on Division Street.

Our property had a barn on it, and it was my job to clean out the barn. I also cleaned the barn at Gage Hill Stables in the North End of Fall River.

Sis always slept downstairs on the couch. My parents and the six males slept upstairs. The brothers slept on single beds. There was only one bathroom downstairs and we had a bed-pot upstairs. When my brothers got older and started drinking, the pot had to be emptied out often. Now you know where the phrase "not a pot to piss in" comes from.

There were many laundries all over Fall River. Like many other families, all our clothing went to a laundry to be washed. It was called a wet wash, and it came back wet. It cost more to dry. When the wash came in, my mother would hang it out to dry. There was a Chinese laundry on Columbia Street that did shirts. No one did their own laundry.

Everybody used the bus. Few people had cars. The buses would go to the Tiverton line and back. If you had the money, you took the bus; otherwise, you walked.

When coal was delivered to the house, my father had the coal company dump the coal in front of the house. We kids would bring the coal along the narrow walkway on the side of the house to a chute in the back of the house. Two of my brothers would tip the team and the coal would go down the chute. It cost nine dollars for a ton of coal and fifty cents to put it down the chute. I moved my share of coal! Every house in Fall River had a coal bin.

My father got truckloads of bobbins delivered to our house to use for kindling. The mills had to get rid of them. But the mills were a haven for cockroaches, so my father kept the bobbins outside, and I brought them in when they were going to be put right into the fire.

We had big crocks downstairs that were full of corned beef preserved in brine. In the wintertime, the brine would freeze, since we didn't have heat downstairs. We had two coal-fired stoves in the house, but no furnace. One stove was in the kitchen and the other was in the parlor.

My mother was always cooking; she was the best cook I know. My mother would make five meat pies at a time. I never, ever, remember going hungry. She was up already when I got up. I went to bed from 8:00 to 9:00 pm and she was still cooking.

The system in those days was to give all of your pay to your parents. It was automatic. Parents would give you back an allowance for the week.

I went to St. Louis School, on Division Street, and Coyle High School, in Taunton. There were about 125 in my graduating class. I wanted to go to B.M.C. Durfee High School, but my mother's brother convinced my mother I should go to Coyle. He had a big influence on her when my father died as she was the youngest in her family.

**Recreation and Entertainment**

The biggest thing for us was the waterfront. We swam in the Taunton River. In those days, there was no combined storm water and sewage. The whole river was a cesspool. We would throw rocks at the turds in the river. The river was the receptacle of all of the waste in Fall River.

The New York boats were still running when I was a kid. We would go down to the King Philip Yacht Club and swim out; everybody on the ship would wave at us.

I remember walking out to the lighthouse when the river was frozen over. The paper did a story on it and, when my father read it, I wasn't able to sit down for a month.

Where the Heritage State Park is now were all coal yards: Staples, Bowen. A group of men kept their boats at wharfs were Point Gloria is now.

As a kid, I was active in the Sea Scouts, now known as the Sea Cadets. The Sea Cadets are now at Battleship Cove. It is now part of the Boy Scouts system. The Sea Scouts had a twenty-six foot sailboat at the King Philip Yacht Club, located just north of South Park [now Kennedy Park] on Mount Hope Bay. When we went there, the yacht club was perched over the water and got flooded at high tide. Later, after the 1954 hurricane washed it away again, it was relocated up the shore further.

The Sea Scouts would go sailing in their boat down to the islands. Once, we lost wind and had to row back from Prudence Island. It was a lot of rowing to get back to the yacht club. After World War II, we got a power boat. I was still active in the Sea Scouts when I went into the service.

The King Philip Yacht Club was our sponsor. We hung around the club. I lived a short distance away. Railroad cars were parked in the rail yard just above the club. The yacht club was responsible for keeping a lot of kids out of trouble, including me.

Eighty percent of my friends were from the Sea Scouts. The other twenty percent were from St. Louis or from Coyle High School. I played football at Coyle. By the time I got home, it was late. At Coyle, we had maybe two hundred people in the stands; at Durfee, during the Thanksgiving Day game, there would be ten thousand people at Alumni Field.

When I was seventeen years old, I got chosen to represent the Northeast Region of the Sea Scouts at a Report to the Nation ceremony in Washington DC. It was 1947 and I got to meet Harry S. Truman, the President of the United States.

In the winter, we would go to South Park and fly a kite. The park was ideal for flying kites because of the hills. It was ideal going skating in the park. Public facilities got a lot of good use. When I was a kid, there was a bandstand within sight of the pavilion. The city had some kind of music on the bandstand every night.

The CYO [Catholic Youth Organization] had a tremendous organization and had its own leagues. Every church had its own team and competed. The CYO league hall was on Anawan Street. The Boys Club had two buildings: one on Pocasset Street for the adult division and one on Anawan Street for the junior division. The Boys Club was the only place to go for recreation. There were no health clubs back then.

I belonged to the junior division of the Boys Club and then, later, went to the young men's division. Durfee High basketball games were played at the Boys Club, because the school didn't have a court. The old Boys Club was all one open space.

**Neighborhood Experiences**

Division Street was ethnically mixed. Portuguese people were principally around us. French were on Bradford Avenue. Polish people were higher up on Division Street.

The Portuguese went to the Santo Christo Church. The Irish went to St. Louis Church. The French went to St. Anne's Church. The Poles went to St. Stanislaus Church.

**Work Life**

When I was in St. Louis School, I would carry lunches to the Firestone workers. Because I owned a bike, I could take eight to ten lunches at a time. I made five cents, which was a lot of money back then.

People would go to a place below where Jerry Remey's is now to get food. My mom would encourage me to do it. Two or three people would want me to walk down there with them to get whatever public assistance food was being given out. They gave me five cents for the use of my team from Division Street. Then they gave me a big block of cheese to bring home. They would give some portion of the food that they got from the place and I would give it to my mom. They got food on a weekly basis.

I delivered papers five days a week and on Saturday. The papers were fourteen cents, and people still held their hand out to get that penny back. I delivered the *Fall River Herald News* from the bottom of Division Street to the top of Division Street, at Bradford Avenue. I would deliver the paper to the third floor. I would ask people on the other floors who weren't getting the papers, "Want the paper?" They would say, "No, I get it when they are done with it." It was passed down the stairs from the third floor to the second to the first. I wished that the person on the first floor got the paper so I wouldn't have to go up the stairs and be able to deliver more papers.

My first adult job was at Bessie Russell's men's store, located next to where the Portuguese Cultural Center is now. I was a stock boy and I was sixteen (you couldn't work before then) and a sophomore in high school. During school, I worked on Friday nights and on Saturday. If school was out, I was allowed to work all day. During Christmas and during other holidays I worked more hours. I boxed clothing, shirts, and such and got ten to fifteen cents an hour.

I next worked for W.T. Manning auto parts distributor on Pocasset Street, where the *Fall River Herald News* parking lot is now. It was the biggest auto parts supply store in the City of Fall River and supplied the other stores. The stock came in by the railroad at the central wharf.

When I got out of the service, I went to work for Stone and Webster at the Montaup Power Plant, making seventy-six dollars a month. I thought I was a millionaire. Then I went to work at the Somerset Police Department for fifty-four dollars a week, six days a week. Even though the pay was lower, it was more secure work and had a better pension plan. I retired from that job as a Captain.

**Military Service**

I was in the Naval Reserve and then went into active service in the Navy.

After Boot Camp, I was assigned to the *USS Hobson*, DMS 26 (Destroyer Mine Sweeper), based at Charleston, South Carolina. Five months later, the *Hobson* sank. DMS vessels would accompany aircraft carriers and pick up any personnel from aircraft that hit the water on taking off or landing.

I was a radio man striker, learning Morse code training in school. A striker is someone who is in training.

When I was a radio man, we were coming back from Guantanamo, Cuba, during a high-speed run. Water was rushing over the bow and came into the radio shack. I had to swab the deck in the shack, which was a small space, not much bigger that a closet. I got hit with 440 volts of DC electricity. If it was AC, I would have been dead, but ships have DC power. I got paralyzed for about seven days and was confined to my bunk when the ship was in Charleston. I wasn't sent to the hospital on land but was kept on my bunk. The ship was tied to a mooring in the harbor. A Corpsman was treating me. I recovered from the paralysis and was put on light duty.

On the night of April 25, 1952, at 10:26 pm, the *Hobson* got hit amidships and the ship broke in two and sank within four minutes. A total of 176 men were lost; 61 survived. Only 9 of those 61 are alive today.

I was asleep in my bunk, called a "fart sack" because the sailors on the four-deck bunks are so close together. When we were hit, I woke up and climbed up a ladder to an available hatch and

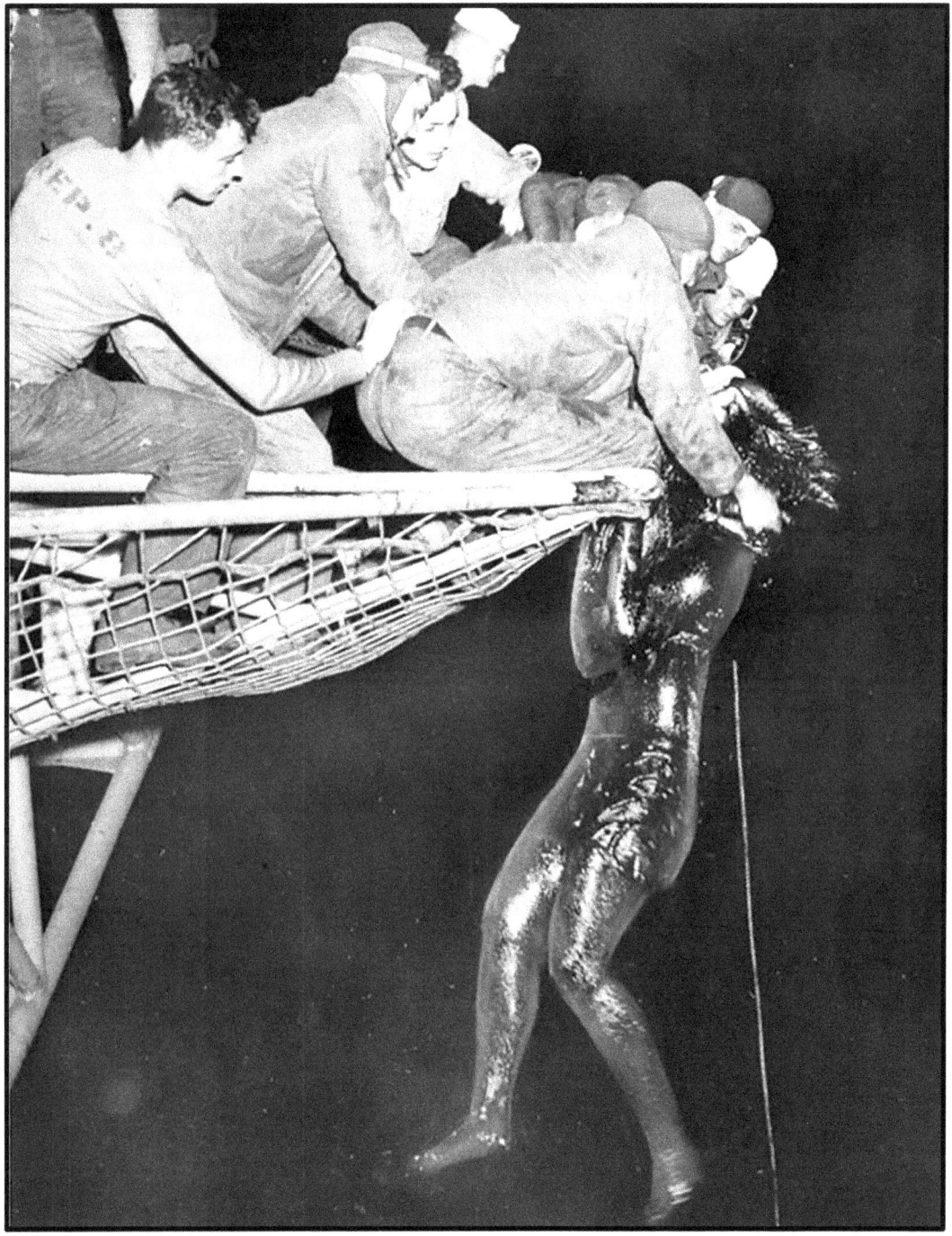

Jim McIntyre, the oil-covered seaman, was plucked from the mid-Atlantic after the collision,
26 April 1952, between the aircraft carrier *USS Wasp*
and the minesweeper *USS Hobson*, and hauled aboard the *Wasp*. 176 lives were lost.
The Granger Collection, New York

went through it to the upper deck. I made it to the stern of the *Hobson* in a dazed condition. I didn't know what was happening. I was on the stern for five to seven minutes before the ship sank. I got to a life raft and was hauled aboard the *USS Wasp*.

The fuel tanks aboard the *Hobson* were refueled with heavy oil that day and were ninety-nine percent full of fuel. The tanks were ruptured by the hit. I was covered in heavy oil; even my own mother wouldn't have recognized me.

Oil kept coming out of my pores for months after that for at least six months. No matter how much you showered or washed in a tub, it just kept coming out. You didn't see it until you put on a clean, white t-shirt and you would have to throw it away. It would be soaked in oil.

For sixty years, I have been going to the Veteran's Administration, first at the Hope Street site in Providence for a year, then to the new building on Chalkstone Boulevard. Every time I would go in for a new rating, I had to prove it was service-connected. They constantly asked for documentation of what happened. I kept saying that the people who know about my accident are among the 176 men at the bottom of the ocean. The Corpsman who treated me went down with the ship. The other people who treated me went down with the ship. I am now ninety percent permanently disabled and compensated at ten percent. It took me sixty years to get to this level of compensation.

Boys Club, 157 Pocasset Street

# Mary Margaret (O'Neill) Melker

*Born in 1928*
*Died on December 12, 2013*

**Family Background**

My parents were Patrick and Sarah (Coogan) O'Neill.

I had two brothers, Cornelius ("Neil" or "Corney" or "Con") and Patrick.

Our family residences were 41 Warburton Street (until the death of my mother) and 156 Linden Street (with aunt and Uncle O'Neill).

My father's siblings were John, Mary (died of tuberculosis), Connie, Maggie, Nora, and Tim. My mother had one brother, Owen Coogan.

My father came from County Cork in Ireland; there are a lot of Irish who came to Fall River from County Cork. When someone came here from Cork, there was usually someone here from their family when they came. I have no idea why O'Neill is spelled with two l's and not one. My mother came from County Monaghan, Castleblayney, just below the border with Northern Ireland. There weren't many people here from County Monaghan.

My husband's grandparents came from the next village over from my family's. His family knew my family. Yet, he had a German name.

My husband's name was Howard Melker and he was seven-eighths Irish.

**Family Life**

When my mother first arrived in this country, her first job was at Danvers State Hospital. When she started working at the Fitchburg parish, the staff gave her a list of groceries to order from the market. She had never encountered a telephone before and when she picked it up she started ordering the various items on the list. She thought that the phone line led to the grocery store. They never got the groceries.

My mother went to a parish in Fitchburg where her uncle was the sexton. Father Feehan was the pastor. When Father Feehan was made the Bishop of the Diocese of Fall River, my mother came to Fall River with him. Bishop Feehan was only the second bishop of the diocese, after Bishop Stang.

In those days, when a wealthy household sold their house and moved, the household staff moved with them. The staff wouldn't have a job otherwise. That was also true of priests when they moved. Bishop Feehan and his staff all moved into the brick house of the bishop's residence on Highland Avenue.

My mother's brother, Owen, had an arranged marriage with the ward of a friend of Bishop Feehan. Her father was a best friend of the bishop. The woman had a Doctorate in Biology from Trinity College. The Irish relatives said that she was the "Doctor of Bugs." In those days, friends of the parents of orphaned children would take in the children as wards.

My father's sister Connie went to Boston because she found Fall River too small and stifling. She went to Boston and married a gentleman's gentleman. My relatives asked what that meant, and they said it was a fancy name for a butler. One of her sisters went to visit her and found that she was a "first class launderette" working for two dollars a week. Once, she sent a relative a wedding present of two dollars, and the relatives were scandalized. "Only two dollars?" But, others pointed out that this represented one week's wages for her.

My mother's position at the Bishop's house was one of the housekeepers. She had lifelong friends from the Bishop's house. The cook there was chief of operations.

I was born here in Fall River at home. Irish girls usually had their first baby in a hospital. My mother's first baby died. She wanted to go back to work, but my dad didn't want her to go back.

Both of my brothers were priests. One brother was named Cornelius. We called him "Neil," later "Con." Others called him "Corney." The other brother was Patrick, who became a monsignor here. There has been a Patrick in every generation in our family since before 1800. My son named his son Alexander and broke the tradition.

I have a small trunk with a high, rounded top that says, "20 Park Street, Fall River, MA," on it. It was the location of Mrs. Dube's rooming house. The Irish went there to live with her. She was an awful cook. The current location of the Belmont Club was once Mrs. Cusick's rooming house. Mrs. Cusick was a wonderful cook. My father's brother Timothy O'Neill was a blacksmith. He stayed at Mrs. Dube's rooming house but went to Mrs. Cusick's for breakfast and dinner. Then he would leave his lunch pail to be filled for the next day and walk back to Mrs. Dube's to room. Later, Tim lived at 156 Linden Street with his sisters Maggie and Nora.

Tim was a blacksmith at the Staples Coal Company, where the Regatta Restaurant was

Bishop Feehan residence, corner of Highland Avenue and New Boston Road

located. Staples Coal Company was managed by Charles Burt, Mrs. Burt's husband. At that time, if something broke on a truck, there were no parts stores. Uncle Tim would replicate the part. Tim had no trouble finding work.

Tim was 6 feet, 4 inches tall and didn't have much to say. He would go to the library to read the Irish papers and, if he saw something interesting, he would cut it out with his pocket knife. My father said, "Tim was apprenticed to the devil."

Tim quit Staples because of a pay slight and because he had cruel supervisors. They got my father to try to have him come back, but Tim retired. He had saved his money. He had let my father invest for him, and he had benefited from it. There was no Social Security then.

Maggie and Nora, my father's sisters, never married and both worked for Mrs. Burt. They both lived on the third floor of Mrs. Burt's house. The Bishop's house on Highland Avenue, where my mother worked, was to the rear of the Burt's house at 47 Underwood Street.

My mother died when Patrick was seven. My father had to keep us together, and we moved in with Aunt Maggie and Uncle Tim. Nora, their sister, had died before we moved in. Maggie and Nora worked for Mrs. Burt, and Maggie retired from there. They had to get permission from the landlord for four more people to move into the house.

When my father came to Fall River, he spent six months working at the Print Works. Mr. and Mrs. Burt owned 47 Underwood Street. Mr. Burt got hit by a train in Warren [Rhode Island] and was killed. Their son had meningitis, and institutionalizing him was out of the question. My father was hired to prevent their son, who was twelve or thirteen years old at the time, from getting hurt or getting into trouble. I remember being afraid of him. The first day on the job, the son hurled a rock at my father. He never did it again. My father quit the Print Works to work for Mrs. Burt full-time. Three of her best friends were Irish people.

All wealthy women in the city had an electric car. This was before gasoline cars came into general use. Mrs. Burt had two cars, the electric car, a limo, and another car for shopping. My father became her chauffeur and general helper, painting, etc. The limo was elegant; I loved to ride in it. Sometimes, I got to ride in back with my father as the chauffeur, pretending that the car was mine and that I was a rich kid.

They would get my father's uniform at a place next to Trinity Church in Boston. It was a gray suit that you could wear to church.

In the summer, Mrs. Burt went to Bristol to rent from the Colt Estate. My father made an apartment above the garage. He put screens in the hay door. The apartment included a dining room, a kitchen, and two bedrooms.

Once a year, my father would take Mrs. Burt and Maggie to the Parker House to have lunch as friends. Maggie was her cook. Mrs. Burt was ahead of her time in many respects.

Mrs. Burt was a Newbury from Taunton. When Mrs. Burt wanted to go to the Chilton Club in Boston, my father would call the Sacred Hearts Academy, where I was in high school, and say, "I need Mary." I guess they were afraid of him, because they let me go. I walked over in my uniform and I would get to go to Boston with them. The ride was boring because all my father and Mrs. Burt talked about was the stock market.

She convinced my father to invest in telephone stock, and he lost all of it. The telephone stock went down to two dollars a share. Mrs. Burt said, "Sell it," but my father said, "No, it will come back; people will need telephones."

Mrs. Burt would go to R.H. Stearns—it was always the first stop—and my father got friendly with the Stearns doorman and got to park the car nearby. Mrs. Burt said, "He's very nice to you," but what she didn't know was that my father was tipping the doorman to get the parking space.

Mrs. Burt always bought hair pins at R.H. Stearns. She would take them from the counter and we would have to walk across the store to the window to see them in the natural light. I thought we were all going to get arrested for shoplifting. However, she had old money stamped on her forehead. She was the very epitome of old money.

I was a walking pain. My father would say, "Do what she says." I never heard her raising her voice; she didn't have to. However, we must have been good kids; we had the run of the house.

When my father came on board as her son's keeper, she had an apartment built over the garage where her son lived. Then we moved into the third floor of the main house. The garage had a turntable in it. We would spend hours spinning the car around. The garage also had a furnace. Cars then wouldn't start if they were not warm. There were three or four rooms above the garage. Later, other owners took the turntable out.

All the houses in the Highlands had domestic help, and they were all Irish. The big thing in Fall River then was the gossip. Below the stairs, they knew everything, but no one said anything about Mrs. Burt. They knew when they had it good. The Diocesan newspaper called the help who lived in the house "living-in girls." All used the spray of the ladies of the house. The Irish girls picked up the ways of the big houses. When Maggie was hired, she bought a solid mahogany table with four leaves that sat twelve. The Irish households were very staid, with furniture that they were used to in the big houses. The Irish girls were devilish card players.

The O'Neill's were very bright people. My brother ran the Catholic school system for the Fall River Diocese. My father and his generation spoke perfect English in Ireland; the English ruled and required it. My father was very knowledgeable and educated. If anyone needed to know something, they asked my father. He could do math in his head; he knew the order of presidents; he was just very smart.

Back then, we had streetcars that came up by here. They came by Robeson Street and Highland Avenue and turned around at Hanover Street. You could go anywhere in the city on the trolleys. If I found a bus pass on Friday evening, I could ride all weekend.

Also back then, the lots went through from Highland Avenue to Hanover Street. This house was built as a wedding present for the daughter of the household that owned the house that the nursery school now owns on Highland.

Tim was the family vintner; he take anything and make it into whiskey.

When we were young, I would crew for my brother Pat during sailing races. He had several racing trophies.

Mrs. Burt was very active socially. One day a week, every Wednesday, she attended a matinée at the Newport Theatre near the Tennis Casino. My dad would bring one of us with him. He would drop them off at the theatre then go someplace with us. When it was time for the theatre to let out, the chauffeurs would get in line with the other chauffeurs in front of the theatre. You wouldn't believe the number of chauffeurs at the theatre. The chauffeurs all knew one another and were always civil to one another. My father would escort the ladies down the stairs and to their houses. We would go into the Forge Casino and get an ice cream. The ice cream there was fifty cents, while it was fifteen cents at Kresge's in Fall River. However, Mrs. Burt would always say, "It's not good if it isn't expensive." We always dressed up. Silence was a requirement. We were not to talk unless spoken to.

One day, my father drove Mrs. Burt to Hudner's Market, located downtown on the corner of South Main Street and Borden Street, where the Dunkin' Donuts is now. There was a sign in the Hudner window that said that bananas were on sale. She asked my father to stop and she got out of the car to take a closer look. My father thought she remained in the car and went up Rock Street. He then noticed that the car door was open. He thought she had fell out. He rushed back to Hudner's and found Mrs. Burt in front of the store holding the bag of bananas.

We called Mrs. Burt "Auntie Burt." She was a staunch Republican and, when Louis Howe's cortège was passing by on Highland Avenue, we asked her, "Auntie Burt, can we see the parade?" She replied, "I wouldn't cross the street to see Louis McKenzie [sic] Howe." His funeral was a big deal. Louis Howe is buried next to Mrs. Burt at Oak Grove Cemetery.

Mrs. Burt treated her help well. Sometimes the *nouveau riche* weren't all that nice to their help, but she came from money. My father bought a house at 41 Warburton Street for six thousand dollars. Mrs. Burt financed it and my father had the payments taken out of his pay every week. When the balance reached one thousand dollars, Mrs. Burt said, "Pat, forget the rest of it." There were kids in practically every house on Warburton Street.

My father was a saver. He told me, "The day I married, I had ten thousand dollars in the bank." I wanted to take piano lessons and go into the Girl Scouts, but my father said, "We can't afford it." We had to have private nurses for my mother.

In 1938, Catholic Memorial Home opened. My father was excited about it. It was the first modern nursing home in the area. It was needed, he said. He didn't want to go into it, though. My brother Patrick said that a woman told him that she loved the place. She praised God for sending her there.

In the winter, some people would put the help out in the street. Not Mrs. Burt. She let the help have the run of the house. Mrs. Burt would go to Pasadena, California, for the winter, from November to April. She went all the way by train. Florida was still in the development stage at that time. I was fascinated by her trunk that she took on the trip. When she was gone, my father would be busy rubbing the silver and keeping the place well. She came back to find everything in order. There was a huge hotel in Pasadena where she stayed; it was once in a movie. There were activities for older people there.

My mother died in 1938, and my father was at the Colt estate during the hurricane in September of that year. I told my brothers, "We could be orphans." One of the gardeners at the estate told my father later that he thought, "Oh Patty, I see you no more." We all lived at the Colt estate in the summer months until school started. The polio epidemic was in force. My brother Patrick took up the art of looking pathetic and got invited to sail by the summer families.

When my mother died, my father was a basket case. He was crazy about her. Mrs. Burt decided that a good therapy for my father was to drive out to California to get her. The 1938 hurricane had ruined her two cars, and she bought two new Buicks to replace them. My father and brother went to pick her up. They were gone about a month. She took the train out there and usually took it back.

When my mother died, the house at 41 Warburton was fully paid. My father simply put the key in it and left it there, vacant, and brought us to live with Aunt Maggie and Uncle Tim. My father wanted my aunts and Tim to move to the house, but they thought that the Highlands would be too isolating. They enjoyed their Sacred Heart neighborhood, with its park and baseball games. That's why parks are so important to a neighborhood.

In 1944, Mrs. Burt died. The garden had been planted in Bristol, and my dad got a ration card with a B rating. That allowed us to get more gas and other necessities. Having a garden helped with your card rating. After Mrs. Burt died, her nephew Mr. Nichols paid my father's salary while he tended to the garden in Bristol. Mrs. Burt's nephew was the manager of Kidder-Peabody in Taunton.

When Mrs. Burt died, everyone wanted to hire my father. The Cummings ladies hired him and got to depend on him. They would call and say, "We need you right away," and the problem would be ants in the kitchen. I remember the Cummings house; it was beautiful. I particularly remember a piece of furniture in the dining room made of the house. It included a sterling coffee, tea and chocolate service on the table.

My brother Neil was a real kid at Ruggles Park. We didn't know how smart Neil was until he went to Coyle. He came home with papers in the 90s and was valedictorian of his class. That was the first time we knew he was smart! I would have flunked algebra if Neil wasn't still at home.

My brother Pat taught at Harvard and Notre Dame. He would say, "Everyone knows me [how intelligent I am] but not the people at home." When he went to Notre Dame, he said, "Do they think that I am going to stay in Indiana if Buzzards Bay calls to me?" Pat was a charmer. When we were in Bristol, he would be on the shore and wealthy people in sail boats would pick him up and say, "That's Pat's boy; he lost his mother," and they would take him to dinner at various houses.

**School Life**

After my mother died, I went to Sacred Heart School. It was a big school, with two classes for each grade and forty-two kids in each classroom.

Tuition at Sacred Heart School was seventy-five dollars for the year, which we gave in seven-dollar-and-fifty-cent installments every month in an envelope. I can remember after Mrs. Burt died, the principal of Sacred Heart School took me aside and said, "I know your father lost his job; tell him that he doesn't have to pay the tuition for a while." My father got angry and offended at that and said, "Did that woman think that I would wait until Mrs. Burt died to find another job?" From then on, he made sure to give the school its tuition at the beginning of every month.

My parents expected all of us to go to college. This started early, in the second grade. I remember saying to myself, "What was all that about?"

**Recreation and Entertainment**

Pat was involved in the neighborhood football league at Ruggles Park. There wasn't an adult involved. There was a big hill there that was good for sledding. The kids were in the park from morning to night. There were CYO [Catholic Youth Organization] competitions there. Ruggles was flooded in the winter for ice-skating. There must have been lights there, otherwise people would have been crashing into one another.

When we sledded on Linden Street past Locust Street, the side streets were blocked off. When the bus came by, we threw snowballs at it as it came through. The Monsignor and his cohorts had a thing going at Linden and Pine Streets, where when cars got stuck on the hill there, they shoveled them out and got paid for it. When that car left, they shoveled the snow back and waited for the next car to get stuck and did it all over again. The Cork people were all for education. It was okay for us to sled as long as we got our homework done.

I'm still friendly with my high school friends at Sacred Hearts Academy, particularly with friends from Snell Street. The Durfee Theatre let out at twenty minutes to 11:00 pm. People going to the south of the city would line up in front of the Granite Block and those going north would line up on the other side. When we lived on Linden Street, we would begin walking home and catch the bus on the way, or we would end up walking all the way home. No one ever bothered me at all or frightened me.

One day a year in the summer we would go to Crescent Park and one day to Rocky Point. That was all. It later surprised me when I found in high school that people could pay a quarter and go there anytime!

At the circus, I was amazed when the elephant lay down with the girl underneath. *Wouldn't he flatten her out?* I thought. Neil and I would be excited whenever the day came to go to the circus when we lived on Warburton Street. Once, he was so excited that he fell on a radiator and split his forehead open from the hairline down. From that time on, he had a neat scar down the middle of his head. It was so in the middle of his forehead that later people would think that it was a furrow in his brow.

**Courtship and Marriage**

My father gave me my mother's wedding ring. He brought it to Monte's Jewelry, across from the Cathedral, and had it sized. He knew them since Mrs. Burt went there. I was married on the same date as my parent's wedding day. We scheduled it for the first Saturday after Easter, when Neil could come home from the seminary. Neil officiated at the wedding.

I was married to my husband Howard on April 19, 1952, at Sacred Heart Church. He was hired by Travelers Insurance a week before I was hired. They sent him to Lawrence. Then, when the Korean War started, they shipped all of the office to Maine and put them in the same National Guard unit. I hated to leave my older brothers. I was going to get married and go to Maine. I hated it. The whole place closed up for the winter. Howard promised me that we would go back to Massachusetts as soon as possible. When the men returned from the war, we were transferred to Boston. He had bought a car for work in Maine, but didn't need it around Boston. He complained that he could have gotten more use out of it if we stayed in Maine or wouldn't have bought it. There were five train stations in Quincy, and it cost only twenty-two cents a trip to Boston. When the man in charge of the Fall River office died, we were transferred and moved back here.

**Work Life**

I worked at Kresge's back counter when I was age fifteen and still a sophomore in high school. The whole back of Kresge's was a counter. At one end were records and at the other end were bird cages and fish and other such items. My father didn't like the idea that I was working there; he was afraid that the entire Navy would come to have me play records for them.

In Grant's 5 & 10 they had a piano. If someone wanted to buy sheet music, the sales person would play the song from the sheet music. It was entertaining; people would come in just to hear the music.

One Saturday, a little kid wanted a fish in the aquarium. I had to move the aquarium to get at the fish and, in doing so, I moved a pipe. That pipe was a drain and, on Monday morning, they came in to find the place flooded.

These were the war years, and I was paid twenty-five cents an hour. When I moved to Cherry and Webb, I made thirty-three cents an hour. At Christmas, Oliver M. Cherry himself handed out five dollars each to us part-time workers. He shook your hand and told you what a good job you were doing. He lived on Madison Street, near Stewart.

I became a card-puncher at the B.M.C. Durfee Bank. I worked sixty hours a week. I loved it. I was locked in a room working when the bank was in the process of being taken over by another bank. We went to the Colonnade Hotel in Boston and were locked in a room. We were treated very well: we had scallops wrapped in bacon and other good meals. Eight months after my husband died, Neil died.

Uncle Tim O'Neill had seven brothers. One stayed back to work the farm and five went to Butte, Montana, to work in the copper mines. I still have the shaving mug of Pat O'Neill, which has his name on it. In those days, the barbershop kept your own shaving mug for you when the barbers shaved you each morning. They made big, big money in the copper mines, but they all ended up with "miner's consumption." Cornelius O'Neill left Montana to come to Fall River when he knew he was dying. Nora accompanied him to Boston, where he took the boat to Ireland. He wanted to go home and die.

All the O'Neill men were tall, about 6 feet. Tim O'Neill, the blacksmith, was particularly tall, over 6 feet and good at what he did. In the early days of vehicles, there were no parts stores and parts sometimes had to be made by a blacksmith. Tim had to produce those parts. He was a blacksmith in Ireland before he came over here as the youngest of seven brothers. Few people who immigrated here had an apprenticeship.

**Neighborhood Experiences**

Bishop Feehan had white, white hair and was a handsome man. When I was in St. Mary's School, the nuns had us practicing how to address him when he came to the school—"Good Morning, Your Excellency," or "Good afternoon, Your Excellency." I remember going downhill in roller skates and passing the bishop as he read his breviary and saying, "Good afternoon, Your Excellency." He must have wondered, "What the hell was that?"

Warburton Street was two blocks long. No house didn't have at least one kid. There was a big crowd of us and we all played together. When my mother died, we moved to Linden Street. The Warburton house remained empty for a number of years, and then my father rented it. He was saving it for me. When I moved to Quincy, he decided to sell it and found that he had to ask me to sign off on it. He didn't think of that.

Mr. James A. Burke Jr. owned the yellow brick house at the corner of Highland Avenue and Hood Street (887 Highland Avenue). He was the superintendent at the Sagamore Mill and agent for Foster Spinning Company. Any seminarian that needed a job for the summer could find one at the Sagamore. Priests were lucky to have family since the Church provided very little for them. Family provided travel for them and things like that.

The boys got their driver's licenses on their sixteenth birthday. The boys taught me how to drive. We were practicing once near St. Luke's Hospital in New Bedford. I was practicing backing up and backed up into a telephone pole. The metal bumper got stuck on the pole, and I couldn't go forward or back. It damaged the bumper. My father wasn't happy and told my brother, "Why were you teaching her to back up into a pole?"

I was twenty-five before I got my license; if you were under twenty-five, you had to pay more for insurance. Everyone had taken the bus to work then, but the bus strike brought it to a head; everyone started driving after that.

In those days, when John Stone drove the ambulance, he got the biggest kid in the neighborhood to bring someone down. When they saw John, the kids would yell out, "Pick me." He let the kids run the siren. They weren't paid! Pat said it was the highlight of his teenage years; Pat said the funeral Mass when John died.

**Ethnic Identity**

Both my mother and father had brogues. If they wanted to say a real insult, they would say it in Gaelic. When I was growing up, you heard a brogue everywhere you went. Lots of girls didn't want to get married then. They had more freedom being single. Did they ever dress up!

I am in contact with my cousins in County Monaghan. I can pick up the phone and have a conversation with my cousin John in Dublin. The old Irish believed in the "mysteries" of life. My relatives in Ireland still do. My father practiced the mysteries. He told us of a woman in his area that had died. Her husband was a good man and would go out with the boys every night while she stayed at home and take care of the children. One day, when the kids were older, she said, "Things are well enough, so I won't be coming home," and she died.

The Irish would always reference the mysteries for why things happened. "God knocked me off my horse," they would say. My husband, insurance claims man that he was, would say, "That's what they all say."

Never heard a word against blacks or Jewish people from my parents, but they didn't like the English. The English were terrible to the Irish in Ireland. My father went back once before he got married and my mother did too. When his parents walked him to the gate as he was leaving, my father later told me, "I looked back at them and knew that I would never see them again."

They couldn't use their own language [Gaelic] in Ireland when the English ruled there. The teachers here didn't take off points for English if a student was French or Portuguese, but they took five points off of my father for his English: being Irish, he was expected to have good English. Here in this country, Gaelic was used to tell jokes about the farmer's daughter, so we kids couldn't understand them.

**Christmas, Holidays, and Special Occasions**

At Christmas, when my mother was alive, she and Neil would wrestle with the Christmas tree lights, where if one light went out, the whole string of lights went out. So you had to go through and test all of the lights one at a time to test them and see if the string would light up again. Santa Claus came to the Warburton house one year; I don't know where he came from. When my mother died, my father got all of our decorations and brought them to the O'Neill's house. It was the first Christmas without my mother. My father called my mother's niece and he picked up presents for we kids. He got a good batch of things. Pat was only seven years old when my mother died. When the pocket doors were opened to the parlor, it was full of gifts. We got gifts from people that we never got gifts from before. Everyone wanted us to have a good Christmas.

When the war started, my father constructed a little stable at Christmas. It was made out of stakes from an orange crate. He went to the 5 & 10s and got wise men and shepherds and put the Christmas tree lights in back of the manger. That was our tree for that year. He did a nice job on the stable; our family has always treasured it, and it has been passed down in the family.

## Downtown

I never wanted to live any place else. Fall River was big enough so that you didn't know everyone else but small enough so that you had a lot of people around. The downtown was wonderful; Van Dykes was heaven on earth. At Christmas, we would get on a bus and go downtown to look at the decorations at McWhirr's. Cherry and Webb's was decorated too. We would walk up and down the street looking at the decorations.

Van Dykes had big square dishes with pickles in them. They were wonderful. We had to stand up at the counter. When I started working at Traveler's, I went to the Eagle's Annex for a chow mein sandwich. I had never seen one before, but I tried it. My father was suspicious of it. He said, "The chickens in Ireland wouldn't eat that stuff."

The lunch counter at Kresge's was wonderful. You could get an ice cream sundae for fifteen cents and a root beer for five cents. Pat and I were cute kids, so they put our root beer into two mugs. Grants was our entertainment. You would go in and someone would be playing the piano. Sometimes they would sing. Sometimes the employees sang.

Downtown wasn't too far from Linden Street.

## Health and Illness

They had bone-setters in Ireland, and no doctors. People took care of themselves. My father had a cure for cuts that were infected or had dirt in them. He would put the white of an egg on gauze and put it over the cut. It drew out the dirt in the cut. When the gauze was taken off, the cut would come out clean. My mother-in-law once got a cut on her finger that had dirt in it that wouldn't come out. Someone had secured a piece of raw bacon on her cut finger. I put some egg white and gauze on her finger and it later came out clean.

When my brother Pat got hit by a car and hurt his leg, he didn't go to the hospital. He was hit by a man test-driving for his license. Instead of feeling sorry for Pat, my relatives said, "Oh, the poor man will be too nervous to get his license." The exception were knees; they were an issue because it affected your ability to work. You couldn't work with a bad knee.

When scarlet fever hit a house, the Health Board put a red card on the door. The polio epidemic was awful. When school started in September, my father kept us in Bristol to avoid getting polio. Pneumonia took a lot of kids.

When I lived in Quincy, my father visited and became sick. He went to visit a Dr. Mahony, who was Black Irish, what my aunt called "Spanish Irish." The doctor loved that he was from the old country and sat my father down on a rocking chair in his office and started laughing it up. My father was seventy or so when he died. People were always waked at home. It was always implied that if you were not waked at home the house was not worthy. I always got dressed for wakes. It seemed like a waste to get dressed up and then have to go home again. I would go to the Cummings house; they would always invite me in.

## The Depression and Prohibition

Owen, my mother's younger brother, was imported to this country to become the bishop's chauffeur. He was a handsome man and died very young at the age of thirty-seven from skin cancer. During Prohibition, the bishop had a consecration to attend in Canada. Canada didn't have Prohibition. When they returned, the customs officials were all French. Uncle Owen had stuffed the car toolbox full of hard liquor. When the Irish staff saw it, they said, "Well done."

**World War II**

When Pearl Harbor was announced over the radio, Pat was emptying the wet garbage can in the back yard. He was about ten at the time and came up the stairs and said to my father, "Dad, I just heard on the Harrington's radio that someone bombed Pearl Harbor." I didn't know what was going on. The family downstairs had a son in the service stationed at Pearl Harbor. They had to sweat it out.

Air raid shelter signs were going up. I started my career at Kresge's, and a woman came in one day in tears. "Why are you crying?" I asked. She replied that she had just sent one of her sons overseas. All movies changed to war movies practically overnight.

The city recruited high school kids to be auxiliary firemen when World War II started. Neal was one of them. My father would worry every time Neal put on his helmet for air raid duty. He though that Hitler would drop a bomb on his son's head.

When my husband died, his feet were still full of shrapnel from the Battle of the Bulge, when he was diving into a foxhole and his boot got a big slice taken out of it.

When we went to Newport with Mrs. Burt, my father would visit his cousins in the Newport fire and police departments. The first question would be, "What do you hear from home?"—meaning Ireland.

The Diocese bought the building on Franklin Street, and it became the USO. I remember that they had an air raid warning system, with young people as volunteers. The firemen went into the war, so they trained the young guys to fight a fire. If a three-family caught fire, it was a big deal.

I remember that they had a submarine at the city pier for the 4th of July. One sailor said to my father, "Do you begrudge me my twenty-one dollars a month?" That's what a private first class made. People couldn't afford to marry.

In Fall River, you knew so many people. You had an identity that you didn't have in big cities. I worked as a teen, and they were glad to have us. I made four hundred dollars in my junior year of high school at thirty-three cents an hour. I graduated in 1946, the first peacetime class. Fall River was a great place to grow up.

**Popular Expressions and Nicknames**

"Full of the chair" (when someone was quite overweight). "He's one size to an elephant" (when someone was very overweight; people in those days were not fat because they walked everywhere). "Laziness, did I ever offend you" (if you were slow to honor a request, as in bringing up the coal from the cellar). "A basket case." If a child was good or bad or smart as their parents, an Irish saying was, "Where would you leave it?"

There were so many Harrington's and Sullivan's. "Dinny the Bow" handled the bow on the Fall River Line. "Handsome Dan" was Representative Sullivan's grandfather. All the policemen and firemen were Irish. "Jack the Lantern" was the lamplighter. "Jack the Woman" took care of old ladies, doing such things as getting them into bed at night. Little people were called "Peanuts." Big people were called "Stretch." In parochial schools, nicknames were not encouraged.

# Delores "Del" Anne (Alves) Mello

*Born on January 3, 1939*

**Family Background**

I was born in my grandmother's house at 640 Lawton Street, delivered by a doctor.

My parents were George (born in Fall River) and Josephine (Martini) Alves (born in Italy).

My father's parents were George, a baker, and Anna (Medeiros) Alves. My mother's mother was named Pasqualine Faggioli Martini.

I have two brothers, George and Manuel.

My husband's name is Gilbert Mello, and we have three children: Gilbert, Christine, and Darlene.

**Family Life**

This house [156 Powell Street] was built in 1939. Almost all of the wood in this house came from the 1938 hurricane. My father and grandfather brought the lumber back from Horseneck Beach.

My parents had eleven dollars in pennies when they were married. My father died when he was forty-two. My mother said that my father didn't know how to hammer a nail but Grandfather taught him how to do everything. They dug the cellar to this house by hand, and they made and poured cement by hand for the foundation. My grandfather was a hod carrier. He helped to build St. Jean's (now Holy Trinity) Church on Stafford Road.

My mother was nine when she came here; she was born in 1911 and came here in 1918. She was only two when my grandfather came. My grandmother was to come in six months time, but the war broke out and she came seven years later. Then they had three more children after she came here. One son, my mother's brother Antone, died after he caught pneumonia when bringing dinner pails to his brothers and sisters working at the mills at the Berkshire-Hathaway Plant A, on Grinnell Street.

My mother went to live Down North at my father's family house on McDonald Street after they were married. My father was from Down North and was delivering bread that morning from his bakery, the George Street Bakery. My mother said, "I'm about to deliver," and my father said, "Can't you wait until I deliver the bread?" The roads were bumpy and it hurt; she gripped the truck's door handles. I was about to come out as they brought my mother up the stairs to my grandmother's house.

My father's family didn't like my mother's family because they were Italian. They spoke only Portuguese in the house, so my mother learned Portuguese there. My mother made twenty dollars a week at the mill, and that twenty dollars went to keep the bakery going. When she had me, they lost the twenty dollars and the bakery. It went out of business. My uncle on my father's side owned the Hope Street Bakery.

My mother went to a one-room schoolhouse in Tiverton [Rhode Island] when she came here. One day, she asked her cousin if she could go to the bathroom, which was an outhouse. The teacher yelled at her for speaking. She was so embarrassed. She spoke only Italian.

I grew up in the country here. I had the greatest childhood ever. All of the roads here were dirt then. My father made a big trench in the side of the road to take the water away. When it rained, my brother and I would put two pieces of sticks in the trench to see which would get to the bottom first. Later, I would use the trench to drive my car over to fix the brakes or change the oil.

My kid brother taught me how to drive. He was thirteen years old and I was seventeen years old. After my father died, I wanted to get my license to take my mother to do her shopping and to go to work. Once, when I thought I saw the cops, I panicked and drove the car in the garage and hit the wall. It was a '53 Nash.

After he lost the bakery, my father went to work at the Torpedo station in Newport [Rhode Island]. He got ruptured there carrying food on to ships, and he couldn't do it anymore. He then went to Brown and Sharp. He started having strokes in his thirties. He had high blood pressure.

Every time my father saved a little money, he would buy a piece of land here. We ended up with three acres, where my brothers built their homes on one of the acres.

At night, we would sit around the radio and my mother would teach us how to crochet and embroider. She taught my brothers too. I could tell which one of us did the stitches: my brother George did tiny stitches, Manny's stitches were medium, and my stitches were the largest.

**Food and Meals**

My mother did all of her own preserving. We kids would argue over who would put the caps on the bottles. When she made ketchup, she would crush the tomatoes and then put them in a cloth bag and hang it on a clothesline. The water would drip out, and she would have her ketchup.

My father would raise a pig a year and slaughter it. The whole family would come over and cut it up and wrap it. We also prepared a half a cow. My mother would make chourico in the cellar. We would wash the intestines and stuff the chourico meat and morcella, which is blood pudding, in the intestines. We would cook *torresmos*, which are fried pieces of pork with fat. They were delicious.

My father had different barns for rabbits, goats, geese, and chickens. There was a different barn for baby chicks. The chicks barn had a big umbrella-shaped hood and a kerosene lamp to make heat. There were fifty or so chicks. Every once in a while, he would let the chicks hatch. The chicken's voice would change and you knew that they only wanted to lay on the eggs until the chicks hatched. That's the stuff kids should see today. Seeing the chicks come out of the egg was amazing. They were wet when they came out, then they fluffed out in about ten minutes.

My mother cooked mostly Portuguese food for my father. He had to have his Portuguese soup at least four times a week. When my father died, she did more American–style cooking. On weekends, we would have a roast. She baked from scratch. My father didn't like music; she would have the Polish Hour on the radio on Sundays when my father was outside in the garden. Mom worked as a weaver in the mill, in Plant A at the Berkshire-Hathaway Mill. It was hard work.

Before we went to bed, my mother would make us very light coffee and sugar and we would break milk crackers into it. The coffee would warm the milk. She didn't want us to have cold milk.

**Recreation and Entertainment**

We would go for rides on Sundays, then go visit my father's sister. Our family and all our relatives would go to Brayton Point Beach, near where the power plant is now. They had a beach there. During the war, the siren would go off at noon at the fire station. My brother would say, "The Japs are coming, the Japs are coming," and I would start crying. My father put black tape on top of his car lights; it was the law during the war.

At school, there was a diamond for games. We played the game with a ball bouncing it in the squares. If you missed it, you had to start over again. "Squeeze the lemon" involved the strongest person standing next to the large, round drainpipe and the rest of the kids lining up against the wall and pushing along the wall to see if we could push the kid out standing next to the pipe. We also played dodge ball, jump rope, and jacks. We would go home for lunch every day.

**Work Life**

I worked at US Luggage on Broadway at the Globe. It closed in 1980. Then I worked part-time for an upholsterer located at the corner of Walnut and Linden Streets, Henry Herz. My youngest child was four at the time. My husband died at age fifty. My mother had a stroke and was invalided after that. She lived for three years after that and passed away. I was at home after that, but I did occasional stitching for an upholsterer.

**Neighborhood Experiences**

I had a pony when I was young; however, one day I fell off the pony and the next day it was gone. My father was concerned about my getting hurt. I never had another horse until I was twenty-one years old. There are houses now where the pony was once kept. My first horse was named Coco, and I loved him very much. I had a great time with him, and he lived to be thirty-two years old.

When my father died, I was seventeen. I had more freedom then; my mom was more lenient. Two men lived at the top of the street: the Thiboutots. Armand was a blacksmith and Meddie painted cars on Slade Street. Armand would let me use his horse anytime I wanted.

Armand was a blacksmith, but he did railing work too. When we would go out to visit them, the women sat together and the men sat in another room. I liked to sit with the men because they had better stories that they told about the war. Mr. Thiboutot had a rough childhood. He said that he would go pick blueberries in Oak Grove Cemetery and see Lizzie Borden pull up with her horse and carriage when she visited her parents' grave. The kids were scared of her.

He would tell of sleeping in bed with no heat, with two brothers at the bottom and two brothers at the top of the bed. His father was mean. He and his brother fell into the ice at Cook Pond and had to hide their clothes when they came home so they wouldn't get hit.

**Christmas, Holidays, and Special Occasions**

At Christmastime, we would go around singing at the doors of relatives. My grandfather played a squawk box and others would have bells and pans and others to make a bass. They would sing "Open the door," and sing back and forth. This was not an Italian tradition. My Italian grandfather played Italian music and my Portuguese grandfather played Portuguese music. My father would drink only on the holidays. He was a happy man then; otherwise, he was always serious and kind of grouchy.

# Leon Menard Jr.

*Born on August 5, 1918*

## Family Background

I was born in Middlebury, Vermont.

My father's name was Leon Menard. He graduated from the University of Vermont Medical School and became a doctor. My mother's name was Rosealma (Florence) Menard. She was a nurse and originally came from New York.

My mother's father was Napoleon Caesar Florence. He had dairy farms in Burlington, Middlebury, and Bristol, Vermont. He furnished milk for the whole district. Milk then was ten cents a quart. He would haul gravel with horses and wagons in Bristol, Vermont, and would buy farms in foreclosure to use for raising hay. He owned a hotel in Burlington, but only for a while.

My mother's mother cooked for several people, including four hands, two sons, and other members of the family. She split her own wood for the stove with an ax. There was a forty-gallon tank on the side of the stove to warm the water. The kitchen table was large; I don't know how they got it in the house. The farm was near a railroad station.

My grandfather Florence had automatic milkers, where the milk was carried to the milk room. It was all whole milk and they would separate it into cream and skimmed milk or leave it whole. They milked two cows at a time. They had a few hundred cows in the barn. I would run the horse-drawn rig to turn over the hay; I tried to use the tractor, but I couldn't turn it over to start it. The urine and other waste from the barn went into a lagoon with floating solids on the top. Once, my brother Paul slipped off of a roof he was playing on and fell into the lagoon. They washed him off in the watering trough. He cried a lot. He was lucky that he fell feet first.

My father's father was Edmund Menard. He was a cabinetmaker by trade and could build a house too.

Both grandfathers spoke French and English and my grandmother spoke only a few English words like "hello," "goodbye," and "thank you." She understood English but did not speak it.

The order of birth in our family was this: Leon Jr. (me), Paul, and Jean.

My wife's name is Anna and we were married on July 28, 1945. We have six children named (in order of birth) Michelle, Leon III, Elizabeth, Stephen, David, and Mary.

## Family Life

Our family home was at 322 Oliver Street (demolished to make way for St. Anne's Credit Union parking lot). My father was a doctor, an obstetrician, in Fall River. My mother was a nurse but didn't work after she was married. However, she did work for the drugstore on the first floor of our house for a few years. My father came from Holyoke and went to a Jesuit college in Montreal. His uncle was a lawyer with an office in the old (pre-1928) Granite Block, and he convinced my father to come to Fall River. My parents moved to Columbia Street in the 1920s and then to Oliver Street.

My mother died when she was forty-four and my father died when he was fifty-five years old.

My father's office was on the first floor of 322 Oliver Street, on a one-story wing on the side of the building. It had a waiting room with two offices. In our building, there was a pharmacy, a pool room, a restaurant, and an auto agency, where Hupmobiles were sold. Lambert's Drug Store was on the [southwest] corner of South Main and Middle Streets, diagonally across from St. Anne's Church. Next to that was a Dodge showroom (right next to our house at South Main and Oliver Street) in front and garage in back. There was also a six-family home—all between Middle and Oliver Streets on South Main Street. At that time, Oliver Street continued across South Main Street into what is now St. Anne's Hospital property.

**Friends**

Al Walley was a friend. Richard St. Dennis (the son of Dr. St. Dennis) was a friend and was lost in an airplane in World War II. Paul Bardsley lived on Oliver Street. I kept my set of electric trains under my bed. Once, I brought them to Paul's house to play with, but we couldn't because he didn't have electricity in his bedroom.

Another friend was Frank Magoni, whose father was also named Frank. Frank Jr.'s mother ran the Downy Flake Donuts Shop. I sold donuts in the shop in the summertime. Frank Jr.'s brother Louis started Magoni's Restaurant. The stove in the middle of the fireplace at Magoni's Restaurant came from my farm in Swansea [Massachusetts].

**School Life**

I attended a kindergarten on Mulberry Street, which doesn't exist now. I then attended first through third grades at the Osborne Street School. Then, when St. Anne's School was built in 1924, I attended fourth and fifth grade there. I went to Henry Lord Junior High from grades six through nine. Then, I went to Durfee [B.M.C. Durfee High School] for one or two years.

The kids at Durfee weren't too serious about education and skipped school a lot. After attendance was taken, we would skip out and hang out on the wall. Once, my father came by and was upset that I wasn't going to school. He sent me to Assumption High School in Worcester, where I boarded and stayed for four years. The brothers at Assumption were strict. We had to take quick showers or the brothers would cut the water off. We got hit a lot. Once, when I left the shower and opened my bathrobe to show someone my suntan, a brother hit me and had me thrown out of school. My father drove me right back to the school and made them take me back.

I went to Worcester Academy for a year, where I graduated near the top of my class.

After Assumption, where both the high school and the college were in the same building, I went to the University of Vermont, where I did two years of pre-med. My father called me home in 1941.

I then went to college at the University of Massachusetts in Amherst. I studied agriculture at the Stockbridge School and then at the university. There were so many veterans at the college that they brought in wooden barracks from Newport and set them up near the football field. The school exploded in population from twelve hundred to twelve thousand students because of the returning vets. I received my Bachelor of Science degree there. Everything was free, courtesy of Uncle Sam. Then I went to Swansea to operate the chicken farm.

## Courtship and Marriage

*Mrs. Menard*: I met Leon when we worked together at the hospital in Terre Haute and got to eat together in the mess hall. We started dating by going to the movies or meeting for lunch. Once, in the mess hall, I started flicking water at him from a glass. He didn't like the fact that his khaki suit was getting wet and said that, if I did it again, he would throw his meringue pie in my face. I did it again, and he did it; he threw the pie in my face. One day, when we were riding our bicycles along the countryside in March, we decided to get off and rest. It was nice, and the apple blossoms were in bloom. A horse came up on the other side of the fence and was swishing his tail. We petted him for a while. Then Leon said, "Will you marry me?" and, just at that moment, the horse let out gas with a loud sound.

## Work Life

*Mr. Menard*: I had a chicken farm in Swansea on Gardners Neck Road for six or seven years. My father owned the land and, when he died, I went to farm on it. I raised about four thousand hens and raised hatching eggs. I lived there and built two buildings. There were several chicken farms in Swansea at that time.

When the state took the farm for the highway, and after a few stints doing odd jobs, I started driving a gasoline truck and did that for ten years. When I ruptured a disc, I couldn't drive anymore. I was out of work for three years. Then I drove a school bus, but the high school kids were too much.

## Health and Illness

My father charged two dollars for an office call, which included meds that he carried in his bag. He even charged two dollars for delivering a baby. When he died, he left a book with a list of names of people who owed him money, but he didn't put any amounts next to the names. Half of the babies that he delivered were at home and half in the hospital. In the morning, he was in the hospital, then he had office calls from 1:00 to 3:00 pm. At night, he worked from 6:00 to 8:00 pm.

My father later developed Hodgkin's lymphoma and had shots that knocked him out for two or three days at a time. He slept in the couch upstairs. One day, a Portuguese woman in her thirties and dressed in black came to the door. She said, "I want to pay your father." I asked my father how much he should ask for and I went down to tell her. She reached into a beat-up purse and started pulling out change: nickels, dimes, and quarters, until she reached two dollars. I asked my father what the money was for. He said for delivering a baby. He said, "If I charged her more, she wouldn't come back. That's all she could afford."

My mother had headaches and high blood pressure. They would bleed her into a bottle and throw the blood away. That's how they treated high blood pressure in those days.

## World War II

I was drafted in February, 1941, and went to Fort Devens and then to Fort Bragg, North Carolina, until June of 1941. Since I had pre-med training, they trained me as a lab, then surgical, technician. I then joined a hospital unit, which worked like a MASH unit but it was mobile. They didn't call them MASH units until the Korean War. Then I was shipped out on a troop ship to Australia, which took forty-two days. We ran out of fresh water and were rationed at one canteen a day, which wasn't much in hot weather. Everyone on the ship got sick.

We stopped in Bora Bora for fresh water, then proceeded to the south of New Zealand to some big city there. We couldn't get off the boat there for three days. Then we were moved to a town outside Melbourne and stayed there for about a month, where we camped on straw mattresses during our summer barracks. Our mobile hospital unit was made into two units, A and B. This was in 1941, before the war started in December.

The hospital unit that I went to be trained with was all southerners; I was the only northerner and draftee, and I got razzed for it. Out of a group of six hundred men, I was the only one who went to med school. Once, when I was giving shots to a few thousand men a day, the southern captain wanted me to hurry up. I was going as fast as I could. He said, "Don't bother changing the needles; it's taking too long; just keep using the same needle again." At lab school, they told us to never use the same needle twice. I refused to do it, and he called in the lieutenant. They got into an argument and went into the other room, where I could hear the shouting. I kept changing the needles. The lieutenant was from Florida, a real gentleman.

We then went to Good Enough Island, in the South Pacific, which was about seven miles long with a 8,500-foot-high mountain on it. The Lever Brothers Soap Company owned the plantation on it. The Japanese had occupied the island and the Australians had wiped them out. The Americans had constructed an airstrip on it. Planes had to come over the mountain and dive bomb into the airfield. We cleared an area for a tent hospital for the training unit. Men started coming in from the battle of Guadalcanal. We had lost a hospital ship to the Japanese and had twelve hundred wounded men and only a hundred beds to put them in. We were wrapping the wounded in blankets and laying them on the ground.

Some Japanese soldiers were still on the island and came out at night to steal food. I was on Good Enough Island for nineteen months in the Hospital Unit.

The Army put up frames for tents. They put the natives to work cutting saplings for the frames with machetes. The natives couldn't use hammers, so they instead used the dull sides of the machetes to drive in spikes into the posts.

When it rained, we could see the rain up in the mountains and we could hear it coming down the mountain. Suddenly, a three-inch stream would become a six-foot stream that would wash trucks away. You had to get out of the way, otherwise you would be gone.

Good Enough Island was a former coconut plantation. The natives there were paid about one and one-half pounds a year. They didn't need much cash, since the men wore only loincloths and the women grass skirts. The girls would line up in the water near the shore of a pond or the ocean and walk toward the shoreline together. As they did this, the fish would move toward the shore and get washed up on the shoreline for the girls to collect.

Everyone had malaria on the island at one time or another. They gave you these yellow pills for it that made you turn yellow. They gave us quinine. I got malaria ten times when I was there.

There were spiders on the island as big as your hand. They would spin these huge webs that even squirrels would get caught in. When the squirrels got caught in the web, the spiders would twirl the squirrels and wind them up in the web.

I was sent back to the United States, partly by boat, and landed in California for five or six days. I worked in the kitchen; they put you wherever they needed you. Then, I took a railroad trip for five days to Boston via Chicago, where stayed overnight on the troop train. The smell in Chicago was terrible, since it was near the cattle pens and the slaughterhouses. Then, we went to Fort Devens for three days and on to Boston and home with my bag of clothes.

# Robert Millerick

*Born on June 16, 1931*
*Died on September 4, 2012*

**Family Background**

I was born at the General Hospital when we lived on Sixteenth Street. I lived there for six weeks, when we moved Down North to 34 Wiley Street. That house burned down a few years ago and there is another house there now.

My parents were Daniel C. and Katherine (Mullins) Millerick. My mother was the aunt of Jimmy Mullins. She was the sister of Jimmy's father. My father was a purser or cashier on the Fall River Line.

I had a grandfather who was born in 1864. He was conceived while my great-grandfather was at home from the Civil War. When the war started, he enlisted in the Third Massachusetts Volunteers and saw action in the Carolinas. He was let out of the service because he had a family with three or four children. Later, when vets were needed badly, the whole regiment re-enlisted.

He saw more action and was captured. Some Pennsylvania miners dug a tunnel under a trench under the Southern works. The mine blew up and formed a crater. The Northern soldiers went through the crater to escape, but the Confederates picked them off as they ran through it. My great-grandfather was shot in the arm. His arm was amputated by the side of the road by a rebel surgeon. He got discharged and had six more children.

Soccer was really big in the city. In 1888, the Fall River Rovers won the National Championship. It was the first national competition and championship. Fall River won against a team from New York City and played the game in New Jersey. My grandfather was the goalie for the team. He was 6 foot, 5 inches tall, and skinny. He worked in the quarries. In those days, you could charge the goalie. A guy named O'Connell from the New York team charged my grandfather and my grandfather threw the attacker over the goal. Fall River won 4-0.

My grandfather was married the next week. He came back on the Fall River Line. His wife to be, my grandmother, was in the crowd at the pier to meet him. A male friend in an Irish brogue told my grandmother, "Well, Mary, I think he's not coming." She replied in her own brogue, "You're lying; I can see his head." He towered above the other people on the boat. After they married, soccer wasn't the place for a married man, and the guy who took my grandfather's place became an All-American.

After World War I, Fall River had the Hose 10, a great soccer team. I guess it was named for a fire company. I had a chain with a Hose 10 medal on it. My aunt's boyfriend was on the team.

My wife is Maureen (Dalton) Millerick and we have two children, Cynthia M. Christy and Karen A. Gariepy.

**Family Life**

My father was the nicest guy in the world. He was tough as nails, though. He was loving to me and my mother. He only hit me once, on the top of my head, when I argued with my mother. I was always arguing with my mother. My father would be reading the paper and I would be arguing with my mother; he would then lower the paper and look over it at me. When he did, I stopped arguing. One day, I said, "Shit!" and he rapped me on the head. He said, "Don't talk like that, and I'll give you three reasons why not: (1) she will be the best friend that you will ever have; (2) she is your mother; and (3) she is my wife, and no one talks to her like that."

My mom was a beauty. Once, a man on the street said something to her and my father asked, "What did that guy say to you?" He was 5 feet, 8 inches, and wiry as hell. He gave the guy a right fist and brought him on the ground. A cop came and asked, "What did he do?" and my father said, "He was wise with Catherine." The cop grabbed the guy by the collar and brought him to the station.

Once, my father dived head-first into the river and got knocked out when he hit an anchor that was below water. My mother helped to fish him out. Later, when they argued, my mother would say, "I should have never pulled you out of the water."

My father's father was a blacksmith. During the war, he was sent to Newport [Rhode Island] at the age of eighty-two to teach some of the foundry and metal work to civilians. His shop was located to the rear of the Lamport building on the waterfront. I once did some wiring at Lamport, and an old timer came by and said that there once was a blacksmith shop there. "Is your name Millerick?" he asked. He said that the blacksmith must have been my grandfather. He brought me to where the blacksmith shop was located. The cobblestones were worn down from the metal wheels of the wagons. He showed me a baler hook and said, "Your grandfather made this."

My father told me a story of when my grandfather was shoeing a mule. To do that, you had to get behind the mule, with your back to his backside, and pull the mule's foot between your legs to get at the bottom of his hoof. The mule pulled his leg back and the partially nailed hoof ripped across my grandfather's apron. My grandfather then took his fist and hit the mule on the head and brought the mule down. "That's how tough your grandfather was," my father said.

The wagons that carried the cotton from the pier up Pocasset Street to the mills above the hill had sprockets on their wheels so that the wagon wouldn't roll down the hill, pulling the horses down the hill with them. When the wagons went up the hill, and were in low gear, you could hear the *click, click, click* of the gears.

My family was born in Ireland but my grandmother was born in England when the family moved there to work in the textile mills. They were there for five years, then moved to the United States. Someone once told her that she was English because she was born in England. She didn't like that and said, "If I was born in a barn, I wouldn't be a horse." She was a great storyteller; she had some great Pat and Mike jokes.

When my grandmother was in the Catholic Memorial Home, I walked from Wiley Street to see my her every Sunday. When I was in the Navy, I was in Ireland and was in a pub when someone was singing "Rose of Tralee." He asked if I knew "Danny Boy" and we sang and harmonized beautifully. As it turns out, I was singing with the grandson of the greatest Irish singer of his generation, John McCormick. My grandmother loved that I sang with the grandson of John McCormick. I had gotten the grandson's card, and I gave it to my grandmother; she loved it.

My grandmother was only 4 feet, 5 inches and my grandfather was 6 feet, 5 inches; they had ten kids.

On St. Patrick's Day, we had corned beef and cabbage. The McDonald's cooked up seventy-five pounds of corned beef in one year. There was always a party on St. Patrick's Day.

**School Life**

At St. Joseph's School, the nuns were very strict. My problem was that I couldn't retain anything. I can do anything; I have rewired my house and designed wings to my house, but I can't read drawings though.

In fourth grade, the sister kept me and three other guys back. We all knew it was going to happen; we acted up a lot and our marks were not what they should have been.

**Recreation and Entertainment**

After school, we changed our clothes and went to North Park to play baseball. When it began to get dark, we played "freed-a-box." This involved five players on two teams. If one guy was caught, he went in the box. Then we would hide. If you got to the box, you freed your team member. If an opposing team member tagged you in the process, you got to go in the box. We also played war. When the street lights came on, we went home.

In the winter, we skated at North Park. The best sledding in the city was on Weetamoe Street, from Highland Avenue all the way down to the cemetery. The police blocked off the side streets. Sometimes, the guys from Thirteenth Street came in with a "bowtop." A bowtop was a short sled that was steered with ice skates. When they showed up, everyone got out of the way. The sled could kill you.

There was a lot to do in the North End. There were hills, skating, the park, the river. I was a terrific swimmer. My favorite diving spot was a rock at high tide at Bliffins Beach. My mom was a championship swimmer. She swam from Sandy Beach to Bliffins Beach. Danny O'Connell's father and John Williamson were on the team. The races between the beaches were held on every Labor Day.

The cop Charlie Dougherty was as Irish as a Patty's Pig. He was at the North End Station. He would bring me home and tell my mom, "You'd better be keepin' a lock on this boy; next time, I'll be usin' the other wooden end of this stick and not the strap." Cops had a long patrol stick that they sometimes put lead in at the tip for crowd control during strikes. The stick had a strap on it so it couldn't be taken away from the cop.

We would take bobbins from the mills and throw them at the wooden fence at the train tunnel. The bobbins stuck in the wood and eventually ruined the wood. They were replaced by the city. We played handball off of the tunnel walls.

In the game of wicket, you would take six soup cans and pile them in a pyramid of three, two and, one cans, and the other team did the same. One team would take a rubber ball and try to knock over the cans. If the ball hit the cans, one of the players ran around in a circle touching the bases until the other team gets the ball.

Lower North Park is where we played baseball as kids. Our team was the St. Joseph's Midgets. One year, we beat the CYO [Catholic Youth Organization] champion team. Boy, were they mad! My brother played for the CYO team.

Some of my buddies would sunbathe on the top of the Slade's Ferry Bridge. When a ship would come up the river, and the drawbridge started opening, they dived into the channel. The sides had piers that were too close to the edge to dive over the edge. Some guys would get on top of the railing on the Brightman Street Bridge and swan dive off of it, head first.

**Work Life**

I spun copper wire for the telephone company for many years and lost all of my fingerprints as a result. I can't grip things now. I was a joiner man and cable splicer with the phone company.

In the Seabees, I was a construction electrician. I was in the Reserves and went to Vietnam in 1968-69, where I was security chief at the base. I served for thirty-seven years in the Federal service, active and inactive. When I was in the service, we went around the world. We went from England to the Arctic Circle. There were four civilians on our ship who were with special operations.

**Neighborhood Experiences**

Hayes Bakery was on the corner of North Main and Hood Streets. During the war, they made potato pies. The pies included small cubes of potatoes and gravy in a great crust. They were wonderful. There wasn't much meat during the war.

My best friend on Wiley Street was Leo Travis. His grandparents were the Cabeceiras who lived over the North Star Bakery. During the feast of the Holy Ghost, we would visit his grandmother. She was always in the parlor, all in black. We would part the beads in the doorway leading to the parlor. She always hugged all three of us. She made sweet bread with the eggs in them at Easter. She would say that the eggs in the bread were only for me: they were "Bobby's eggs."

Leo's mother would make Portuguese food for me. She would make a Portuguese roll and bake it stuffed with chourico, peppers, dressing, and other things. They were wonderful. I have never had anything quite like them since. His father, Manny, owned a 1937 Plymouth, and when he sold it, it was like new; he was the nicest man. We would go to the St. Michael's bazaar and have favas; we looked forward to it all year.

The parts of the North End were the North End, the Village, Steep Brook, and Mechanicsville. On my corner alone, we had Irish, Greek, Italian, French, Portuguese—and we all got along.

The Fourniers and Tessiers lived on Short Street, to the rear of George Street, near Davol. Lima's Market was on the northwest corner of Oregon and Cory Streets. The Lima's were a fine family; my mother traded there a lot. We liked the girls there. The Thompson family lived kitty corner from Lima's Market. There was Kenny, Billy, Jane, Eddy, and Frankie. They lived in front, and the Torres family lived in back. In 1948, I was a junior and wanted to quit school. Sgt. Grogan, an Army recruiter, said no, stay in school. He lived in a long cottage on Cory Street.

On the 4th of July, [a friend] showed up on Wiley Street with a great big bag of fireworks. There was a carbide cannon that looked like crushed coal. When it fired, it sounded like a machine gun. We had rockets and fired them right on Wiley Street. One rocket had a parachute on it that landed in a tree. I went to get it. My brother said, "Watch out; it's hot." It was. Another time, my brother brought two "salutes" home. He lit them and threw them in the street. Once he lit it and gave it to me to throw. I didn't throw it fast enough and it went off in my hand. It peeled off the skin on three fingers of my hand. My mother put the fingers in soft butter. The next day, we were going on a relative's boat and I dipped the fingers in the salt water. The salt water healed them.

One morning at 11:00 am, we heard a boom and the school building shook. A tanker at Shell Oil had exploded. One person who was on the deck was launched into the middle of the river. When they were towing the ship out and it approached the Brightman Street Bridge, we went to the bridge to see it as it passed. The ship had a big bubble in the middle of it; it had to be an explosion that occurred in the ship's hold.

At the southwest corner of Brightman and McDonald Streets, where the convenience store is now, was Leo's Ice Cream. The pistachio ice cream there was my favorite. We would leave there with our ice cream cones and go to the bridge to sit on one of the eight benches that were on the bridge. There was a cart that sold peanuts on Brightman Street outside Leo's. We would take our peanuts, eat them on the benches, and throw the peanuts on the road. The wind would blow them away. My mother would then take us walking to the Somerset side. The benches disappeared during the war, I guess for scrap for the war effort.

We knew everyone in the Wiley Street area, from Hood to Almy Streets.

The Allenson family was all over the North End. There were Allensons on the corner of Hood and Wiley Streets. Mrs. Westall lived nearby. There were "Jickies" all over [slang for English people]. One of our sayings was, "We beat the Jicks with peggy sticks, hooray for Cox's Army." Cox was an Irish fighter.

There was a Ward family in the neighborhood. Their father was a policeman. Their son, John, was killed flying a bomber over Europe. Their son, Jimmy, was a radio operator on a sub that went into Tokyo harbor. A famous story of his was when his sub went into Tokyo harbor, they put up their periscope and watched a horse race in the city.

The minister's daughter at the Park United Church would open the blinds when she undressed. The boys—and the girls—watched. She was sent away from the church.

We watched as a guy built a thirty-five-foot boat in the garage in the back of the Lima property at the northeast corner of President Avenue and North Main Street.

In the neighborhood, Mike had an Irish Wolfhound that was always getting away. The dog was so big he could put his paws on the roof of a car. After being called again on a complaint, a cop said, "This is the last time; keep your goat in the yard or I'll shoot the bastard."

My father told me that the first mail truck robbery took place in Fall River near the corner of North Main and Odd Streets, on French's Hill.

The North End trolley went all the way to Bliffins Beach and then turned around. I rode the last trolley from the North End to downtown. The trolley driver told me that it was the last ride. Then the buses took over. They ripped up all the trolley tracks for the war. Beautiful cobblestones came out too.

**Health and Illness**

For illnesses, the standard cure was gargling with lemon in lukewarm water with salt. Castor oil was used a lot and so was Father John's Medicine. There was also chicken soup, called "Jewish Penicillin."

Jimmy Mullins and my other male cousins made my grandmother's wake a real Irish wake. All of the cousins—the whole clan—were there. We said, "Let's go to Mitchell's Café." We did, and we came back drunk. My mother was scandalized. But we said, "This is what Grandmother would have done."

**The Depression**

On the corner of George and Lindsey Streets was the WPA [Works Progress Administration] store. My mother sent the kids; she didn't want to go herself. They gave you a coupon book and you tore out the pages as you purchased things there. On the shelves were brown paper bags with sugar, flour, corn meal, peas, and potatoes. While you were there, they would fill up the bags for you. We would go there frequently. They had the old-fashioned high shoes there. One time, I got shoes there and they asked me how they fit. They were too large for me. I said, "I can turn around in them three times before they move." I wore my sneakers until the rubber wore off and the canvas showed.

At Christmas, the WPA ran a show at the Empire Theatre with a Santa Claus. They gave away a bag of hard candy when you left the show. It was a good show. When Santa Claus came near us, both me and my brother recognized that it was our father. He surprised us! We were about to say, "It's Dad!" when he said, "Shush!"

Our father tried to get work as a bricklayer at a place on Borden Street. He climbed a ladder to show them how he could do it and he fell off and broke his leg. He was laid up at home; my mother was not happy. We ate a lot of soup in those days.

During the Depression, we had a neighbor with five daughters and I remember my mother bringing a large pail of soup to them. Every neighbor helped one another in those days. We had little, but it was a good, happy home.

During the Depression, the WPA were constructing concrete sidewalks. Most of the sidewalks before that were made from coal cinders from stoves. They made the sidewalks from a portable cement mixer that we played in at night. The local beat cop, Charlie Dougherty, chased us out.

The CCC [Civilian Conservation Corps] camps were in the Reservation. They cleaned that place out; there was nothing left but the trees. My mother's first cousin from New York City, Martin Melchern, worked in a CCC camp in Montana. He later became a New York State policeman. He was a handsome guy; my grandmother said that if she were younger, she would marry him.

**The Fall River Line**
In 1936, I took my first trip on a Fall River Line boat to New York City. My father got my mother free passes on the line. There was a wedding party on the boat and they were all dressed in tuxedos. One guy was drunk as a skunk. My mother was holding my hand when this guy says to a woman, "Don't worry, I'll see you on Saturday." He then got on the railing and jumped overboard and started swimming to a pier. My mom and another man started yelling, "Man overboard!" and the crew got boats into the water and brought him out and to the shore.

In 1937, there was a strike and my mother said to my father, "What are we going to do now?" He worked on a freighter for a while.

On the Fall River boats, my father introduced me to James Cagney, Paul Whitman, Mal Hallet (a band leader who was originally with Whitman), and others. A trip to the engine room was a feast. You could eat off of the engines, it was so clean. The brass was spotless. The whole ship was clean.

The stewards in the dining room were all black. Clarence Haskins was one. Later, he was a cook at the Louis Hand cafeteria. Once, I went there and asked for Clarence. He came out and was black as coal. He asked me if I was Danny Millerick's son, and I said yes. "What are you eating?" he asked. He then made me a big plate of meat and potatoes with all kinds of fixings, all for free.

There was also a steward on the boats that we called "Stick-em-up." When I was a kid in the dining room of the Fall River Line, I had a little pistol. I took the gun and poked it into a passing black waiter. The tray of food that he was carrying fell and the food flew all over the place. I didn't know what I was doing. My father was counting money at the cashier's counter and got angry at the waiter. My mother got angry at me, and I got holy hell from both of them. The next Christmas,

I got a box in the mail measuring about twelve inches by twelve inches. I opened it up and inside was a two-engine red and green airplane. The card inside said, "Have a Merry Christmas from Stick-em-up."

George Smoke cleaned the staterooms on the Fall River Line and later opened a cleaners in the city.

My father's top pay was seventeen dollars a week on the Fall River Line. The fellow who owned Connor's Travel Agency in the city was my father's boss.

The Fall River Line steamers tied up at Pier 14 and Pier 28 in New York City. The Pier 14 bar on Bedford Street in Fall River was where the black staff of the Fall River boats hung out.

I remember the smell when the paddle-wheels of the Fall River Line steamers started. It was a nice smell; it wasn't a mechanical or salt water smell; it was just nice. My wife remembers the smell also. My father was on the *Priscilla* and the *Commonwealth*. On my first trip on the boats, I slept in a stateroom with my mother. A pipe was next to my bunk that went from the floor to the ceiling. The boats left Fall River at 7:30 pm and arrived in New York at 5:30 in the morning. At 7:00 or 7:30 am, people would disembark. A row of checker cabs would be waiting for people on the pier. At 5:30 am, the boat whistle blew. The pipe next to my bed carried the whistle sound from the engine room to the stack. It was so loud that I started crying. It really scared me. My mother said, "Baby, baby, it's all right."

In New York, we would see the crew practicing life preserving in boats. There were many life preservers on all of the Fall River boats.

We would go from the boat to the train station and take the train to Jersey City, New Jersey, where my aunt and uncle lived. My uncle was Stewart Sowersby, of the family that owns the antique and auctioneering business on Durfee Street. He worked for a paint company in New Jersey and was a union organizer. My aunt worked for the Colgate Company and gave us toothbrushes and soap to bring home. We would leave Friday night and come home on Monday morning.

One of the Fall River boats was used at Pearl Harbor as a transit boat. My father knew the name of it. My brother slept on it when he was stationed there during the war.

There was a steering wheel fore and aft. The steering wheel in the aft was disengaged. When someone needed it to move the boat out, it was engaged.

**World War II**
The older guys from St. James and St. Joseph's hung out at the corner of North Main and Hood Streets. On December 5th and 6th, 1941, the corner was full of guys; on December 8th, the corner was empty. Ninety-nine percent of the guys on the corner enlisted. The same with the guys who hung out at North Main and Stewart Streets. There was patriotism everywhere.

During the war, the city would have a paper drive. We collected papers and piled them on the corner. We would go all over the place picking up papers. We brought the papers to the rail depot on Rodman Street, next to McKenzie and Winslow. We also picked up aluminum scrap for the war effort. All the young corner kids, aged thirteen and fourteen, did it.

Where Coca Cola was on Davol Street [north of the Mechanics Mill] was a scrap yard then. We had scrap drives. The guy at the yard would tell us where to throw it. They had a lot of World War I stuff, like rifles, pistols, and helmets. Some pots and pans were brand new. There was a sign there that said, "This time, not to Japan." Before the war, all our scrap iron went to Japan and came back as weapons used against our boys.

If a house had a blue star in the window, it meant that the family had a soldier in the service. If it was a gold star, it meant that a serviceman was killed in action. The stars were about twelve inches in diameter. There were blackouts during the war. When the siren went off, all lights were to go out. Street wardens enforced this and would say, "Put out that light." No lights were allowed anywhere. One day, when my friend Leo Travis broke his arm, we went by taxi to St. Anne's Hospital with Leo's mother. The doctor took Leo and his mother into the next room and left me in the dark. I was only thirteen years old and scared to be in the hospital in the dark.

Two Navy fighter planes crashed in the area. One came too close. It went spiraling out of control over Somerset and crashed into Pearce's Beach. The pilot was ejected and was okay. The other pilot went toward Assonet and crashed into a stone wall near where the Elks is now, then Allen's Orchard. The pilot was cut in half by the belts. The FBI and Naval Intelligence came to retrieve the plane's contents. Of six machine guns on the plane, only five were recovered. The other was missing from the plane. They were led to one of the Noverca boys at Steep Brook, who said that he had found a long pipe. They asked him, "Where is this pipe?" He said, "It's over there," and sure enough, it was the mission machine gun.

Another time, the engine of a B-25 bomber quit over the Taunton River. We saw it go overhead. The crew got out, and the plane crashed in Assonet.

Brad Bradberry manned a machine gun in back of a torpedo bomber. His outfit was on a carrier at Quonset and was ordered to the Pacific. Before he left, he flew over the city and waved his wings and flew between the two towers of St. Mathieu's Church. Because of this, he was restricted from flying for thirty days. As it turns out, it took thirty days to get to the Pacific. Ha!

Waste kitchen grease was used to make gunpowder or some other vital war use, so wives filled coffee cans with it, brought it to the market to be weighed, and got redemption stamps for sugar and other stuff for it. Shoes, meat, sugar, and gas were rationed.

The Brightman Street Bridge was a vital link on Route 6 between Camp Edwards on the Cape and the inland. The state National Guard guarded it at night. Once, when an Army unit was about to cross it, there was an exercise where the National Guard, who were mostly World War I veterans, stopped the Army from crossing the bridge. It was embarrassing for the Army.

When my brother had just come home from the Pacific, he had a stack of records that he had played all through the Pacific. The records were of all the popular standards of that time and he loved to play them. He put the stack of records on the bench and we hugged. I then sat down on the records and broke them. They survived the Pacific but not me.

I was in the service from 1945 to 1947 and then went into the National Guard until 1948.

## Miscellaneous Memories

Roosevelt came to Fall River I believe during the Wilkie campaign. Me and Charlie Bert went to South Park [now Kennedy Park] to see him and went up into the trees to get a better look. The Secret Service told us to get down from the trees. The Secret Service were all over the city, on roofs and everywhere. They even welded the manholes shut along the route that Roosevelt traveled in the city. Years later, when we needed to get in the manholes to do some work for the telephone company, we had to break the welds to get into the manholes.

## Popular Expressions

"Tell it to the Marines."

# John S. Mitchell

*Born on July 10, 1928*
*Died on April 7, 2013*

## Family Background

My parents were John S. Mitchell Sr. and Helen "Ellie" (O'Brien) Mitchell. I had a brother, Robert, and have a sister, Helen (Mitchell) Sullivan.

My father's parents were Sylvester and Margaret (Hurley) Mitchell. Sylvester Mitchell died in 1929. He was a foreman down at the pier. My mother's parents were Thomas Edward (1866-1950) and Bridget (O'Laughlin) O'Brien (1869-1944). The O'Brien family lived Down North at 106 Jones Street.

My father had three sisters: Bessie (Elizabeth), Mary, and Margaret. Bessie and Mary were twins—one worked at Cherry and Webb and one worked at Liggett's in the Granite Block.

My mother had eight brothers and sisters: Gertrude, Father Edward L., Agnes E., M. Madeline Sullivan (was a Yeomanette in World War I, based in Newport), Francis X., Hannah M., Julia F. O'Toole (her husband was Superintendent of Schools in Somerset for many years), and Louise T.

My brother Robert served in the Navy in the Pacific, moved to the West Coast, returned to Fall River, and started a finance business.

My younger sister Helen's husband was killed in 1954 while he was doing repairs on a telephone pole after Hurricane Carol. They had a ten-week-old boy at the time. She remarried and, after four or five kids, she went to SMU [Southeastern Massachusetts University, now UMass Dartmouth] at nights and became an ESL [English as a Second Language] teacher and then became the director of the program at Bristol Community College [in Fall River].

Our first home was on Whipple Street, then we moved to 111 Cottage Street.

My wife is Lillian (Kuzniar) Mitchell and we have four children: John R. (attorney and former mayor of Fall River), Jeffrey E., Judith A. (Mitchell) Slavinski, and June (Mitchell) Palmer.

## Family Life

My father got hurt when he was young and always walked with a limp. He loved his pipe. He brought us up because my mother died in 1941, when I was twelve years old. He had many opportunities to go to work in Newport, but he wouldn't leave us. We were all in grammar school. Our grandmother was upstairs, but she was sick in bed. Our two aunts were working. My aunt Gertie took care of my mother and took her in when she had multiple bouts of cancer. Gertie lived on Read Street and was a nurse at the City Hospital. Gertie also took my sister in a bit; I stayed with my father.

My father was an office worker on the Fall River Line until 1937. After that, he opened his insurance business office in our home on Cottage Street. He loved to go to South Park [now Kennedy Park] to watch the ballgames. He ran for state representative in 1936 but didn't get in.

My mother was a school teacher and went to Bridgewater Normal School. Aunt Gert went to nursing school. Aunt Agnes was a hygienist, and the first woman in the area to do this. Uncle

Frank was an engineer and Aunts Hannah and Julia were teachers. Uncle Edward was the chaplain for the New Bedford prison and chaplain for St. Mary's Orphanage next to the prison. He also ran the Cathedral Camp until the war. Then the camp was taken over by the Army to train the Military Police. Some of the O'Brien family worked there. I worked there the last summer before the war during a priests' retreat. Father Edward O'Brien was one of the first Irish kids in the neighborhood to go to college. The neighborhood had a torchlight parade to the train station on North Main Street when he was going off to Niagara College.

On every holiday, we went to the O'Brien's house at 106 Jones Street. My father brought his 1928 Essex Super Six car to Jones Street to be put up for the winter. They put it up on blocks and drained the radiator; there was no anti-freeze. In April, he put it back on the road. When the war came along, my father put it at Dr. O'Brien's on Ridge Street. There were few garages then. When we went to look at it, kids had gotten at it. It was built like a tank.

**Friends**

We had a club that met at the garage of Phil Clorite's house. The garage was the hideout for all of us in the neighborhood. The Clorites owned Clorite's Fruit Market, across from the Durfee Theatre. They sold fancy fruit baskets and also delivered them. Our gang included Jimmy Harrington, Dick Hurley (his father was the city's Veteran's Agent in the 1920s and 1930s), Jim Mullins, Joe Falvey, Raoul Gagnon, Johnny Cox, Billy Harrington, and Richard Bolger.

Our gang would hang around in front of Nick Mitchell's. People from St. Mary's, St. Anne's, St. Louis, and Santo Christo hung out in front of the drugstore. Some neighborhoods had junior football teams. The Flint had the Rough Riders and our neighborhood had the Ramblers.

Dick Hurley was quite a character. One night in 1945, we went out; the next morning he was gone. I found out that he had enlisted in the Navy. He didn't tell me a thing about it. He did two tours in the Navy. The next time I saw him, he was on shore patrol at the Boston Braves park. He hated the cold and then graduated from the University of Miami and lived in Florida for a while. He toured the world in the Navy and would send us Christmas cards every year. He then became a professional caddy in Florida. Then we got a card from Fort Ord and found out that he joined the Army, and stayed in for two stints. When he was young, he talked very fast, and you couldn't understand what he was saying, except me. He was a character.

**School Life**

I went to St. Mary's School all the way. I was tall for my age. A classmate of mine was a little sickly. In the seventh and eighth grades, I won the honor of giving him a piggyback from the first floor to the second floor. He was always going to the bathroom. He wore me out. They always called me to do it. The kid would pull my ears and say how nice I was to give him a lift. He was laughing all the time.

**Recreation and Entertainment**

There were not many cars then and in the winter we sledded on the city streets. The side streets were blocked off. We sledded just about every night. In the summer, my relatives worked mostly downtown, and Wednesdays were a half-day, so on Wednesdays we would go to Newport to Second Beach in my father's Essex Super Six car. We put up newspaper on the car windows and changed in the car. There were quite a few people in the car. Other times, on Saturday or Sunday, two or three family cars would go to Horseneck Beach. I would get sunburned badly and paid for it. Before the 1938 hurricane, there was not much of a public beach at Horseneck; mostly, there were private cottages there.

**Courtship and Marriage**

I met Lilla downtown, when she worked at Lord's Dress Shop. I saw her on the street and waited for her one night. We dated and that was that.

**Work Life**

When I was young, I worked at the circus grounds. I seem to remember carrying water a lot. We would run the stakes where they were going to be put. We kids would go down there early in the morning to see if they were hiring. It was tough work; they got their dollar from us. Most of the kids left early.

I worked at the Empire Theatre when they were having a lot of stage shows during and early in the war. Bill Cannon was a manager. They would have service benefits, USOs. They would sell the house out. We looked like Marine generals with our uniforms and pressed collars and fronts. I did that a year. Mike lived in the Empire. He was a watchman and would go and put out posters. He would show us the back of the stage, where the stage fronts were hollowed out. It was scary.

I also worked on the second floor of a garage on Ridge Street cracking open walnuts. The garage had a store in front that had a company that sold meat slicers. Cote stored pianos on the second floor. Cars were stored in back. We kids were nut-crackers, smashing walnuts to get the meat out. We could eat all we want, but the owner knew that we would get sick of them quickly, and he was right. The owner of the place had a business of providing walnuts to drug store counters and ice cream shops to put on sundaes and such. It was a perfect job for kids.

I also worked at Wagner Hat on Pocasset Street after high school was out. I would pack up the hats being shipped out. This was in the Darwood Mills on the top floor. They were men's straw hats for the summer, or "Sailor's Straw Hats." The machines pressed the straw around a mold and then add a band. The hats didn't take the rain too well. If they got wet, whey would flap around your ears.

I worked for a Mr. Cox, an iceman. He bought up ice trucks and stayed only in the ice business. Other ice dealers started selling oil in the winter and ice in the summer. I worked part-time for him early in the war and only the few heavy business days in the week, usually weekends. I worked for him for two summers.

I was also worked the counter at Bellefeuille's Drug Store, where Mitchell's Drug Store was later. Bellefeuille's was not so much a drug store, since they sold mostly ice cream. When there were two baseball games going in South Park, you couldn't move in the place. There were twenty-five electric frappe mixers going at the same time; it sounded like a motor boat. Hundreds of people watched the games at South Park; with the rationing of gas during the war, you couldn't go anywhere.

**Neighborhood Experiences**

One morning, my mom sent me to get a loaf of bread at the market. The fellow inside said, "John, I'll be right with you." He then went into the phone booth—and fell asleep. I left without the bread.

—*Herald News Photo*

**RAMBLERS FIND IT DIFFICULT TO GET OPPONENTS:** Most football teams have trouble beating their opponents, but the only real trouble the Ramblers have had this season is inducing teams to play them. This team, which plays its home games at the South Park, has not met defeat, and according to the boys their list of victories would be much longer if several opponents hadn't taken run-out powders after arranging games. First row, left to right—Jim Harrington (co-captain), Bob Murphy, Bill Harrington, Dick Bolger; middle—Walt Wilson, Jim Mullen, Jack Manning, Bob Flannery, Bill O'Donnell, Joe Falvey; rear—Phil Clorite, Raoul Gagnon, Jack Mitchell, Jack Hall (co-captain), Jack Cox.

In winter, the streets that were mainly plowed were bus routes. The bus company plowed them. The side streets were rarely plowed.

My father would go to the Jewish Convalescent Home on Robeson Street to help put up lights and do other errands that they couldn't do on the Jewish holy days.

**Christmas, Holidays, and Special Occasions**

We would have our own Christmas at our house, then go to the O'Brien's house [at 106 Jones Street] later in the day. Their house was full of family. There was always a present for us; our aunties were good to us.

**Religious Life**

Many kids at St. Mary's were altar boys, about thirty to forty of us. The church provided the cassocks and supplies. I got a pair of shoes from it. I was an altar boy for five or six years. I took the place of John O'Brien in carrying the crucifix down the aisle of the church because I was the tallest. St. Mary's Father Sullivan went into the service as a chaplain. Father McCarthy was a good golfer: we always knew his Mass would be short on Sundays in good weather; we always knew where he was going.

Once, after confession, the priest surprised me by asking me, "John, go down to the corner and get me a malted; here's the money." I was ten years old; I was surprised that he knew who I was.

**Nicknames**

Everybody had a nickname. Jimmy Harrington was "Haygo," Jack Mannon was "Captain Jack," Raul Gagnon was "Tubba," and Lenny called me "Splint."

**Health and Illness**

About sixth grade, I got streptococcus of the kidney and later pneumonia. My mother had just died a short time earlier. Dr. O'Brien came over the house, examined me, put me on his shoulders, carried me to his car, and brought me to St. Anne's Hospital. I tinkled black pee. One of the things I had to do to get over it was to drink lots of water. Grandmother Bridget said to me, "I will give you a nickel for every glass of water you drink." My sister was jealous of that and still reminds me of it. I was one of the first persons on sulfur drugs. Because I was in the hospital, I lost a year of school.

We didn't drink cold beverages; the old timers didn't believe in it. Even beer was warm.

Ginger brandy or whiskey were often given for ailments. When you were sick, Nick Mitchell would come up with an invention of his to cure it.

**World War II**

My father became an air raid warden during the war. I was a messenger and delivered water tanks in case we were fire bombed. I got to wear a helmet that said "Messenger" on it. We would make sure that people had their shades down. Everyone wanted to be a messenger, but my father was the warden and I got it.

# John Moriarty

*Born on September 30, 1930*

**Family Background**

I was born at 417 Bedford Street, on the third floor. A doctor delivered me and my sisters at home.

My parents were John J. and Fabiola ("Bella") (Ripeau) Moriarty. I have two sisters, Helen and Frances.

My father's parents were John W. and Eliza (Harrington) Moriarty. My mother's parents were Alphonse and Leda (Brasley) Ripeau. My mother's family was in North America for seven generations; however, she was the first generation born in the United States.

My father had one sister, Eliza (known as Lila), and my mother was an only child.

**Family Life**

My mother was born in New Hampshire when her father was working there. He was a loom fixer and worked wherever there wasn't a strike. He didn't want to get involved in strike-breaking. If a strike was coming, he would pack up the family and go to Lowell or New Hampshire or anyplace to get work. He always got work because loom fixers were always in demand.

When my parents married in the 1920s, my father's family was not happy that an Irish family was marrying into a French family. This was called a "mixed marriage." My father's family wanted him to marry an Irish girl. My mother had to be interviewed by the matriarch of the Harrington family, Aunt Nora Mitchell. She was not the oldest, but she was the matriarch. My father's parents were dead by that time. Nora Mitchell's husband, Robert or "Rob," was a captain in the fire department, stationed on Bedford Street.

Aunt Nora was a bit of a rebel herself. She married a Presbyterian ("At least he was not a Frenchman."). Nora had a house on Oak Street, which had been her mother-in-law's house. When her mother-in-law died, she moved into that house at 34 Oak Street. That area was mostly Lace-Curtain Irish, with some Shanty Irish. Robert is buried at the North Burial Ground, with the other Presbyterians, and Nora is buried at St. Patrick's Cemetery.

In the early 1900s, the Harringtons lived on Plain Street, which was an Irish neighborhood then. The Columbia Street area had mostly Shanty Irish. The Lace Curtain Irish had lace curtains in the windows and were concerned with appearances. Appearances were everything.

We ate at home all the time. We had plain food. My mother was not a fancy cook. A big event was fish and chips. There was a fish and chips place on Bedford Street, between Seventh and Eighth Streets. They wrapped the fish and chips in newspapers. Where the courthouse is now, at the northeast corner of Bedford and Rock Streets, was a Chinese restaurant. Aunt Lila would take us there for a chow mein sandwich. From the old police station to the corner of Rock Street were all stores.

I didn't know many people outside of family.

My nickname has been "Professor" all my life, even in high school.

We never ate meat on Friday. We never ate anything special during Lent. On Easter, we had eggs, but then we had eggs every Sunday.

At Christmas, we had a tree in the bay window. Our Christmas shopping occurred at Woolworth's or Newbury's. My aunt always referred to Woolworth's as E.P. Charlton's. The "real" Santa Clause was at McWhirr's, downstairs.

Back in the 1940s, we all spent a good deal of time on figuring out how to get out of the city for good. I said, "I'm never coming back to this place." Some years after my mother died, I did come back. It was such a different city. Looking back, the city that I grew up in seemed like Camelot. It was a nice place: cleaner, friendlier, and with much less crime.

**Work Life**

We didn't know we were poor because everyone was poor. We didn't think about it. We were fortunate that both our parents had jobs. My father was

John Moriarty and sister at Ocean Grove

a chauffeur in the 1920s for William J. Dunn. Billy Dunn was the richest man in town. He owned the Academy Building and several theatres. He also owned the *New Bedford Standard-Times* and the land on which the *Herald-News* building was located. He also owned the Hotel Mellen and lots of real estate in Fall River and New Bedford.

My father had to be on call when needed. Sometimes, he would get a call in the middle of the night to come pick up Dunn at his house in Portsmouth [Rhode Island]. My father kept Dunn's Lincoln limousine around the corner in a garage. Off they would go. If anyone passed them on the road, Dunn would say, "What kind of car is that? Let's get one." My mother learned how to drive in the Lincoln limo. After driving that huge car, she said, every other car felt like a toy.

Dunn started out as a junk man and, early in the 1920s, managed to get a contract to dismantle and remove textile mill machinery. They couldn't sell the machinery because it was out of date. He made a fortune in junk. He started buying everything. Every time he would buy a property, he would mortgage it to buy something else. If he wanted to buy a property, he often would not do it himself, since the price would go up, so he often used my father as a straw, including when he bought a parking lot on Third Street. When the crash came, the banks started calling in the mortgages and Dunn's empire came down. He ended his life in his own hotel, the Mellen.

Years later, I remember one of Dunn's sons coming to the house to see my father to get him to sign papers releasing his interest in a property that he had "bought" for Dunn. After working for Dunn, my father went to work for Harry Monks as the mayor's chauffeur; that was when pols had chauffeurs.

While in high school, during the summers I worked at the Willow Tree Dairy, an ice cream stand on Bedford Street, east of Twelfth Street, on a lot next to the gas station. I started there one summer and the next summer the building was moved to the Narrows and became the Carnival Drive-In. The Willow Tree Dairy moved to another building in front of the Pilgrim Mill on Pleasant Street, near where Louis Hand curtain factory was located. The building was shaped like a milk can.

One summer, for some reason, I didn't work there and, instead, worked behind the soda fountain at Letourneau's Drug Store on Pleasant Street. Dr. Letourneau was the pharmacist and was a nice man. He wrote a letter of recommendation for me to the New England Conservatory.

**Neighborhood Experiences**
My family lived at 429 Bedford Street, between Tenth and Eleventh Streets. That part of Bedford Street was a pleasant place then. The Pepperell Mills kept up their property beautifully, with a grassy area in front and a white fence around the property. Dr. Crispo lived next door at 439 Bedford Street, next to the house where I grew up. His son became a lawyer. One of his daughters, Angelina, taught at Durfee [B.M.C. Durfee High School]. E.P. Francis had owned our house. He was the owner of the Francis Bottling Company, which was around the corner on Eleventh Street. The next blocks, now decimated, had houses down Bedford Street as far as Sixth Street.

Saloons were on the corners, and we walked by them gingerly. The Golden Pheasant was on one corner and had a "Ladies Entrance." There were a couple of good grocery stores nearby, one on the corner of Bedford and Eighth Streets called Letendre and Boule's, and one on the corner of Bedford and Seventh Streets, called Grozen's Grocery Store. This is where we went shopping for groceries.

Eighth Street, between Pleasant and Bedford Streets, was a wall-to-wall tough area. It consisted of three- and four-story tenements. The kids were tough there, in a different sort of way than now, but you didn't want to get into an argument with them. You got past Eighth as quickly as possible; I never went down Eighth Street. There were lots of other kids in the neighborhood; it was a real neighborhood, except for Eighth Street. The rest of the neighborhood was not tough.

Charlie Howayeck, the grandfather of Gary Howayeck, owned a saloon on the corner of Ninth and Bedford Streets. The Howayecks lived upstairs above the barroom. Charlie was his own bouncer. He took care of problem patrons by himself. On the corner of Bedford and Seventh Street was the Black and Silver Grill. I think it later became the Pier 14. We kids would point to a window above the bar where a woman once hanged herself.

Outside of the Black and Silver Grill was a skinny colored (that's what we called black people back then) guy who sold hot dogs from a highly-polished copper cart. It was always gleaming. He was always cheerful and nice.

There were some gypsies on Bedford Street, between Seventh and Eighth Streets, but they were not there all the time.

On the corner of 417 Bedford and Tenth Streets were stores with three stories of apartments above. Around 1933 or 1934, the house next door had been subdivided and we moved there;

my mother wanted a first-floor apartment. For a while, my parents had a variety store on the southeast corner of Tenth and Bedford Streets.

Tenth Street had three junkyards. The biggest was Powell's in back of 417 Bedford Street, and it was very big. My grandfather would take me there during World War II to get manure for my Victory Garden. The yard had horses that pulled the junk wagons around the neighborhoods. The junkyard had big bailing machines. On the same side of the street, there was a smaller junkyard where my sister and I would bring balls of tin foil to sell. We would go all the way down Bedford Street, picking up empty cigarette packages. We would then peel off the foil from the interior paper and ball it up. My mother found out and had a fit. "You took those out of the gutter?" she asked.

Also on Tenth Street, there was another yard that took recycled bottles. There were piles of bottles, and I was fascinated to see the piles of bottles through the fence. People today think that recycling is a recent idea. But everything was recycled then. There was also a Shell gas station at Tenth and Bedford, on the corner.

Columbus Day was a big thing on Bedford Street in the Italian neighborhood. They had big fireworks at Columbus Park. It was something we never missed. Their fireworks were elaborate, with the ending including "picture" fireworks.

My mother said that she wouldn't be caught dead living "Up the Flint." She thought it was so déclassé. Later in life, when she moved to a new house on North Eastern Avenue, she said, "I never thought I'd be living in the Flint."

When they were tearing down the old City Hall and city government moved to the Hotel Mellen, Leo Martin was a city councilor. His wife, Ida, was a cousin of my mother. Leo was a fixture in Corky Row. They said that when it came time for Leo to attend his first city council meeting at the Mellen, he had no idea where to go and had to be picked up by a car because he had never been north of Bedford Street!

## Downtown

We would go downtown every Saturday morning. My mother would take my sister Helen and me to have blueberry muffins at the Woolworth's counter. Everyone went downtown on Saturday.

My mother had been an usherette (that's what they called them) at the Academy Theatre. All the seating was assigned and the tickets were numbered. She said that you had to learn the alphabet backward. Billy Dunn owned the theatre, and that is how my mother and father met. They married and, like many other newly-married couples, they took the Fall River Line to New York City and went on to Niagara Falls.

The Durfee Theatre was the place. The Empire also. There was the Premier Theatre on the corner of Rock and Bedford Streets, but it burned down in the fire of 1928. We also went to the Plaza Theatre on Saturday to get their dishes. I would go with my grandmother; she liked the cowboy films.

## Fall River Lore

A story about 511 Rock Street: One day, I got a call from Michael Martins about a Mrs. Mary Borden Williams who was visiting the Historical Society. She was the granddaughter of Richard B. Borden (son of the grand patriarch, Colonel Richard Borden), who bought the house from Joseph Remington in 1863. Remington built the house in 1858. I thought she might be 110 or so, but the three generations married late and had their children late.

She came to the house, and I asked her why there were so many pin-prick holes in the door frame in the butler's pantry. She said that no one went into the kitchen except the servants. The door to the kitchen was closed all of the time. This was in the 1930s, when she lived here as a little girl for two years. She said that Mrs. Borden (Mrs. Richard B. Borden) didn't go into the kitchen but left instructions for the cook and servants by tacking messages to the door frame of the butler's pantry. Charles N. Borden and his wife (the parents of Mrs. Williams) lived here at that time (c. 1934).

**The Fall River Line**

When I was about four, a friend of my mother's got married, and the newlyweds took the *Priscilla* to New York. My mother took me and my baby sister on the boat to see them off at the dock. However, she didn't hear the announcement, "All ashore that's going ashore." The boat started moving and my mother began to panic. They put us off in Newport and we took a Short Line bus back to Fall River.

**Health and Illness**

Paregoric was rubbed on babies' gums when they were teething. It was a kind of dope that numbed the gums. It is now outlawed for that purpose. For colds and other ailments, my grandmother would give us hot tea, with hot whiskey added to the tea and honey and lemon juice. Then, you would go to bed right away. It would kill anything. If you woke up alive, you were cured. Mustard plasters were another home remedy.

French wakes could be a little raucous, whether at home or at a funeral parlor. Someone would sneak booze in and there would be an occasional fist-fight. The Irish wakes were a little more subdued. We had funeral parlor directors in our family: we were related to Jeffrey Sullivan and to the directors of the Hendricks Funeral Home on South Main Street.

**School Life**

I went to Sacred Heart School on Linden Street (it was new then) for all eight grades; I then went to Durfee. There is a plaque outside of the school with the names of parishioners who went off to World War I. My father's name is on the plaque.

The priests kept tabs on everyone. Before I went to school, the priest from St. Roch's Church came to visit my mother. My parents were married at St. Roch's, which was a French church. All of the Eighth Street French kids went to St. Roch's School, which was located in the basement of the church. Half of the day the kids were taught in French and the other half in English. My mother said no, that she wanted me to grow up to be an American. I would go to an Irish school. She had ideals. The priest was not happy.

Sacred Heart School had good nuns (Holy Union Sisters) who were devoted teachers. Many had master's degrees, whereas many of the public school teachers then had two-year normal school degrees, not even bachelor's degrees.

There were cliques at Durfee. The Yankee kids kept to themselves. The Jewish kids from the "Jewish Highlands" also had their own clique. Then there were the rest of us. My friends were mostly from the music organizations.

## Friends

Larry Lesser became president of the New England Conservatory, stepped down, and, when his successor left the position after a brief term, became president again. His father was born in Fall River, and his grandparents lived on Pearl Street, in the Jewish neighborhood near the synagogue. Larry was a cellist and a protégé of Piatigorski.

Bill Seymour lived in Fall River as a youngster and later became president of the Boston Conservatory. His father was a minister at the Primitive Methodist Church, on Plymouth Avenue. Bill is a graduate of Durfee High and was a freshman at Durfee in 1947-48 when I was a senior. It is remarkable that two leaders of these music institutions had their roots in Fall River.

Janet Parker and I were on the debate team. Phil Jamoulis and David DeLaura were on the other team. We went through all of the stages together. In the finals, it was their team against ours. The subject was, "Should the Communist Party be legalized in the U.S.?" We had the positive and they had the negative. The judge was Rev. Lester Hall. Fr. Hall was a curate at Sacred Heart parish. We lost. Because of the topic, it was stacked against us. This was in 1947, just before the McCarthy scare. Janet and I worked hard on it. I thought that my Sacred Heart connection would work for me, but it didn't.

While I was doing my research for the debate, I contacted the Communist Party for information. However, I kept getting mail from them, and my father had a fit. At that time, he worked for the Navy and was afraid that someone would find out about the mail and he would lose his job.

Janet and I were the two top seniors at Durfee in 1948. I was the top and Janet was second. Janet edited the school paper for two years and later went to law school.

## Music

My memory of Angus Bailey is my performance debut at the age of four, when I performed in the Academy Building on WSAR [radio]. I was standing on a table to reach the microphone, singing, "How Much is that Doggie in the Window?"

I started to learn to play the piano when I was ten years old, in 1940. I took to it quickly. I had private lessons at the convent that was across the street here [from 511 Rock Street] when the Holy Union Sisters owned the Flint mansion. Our music teacher would send some of her better students to social clubs to play for the members, and it was good performance experience. Our teacher, Sr. Stephen Mary, a nun, was a graduate of the New England Conservatory and a really good teacher. I never had to unlearn what she taught me. She was an organizer, and formed an orchestra of nuns. She raised the funds to build a music building at the Sacred Hearts Academy at the top of Linden Street, near Prospect Street.

When I was in high school, I formed a dance band called The Stardusters. We played at weddings, anniversaries, everything. We played in every hall in this town—the Lusitano, on Pleasant Street, the Moose Hall, on South Main Street, the Eagles' Hall, off of High Street, the Sons of Italy Hall, on Cove Street, and the hall in the basement of the Royal Theatre, on Brightman Street. I started the band in 1947 and continued it until 1950 or 1951. When I went to the NEC [New England Conservatory], I would come down on weekends to teach kids piano and play in the band in the evenings. Ron Lowenstein and his brother Eliot were pupils of mine, as was Beverly Padelford (Doctor Padelford's daughter), the Poirier twins from County Street, and Mike Strickman (son of Leo and Marge Strickman). At the end of the evening, after playing a dance job,

July 13, 1947, The Stardusters.
*L to R*: Ray Hogveira, Joseph Mendona, John Moriarty, and Ed Soares

we would let off steam by going to Mark You's Restaurant to have a chow mein sandwich, or to Fa-Neek's to have a hot dog. My father always waited up for me. "Why are you so late?" he would ask, and I would reply, "We had to go for a chow mein sandwich."

Phil Jamoulis was also in high school with me. He had an orchestra he called Swing and Sway with Philip J.

One of my high school years, when I rode the bus to the NEC for piano lessons, Rose Sullivan also rode the bus. Her husband, Jeffrey Sullivan, an undertaker, had died, and she was going to school in Boston to get an embalmer's license. We would sit on the bus together, doing our homework. Her son, Jeff Sullivan, is a distant cousin.

Durfee at that time was still a very good school. It had good, devoted teachers. Helen Ladd was the music teacher and a New England Conservatory graduate. She was a dynamo. When I first went to Durfee, I approached Miss Ladd and said that I wanted to be in the orchestra. She said that the orchestra had no piano position, but then she asked me, "How about learning the double bass?" Victoria Eisenberg gave me free lessons in double bass. Ladd got Francis Findlay down from NEC to teach a class.

The Durfee orchestra was first class. We went to music festivals and always took first place. We played difficult works by Hayden and Beethoven. Helen Ladd had standards. She didn't help only me; she helped anyone who she thought might have potential.

Bernard Chebot was a Durfee student under Ladd who went on to the Julliard. A cellist from Durfee named Virginia Mello went on to the New York Philharmonic. Joe Raposo was another one of her kids. He came after me. He attended Durfee after I graduated. Helen Ladd also mentored Bill Seymour, who later became president of the Boston Conservatory.

Helen Ladd started a string program in the grammar schools as a way to get kids playing the violin. Eventually, she would have some of them switch to viola or cello. This provided her with a steady influx of musicians for her high school orchestra. She had so many violins that she had a real string section.

She also started boys' glee clubs (the girls could take care of themselves, she said). Every grammar school had a glee club. This got the boys to stay in music as their voices changed. During class time, I would go out with her to the grammar schools. By high school, she had a full mixed chorus. During my junior and senior years, I played for the rehearsals of the glee clubs. They had their final concerts at the Durfee Theatre.

Helen Ladd led rather than pushed. She was a devoted teacher without being "devoted." She just did it. She would take me and a fellow student to Boston for concerts. She brought me up to NEC to audition for one of the top piano teachers there, on her own time! And he accepted me.

I entered the New England Conservatory as a music major with the intention of teaching in the public schools. However, after one semester, I switched to a Performance Major in piano. I graduated at the top of my class and was awarded the Chadwick Medal, the biggest undergraduate award. I stayed on for a year, treading water. I was officially in the masters program and did coaching of singers in Boston.

At the end of the year, a friend of mine told me that Brandeis was going to be opening a graduate school of music. I went to the university and met Irving Fine, who was to be head of the graduate school. He said, "We're not set up for a performance major, but we do need someone to play the piano," and he set up a course for me. I was living in Boston at the time and, toward the end of the year, I was informed that I was awarded the Frank Huntington Beebe Award for European Study, which would allow me to study in Europe for a year.

I went to Europe to spend half of the year in Italy and half of the year in Paris. I studied piano in Italy and in Paris studied French vocal music with Pierre Bernac, the great recitalist. Toward the end of the year, as the award money ran out, I heard that there was an opening in the NEC faculty for a vocal coach. I wrote the president to apply for it, got the position and returned to NEC. This was in 1955.

In 1961, I left NEC and went to Santa Fe to become the Artistic Administrator of the Santa Fe Opera, where I had been working during the summers since 1959. In 1965, I left the Santa Fe Opera and returned to NEC.

In 1973, I went to the Boston Conservatory to form an opera department there. It was so successful that the NEC joined it. It was one joint opera department for the two schools.

In 1989, NEC wanted its own opera department, so I went back to NEC to become head of the new department.

The Central City Opera in Colorado was once famous, from the 1930s to the 1960s. Its theatre was built in 1878 by Welsh miners. Central City in the nineteenth century was a gold mining

Miss Helen Ladd, Class Day, June 15, 1948

town that had recovered the surface gold and then had to go underground to mine for more gold. Welsh and Cornish miners were brought in to do deep-rock mining after all the surface gold had been gathered. The Welsh and Cornish are avid music lovers and singers and built the stone opera house.

In the 1970s, the Central City Opera fell on hard times. The board of the Opera Association, mostly from Denver, asked me to come to revitalize the company. I said yes if they had good on-site year-round management, as I did not want to leave my position in Boston. The company was in bad shape, but I brought it back. It took three years. I needed someone to assist me with secretarial duties related to the opera. I looked all over and finally found a retired nun across the [Rock] street who was a great secretary. I have traveled to Central City for many years; this year will be my last, as I am retiring as head of the opera festival.

# Diamantina "Diane" Motta

*Born on April 26, 1929*
*Died on June 5, 2011*

**Family Background**

My parents were Manuel ("M & M") and Diamantina (Barboza) Motta.

My father's parents were Augustino and Elvira Motta. My mother's parents were Frank and Theresa (Vincent) Barboza.

My father's siblings were Olive, Estrella, Hilda (called Eva), Freddy, and John.

My mother's siblings were Virginia, Manuel (called Bob), Richard, Mary, Joseph, and Gilda (who was a twin; the other twin died).

I have three sisters—Dorothy ("Dotty"), Donarta ("Doris"), and Dolores ("Curly").

**Family Life**

We lived on the second floor of a two-family cottage at 23 George Street, one house up from Davol Street. It was owned by our mother's parents.

Grandfather Motta was a tall man and very straight. He worked as a bartender at a bar in Swansea [Massachusetts], where they lived.

Grandfather Barboza was a sweetheart. When he visited, he would show us a dime and say, "If you put this dime in the dirt, it will grow to be a quarter next week." It never missed. He made us believe it. He would watch where we dug in the dime and then put a quarter there. He didn't like to dress up. He loved his overalls and always wore a floppy old hat.

I never saw Grandmother Barboza without a clean starched dress and apron. She did all the cooking for the farm hands. She got up at 5:00 am to cook for them and the family. She cooked three meals every day.

She hated that she didn't stay in school to read and write, but she didn't want to wait to leave Portugal. My grandmother's mother in Portugal seems to have had some money, and was better off than most. My mother and aunt Virginia cleaned my grandmother's house.

All of the Barbozas had curly hair, including the boys. My mother had naturally curly hair, and she went to a black woman who had a shop on Bedford Street and knew how to cut curly hair. The Barbozas also had either blue or hazel eyes. My grandmother's eyes were blue and my grandfather's were hazel. My grandmother's eyes would turn purple when she was angry. Uncle Richard was quiet; he was no ladies man. He had auburn hair, blue eyes, and light skin.

My grandmother went to Portugal by ship every year. She brought a trunk full of clothes. She would cut the tags off of new clothes to avoid customs duties. I would go with her to the travel agent on Bay Street to get her tickets and to do customs slips.

We would all go up to Boston to see her off. We stayed until the ship was this small [showing fingers separated by an inch]. I was my grandmother's pet; she dressed me up. I could have gone to Portugal with her every summer if I wanted to go, but I could never leave my mother.

On Sundays, we went to the farm, called Hillside Farm, in Assonet to have dinner. My grandmother cooked two roasting pans full with meat or chicken. An uncle would come in a convertible to bring us to the farm or our grandfather would pick us up. We never left the farm hungry. If we were good, there was an ice cream man that came to the farm in a horse and buggy. All the kids would come running to get their ice cream. My grandmother paid for all of it.

The tables downstairs in the basement, where daily meals were served, had oilcloth on them instead of tablecloths. Chourico was kept in lard in big ceramic crocks and stored with a lid in the basement back room. Ivy grew on the ceiling of the basement room.

My grandmother was also very artistic. She would make paper flowers and arrangements. She would also put a small hole in egg shells and drain out the eggs, including the whole yolks, and used the eggs later. I'll never know how she did that. She then painted the egg shells and put wire in them and made arrangements in pots with them, like a flower arrangement. She also took dried corks and put them on a string and hung them on doorways. Her doorways upstairs were decorated with pretty hanging beadwork that she made.

She said that the wealthy women in Portugal wore long black capes with hoods when they went out. The hoods were deep, so you couldn't see the faces of the women. That way, a woman could stay hidden if she didn't want to recognize you or she didn't want to be seen. If she wanted you to see her, she would open the hood. White capes were worn by girls under the age of eighteen. My grandmother would say, "If you're bad, I'm calling the *vaya de capra*," the old lady with the cape.

Sometimes Curly and I would go with my grandfather or uncles to the Boston farmer's market. We would get up at 3:00 am and ride in the back of the truck with the tomatoes and other vegetables that they were delivering. Curly was twenty-two pounds and I was twenty-three pounds. My grandfather made everything fun. He was not much of a driver; he was more comfortable driving a horse and buggy. When we would stop, he would buy us candy. "Buy that candy," he would say, "It's more money and it's better." When he said that in front of my grandmother, she showed that she didn't like that very much.

Men liked my grandmother and would look her over. I would tell her that a man nearby was checking her out, and she would say to me, "Come here," and she would pinch my fingers. She hurt!

Every fall, the family had to go to the farm to kill and dress pigs. It smelled awful. I couldn't stand it. They would cut the heads off the pigs. Everyone wore bandannas, like gypsies, so their hair wouldn't get into the meat. My grandmother washed the guts so clean as if she was going to wear them. Doctor Mason bought a pig each year from my grandmother and had her prepare the meat: roasts, chops, etc.

There were three cottages near the entrance to the farm. They were for farm hands or visiting family members. They had no water or electricity. The men had to get a pot of water at the house and bring it back and put it in a tub to wash in the morning. My grandmother would go make and change the beds. Some of the farm workers my grandparents brought from Portugal, and they had free room and board. They had to pay back my grandparents what they owed them by working on the farm.

We had a big tub to take baths in. We warmed up the water on the stove. We partially filled the tub in the sink, then put it on the floor and completed filling it fully using a dish pan. The filled tub was heavy, and it took two people to empty it. We washed up in the narrow pantry. A cloth was put over the entrance to the pantry when people were washing.

Aunt Virginia lived downstairs. She worked in the sewing shops, which was difficult work. She was a good sister and helped a lot. During the war, the sewing shop where she worked didn't operate, but the mills were working. She would take care of us and helped us with making food such as stews and beans for both the kids and mom. When she moved to Westport, Dotty moved in downstairs.

Our chores were emptying wastebaskets, cleaning the stairs, and making our beds. We didn't leave dirty dishes. Dotty and Doris had the hardest work. When my father called for us from the pantry window, we had to answer the third time when he called.

Many people came to the street or door to sell things, mostly Jews. My mother traded from a Jew who sold blankets, spreads, and things like that. Every Jew who traded in the North End spoke Portuguese.

One Jew was named Melisa because he had one eye closed. His nephew was called Barney, who sold clothing door to door; his wife was pretty and nice and had a store on the [northeast] corner of North Main and Hood Streets.

**Friends**

I took piano lessons from the father of Joe Raposo of *Sesame Street*. Curly took violin lessons from him. I once told Lorraine, "Want to see me play the piano?" and I pretended to play our player piano. At one point, Lorraine said, "I think I see keys moving that you aren't playing." I think Mr. Raposo lived in the North End, but we went downtown for the lessons. He had an upstairs studio downtown.

Up George Street lived Alice Nunes. She and I walked to school together. We were not afraid to walk the streets.

**Food and Meals**

On Fridays, we always had fish. My mother fried flatfish, served with hot pepper rings and hot bread, from Silvia's North Star Bakery next door.

For breakfast, my father would go to the baker on Brightman Street for cinnamon buns. He loved sweets. I would come home for lunch with Curly from the Borden School.

For a snack, my father would have milk crackers or butter thins with milk, or else cut-up white bread with milk and sugar over it; he had ulcers. We always had plenty of food at home.

Every Thursday, my grandmother made white cheese and Portuguese boule or bread and would have it brought to us. She was very generous.

**School Life**

My father would never send us to Catholic schools, only public. We went to the Borden School in North Park. Miss Burns was our first grade teacher. She had "finger waves" in her hair, which was the fashion then.

During the week, we went home for lunch. On Fridays, we bought our lunch. We bought our tickets at school. I still remember those red tickets. They were red and five cents each. If you bought fifteen cents worth, you gave them three red tickets. If it rained, my father got a cab for us and as many kids as it could fit.

### Recreation and Entertainment

My father played the big bass drum for the Republican Club marching band and played in parades. My father loved parades. The drum ended up in the attic. [The Republican Club was a Portuguese club honoring the revolution in Portugal].

We jumped rope, played marbles, and played with cut-out dolls taken from cut-up books. We played in the yard or could go to other's yards. We were the only girls with sleds in the area. We went to North Park to slide and to skate and went to Lincoln Park to roller skate.

Dotty played the accordion, Doris played the cymbals, I played the piano, and Curly played the violin. We all took lessons.

### Work Life

My mother worked in the mills all her life, first in the Sagamore Mills, then in the Foster Mill until it closed. Mom's lunch was always two squares (raisin, fig or lemon, she liked them all) and a quart of milk. She walked to and from work. Later, my friend Andy picked her up every day at 11:00 pm for ten years.

The mills were hot, and she would put a dress in a bag and change from her street clothes to her work dress and then change back again after work. She shook out her work dress when she got home. When she ended her shift, she looked like a ghost, she was so covered with cotton. She was very particular about her appearance and always looked well-dressed.

My father worked as a bartender. My father was proud to be an American and couldn't stand the Portuguese. He hated that they spoke Portuguese.

When my father came home from work, my mother would have a few peeled hard-boiled eggs waiting for him and a glass of milk and a few scoops of ice cream.

My first job was working as a waitress at sixteen years old at the Granite Block Spa for Mr. Konas, a Greek. Most of the people who worked there were Greek, except for three waitresses.

### Neighborhood Experiences

North Star Bakery was next door (on the east) to our house at 23 George Street. Fresh bread was baked there every day; the smell was wonderful. There was always a line out the door on Sunday mornings. Joe Silvia owned the bakery; he was wonderful. His three sons helped him operate the bakery. The Silvias lived in the back of the bakery on the first floor. Long-term tenants lived on the second floor. Two old maids and their mother lived on the third floor. One of the daughters was married when she was advanced in age.

We were very friendly with the Vincents, who lived across the street. Lorraine's husband, Moe, was a decent person. He was one hundred percent Irish but spoke Portuguese so well. He worked at the St. Michael's Credit Union on North Main Street. The Dupres, who were French, lived in the next yard, in back.

Every week, my father would drop off the grocery list to the Red and White Market on Lindsey Street. They charged a quarter to deliver the groceries. Henry Baldier delivered them. He was friendly and a hot ticket. He would make you laugh. He was very skinny. On one cold day, he was frozen and said, "Look at me; I'm blue."

One day he said, "Someday, I'm going to get a real job." We said, "Why? Marry an old lady." And he said, "Oh, please."

The fish man would come down the street on Fridays, yelling, "Peche!" Vegetables such as corn and string beans were also sold from trucks. Women knew them and would open their windows and talk with them and tell them what they wanted.

The Wilkinson Gas Station was at the [northeast] corner of Davol and George Streets. A father and his two sons operated it. Then the Carvalhos took it over; they were nice people. It was an Amoco station.

There was a pool parlor on the [northeast] corner of George Street and Leonard Street. Freddy Lima hung out there. He loved to sing the song "Cherry Berry Bee." Lots of guys hung out there. Fonseca owned the house next to it; he had lots of daughters.

There was a cobbler called "Corky" on George Street, near the tracks. The newspaper had a write-up about him later. No one could do my father's shoes but Corky. My father always wore spats, gloves, and a derby hat. He was very particular about his appearance. He had gray, tan, and black spats. They went over the shoe and under the pants.

**Christmas, Holidays, and Special Occasions**
My grandmother made holidays very happy. The whole family came. She kept the family together. She did things the right way. Christmas on the farm was the prettiest sight you could see. My grandmother had three big trees on the first floor, all decorated. She had gifts for everybody. She would have a doll or some other toy that we liked. There were a lot of grandkids by then.

During Christmas, the Portuguese would go door to door playing guitars and singing. The people in the house would open the door and offer them a drink. They would then go to another house.

At Easter, my grandmother made us Easter baskets. They would include a toy, marshmallow eggs, colored eggs, marshmallow bunnies, and things like that. She even made the small baskets. My mother continued with the baskets.

**Religious Life**
My grandmother was very religious; we would go to church to light candles and pray. My grandmother was very generous. For her own soul, she sent money to the Azores to pay for dressing a girl and boy for First Holy Communion. It was a tradition for people to donate money to pay for dressing poor children for their First Communion.

**Health and Illness**
Little Bobby died of diphtheria when he was four years old. I remember his little white coffin. My grandfather Barboza was behind a tree at the cemetery crying his heart out. That was his love. Bobby is buried at Notre Dame Cemetery.

If we had a cold, my mother would put water in a saucepan, add the juice of a lemon, sugar, and plain brandy, and heated it. A shot of that and you slept all night. For a sore throat, she would rub our throats with Vicks and wrap our necks with rags or a hand towel.

Curly was a finicky eater. My mother told the story of when Curly was sick with some vitamin deficiency and Dr. Lewis recommended to my mother that she give Curly tomato juice to cure her. My mother wasn't familiar with canned tomato juice and instead squeezed tomatoes and had Curly drink it. Later, when the doctor asked if Curly was drinking tomato juice, she explained how she prepared it. The doctor was surprised and said, "Well, if she is drinking it, keep doing it."

Dr. Lewis had a long neck. Once, he told Curly that he would cut her belly open and take out the pennies. My father was angry and called him "that hawk with the long neck." Curly was my father's favorite and loved to show her off.

**Hurricane of 1938**

During the 1938 hurricane, I ran all the way home from the Borden School, with Curly in back of me. Curly fell, and I had to backtrack and pick her up. We made it home, but trees were coming down everywhere.

**World War II**

When Pearl Harbor was announced, my grandmother wanted to go to St. Anne's Hospital to see baby Freddy and Doris. We were going to see Doris first, then the baby. Freddy was born two days before Pearl Harbor.

Albert [Dotty's husband] got drafted during the war. Dotty went to live at the Vincent's house across the street on the first floor. Dotty had Bobby in "the block" [a wooden row housing structure] a few houses up George Street.

Silk stockings were rationed during the war, but my mother never went without. My father would give out free shots and, when he came home, would take bags of nylons from here and here [either side of his chest] and here [his pants]. My mother never ran out of them. He would tell my mother, "Don't give any to her [me] until she cuts the claws [my nails]."

**Popular Expressions**

"Hubba, hubba, ding ding, you've got everything."

# James Mullins

*Born on November 24, 1928*

## Family Background

I was born in our house on Sixteenth Street.

My parents were James E. (born in 1892) and Annie (Wetherall) Mullins.

My father's parents were John Mullins, who arrived in the United States in the 1880s, and Mary (Connelly) Mullins. Her family moved from Ireland to Liverpool and then to Manchester to work in the cotton mills in England.

Our family came from Port Láirge (Waterford), in southeastern Ireland.

My mother's father left his wife, Catherine (Collins) Wetherall, for a young woman and moved to Taunton, Massachusetts.

My father's siblings were Catherine Millerick, Margaret Hill, Helen Murray, Thomas, and Peter (who died in World War I of influenza in 1918, at the training station in Newport, Rhode Island).

I had five sisters who lived into adulthood: Catherine M. Ryan, Eileen M. Sutherland, Anna Mullins, Ruth M. Mosley, and Claire Mullins.

My wife is Virginia (Pacheco) Mullins.

## Family Life

My grandfather, John Mullins, was a dynamiter and worked in the quarry when he first came here. He then went to work at the gas company on Bay Street, then to the city's Street Department, handling a shovel. The city wanted City Hall to be clear of snow so people could come in to conduct their business. He lived on Jencks Street in the Flint and, when it snowed at night, walked downtown with his shovel to clean the sidewalks. He cleaned the sidewalk, then walked back to his house to start work the next day.

My grandfather Mullins was a big man and was known as Big Jack. He had the "Irish virus." He wouldn't drink for three months, then saved his money and went on a bender for thirty days. He would be totally out of it during that time.

People call me Jim or Jimmy. When I was in the Navy, I was called Moon Mullins, after the comic strip of that name. The southern servicemen thought that was my real name, since they were not familiar with the comic strip.

I had six sisters. One died when she was three or four years old when she pulled a pan of hot water down from the stove and scalded herself and died. My parents never got over it. Later, doctors told my parents that if that had happened later she could have been saved. My sister Anna died in 1950. She was a nurse who was to be married in October but died in July of leukemia. She was buried in her wedding dress. Claire, my youngest sister, was a nurse at St. Anne's Hospital and became the Assistant Lead Nurse there. A few years ago, we heard Barney Frank speak at the Fall River Public Library, and he mentioned that there was a shortage of nurses locally, yet many persons couldn't afford to go to Bristol Community College's nursing school. I took twenty-five thousand dollars out of Claire's estate that she left to me and formed the Mullins Family Nursing Scholarship in her memory.

All my sisters took piano lessons, and while they did, I memorized the lessons and the music. My father played the piano. Every night, we would gather around our piano and sing. We knew all of the World War I songs, including songs from the 1890s that my father's family knew. I am self-taught on the piano and now know about a thousand old twentieth century songs by ear. I own a few hundred books on twentieth century music and musicians.

Coal was brought into the house by chute, but on Whipple Street, coal had to be brought in by men with canvas bags on their backs. It sometimes took all morning to bring in the coal. We had central heating, but there was only one radiator upstairs in the hallway; there were no radiators in the bedrooms.

From Sixteenth Street, we moved to 298 Third Street, across the street from St. Mary's School and next to Remy the Mover.

From Third Street, we moved to Farnham Street for five or six years, to a two-decker. My mother was concerned that my father was too tempted by the three bars between City Hall and our house. She thought that my father would avoid the temptation by taking the bus at City Hall to Farnham Street. From there, I walked to my job on Hathaway Street on the Taunton River.

Then Mike Breen was selling his house at the northeastern corner of Eastern Avenue and New Boston Road. A real estate agent told my parents about it and they bought it and they, my sister Claire and I moved in.

**Food and Meals**

In winter, we ate Oatmeal for breakfast. In the summer, we had cornflakes, or corn puffs, etc. When we got weevils in our corn flakes, mom wouldn't throw it out but just scooped the weevils out of the bowl. On weekends, we would have bacon and eggs and toast or pancakes or waffles. We would have coca and milk with it. We would have fish on Fridays or Campbell's vegetable soup. There was an excellent fish and chips place on Morgan Street. On Saturdays, we had franks and beans. Sundays, we had a roast or ham, with pea soup on Monday or Tuesday made from the ham. Other meals were hamburger or baked sausage.

**School Life**

Even though I went to school across the street at St. Mary's, I was late every day.

There was no phone in the school, so the nuns would send a kid over to use the phone when they needed to call someone.

The nuns would whack us across the face if we did something. They knew that if we went home and complained to our parents, we would get another whack and they would ask, "What did you do to the sister?"

In grammar school, we had confessions every week; since I didn't have anything worth confessing, I usually had to make something up.

For many families, if you were big enough you were taken out of school and went into the mills. Someone would tell a parent, "He's big enough; he could be earning fifty cents a week as a sweeper."

I was the senior class president of Durfee [B.M.C. Durfee High School] in 1946. That was a big deal since I was a tech student and only students in the regular program at Durfee became class presidents. Someone asked me to run in my freshman year, but a teacher advised my not to do it yet. However, I was asked again to run in my senior year, and I won the election. The teachers were furious.

**Recreation and Entertainment**

We would go to Lannigan's Beach on the bus or down to Island Park [Cashman's Park, Portsmouth, Rhode Island] to swim. Before the war, I went to Watuppa Pond to fish with my father. We played pickup ball or would go to Portsmouth to roller skate. Church groups would hire a bus to bring a group to Portsmouth. We mostly played games in the neighborhood, like red rover, basketball, or baseball—or we would play roller hockey on Cottage Street, where there were few cars.

We played dodge ball, hide and go seek, and roller-skated. We had to stay close to home. The WPA [Works Progress Administration] put in new sidewalks on Hamlet Street that were smoother than what we had in our area, so we went there: it was great for roller-skating. We played roller hockey on Cottage Street between Whipple and Second Streets. In the winter, we would slide from Whipple to Cottage, past Ridge to South Main Street. If there was a lot of snow and we got a good head of steam, we could cross South Main Street and go down Division Street or Hunter Street. My sisters would go skating at South Park [now Kennedy Park].

Across from our house on Second Street was the Reed Garage. They spray painted cars there, and kids would come in when they were spray painting. We would breath the spray paint in and come out of the garage and spit out the color they were painting the car, yellow or green or whatever. We got a big kick out of it.

We played at the St. Mary's School playground or at South Park. I played with the CYO [Catholic Youth Organization] basketball team in 1942. During games, we would push our opponents up against the hot steam pipes that lined the wall and burnt their asses. My grandkids now play in the same CYO court that I played in years ago. The heat pipes are covered now.

Father Thompson and Father McCarthy coached the teams at St. Mary's. Fr. McCarthy didn't want us hitting tennis balls against walls since it would hurt our arms for baseball. We played two-handed football in St. Mary's schoolyard, which was surrounded by an iron fence and had a surface of rocks and gravel. Black Mac. That's what we called Father McCarthy at St. Mary's. He was a dark Irish.

We also played in the Davenport School yard at Fourth and Branch Streets. One of my earliest recollections was the school burning. My father looked out of the backyard doorway and said, "The suns coming up from the wrong direction." I ran to the area and a cop was clearing people away. However, I hid in a doorway of a barbershop, and he didn't see me, and I was able to see the fire.

During my high school days, we hung around The Nonpareil with five or six guys; we would go to Lincoln Park or the Roseland Ballroom in Taunton. The problem with Roseland is that, if you met a girl from East Providence or North Quincy, you would have a problem meeting the girl again since no one had a car.

We would also go to Urban's Polish Picnic up on Stafford Road. Luke Urban's brother owned it. There were two buildings there, one with a bar.

Davenport School on 118 Branch Street, corner of Fourth Street

**Courtship and Marriage**

The families of my mother and father lived in the Flint. They met in school. The first time my father saw my mother, he threw a snowball at her; she said it was a rock. He became a chief in the Navy in World War I. He was called a "Kaiser Man," which is what they called men who got promoted during the war. He left from the Boston Navy Yard and spent most of his time during the war in the tropics. He and my mom were married during World War I.

I met my wife at Lincoln Park dancing. I knew her brother and went to high school with him.

**Work Life**

From 1909 to 1922, my father was in the Navy. He was the last enlisted man to go into the reserves. He got a call in 1940 to go back into the Navy. "How can they call you now; you are older with kids," my mother told him. In 1940, he went back into the Navy until 1945. He was stationed in Cuba and went around Central America to places like Nicaragua.

My father was assistant City Auditor before World War II. When he got out of the Navy after another stint in the war, there was another person doing the job, even though he was a vet and the job should have been reserved for him. He took the Civil Service exam and ended up taking the Treasurer's job in 1945-46. The Treasurer-Collector positions were combined in those days. He retired in the 1960s. There were no computers in those days; it was all done by pencil and paper. I remember him bringing home reams of paper on weekends to go over. He got fifty dollars extra to do the city's budget; imagine!

He ran the office like a ship. The city had a poll tax then of two dollars. If you didn't pay it in time, it went up to five dollars, then to seven dollars and fifty cents. One guy came in one day and started making a loud fuss and complaining about the tax and said he wouldn't pay it. The sheriff was in the building and my father said, "Sheriff, put the cuffs on this son of a bitch." The guy backed off and said, "Wait a minute; I'll pay it."

After I got out of the Navy, someone referred me to a job opening at the electric company. I got an interview, and the person there asked if I knew anything about switchboards. I thought he was talking about telephone switchboards and told him I could handle one. However, it was a switching station that sent power to various substations in the city. I worked my way up, became an officer in the union and, twelve years later, became a supervisor. Becoming a supervisor within such a short time was unheard of, but my superior died unexpectedly one day while he was home for lunch, and I was next in line for the job. I went from maintenance to electrical operations and became supervisor of maintenance and testing. They needed someone to do the testing, and I did it. I became in charge of the maintenance department. I started at sixteen dollars a week and ended making over a thousand dollars a week when I retired in 1999.

Getting a job then depended on who you knew, your religion and the associations that you belonged to; when going for a job, you were told, "Be sure to wear a Knights of Columbus button."

**Neighborhood Experiences**
There were mostly Irish and Portuguese on Sixteenth Street. The first Portuguese policeman in the city was from the Ponce family on Sixteenth Street.

We then moved to Second Street. The City Barn was on Morgan Street, between Second and Whipple Streets, where the O'Brien elderly apartments are now. There was a big administration building in the middle of the lot and compartments were they kept horses and street materials. It also included a blacksmith or welding shop. Our house on Second Street was two houses up the hill on Second Street on the same side as the barn.

We kids could see the blacksmith at work inside the shop. When my wagon yolk broke, my father said to ask for Mr. Moxie Monroe. He would fix it. He did; he welded the yoke on my wagon. Kids could bring in roller skates and he would repair them.

In the middle of the yard was the building where the foreman was located. Depending on the foreman on duty, kids could come in and play in the yard. About halfway up the Second Street wooden fence was a stack of sewer manholes, with ladder rungs inside them. We kids would play submarine inside, with the engine room below and the submarine "lookout" at the top of the manhole.

When we kids came back from school, we would stop by the City Barn and look in the big windows that were three of four feet off of the ground. We would hang off of the windows to see the blacksmith. We would watch him work the bellows, with its big fire, as he hammered away at the horseshoes, with sparks flying. The blacksmith had on a leather apron and was bare from the waist up.

In early 1936 or 1937, my family moved into a cottage at the corner of Second and Branch Streets, next to the Corky Row Club. Next door, there was a Chinese laundry. Mr. Hawthorne lived next door; he was the manager of the Shell Oil terminal. At the corner of Third and Branch Streets lived the O'Loughlans, who owned a variety store there. Minnie O'Loughlan was a big woman and when she died, and after the wake, they couldn't get her coffin down the stairs from the third floor. So they brought in a rig and took out a window and lowered her coffin to the street with a rig. It was a big event in the neighborhood.

Diagonally across from the Corky Row Club was DePaola's cobbler shop, and later an Italian restaurant. At the corner of Second and Branch Streets was Dr. Lowney's office. The French convent was up the hill, and two houses up from the convent was Frank Duffy of Duffy's Drugstore. Ed Monarch was our mailman. The Gallery sisters lived up the street. Their father, Admiral Gallery, was honored for capturing a German submarine in World War II. Corky Row then was a semi-affluent middle class area.

The nuns from St. Mary's School would walk the school kids in a line past our house. The nuns would later say that they knew how old I was by my height because I looked out the window at the line of nuns and kids going by.

Mr. Vautrin was a carpenter and had five sons and five daughters. He always wore overalls and a cap. My father always wore a suit and a tie. They lived across the street from us. At 110 Whipple Street, next to the Vautrins, was a three-decker where Fire Chief Holmes lived. Next to him was Charlie Connors, a crippled carpenter who worked in his back yard and did his carpentry work from his wheelchair.

Opposite the City Yard's blacksmith shop was Freddy Burns' gas station, with two pumps. Next to that was Jack Brady's electrical shop, with cables and trucks. O'Rourke's Funeral Home was on the corner of Second and Cottage Streets. A second-hand store was next to it, followed by three-tenements until the City Yard. L and B Market, owned by the Monarch family, was across the street from the funeral home.

The Nagles lived up on Second Street. Bob Nagle became the Superintendent of Schools. His sisters were teachers. His brother Hillard was a customs inspector in Boston. On Whipple Street lived Terrance Lomax, a lawyer and city councilor. He was one of the most prominent persons in the neighborhood.

Up the street from 110 Whipple was the Diskin family. Grandfather Diskin was a Civil War veteran. He had a full white beard but with brown around his mouth from tobacco. One of the Diskins was a salesman at Bessie Russell, a men's clothing store on Main Street. He was called "The Duke" because he was always dressed up. Judge Hanify lived in the next house.

Next door on Whipple Street was Dr. Rubinstein. The Bolger family was next; they had three brothers: Richard, Eddy, and George. Richard went into real estate, Eddy became an electrical engineer, and George became a lawyer. In the back yard next to the Hoyles were the Lowneys. They had the only car in the neighborhood. Later, in the 1930s and 1940s, we had one.

On the corner of Whipple and Cottage Streets was a police call box. Policemen had a route and a beat. If the police headquarters wanted to get in touch with a patrolman, the blue light on the top of the box would blink. Sometimes, the cop would lift kids up to speak into the phone. The cop at the other end of the phone would say, "Who is this? Get the patrolman on the line." The kids would say, "We want Santa Claus."

The cops lived in the neighborhood and knew everyone. If you went outside your neighborhood, a cop would ask you who you were and where you lived. If you said you were going to your aunt's house, he would ask, "What's the name of your aunt? Where does she live?" When I was a kid, I didn't go beyond Cottage Street. When we kids would climb apple trees and shake them for apples, the neighbors would call the cops.

The Deaconess Home was on Whipple Street and backed up on Second Street. French nuns lived in back of the home. Deaconess Home was a place where single girls could live when they were away from their families.

There were some characters in the neighborhood. Every Saturday, a drunk would walk up Second Street, alternating one foot in the gutter and one foot on the sidewalk. There was a grandmother who went out and picked up the fresh horse manure with her bare hands to use in her rose garden. One man, who lived at Whipple and Cottage Streets, walked his Irish Wolfhound dog on a leash. When kids passed the dog, he would put slack the leash, and the dog would lunge at the kids. Danny Harrigan was the local gay guy who wore green pants and a lavender shirt and a pork pie hat. He was known as "Mr. Rainbow."

One of the big things that happened in the neighborhood was when all the neighbors came out when the milkman changed tires from iron to rubber wheels. We couldn't hear the milkman coming any longer. The horses knew the stops along the route. When the milkman got off the wagon, the horse would go to the next stop. However, when old horses were bought from the Fire Department, the horses would take off on the milkmen when they heard the fire trucks go by.

The knife sharpener had a grimy, dirty wagon. It looked spooky, and we stayed away on the curb from him.

In those days, we got mail twice a day and the stamps cost only a penny.

The police came to the door every year to take the census. When a policeman came to the house, it could mean trouble, so when a cop came in the yard, the saying was, "He better be taking the census."

Champagne's Bakery on Fourth Street made wonderful beans on Saturday; there were lines around the block to get them. They made great cream puffs too. Across the street from the bakery was the British Club, where the old timers sat on the porch drinking their pints of beer. We Irish would walk by and give them the finger.

On the 4th of July, there was an annual bonfire at the corner of Third and Branch Streets, outside the Corky Row Club. Adults and kids would bring debris, fences, and all kinds of stuff and piled it in the street and set it on fire. Some kids even took a boat from someone's yard and brought it to the bonfire and burned it. It's crazy, when you think of all of the wooden buildings in the area. When the cops and firemen came to put out the fire, we all booed them.

There was a whole group of men who came out of World War II who went into the Civil Service: cops, firemen, postal workers.

One of the stories that was passed around is the time the city took down the statue of Lafayette at Lafayette Park. The mayor had a beef with a person who lived across the street, and when they put the statue back, they reversed it so that the ass of Lafayette's horse was facing the guy's house.

Dr. Griffin lived at Spring and Third Streets.

John Collias, the brother of Attorney Peter Collias, became a courier for the US State Department. He would fly all over the world with a bag handcuffed to him. He would take the bag to England, then they would tell him to go to Paris, then from Paris to Ankara, Turkey, one after the other.

There were bookies all over the place, including cops. Charlie Arruda, a cop, owned a big car and always had a blond on his arm; he was a bookie. Cops walked the beat; there were no cop cars until the 1930s. Cops wore slickers.

My father made small amounts of beer. Once, he put the beer in back of the piano to ferment. One of the corks popped and the beer went all over the floor. My mother was furious.

You could get a prescription for a pint of brandy for medicinal purposes if the druggist knew you. But only for "medicinal" purposes.

There bootleggers all over Fall River, especially among the Portuguese and French, who made wine and beer. The Portuguese also made cachaça, or moonshine. The rule was that you never bought moonshine from someone that you didn't know; it could kill you. You had to be careful about moonshine in those days and know who made it. Lead from the barrel's parts could leak into the moonshine and poison you.

A group of drunks hung out at Bigberry. There were some shacks there and they called it "Bum's Park." Once, in the 1940s, they drank a gallon of anti-freeze after straining it. One man came back the next morning looking for more and found all five dead.

**Christmas, Holidays, and Special Occasions**

At Christmas, our aunt put up a stocking for each of us. The stockings included animal crackers and a fifty-cent piece in the toe. One year, I got a cardboard fort with toy soldiers and artillery. We mostly got clothes, socks, shirts, and pants.

At Halloween, we would put soap on windows and ring doorbells and would go trick or treating.

**Religious Life**

The parish priest also came to take the church's census. He would ask, "Who has marriage plans? Is anyone going with a Protestant?" In first and second grade, the nuns would tell us, "Don't go with a Protestant because you might marry them and have a mixed marriage." There was a famous doctor in the city, and the nuns sang his praises and then said, "Too bad, he's a Protestant and going to hell." When Protestants went by St. Mary's School, they would taunt us and the nuns would have to close the shades.

Once, when I went to confession, the confession box opened and it was Father _____, with booze on his breath. He said, "Jimmy, go to the corner and get me a *Record*. I want to check the races." Bishop Cassidy wouldn't allow liquor in the rectory.

**Health and Illness**

When my father arrived at the Fall River train station on North Main Street following World War I, his sisters were at the train station. He asked how they knew he was coming home, and they told him that they were actually waiting for the coffin of his younger brother Peter. Peter's body was on the same train as my father.

The obituary page in the newspaper was called "The Irish Sports Page." Wakes were held in the home. It was the custom to have someone stay with the body all night so it wouldn't be alone. There would be food and drink. When my parents saw the obituary of someone, they would say, "They came to ours, so we should go to theirs."

When I was young, they treated an earache by taking a small bottle, filling it with hot water, and wrapping a flannel cloth around it. Then you held it to your ear.

One old remedy that my father told of was, in case of a leg cut, to take cobwebs from under the sink and put them on the wound. It sounds like a good way to get an infection. Poultices were also used. Phisicks were popular and prunes to keep your system going. For colds, the drug stores carried Creo-Turpin, which had a high alcohol content. It burned as it went down. It was taken

St. Mary's schoolyard gang, c. 1941
*Standing, L to R:* Billy Whipp, John Russell, "Boody" Kennedy, Donald Griffin, Leonard Smith, "Buddy" Lingard
*Seated, L to R:* Tommy Comiskey, Jimmy Mullins

two or three times a day. Drunks would drink it when they couldn't get liquor. Milk of Magnesia was used as a laxative. Applesauce and dry toast were taken to cure diarrhea.

Only in emergencies did a doctor come to a house. People were afraid of doctors. The saying went, "First the doctor, then the priest."

Grandmother Mary was one of the first patients at the Catholic Memorial Home. My father would visit her and slip a pint of brandy under her pillow. Once, she got hit by a bus outside of St. Joseph's Church, but she was okay. My mother was in an Eastern Mass Street Railway bus once when it got into an accident and she was thrown forward and hit the cash box. The company kept after her to sign a waiver, but she didn't want to bother anyone and wouldn't sign, even after many visits by the company representatives.

## The Depression

Once, my father put up an NRA [National Reconstruction Act] sign on our window in the front room. That was before the Supreme Court overturned it. The WPA [Works Progress Administration] was great; it gave tradesmen a chance to work at least a few days a week. To get a day job in the WPA, you had to be at South Park at 6:00 am to catch the truck. It was an open-bed truck that went to Camp Devens. If it rained, you got wet; if it was snowing, you got snowed on. Mary Sullivan and Peggy O'Brien taught kids singing and dancing at the Borden School on Morgan Street.

Every evening at 5:00 pm, the nuns at the French convent brought out a pot of steaming soup and loaves of bread for the poor. Around Fourth, Fifth, and John Streets lived poorer people. I remember a little girl walking by with her father on a cold day with a dress on and no coat. People would walk down the street with a container of soup and a loaf of bread under their arm. My father would tell me, "This is what happens when you don't go to school." My father and mother didn't want me to work in the mills. They wanted us to graduate from high school, get a diploma, and get a civil service job. That was their idea of success.

## Hurricane of 1938

Before the 1938 hurricane, St. Mary's schoolyard had monstrous trees all around the block. They all came down during the hurricane. Kids played on the downed trees. Plate glass windows blew out and our lights were out for several days. The National Guard was stationed downtown to prevent looting. Orders were to shoot looters on sight. We didn't have any damage to our house, but the windows were rattling. We gathered in the kitchen away from the front windows and ate by candlelight for a few nights.

## Nicknames

Some of the nicknames in the neighborhood were: Hannah the Man (a masculine woman in the neighborhood); Mertie the Dog; Dinny the Bow (a watchman on the Fall River Line); Mike and Dan the Broom (street sweepers); Handsome Dan (Austin Sullivan's father); and Drunken Tim. Imagine how bad a drinker you had to be in an Irish neighborhood to get this name.

It was common for a father in Ireland to go to America, where he would send money for the wife and kids. Sometimes, though, they never heard from him again. However, on occasion, the wife and kids would show up on his doorstep.

## Irish Sayings

My mother had a saying for those persons who go to church but are hypocrites and don't follow the Church's teachings. She would say, "The nearer to the altar, the further from God." When someone was visiting and you wanted to be a little discreet when you asked if they wanted a shot of whiskey, you would say, "Would you like a 'drop of the creature?'" A saying for women of suspect morals was, "She was no better than she should have been."

# Robert G. Nolan

*Born in 1931*

**Family Background**

I was born in New Jersey.

My parents were George and Margaret (Tolan) Nolan (both born in County Claire, Ireland). My father's parents were George and Bertha Nolan.

I have a brother named John ("Jack"), born in 1939.

My wife is Nancy Nolan.

**Family Life**

At one point, we lived at 58 Branch Street and paid a dollar and seventy-five cents a week in rent. Across the street, at 61 Branch Street, the rent was twenty-five cents cheaper for a similar apartment. So, my father, mother, and me moved across the street to 61 Branch Street on the first floor, where the Corky Row Club is today, but then it was a tenement house.

My father was an iron-worker and rigger and had difficulty finding work in the city; they were living on the margins in the 1930s. So, the whole family of Nolans moved to Newark and the New York area. I was born when they were living in New Jersey. My father worked on bridges as a rigger or any work he could get. In 1933, there was no more work in New York or New Jersey, so most of the family came back to Fall River.

When we returned here from New Jersey, there was no construction here. My father was short and stocky. He was approached by a rigger and asked, "Are you looking for work?" He started working as a rigger and worked during the Depression in different places. In World War II, he worked in Rhode Island at the Seabee base. He was active in the Iron Workers' union. He worked putting up electrical towers at the Montaup Power Plant and worked on the Braga Bridge.

My father died at the age of fifty-eight. He had a sixth grade education and was one of eight kids. He was the oldest. He may not have had an education, but he knew his way around blueprints. I'd come home with my high school report card and he'd look at it. Then he'd say something like, "Say something to me in Algebra." Wise guy!

We didn't know where poor people lived. The tenements was were everybody lived. It was the way things were. I didn't know until years later that we were in dire straits.

Corky Row was the best example of a non-biological extended family in the world in this way: It was every parent's responsibility to see that every kid in the neighborhood was in the straight and narrow. An extended family in the best sense of the word. There was a sense that every family took care of every other family. Children respected that and them. It could have been an ethnic thing, an Irish thing, maybe. Protecting us against the world. Or, it was the right thing to do. But, it was true for all of the ethnic kids. The policeman on the beat sent the kids home if they were acting up or it was late.

Most of us were paperboys. We would collect on Saturday morning and deliver in the afternoon. Once, when I was delivering my papers, a lady asked me to come into the apartment and said, "Hey Bobby, take care of the baby while I go to the store."

They were all characters and jokers. A guy named Herby was always in trouble with the police, petty stuff. As a joke once, we yelled out, "Hey, there's a cop," and we all started running with Herby down six blocks. At that point, Herby stopped. "What's the matter, Herby?" we asked. He said, "I didn't do anything today."

Parents then whacked their kids; today, they would be arrested for abuse.

We owned a tenement house on Fourth Street and one night, when I was coming out of Midnight Mass, a friend came up to me and said, "There's a fire up there." We walked up the street and then I realized it was my house. Smoke was coming out of the house. "Where's Jack?" I asked. One of the members of the Griffin family had grabbed Jack (my younger brother) and brought him to their house at the corner of Fourth and Branch Street. My father told me, "Go down to the Griffins and get Jack." When I got there, he didn't want to leave and said, "No, I want to stay with the Griffins."

## Neighborhood Experiences

Next door to 61 Branch Street was Booth's Market, on the corner of Branch and Third Streets, where the Corky Row Club is now. Third and Branch was my stomping ground. I was there before there was a Corky Row Club. We would hang out on the corner and look into the market as they were cutting meat for sale.

Champagne's Bakery had fabulous pastry. Their beans were to die for. Every Saturday, there would be a line up to the bakery. Joe Champagne was in my father's generation.

Horses delivered ice and milk and picked up rags in the neighborhood. Horses pulled wagons. There was a weight attached to the harness of the horse's head. When the driver got off to deliver ice or milk, he took the weight off of the wagon and put it on the ground so the horse wouldn't move. The kids would pick up the weight and put it on the wagon and give the horse a whack. Then we'd confess to Fr. McCarthy.

The horses left droppings; you had to watch where you walked.

The neighborhood was very multi-ethnic; it wasn't just Irish. At the Davenport School, down Branch Street on the corner of Second Street, was Mr. Wong's Laundry. The next house was the Litos' house. Mr. Litos was prosperous. He owned Royal Distributors on Pleasant Street. They spoke Greek in the house. At Third and Branch, on the left side, was Mr. DePaola's Cobbler Shop. He spoke Italian; I could hear it. On the south side of Third and Branch was O'Loughlans' Variety Store. Mr. O'Loughlan spoke English with Gaelic tones. So, within a block, there were the sounds of Chinese, Greek, Italian, and Irish.

Next to our house, the next garage over, lived Manny Soares. His wife knew no English. At Fourth and Branch, on the north side, was a store owned by Tabbit Mousa, who was Lebanese. He spoke Arabic and English. At the Davenport School, on the next corner on the west side, was Lambert's Variety Store. He was Mayor Lambert's grandfather. He spoke French. On the opposite corner was Iwansky's Market, still in operation today as Jarek's Market. Polish was spoken there. Across the street was a Jewish tailor; Hebrew was spoken there. There was Vailliancourt the barber. It was a melting pot, but everything worked well.

The name Corky Row came from four houses that were built on Branch Street, where "the Corks" lived. The houses were built by the Holland family, who were from County Cork.

The position of president of the Corky Row Club has been held by persons with various nationalities.

**School Life**

I went to the Bishop Stang Day Nursery and Kindergarten, which was located to the rear of the Lizzie Borden house. Then I went to St. Mary's School. I learned for two reasons: not to disappoint my parents and not to incur the wrath of the nuns.

**Religious Life**

There was a sense of responsibility instilled by my family and the church. We were expected to work as soon as we could. It was the Depression. You were just chipping in. I set up pins in a bowling alley.

Paul Solomon and Pat Lowney were best friends in Corky Row. Paul was Jewish. When Pat Lowney was serving as an altar boy at St. Mary's, he would bring Paul with him to Mass, and Paul got familiar with the ritual. One day, Pat's fellow altar boy didn't show. When that happened, usually a boy in the church would substitute. Pat said to the priest, "Father, my friend can serve." Paul put on the cassock and he served the Mass with Pat. He knew all the responses because he was in the church so often. People in the church said, "Isn't that Paul Solomon?"

**Recreation and Entertainment**

We weren't allowed to sit in the house. We had to go out and play. We kept moving. I learned how to play baseball, peggy ball, boxing. You were expected to be playing and active.

St. Mary's had a baseball team and a football team. There was also a barroom softball team. Mitchell's Café had a softball team. Liberty Café had a team. Crowley's Café had a baseball team. There was the CYO [Catholic Youth Organization] league and the Boys Club league. The Corky Row had a football team. We played football all over the city. Bob Nagle was a referee. George Belanger was a captain of the football team. We later had our sand lot football teams.

The City Barn [at Second and Morgan Streets] was our playground. We jumped in the sand piles. The horse barn was there in the 1930s.

We would go to the Plaza to see cowboys on Saturday. It was on South Main Street, opposite Morgan Street. Kids had to check their toy guns at the counter. The show was ten cents on Saturday. Roy Rogers and Trigger and the Three Stooges were regular shows. We had a few cents for candy. We were in heaven.

*Additional materials:* Two volumes titled *Corky Row, 1936-1986*, available in the Fall River Public Library, prepared by Mr. Nolan and several others. The Addendum to the two volumes was provided at the interview.

# Mary Novo

*Born on November 19, 1944*

**Family Background**

I was born on São Miguel Island, Azores, to Manuel F. and Helena O. Amaral, and came to Fall River at the age of seven.

My dad, Manuel, was born in Fall River, Massachusetts, on August 17, 1917. He had a brother named Alipio Amaral, who was also born in Fall River. My grandmother was widowed. During the Great Depression she went back to her country (Azores) with her two sons. My dad was nine; my uncle was seven.

My dad married Helena in the Azores on January 15, 1939. My brother Manuel was born December 4, 1939, my sister Mary was born April 12, 1941, then my sister Marcelina was born December 20, 1942.

My sister Mary died in the Azores while walking with my mom in the street. There were no cars then, just bulls pulling carts. The bull charged after my sister because she had a red dress on. Mary didn't die right away, but passed away due to internal hemorrhaging. Then I was born and they named me Mary Helen. Then my brother Joaquim was born July 20, 1948.

So in 1950, my dad came to America by himself, to put up home on Flint Street, thanks to Manuel Rogers from the Rogers funeral home that sponsored us all to come to the United States, and to Edward Farhinas, that lent the money for the airfare.

My husband is Joseph Novo and we have three children: Joseph III, Manuel ("Manny"), and Carrie Marie.

**Family Life**

In 1951, we all joined my dad in Fall River. My Mom was thirty-four, Manuel was twelve, Marcelina was nine, I was seven, and Joaquim was three. We arrived in Boston on December 25, 1951, Christmas day. It was freezing and we had no coats to wear. We went to Flint Street to live. We didn't stay too long in one house. We moved to 385 Alden Street. We lived over a poolroom, where the owner had only one arm.

Then we moved to Everett Street. I loved that house. We had a mountain where we played all day with sleds, and making igloos and snowmen with the snow. Then finally, we moved to 552 Alden Street, where the landlord asked my parents to buy the house without putting any money down, just collect the rents and give it to him to be deducted from the mortgage.

We wanted to go to school, but didn't have any boots or coats, so St. Vincent de Paul [charity] bought us all coats, boots, and food—for which we are all grateful.

My mom had lace curtains that she stretched on what was called cool frames. The curtains were stretched on nails located along the frames. Me and my sister had to stretch the curtains on the frame after my mother washed them.

## Health and Illness

Mint tea was used to cure everything. Portuguese soup included mint for the Holy Ghost Feast. My mom, when she came down with pneumonia, was kept in an oxygen tank. Dr. Resnick gave penicillin to my mom to get her out of her pneumonia, and it worked. This was in the early 1950s when penicillin was new.

## Food and Meals

Every year we would kill a pig to help feed the family for the winter months. We would go out to a farm, pick a pig, and tag it, for which we would feed it corn for the next three months (to clean out and tenderize the meat). In the fall (October or November), when the weather got colder, the men would get up very early and go to the farm to kill the pig.

The night before the pig killing, the women worked hard preparing: peeling onions, washing the intestines from a cow with oranges, then turning the intestines inside-out under running water.

It would take six men to hold it down. One man would stab it and drain out its blood before the blood coagulated, then rush the blood to the house. This blood was used to make morcella, a (spiced pork-blood sausage).

On the day of the slaughter, they brought the pig home, hung it in the cellar, opened it up to cool down the meat, then cut it all into big pieces, skinned it, marinaded the meat for chourico and *torresmos*—crispy fried pork rinds, much savored as snacks, were made from pork fat preserved in salt (salt pork), which was traditionally fried to render the lard—salted all the bones, and kept the lard to cook. The chourico was sent out to be smoked.

We used a funnel to fill the cow intestines to make chourico sausage. We kept pushing it down until it was full. My mom would separate the meat in casings and prick the casing with a pin so the air would slide out, and then it was over-tied with a string. After all this was done, it was all sent to a man to be smoked. In those days we didn't think of freezers, so when the chourico came home it was put in a big crock and layered with the lard from the pig.

My mom would buy old chickens and we would have to pluck them in warm water. She used them in soup. What a smell! My mom would take the feet of the chickens and burn off the feathers on the feet by putting them over the gas burner. I hated that smell; it was awful.

## Neighborhood Experiences

Manuel Rogers Funeral Home on North Main Street sponsored all of the Portuguese immigrants to come over from Portugal. Edward Farinha Agency on Eastern Avenue lent the money for the immigrants to come over and told them to pay in the long run. Mr. Cruz's grocery store on Alden Street would let you feed your family and told them to pay when they could.

Father Resendes was the pastor of the Espirito Santo Church and was greatly devoted to the parish. As a student in Espirito Santo School, I remember going with the nuns to Lincoln Park. Mary Fonseca's mother, Mrs. Leit, had a store at the bottom of Webster Street and Alden Street. My mother would go buy curtains, bedspreads, all things for the house and would pay a dollar down and a dollar every week. Ross Jewelry on Pleasant Street is where I would buy dishes or a guitar there and pay a dollar down and a dollar a week.

**School Life**

Although I was seven years old, I went to kindergarten. I had a lovely teacher named Miss Mary Cabral, who was an angel. School tuition was twenty-five cents and the nuns knew we had no money. For all four of us, it cost a dollar, so they didn't even ask us to pay.

I remember my school years with the nuns. They were very strict, but at the end of the school year, they would bring us to Lincoln Park [North Dartmouth, Massachusetts]. We didn't have any money for the rides, so they gave us tokens and told us to go on the rides. That was fun. I didn't like the big roller-coaster. This school means so much to me. My dad and mother-in-law went to this school.

**Religious Life**

The pastor at Espirito Santo Church was Father Manuel Travassos. He died shortly before Christmas. I remember him being laid out in the middle of the church on December 20, 1953, on my sister's birthday. Then Father John Resendes became pastor; very strict, but his sermons were sincere and heartfelt. He loved to sing a lot.

The week of the Feast of the Holy Spirit, my dad would dye sawdust all bright colors and put up flags all around the properties. On the morning of the Feast, all the family would get together, put the wooden frames down in the middle of the street, then fill in the frames with the bight colored sawdust, which formed beautiful designs. In the border of the design, we would mix fresh mint and lilacs, so a wonderful fragrance.

On the porches, we hung our best bedspreads as a sign of respect and great admiration for the Feast of the Holy Spirit. My husband, Joseph Novo, and I were the last ones to be married in Espirito Santo Church on September 7, 1963.

# Valentine Samuel Palmer Jr.

*Born on November 27, 1921*
*Died on March 30, 2011*

### Family Background

My parents were Valentine Samuel and Nellie (Ashworth) Palmer. My siblings are/were James, William, Murial, and Florence, who died in the scarlet fever epidemic.

I was the fifth Valentine in a row; however, when an earlier Valentine was being christened, the baby was making a fuss and an aunt became flustered and told the minister a different middle name from Samuel.

My wife is Margaret Mary (Howe) Palmer. We have four children: Russell, Brian, Kevin, and Janet.

Wilbur, in his *First Families of Little Compton*, says that the Palmer family came over in 1620 on the *Ann*, the ship that came after the *Mayflower*.

### Family Life

I was born on the corner of Diman Street and Bradford Avenue, directly across from South Park [now Kennedy Park], where the cannon is located. We lived there until I was six. I went to the Longfellow School. From there, we moved to McCloskey Street (in the low twenties; the second house in from the corner on the left-hand side) and then to Westport [Massachusetts], at the Greenwood Park until fifth grade. We then went back to Fall River and lived off of County Street, at 14 Clayton Street, near the Narrows. From there, we got caught up in an epidemic of scarlet fever.

Then we moved to the corner of Whipple and Cottage Streets, in a place that was infested with bedbugs. They were all over the place; my poor mother did her best to clean the place up. Then we moved to Park Street, next to the Dominican Academy. There, I went to the Osborn School on Osborne Street. From there, we moved to 50 Bradford Avenue (where we lived on the second floor and attic), where I went to school at a school on Williams Street for the seventh and eighth grades. From there, we moved to 50 Globe Street, on the first floor. The Globe Street house was off of Bay Street, right after a side street.

My father was an auto mechanic and had a drinking problem. Many people owed him money. When the fire of 1928 burned Pomfret's Bakery, someone asked the owner what he was going to do with the baking equipment in the bakery, which was damaged in the fire. This person said, "I'll take it off of your hands." Pomfret sold it for pennies on the dollar. The owner sold the equipment for scrap, which included bread mixers, conveyors, and other baking equipment. My father got down there and worked on the equipment and got it all working again. My father was well-known around town.

My father was the best mechanic in the city. When he was about to go work at an auto dealership on President Avenue, Dan Dennis of the Packard Agency was angry because his clients were threatening to go with my father.

Osborn School at 160 Osborn Street

When I came back from the service, my wife and I moved to 149 Tecumseh Street, on the second floor. We had one bedroom, her mother had the other, and her sister the other. Her oldest brother was in the Navy. Later, we moved to 43 Tecumseh Street, where all my wife's relations lived, next to a grocery store.

**Food and Meals**
I had Quaker Oats and cream of wheat for breakfast. We never used butter as a regular spread all my life. We got into margarine. The margarine looked like a brick of lard. It was pure white. It came with a capsule that you had to open and mix with the brick of margarine. This made it yellow and masked the fact that it was margarine. If dad got some red dye in his margarine, he was unhappy. My job was to mash and mix the dye into the soft margarine. The first capsules were liquid, then later a powder. As a consequence, the only place that I got butter was someplace else.

Mom made big meals like oxtail soup in big pans. She would put in potatoes, carrots, turnips, and the oxtail and let it cook. The vegetables disintegrated and the result was fourteen quarts of food for the family. It was good!

We had blue enamel pans that I mixed bread in. I mixed flour, yeast, and powered milk to make one pound of bread. I bought yeast at a bakery shop on Stafford Road, across from the fire station. The yeast came in a big block. I mixed it and put in the bed with an electric blanket over it. When it rose, I beat it down and put it back in bed. This method resulted in halving the time it took for the bread to rise. Then I put the dough in bread pans and made fifteen loaves of bread. Whenever I make bread, my oldest son arrives the next day, even when no one tells him about it.

There was a market on the northwest corner of Columbia and South Main Streets. Mom would say, "We need meats," and then would say, "Take this two dollar bill and give the manager the bill and he will know what to do." "What will I buy with it?" I asked. She just said, "Go for a walk down South Main Street," and I did. In about an hour, I came back and got a large bag of groceries. It was guaranteed that there would be a large ox tail in the bag. It would go a long way.

I loved "Long-John" donuts, which were long donuts that had cream and jelly on the top. I would walk down to Pomfret's and they would hand me a Long-John as I walked in.

**School Life**

In high school, I read constantly. At one point, I was told by the librarian, "Sorry, Mr. Palmer, but you can't take out any more books. We don't consider it proper for a fellow to take out books just to impress the girls." I had three books with me that I had for two days. I told her to take one of the books, open it, and tell me the page and the first sentence. I told her what the rest of the chapter was and what it was all about. I would take books into the bathroom to read.

I read lots of Zane Grey. The teacher said to me, "No more Zane Grey for book reports." So I submitted a report on the book *Hopalong Cassidy and the Bar 20 Cowboy*. I told her, "Ma'am, you said no more Zane Grey, not no more westerns." I gave a book report on *The Trail of the Lonesome Pine*; I can't remember the name of the author. [*Editors note*: the author was John Fox Jr.]

**Recreation and Entertainment**

We played peggy ball, which required a flat board with a depression on one end of the top of the board to hold the ball and, on the bottom side, a stick attached to the board to act as a fulcrum. Whoever hit the ball had to declare how far it was away in yards. I was the jumper, since I had long legs. If you had long legs and you could jump over the ball, you won fifteen cents a jump. In those days, there was so much to do.

When we lived on Bradford Avenue, I had to walk to Durfee High School [B.M.C. Durfee High School]. We could get into trouble easily through gimmicks. We would take rubber bands and paper clips and snap them at the girl's bottoms to get their attention.

We were members of St. John's Episcopal Church on Middle Street, which was part of a large basketball league. I played basketball all over the city. At one point, the doctor told me that I had to quit two teams or end up in the hospital. I was playing for five or six teams at the time. On the northeast corner of South Main and Rodman Streets, there was a gym on one of the upper floors and we played basketball there.

I was the president of the Scarab Society. A scarab is an Egyptian beetle that self-perpetuates itself. The group was for kids fourteen to eighteen years old in the church. We played pool on the pool table in the basement and billiards. We made money by selling tickets to the roller skating rink in Portsmouth [Rhode Island]. They ran buses once a week from the city to the rink. We got ten cents for every passenger and we would get full bus-loads. I got in free to roller skate. We alternated selling tickets with St. Stephen's Church on South Main Street, near Penn Street. If they had a bazaar, we went to it and they came to ours.

We spent hours and hours ice skating on the South Park pond. When I was about sixteen years old, we hung around South Park near St. John's Church. The church had two bowling alleys. I would set pins when the church had bazaars. I would get two cents a string. The pins came up from the bottom of the floor.

We kids would horse around in South Park and be noisy. The policeman would come by and walk around us and hold his billy club in his hand and whack me in the butt. He would then say, "Okay, Palmer, get these kids out of here." Imagine a cop hitting a kid today?

I got invited to leave the choir. I had joined to get close to the girls. I went to a few choir rehearsals and, on the third, went to my locker and there was nothing in the locker. The choirmaster told me, "No hard feelings, Mr. Palmer, but it's the consensus of opinion that your voice doesn't quite blend with the choir." My mother said, "You can't carry a tune in a bucket."

At 50 Bradford Avenue, there was a window facing the park in the attic. We would go up with a spotlight and hit the button and the light would go on. When lovers would come into the park, we would wait until there was some mugging going on (or maybe sex) and put the spot on and then off. They would panic and wouldn't know where the light was coming from. One day, dad was coming home and saw us. He came to the attic and that was the end of it.

I learned how to ski at South Park. We would ski from Bradford Avenue to Middle Street, where the swimming pool is now. I spent hours in the park.

I am one of the many kids who tried to move Rolling Rock. We cleaned out underneath the rock and used sticks to pry it. There must have been thousands of kids who tried to move it down County Street.

**Neighborhood Experiences**

Frank Mercier had a cottage on Main Road in Tiverton. He bought turkeys for Thanksgiving from an outfit that was up on Slade Street. They had a big barn there. They would take the turkeys down to his place, hang them up by the feet, and reach in the beak to cut the blood vessels. If you killed them this way, it loosened the feathers. If you cut their heads off, the feathers would be difficult to get out. His cellar was three feet deep in turkey feathers.

There was a Kosher meat house on Ferry Street. If the turkeys were to be kosher, they had to go there to be killed and cleaned and plucked. Then, they gave them back to us with the Kosher label on them. On each leg was a tag with the name of the person who paid for them.

**Courtship and Marriage**

I met my wife when I worked at Firestone. She assembled the aircraft gas tanks. There were three guys and ten to twelve girls on each shift. I was the boss. She had just finished assembling a tank and signed her name on it. "Do you sign everything you do?" I asked. "I'm proud of everything that I do, so why don't you just get lost?" I went to my buddy and asked, "Who is the brunette?" I told him what happened. "Stay away from my girls," he said. She worked for him.

Two weeks later, she came over and sat next to me when I was doing an inventory. She started playing with my hand. I said, "What's going on here?" "Nothing," she said, "I just thought I'd come over to talk. Do you want to talk to me?" I was flustered and got red. When I found out she was playing games, I made a date with her. She lived on Tecumseh Street. We stopped for a malt after a movie at the Durfee Theatre.

Moxie the cabbie at City Hall Cab was waiting at the gate for me one night, as he always did. "I've got a date," I told him. "Okay, Fanny Farmers or Tecumseh Street?" he would ask, "Which is it?" When I got to her place, she had taken off.

When I punched in at 5:00 the next day, I saw her and said hi, but she walked right by me. She was icicles. I realized that the date was for the previous day, and I forgot about it. I didn't realize it. She punches in and looks at my card and sees that I had punched in at 2:00 am. "Where were you last night?" she asked. "O hell, we had a date last night." I explained that someone from Akron showed up last night and I had to be here. We didn't start off on the best foot.

**Work Life**

Frank Mercier had a grocery store next to Nick's Hot Dogs on South Main Street. His father was a chauffeur for E.P. Charlton. I got paid to deliver groceries at the store. Once, I lost a two-dollar bill in the area and I searched for hours trying to find it; it was my week's wages.

I was working by then in the River Mills off of Bay Street, near the Globe Mills. There was a pond nearby that froze in the winter. Since I worked the night shift and didn't want to wake my family by coming home in the early morning, I brought my skates to work and skated on the pond after work until I was ready to go home. From there, I went to Firestone Rubber and worked there for more than thirty years.

When I worked at Firestone, I was a supervisor in charge and worked two shifts. I got sixty-four cents an hour, which was big money then. We made aircraft gas tanks that came in two sections. This was to avoid having gas slosh around and cause destabilizing movement in airplanes. Each tank was about three feet long and they came in three sections. The tanks had woven cloth inside and holes to allow gas to go between sections gradually. The rubber cloth was self-sealing. When the gas tank was hit, the rubber would create a seal and prevent fuel from escaping.

I took severance pay from Firestone and went to work for the Foxboro Company in Attleboro. I worked there one year. It was a great place to work. Foxboro was like a tribe. Cars at work on Fridays had canoes on them. On Saturday morning, we would go to the river and the men would get on the canoes and the women would drive down and have lunch waiting for us at the place where we were going to stop. We did this two or three times a month.

## Health and Illness

A wealthy gentleman from Tiverton would come to South Park and take pictures of kids. Then he would return and give the pictures he took to the kids. This was the only picture of my brother Bobby, who died at the age of six. He died at City Hospital on Robeson Street from a ruptured appendix. We were on welfare at the time. The family physician changed the prescription and he got Bobby walking again. Then, the city doctor came in and changed the prescription back and Bobby died a few days later. This was before antibiotics and penicillin.

When we were at 14 Clayton Street, all the kids got scarlet fever and everyone in the house was quarantined. The five kids in our family each got it, one at a time. I was out of school for ten weeks in the fifth grade. By the time I was over it, the school year was almost over and I stayed back. I went into the General Hospital, the place for contagious diseases. My sister Florence was there at the same time. One day, I saw a white hearse take someone away. I didn't know until later that it was Florence.

## World War II and Military Service

While at Firestone, I got drafted. I could have gotten an exemption, but didn't take it. I was 6 feet, 2 inches tall, 154 pounds, and skinny. I checked in at the Union Hospital for the exam. The Army sent me to radio school in Sioux Falls, South Dakota, and then to Boca Raton, Florida, for radar school for a few months. Then they sent me to Alaska, where the temperature was fifty-four below zero. My blood was still thin from Florida. I learned never to pick up anything without your gloves on, otherwise it stuck to you. If your buddy got frostbite, you got court-martialed, because the Army reasoned that you should have taken care of your buddy and prevented it.

I spent thirty-five years in the military and never left the United States once. The Japanese were in Alaska when I got there, on the outer islands. I traveled the entire length of the Alcan Highway from Dawson Creek, Canada, to Fairbanks, Alaska—about fifteen hundred miles. It was dangerous at times, especially in winter. The road was very narrow and was touch and go at times.

After World War II, I went to Hanscom Field in Lexington. I joined the Air Force Reserves and was called up for Korea. I went to Roswell, New Mexico, to the unit that had dropped both atom bombs on Japan. I ran the finances for the Hanscom Field reserve unit. The reserve unit got an allocation of funds at the first of the year and that had to be allocated to parts of the aircraft. Fuel was a big one.

## Significant Events

One night, Jimmy Stott and I got out of the Durfee Theatre, and we looked down Central Street. Firestone was on fire. When we got to the gate, they let us in since I was the supervisor for two night shifts, even though I was only nineteen years old. We saw young Harvey Firestone covered in dirt and working to put out the fire. Firestone was the largest storehouse of rubber of any place in the United States, and this was wartime. The firemen asked us to take a rope and go on the roof so the hose could be attached to it and the hose brought on the roof to put water on it. It was a challenge to get up there, but we did; however, the wall of an abutting building fell down and we couldn't make the connection. We got down and said that we couldn't do it. My mom later said that she saw some crazy people up on the roof trying to do something; when she found out it was me, she almost went crazy.

# James Stephen Panos

*Born on April 17, 1933*
*Died on August 31, 2012*

**Family Background**

I was born at St. Anne's Hospital. My parents were Stephen F. and Maria S. (Kalogiannis) Panos.

Kalogiannis means "good John." On the same island where my mother's family came from there was also a family named "bad John" (Kakogiannis). I wonder what the story is behind that! Panos is not a shortened name; it is the possessive of the Greek God Pan, the god of fields and streams.

My father's father was Frangulis (Frank) Panos. My mother's father's was Demetrios Kalogiannis.

My name in Greek is Demetrios. All Demetrios' became James. There is no connection between Demetrios and James. At the port of entry, the authorities changed the names. Demetrios was shortened to Deemi, which maybe sounded like Jimmy and therefore James.

My brother's name was Frank.

My wife's was Margaret (Mullaney) Panos and we have two children: Christopher and Alexander (called Lex, after Lex King Souter).

**Family Life**

Before I was born, my family lived in the Flint. About 1933, we moved to the second floor of a three-decker at 502 South Main Street, on the corner of South Street. On the first floor of that building was another Greek family, the Stavros family. On the third floor were Mr. and Mrs. Limoges, who were very nice people.

I stayed at the South Main Street address until 1948. Then, in the fall of my junior year at Durfee [B.M.C. Durfee High School], we moved to 246 Cherry Street, the second house from the corner of North Main Street. Dr. Dionne was on the corner, where the Belfords later had their law practice. The house was a three-decker stucco that Dr. Dionne sold to my father. We lived on the second floor and the William McConnell family lived on the first floor. They were a wonderful family. Several different families lived on the third floor.

I lived there until Peg and I were married in 1962, and we moved to the second floor of Cherry Street. Later, we bought a house at 715 High Street, on the northeast corner of French and High Streets.

My father was a candy-maker. He came to this country in the 1890s. He was thirteen or fourteen years old at the time and came to join his uncle Nicholas Panos, who was a partner with James Bounakes, who was quite an entrepreneur. The two had partnered to start a restaurant and ice cream parlor in the Flint. The Nonpareil ice cream parlor in downtown was Bounakes' store. He was a prime mover in the Greek community. He helped form the first St. Demetrios Church on Cherry Street, behind the Quequechan Club.

My father learned candy making and ice cream making from his uncle. He was so successful that he opened a second store. Both stores were up in the Flint. Then, my father went back to Greece to find a wife to marry. He left the store in the care of someone (who shall remain unnamed) with a good-sized bank account, ample supplies, and a well-stocked store. He married my mother in Greece and stayed in Greece a year. When he came back, he found the store empty of supplies, the bank account empty, and a mound of bills.

He rolled up his sleeves, closed one store and concentrated on the other. He got things going again. He paid the bills and was ready to make a successful career. Then the Depression hit. He closed the store and moved to South Main Street to a house that was in foreclosure and the bank was renting out tenements. It was an unheated cold water flat. There was a central heating system, but it was not usable. He had a stove put in the living areas to heat the house; the bedrooms were cold, but we were healthy.

He then went to work for Peter's Candies in the Granite Block and worked for him for many years. Peter Stevens was the owner. At one point, my father went to Peter's Candies Monday through Friday, go to the bus station at the Granite Block, got on the bus and went to Beverly, Massachusetts, and made candy there for a friend on the weekends. The friend's name was John Sanidas.

My father made candy all day Saturday and slept in a flat over the store. On Sunday morning, he would then go to Pawtucket, Rhode Island, and make candy for another friend. The Pawtucket place was a drugstore that had a soda fountain and sold fresh candy. On Sunday night, he would take another bus and return to Fall River to start another week. He was a remarkable man and an exemplar for my brother and me.

B.M.C. Durfee High School, Rock Street

My first cousin Zoe and I played in a skiff and would go to Long Wharf and back. It was fun. Every once in a while, we would come across lobster "cars," which were big storage boxes that allowed lobsters to stay fresh in salt water. The families would sometimes go on picnics on a boat to places like the Lobster Pot in Bristol, with lobster cars in tow. The ladies packed a lunch, which included bread, boiled eggs, feta cheese, and cold drinks.

We would spend half the summer in Newport, Rhode Island, and the other half in New London, Connecticut, where Zoe's family lived. Zoe's father, George Kalogine, was my uncle on my mother's side and my godfather. In New London, we had many Greek friends. That city had a special flavor for me. Like Newport, it was busy with sailors because of the submarine station. My godfather ran a tavern downtown called The Tavern Bar and Grill, on Bank Street.

**Food and Meals**

During school days, we had coffee and toast for breakfast, with some cod liver oil and a wedge of orange to kill the taste of the oil. It was good for you, as we now know it has Omega-3 in it. Mom also had eggs and oatmeal, but I ignored them. Lunch was a hearty soup and fresh bread and yogurt or rice pudding. There was always yogurt and rice pudding in the icebox. Our first refrigerator was a Sears, and we were delighted to have it. There was no more worry about getting ice.

**School Life**

At five, I went to the Robeson School on Columbia Street, at the bottom of Grant Street. That was the original location of the building that houses the Fall River Historical Society. The house was Andrew Robeson's house and he later gave the land to the city. From there, I went to the McDonough School, where the apartment house is now, on the corner of William and Fountain Streets. I stayed there until eighth grade. Andrew L. Duffy was the principal; he was a fine gentleman.

**Recreation and Entertainment**

In the summertime, we had relatives and friends who lived in Newport. Our relatives on our mother's side were fishermen or lobster men and lived on Long Wharf on the third floor of the Newport Oil Company building, next to the Naval Base. They had no electricity, no gas for cooking, an old wood-burning stove that my mom and aunt cooked on, and all kinds of seafood, fish fresh from the sea, and lobsters.

There were five fishermen in the family, four brothers and a nephew. They had three boats, one called *Mary*, one *Four Brothers*, and a third whose name I can't remember. The third boat was a catboat that belonged to one of the brothers who was independent and fished for lobsters by himself. Within three blocks, there were all kinds of relatives and friends who were wonderful and engaging people. One couple owned a bar and grill opposite the Long Wharf, and they lived on the second floor. He fished in the morning and came in to run the bar in the afternoon. The place was busy with sailors and other people.

The Second Story Theatre Company in Warren [Rhode Island] originally began in Newport in the same building as the bar. When the rents got too high, they moved to Warren to the second story of the American Legion Hall.

**Courtship and Marriage**
Peg and I were married in the Catholic Church. However, the Church didn't allow a second ceremony in another denomination. Therefore, I was excommunicated from the Greek Orthodox Church by none other than Father Peter Stephanopoulos (George's father). He was upset that I was active in the church and then moved outside it. A few years later, the Catholic Church changed its position on second ceremonies and Peg persuaded me that I should be married in the Greek Orthodox Church. We were married in the Greek Church by none other than Father Stephanopoulos. When we were living in the High Street house and when our son Christopher was two, he was playing in the yard one day. He was very bright and spoke early. Christopher walked up to the neighbors who were walking by and said, "Hello," and they responded, "Hello," and then he said, "You know what? My parents are getting married this weekend." Luckily, they were neighbors that we knew, so they knew the full story.

Peg and I met when we both taught in the English Department at Durfee. After college, I went to Durfee to teach when Ambrose Keeley was the principal. He was a wonderful man. I taught for one year and then got my draft notice. I was in the service for two years. Meanwhile, Peg got hired to teach in the English Department. When I got out of the service and returned to Durfee, Peg had been teaching there for a year.

I decided to take a year off and went to Brown with a fellowship for one year. I took all courses there to get a masters degree. Meanwhile, Peg took Masters level classes in English at Brown. We would meet and chat occasionally on the Brown campus. When the fellowship was over, I went back to Durfee and said to Peg, "You know, there's a lecture being given at Brown on Greek romance; would you like to go?" We had dinner on the way at Eileen Darlings, and that evening was when one of the debates between Nixon and Kennedy was on television. We stayed watching the debates and were too late to go to the lecture. I said, "Let's go to Newport." Peg would say later, "I didn't get the lecture, but I got the lab."

From that time, we were inseparable. We corrected papers together. Peg's mother owned a house at the corner of Florence and Robeson Streets, 303 Florence Street. We would sit at the library table in Peg's house correcting papers, trading comments on the papers. Peg was a bright light from heaven for me; I miss her every minute.

We named our second son Alexander, with the nickname of Lex, after Lex King Souter. I heard Lex King Souter speak once and couldn't get him out of my mind.

When Peg and I visited Greece, we spent a month there and visited the island of Skiathos, where my parents came from. We met two cousins, one from my father's side and one from my mother's side. We were able to see the houses where my mother and father were brought up and the church where they were married. I always told Peg, "I'm Irish by affection."

Peg and my father got along very well. My father was instrumental (enthusiastically supported by Peg) in getting us married in the Greek Church. He loved Peg.

**Neighborhood Experiences**
There was an A&P on South Main Street in the block just south of South Street on the west side of South Main, about across from Nick's Coney Island Hot Dogs. You had to grab items in the A&P with a hook and put them in a basket. The cashier computed the items on a paper bag; he was always accurate. There was a small Lebanese store on the corner of South Main and Morgan Streets called Koohey's. A supermarket opened up on the corner of South Main and Columbia

Streets, where the restaurant is now. It was called White's Supermarket. Theresa's Bakery was where the Terminal Bakery is now. I loved their lemon squares. There was also a cobbler just north of the A&P. He was Lebanese and a nice man who did a good job on shoes. The shoes came out of his shop looking like new. He polished them to look spanking new.

I remember Teddy Mitchell, who worked for The Nonpareil ice cream parlor on 135 S. Main Street, owned by Mrs. Zoe Bounakes. He was always with a laugh and a joke. He would take a frappe in the metal containers, take it off the machine, toss it in the air, and catch it without missing a drop. He also did this at Mitchell's Pharmacy, near South Park [now Kennedy Park].

Fall River was a very family-oriented city. All the education that I needed I got from my education at Robeson, McDonough, and Durfee. I learned a lot from the Greek School. I had four years of Latin as well.

**Religious Life**

My mother held the fort, kept the boys in line, kept the house, made sure we went to school, to Greek School, to church, and to Sunday School. The priest at St. Demetrios Church was Father Comninos. He was a wonderful priest. He had an appreciation for aesthetics and history and an appreciation for his communicants. He was from Greece and was very learned and taught Greek School and Sunday School. He was well-liked by the entire community.

The Greek Church owned the house on Hood Street that Father Stephanopoulos lived in and that was where they lived when George was born. The church later sold that house and bought a house for its priest's residence at the northwest corner of Highland Avenue and Stewart Street.

**Military Service**

I had basic training at Fort Dix in New Jersey. The Army sent me down to advanced infantry training to Fort Bragg, North Carolina. At that time, the Army thought that if they gave you eight weeks of paratrooper training, you wouldn't mind going in for an additional three weeks to be a paratrooper. On that thinking, they sent down the whole unit to Fort Bragg. Only one person went on to the paratrooper school.

At the time, I was assigned to the 325th Army Infantry Regiment. The company commander was a man who had a masters degree in psychology and a PhD. He decided that he wanted to give me responsibility for communications and information for the company. That excused me from all of the training—including the physical training at the company. Strangely enough, when I took my physical tests, I passed them all.

They had to decide what to do with us. They shipped a number of us off to the 50th Signal Battalion, which was part of a major Army group going to King Cole maneuvers. The place was snake-infested and awful. At that time, I had also made application to the Army Education Center to teach. There were large-scale GED and college programs going on. The captain in charge of the office that reviewed these applications was not moving fast enough to process my application. Master Sergeant Bolski was sympathetic to my plight. His son was studying for his doctorate in chemistry. He didn't get into an argument with the captain but spoke with the other master sergeants and got things speeded up. The result was that I was transferred to headquarters the very day before the battalion left for Louisiana.

It was a wonderful experience. The classes consisted of non-commissioned officers whose categories were running out, so that if they didn't have a high school degree by a certain time they were out of the Army. Great numbers, therefore, signed up to get their GEDs. I had wonderful and committed students.

At one point, I was teaching in a converted World War II barracks. At the end of each week, I was responsible for and had to be sure that each building was "standing tall." I would say to my master sergeants, "It's time to get this place in shape." They replied, "Yes, private, it's time." They had the place in ship-shape in an hour. I spent the next nineteen months doing that, from 1956 to 1958.

During this time, my mother died. The master sergeant, an older, kindly person, came down to tell me about it. He arranged leave for me. I had a '46 Plymouth and it took nineteen hours to get to Fall River. I spent the week with my father and brother and drove back down and arrived Saturday evening. In the morning, I woke up to the sound of barrel drums; the 82nd Division band was next to us. It was like a dream world.

**Miscellaneous Memories**

When Lizzie Borden was dying in the hospital, Doctor Morton was her physician. Dr. Morton's daughter Nancy (now Nancy Barnes) was born in the hospital at the same time. Lizzie asked to see the baby and it was brought to her and she held Nancy.

We have a group called the Romeos, who meet once a month. They are a group of old associates. We choose a new site to meet every month. We sometimes get up to sixteen people attending, but usually ten to twelve. We have "serious" discussions where we resolve all of the problems of the world, and then we walk out not having to do anything about it. There is also a Westport group that meets, but they are more formal and have speakers.

# Aurora (D'Adamo) Perry

*Born on June 11, 1933*

**Family Background**

I was born at Union Hospital. My parents were Federico and Vincenza (Lucciola) D'Adamo

My mother and father were both from Italy. They came from a farm village named Castelforte, which is somewhere between Rome and Naples. My mother was one of ten, half of whom migrated here. My dad came here when he was fourteen or fifteen years old with a bunch of cousins. When he went back to visit his mother, he was of draft age and served in the Italian Army in World War I. My mother's sister was married to his brother. My father came back here and went back to visit his brother and married my mother in Italy. Then they both came to the United States. They arrived here about 1930.

When dad came from Italy, he went to Holy Rosary Church. At that time, there was an Italian Methodist Church on Plain Street and they held social events for young people. He liked it and went to services, which were in Italian and English. The church is now converted to a home. Later, when my mother came over, she also joined the church. My aunt lived at 114 Plain Street, next door to the church and learned Portuguese very well. He name was Vittoria D'Adamo and she was my godmother. I did a lot with her because she drove a car and my parents didn't. She died young, at fifty-six years old.

I have one sibling, Anthony (born in 1931, when we lived at 1090 Bedford Street).

My husband is Edward Perry and we have two children, Deborah Ozug and Donna Perry. We also have two grandchildren, Nicholas and Jenny Ozug.

Our residences in Fall River were: 1088 Bedford Street, second floor; 230 Healey Street, first floor; 1090 Bedford Street, after marriage (mother on the first floor and we were on the second); 163 Savoie Street (that we built); and 1144 Bedford Street, first floor. My brother owned this house; I bought it from him.

**Family Life**

We sat on our front porches and talked with neighbors. No one had much money after the Depression. Our social lives were limited. We had a happy childhood, with not many frills. As long as you had clothes on you back and food on the table, you were in good shape. We had a good life.

Whatever was put in front of us, we ate. There was no such thing as favorite foods that our mothers made for us. Having favorite foods is a new concept of this generation; we ate what our mother's gave us.

When I was born, we lived at 1088 Bedford Street, on the second floor, above my father's first barbershop. His other barber shops were at 1080 and 1090 Bedford Street. Tony DeBonis owned a cobbler shop nearby.

My father was self-taught. He would write to the *Providence Journal* or the *Fall River Herald*

*News* and they would respond to his questions he had about the population of India and things like that. When we died, we found stacks of letters from newspapers responding to his questions.

My father was a barber until he was ninety-six years old and died when he was one hundred. My dad was into the community. He belonged to the Sons of Italy and other Italian organizations. He was active in Columbus Day activities. I am currently active in the Italian-American War Veterans.

My father had a huge garden in back of this house. He loved his garden. It was very orderly, with neat rows and carefully cultivated. He grew huge tomatoes and zucchini. We either ate from the garden or ate from produce that was canned from the garden. He had a pear tree, and we bottled the pears. He had fig trees and a grape vine but didn't make wine. It wasn't worth it, he said, although he liked wine. He loved his back yard. In his later years, the garden was his life.

My mother didn't work for the first seven years; after we went to school, she went to work in the shops, at Har-Lee's mostly. My father loved to cook. I would come home from school for lunch. My mother couldn't read or write, but she was determined to speak English. We would go to a "show" (a movie) once a month. She collected the dishes that the theatres gave out. She liked musicals. My mother died in 1986.

We never dressed up for Halloween; it was not a big deal then. I do remember having to wash eggs off the barbershop windows the next day. We never had New Year's celebrations. I don't remember getting Christmas gifts. We never had birthday parties or sent birthday cards.

## Food and Meals

For meals, we had chicken, stuffed eggplant, macaroni, salads, Italian bread. My mom made a mean raisin square. We didn't have many desserts. For breakfast, we had a slice of toast and coffee, maybe biscuits. On Christmas eve, we had an all-fish meal, including smelts and baccalau.

At Easter, the women made braided sweet bread. That is all that we got; there were no bunnies. Pastere, or rice pie, was also made at Easter. It was made with rice and ricotta cheese. We gave it to people who were good to my mother.

## School Life

I went to the Dubuque School and then to the Davis School for seventh to ninth grades, where the Bishop Eid Apartments are now. Then I went to Durfee [B.M.C. Durfee High School]. I loved school and I did well. I was on the Honor Roll for most of my school years. I took Italian and Spanish. They had the best sports programs.

My mother and father were emphatic that we were going to get a good education, especially my mother. My brother graduated from Durfee in 1949, then went on to Bryant for a degree in accounting. I went on to the Thibodeau Business School. My mother was a stickler that both of us were going to get an education. In those days, Portuguese and Italian kids went to work at sixteen years old. Guys who went into the service could take advantage of the GI Bill.

## Recreation and Entertainment

Our recreation was limited. We went to Fogland [Tiverton, Rhode Island] to the beach there.

On the western side of Oak Grove Avenue, where the Crestwood Nursing Home is now, there was F and B Cone Company, owned by Lebanese. It was a sugar cone manufacturer and, when we were kids, we would go there and they would give us a bag of broken sugar cones for five cents. It was a real treat. When we had ice cream in a cone, we thought that was really special. On Sunday, we would go to the shop that was on the northwest corner of Eastern Avenue and County Street and get an ice cream cone and sit at Lafayette Park. It was our treat on Sunday afternoons.

Everyone went to Lincoln Park [North Dartmouth, Massachusetts]. Before that, we went to The Casino on Morgan Street. When Durfee let out, we walked down Rock Street to Rector's Spa to get a cup of coffee. Rector's Spa was located on the northwest corner of Bedford and Troy Streets.

**Work Life**

One day, my father said, "I'm going to give you the best birthday gift of your life." He gave me an accordion. When I was sixteen, I started playing the accordion and the organ. I worked seven days a week.

When the guys went to war, I played the accordion with a Polish band. I taught accordion for twenty-eight years, including at the Shoob School of Music. I played the organ at the original Quarry Street Methodist Church and now fill in for organists. Ray Garowski (who was Portuguese) had a fourteen-piece Polish band. It was fun. All of a sudden, the accordion became famous.

WSAR [radio] once had its home in the Academy Building. At that time, they had a Kiddie Hour, where kids performed. I played accordion on the show. Yolanda Breault played the piano. She taught me chords later. When I was in high school, I had a program of my own, where I sang

Davis School, 33 Quequechan Street

and played the accordion. I also had a show on the WALE radio station and played the accordion for half an hour. It was on Wednesdays at 4:00 or 4:30 pm.

My first job was at Har-Lee Manufacturing dress shop in the main office. I worked there for three years. I made thirty-two dollars, gross, and twenty-eight dollars, net, and gave my mother twenty dollars. Then I worked at a retail store that my cousin owned on Purchase Street in New Bedford. From there, I got married and taught the organ. My future husband's friend introduced us when I worked in New Bedford.

My husband was a commercial fisherman and owed two scallopers out of New Bedford. The boats were named *Geraldine* and *Bountiful*. My husband and I owned the Flint Fish Market at one time. It wasn't our thing to work inside, so we sold it.

**Neighborhood Experiences**

There were many activities around Columbus Day. We had a ball on Friday, a dinner on Saturday, a parade on Sunday, and fireworks. Then we had a get-together at my house after. On Monday, we had a Mass at Holy Rosary Church then a ceremony at Battleship Cove. The weekend included field games, a greasy pole, road races, one-legged races, and a parade of costumes. Music was provided by the Fall River Musicians' Union until 8:00 pm. Then we went to friends' houses. It was then moved to North Park but the costs escalated, with insurance and all that. The Sons of Italy took it over and the Italian-American War Vets.

Next door, on the northwest corner Bedford Street and Oak Grove Avenue, was the Horvitz Variety Store and fruit market. On the opposite side of the street was Oak Grove Pharmacy, on the southwest corner of Oak Grove and Bedford. A Laundromat was on the northeast corner of Bedford and Oak Grove for fifty years, until recently. On the next corner, on Bedford and Covel, was Smith's Market. On the northwest corner of Bedford and Quarry Streets was the Hood Dairy. Columbus Café was across the street on the southwest corner of Bedford and Quarry. The Marconi Club was on the northwest corner of Bedford and Johnson Streets, where the Portuguese restaurant is now. The Macaroni Shop was there forever. Mr. Favio owned it (he died when he was one hundred years old), then Romeo Cittolini. It was then sold to the Boys Club to allow them to expand. The Brown School was where the Boys Club is now.

**World War II**

During World War II, my father was an Air Raid Warden. We lived on Healy Street at the time. He would walk up and down the street, billy-club in hand, with his black and white hat. We had to have stamps for things like butter. There was pandemonium in the city when the war was over.

# August "James" Petrucci

*Born on February 22, 1920*
*Died on August 15, 2014*

**Family Background**

I was born in Compolito, Italy. I was eight years old when I arrived in the United States. I have three brothers and sisters: Ersilia (born 1914), Pierina (born 1916), and Vincenzo.

My wife is Theresa (Petrillo) Petrucci [Theresa's interview follows this one in the book] and we have a son named Joseph.

**Family Life**

My father had come here in 1914 or 1916. He and his brother came here. When World War I broke out, he went back to Italy and fought in the Italian Army. Then he returned. Then he went back to Italy again. That's when I was born. Then, when he came back, he called us over. We came over on a ship named the *Saturnia*. The big shots were on top and we were even with the water line. Me and my two sisters were in one room. It took about three to four weeks to come over. Once on the ship, another kid was pushing me around the boat in a cart. He pushed me into an iron pole, and I got hurt in the leg. I had to go into the medical room for stitches. At Ellis Island, they asked what happened. My father was to have picked us up, but he didn't show up, so we had to stay overnight until he picked us up to go to Fall River.

**Recreation and Entertainment**

We would go mushrooming in Dartmouth. No one would tell you where their place was. We would be in the fields at 4:00 am yelling, "There's one, there's one!" We would come home with four bushels of mushrooms.

The New York Giants were big in Fall River in the 40s and 50s, before the Patriots. Tony DiNucci went to school with the owner of the Giants. The Roma would run trips to New York with sandwiches and beer and rent a whole car of the train. When they got to the hotel, they put the beer in a bathtub and go out all night. When they got back, they would talk about it. Then, they would go to the game the next day on Sunday.

They would leave Providence Saturday in the morning at 6:00 am and arrive in New York about 10:00 am and then go to the hotel. They let us bring beer into the hotel. We had totes with ice and beer. Everyone would go into Al Petrillo's room and tell stories. We would go once a month until the football season was over.

I have a scar on my head that I got when I jumped into the Beattie Quarry when I was fourteen years old. There were rock shelves in the quarry. I got onto a shelf and dived in and cut my head. When my mother saw it, we went to Dr. Mangione on Bedford Street; I got twelve stitches.

There was a wire at the quarry that ran from the top to the bottom of the quarry. We kids would get up on a pole, grab the wire with a piece of rubber hose or something else, then slide down into the water.

## Prohibition

I once stole a gallon of wine from my father's basement and brought it to the Holy Rosary Church basement and me and my friends drank it there. My father would make moonshine in a copper kettle. He once said to me, "You watch that." Instead, I went to the park and, two hours later, it almost blew up. I now make my own anisette by buying the alcohol and the flavoring and mixing them.

When we lived on Quarry Street, my father made champagne in the basement. He would cork the bottles and bury them in the dirt. One time, my father went down and came back all wet. The champagne bottles popped and drenched him. We made a thousand gallons of wine in those days.

## Work Life

When I was sixteen years old and worked at the Pepperell Mills, I would take waste cotton and bag it and bring it home and make mattresses with it for our house. I still have the bed that we brought from Italy. Then I worked in construction. I worked as a truck driver for Sterling Beverages delivering Knickerbocker Beer.

I was in a CCC [Civilian Conservation Corps] camp in New Hampshire for about a year when I was sixteen or seventeen years old. We cleaned the streets and worked in people's yards in the nearby town. We cut trees down and things like that. We lived in barracks, it was regimented like the Army.

## World War II

In 1942, I was drafted and stayed in until 1947 or 1948. I went to the Carolinas first for six months, then to Washington State for a few weeks. Then I took the boat to Hawaii for one and one-half years. Then I was at Iwo Jima. When the war was over, I went to Osaka, Japan. I was there for eight months helping to disarm the Japanese. Then, we were discharged and sent home.

# Theresa (Pretrillo) Petrucci

*Born on December 1, 1926*

*In attendance were Terri Petrucci, James Petrucci, and Antoniette (Terri's sister). Antoinette's comments are marked with her name, all other text is from Theresa.*

**Family Background**

My parents were Salvatore and Alexandrina (Maddaleno) Petrillo.

I have five brothers and sisters: Mary (born 1915), Adolph ("Al" born 1916), Jessie (born 1924), Antoinette (born 1925), and Salvatore ("Sal" born 1928). Mary and Adolph were from a previous marriage; their mother died.

We were born at 62 Quarry Street, at the corner of St. Germaine Street, on the second floor. We lived at 22 St. Germain Street, then moved to 14 St. Germain Street after we were married. It was the same building but a different door.

My husband is August Petrucci [August's interview precedes this one in the book] and we have a son named Joseph.

**Family Life**

Our parents were strict, my father especially; we had to abide by the rules. Our life revolved around family, food, and friends. It was our Italian motto. Before he had the Roma Café, my father sold ice, coal, and wood. My mother never worked outside the house.

Lots of grandparents lived with family. If you had ten kids, their friends came to the house.

At night, we would say the rosary. My husband's mother came over to say the rosary. My father had a good voice and sang all the time. My mother once heard this guy singing in the street and thought, "He's never home; but my father was in bed with her."

People visited a lot. Before, whole families would drop in. No one called before they came.

*Antoinette:* We had a coal stove. One night, my mother woke us up. The house was full of smoke. She couldn't find the door to get out. She was calling everyone in the family. We were getting smoke inhalation and almost died. The flue to the stove had moved. Once, my mother put the meat of a rabbit out the window in a pan to keep it cold. A man that lived near us got a ladder and climbed up to the pan and took it out of the pan. He was going to cook it and serve it to us. But, he slipped and went through the first floor window. My mother still wanted the rabbit back. He gave it back. Pasta with gravy was cheap. If you ran out you could keep adding water.

**Food and Meals**

*Antoinette:* We had nothing exciting for food. For breakfast, we had milk crackers with milk or coffee. For lunch, we had leftovers. We had a lot of custards. Supper depended on the day: On Monday, we had greens; on Tuesday, we had pasta; on Wednesday, greens; on Thursday, pasta; on Friday, eggs, rice or mashed potatoes, since it was a Fast Day. Saturday, we had chicken soup.

*Antoinette:* My mother killed the chickens. Once, when she didn't do it right, the chicken hopped all over the place. We had to dunk the chicken in hot water to pluck the feathers. It was horrible and smelly. Then we had to take out the intestines. We made our own Italian sausage and hung it to dry in the cold breezeway. When the sausage was dried, we put the dried sausage in oil. That way, we had it all year. We picked blueberries where the water works is and my mother preserved them. We also preserved peppers in vinegar. We preserved everything from the garden, including tomatoes, string beans, carrots, and peppers. We would par boil the string beans and add salt and sugar. We would make a vegetable salad in jars.

We made our own vinegar out of the little wine left over. To make the vinegar, we used a vinegar starter called "mother." Any wine that we had left over, we put in with the starter. I still have the wine press that my father used. After we ground the grapes, we let it sit and turned it every few days. Then we squeezed the juice, let it rest, and put it in five gallon jugs until clear.

**School Life**

We went to the Brown School on Bedford Street, where the Boys and Girls Club is now. The third grade teacher used to stick her fingernail in your chin and shake it if you were bad.

**Recreation and Entertainment**

We played hide and seek and house. There was a house on St. Germain Street that had an empty tenement that my father owned and we girls would play house there. We had a ladder and if you went to the top, you went to New York; to the bottom and you went to Providence or Boston.

We would slide down Bowler Street with our sleds; we made snowmen and had snowball fights.

Under our grapevines, we had parties and played cards. We sang and danced the Tarantella. My father owned the Roma Café and would come home late at night. He would bring men home and my mother would have to get up and cook and get wine for them. We kids had to get up and sing for the men. Then my father would then say, "Back to bed."

Everyone knew everyone. We had dances at the Sons of Italy Hall. We played cards Tuesday nights for forty years—it was all women. Sometimes we would have couples. We also had dances and New Year's Eve parties. We did all of the cooking down at the church. We were involved with the Feast every year, and I was president of the guild twice.

Kids would hang out at Columbus Park until 2:00 am to talk and kid. One year, Holy Rosary won the baseball championship. We never went to the circus. There was a circus at the Bigberry stadium during the 1920s, I think. We went to Ocean Grove [Swansea, Massachusetts] with plenty of family, relatives, and friends and lots of food.

We made a party out of everything. When we made wine, everyone came. The grapes had to be plucked off of the stems, and everyone helped. When we made cookies for weddings, we made a party out of that. This house was a party house. We didn't need much reason to have a party.

Radio shows that we liked included "The Shadow Knows" and "Major Bowles."

*Antoinette:* The son of one of our neighbors died swimming in Beattie's quarry. He carried his son home. The boy's mother lost her mind a little. Two French kids died in the quarry. They say that there are two kids still in the quarry.

*Antoinette:* Columbus Day was a big event. We had fireworks, a greasy pole, and things like

Terri Petrucci

that. There was a salami and a five dollar bill on top of the pole. The smart ones would let the others go first and take the grease off of the pole.

**Courtship and Marriage**

Jim's family lived next door to us. He was a good guy and had a car. He took us riding. One time, he asked me to go to a [Boston] Braves game. On the way, he asked me, "Want to learn how to drive?" and put his arms around me. We got pulled over. The policeman said, "If you want to make love, go up that road." He never dropped me off on St. Germain Street. I was going to break up with him. He was a great guy, though, and we finally got married. We were married at the Holy Rosary Church and had our reception at the Sons of Italy Hall on Covel Street.

**Work Life**

We kids would go to the barn and bag the wood, which we got two cents a bag for. My father had a horse and wagon. One time, my brother left the door open and the horse ran away. Another time, a horse had to be shot. In 1938, he bought the Roma Café when coal and wood were no longer used much. The Roma Café was at the corner of Second and Pleasant Streets in the basement of the Academy Building. Paul Woltman was across the street. My brother Al took it over when my father died in 1942.

I worked in the 5 & 10 in the Flint then in sewing shops. I was a cafeteria worker at [B.M.C] Durfee High School and retired in 1997.

*Antoinette:* I worked at Shelburne Shirt for thirty-five years. Then, I was the lunch lady at the Small School for twenty-eight years until the school closed.

**Neighborhood Experiences**

When the Merchant's Mill burned on Thirteenth Street, it was a big fire. Logs flew over Quarry and St. Germain Streets and burned a four-tenement down. There were two old French women who didn't want to get out. My brother Al and Joe Ricci went in and carried them out.

Shops in the area included the Macaroni Shop, where the Boys and Girls Club is now. Across the street from that was the cobbler shop of John Vavala. Diagonally across from Hood's Dairy was Mirra's Market, on the southeast corner of Bedford and Quarry Streets. Mauretti's Market was at 930 Bedford Street. The Columbus Café was across from Hood's on the southwest corner of Bedford and Quarry Streets.

The Columbus Club was where Graham's Hot Dogs is now on Bedford Street. The Marconi Club was on the northwest corner of Bedford and Johnston Streets, where the Portuguese Club

Merchant Street downed in the 1938 hurricane,
with the Brown School in the background

is now. Leo's Market was across Columbus Park on Bedford Street. On the corner of Oak Grove Avenue and Bedford Street was a little market.

The A&P market was next to where the Oak Grove Pharmacy was on the southwest corner of Bedford and Haffards Streets. The owner of the pharmacy lived on Chavenson Street. S&B Cone Shop was across from the Crawford Nursing Home on Oak Grove Avenue. On the northeast corner of Bedford and Oak Grove was a gas station (where the laundromat was until recently). Where the Boys and Girls Club is now was where the Brown School once was. Al Vita had a dry cleaning shop.

The Rag Man was called "Skelly the Goal-Tender." He lived on Healy Street and would yell out, "Rags, rags!" We were afraid of him. We also had the fish man and the vegetable man come by and a man who sharpened knives and scissors.

**Christmas, Holidays, and Special Occasions**

*Antoinette:* We had no car. Every Christmas Eve, we would go the Imbriglios and the Pascarinos in Tiverton, Rhode Island, to decorate their trees. There were all Italians were we lived. People stayed in their homes for a long time.

On Christmas Eve, we made seven fishes made different ways, including eels. We would also get together on Easter, although we now do it on Palm Sunday, since families want to be together on Easter. I would make bread and ricotta pie and meat. We would have about forty people over to the house on Palm Sunday.

On Christmas Day, we would make capon chicken and pasta. On Thanksgiving, we would never have just the turkey and vegetables. We also had antipasto, soup, pasta, then the turkey. We had hot chestnuts all the time.

*Antoinette:* On New Years, we made lentil soup. For Easter, there was a sweet bread, a rice pie, a noodle pie, a meat omelet, Italian cold cuts, and cookies. My mother made the sweet bread in the shape of an 8; we called it a doll with an egg. She made one large sweet bread with eggs on top with a ribbon around it. At Easter, the head of the house would take a palm, dip it in holy water, and go around the table blessing everyone at the table. Then he would go around and bless the whole house. We would give a palm to everyone on Easter (now Palm Sunday) and some would kiss the palm and some would kneel down in front of their father and ask forgiveness.

**Health and Illness**

I once fell off the wheel of a wagon and got a cut from a broken bottle. I got a scar from it. I didn't have any stitches. Mrs. Fiori took care of it. She wasn't a doctor or a nurse but a lady that was smarter than our mothers and took care of us.

Some of the illnesses we had were mumps and measles. For mumps, a scarf was put over our heads. For measles, we were put in bed with the shades down and in darkness. For casts, my mother would take cotton from the beds and spread it on the area and beat up eggs to put over the cotton. For colds, our mother made boiled prunes, figs, apples and honey to drink. For headaches, they sliced potatoes, put them on your forehead, and kept them in place with a cloth tied around your head.

To ward off the evil eye, water was put in a plate and oil dropped in it with a spoon, four drops in a cross. You would make the sign of the cross three times and, if a ring appeared in the water, someone was giving you the evil eye. You had to learn this ritual only on Christmas Eve.

My father was waked in his house, and the men stayed up all night while he was laid out. One of these men, Mr. Porcelli, fell asleep and started snoring. My aunt put some flour in a cup and when he sniffed up the powder, he woke up coughing. Everyone woke up and started laughing. They did things like that to wake you up.

**Popular Expressions**
"Che sara, sara, what will be will be" was one of our sayings.

South Main Street looking north

# Frank Pontes

*Born on November 12, 1927*
*Died on July 30, 2013*

**Family Background**

My parents were Manuel Rego (from São Miguel Island, Azores) and Maria (Cambra) Pontes. I have a brother, Manuel Pontes, and a step-sister, Rose Pavao.

I am married to Lorraine (Fernandes) Pontes [Lorraine's interview follows this one in the book] and we have two children, Cheryl Trask and Frank Pontes.

**Family Life**

I came from the Flint, Choate Street. My father owned a grocery store on the first floor of the building. My father bought houses, but my mother lost everything when he died. She tried to keep it going, but she couldn't. He went bankrupt because people couldn't pay their IOU's. We had to do without. I was sixteen or seventeen years old when we found a book of the people that owed him rent and grocery money in the thousands of dollars.

My father died a month before I was born. My mother was a good cook. We were on welfare and I would have to go in line and wait for a bag of food. We would make donuts or bread. I would bring a few donuts to neighbors and they would give me peaches or anything that they had to share from their garden. My brother was an epileptic and had polio at the age of six. My mom had to stay home to take care of him. She took care of eight to ten kids for whatever their parents could give.

Everyone talked to and loved my mom because she was a good woman. Everyone thought she was Irish because of her light features and white hair. She was a beautiful woman.

No one had money. My brother had to go to Mass General Hospital every month, and a Mr. Silvia came up to my mother and offered to bring him to Boston and take him back. He did this for years! He lived comfortably but, if it wasn't for him, we wouldn't have been able to get my brother to the hospital. He was an insurance man and owned a car. We didn't have to tell him when an appointment was coming up; he would contact us. He was a good man.

Once, I was untying a newspaper bundle, and the wire went into my eye. I became blind in that eye. The Boston hospital wanted to remove the eye, but my mother said no.

All my uncles and aunts lived far away. Uncle John lived in Westport [Massachusetts], building stone walls for the Tripp family. He built a lot of the walls that are near UMass Dartmouth. He was a skinny man, but strong. I worked with him one summer and quit; the job was too tough.

**Friends**

David Souza was my best friend. He had three older brothers so he had a little money to buy things that I couldn't afford. For Christmas, he would give me roller skates that he didn't need anymore. I really took care of those. He gave me his bike. It was like, "Wow!" I painted it and took care of it. There were no such things as toys then.

Frank Pontes with his mother on Frank's confirmation day

Once, we all went to upstate New York for a wedding. The father of the bride, "Clarkie" Souza, had a big family. The groom, who had lots of money, rented an inn for eighty of us to stay in. "Clarkie" started buying screwdrivers for Lorraine, then ordered more. Lorraine then took over the microphone and started singing. She was mortified the next day. It was a three-day blowout. The groom came in kilts, and the bride's mother was scandalized.

John "Clarkie" Souza made it to the Soccer World Cup for the United States. It was the first time that the United States won over England. He is in the soccer hall of fame. He lived in the second house over on Choate Street.

**Food and Meals**

My mother preserved food. My uncle had a garden and he gave us turnips, carrots, and cabbage. Every day we had soup, soup, soup. Every day.

I worked for Benny Correia for no money. He gave me one piece of fish or crabs. He had no refrigeration to keep them over, since he sold fish from a horse and wagon. Anything that was left over from Saturday we could take home.

My mother made pastries later when we had more money. She made pastries for the church feasts. She made a big sweet bread in the shape of a leg because my brother had polio, and the church would auction it off. She did this more than once. We had a grapevine in our yard, and my mother made jams and did canning in the cellar. When we were out, she picked blackberries on the road to make preserves.

I worked at Silvia's Bakery on the corner of Everett and Alden Streets. I would empty out the truck. On Sunday mornings, he would give me one Portuguese bread and two squares. Sunday breakfast was slices of Portuguese bread with jam and squares cut into six pieces.

Even though my mom had little, if there was anything left over, she would give it to someone. When the grapes came out, she gave grapes to everyone in the neighborhood. Then she would bring them jam. In turn, we would get corn, sweet peppers, and other vegetables from others who had gardens.

I loved to go to wakes, which were held in the home for three days. They would have malasadas, cup cakes, brownies; after prayers, we would all eat. My mother would tell me, "Don't eat more than one."

**School Life**
I went to Espirito Santo School, then to Watson, then to work.

**Recreation and Entertainment**
I was always a champion roller skater with the skates that my friend gave me.

For games, we would put three cans in the street, then roll a ball down the street. If the ball hit one of the cans, you would have a shot at hitting the ball with the stick.

We would sled down the Choate Street hill. Policemen stood on the bottom of Alden Street to stop traffic and allowed us to go down the hill.

Music was our thing. When no bands played, we would go to Lorraine's house to practice. We were never too tired to dance. We were too tired to go to work. We would come home at 1:30 am and get up at 6:00 am to go to work. My mother would ask, "How do you do it?"

Donald Facciano borrowed my bass made out of a wash tub and played it in his band at Lincoln Park [North Dartmouth, Massachusetts]. Eddie King would come with us all the time. "Let's start practicing," he would say.

Once we played "Name That Tune" on the phone with the prize being S&H Green stamps redeemed at Walter's Super Gas Station. One of our friends guessed it and Lorraine had to call her up and tell her not to go and get the prize.

Lorraine's uncle, Manuel Perry, could play string instruments and the accordion. I played with him at the St. John's Club for a few years. I would whistle while playing and the band tuned up while I whistled. I got paid five dollars and came home broke after I bought food and drinks for me and the others.

Joe Souza, a friend of ours, had a quonset hut on the South Watuppa. It was one big room for music and dancing. We got a sailboat and sang and played all up and down the pond. People called from the shore requesting songs for us to sing. We would go up and down the pond with our guitar and accordion, with people shouting out sing this song or that song. We did this a lot on the pond.

At the bottom of Newhall Street, on the pond, lived eight to ten nuns. The nuns would wave their hands when they saw us. They wanted a ride in the sailboat. It was a rough day, but they still wanted to go. We took four of them. They wanted us to tip the boat and go fast. We almost got water in the boat. One nun was alone, praying up a storm.

Once, Eddie King took out the sailboat and didn't put the keel down. All the girls in the boat went in the water, pocketbooks and all. Another time, Eddie got in a canoe when there was a squall coming up. He didn't know that there was a hole in the canoe. As the canoe sank, by and by, we saw only his nose. We had good times with no drinking.

**Courtship and Marriage**

Lorraine and I had a wonderful courtship. She was witty, and we both enjoyed each other's love for dancing and fun but, most of all, our love for each other. We were married in Polish National Catholic Church, since I was divorced from a previous marriage. Our reception was held in the Young Nationals Club, off of Bedford Street. Lorraine's mom and dad made all the food. We had about eighty-five people or more. We had lots of food, fun, and dancing. Lorraine's mom made her wedding gown and trousseau.

**Work Life**

I began work in the Howard Arthur Mills, but I worked in construction all my life until I was over fifty. My first job was at Quonset Point building a restaurant. That took three to four years. Then, there were two seasons for road work, one when you worked and one when you didn't, in the wintertime. I had no car then, and when my ride got laid off, I had to leave also. Then I went to work for Tommy Kidd, Contractor. Lorraine's uncle worked for him. I worked for him for ten years. I did everything involved with civil engineering. Then I went to work for Robert Germaine, doing telephone company work.

I next worked for LaFlamme Development, preparing subdivision sites for water, sewer, and gas lines. I worked there for five years and quit in 1963. Then I went the Brayton Point Power Plant and worked there for eighteen years doing breakdown work. I worked my way up to foreman. It was more steady work. I retired in 1989.

In my construction jobs, I've been buried four or five times in cave-ins. After one cave-in, I was in the hospital for over a month.

**The Depression**

The welfare place was in the back of the mills on Alden Street where Shelburne Shirt was. Once a week, on Fridays, they would give us potatoes, rotten cabbage, food in bags that were left there for too long. I would wait from 7:00 am to 3:00 pm. The older kids kept pushing me aside and, by the time I got there, nothing was left. My mom got a dollar a week from welfare.

My mother would crochet the edges of handkerchiefs to sell. I would go around selling them at fifteen cents each. That was all you could get in those days.

**World War II**

I went into the service in 1946 but was still considered a World War II veteran. Japanese soldiers on the islands didn't know or didn't accept that the war was over and wouldn't come out of their caves. We had to shoot flame throwers into the caves to get them out. They ran out. We were in Japan when it experienced the biggest earthquake in 1947. I escorted the Emperor to visit the countryside and Hiroshima. The destruction there was unbelievable.

# Lorraine (Fernandes) Pontes

*Born on February 17, 1930*

**Family Background**

My parents were Manuel and Irene (Pereira) Fernandes. My father was born in Portugal in a town near the border with Spain. My mother was born on São Miguel Island, Azores, and came here when she was eight years old.

My father's father was a tailor and moved from Portugal to Brazil. In Portugal, all property is divided among the wife and children. My grandfather's brother farmed my grandfather's land.

I am married to Frank Pontes [Frank's interview precedes this one in the book] and we have two children, Cheryl Trask and Frank Pontes.

When we first got married, we lived with my mom and dad. We then moved to the second floor of 61 Dickinson. My parents were getting on in years and asked us if they bought 32 Dickinson Street, would we move there to be close to them. We said yes because we were always close. I never left my parents and we took care of them in their later years.

**Family Life**

When my father was eighteen years old, he came to the United States and landed in New York. He worked for a time in New York City, then he worked in the steel mills. Then he worked on the Fall River Line. That's how he met my mom. Following that, he got a job on the Martha's Vineyard ferries, working in the engine room. The Martha's Vineyard ferries in those days were luxurious, not what they are like today.

He bought his first car about 1945 and, when he brought it home, told my mother, "Look out the window; It's yours. I bought it for you to take the kids out." It was a Studebaker. "Learn how to drive," he said.

I was born on Columbia Street next to the Doran School. My parents had a restaurant at 76 Columbia Street where the Columbia Bakery is now. My father fed everyone there. The Iron Works workers would bring their pails to fill up. During the Depression, he still fed them. Then he lost his restaurant.

Then we moved to 370 Ferry Street. My mother always worked at Schneierson & Sons. She would walk from Ferry Street all the way up to Broadway to the Globe Mills. My father took jobs wherever he could get them. My mom would come home and make something to eat. Then she would sit at the sewing machine to make dresses, bed spreads, and drapes; everything. We never went on welfare.

Everyone was equal; by that I mean that everyone was poor. We were neighborly and close. We watched out for each other. People were helpful. No one had money so no one was jealous of one another. People would chip in and help one another.

We had only one stove, a pot-bellied coal stove. In the winter, we would close off half of the tenement. We bathed in galvanized tubs that were put in front of the stove. I was washed in the

Lorraine Pontes as a flower girl at a family wedding

tub first and then my brother in the same water. The water was heated on the stove.

We had the old-fashioned iceboxes. The iceman came in his truck with ice. We would put a sign in the window that read ICE. There was a coffee man that came around and sold ground coffee. The fish man and the chicken man came in their horse and wagons and blew their horn or rang their bell to let people know they were there.

We had a good life. We had no bikes. The kids played all kinds of games in the yard. For those kids who had roller skates, they roller skated. We would toboggan down Columbia Street, all the way down Columbia Street.

If we didn't go to church, we couldn't go anywhere on Sunday.

We lived on Ferry Street until I was twenty. Then we moved to Old Fall River Road in Dartmouth [Massachusetts] for one or two years. I didn't drive then; I didn't get my license until I was twenty-nine. A cousin took me back and forth to Fall River.

We took in Frank's brother after his mother died for two years, but it was too much. The doctor said that I needed to do something about it because I would have had a breakdown. Then, Francis Olivera from Columbia Street helped us get a bed in a home. Frank's brother had many seizures all night. He had severe case of epilepsy. Our girl was three years and the boy was three months.

My father lived to be ninety-two. He worked on the *Priscilla* in the engine room as an engineer for quite a few years. He loved the job. My uncle Jack Martin also worked on the Fall River Line. After my father got married, it was tough going back and forth on the boats and being away from home. That's when he went to work on the Martha's Vineyard ferries. James Cagney had a cottage on Martha's Vineyard, and he would take the ferry there. He wouldn't go upstairs but stayed by his beach wagon below. My father said to me, "Do you want to meet him," and he brought me to see him. Cagney didn't say much, only, "Uh, huh." I asked him, "How are you?" and he just said "Uh, huh."

My grandmother was tough in a way. She took care of my brother and me and our aunts and the four children that she cared for during the day. My mother would leave lunch and cake for my brother and me and my grandmother would share it with the others. When we left to go back to school after lunch, she would give us a knock on the head and say in Portuguese, "Use your head." She would say the rosary every day with us at lunchtime.

She couldn't read or write but had a telephone. She had a notebook next to the phone that had pictures and numbers next to each picture. Every family member had a picture. If she wanted to call her brother at his Westport farm, there would be a cow next to his number, and so forth.

My grandmother had the old irons that you warmed up by putting on coal stoves. She would teach me how to iron bead spreads.

During the war, when my aunts' husbands came into port, they went to visit them, and I would sleep over with my grandmother. When it stormed, with thunder and lightening, we had to turn our shoes over and say a certain prayer. Instead of pillows, she had round bolts. She lived on the third floor with us at 370 Ferry Street.

My grandmother made butter from cream. She would take a quart Mason jar full of cream and then roll it back and forth on your thighs until it became thick. She would put salt in it, and the result was white butter. That's all that you did. It was like the soft white butter that they sell today. We kids would help her roll the jar.

We had big porches, and when we washed curtains, we would stretch them on wooden frames with pins on them and put them on the porch to dry.

My mother made all of my clothes. I never bought clothes until I was married. I had three parties for my twenty-first birthday.

**Friends**

I had a friend, Dolores Perry, who lived on Ferry Street in the next house, whose mom washed the pews in the church. When we would go over her house, she would give us a slice of bread and butter with sugar on it. She was a sweetheart.

A friend of ours, Eddie King, who was Portuguese, was a fireman. One New Years Eve, he was working at the Bedford Street station downtown. We were living at 32 Dickinson Street at the time and had gone to bed. All of a sudden there were all kinds of lights outside. Frank said, "What's going on?" and we looked out the window to see Eddie on the hook and ladder. He yelled out, "Happy New Year!"

Every Friday, Eddie would come to our door at 2:00 am. I'd get up and he would say, "This is the only restaurant that's open all night long." He stopped at the Jewish bakery on Robeson Street and would bring bread and bagels. Every Friday. He became our daughter's godfather.

**Food and Meals**

My mom would bake a lot and preserve food. She would make sweet bread, and there was always a pot of tea on the wood and coal stoves. Tea was a big thing. She would make goat cheese, massa, and bread pudding. My mother and father were great cooks.

To make sweet bread, you had to put it in a large deep pan; place a blanket over the pan, and keep kneading it. The pan was placed on a chair in back of the stove so the heat would make the dough rise. My father made a good bacalhau.

My father killed a pig in the back yard here. We made chourico and morcella here in the basement. In Portugal, they hung cow meat in the basement and there was never such a thing as salmonella. We didn't know what lobster or broccoli was as kids. Kale, peas, carrots, and corn were the only vegetables that we had as kids. For breakfast, we had milk crackers and coffee.

## School Life

I walked to the Doran School, from kindergarten to fifth grade. There were twenty-four to thirty kids in the classes. You could hear a pin drop; the kids were very attentive. We came home for lunch and then went back. We had nice teachers; we were taught well. From there, we went to the McDonough School from six to eighth grades and walked there also. I went to Durfee [B.M.C. Durfee High School] but left to help my folks.

## Recreation and Entertainment

My mom never bought us a bike; it was too dangerous. At age seventeen, I started dancing at The Casino on Morgan Street. Kids from each neighborhood stood in different parts of The Casino. It was all live music. Some big bands came there, including Lionel Hampton, Gene Krupa, and many other big bands that played there three and four times a week. When that closed, we went to Lincoln Park [North Dartmouth, Massachusetts] to dance. All the great bands played at Lincoln Park, including Tommy Dorsey, Lionel Hampton, Stan Kenton, and Xavier Cugat. Our first date was at the Lincoln Park Ballroom and Woody Herman was playing that night.

In the late 40s, we would go to the Celebrity Club in Providence to see stars like Ella Fitzgerald, Sarah Vaughn, Nat King Cole, Dizzy Gillespie, Billy Epstein, and the Mills Brothers. The club was owned by Paul Philipi.

Once, my father was at Fa-Neeck's on Stafford Road and played there until midnight. Then he said, "Let's go to my daughter's house." They came and played some more until the morning. It was a good thing that our neighbors downstairs were good about it. Our kids loved the music.

One New Year's Eve, our daughter had strep throat. We called Dr. Cronin, and he said that he would be there that night. "On New Year's Eve?" we asked. He said, "So?" We had company when he arrived and were playing music. He enjoyed listening to the music and stayed for a while; he hated to go. Meanwhile, his wife was waiting in the car, since they were going to a party. He looked at our daughter and said, "Strep throat!" He was a great doctor.

George Ferreira was a keyboard player and joined our neighbor's band. They practiced in our neighbor's garage. Dave Felix, our neighbor's son, was the leader, and his mom and dad supported them. Their names are Manuel and Alice Felix. My son would go there to hear them practice and we got to know all of the band members well. They were great kids. George always said that he would be a star someday and, a few years later, the band broke up and George went on to become a star. George became a friend to all of us. He was born in Portugal and came to America and resided in the Flint with his mom and dad and siblings. He is now popular all over the world and is on the Portuguese television channel a lot. He's very popular in France.

When we had the Holy Ghost in the house, there were people at home every night.

We always had a set of drums set up in the house. When we were married and lived at 32 Dickinson Street house, the guys would be practicing until 3:00 in the morning. When 32 Dickinson Street came up for sale, my father said, "If I buy it, will you move there." We said yes. After my parents died, this house was left to me.

## Courtship and Marriage

I first saw Frank at the Calumet Club, which was at the corner of South Main, Columbia, and Rodman Streets. We met at the Lincoln Park Ballroom and started to dance and have been dancing ever since.

## Work Life

I started working in the garment industry at a place called A&A on Pleasant Street. I walked to and from work. I couldn't afford bus fare. I first worked at Bayside, a maker of cheaper garments. Then to Gen Mar, then to Beacon, and then to the Hallmark Card Store in Somerset. I was the manager there. I left there to take care of my dad.

## Neighborhood Experiences

The Krasnow Drug Store was at the corner of Ferry and Canal Streets. Once in a while, we would go there for an ice cream with jimmies on it for five cents.

There were lots of grocery stores on Columbia Street. They put everything "on the book." You paid what you could. People were so thankful and helpful. When my father and mother found a family in need, they would buy bags of groceries and bring it to them.

Everyone had front porches, and we would converse with neighbors across the street.

Manuel Fernandes, his wife, Irene (Pereira) Fernandes, son Dennis, and daughter Lorraine Pontes

## Christmas, Holidays, and Special Occasions

My mom was my best friend. My father was humorous and funny. We always had music in our house. My grandfather would go around caroling (he died at forty-eight) and my uncle took it up. My uncle married an Italian woman and they were playing music all the time. I would sing, Frank would play the guitar, and someone would play spoons. Frank made a bass out of a galvanized round washtub. We still have it. We wrote the name of our group on it: "The La La Gang."

When we went caroling, we picked up people as we went along. We would have seven cars at the end of the night. We would go caroling all night. The last house made breakfast. We went to Midnight Mass; we never missed that. If Christmas was on a Monday, we went caroling all three days, from Saturday to Monday.

There were some funny moments, like when one guy kept singing on the other side of the door and wouldn't let us in; he kept us singing too long. Usually, we would take one drink and then leave, but one guy didn't want us to leave. He didn't want us to go, but we had to go to other houses. Once, we went to the Highlands to someone we didn't know just to see what would happen. It was George Oliveira of Oliveira Insurance. He wouldn't let us leave and gave us each a bottle of wine.

One Jewish fellow was married to one of David Souza's daughters; he owned a Dunkin' Donuts in New Bedford. After his celebration of Hanukkah, he cleared off the table of the Kosher food and brought in the chourico, linguica, and the other Portuguese food.

City Councilor Linda Pereira's mother came to sing at our door; she had a beautiful voice. She sang Portuguese carols. Linda's father, Freddy, also came.

The words to the caroling music are somewhat like this:

> Dear lady of the house,
> We are here at your door. (Repeat)
> We would like a small drink, a small drink of wine.
> La, la; la, la; la, la; la.
> Dear lady of the house, please open your door (door would open).
> Dear lady, would you give us permission to come in.

She would then give us permission to enter and we would eat and sing a few more songs, then go on to another house.

The real Portuguese ad lib it.

One year, after Christmas, we were sleeping when we heard people singing and playing Portuguese Christmas carols at the door. We said, "We better get up." The music stopped. We opened the door and it was Everett Silvia and his wife. He had tape recorded the music and plugged the tape recorder into a light socket. It sounded like a big band of people.

## Downtown

Downtown was great back then. We had five theatres downtown: the Durfee, the Capitol, the Empire, the Embassy, and the Plaza. There were beautiful stores like the Parisian Dress Shop, Cherry and Webb, McWhirr's, Bessy Russell (a men's store), 5 & 10s like Woolworth, and Kresege.

## The Depression

My grandmother was on welfare. We walked all the way from Ferry Street to the Weetamoe Mills in Border City Down North and walked back again with bags. I spoke Portuguese and English and interpreted for my grandmother because she couldn't speak English. My mom made pillow cases out of the welfare food bags.

## World War II

I was very young, in my teens, but I can remember the bombing of Pearl Harbor and the declaration of war when President Franklin Roosevelt talked on the radio. We all cried. All of my uncles joined the Navy. Frank went into the Army in 1946 and went to Japan. They had to find the Japanese who were in the bunkers in the hills.

# Daniel Reddy

*Born in 1930*

**Family Background**

My parents were Eugene and Dorothy (McViney) Reddy. My mother was related to Bishop McVinney of Providence, but her side of the family spelled their name with one "n." The family came from Prince Edward Island, Canada.

My father's parents were Frank and Margaret (Duffy) Reddy ("Maggie"). My mother's mother was Elizabeth Doherty.

I have six siblings: Eugene Reddy (known as "Ray"); Eileen Reddy (who became a nun); Gertrude; William; Regina; and Elizabeth ("Betty").

Our family residence was at 939 Bedford Street, located at the end of Wall Street.

**Family Life**

My father was a loom fixer. My brothers and I played a lot of ball. He was a good father and watched all of our games.

My father raised canaries. Only the male canaries sang. He whitewashed the unoccupied attic of one of the Bedford Street properties and put the uncaged canaries in the attic. One day, one of my aunts opened a window in the attic, and that was the end of the canaries.

The Doherty's owned three houses on Bedford Street. My great-grandfather Doherty had a barn on Healy Street where Rachelin's junk yard was located. I never knew him, because I was two when he died. He operated his teaming and livery business from the barn. Hemingway Movers later bought the business from my grandfather Doherty.

My great-grandfather delivered most of the gravestones to St. Patrick's Cemetery. The Doherty's have one of the largest monuments in St. Patrick's, which includes over ninety plots in the lot. The monument is near the front of the cemetery and has a Celtic cross on the top of it.

The house at 939 Bedford Street was a six-family. On the east side of the house, the first floor was occupied by the Noonan's (Mrs. Noonan was a Doherty); the second floor was occupied by Grandmother Doherty; and the third floor was occupied by Aunt Catherine. On the west side, the first floor was occupied by Uncle John Doherty; the second floor by the Reddy family; and the third floor by Grandmother Reddy. East of 939 Bedford was a two-family house owned by the family. On the first floor lived Rosie and Lizzie Doherty. Lizzie was friends with Lizzie Borden. The attic of this house is where my father kept his canaries. The cottage had a Bedford Street address but fronted on Healy Street in back.

My great-grandfather and then my grandfather owned a teaming business. His teams carried the stones from Beattie's Ledge to St. Patrick's Cemetery; the stones were used to build the wall around St. Patrick's. They also carried memorial stones to St. Patrick's.

My grandmother would go to Van Dykes for the butter during World War II. She was a good customer, and he would save two pounds of butter every week. My grandmother ate butter with a spoon, and still lived to be eighty-four years old. She would put out for herself a dish of butter and a can of snuff.

One day, when it was raining, she said, "Danny, come up here," and gave me five pennies to take the bus. I gave the bus driver the five pennies, and he threw them out the door and wouldn't let me on the bus. Back then, they called pennies "coppers." The next day, my grandmother got on the bus and grabbed the bus driver by the tie. She said, "Next time you do that, I will wring your neck."

I brought up my grandmother's coal for her house, and she gave me ten cents a week. I delivered groceries for the A&P on Bedford Street for a dollar a week. My grandmother got all upset that I was being paid so little. Although she was 5 feet, 2 inches tall, she went to the store manager and said that she would "wipe the floor" with him if he didn't do something about this. They then doubled my salary to two dollars a week.

My grandmother came here from Ireland, north of Dublin. She lost a brother coming over on the boat. His name was Willie. He got separated from the family on the boat and they never found him. My grandmother worked in the mill. I carried the dinner pails for my grandfather and father who both worked in a mill at the end of Quarry Street, south of Pleasant Street. They wouldn't let me cross Pleasant Street, so they met me on Pleasant Street every day to take the pails.

**Friends**

The Columbus Day festival included a greasy pole. Jim Primo ("Stuffy") was usually the winner. On top of the pole was a large heavy Italian sausage. It was worth about five dollars. Stuffy won it every time. He wrapped a sweater around the pole and went right up. The pole was about forty feet high.

Some of my friends were Anthony Veronese ("Mush"), Johnny Conforti (whose nickname was "Zip;" he later played baseball for Coyle High School). All of the Italian players who played baseball at Columbus Park were great players.

**Nicknames**

Jim Primo was "Stuffy." Andrew Primo was "Honey." My brother William Reddy was "Wild Bill." I was called "Sparky" and, to this day, people still call me by that name. I got the name from my older brother, who is three and one-half years older than me. In the Catholic schools, you had to go home for lunch. Sacred Heart School was a fifteen- to twenty-minute walk from our house, and I was slow. There was a popular cartoon at that time called "Barney Google and Spark Plug," and my brother would say, "Come on, Sparky; let's go." The name stuck. My son-in-law, Paul LeCompte, who works as a framer at Riverside Art, once found an old newspaper in the back of a picture to be reframed and it included a cartoon of "Barney Google and Spark Plug." He framed it and gave it to me.

**Food and Meals**

When I was in school, my mother had the same menu every week for Monday through Friday. Friday was grilled cheese and fish. I didn't like fish, so I got Campbell's tomato soup and crackers. On Thursday, we had beef stew. Another day, we had spaghetti. On Sundays, we would have a pork roast or smoked shoulder, sometimes a meatloaf. We ate a lot of Italian food, since my mother grew up in an Italian neighborhood.

**School Life**

I went to Sacred Heart School. We were members of the Immaculate Conception parish, but Quarry Street was the dividing line between the parishes. If you lived within the parish boundary, you went to Sacred Heart School for free. Since I lived outside the boundary, my family paid twenty-five cents a week for me to go there. There were seven kids in the family, and we always had three children in the school.

My brother Bill missed school so often that my father had to go to court. Bill wouldn't come home until my father left for work. Bill later became a policeman. Bill was my hero; he was great at baseball and could knock the ball out of Columbus Park.

**Recreation and Entertainment**

I played outside at Columbus Park most of the time. We would play games like buck, buck. On Sunday mornings after church, Columbus Park was a big peggy ball place for teenagers.

In those days, you belonged to the parish of your mother's nationality. I couldn't play for Holy Rosary, even though I lived a block away, because we were Irish. John Potota had to play for Notre Dame, since his mother was French. I would have preferred to play with my neighborhood friends, but I had to play for the Sacred Heart team. However, I made a lot of friends there too, so that was an advantage.

The Sacred Heart School won the Catholic School Baseball Championship in 1945, when I was in the eighth grade. "Skippy" Lewis was one of our teammates and became a Triple A player. He was later injured, and coached after that.

CYO [Catholic Youth Organization] was good. There were northern and southern divisions of the CYO in Fall River. Sacred Heart played against St. Mary's, St. Joseph's, and many others.

We went to both Sandy Beach and Bliffins Beach, but mostly to Bliffins. I was a good swimmer. Bliffins had a high diving platform, forty feet at the highest diving board, and two or three different levels. Jack Mercer and his two sisters were great swimmers and raced locally. They were called "The Swimming Mercers."

**Courtship and Marriage**

I met my wife while taking a swimming test at Houghton's Pond. I went to a dance that night, and her brother introduced me to her. That began a three and a half year romance. If I had the dollar and thirty-five cents, I took the bus to Mattapan, where she lived. If I didn't, I hitch-hiked from Fall River to Mattapan Square and back.

I was in the Naval Air Reserves. I met my wife when I was eighteen years old, when we were at Boot Camp at Squantum in Hingham. Her brother drove her down. When I started dating her, I rang the doorbell and there would be boyfriends around in the house. I never owned a car, so her brother drove her down to Fall River when she came down. Her brother finally bought us a car; he was sick of driving us around.

**Work Life**

I delivered papers, both the morning and evening editions, My route included all the way up to County Street to Tremont Street. I did this in the sixth and seventh grades. I made ninety-two cents a week, and I turned all of it in to the family. Later, I delivered groceries for the A&P market on Bedford Street.

I joined the Naval Reserves at the age of seventeen. My brother Eugene had a job at the Newport Naval Base, and he got me a job there. I worked there for forty-two years, first as a draftsman and then as a sub technician. I've been on more submarines than many Navy men.

**Neighborhood Experiences**

I played in Columbus Park, which was right across Bedford Street from our house. I played baseball a lot, and I held my own.

Columbus Day was always a big thing. We always had guests that night. I lived in the Italian district, and it was a great experience.

We ate mackerel fish all the time; I hated fish. There was a fish wagon drawn by a horse that came down Healy Street every week (to avoid the trolley's on Bedford Street) where fish was sold from the wagon. They sold the whole fish; if you wanted it filleted or cleaned, you had to pay extra. The iceman and rag man also came up the street.

Marzilli's Bakery had their wood oven on the Bedford Street side of the store. We sometimes had to close our windows because the smoke would blow in the windows.

My grandmother got a twenty-five cent piece of ice. My mother had a nice icebox; she got a refrigerator when they first came out.

Mash's grandfather made wine. On VJ Day, Mash and I consumed some of the wine. We were fifteen years old.

**Christmas, Holidays, and Special Occasions**

We were poor, but we always got a toy at Christmas. My father bought coal, and with every unit of coal, you were given 200 S&H Green Stamps. My first sled was bought with S&H Green Stamps. There was a shop on Borden Street where you could cash in your stamps. My brother Bill and I shared a lot of Christmas presents. I got the bike because of my paper route. Bill became a police officer and later a detective here in Fall River. He had the #1 badge. He loved the job and never wanted to retire; he loved to talk.

**Health and Illness**

Every Friday, my grandmother gave us something to clean us out. She would call out, "Line up; we have to clean you out." It tasted terrible. My father got pneumonia when I was thirteen. It was very bad. They set up an oxygen tank in the room. He was released from the hospital on my fourteenth birthday.

**The Fall River Line**

My mom's brother, Leo Doherty, was once coming back from New York on the Fall River Line. On a dare, he got on the railing and jumped overboard. He swam all the way back to Fall River. It got publicized and many people were waiting for him—including my grandfather—when he swam back to the city. When he got off of the boat he was greeted with a punch from my grandfather. All of my mother's family were good swimmers. Leo was handsome and a charmer; he looked like Errol Flynn. He has some pretty wealthy girlfriends, and was married five times; my mother was not too proud of it. When he was broke, he always came back to live with my mother.

# Helen (Franco) Rocha

*Born in 1925*

**Family Background**

My parents Miguel Moniz and Mariana Franco.

My father's siblings were Manuel, Joao, Jose, Antonio, and Maria.

My mother's siblings were Maria, Guilheranna, Maria Jose, Isabella, Matilde, Victoria, and Antonio.

My siblings are Michael, John, Manuel ("Manny"), Mario ("Morty"), Clotilde ("Tillie"), Charles, Ignez (which she changed to Agnes and then to Irene), Mary, and Arthur ("Archie").

My husband is Antone Rocha and we have seven children: Helena, Anthony, Marian, David, Phillip, Paul, and John.

**Family Life**

My mother and her family came here from the old country. My grandmother got sick on the voyage. They arrived during Holy Week and she died on Good Friday. They settled in the Flint on Raymond Street. At the time, the Flint was French. Each ethnic group got picked on: whoever came last got picked on. The Portuguese were called "Portagee Stink Fish!" by the French. My aunt knew it was a derogatory term and wanted to say something back. Someone taught her to say, "You stink shit!"

I was born on the first floor of 95 Healy Street, in the middle bedroom. My birth was the first time that my mother had a doctor deliver one of her babies; all of the seven others before me were delivered by a midwife.

I was delivered by Dr. Boylan, who forgot to register me at city hall, so my birth was never recorded. When I was getting married, I had to go to the City Hall to get my birth certificate. But they said I wasn't registered. I had to go to the parish to get my baptism certificate. If I hadn't been baptized, I wouldn't have had proof of my birth. What's funny about this is that Dr. Boylan became the medical examiner for the city for years and years.

I was a breech baby, and my father told me that Dr. Boylan told him that both my mother and I were going to die. My father prayed to St. Anthony to spare us, and he did. My father promised to say prayers every night for the rest of his life if we were saved, and he did. He said the Our Father, the Hail Mary, and the Gloria.

When I first started school, my father worked in the Flint Mills. My two older sisters would go home for lunch. My mother would make my father's lunch pail and carried it to the mill. The first time I stepped into the mill—I was in kindergarten then—I was terrified. The sound of the machinery was so loud! I just stood there, frightened.

My mother didn't know how to read and write, but she picked up English very well, probably in the mills.

We had so much fun and laughed so much. There were three bedrooms in our house. Three slept in one bedroom, two in another, and the two older sisters slept in the other bedroom. My sister and I slept in a day bed in the kitchen. As brothers or sisters left the house, we would move up to the better beds.

When you're a kid, you don't realize certain things. When you are older, you realize how fortunate you were. I didn't feel poor; my father had a garden and my mother was a good cook.

I never had a birthday party until I was eighteen years old. No one got birthday cards. We didn't miss it or were offended by it; it just was that way. Our Christmas was simple. Our parents hung stockings out, with an orange and an apple in the bottom—after that, walnuts and mixed nuts. At school, we got a little box of Christmas candy.

Our icebox had a swinging flap door in front of the box on the bottom. Behind the door was the drain pan. A drain pipe came down to the pan from the ice compartment. If you forgot to empty the pan, there would be a mess.

We had a clothes line from the house to a large pole in the back yard. When my mother lived on Quarry Street, she had clothes on the outdoor line, and it rained and froze overnight. In the morning, the woman who owned the house (a Protestant) told my mother to take the clothes off the line, since it was Sunday. You couldn't have clothes on the line on Sundays. My mother's hands were frozen from taking the clothes off of the line.

My father taught me my ABC's in English and my prayers in Portuguese. My father was a wonderful father. The youngest would get his dinner pail when he came in the door after work. Whenever he had a dessert of fruit, he brought it home for the youngest child. I loved and looked forward to that little treat.

My father worked at the Flint Mill; that was the last mill that he worked in. He retired when he got respiratory problems from breathing in cotton dust. He also lost part of his hearing; many people in the mills did. He was a loom-fixer and went to Bradford Durfee Tech to learn loom-fixing.

My brother Arthur and sister Irene graduated from Bradford Durfee Tech. Irene was the first woman accepted to Bradford Durfee Tech. She designed the first colored sheets.

My mother was wise; what a wise woman. For a woman who couldn't read or write (although she spoke English well), she was really "cool."

My mother never swore at us; never, never. But, if something got her angry enough, she would swear. One day, I was in the bedroom and she was in the kitchen. I heard her say, "That little bastard." I ran in and she said, "Look at that." One of my brothers lived upstairs, and one of my nieces was sitting on the curb. A boy who lived in the next house comes by with an ear of corn. My niece asks, "Can I have bite?" The boy says, "No!" He took another bite of the corn and rubbed the ear of corn in the dirt in the gutter. My mother was angry. "I wish I had some fruit in the house," she said. Right then, a fruit peddler came down the road. She went out to the cart and bought some bananas. She peeled a banana and gave it to Ronnie, the girl. The boy says, "*Vavo*, can I have one?" "No," she said, "You wouldn't give her a bite of your corn, now you watch her eat the banana." I later met the boy (now grown) who hadn't given Ronnie a bite of his corn. He still remembered the event. He told me, "Your mother wouldn't give me a banana."

My brother had eight kids and he had them all in a singing group called the Singing Franco Family. They were quite popular and well-known in this area.

**Neighborhood Experiences**

Healy Street was a great street. In addition to number 95, our lot also had 101 Healy. About three feet away from the house was a fence and after that was a meadow and David Rachelin's junk yard. He was a very nice man. After the junkyard was a meadow and then the Stafford Mills beyond. I think it was Bowler Street. From Bowler Street were the mills and then County Street.

I walked from our house to the Espirito Santo School, exactly one mile. At that time, the Quequechan River ran right up to the schoolyard. We never had a car, and it was impractical to take the bus to the school because we would have to take the bus downtown and then back up Pleasant Street.

When the Prince Henry statue was erected on Eastern Avenue in the 1940s, it was a big issue. The French were very hostile to it. When I was going to the Portuguese school, the parents were immigrants. The kids were second generation, and most of the kids spoke broken English because their parents spoke Portuguese at home. The French always spoke French, not English. The French always spoke French to one another when you passed them.

There was a house two houses away from us on Healy Street. At one time, it was a nice house owned by an Italian family. Then other people came in. Then, one Saturday morning, a "Black Mariah" (a police van) came up. Two old ladies lived on the top floor of the two and one-half story house. When I got there, neighbors were clustered around the house. The two old ladies were drunk and naked. The police brought them down in blankets and put them in the Black Mariah. I was ten at the time.

The peddlers came with hand carts. The push carts had big shallow boxes on the carts that carried fruits and vegetables. Other carts bought rags. Jewish peddlers would yell out, "Rag Man! Got any rags?" There was a fish man and an iceman who also came by. Most of the peddlers had push carts.

**Downtown**

Fall River was such a thriving town. It was wonderful. We had a classy downtown with stores like McWhirr's and Cherry and Webb's. There was a grandeur about Cherry's; it had a beautiful staircase. The salespeople were dressed nicely and were always helpful.

McWhirr's was a unique store. You could buy anything there, from a pin to a piano. You could go on an elevator to the upper floors. On the first floor was a lending library, where you could pay a few cents to borrow a book. A post office was also on the basement floor. You could mail your packages right there. Older and younger women worked at McWhirr's. The cashiers didn't handle money; they would put the money into a vacuum tube and it would travel on the track to the offices, and the change sent down. They had a nice lunch counter, where they served hot lunches on real plates as well as the other lunch items. It was convenient for you if you were shopping and wanted lunch.

At Grant's 5 & 10 there was a piano as you walked in the door, with someone playing the tunes of the day. If you wanted to buy a sheet of music, this person would play the music for you. Downstairs, Grant's sold housewares, kitchenware, fabric, and anything for sewing. Other downtown 5 & 10s were Kresge's, Woolworth's, and Newbury's. They later had a store called the Enterprise. There was no self-service; you got waited on by a person. There were quite a few shoe stores downtown.

I felt safe in Fall River. I would go to the movies alone. There were continuous cartoons, the

"March of Time," and the main feature. If I wanted to, I could stay there, since the movies ran continuously. The movies ended about 11:00 pm or midnight. I walked from the Durfee Theatre all the way home. I was a fast walker. Bedford Street was lined with bars then and there was always a gang of young guys hanging out in front of the bars. If one of the guys swore, someone would say, "Hey, watch it; here comes a girl." I never felt threatened or uncomfortable.

**Recreation and Entertainment**

The most elegant theatre was the Durfee Theatre. When you went into the main lobby, there was a beautiful staircase going up to the balconies. It had a very long lobby, with all of the coming attractions shown in posters in glass cases. The ushers were in uniforms. The Durfee was designed after the Alhambra Palace and had a goldfish pool that everyone stopped to admire. There was also the Empire, the Capitol, and the Academy, which was once an opera house. After Rodman Street, there was the Plaza and the Park Theatres.

Every Saturday, there were serials such as *Flash Gordon*. I hated the Three Stooges, although I love them now.

The first movie that I saw I think was the first talking movie. One of my brothers played the organ at the church. One brother took me to the movies, and I was too small to see anything from the seat so they put me on the arm of the chair. When someone started singing a song in the movie, I started singing it with them. At the end of the song, I got applause from the audience. I was too young to be embarrassed.

For games, we played kick the can, hide and seek. There were no toys. We made our own kites with small pieces of wood and newspaper. Rags were used for tails on the kites. We had this goofy game where we took a piece of broken glass, put a piece of glass over a piece cut out of a cartoon, then we would bury it. Then, we would forget where we buried it. I don't know why we did it.

**School Life**

In the Portuguese school, we spoke English. When I was in kindergarten to third grades, I spoke better English than the other kids. They would call me "show-offa." The kids of Portuguese parents tried to learn English, but the French were very clannish.

From eighth grade, I went to Durfee [B.M.C. Durfee High School] in 1940 for one year, then to Jesus Marie Academy. I loved it. The classes were only twenty in size.

**Religious Life**

Notre Dame Church was beautiful. Even though I went to Jesus Marie Academy, I didn't go to Notre Dame Church. One year, I went to Midnight Mass at Notre Dame. The Prevost choir and the brothers were singing. There were about 150 to 200 voices. The church was lit in a blaze of light. It was quite impressive. When the choir sang, there was not a dry eye in the church. It was so magnificent, so beautiful. If there is a heaven, that was the closest I came to it.

**Prohibition**

An uncle of mine was a rum-runner. My father and his brother made wine for the house. My brother won a soccer scholarship to Northeastern University. He made root beer at home. I loved to watch him siphon the root beer from the barrel to the bottles and to put the caps on the bottle.

**Food and Meals**

My mother was a very good cook. My father kept chickens. We had a four-stall garage in the back yard, and he kept two of the stalls for the chickens. He raised chicks there and got eggs from the chickens. He had a garden in back of the house and to the side of the garage. In March, he would put up a cold frame made of the old-style windows from a house.

He planted seeds in March, and we would have fresh vegetables all year long. The boys helped him with the garden. We had kale, cabbage, potatoes, peppers (red-hot peppers to make pimento-muida), and Bell peppers. We always had mint. I always brought mint to my mother every time I came back from the garden; she loved the smell of mint.

**Work Life**

I worked at Seal Sac for two summers. They made plastic bowl covers and garment bags and stuff like that. This was in 1942 and 1943. They were in the fifth floor of the Union Mill, where Prima Care is now. As a student, I worked at Margaret's Bakery on Pleasant Street in the Flint. I also worked at McClellan's 5 & 10 in the Flint and at Kresge's.

**World War II**

When Pearl Harbor happened, I was at home on a Sunday. I didn't realize the impact then. I had never lived through a war. I only learned of wars through history at school. I didn't realize the impact of war.

I joined the USO on Franklin Street. There was dancing there, with music by various orchestras or from a juke box. There was a big dance area inside and a kitchen for coffee and donuts. The boys were from all over the country. Many were far from home. They were usually polite. One Christmas, my mother asked me, "Go down to the club and see if anyone would like to come to dinner." There was one fellow there sitting on a couch. "Are you going anywhere for dinner?" I asked. He said, "No." So, I asked him to join us. The streets were deserted, but there were three sailors hanging around the 5 & 10s. I asked the guy to go up to them and ask them to come to dinner. "All three?" he asked. "Yes." They weren't so sure, but we ended getting into a cab and went home.

My brother also came home with a serviceman who was stationed with him at Devens. So, we had six servicemen and six in our family. One of the servicemen had a tooth extracted earlier in the week and, being hungry, ate like he never ate before. At the end of the meal, the guys asked for dish towels, put them in their belts to make aprons, and did the dishes. It was wonderful, just wonderful.

One evening, I went to Ventura's Drug Store. Two sailors were standing outside the drugstore. It was unusual to see sailors up here, this far from downtown. Sailors loved chow mein sandwiches at the China Royal. So, when I came out of the drug store, I said, "Hi!" "Looking for someone?" They said no. "Would you like to come to my house for coffee?" They had coffee with us, and later they would drop by every now and then for coffee and to visit—John Harris and John Pratt.

One night, there was a car parked in front of our house when I came home. It was the two sailors. "No one is home!" they said. My parents were always home, but this time they weren't. "Want to go for a ride?" they asked. We passed by a bar on the corner of South Main and Columbia Streets and they asked, "Do you ever go in there?" and I said no. They said, "You better not!" They treated me like a sister.

The boy that I picked up at Christmas at the USO was named Dave Ringle. He bought a junky car later and asked me to go for a ride. I got in and we went for a ride to my aunt's farm in Westport [Massachusetts]. The car made an awful noise. As we passed the Howard Johnson's at Pleasant and County Streets, everyone came out to see where the loud noise was coming from. It drew crowds.

My sister Tillie married a fellow who went in the Navy. He started from Boston and was transferred to the State of Washington. Sis went out there with him. I came home from school one day and Dave Ringle was in the living room, laying on the couch. He said, "Tillie left today." And he added, " She told me to give you something." He then kissed me on the temple, like a brother.

There was a girl next door called Elkie who would stand by the gate. I introduced Dave to Elkie. He then said, "Elkie and I are going to the movies." He never thought to invite me because he thought of me as his sister. We would go bowling or to a movie. He was a nice guy; he was never away from home before.

One day, I got a letter from a marine, Dick Merkle. It had one dollar inside. His aunt was a nun. He wanted to say a Mass for special intentions. I went to Holy Rosary Church and showed the letter to the priest. A few days later, I got another letter from Dick with another dollar in it saying that the special intentions were granted. The dollar was for me.

Another boy wanted to marry me and send me back to his mama in Oklahoma. No way!

We always had "Red Sea Balsam" in the house to use on cuts. The balsam was put on the cut and a warm cloth was put over it. One day, my mother had to leave my brother Charlie to help a neighbor whose baby was choking on a piece of apple. When she got back, Charlie had torn his stomach on a nail that stuck out of a wood box. She put the balsam on the cut with the warm cloth on top and put him to bed. My father came home, didn't see the baby, and asked "Where's the baby?" He's in bed, my mother said, and explained the accident. My mother showed him the cut on Charlie, and my father fainted dead away.

One of my brothers would drink the Red Sea Balsam right from the bottle for a cold. Years later, I saw a display of the balsam in Braz's Market in Somerset, on a bottom shelf. The bottle was unmistakable, with its octagon-shaped bottle and a sail on the label. "Oh, my God," I said. "I haven't seen this in years." When I read the label, it said, "For external use only." My mom couldn't read, and my brother didn't die.

My sister, who once was a WAC [Women's Army Corps], had an antique shop on Plymouth Avenue. The two of us heard on the radio that we had won the war. Once this happened, all the churches were to open and to have a thanksgiving mass. We went to the nearest church, St. Mary's, and tried to get in but it was too mobbed with people. As the people left the church, a sailor was in the back of the church. We noticed that he seemed to be crying and we went up to see what was the matter. He said that his family was destroyed by the bombing of Pearl Harbor. We both asked him if he would come to our house for a cup of coffee. He said that he would. After that, we never heard from him again.

# Angelo Stavros

*Born on January 29, 1933*

**Family Background**

I was born at St. Anne's Hospital. My parents were James Arthur and Helen (Miller) Stavros (Greek ancestry).

My siblings were Diane S. Joiner (a Marine), Neove Leary (who had four children and was a cashier at Woolworth's for many years), Nancy S. Kramer (who worked at the *Fall River Herald News*), and Marion S. Bwedder.

My wife is Cremilde (Torres) Stavros [Cremilde's interview follows this one in the book].

**Family Life**

My father was outgoing. He and his brother opened up a fruit store downtown, but it was destroyed in the 1928 fire. He was located where the First Fed Bank was on the corner of Bedford and North Main Streets (northeast corner). He lost everything; he had no insurance. He then went to work for Central Lunch. He came to this country when he was seventeen; my mother was fifteen when she came over. My father was a wonderful man; he died of a stroke. My mother was a seamstress.

We lived on the corner of South Main and South Streets, at 16 South Street, on the first floor. The family of Jim Panos lived on the second floor. There was a French family on the third floor, but two or three families moved in and out. People took pride in their homes.

**School Life**

I would go to Greek School on Monday, Wednesday, and Friday. Monday and Wednesday were for learning Greek and Friday was for religious teaching. My parents taught us the value of education. Discipline and respect were taught in the home. Values were important.

In the 1940s, I attended the Robeson School on Columbia Street, then the John J. McDonough School, and on to [B.M.C.] Durfee High School. I played basketball for Durfee. After graduation, I went on to the Navy for three and one-half years. Then back to school.

**Neighborhood Experiences**

It was a totally mixed ethnic neighborhood. Every ethnic group went to our own churches. There were ethnic rivalries.

In the 1950s, I, and most of my friends, congregated at the State Lunch, next to the Durfee Theatre. Most of the downtown diners were owned by Greeks: the State Lunch, the Central Lunch, Rector's Spa, Nira's, Star Lunch, and The Nonpareil ice cream parlor. James Marvelis owned the Central Lunch, where my father worked after the 1928 fire.

Nick Pappas owned Nick's Coney Island Hot Dogs. At the corner of South Main Street and Morgan Street was the Capitol News, also owned by Greeks, the Litos family. An ice cream parlor near South Park [now Kennedy Park] that later became Mitchell's Drug Store, owned by Nick Mitchell's father. Bounakas owned The Nonpareil. The Granite Block Spa was owned by the Konas family. The Bijou Restaurant north of the Public Library was owned by James Gianakis. The Bijou Theatre was next door. George Charos Coney Island Hot Dogs place was located on Pleasant Street, where it is today. Those were the only two Coney Island hot dog places in the city then.

On Saturdays, we would go downtown to Kresge's and Woolworth's. Downtown was so busy you had to walk on the streets. We would go to Kennedy's and to Van Dykes, located across the street; they had great sandwiches.

Where we grew up, there were only three or four Greek families. Most Greek families lived near the Greek Church that was located on Cherry Street. We would go to Greek picnics off of Stafford Road in Westport [Massachusetts].

**Food and Meals**

In the morning, we would have a normal breakfast. On Sundays, we would have chicken. Then it was boiled to make chicken broth and soup. We also had a dish with chicken livers. We had chicken every Sunday and lamb every fourth Sunday. On Greek holidays we had lamb.

**Religious Life**

The father of George Stephanopoulos was the pastor of the Greek Church here for two or three years.

During Lent, we would fast, then after the Mass on Saturday night, come home and have a big meal after church. We would march outside with the candles and walked the candles home and tried to keep them from going out. One of the traditions was to color eggs red and then hit them against another person's egg, from oldest to the youngest. The winner was the person with the last unbroken egg.

**Courtship and Marriage**

Our courtship involved going out to movies at theatres; I then went into the Navy and we corresponded. I played basketball in the Navy. Most of us went to Horseneck Beach to the Spindrift, which was located on the other side of the river, between the old bridge and where the new bridge is now.

# Cremilde "Millie" (Torres) Stavros

*Born on March 29, 1930*

**Family Background**

I was born at home at 46 Oregon Street, corner of Cory Street. My parents were Joseph R. and Mary (Reis) Torres.

My husband is Angelo Stavros [Angelo's interview precedes this one in the book].

**Family Life**

My parents were wonderful people. My mother worked in the Narragansett Mill. My father had a milk cart when he was very young. It was a horse and cart and he delivered food pails in the factory and they would buy them. My father and his brothers had the garbage contract with the city for sixteen years. My father was hard working. He had three brothers and one sister. Together, they worked as a team, owning a grocery store, four tenement houses, and a garbage collection business. They were known as The Torres Brothers.

My father made wine all the time, and one of my aunts, a single woman at the time, made fruit liquors. He was always active. He developed cancer and went to Boston for radiation; the doctors there said, "You have the heart of a young man."

My mother was very smart. She was not an educated woman (few were in those days), but she could do anything she set her mind to. All my friends loved her. She was respected by her friends and relatives. She could knit, sew, crochet, and embroider (not her favorite thing). She made all our clothes. Mom and sister Lea knitted coats, hats, mittens, and sweaters. She knitted many of her own hats and purses (I still have some). She loved to read and look at magazines. My sister Lea and I were very close. She married Gil Olivera of Olivera Insurance.

My aunt Mary Torres would make candy out of tea. We would cut up pastel tissue paper and all sit around her dining room table and she would cut a piece of the candy and roll it in the tissue paper and twist each end. These were prepared for May and Easter. She had a roller piano and we would gather around the piano and sing all the songs.

The Torres family donated a stained glass window at St. Michael's Church and contributed some of the funds to have the new St. Michael's School built and also donated to the St. Michael's School, at Lindsey and George Streets.

**Friends**

The Torres and the family of Juliet Meyrelles were best friends. They had a big cherry tree in their yard, and we would go in the attic and eat cherries. I was jealous that we didn't have an attic in our house. They lived on Burns Street in a two-family house. Juliet was very pretty, with blond hair and blue eyes. She was always beautifully dressed; her mother made all of her clothes. She loved to laugh and tell jokes and was extremely outgoing. She was an only child and always wished that she had a brother or sister. She was much more daring than I was.

The Rochas were a large family with many children. Rita was my best friend. Her sister Amelia was afraid of my sister Lea. Rita lived across the street from me. Louis is still living. He married a girl Irene who lived on our street. His wife's brother was killed in the Pearl Harbor attack; he was a pilot. Another brother was killed in World War II.

The neighborhood was like family. You lived with your parents until the day you were married. You stayed in sight.

**Food and Meals**

We sat down as a family for dinner daily. My mother cooked my father's favorite foods. His favorite meat was pork (as is mine). We ate a lot of Portuguese soup. She added chourico to many things. We all loved and ate many crabs. My father made clam boils in a big copper pan outside on a roaring fire at our summer home. At the dinner table, we talked about happenings in the family, in the neighborhood, in church, and in school.

My mother made so many wonderful and beautifully decorated cookies. When my sister and I started our own families, she began decorating a Christmas tree that consisted of all cookies.

**School Life**

I went to St. Michael's School, Morton Junior High, and [B.M.C.] Durfee High School, and sang in their choirs. I would get very nervous, though, if I had to sing solo in front of an audience. Once, I sang for Mayor Grant, and I got so nervous that nothing came out. For my first solo, I sang "Green Eyes" at the St. Michael's Church bazaar.

At St. Mathieu's School, the nuns taught only in French. At St. Michael's School, we were taught in English but had Portuguese twice a week. We never spoke Portuguese outside of home.

I had wonderful memories of my high school days at Durfee. My friends and I attended all the games (football, basketball, baseball) and we fell in love with all the heroes. I was also a Durfee cheerleader. We went to the proms every year and talked on the phone for hours. I packed nine people in my car after graduation. We danced at the Tip Toppers, the Hi Coeds, and the YMCA.

**Recreation and Entertainment**

Juliet Meyrelles, Rita Rocha, and I would play movies: we would act, sing, and then burst out laughing. I liked to play and imitate Shirley Temple; I had a Shirley Temple doll. On rainy days, we would look out the window and wave, make pictures on the window, and act silly.

We did all of the things that children did in those days: ride bikes, roller skate, skip rope, hide and seek, and talked about school, the things we liked and disliked.

We would go to the Newport [Rhode Island] beaches and my father would go fishing while the others would go swimming. North Park had the pond were we could wet our feet. We would also go down to Bliffins Beach. On weekends, we would go to Sandy Beach by car. We played marbles; I had a big box of marbles. During my high school days, my parents owned a summer cottage on East Beach in Westport [Massachusetts].

My father was an indoor roller skater, but my mother did not skate. He took us roller skating to the Portsmouth [Rhode Island] Roller Rink. My mother made us skating outfits. My father played cards with friends at the Republican Club.

My mother wanted her daughters to have music lessons. My sister played the piano and I took voice lessons, violin, and tap dancing. She was so proud of us; we were her life.

Our family went to the 1938 World's Fair in New York City. I was eight years old and my sister was thirteen. I remember very well a man saying that we would have televisions in our homes some day. My father said, "Not in my lifetime." When we bought our first television set, he couldn't believe it. He loved Milton Berle. When the TV was on, he didn't want us to talk. He enjoyed all of the rides at the World's Fair; my mother would not go on any of them; she sat in the vineyard. He loved New York and loved to dance; my mother was too shy. He was very honest and generous.

**Courtship and Marriage**

We met at Lincoln Park. All the boys and girls went there to dance in the ballroom. My mom was not happy that I went there. We were to be married in the rectory by Father Silvia, since Angelo was not Catholic. I didn't like the idea, since it was a cramped space. Father Silvia said, "That's what you get for marrying a non-Catholic." My father said, "Don't worry about it; I'll take care of it." My father intervened, and we got married in the church. In those days, if you were Portuguese, you married Portuguese, or an Irish person married an Irish person.

**Work Life**

After graduating from Bryant College, I worked in the office at the Arkwright warehouse—United Merchants. I left after five years to have my first child and decided to go back to school. I went to Roger Williams College for a Bachelor of Arts degree and became a full-time teacher at the Girls Vocational School on Morgan Street and at Durfee High School. I loved teaching. I had found my vocation. The students I taught (most) were great kids. I missed them when I retired. I taught in the Business Department, which no longer exists.

**Neighborhood Experiences**

The neighborhood held an annual "matança." Pigs were brought from a slaughterhouse and a matança resurrected. Families and friends gathered together to cut up meat and made chourico, morcella, and various other things. Food was served and music was played. People with grape arbors brought grapes. The youngsters in the family would bring some of the food to neighbors and would receive one dollar as a tip.

Stores in the neighborhood included the Shalloo Market, owned by the father of Monsignor Shalloo. It was located next to the mill on Oregon Street. The Shalloos lived next to us. Father Shalloo was in the seminary when I was young, so I didn't know him. My parents and the entire neighborhood went to his ordination. My father and three of his brothers gave a sterling silver tea set to him at his ordination. His sister, Marie Shalloo, taught German and other languages at Durfee and was an advisor.

Michael's Chourico was way up on Lindsey Street, next to and to the rear of the Republican Club. The North Star Bakery was owned by the Silvia family.

The Lima grocery store was diagonally across the street from our house. We went there often. Mrs. Lima was a very pleasant woman. My mother would tell the story of older Isabelle. She was engaged to be married, but her fiancé died. She was engaged twice, but both her fiancés died before the wedding. She had a trunk full of things for her marriage. Later in life, she married a Mr. Pavao. The Lima family owned the building with the store and the house next to it.

I would cross the railroad tracks to get to the bus line. I walked the tracks when it was pitch black late at night to get home and was never afraid of anything. It was a short cut home. In those days, you did it and didn't blink an eyelash.

**Christmas, Holidays, and Special Occasions**

In my childhood days, my mother would say, while decorating the tree, "Remember the tinsel goes on one by one." My sister Lea and I always had an abundance of toys. Visiting relatives was fun. I had many cousins. There was never a dull moment. We didn't have to drive because we all lived in the same yard. There was so much to do. Two of my cousins played the piano by ear; they never took lessons and couldn't read a note. They played Christmas carols and the rest of us sang. On Christmas eve, groups of people would come around with their guitars and sing Portuguese songs.

**Health and Illness**

My mother's sister's husband got influenza during the great epidemic in 1918 and died of it. Their son of four or five years also died of it. They are buried together at St. Patrick's Cemetery. Their daughter got pneumonia just before graduating from Durfee and died from it in 1938. I still put flowers on their grave.

My mother said that it was a daily occurrence to see people coming out of their houses in shrouds. Everyone was terrified of it. No one knew who would be next. There were not enough doctors, and there was no cure for the influenza. My grandfather told his wife, "Let's go back to Portugal." They did it with the exception of my mother, who was about to marry, and her oldest sister, who was already married. Her sisters and one brother returned to this country as married couples with children after many years.

**The Depression**

My father owned a grocery store on Lindsey Street during the Depression called the Torres Brothers Market. He sent baskets of food to people; otherwise they would have starved. Later, in a drawer in his desk, he had rolls of paper. I asked him what they were for, and he said that they were the bills of the people who were sent baskets of food. Some paid him back, but others didn't. Many people said, "If it wasn't for your father, we would have starved to death."

**Popular Expressions**

"In the blink of an eyelash."
"Give me some skin."
"Shake a leg (make it fast)."
"Cut it out."

# Elizabeth "Betty" (Turner) Sullivan

*Born on August 11, 1929*

## Family Background

My parents were Leo and Loretta (Smith) Turner. My father's parents were John and Esther Turner. My mother's parents were Thomas and Elizabeth (Cassidy) Smith.

My father's siblings were Irene, Arthur Joseph, and Raymond. My mother's siblings were Mary, Ellen, Thomas, and Rita.

I had one brother named Jackie, who died at ten months.

My husband is John Joseph Sullivan and we have two children, Patrick Michael and Elizabeth May.

## Family Life

Grandmother Elizabeth (Cassidy) Smith came from Ireland in 1880. She was born in Ireland about 1875. Her father, my great-grandfather, was a mason and built the old Sacred Heart School. Her mother died in childbirth. She had an older brother, John, and an older sister, Mary (Aunt Polly), who later married Joshua Nuttal. I loved him; he was a wonderful person. They had three children who all died in their 30s from TB [tuberculosis].

The father of my grandmother, John Cassidy, came from Bradford, Yorkshire, but disappeared. He was said to have been killed while working on the train tracks.

Aunt May [Mary (Harrington) Lovett] was born in 1902, my mother was born in 1903, Aunt Rose [Rose (Harrington) Sullivan] was born in 1904 or 1905.

After her husband disappeared, Tom Smith's mother (Mary O'Brien) moved in with her brothers James and Michael and kept house for them. When Tom wanted to get married, his mother said, "You are going to take the children [in St. Vincent's] with you." The oldest, John, married and moved out of the house. Aunt Polly also moved out after she married Uncle Joshua. After Tom and Lizzie married, the newlyweds took in children living at St. Vincent's (Rose, Willy, Eddie, and Josie) and the couple raised them. I believe they were living in the Tremont Street area at that time. Great Aunt Rose married Thomas Harrington and had two daughters and a son. Their son Bill was in the first graduating class from Providence College.

We called our mother's cousins "aunts": Aunt Rose Cassidy Harrington, May Harrington Lovett, and Rose Harrington Sullivan.

My maternal grandfather and grandmother [Thomas Smith and Elizabeth (Cassidy) Smith] ran and lived at the Mellen Hotel Annex, now the Belmont Club on Franklin Street. They had started in the Flint working in the mills and then moved to a rooming house at the [southeast corner of] North Main and Pine Streets, across from and south of the YMCA, living above the Pierce Paint Store. Mary Melker's father and uncle came from Ireland to work as chauffeurs and lived in the same boarding house. There was a fire at the boarding house and my grandparents then moved to the Mellen Hotel Annex.

My mother was married in 1925 when she lived at the Mellen Annex. My husband's mom was a Smith also. They were Walter and Annie Smith and lived on Pear Street.

I was conceived at the Belmont Club, where the piano is now, and where my parents had their bedroom when the club was the Mellen Hotel Annex. I was born at the General Hospital. My family lived in the back of the Annex. I remember a rocking chair in the back yard. My uncle Josh, Polly's husband, would take me out walking. We would sit on a wall behind the bank and watch them build the new post office. Their children died as young adults. I was the only child in the whole family for about ten years. The others were young adults.

There was a man who boarded at the Mellen Annex who was called "Sargent," having been in World War I. He was not a typical Fall River person. He had a Southern accent and was tall and thin. A lady was also a boarder at the Annex. Her name was Ellen and she was prim and proper. I think they were married later on.

We lived at the Mellen Hotel Annex until I was three years old. My mom had lived there with her parents for five to ten years. My grandmother did the cooking there and my grandfather took care of the place. My mother did the housework. After my mother was married, she and her mother would have a spat between the two and my mother and father would go to a tenement, then go back to the Annex again.

The Brennan's bought the Annex in 1933 when it became the Belmont Club, so I presume that's when we left.

Following that, from three to five years, I lived at the top of Franklin Street, at the corner of Grove Street. At the age of five, we moved to Seabury Street, south of Sacred Heart Church, in a four-tenement house in back.

From Seabury Street, we moved to Meadow Street at the bottom of Cherry Street, below the tracks on the third floor. From there, we moved to the corner of Meadow and Pine Streets to a house that is gone now. My grandmother had moved down to Meadow Street. I walked all the way from Meadow Street to Sacred Heart School and back to lunch and then back to school again and then back home. My mother paid a little girl five cents a day to accompany me to school. After that, we moved to a house on High Street near Durfee High School.

My brother died, so I was the only child. I got everything, even through the Depression. I was the queen of the family, the absolute center of the universe. This gave me a very strong will. When I was small, I was bathed in a tub that was put in the sink. My father would go to the Y to shower, and my mother would go to her mother's house to take a bath.

My mother told me that when she heard the fire engines during the 1928 fire, she walked down to the library steps with my father in her nightgown, with a fur coat over her nightgown. She and my father watched the fire sitting on the steps of the library.

When I was ten years old, we moved to 910 Locust Street. Then we moved to Ocean Grove [Swansea, Massachusetts] for three years to live with my grandmother, who had bought a house there. My grandmother had rented a cottage at Ocean Grove and liked it so much she bought a house directly across the street from the church. I still went to Sacred Heart School but paid one dollar a month for tuition because I was now out of the district. My father drove me in; he worked for Hemingway driving a truck. I would take the bus home. This was 1940 to 1943.

We stayed at Ocean Grove for three years. My mother didn't like it. My grandmother bought another house on another street in Ocean Grove. Then, my grandparents came back to Fall River for a while.

When I got married, my grandmother was living in Ocean Grove. My reception was at the top of Gardners Neck Road. I changed into my going away clothes at grandmother's cottage.

We next moved to a house at the corner of Linden and Cherry Streets. The house is still there. From there, we moved to Elm Street, in a little house below Durfee Street.

I loved Uncle Herman; he was so much fun. He played the guitar or banjo while singing German songs. He was part German; I think his father was German. He married my mother's cousin Nellie. When they lived on Warburton Street for a while, he had chickens in his back yard. My father loved Uncle Herman because he made him laugh.

One of my grandmother's sayings was "Eee, by gum!"

We would go to my grandmother's house and sing English songs from Yorkshire that she brought from England. I still remember the song and lyrics; I memorized the songs mostly. My grandmother was short, fat, and sweet. She came over when she was seven, but she didn't have an accent. She was eighty when she died.

Our English food included Black Pudding [a blood pudding] and tripe. We bought our English food at Hudner's Market downtown, at the corner of South Main and Borden Streets. They had all of the English food.

**School Life**

At the Sacred Heart School, there were forty-eight persons to a class. There were forty-two chairs bolted to the floor and every classroom had six loose chairs in the back of the room. I don't know how the nuns did it with such a large class size. There was one teacher to a classroom; as a teacher myself, I don't know how they did it.

The students who stood out were given special privileges by the nuns. John Moriarty and I were at that level. We were both at the top of our class. John was one year behind me, I think. We were sent to the store or to take notes to this one or that one. I loved it. I got 100s in everything. I would be sent to the Sacred Hearts Convent on Rock Street to walk the music teacher to the Sacred Heart School for music instruction. Nuns were not allowed to walk on the street alone.

No one paid for school; the parish paid for it. The parish seat money paid for it, I guess. Seat money consisted of every adult paying twenty-five cents at the church door. A man at the door had a pile of quarters to change dollar bills. Everyone paid their twenty-five cents every time they attended church.

I went to the Sacred Heart School, Sacred Hearts Academy, Katherine Gibbs, Stonehill College (in my thirties; I was the oldest student in the school back then), and Brown University for graduate school.

Teachers were not allowed to marry in Fall River until World War II. The men were gone then. Women teachers had to retire when they married. I guess they were afraid that the students would see female pregnant teachers. Men could be married and still teach. In high school, the teachers were mostly men.

When I graduated from Katherine Gibbs, I was interviewed for a job at the Gas Company. They wouldn't take me because I had an engagement ring on my finger. This was in 1948.

Both of my "aunts" (actually my mother's cousins) Rose and May went to Fitchburg Teachers College. My mother went only as far as sixth grade in school.

Thomas, my mother's younger brother, studied for the priesthood at St. Charles College in Maryland for two years and then at a seminary in Rome for two years. When he came back, he didn't continue it; he didn't like it. He then went to work in the post office. He was the only person in the family with a college degree until I came along. I have a masters from Brown and a doctorate.

**Recreation and Entertainment**

We played a game called "Tony Chestnut." It was played with a jackknife. Tony Chestnut stood for toe, knee, chest, nut. First you flipped the knife from your toe so that the blade would stick in the ground. If it didn't stick in the ground, you were out. If it stuck in the ground, then you flipped the knife from your knee. Then your chest. Then your forehead (nut). If you made it to the end, you won. In the schoolyard, we played jump-rope with double loops. Eileen Darcy and I rode our bicycles in Oak Grove Cemetery.

When I was about eight, my father was driving a truck. He would collect pieces of canvas on his route and brought them home to my mother. My mother had a sewing machine and my father made a pattern of a tent with all different shades. My mother made a big tent on her sewing machine. We would go to the beach every week in the summer, to Fogland [Tiverton, Rhode Island], and Helen and I went swimming. Uncle Herman and my father went fishing. My father bought a boat, and my mother made a sail and a jib for it. From eleven to fourteen years old, I sailed from it. That's how I learned to sail. When I was at Cathedral Camp, I taught sailing.

**Courtship and Marriage**

From Ocean Grove, we moved back to Fall River to the third floor of 11 Garden Street. When I was fifteen years old and coming back home one day from confirmation class with a few friends (I was then a freshman at Sacred Hearts Academy), we stopped at Murray's Drugstore, at the corner of New Boston Road and Madison Street, for a soda. A woman who was working on the soda fountain said, "Any of you girls looking for a job?" It was two dollars a day for five hours a day, from 1:00 to 6:00 pm. I said, "Yes, I'd like to do it." So, I got the job. I was then a freshman at Sacred Hearts Academy.

I worked there for a few years, every other day, after school from 2:30 to 6:00 pm. That's where I met my husband. Guys would meet outside the drugstore on Sunday afternoon. In the daytime, young kids from twelve to fifteen years old would meet there. They would come in and out and buy candy or magazines. In the evenings, after 7:00 pm, older guys would meet there and hang out. They were polite and held the door for people coming in. Sometimes, they would come in.

I worked there on Sundays, when the older boys were there. "Bugsy" Dow, Jack Deplich, and John Sullivan (who I later married) hung out there. This was about 1945 or 1946. One weekday, I had gone to the library and my mother asked me to stop by the drugstore to get a coffee cabinet and bring it home. I got off of the bus in front of the drugstore and went in and got the coffee cabinet. Principal Carroll of Durfee and his wife were there waiting for a prescription. "We'll drive you home," they said. They lived a few houses away from us on Garden Street.

Bugsy Dow opened the door and asked me to come out. I came out and said hi and he said, "Someone wants to ask you something," and motioned to John Sullivan. "What do you want to ask me?" I said. He got red in the face and was blushing. Bugsy then said, "He wants to ask you if he can walk home with you." "Sorry," I said, "I'm going home with the Carrolls. But, I'm working tomorrow." "When?" he asked. "Until 6:00."

When they were in the drugstore, my mother and Aunt Nellie would say, "See that fellow there? He's pretending to read a magazine but he has a crush on Betty." He came the next day and walked me home. He went into the Army the next morning. He sent me post cards from basic training. On the third card he wrote, "You don't know it yet, but you are going to be my future wife." I was shocked! I was fifteen and he was eighteen at the time.

John went into the service on the day that Roosevelt died, on April 12, 1945. I was a sophomore at Sacred Hearts Academy. The war was almost over. He never left the country. He was stationed at all of the POI's [Points of Embarkation] and they would keep moving him around. He had problems with his feet. He came out of the service in December of 1946.

I was getting all these letters from basic training and my mother was reading them. My aunt Mamie had a gift shop on New Boston Road, Mary's Gift Shop, and my mother called her to ask, "He lives on Walnut Street and his name is Sullivan. What do you know about the family?" Aunt Mamie said that yes, she knows the family, and goes on to describe the Sullivan family. The whole thing was settled right then. "They are a wonderful family," Aunt Mamie said. John's background was an open book to my mother. If my mother didn't know about that background, she wouldn't have approved.

It turns out that in 1920, John's grandfather, Dennis Sullivan, and my grandfather, Thomas Smith, were arrested together in Westport, along with "Clipper Jack" (John's uncle) and Aunt Mamie's husband, Henry Boulds, and his father. They were arrested for cock-fighting, which was illegal. The birds were from his grandfather's place on Grinnell Street in the city. They had a secret place in the woods where they would go to. They ended up in the Westport jail. My aunt Ella was getting married the next day, but her father didn't come home. The family was upset and worried.

Three months after entering the Army in 1945, when John was on leave from basic training, he was going out with the guys on Saturday and called me. "Can I take you to church on Sunday?" He met me at the corner of Hanover and New Boston Road. I told my mother and met him on the corner the next day and we walked to Holy Name Church. My mother and her cousin Nellie sat several rows behind us. Our first date was going to Mass! When we came out of the church, I introduced him to my mother and Aunt Nellie. He asked me if I would come to his house for dinner. I asked my mom if that was okay.

Once, I came into Fall River to go horseback riding at Gage Hill Farm on upper North Main Street. Others were there, including Jack Delaney, Henry France, and others. Henry had gotten off of his horse and was chasing it down North Main Street. In those days there were woods and trails all along that part of North Main Street.

That's how I met Jack Delaney. Jack and John Sullivan were good friends. Later, when Jack had a car, he dated various girls. John didn't have a car or a license, so we would go on dates with Jack and his girlfriends. Once, Jack didn't have a date, so we begged Marion to go out with him. If he didn't go on a date, we wouldn't have a car, and we would be stuck. "Just this once," we asked. Then they kept dating. Marion was the maid of honor at our wedding, and Jack was the best man.

After we had been dating for three years, John took me to Mell's Jewelry Store when I was eighteen years old, and he bought me a diamond. He didn't have any money, and paid two dollars a week for it. That's how people got things at that time. He didn't give the ring to me right away.

One day, he took me to St. Mary's Church. There were a few old ladies saying the rosary in the church. He brought me to the altar rail and we knelt down and he said something like, "You know I love you, and I want you to be my wife," and he gave me the ring. It was in the middle of the afternoon.

**Work Life**

My grandmother went to work in the mills at the age of thirteen. She had to stand on a stool to reach the looms. Since her mother died in childbirth, she took care of her three brothers and sister. Since she worked, she couldn't take care of the kids and put them in St. Vincent's Orphanage. She would visit them every Saturday with a quarter for the kids. The kids would plead, "Please take us home," but she couldn't. She lived in a small space and worked twelve hours a day, from 6:00 am to 6:00 pm. She never saw daylight except in the summer.

My grandmother worked in the mill with a girl named Eliza Britland (who later married Joe Pomfret, the baker). My grandmother was so poor that she carried an empty dinner pail and pretended that she carried food in it. Liz knew that my grandmother didn't have food in the pail and asked her mother to put a double serving in her dinner pail. She then told my grandmother, "Please take some of this food because I can't eat it all. My mother won't like it if I take it home."

John and I were at Cathedral Camp for seven years, from 1966 to 1973. I have a drawer-full of the songs that we sang there. Three or four of us would sing them or chant them. I worked in the office and taught sailing and John mowed the lawn. We loved it. We had a cottage up in the woods. We had a beer machine that dispensed draft beer. I don't know when we got the machine, but it made it to the cottage every summer. We got a keg for it and put a mayo jar that people threw quarters into. Our door was open, and people came in and out. We even had our own beach. There was a big beach at the camp and our small beach.

We had loads of fun. There was an old oak table at the cottage where the gang would play cards. There were two bedrooms upstairs, and the seminarians would come to stay on their days off from the rectory. They stayed at the camp overnight. I could get anything I wanted from the cook and take it up to the cottage.

It was so much fun; every day was different. We never knew what would happen next. Mass was said every day. John's brother, Father Walter Sullivan, was in charge of Cathedral Camp. Walter was great; he knew what was right. I conferred with him about all of my life decisions. I remember teaching him how to waltz in his mother's kitchen. He had been in the service and in college and was engaged at the time.

**The Depression and Prohibition**

My grandfather made home brew in the cellar of the house at the top of Franklin Street, on the corner of Grove. Every once in a while, there would be explosions in the cellar. My grandfather gave me a bit of home brew and I liked it. After the repeal of Prohibition, Rhode Island allowed alcohol before Massachusetts did, so Uncle Henry, my father and mother, grandfather and grandmother, Aunt Mamie, and me went to Warren [Rhode Island] to a place called Goes. I was sipping their beers, so they gave me a glass.

At the time, we were living at the bottom of Cherry Street and I was in first grade. When we got home, I was whining and cranky. My mother said to my father, "I knew she shouldn't have gone there. She's got a crying jag on." In school the next day, I told the nun the story. I don't know how it came about but I told the class the whole story. "I was given beer with my grandfather and grandmother and came home and had a crying jag." Marion Delaney went home and told her mom at lunch. "Do you know what Betty Turner told the class?" Her mother called Aunt Mame. They were ready to kill me. The family was in a dither. "How can we face the world?" I have never let Marion live that down.

# Paul Lawton Sunderland

*Born on December 24, 1925*

**Family Background**

My parents were Charles Willett (born in 1882) and Rosella (Cornell) Sunderland (born in 1887).

My father's parents were Willet Hershel (born in 1861) and Cora Estelle (Bliss) Sunderland (born in 1860). My father's brothers were Frank Herschel, born in 1879 (his wife was Emily Place), and George Smith, born in 1884 (his wife was Katherine Staincliffe).

My mother was an orphan. She never knew who her natural parents were. At the age of four, she was driven by carriage to the home of her foster mother, Susan (Lawton) Miller. Mrs. Miller's husband died while she was pregnant with her daughter, Bessie. My mother was Irish but was brought up as a Yankee Protestant. Mrs. Miller lived at 16 Baldwin Street and died in 1917.

On my father's side, my grandparents were divorced. My grandmother never married again, but my grandfather did and moved back to Warwick, Rhode Island, where he was from. My grandmother on my father's side came from Bliss Four Corners in Tiverton, Rhode Island. The grandfather of my grandmother started the grocery store at Bliss Four Corners. The store was recently torn down to make way for a new bank building.

I am the youngest in the family. In descending order of birth, my brothers and sisters are: Helene (born 1909); Edna (born 1912); Charlie (born 1915); Herschel (born 1917); and Walter (born 1919).

My wife is Jean (Wordell) Sunderland.

**Family Life**

My father was locomotive engineer as were his two brothers Frank and George. They were employed by the Old Colony Railroad, which later became a division of the New York, New Haven, and Hartford Railroad.

My father was demoted temporarily during the Depression to fireman because of reduced rail activity and low position on the seniority list. As rail business increased, he regained his status as an engineer, as fill-in for regular staff. As he gained higher position in seniority, he was able to bid on and secure a regular job. He was fortunate to have a regular income during hard times.

At one time, my father was the fireman on the Boat Train, so called because, on its last run of the day, it carried passengers from Boston to the New York boat sailing from Fall River overnight to New York. When we heard the train whistle as it approached up the tracks from our home, my brother Charlie would take me by car to the Fall River Line wharf. After the passengers detrained, I would wait for my father's signal for me to board the locomotive for a ride over to the roundhouse, where Charlie would pick us up to take us home. That locomotive ride was very exciting to me.

I remember my father treated the family to two great events in my young years. One was the annual banquet for the Brotherhood of Locomotive Engineers and Firemen at Roseland Dance Hall in Taunton [Massachusetts]. The caterer was the Hi Hat Caterers that served a turkey dinner. I remember the banana fritters were delicious. The other was the boat ride to Nantucket. The family was wakened at a very early hour to take the trolley ride after breakfast to the Fall River depot for a train ride to Taunton, where we switched trains for the trip to New Bedford to board the boat. The boat made stops at Woods Hole and two places on Martha's Vineyard before we arrived at Nantucket for a dinner in a restaurant. We returned to New Bedford and boarded the intercity trolley to Fall River and home. I remember some family member carried me up the hill to the house, for at some point on the last leg of the trip I had fallen asleep.

My mother remained at home. When she was young, she worked in the textile mills then became a telephone operator. She became friendly with my father's aunt and the aunt arranged for the two of them to get to know one another. They were married in 1908.

In 1922, my father bought the house in Steep Brook at 3555 North Main Street. After my father died in 1947, my sister Helene became co-owner with my mother of the house and bore all of the expenses. She remained there until her death in 1989. The house was sold outside the family. Thomas Thurston built the house in 1704. He, coincidentally, was a direct ancestor of my wife.

I never learned how to skate because I had a paper route, which came down to me from my brothers. I never had a chance to go skating. I had forty to fifty customers and they were spread out all along North Main Street, which was sparsely populated then. I got a brand new bike to use on my paper route. Herschel would take my bike on Sundays to go on bike rides with Walter and others. He got a smaller sprocket to give him more speed, but it was tougher for me to pedal.

Helene attended Westfield Normal School and secured a teaching job in Little Compton [Rhode Island] in 1928. She taught in a one-room school. When the Josephine Wilbur School was completed, she taught second grade there until her retirement in 1970. When I was in second grade, she took me with her to school for a day when the Fall River schools had spring vacation at a different week than Little Compton.

Ever since Edna was a young girl, she had a burning desire to get a good education. She left home to live with a family on the East Side of Providence as a live-in maid. She graduated from Hope High School and continued her education at Pembroke College, graduating in 1933.

Edna got my brother Charlie a job as a chauffeur with a family that lived in Barrington [Rhode Island] and summered at their cottage at Sakonnet Point in Little Compton. He graduated from Barrington High School.

Blake's Market was at the northwest corner of Wilson Road and North Main Street. Herschel worked for Blake's clerking and delivering orders. They had horses in a stable in the rear of the property, cared for by and older man, Pete Brooks. Hersh spent his spare time with Pete and the horses.

Walter worked for Bill Davis on his farm on Lewin Street, milking cows and other farm work. When Hersh and Walt came home from work, our mother had the pleasure of smelling the odors of horse and cow manure.

All three of my brothers went to Bradford Durfee Textile School. When Charlie graduated, he had a very difficult time finding a job due to the Depression. He finally found one with a typesetting company located in Providence. When another opening occurred, he advised Hersh to take it, which Hersh did.

After Edna graduated from Pembroke, she had the same problem of finding a job and accepted a clerking job at Gladdings Department Store in Providence. She finally landed a position at the State Health Clinic for pregnant women. She had an apartment on the east side of Providence and invited her brothers to live with her.

When Edna married, her brothers could not afford to pay the rent. They came home to live. My mother financed a car for their transportation that was paid for by taking in riders for their transportation to and from work in Providence.

Charlie, being the oldest, took charge of the vehicle, using it for his exclusive use for dating girls. My mother called him "good time Charlie" for he loved dancing and was fun-loving.

Walt graduated from the textile course. He got a job with the Berkshire Fine Spinning Company in the efficiency department, doing time studies and related work in the various plants in New England. He was drafted in the early peace-time draft in September, 1941, eventually joining the newly-formed 6th Armored Division. Later, the other two brothers were also drafted. Charlie was accepted for officers' training and became a lieutenant in the Army Air Corps. He ended up in charge of a mobile machine shop near Foggia, Italy.

**School Life**

I attended the Wiley School for grammar school years, grades one to six, then went to Morton Junior High School for grades seven to nine, and on to [B.M.C.] Durfee High School. My older siblings went to the old Steep Brook School at the bottom of Ashley Lane on North Main Street. This is where the Border City lots were located, west and north of the school, where Steep Brook fell into a large tank and piped by gravity to the Border City Mills for fresh water.

In April, 1943, in my senior year at Durfee High School, the seniors were invited to take an examination administered nationally by the U.S. Government for selection for further education at a college chosen by the Armed Services. Each participant was given the option of selecting the Army or the Navy. I chose the Army.

Apparently, the government was preparing for a long war and wanted to make sure that there would be college-educated people in the future. College private enrollment was down because of the war. Edna encouraged me to get a college education. I applied and was accepted at Brown University. During the war years, colleges were offering three semesters a year to speed up time required to obtain a degree.

The semester started in July. After a few weeks of studies, I received a notice from the United States Army saying that, if I was still interested in a college education, to join the Army. Since I was under age at seventeen, I was assigned to the Enlisted Reserve on July 28th. In a few days, I received notice to report to Harvard in September. I immediately withdrew from Brown.

**Recreation and Entertainment**

We played baseball in the Border City lots and the ship lots. In the spring, the boys would set the lot on fire to clear out the old grass. People always blamed it on the train's coal-fired steam engine coming through. An older kid set the fire with a matchbook. Then he went back to the Four Corners and counted the minutes before the fire engines arrived.

Saturday morning we would go to the Durfee Theatre by bus. It cost ten cents for the 10:00 am program (fifteen cents in the afternoon) for a double feature, the Movietone News, and comics. I had to go home in the afternoon to do my paper route.

In the winter, we would slide all the way down Wilson Road. We used what was called a bulltop. Two bulltops were connected by a plank and steered by a skate. Someone had to stop traffic on North Main Street as we came down. At the end of Wilson Road, they had to create bare ground and a snow embankment to stop the sleds.

Lannigan's Beach was where Hancock's Marine operation is now. Bliffins came in later north of Lannigan's and had a better beach. Ed Bliffins had a ninety-nine year lease from the Millard family. There was a fence between the beaches that went from the water to the railroad line. Lannigan's Beach went out of business, but they put up a hot dog stand at the entrance to Bliffins Beach.

Between Bliffins Beach and Bessie's Beach was a wharf, called Miller's Wharf. Charlie Millard owned it. Bessie's Beach was in the Millard family. It included several shacks or summer places. When we went swimming there, we didn't have towels like the kids of today; to dry out after swimming, we would stand next to Bessie's tar paper shack and dried out in the reflected heat. Bessie was my mother's foster sister.

On Labor Day, there was a swim race from Sandy Beach to Bliffins Beach. The Mercer Family were great swimmers. Eva Davis was a swimmer and Margaret Clayton also.

Bessie's Beach was named for Bessie Simmons. She was a big woman. She couldn't swim but she could float. Once she floated out to the country club and couldn't get back. A boat was sent for her, but she was too big and would swamp the boat if she tried to get in. So she had to be towed back to shore.

Clark Shaw built a concrete outdoor bowling alley along what is River Street now, which was once owned by the Clarks. It was between Clark Street and the water. River Street was parallel to the river. I was the pin boy and my pay was free games.

We had a cherry tree in our yard, which I would shimmy up and shimmy down. Walter would shimmy up the tree and then get down by swinging down from branch to branch. His friend Warren Dewhurst said that he could charge for the show.

**Work Life**

The Canedy family of Canedy Opticians lived in the neighborhood. There was a wholesaler of lenses called MacLeod who was looking for someone to deliver his lenses. The local opticians did the fitting of the frames, while MacLeod ground the lenses. It paid a little more than the paper route, but it included a one-dollar weekly bus pass. I made six cents a customer on the paper route, or about two dollars and seventy-five cents. MacLeod paid me four dollars, plus the pass.

The ICT bus would come in from Providence and stop at the terminal, which was a below ground-level room across from the southeast corner of City Hall. A kid would get off of the bus, give me a satchel of lenses, then get back on the bus to make his deliveries in New Bedford. I would then go to the Flint and other places to deliver the lenses. On his way back from New Bedford to Providence, the kid would pick up the satchel and take it with him. Every Thanksgiving, I would visit the MacLeod shop and they gave me a turkey.

My brother Walter was drafted in September, 1941. Later, in 1942, my other two brothers got drafted. All of them came back. Edna's husband, Robinson O. Bellin, came back from the Army, also, and was in the OSS [Office of Strategic Services] because he knew languages. She met him at Brown.

After the war, Charlie and Herschel continued typesetting, and Herschel landed a decent job

Home of Richard and Ruby Parlow, 3555 North Main Street, Fall River

at the *Fall River Herald News*. Before the war, Charlie had a job at Brown and Sharp. Charlie then went to the Norwood Press (publishers of books) on Route 1 near Boston that later folded; then he went to Williams Press in Albany [New York] and moved there. Now, I have only one sibling left, Walter, who lives in Assonet.

After the war, I returned to Brown and got my degree in mechanical engineering. Since the market was crowded with college grads then, it took a while to find a job. South of my house was the home of Bill Kerrigan (father of Bill Kerrigan), who worked for the Unemployment Office. He said that he would look out for a job for me. I went to McWhirr's for Christmas presents and asked Mr. Thompson for a job. He listened but there were no openings. A job opened up at Davis Screen Printing and I took it for two months.

From there, I went to Fram Filters in East Providence. I worked the midnight to 8:00 am shift and tested filters, including Fram's and the filters from other companies. However, I had to have a car to work these hours and bought a 1937 Ford Coupe for seventy-five dollars. It was my first car.

The following August, I was offered a job at Montaup Electric [Somerset, Massachusetts] and started there on October 1st. I worked there and at an associated company until I retired in 1987. When I came out of the service, an ordinary person got forty dollars a week; with my engineering degree, I got sixty-dollars a week at Montaup.

There were a lot of changes in the industry while I was at Montaup. Montaup was owned by three utilities that Montaup supplied with power: Fall River Light Company, Brockton Edison, and the Blackstone Valley Gas and Electric Company. They together formed Eastern Utilities that

Blacksmith carriage shop, North Main Street, near Wilson Road, Steep Brook, Fall River

became the dominant organization. They then modernized by establishing a service corporation that took away functions from other companies to do it cheaper, such as accounting, engineering, etc.

**Neighborhood Experiences**

In the 1700s, David Wilson purchased land in East Fall River with a good stand of timber on it. When the trees were harvested, the logs were hauled down Yellow Hill Road and Wilson Road to a wharf on the Taunton River to be loaded on ships and transported to Newport for sale. His son, Hezekiah, ran the operation at the river. Eventually, the family entered the coal business, located at the end of Cove Street on the river. During my time, David's descendant, Harry, was the owner of the coal company. Harry lived at the southeast corner of Wilson Road and North Main Street.

Ships were built at the ship lots at the shore behind the North Christian Church. According to local folklore, hulls were fabricated at a location beyond the top of Wilson Road and hauled down to the ship lots for final construction and launching of the ships. Gideon Hathaway lived on Wilson Road where a family cemetery and Hathaway Commons Condominiums are now located.

In 1754, Gideon purchased a house on North Main Street in the vicinity of the ship lots. Apparently, Gideon purchased this property to house one of his sons. Gideon is described as a Boatsman in this deed. In his will drawn in 1790, he granted this property jointly to his sons Robert and Elisha. When Robert died intestate in 1812, the court appointed a committee of appraisers to split the property between the two sons. Robert's widow was given the house and ninety rods of land. Robert's widow left the property to her children. Her son George, who is described as a shipwright in deeds granting rights in the property to him by various other heirs, continued to live there. One can assume from deeds describing Gideon as a Boatsman and his grandson as a Shipwright that the Hathaway family was prominent in the construction of the hulls at the Wilson Road location and final fabrication at the ship lots.

The Thurston family owned three houses north of the church on the west side of North Main Street and the large house north of our house on the east side. Charles Thurston (b. 1849) lived in the southernmost house, a full Cape. He was a cabinet-maker and had a shop down behind his house. He provided wrought iron wagon tires for hoops and stilts for children to play with. He also made woven wooden baskets that we used to pick wild blueberries and huckleberries.

The second, a half-Cape, was rented, and a Civil War veteran lived there. I remember seeing him sitting on the porch on the side of the house on a nice sunny day.

The third, a full-Cape, is where Arthur Thurston lived. He had a small barn where he kept a horse and wagon. He used to hitch her up and take Charles up to a wood lot for firewood. My father used to call on him to plow our vegetable garden in the spring.

Two sisters, Carrie and Ellen Thurston, lived in the large house. They raised chickens for a living, selling eggs and chickens.

I played with a kid who lived two houses down from our house named Abram Simmons Jr. He and his father were namesakes for Captain Abram G. Simmons, who captained ships of the Fall River Line and were somehow related. The captain's brother, Hiram, was in charge of the Steep Brook railroad station at the foot of Wilson Road. I remember playing with some kids in the area where the old station must have stood. We found some old coins in the sand and foolishly bought candy at Codega's Variety Store at the northeast corner of North Main Street and Wilson Road. The coins probably fell through the cracks in the station's flooring.

William Z. Canedy of Steep Brook was a deck officer with the Fall River Line. John Connor lived at the bottom of Stage Hill. He was a quartermaster on the Fall River Line. I remember when he died; he was laid out in his house.

The Clark's owned the sawmill and icehouse on the pond formed by Steep Brook, and they were also merchants of ice and sold wood on North Main Street. There was a carriage shop and a blacksmith shop in earlier days on the brook. Kids skated on the mill pond when I was young. Later, people dumped cars off of the steep embankment below the mill dam. We kids would strip off the rubber tires from these cars and sell them to the gas station at the Four Corners. We got a penny a pound for the rubber.

The last farm in Fall River was the Wordell Farm, a dairy farm. I hung around with Norman Wordell. He had two older and three younger sisters. When I returned from the service, I noticed Jean more and, years later, asked her to marry me. We were married at North Christian Church.

The Thurston Club put on a reception for us in the parish hall. The club was started in the early 1920s by Ellen Thurston. It was originally called the Swastika Club, since that had an association with the American Indians, which regarded the sign as good luck. When Hitler took that name, they renamed the club for Ellen Thurston.

The Harry Holt house was at 3775 North Main Street. Holt was born in 1862 and was a carpenter. He had an extensive flower garden on the south side of the house; he kept the beds very neat. He would supply flowers for the Sunday service at church.

Holt claimed the cove in front of his house as his own. It was called Thurston's Cove. The railroad built a causeway with a small culvert across the cove when they constructed the railroad. Over time, the cove was filled by rubbish. The cove originally came up to North Main Street. My brother Charlie went to get a cart full of wood there and Harry Holt came out and said, "That's my wood." Charlie flung the wood as far as he could.

Harry Holt would go eeling in winter, sometimes with my brother Walter. He would fill a barrel up and send it down overnight to New York's Fulton Street Fish Market via the Fall River Line boats. We would have ours at home; we would skin them and fry them in corn meal. We would have johnnycakes with them. Harry would hunt, too; whatever he caught, he made a stew of it. Harry came to our wedding on April 3, 1954, and died the next month at the age of ninety-two.

There were frequent summer lawn parties in Steep Brook. They were run by the church societies. They included cake sales and such. My mother made aprons for the parties.

Sam Lewin, who lived on Lewin Street, was a savant. You could ask him any question related to numbers and he would know the answer. His sister Lidia would feed him every day.

The wall in front of a house on North Main Street has a stone wall that veers away from North Main Street and follows the old layout of the street.

Steep Brook in the North End of Fall River

# Elisabeth "Libby" (Hammond) Thompson

**Family Background**

My parents were Thomas W. and Carolyn (McCarthy) Hammond.

My father's parents were Patrick and Mary (Martin) Hammond. My mother's parents were Dr. Eugene Ambrose and Carrie (Langley) McCarthy.

The McCarthy residence was at 896 Highland Avenue in Fall River. The Hammond residence was at 96 Colfax Street in Fall River.

My father's siblings were Joseph, James, Elizabeth Clemmey, Mary Farrissey, and Catherine Murphy. My mother's siblings were Elinor Lee, Virginia Murphy, Dorothy, and Eugene.

I have two siblings, Carolyn and Tom.

My husband is Raymond Thompson. [Raymond's interview follows this one in the book]

**Family Life**

I grew up at our home at 896 Highland Avenue. My mother's father, an orthopedic surgeon and founder of Rocky Farm Camp for crippled children in Middletown, Rhode Island, built the house. He contracted tuberculosis, but continued to practice medicine with one lung. His wife drove the first electric car in Fall River. Grandfather McCarthy lost one hundred thousand dollars in the stock market crash.

My brother, sister, and I attended the Highland School, Morton Jr. High, and [B.M.C.]Durfee High School. We walked everywhere, including to neighborhood stores and to school and back home. Such stores were Jaffe's Drug Store, Dexter's Fruit Market, the Highland 5 & 10, McFarland's Bakery, and Rene's Market for freshly ground hamburger.

We played at North Park, including ice skating and sledding in the winter. In the summertime, when Morton had its vacation, we went to the beaches and packed lunches and had a grand time playing in the ocean. We were always outside playing sports, riding bicycles, or roller skating.

Mom and Dad came from different backgrounds, but met at Durfee High. Dad left school to go to work as his family was poor. But he went back to high school where he and Mom met and graduated in 1932.

Dad says that his life growing up was comparable to the book *Angel's Ashes*, by Frank McCourt. While in elementary school, Dad would carry lunch pails to his dad and other mill workers. Dad went on to Providence College and received a master's degree from Boston University.

My dad's parents lived on Colfax Street for years. My grandfather would work (occasionally), since he had six mouths to feed and not much money. My dad hitched to Providence College with Ed Jaffee of J and J Box Corporation. He told his truck drivers that they should give Fall River hitch-hikers a ride when they needed one.

My father played football for Providence College. He was frozen he said. He pleaded with the Providence College fathers to give him a room, but they couldn't do it. He was too close to the school.

The house at 896 Highland Avenue was big and the same families lived there. Lois and Eugene McCarthy lived on the third floor and we lived on the first floor. Aunt Dorothy's "Dolly" lived in New York City and came home for holidays. She scheduled the cameramen at ABC in New York.

I would go to the Prevost basketball games; my father was the basketball coach at the Prevost games. My sister and I would cheer for the team. There were no girls at Prevost High School.

We would go sledding on Weetamoe Street toward where Durfee is now or go sledding at North Park. We slid down "Snake Hill" through pine trees that began at the Jewish War Vets monument. In the wintertime, the park department filled the water pool for skating. We had to be in by 9:00 pm.

We would all go to the Alumni Field for football and baseball games and track meets for Durfee. The Durfee High School kids had to walk to the Alumni Field to practice. We walked everywhere or took the bus.

We took a Robeson and Weetamoe bus to get downtown.

When Mom was older, she had a maid and a cook. They had butter and sugar when no one else did. The Hammond apartment was so cold. We could barely afford heat and had to make do with space heaters and filled the tank with kerosene from the cellar. When they had dinners, the sandwiches were often made with onion and cheese.

When Bud and I were dating, my grandmother would call Bud for a ride home from McWhirr's. My grandmother would go to all the 5 & 10s to buy cashew nuts. Langley Street was named for my grandmother's father.

My mom (Carolyn Hammond) was a librarian at the School of Nursing at St. Anne's Hospital for twenty years. At the end of her career, she was librarian for all three hospitals. The city had five hospitals, including the TB (tuberculosis) hospital.

Mom would get a month's vacation in August. We would all go to the beach. Dad moonlighted as a painter and worked for Coca-Cola loading and unloading. He also cleaned the tanks at Shell Oil.

# Raymond "Bud" Thompson

*Born on February 6, 1942*

**Family Background**

My parents were Raymond S. and Elizabeth E. (Pettey) Thompson. My father's sister is Tom Cottrell's mother, so he is my cousin. My father's father was Richard S. Thompson. My mother's parents were named Sisson.

My father thought he was Welsh, but he found out later that the family left Wales by way of Tralee [the county town of County Kerry in the south-west of Ireland] in Ireland. As a result of this, the immigration authorities put in the family's papers that they were Irish. When my father found out, he almost died. The family's ancestors left Tralee in the 1600s in the boat that followed the *Mayflower*. The name Thompson without the p is Scottish. Thompson with a p is English or Welsh.

My mother's family were gentlemen farmers. My mother's family name was originally Pettii, Italian in origin, but it "evolved" into Pettey. The city bought one side of Blossom Road (but not the other) from the Pettey family for the Reservation, to protect the city's water supply at North Watuppa Pond. However, it came with a life tenancy provision, where the Petteys could live there as long as there was a male Pettey living on the property. As a result, the Petteys have managed to see to it that a male Pettey moves into the property whenever an elder male passes on.

I was an only child; there are two sisters and one brother from a previous marriage.

My wife is Elisabeth "Libby" (Hammond) Thompson [Libby's interview precedes this one in the book].

**Family Life**

I grew up at 249 Oakland Street, at the intersection with Florence Street.

My father graduated from Yale in 1917. Few people from the city went to Yale in those days. He also graduated from Phillips Andover Academy. Everyone in the Thompson family went to good-name schools.

My grandfather was distant but loved his grandkids. When I would visit with him at his office, he would reach in back of my ear and say, "What's this?" and take out a quarter from my ear. I asked him how he did it, but he said that it was his secret. "I don't do it too often," he said.

My father's family lived in the house later owned by Doctor Elias, on the southeast corner of Highland Avenue and Weetamoe Streets. The front parlor was Grandfather's domain. We couldn't go in it. On the day I graduated from Durfee, my parents brought me to see him, and I finally got to sit in the parlor with him.

On Sundays, my father would pick up my grandfather to go for a ride. I would sit in the back seat between my father and grandfather. My grandfather was always cold, so we always had to keep the windows closed, even in July. He loved his cigars and smoked in the car. By the time the trip was over, my eyes were closed and as red as this pen.

My wife Libby's father, Tom Hammond, my father-in-law, was the principal of Durfee for many years. His father worked in the Pepperell Mills. He lived with us for a few years during the latter part of his life. He grew up on Covel Street, one of the few Irish in that area. He was determined to go to college and hitchhiked from his house to Providence College every day. After sports practice and other activities, he always got home late every day. Edwin Jaffe or Selwin Epstein directed his drivers to pick up any young men hitchhiking to Fall River and bring them home, preferably to their door. When Tom got home late, his usual meal was a cheese and onion sandwich. Later, when we would have cookouts at our house, we would ask him if he wanted onion on his hamburgers, and he would say, "No, I've had enough onions in my life; I don't want any more onions." Libby grew up on 896 Highland Avenue, next door to the house her grandfather Langley built.

The Hammonds were a family of achievers; Tom's brother James became the president of Fitchburg College and later Chancellor of Education for Massachusetts. His other brother lied about his age and joined three services during the war. Tom's sisters all did well in business. One sister went to Thibodeau Business School on Covel Street, next to the Sons of Italy Hall. This was when women were first becoming secretaries; before that the profession was for men only.

My dad was a cotton broker and lost everything in the Depression. Then he went to work at McWhirr's. He was the youngest son in the Thompson family and therefore didn't get much when my grandfather died.

The biggest day of the year for my mother's family on Blossom Road was when the Sears Roebuck catalog arrived. It was placed in the kitchen and the bible was placed in the parlor. When someone went to the outhouse, they took a page of the catalog with them. To the family, the catalog was more important than the bible.

When I as a kid of ten or so, my father rented a summer cottage in Westport on Cadman's Neck that had a crank phone that hung on the wall. It had five different rings, signifying that there were five different party lines. After the '54 hurricane, salt water went over the well, making it unusable, and we had to move out.

It was common in Westport for the townies to take advantage of the summer people. The first Lees Market had a lever on its cash registers that gave two different prices. If you were a local, the clerk pulled a lever and a lower price was given for goods. One time, my sis from out-of-town visited and asked me to go shopping for her at Lees so she could get the lower price. Doctors also charged different fees to the summer people. St. Jean the Baptist Church took a second collection in the summertime to pay for the fuel bill in the winter.

**School Life**

I went to the Highland School and then to Morton and to Durfee [B.M.C. Durfee High School]. I graduated from Durfee College, which later became UMass Dartmouth, and from Boston State College, which later became UMass Boston. I received my BS in Business Administration, with a minor in personnel management and industrial relations. My masters is in education with a history major.

One of the negative aspects of school was learning how to write right-handed. I was lucky to get into college, but now I have a masters degree and have taught for over forty years.

**Recreation and Entertainment**

Before television, we were always playing outside. We played baseball at the Little League field behind the Highland School. We played baseball day and night, at that field and at North Park. We played football and basketball in the street. We were always playing sports or riding a bike. In the wintertime, we skated at North Park or sledded down Weetamoe Street.

**Downtown**

Some of the places that I went to downtown were Fraze's Sporting Goods, Ashton's Sporting Goods, The Music Box, the Hub Pool Room, Rector's Spa, and Central Lunch, which was later the Roma Café. During the week, I would go there for things like dentist appointments. On Saturdays, I would go to the bowling alley to set up pins, where I made money for lunch at the China Royal, go to a movie, or go to McWhirr's to get a ride home.

Before vacuum tubes were introduced at McWhirr's, three kids ran to the third floor and back to make change for customers. My grandfather Thompson started at McWhirr's as a runner.

James Mahoney left McWhirr's to start the Star Store in New Bedford. His descendants ran the store until it closed.

Samuel Hyde also started at McWhirr's. He went to Portland, Maine, to start a store there. It failed. One of his sons came back to Fall River and became a floor walker at McWhirr's. Samuel Hyde had an estate at New Boston Road and Hyde Street. The white house there was part of the estate.

When Mr. McWhirr died, Asa Mills became president, followed by his son, who became president. The Mills family controlled fifty-one percent of the firm and the Thompsons controlled forty-nine percent.

McWhirr's had no credit policy. You could pay any amount to keep up. They delivered anywhere in Fall River and the surrounding towns. They would deliver the next day following an order or purchase. If you examined the goods delivered and it was not to your liking, you could give it back to the delivery boy and he would deliver the replacement goods the next day.

McWhirr's had a radio show on one of the local stations. During Christmas season, Santa Claus would recite the names of all of the kids who were good. One year, I was sick and couldn't go in to see Santa. One day, my father brought home Santa to visit with me. Was I ever surprised! I couldn't believe it. He took my Christmas list with him. The next day, Santa said on the radio show, "I want to mention a sick boy, Bud Thompson, that I met and Bud, I hope that you're feeling well." I couldn't believe that he said that.

Half of the wedding gifts in the city were from McWhirr's.

**Neighborhood Experiences**

My father grew up on South Beach Street, south of South Park [now Kennedy Park]. He remembered kids going down the hill with wagons full of dinner pails for relatives working in the mills. Hot water was in the lowest compartment, and above that was a hot meal. In the top compartment was a roll and a tea bag. They used the hot water to make tea.

There was a Jewish synagogue at Pearl Street, near Columbia Street. There was a concentration there of Jewish immigrants. This area was mostly second-generation Jewish. We had the only Christmas tree on the street. The extended "McWhirr family" also lived in this neighborhood. The area between our house and the Tansey School was mostly woods; you could get lost trying to get from my house to the school. Oakland then stopped at Florence Street. I believe that this area was part of Leemingville. The new construction that occurred east of here became an enclave of Jewish people.

A Mr. Gittleman owned a record store in downtown Fall River. One day, a sailor from Newport came in and bought a record for his girlfriend. Mr. Gittleman asked why he was buying the record here and not in the Newport PX. The sailor replied that the PX didn't sell records. That got Mr. Gittleman to contact US Representative Joe Martin. The result was that Mr. Gittleman got the contract to sell records to all of the PX's throughout the world. Gittleman Auditorium at the Robeson Street synagogue is named after him.

Isadore Gragnani, the Coca Cola mogul, was a distinguished alumnus of Durfee. He gave millions to Providence College.

Louis (Zip) Freedman's family owned US Records just over the river, next to the Somerset Bowling Alley. He was experiencing a lot of employee theft of records. Stacks of records were being taken, and he asked my father what to do about it. My father suggested that he allow each employee to take one record each week, but that what they took would have to be marked down in an inventory book. The result was that the amount of theft reduced significantly.

The Jaffes of J & J Corrugated Box Company made paper tubes for the textile industry, then went on to make boxes for the needle trade. You could go to Anderson Little and have a custom-made suit created for just one hundred and fifty dollars. Bradley Scott in the South End made all the suits for Johnny Carson. The Pepperell Mills made sheets that were used all over the country. Selwin Epstein started Shelburne Shirt Company. He went to New York, copied a shirt and brought it back and sold it for less. He pirated the design; you can't patent a sleeve, I guess.

In the Kerr Mills, in the brick building with buttresses, there was an exhaust fan system in the basement that drew moist air to keep the cotton moist. The air was blown up the buttresses, which were hollow, to each floor that needed the moist air. It was said that these air tunnels were a critical factor in the quick spread of the fire that destroyed the building.

The steep streets leading from the waterfront to the upper mills were made of cobblestones and had cobblestone risers in the middle to give horses more traction going up or down the hill in winter.

When bales of cotton were brought to a mill, they were hoisted up to the top floor by toughs from the neighborhood. The bales weighed up to 500 pounds each. The heaviest went to the top floor, then down to process, and then out the door to be sent to New York. The bales were then opened and spread out on the floor and the debris and other foreign matter were picked out. The cotton was then brought to the next lowest floor for spinning. Then the thread was brought down another floor for weaving, then to the first floor for storing and moving out and loading on to teams and on to the New York boats.

**Courtship and Marriage**

I imagine my mother and father met at McWhirr's, since she worked there. I met Libby when we were set up by friends. Since I was in grad school, we dated on weekends. We would go to concerts and restaurants. We were married in Holy Name Church on June 24, 1967 (I converted).

**Work Life**

I didn't have a part-time job before college, since my father did well at McWhirr's. When I needed something, I went to McWhirr's and charged it. If I needed sports equipment, I went to Fraze's Sporting Goods and charged it. However, I would help neighbors shovel snow and things like that.

I applied for a job at McWhirr's but my aunts and uncles opposed it; they said it would take away from their dividends. I went to Remy Moving on Third Street and got a temp job as a mover. My first moving job for the company was in downtown New York City. The next day, they called and asked if I could come in to go on a job in Albany. I got ninety cents an hour. I was short enough to get on my hands and knees under a piano and lift it up with my back while they unscrewed the legs. I also carried refrigerators on my back. Being short was an advantage as a mover.

Then I went to Child World to work after school at 4:00 pm. They closed at 10:00 pm, but if a truck came in at night, the merchandise had to be unloaded, put on the shelves, and priced. When this happened, we could be there until early in the morning, sometimes until 2:00 or 3:00 in the morning. Then I would have to leave for school at 7:30 am.

Sometimes, I worked at Moby Dick to cook lobster and steamers. I would get there at 8:00 am to clean the clams for the evening. When I took the clams out of the river, they smelled and I was surrounded by gnats. Since I also smelled from the clams, they surrounded my head. Old man Judson came down and said, "Why don't I give you something to keep the gnats away." So, he gave me stale packs of Camels that he couldn't sell in the restaurant to smoke and ward off the gnats. That got me addicted to smoking two packs of cigarettes a day, and now I have COPD.

Judson at the Moby Dick trusted me and had me do errands for him. He would have me deposit cash from the restaurant at his bank in Fairhaven on Route 6. Once, during dinner hour, he asked me to go to his house on Main Road and get stacks of one, five, and ten dollar bills. He said to go to one of the bedrooms and look in one of the twin beds. "How will I get in?" I asked. He said, "The door is open." Sure enough, the door was open and I went to the twin beds and there in a drawer under the beds were stacks of bills, right where he said they would be found. I took the bills that he said he wanted, closed the drawer and went back to the restaurant.

I got a job at Henry Lord in 1965 and retired from Durfee in 2003. I worked for thirty-seven and one-half years at Henry Lord, Morton, and Durfee.

**Religious Life**

I was a member of the First Congregational Church and then the Union Methodist Church. After we were married, we attended Holy Name Church. My pastors were Lex King Souter, Homer Ginns, and Msgr. Shalloo, and Msgr. Stanton.

I was told as a child that if I was bad, the gypsies would get me.

# Leo Thorpe

*Born on Jun 5, 1932*
*Died on June 3, 2012*

## Family Background

My parents were James (born in England) and Bridget Thorpe (born on Plymouth Avenue in a house just north of Globe Street). My mother was one of fourteen children and my father was an only child.

My father's mother came from Hartlespool, England. My mother's family was from County Mayo in Ireland.

When my parents married, during World War I, my mother lost her citizenship for marrying a foreigner and didn't get it back until the 1930s. She found this out when she went to vote and was refused.

I have eight brothers and sisters. My parent's home at 144 Fenner Street had only three rooms, with three bedrooms in the attic for the kids. A room was added later in front.

My father worked for Pierce Arrow, repairing cars, and had a shop on Belleview Avenue in Newport [Rhode Island]. When Ford bought out Pierce Arrow, my father was asked to stay on to run the shop, but he said "No, my kids come first." He then went to work in a machine shop in Fall River.

## Family Life

We lived in the kitchen and sat around the table. That was where the heat was. We had no central heat.

Any home that you went in, there was a chair by the entrance door. Visitors were expected to sit here unless otherwise invited to go into other parts of the house. There were parlors in many homes and you were not to go into bedrooms. The visitor would sit and wait there until they left with a member of the house.

Kids made May baskets for their mothers on May Day. The "baskets" were made of cardboard boxes covered with elaborate crepe paper. They included artificial flowers of crepe paper, food from the kitchen, or candy.

On Sunday night, dirty laundry was put out in a bag. Monday morning, it would return cleaned but wet. The laundry was then hung on a line to dry. There was no hot water in the house to wash clothes, except what was heated on the stove.

We thought we were rich when we got a pot burner, a sort of kerosene space heater, to heat the house. When we got rid of the coal stove, the gas stove was used for cooking. The kerosene burner consisted of dripping kerosene that fell into a pan. My job was to go get the kerosene in the basement using a large metal container commonly used for gasoline. Invariably, I would trip on the top stair and spill kerosene on myself, resulting in me smelling of kerosene all of the school day.

My aunt had a combination gas (for cooking) and kerosene (for heating) stove.

For larger buildings, all central heating was by coal. Gas was rarely used for heating.

We had one set of clothes for school and one for Sunday. My mother would go to the Outlet Department Store in Providence to shop for school.

We had plenty of play clothes. Everyone wore knickers in primary school. I finally got my first pair of long pants when I graduated from grammar school. I got everything second-hand because I was last in line of the kids. It was special when I got a pencil that was new and that hadn't yet been sharpened and that had a flat end.

Everyone wore hats then.

Many things were delivered to the home. These included bread, milk, eggs, ice, laundry, fruit, and fish on Friday. The fish man would blow his horn and all the Portuguese ladies would come out with their metal porcelain dish pans to hold the fish that they bought.

We would burn trash in the yard; we never put barrels out on the street for pickup. Garbage men came by to pick up "swill" which was fed to pigs in local piggeries. It was gross, but we ate those pork chops.

Some things never change; my daughter bought a house on Birch Street, off of South Main Street, and their neighbors keep chickens, with two neighbors sharing a rooster. They keep the place spotless.

When I was fifteen, my mother had a stroke. Back then, there was no therapy as there is today. Everywhere she went for the last five years of her life, my sister and I went with her.

Our first phone was installed in the late 30s. Our number was 68R. You would have to pick up the phone and give the operator the number you were calling. Once, I waited for my friend to call on his new phone and my friend was waiting for me to call and as a result no one called all night.

**Recreation and Entertainment**

Street games included kick the can, free the goal, red light, pee wee, and bowl-a-wicket. For bowl-a-wicket, the ends of orange crates were removed and these end pieces were used as free-standing backboards. The object of the game was to knock over your opponent's backboard with a ball and for you to prevent this from happening while attacking your opponent's backboard. Old broom handles were used to hit the ball.

Pee wee was played by taking a small piece of wood, throwing it into the air, then using a broom stick to hit it. Broom sticks were gold. Everyone had a bag of marbles, perhaps a jump rope or a French rope (with two ropes).

Almost everyone used evaporated milk for coffee, both because people preferred it and because it didn't need refrigeration—it was used up quickly.

We would take a can, crunch it in the middle, and put it on your heels. It would make a *clicky-clack* noise.

Go-carts were made by putting skate wheels on 2x4s and fastening an orange crate on top. Other activities were kite flying and ice skating on Cook Pond in the winter.

One of my aunts had a car and would bring us to Colonel Green's estate in Dartmouth (son of Hetty Green). He would put an amplified radio on the front lawn of the main house and invite the public to listen to radio programs and be entertained. I went several times. Radios were a luxury then and unusual in the 1930s.

There was an amusement park at Sandy Beach, put by the trolley company. Trolley companies put amusement parks at the end of their lines to expand their revenue. Lincoln Park [North

Dartmouth, Massachusetts] was at the end of the trolley line from Fall River. Its track ran along the center line of Route 6 and would turn around at the park.

A race track, hotel, and resort was located where the old St. Vincent's Home was located on North Main Street [Forest Hill Gardens].

Our neighborhood theatre was the Park Theatre, located at Globe Corners at the southwestern corner of South Main and Globe Streets, where Dunkin' Donuts is now. The Park was designed by Maude Darling Parlin, the architect who designed the Durfee Theatre. Dish days at the Park were on Wednesdays. Saturday shows included two movies, cartoons, and previews.

The city's theatres included the Durfee, Embassy, Academy, Empire, Plaza, Capital, Park, Strand, Royal, Center, and the Bijou. The Durfee organ would rise on a platform in front of the stage. The Empire was a vaudeville theatre. On Tuesday afternoons, there would be two movies and two Vaudeville acts. The Academy of Music stage could be extended to make a ballroom floor.

When the circus came, putting up the tent was a big thing. It was wonderful to watch the elephants raise the center pole and the canvas tent. A circle of men would pound in the stakes, with each taking turns hitting the stake with a sledge hammer.

Some of the rides were very simple. I remember one where a row boat was suspended between two tripods that supported the boat with ropes. The ride consisted of two persons in the boat alternating in pulling two ropes to make the boat go back and forth. Lincoln Park had cages that worked almost the same way.

One day, at the set-up of the circus, I had a push-up ice cream cone in a paper cone, and I was having trouble pushing the ice cream up the cone. Suddenly this big gray thing swooped it out of my hand and the elephant ate it. Carnivals were usually all week long, with side-shows. Popcorn was popped at the carnivals by putting kernels in a wire basket that would swing back and forth over the flame. Cotton candy was always available.

Dancing was very popular in the city and was a main source of entertainment for mill workers. Every neighborhood had one or more fraternal halls that were used for dancing. On East Main Street, there were two halls in the brick building. Dance-a-thons were held regularly in my mother's era in the 1920s.

We would also go to Island Park [Cashman's Park, Portsmouth, Rhode Island] to the amusement park there. There was a roller skating rink and a roller coaster there, among other things. The park was at the end of the trolley line from Newport. Roller skating rinks were at Island Park, Lincoln Park, Portsmouth, and The Casino on Morgan Street.

We would sneak in to the midget car races at Bigberry Stadium and at the Ponta Delgada site on Shove Street. We would be disappointed if there wasn't a crash.

Parochial schools would sponsor teen dances and plays using students.

A local gas station owner, on his own, would show movies on top of his building once a week.

Dollar days at Lincoln Park in the 1950s allowed persons to ride the amusements all day for only a dollar.

## Christmas, Holidays, and Special Occasions

At Christmas, we would take excursions to view the decorated window displays at McWhirr's Department Store. We would also take annual trips to see the Christmas decorations at the Taunton Green. We would watch to see who had the first tree starting around the 20th.

Everyone wore a carnation on Mother's Day, a red one if mother was living and a white one if deceased. The Irish would wear a green ribbon on St. Patrick's Day, almost as a sign of protest (No Irish Permitted).

On Memorial Day, the cemeteries were mobbed with people. The gates to cemeteries were shut to prevent too many autos in the cemeteries. Police were needed to provide crowd control.

The week before Memorial Day, I would carry dirt in a wagon up Laurel Street to fill in the family graves in the "Briar's Den" at St. Mary's Cemetery, behind what is now Shaw's Market. The Church neglected the lots in 1926.

We couldn't do any manual labor on Sundays; it was forbidden by the Catholic Church. People went for walks, to the Narrows, to the Stone Bridge in Tiverton [Rhode Island], and to the North End. My sisters would walk to the Stone Bridge regularly.

There was no trick-or-treating on Halloween. We soaped windows and did pranks like removing gates and moving outhouses back a few feet. We burned cork to make black-face masks and we bobbed for apples or apples suspended from a string. The First National Bank on South Main Street allowed us to soap their windows. We had no costumes; none were available.

**Neighborhood Experiences**

Steep streets like Lincoln Avenue were closed by the city following snow storms because cars couldn't get up them. Only the bus company plowed their routes; the city didn't plow.

There was no anti-freeze as we know it today. Buses would run from 5:00 am to 11:00 pm every day. When they were finished, they would go to the Stafford Road terminal garage and left running all night so their systems wouldn't freeze. The garage wasn't heated. This information came from Ed Berube, who was a bus driver and whose father delivered bread to my house. Ed would work on Saturdays and spent time talking to my parents. Ed was later appointed postmaster general by the newly-elected President John F. Kennedy.

Cars would be put up on blocks for the winter to prevent their tires from rotting, and their liquids were drained out to prevent freezing. Anti-freeze as we know it today was not available.

Coal ash would be spread on sidewalks to provide traction during icy conditions.

I remember paying fifty cents for a car inspection.

In the 40s, Mom would get a dollar pass on the bus, which would allow you to ride anywhere all day. Sometimes, she would ride to Boston in the morning to do shopping and be home to make lunch.

When I rode the bus as a kid, French women would be speaking English, but when an Irishman boarded the bus, they immediately switch to speaking French. The French and the Irish didn't get along.

There were Leddy's Bakery, Margie's Bakery, and Edwards Bakery, on East Main Street. The bakeries cut the ends off of raisin and apple squares, and we could buy a bag of the ends from Edwards Bakery for ten cents. We could get fruit pies all week long. A layer cake was twenty-five cents; if frosted on the sides, the cake was thirty cents. It had a cherry on top.

Chinese restaurants were everywhere. There was a Young's Chow Mein place on South Main Street and another Chinese restaurant upstairs at the corner of East Main and Hamlet Streets. On South Main Street at Columbia (on the southwest corner where the cobbler is now) there was another Chinese restaurant on the second floor. There was a Chinese restaurant on the second floor above the Empire Theatre downtown.

Where South Main Street and Broadway come together at Globe Corners, where the Shell gas station is now, there was a railroad car diner.

There were many drug stores and all had soda fountains. The Globe had two ice cream shops, the Sugar Bowl and The Nonpareil, and just as many fruit stands.

The old police station site was once the location of the Blue Light Hotel.

The canvas for the Notre Dame Church ceilings were painted in a studio on East Main Street by Crenimi. Other of his canvases are in the rotunda in the main library.

There were flower vendors in the downtown (on Saturday night); a corsage vendor had a stand on Second Street off of South Main Street. Downtown stores closed on Wednesday afternoon.

There was a Settlement House at 334 Tuttle Street that was established by the King Philip Mill. The district nurse visited there as did a doctor occasionally. There showers and a library there also. My mother started a women's guild there, and then started one at St. Patrick's Church. Christmas bazaars were held there. The "White Nuns" or Sisters of the Poor, visited the sick in the neighborhood.

There were so many bars on Pleasant Street, one on every corner, that it was said that if you started drinking at the bar next to City Hall and had one beer at each bar along Pleasant Street, you would never make it to the last bar.

My grandmother was in the habit of stopping at a bar on her way home from the mill to get her lunch pail filled with beer. Once, she came across the parish priest and she tried to hide the pail of beer. He wasn't fooled and said after a while, "Get home before your beer gets warm."

**Food and Meals**

In the morning, we would always have hot cereal on the stove in a double boiler, including oatmeal, cream of wheat, etc. We never had boxed cereal, except Corn Flakes, Puffed Rice, Rice Krispies, and Shredded Wheat. There were no sugar cereals.

We put butter on bread, sprinkled sugar on it, cut it into cubes, then put it in a bowl and poured milk over. We also put hot water over stale brown bread to make a cereal. Karo Syrup or molasses was put on bread also.

We had fish every Friday, either at home or at the local fish and chips place. Hartley's provided meat pies; they have been at that location for over 100 years. Women had to go shopping every day because of the lack of refrigeration.

**Religious Life**

Every August 15th, we had to go into the water. "There is a blessing in the water," my mother would say. No one knows where this religious rite came from, perhaps from the blessing of the fleet. I was an alter boy from kindergarten to the third year of high school (and never got molested). The priests were considered gods. Only later that we learned that nuns were just people, just women.

**The Depression**

We didn't know we were poor. Nobody had anything. We didn't lock our doors because we had nothing to steal. The only thing of value in our house was a clock. Our dishes were mismatched. Some people in other neighborhoods would steal clothes off of the line, which was a common occurrence.

Sometimes people stood out because they were really poor. I remember a woman with two kids with old clothes. The kids had what we called "welfare glasses," which had round wire rims.

We never threw glass gallon jugs out, but saved them in the basement. In the spring, a woman from Korman Water Bleach Company would come and buy the jugs for five or ten cents each, depending on the size. A rag man also came buy and purchased rags, which were eventually used for making paper.

Women never had their hair done; would cost too much.

**Work Life**

When my mother had me, she worked in the textile mill. She had thirty days to have me and get back to work or she would lose her job. My father was out of work for most of the 30s. The older kids had to work to support the family.

People didn't have enough to have a soup or stew and a meal in one pail. Tea was put in the bottom of the pail.

**Hurricane of 1938**

When I came home from St. Patrick's school, I remember a kerosene lamp being on because the lights went out, and stayed out for a week. The home across the street lost its roof. I saw a priest crying on the steps of St. Patrick's Church because the hurricane had blown a hole in the roof of the rear section of the church. We went to Somerset to see the tanker that had been stranded on land.

**World War II**

During the war, rationing was in place. We would go to Stop and Shop and wait in line for certain items like bananas, sugar, and butter. Once someone yelled, "They have bananas at A&P," and we had to decide to keep our place in line or run to the A&P.

**Miscellaneous Memories**

Thomas Edison personally lit the street lights for the downtown.

Indians were alleged to have crushed their enemies under the Rolling Rock. The pedestal for the Rolling Rock was formed by the quarrying around the rock and leaving the pedestal and rock behind.

The Lafayette statue at Lafayette Park was at the insistence of the French community, and the story goes that the statue was originally places so that the rear of the horse was facing Eastern Avenue and French residents. City officials, allegedly, did this to get back at the French. It was later reversed.

There was a jail, later an old folks home, where the sewage treatment plant is now. It was called Bayside.

# Robert Eaton Vernon

*Born on November 3, 1910*
*Died on November 21, 2011*

*During this interview, Mary Ann Wordell was in attendance.*

**Family Background**

I was born in a house just north of Beattie's house, the large white house on Highland Avenue, near the water tank across from the priests' residence at Catholic Memorial Home. Beattie was the first auto dealer in the city and was an engineer; he would often go to places as far as Colorado to get the designs to make parts for obsolete machinery. My family stayed there until I was one year old, when we moved to 990 Wilson Road, on the north side of Wilson Road opposite the end of Meridian Street. Our house was built of second-hand lumber from a building that was demolished in the South End.

My parents were John William and Emiline (Holehouse) Vernon.

Both my father and mother's families came from England. My father was brought from England as a young boy, without his mother, and his father settled him with various cousins who lived on Brightman Street. My paternal grandmother was an Eaton and came from the Eaton Coal Mining family in Wales. The Vernon name came from a town in France. When my ancestors came to England, they were required to have a last name, so they took the name of their former town.

I don't remember much about my mother's side of the family, the Holehouse side, except that my grandmother, my mother's mother, was a Quaker. My grandfather, my mother's father, came from England and served in the Civil War. He has held prisoner at the famous Andersonville Prison, and his name is included in the Civil War memorial in Oak Grove Cemetery.

My father was a loom fixer all of his life, and worked mostly at the Narragansett Mill. When the mills were not in operation, he worked for John Brightman for a few winters. Most of the Vernons were bosses in the mills, except my father. My mother worked in the mill until she had my brother, her first child.

I had one brother, who was eight years older than I was.

**Family Life**

I was very sickly as a kid until I left home, when my health improved. The doctor said that my sickness was due to the water that we drank. That water came from a cistern that caught rainwater from the roof. That water was filtered through brick filters, but it contained such things as bird droppings and other contaminants. We also had lead pipes back then. The doctor said that we should buy bottled or spring water, but my parents felt that was too much of a bother.

I never played games like other kids because I was too sickly. One winter, I was sick with colds and other ailments and stayed home all winter. My teacher brought my school lessons home to me all year. My mother loaded me with castor oil, and I hated the damned stuff. She gave me mineral oil later, which at least didn't have the foul taste of castor oil. I was also given Epsom salts, also for constipation.

When I was an adult, I drank a gallon of raw milk a day. I worked for two dairies in Louisiana that shipped milk to New Orleans. I ran the receiving section where the farmers brought in their milk. I would buy my own milk and bring it in to drink, but then the manager said, you don't have to buy your own milk; use what we have here.

We had cousins in Tiverton [Rhode Island] named Fish. Horace Fish was the head of the family and was a fisherman. He was a jack of all trades and could do anything, including shoeing his own horses. I believe that Fish Road is named for the family.

I attended the Church of Hard Knocks. I attended the North Methodist Church, near Noverca's Sawmill, a few times, but that's all. I learned the King James bible on my own. My father kept the bible and books on Shakespeare and such authors in a locked cabinet with glass doors. My father would tell me, "Don't touch those books!" When my father was downtown, I would take the key (I knew where my mother kept it) and would take out the bible and read it.

There were no gas lines on Meridian Street, so for light we continued to use kerosene lamps and lanterns until electricity came to the neighborhood.

We heated with wood and coal that fed the old black kitchen ranges that were also cook stoves. After my parents died, and I inherited the property, one of the first things that I noticed is that the paint on the wainscoting behind the oil stove in the kitchen was blistered. In order to have more room in the kitchen, my father had put the stove too close to the wall. I added a tin sheet between the stove and the wall as fire protection.

My father took chances with electricity, too. When I moved into the house, I kept hearing a *click, click* noise in the basement. It was the BX wire short-circuiting. My father had put a nickel in back of the fuses to keep them from blowing out!

**School Life**

I went to a one-room school on Meridian Street from first through sixth grade. The school was called the Upper New Boston School. There was a Lower New Boston School on the north side of New Boston Road that was later moved to Freelove Street. That school was two stories. When the Highland School opened, I went there for seventh and eighth grades, although I didn't graduate from grammar school. A Chevy and a Model T bus brought us to the Highland School.

There were two teachers at the school. Miss Davenport taught the first four grades and Louise Allen taught the last four grades. Miss Allen was also the principal. Miss Davenport was the daughter of a farm family, the Davenports, on Meridian Street.

The schoolhouse was one room that originally had outhouses. Some of the older boys once tipped over the boys' outhouse. When I was there, the city put in water and sewer lines that ended at the school. On the southwest corner of the schoolroom was the girls' toilet and on the northeast corner was the boys' toilet.

In one corner of the room was a flat-topped cast iron pot-bellied stove. Indians from the Reservation—I believe it was the Perrys—would bring wood to the school to keep us warm. We brought our lunch to school.

There were forty-eight students in that one room for all eight grades. Ernest King was a classmate. His family had the King Florist and owned a greenhouse at the end of Meridian Street at New Boston Road. Bob Reed was also a classmate and his family also had a greenhouse on

Meridian Street. The Reed family was big and included George (Poley), Walter and Frankie (Punk). One Read sister wanted to marry a fellow and asked my advice. John Brightman and his brother Preston were my classmates. They had two sisters, Eleanor and Gladys, who were also in school with me.

Eleanor Brightman later bought the school and converted it into her home. Eleanor enlarged the building so that it is no longer recognizable as an old school.

The school had a flag pole at the front peak of the roof. The teacher would ring us in the morning and following recess with a large hand-held bell. There was a plank walk to the school and stone walls with capstones on either side of the lot.

One recess, the older boys went to the Brightman's farm and tied Preston Brightman—a big stocky kid—to a big apple tree and left him there. When the teacher rang the recess bell, she asked, "Where is Preston?" The boys confessed that he was tied to a tree, and they had to go untie him. Preston's sister Eleanor was the one who later bought the school.

The Hayworths lived on the last house going east and on the south side of Wilson Road. Across Wilson Road was another Hayworth house, which is now part of the industrial park. The Lamberts also lived in that area, and one of the Lambert boys was a classmate. They later moved to Maine.

Nelson Peckham came to the school from his home on Blossom Road. Owen McGowan came to school from his home on Bell Rock Road in a horse and buggy. He had two sisters. Patrick McGowan was his father.

Patrick McGowan also brought the Shepard children to school. Old man Shepard was killed in a forest fire when he tried to take a short cut to Bell Rock Road. He got caught in the fire and was burned alive.

Sex is not new in school. When I was twelve years old and in grammar school, a girl and fellow classmate approached me and asked me to have sex with her. I said no, we were too young. What could be the consequences? What if children resulted? So, sex in the schools is not a new issue.

After grammar school, I attended Bristol Aggie school in Dighton [Massachusetts]. I got there by getting on the train at the Steep Brook station at the end of Wilson Road and got off at the Segregansett Station right at the school. When I lived at the school for the last two years, my health improved markedly. I didn't graduate there and stayed until I was seventeen.

When I was attending Bristol Aggie, a fire occurred at the school. As a result, the junior and senior classes had to have their classes in a trailer until repairs were made to the school. The other two grades could meet in the main school building. The older kids in the class would have fun by perching a small pail of water on the slightly-opened door, so that kids would get doused when they opened the door. Once, the superintendent of the school, Mr. Gilbert, suddenly approached the trailer, and the boys scrambled to get the pail off of the door, which they did just in time. All hell would have broken loose if the pail of water had fallen on Mr. Gilbert.

I lived in the dorm at Aggie, and there was the usual pranks that kids played on one another. One of them involved putting a bottle of water in a person's bed with a stopper on it with a string that attached to the bed. When the person got in bed, he pulled the stopper and got his bed wet. Sometimes, these pranks can get serious. The son of the Pearson Milk Farm family on Meridian Street (where the golf course was located) was killed at college when his roommates wired his bed to give him a shock but instead electrocuted him.

I went to Aggie with John Bonner, the florist, Red Barnett, the boxer, and John's older brother. John was in the same class as I was at the Highland School.

**Neighborhood Experiences**

Our neighbors on Wilson road were the Desmarises, the Haywards, the Kings, the Brightmans, the Bragas, the Pearsons, the Ferreiras, the Viveiroses, and Joe Gladu.

Pond Hill is the hill that begins near Meridian Street and goes down to North Watuppa Pond. The Davis family had an apple orchard on Pond Hill on either side of Wilson Road, where the industrial park is now, and they also had a big orchard south of Wilson Road. Sometimes, the nuns from St. Vincent's Orphanage would bring their kids to pick apples in the Davis orchard.

There was a bridal path along the pond that went to Wilson Road; the bridal path is still there. The Davis family also had a wharf on North Watuppa Pond, as did many other families, until the Water Board took all of the property on the pond to protect the city's water supply.

The Davis family also operated a saw mill on Blossom Road that was powered by water power from one of the brooks that flowed into North Watuppa. The foundations of the saw mill are still there.

When I was a kid, the northern part of North Watuppa Pond, north of the causeway, was all marsh before the dam was put in. Many people picked blueberries there and sold them to bakeries in the city. People picked pails of blueberries there.

Wilson Road was a dirt road then, and the city would hire farmers to scrape the roads to fill in the potholes.

Trucks hauled sand and gravel from McGowan's gravel pits on Bell Rock Road. The pits are still there, but the land was sold to the city as part of the Reservation. In those early days, trucks didn't have a drive shaft but had chains on one or two sides of the trucks wheels. When the trucks went by, they made a hell of a racket; you could hear them coming from quite a distance. When the trucks were a half-mile away, we would say, "Here comes McGowan."

There was a watering through on the western side of Meridian Street, near the one-room schoolhouse. When the water line was extended to the schoolhouse, the watering through was moved to Wilson Road.

Everyone walked then; I walked until I was ninety. If you wanted to go downtown, you got on a trolley.

I once found the wild orchid arathusa in Stump Pond, north of North Watuppa Pond.

Jesse Costa had a farm off of Driftwood Street and drove his horse and buggy with its big sun shade. He would go to the foot of Plymouth Avenue [where Pleasant Street intersects] and sell his produce there. Ike Cleveland also lived in that area, Driftwood Street was once called Cleveland Lane. Brookside Street nearby was once called Pearce's Lane. [Mary Ann Wordell mentioned here that her grandmother named the way Brookside Street]. The Clevelands had a greenhouse on Driftwood Street.

*Mary Ann Wordell:* I remember Tom Fleming, who had a dog act that he brought on the stage of the Academy Theatre. He worked in the mill and was known for walking on his hands down the mill banisters. Everyone was afraid that he would fall down and be caught in the machines. He was very clever.

*Robert E. Vernon:* Martha Brightman lived in a home east of Bob's on Wilson Road. Her husband was named "Skunk Brightman" because he trapped skunks, mostly in Assonet. Skunks were used for fur. When he went on a bus or train, no one would sit next to him because he stank so much.

*Mary Ann Wordell:* Martha Brightman owned a lot of land in the area, and some people believe that Martha Street is named for her.

*Robert E. Vernon:* My brother would go trapping all over, for muskrats and other fur-bearing animals. He brought the skins to Butcher's Rendering Co. in the city, who would prepare the skins and sell them.

There are a lot of muskrats in North Watuppa Pond, north of the causeway. Their nests look like huts, with the entrances underwater. My mother owned a Model T Ford and when we crossed the Wilson Road causeway, she once said, as she looked at the huts, "I wonder who is putting all of those piles of horse manure on the pond."

There once was an inn where Davis had his farm on Wilson Road. It was on an old buggy road and it came out at Bell Rock Road. It was where Parker's farm was near the Fox's farm. There was a legend that treasure was buried near the inn. People thought that the inn owner had money, and they would come out at night with lanterns to dig for the treasure.

**Work Life**

During the Depression, when the mills shut down, my father worked for the Brightman saw mill family and cut cedar trees in the Hockomock Swamp. Brightman sold a lot of tall cedar poles that were used for holding washing lines; those cedar poles were as tall as the three-story tenements where they were used.

In the Hockomock Swamp, horses would pull an unmanned sled of sawn logs out a narrow trail to the waiting trucks. Then, the sled would be unload and the unattended horses would go back again to the cutting site, about a half-mile into the swamp, to load up again. They did this for weeks. One time, we were waiting and waiting for the horses, but they didn't come back. After searching for a while, we discovered that they had gone off on a side trail for some reason and disappeared. We polled the site, but couldn't find anything.

That site where the horses disappeared was a deep area where peat was once excavated for use in ballast in ships returning to England after leaving Taunton. It was one of those places where they had dug all of the peat out. Never saw the horses or the sled again.

I worked for the Davis Sawmill. We would clear out logs that had been downed by storms or American chestnut trees killed by the chestnut blight. Alan Davis dragged out each log with a few horses. The chestnut wood was used for fence posts. It was said that a granite post would last for 100 years and a chestnut post a year longer than that. Chestnut was used to split rail fences because it split with a clean cut. We also cut pine and hemlock.

Generally, wood was gotten out of the Reservation by sleds. The Kings cut logs off of Indian Town Road and Blossom Road and used train tracks to bring logs out to the trucks. Ernest and Peewee King both logged the Reservation. There were piles and piles of wood on each side of Yellow Hill Road, which was dirt then. During the Depression, the Kings uses wood to heat their greenhouses, since they couldn't afford coal.

In the swamps, we cut cedar. We cut a lot of cedars in the Hockomock Swamp north of Taunton. We also cut cedars in the pond north of the Wilson Road causeway; the stumps were visible for years. The cedars went to the Hershoff's mill in Taunton.

When I was seventeen, I went to Connecticut to visit a friend and got a job at a dog kennel.

The boarding kennel had 100 dogs and served such persons as A.C. Gilbert, who developed the Gilbert model trains. The first day there, I stayed overnight and remained there. The owner, a Mr. Katz, also raised pheasant for hunting.

I was going to work for Garelick in Franklin when he first bought a farm there. But when I found out that the Bock Farm in Walpole had a team of Percheron horses, I went to work there. The Bock Farm had about 100 cows. We would use the Percherons to clear land in the forest. Percherons were bred by the French for military use, hauling military armaments.

As soon as the Percherons heard Henry Bock's voice, they became afraid and jumpy, and I had to hold the reins to keep them in check. Bock was known for being rough on the horses when he held the reins.

I also worked in the old Kerr Mill, putting cloth in vats to dye them. Later, I worked at Aluminum Adonizing located at the Bleachery Mill. During World War II, I went to work at the Firestone Mill making gas masks.

On my way to the first day of work at the dog kennel in Connecticut, I was walking down the road when a huge Mastiff was coming towards me. He was not looking to the right or left but up in the air. I kept my eye on him. As we approached one another, the dog leaped at my throat. I dodged him, but he still ripped my new blue shirt that I had bought for my first day of work. But after he lunged at me, he continued down the road. No one knew whose dog it was. Dogs with rabbis will often travel for miles before they fall down and die. I've been a lucky person, but I was very lucky that day!

**Relationship with Nature**

From my reading of the bible, I learned a reverence for all of life, whether animals, trees, or whatever. We have a purpose in life, but we're too stupid to know what it is.

I have loved animals all of my life. When a bee would be caught in the house and trying to get out of the window, my mother would say, "Kill it!" But instead, I would take it by its wings and let it out of the house. When a spider would be coming down its strand as it made its web, I would play with the spider and make it "hop" down.

Wild animals would come right up to me. Once, when I was working in the garden, a snake came right up to me.

I guess I was like a father or brother to many kids in the neighborhood. For example, the Mitchell kids adopted me as their father figure, because of problems at home and their overly strict father. I would let the several kids in the family come to my house and let them play music in one of the rooms and dance if they liked. I bought a phonograph for them. I would also take the car-full of kids on a ride to the movies or for ice cream. Sometimes, we would go to the Assonet Inn for a dinner.

Once on a trip to Assonet, we passed by a watermelon stand and the kids yelled out, "Stop!" but I kept on going saying that, "Watermelons will make you sick." But then, I made a U-turn and stopped at the stand. I said, "I was just teasing you; I like watermelons."

*Mary Ann Wordell*: Bob has never been married or had kids, but lots of young people think the world of him. When I had his ninetieth birthday party for him, about ten to twelve persons came to celebrate with him. William Mitchell, one of the kids, became a policeman and thinks the world of Bob. He now works with troubled kids.

*Robert E. Vernon:* I moved wasp and hornet nests out into the woods in a manner in which they would not be disturbed. I tied the nest up with a string, moved it, then a half-hour later, when the bees had calmed down from being moved, I would take the string off and they would come out and were quiet.

When I walked through the woods, there were many high-bush blueberries and I picked berries as I went through the woods. At one point, there was a nest of yellow-jackets in the bushes, but kids got to it later and destroyed it and the nest was empty.

I kept honey bees for a while and I worked for a farm that kept honey bees. One of the brothers on the farm was in charge of the honeybees. The bees would swarm and sometimes I would have to catch the hive for him. He would knock the hive off of the tree and I would hold a bushel basket and catch the swarming hive. Once, a nephew on the farm knocked the hive so that the swarm fell on me instead of the basket. I got stung, but I held the basket so that I caught most of the swarm and rushed to the hive. The nephew started to run and the bees went after him and he got stung.

White-faced hornets build their nests in the woods. The Chinese learned how to make paper from bees. They watched how bees would chew wood to make paper for their hives and combs.

**Hurricane of 1938**

I was in-between jobs then and living on Wilson Road. The wind was blowing something fierce. Some people were saying that it was okay, it was just a storm. But as I stood in the window, I saw big limbs from the oak tree were breaking right off. There was a big hickory tree in the yard and it was leaning heavily in the wind. These trees have a long tap root and the tree kept resisting the wind; but finally it went down. Many trees were blown down.

# Sumner James Waring Jr.

*Born in 1936*
*Died on October 6, 2010*

**Family Background**

I was born at Truesdale Hospital. My parents were Sumner J. Waring Sr. and Louise (Borden) Waring.

My father was one of the main leaders in Fall River when the textile mills were here. My mother's family owned the Barnard Mill in the Flint. Her father was a cotton broker. He was Nathaniel B. Borden Jr., the grandson of the third mayor of the city who was also the first United States Congressman from our area.

My father's parents were James H. Waring and Nelly (Andrews) Waring. My mother's parents were Nathaniel B. Borden Jr. and Annie R. Borden. Both grandparents were very special, loving people, devoted to their families and the community.

I have had two sisters, Barbara Chamberlain (deceased) and Sally Buffinton.

My wife is Elizabeth "Liz" A. (Westgate) Waring.

**Family Life**

I was born two months prematurely. In those days, it was a death sentence to be delivered at seven months. However, my father was a close friend of Dr. Truesdale, Dr. Atwood, and Dr. Mason, all very excellent doctors. They kept me alive by feeding me with an eye-dropper. The only reason I survived was because I liked to eat. I was in the hospital for three months.

Our family lived at 429 Stewart Street, the stucco house between Robeson and Madison Streets.

My father was called Sumner and I was called Jim at home. However, at school I had to use my first name, Sumner. My French teacher at Morton liked the name Sumner. Why not use Sumner, she said, giving Sum-ner' a heavy French accent.

I broke my leg accidentally in the third grade when I was nine. A lady had a flat tire on Robeson Street, where the synagogue is now. My foot went under a tree root that was exposed on the dirt sidewalk in front of the synagogue, and I kept going but my leg didn't. Dr. Hussey put me in a full body cast for three months. My father and mother home schooled me until I was able to go back to school. Miss Lake, my third grade teacher, would come to our home every week to check on me. She did this voluntarily, with no extra pay; she couldn't do that today. My parents offered to pay her, but she wouldn't take it.

I grew up during an interesting challenging span of years, as we recovered from the Depression, entered into World War II, experienced prosperity thereafter only to be confronted by the Korean Conflicts, then the Kennedy years, which initiated the "new" America, space exploration, television, the assassination of the Kennedy brothers and Martin Luther King Jr., President Johnson's "Great Society," and the Vietnam War. However, the American grit, determination, and spirit prevailed in Fall River as did it in so many other parts of our country.

We were a settled, conservative family, content to entertain ourselves with games, reading, movies, dinner with family, sports, summer vacation activities, and sports as both spectators and participants. Church and faith were important in our lives.

My parents and grandparents evolved from the late nineteenth and early twentieth century childhood, education, work experience, and the enormous changes in travel, transportation, comforts, and educational opportunity, respectively. Those were the years spanning Fall River's greatest prosperity. They each had magnificent links to family and friends who were major parts of those times in terms of business, the profession, education, and government. Veterans of the Civil War were still living so that history was very real to them and thus to us as the stories were handed down to our generation. So, too, were the many within our family who immigrated in the early 1800s. We all felt connected in an appreciative, prideful manner.

The Cotton Centennial in 1912 was the highlight of their early lives, celebrating Fall River's most prosperous time. The Old Fall River Line was a constant source of pride and interesting stories. Motion pictures became an enormous source of pleasure to us all.

The personalities of my parents and grandparents were fun loving, appreciative, and considerate of others. They welcomed progress, loved the arts, and were highly-respected.

My earliest memories have been previously summarized. I was and continue to be a Fall Riverite and treasure the friendships which continue to be mine.

## School Life

I went to pre-primary school at Mrs. Pierce's Pre-Primary School, which was located on Prospect Street, between June and Rock Streets. It was a private school, since there were no public pre-primary grades then. I then went to the Highland School, then to Morton through ninth grade. From there, I went to the Choate School in Connecticut. Then I graduated from Babson College in 1958. From there, I attended funeral service school in Boston.

I walked to school, came home for lunch, and walked back to school again. At 3:15 pm, I was able to play pick-up games with friends. The Cherrys had a basketball hoop on their garage where we played. These were good friendships; I was able to mix with folks that went beyond school.

I then went to Morton and walked up and down the hill to school. I went from a neighborhood environment to an expanded society at Morton, an expanded universe of people. I got a great education there.

I went to Choate for the last three years of high school. Every time I had to write a paper, Fall River was the reference. I was privileged to go to Choate; my father made a lot of sacrifices for me to go there. Harry Smalley, the principal at Morton, spoke to my parents about my going to a private school. He saw the potential in me. "He has it," Harry said.

Choate was quite a different atmosphere. I had a teacher of history who was a classmate of John Kennedy's (JFK was a graduate of Choate). We had to write about our home state senatorial election. Mine was about Kennedy running for the senate. In doing research for the paper, I had a chance to interview all of the old teachers of Kennedy, some of whom were involved in the campaign. When I finished with all of the interviews, the paper was a 99-page thesis. I got an "A" on it. From then on, I became very interested in the Kennedys all my life. In the paper, I said that it wouldn't surprise me if Kennedy became president one day. My history teacher was a Democrat and a classmate of JFK at Choate and at Harvard University.

Connecticut Senator Dodd and Illinois Governor Adlai Stevenson came to the school to speak. Several years before I attended Choate, John Kennedy came back to say that no school was doing a good enough job of encouraging young people to participate in public life and politics. This led to the creation of the course that I attended and where I wrote the thesis.

Choate inspired me to get involved in the community. Early in my career, I became the youngest president of a Chamber of Commerce in the United States at that time. I was fortunate to have numerous friends and classmates at Choate who became leaders in business, education, the professions, labor and politics.

**Recreation and Entertainment**

A group of us from Morton would come home after school and play basketball. Mr. Cherry put a basketball court in his garage driveway. We played baseball and pickup football at North Park. Phil Hudner came home from Andover Academy with a lacrosse stick. Before that, I never saw one. I never saw much scholastic soccer until Choate. There, they had kids from Brazil and Cuba. You should have seen these guys play soccer. At that time, professional soccer teams in Fall River were on the wane after their peak in the 1920s and 1930s. The original soccer players got older in the 1940s and 1950s. Lots of Scottish families played soccer. Wrestling was not a big sport here, but it was huge at Choate. Kids took all kinds of pains to keep within their weight class; after that, the guys would eat anything.

One of the fun pals of my life was my father's funeral director associate, Russell McIlwaine. He was a great athlete at Durfee [B.M.C. Durfee High School] in the early 1930s. He was to have gone to college, but the Depression came. He worked for my father and lived in a two-decker on New Boston Road. Longtime Durfee high school coach Luke Urban came and took an apartment in Russell's house and stayed there until his retirement. Urban had a temper. I would hear Urban and Russell talk. Urban had a lot of stories to tell, and he never spared words. Russell played football, baseball, and basketball. He could score big even before they introduced the center jump. Scores of thirty-five were considered high at that time. Not now. Russell lived on Terrace Street, between Snell and Buffinton Streets. He had to walk to high school in the morning, then to the Boys Club downtown for practice or to Alumni Field, then walk back home again.

We would go sledding down President Avenue; they would close it off for a few hours for us. Snake Hill at North Park was also good sledding. Stewart Street was also closed off; it was too steep to plow. The Eastern Mass Street Railway plowed the streets on their routes; otherwise, other streets often didn't get plowed. Both South and North Watuppa had good skating.

My father would take me to see the elephants come off of the circus train. We would watch the trains come in to the round house where Tillotson is now and after leaving passengers off at the Old Fall River Line. I can remember seeing the boats come in; they were then a source of shipping freight to New York, in addition to passengers.

**Friends**

My friends included Michael Cherry, Brud Larocque (who went to Houston to a major oil company, in which he played a major role), Pat Crowther, (his father was a prominent lawyer), Phil Hudner, Bobby Mello (of Adams Street), Frank Hanson, and Billy Smith. Also Neil and King Hawes, Dr. Hawes' sons, and his daughter Ann, and Drew Cherry of the Cherry and Webbs. Linda McAdams, daughter of Dr. James McAdams, was also a friend, as does Joe Feitelberg continue to be.

## Neighborhood Experiences

When the garment folks came to Fall River in the 1930s, many lived in the Highlands. They were very successful. There were also professionals and people like the owners of McWhirr's and Cherry and Webb, who lived nearby. Mr. Thompson taught me how to play chess and cribbage. One night, when I was eleven or twelve years old, Mr. Thompson asked me if I wanted to play cribbage. He enjoyed teaching me. Our cribbage foursome included James Cottrell, Thomas Palmer, Mr. Thompson, and me. The senior folks then always had time for children.

The Thompson and Mills families owned the R.A. McWhirr Company.

From Maple Street up, the Highlands were sparsely developed. The road system didn't get into place until the 1930s and 1940s. Many residents from the Steep Brook and Wilson Road area worked at the Sagamore Mills, owned by the Brayton family.

My mother walked down French Street and had to walk past Lizzie Borden's house. [Maplecroft]. Lizzie had a small dog that would come out and nip at my mother's heels. Thus, mother was not fond of dogs.

Being born and residing in Fall River has provided a tremendous strength that has remained with me well into college and when I returned here. It prepared me for life. There is such a diverse culture here. There is virtually every faith, tradition, and language spoken here. I remember taking a bus from the Academy Building up to Robeson Street. There were mostly foreign languages being spoken in the bus. When we reached the corner of Bedford and Robeson, the Portuguese got off and you didn't hear any more Portuguese in the bus, only French being spoken. Then, further up the hill, the French got off and all you heard was English being spoken.

It was a way of emphasizing what a wonderful community this is. It is full of hard-working, self-reliant people, good people to have working for and with you. And they are still there. It was and remains a loving community.

However, as in most communities, there were divisions between people based on their economic and cultural status and where they worked.

Most of the city's neighborhoods were built around the clusters of mills that were built in the city. Then the churches and schools followed, all within walking distance. The Pepperell Manufacturing Company was an enormous complex. The American Thread Company employed four to five thousand employees at one time. The American Print Works had about five thousand employees. The Sagamore Manufacturing Company and the Durfee Mills were huge employers.

The city has seen horrendous economic conditions. First, the textile industry went south, then the garment industry went away. Through it all, people have kept their spirits up. The banks here were helpful and tried to keep people in their houses as much as they could. There always has been a great deal of profound sensitivity to the needs of the people. When the skills could not be employed in the city, residents have gone out of the area and out of the state, to as far as the Electric Boat Company in New London, Connecticut. Skilled folks did well, but they had to travel for it after the departure of the textile mills.

## Food and Meals

For breakfast, we had cereal and eggs. When I came home for lunch from school, we had a noon meal like a dinner. During weekdays, we had a nice dinner, with always fish on Friday. Baked beans and brown bread on Saturdays. On Sunday night, we had sandwiches or chow mein sandwiches from the old Eagle Restaurant.

**Courtship and Marriage**

My father and mother met in high school at a dance. They also had been neighbors.

I met my wife when I was the guest speaker as President of the Chamber of Commerce at a meeting of the Junior League of Fall River.

We were married on September 25, 1965, in Fall River's First Congregational Church. We had a 7:00 pm wedding with our reception in the former Women's Club. Michael Cherry was my best man, and it was a beautiful day. The reception was beautiful, after which we left from the Fall River Airport in a helicopter for Boston, before leaving the following Monday for Portugal.

**Work Life**

My first job was as a stock boy summers at the R.A. McWhirr Company. I got to meet a lot of people from all over and all walks of life. The guy that ran the stock department was a Mr. Chevalier. He kept the place in good order. Every day, he had a tomato with his lunch. He put salt and pepper on it. He was demanding but a good worker.

Fred Spriggs had been a superintendent in the postal service in England and he became head of the stock room at McWhirr's. One of his children moved here and he followed. He had a great accent and would often say, "Blimey!" Every day, after work, he would stop at the Acorn Café on Borden Street and get a shot of whiskey and a beer.

We bought a property on the approach to White's Restaurant in Westport. The old house on it was supposed to have been built on an old burial ground. Every Halloween, someone would break into the house to try to exorcise the ghosts that were supposedly there. One night, the police got a call that four kids had broken into the house and were on the second floor. The police came in the house and started up the stairs. The kids were working a Ouija board. One of the police radios went off as they were on the stairs and the terrified kids ran down the stairs and into the arms of the cops.

When the Braga Bridge was opened, our Chamber of Commerce executive Bob Murray had the idea to have an Easter Parade over the bridge. Fall River and Somerset people met in the middle of the bridge.

**Christmas, Holidays, and Special Occasions**

Christmas and Easter in my home were always festive. We also went to my grandparents homes on Christmas Eve after attending a candlelight service at church. Easter was fun as we were welcoming spring while honoring Christ and everyone we dressed as elegantly as possible within their various budgets. Family linkage was so enjoyable leading to treasured memories.

Weddings are such a celebration within life and funerals a celebration of life. Life being such a two-sided coin of joy and sorrow emphasizing that we cannot have one without the other. The rites and ceremonies involved in weddings and funerals have changed a great deal through the years, each becoming more personalized. The religious structure for each is not now the sole place where they are held. In the case of wakes and funerals, the home is seldom used any longer as was almost solely the case for wakes in earlier years up to about 1940. The officiate may not be a clergyperson these days. However, faith and respect for a higher being continues to prevail although evidenced in many and varied forms.

## Downtown

Downtown was the center of social, recreational and shopping activity until the mid-1950s.

Hudner's Market had stores on South Main Street, North Main Street, and on New Boston Road. The theatres downtown included the Durfee, the Empire, the Center, the Embassy (on Franklin Street), and the Academy. I remember watching the wrestling matches at the Academy, where they played every Friday. When the referee pounded on the mat, a cloud of dust would rise out of the mat.

The shops I remember are numerous, including McWhirr's, Cherry and Webb, The Hub, E.S. Brown, Sears and Roebucks, Paul Woltman's, Walter C. Fraze Company, Central Dry, Mohican Restaurant, the 5 & 10 stores, Van Dykes, Hudner Market, Peter's Candy, Fanny Farmers, Granite Spa, Rector's Spa, Mullen Brothers, Plante Jewelers, Cascade Pharmacy, Grand Central Market, Al Davis' Men Store, and on they go. It is important to note that none remain downtown.

## Religious Life

Rev. Dr. Lex King Souter was the pastor of the First Congregational Church. He dedicated himself to outreach of the church and was a community activist. We would meet on Sunday night as a youth forum at the church. With Rabbi Sam Ruderman and Msgr. Boyd, the three of them did a good deal to advance understanding of, cooperation, and respect for all faiths. The Souter Center on Saturday had a basketball league. Everyone in the community benefited from the interaction that Souter fostered.

In World War II, Rev. Souter went into the Air Corps, in the intelligence unit. He counseled pilots and crews before they took off for battle. When he was young, he was the wrestler Masked Marvel, a fact not generally known. He died in his mid-fifties of a heart condition. He was the first to have open heart surgery. Reverend Charles Smith was in the seminary and came in as an interim minister with Rev. Bob Lawrence. They were Souter's disciples.

## Health and Illness

For colds, my mother rubbed my chest with Vick's VapoRub. Also Ben Gay.

Wreaths were used on doors when wakes were still held in homes. The first funeral homes didn't happen until the beginning of the twentieth century, and they really didn't start until the 1920s to the 1940s. Wakes in funeral homes were demanded by the public. New homes were too small to get caskets through the door.

The first funeral homes were in storefronts. My father's first funeral home was in a storefront that was shared with a furniture store. They split, with the furniture store going one way and the funeral home going another. Only the big houses kept up the tradition of having wakes at home.

Prevalent illnesses were much the same as today unless inoculation caused them to be fewer in number. We can't seem to get rid of the common cold. They are, however, treated more on an out-patient basis and at home with a lesser need for going to the hospital.

Polio was the main scare of my youth until the development of the Salk vaccine. The iron lung became the treatment for the most severe cases and death often resulted. The measles, chicken pox, and scarlet fever were some of the major contagious diseases. Home remedies being inhalers, honey, rubbing alcohol, and other such applications such as Vicks, etc. Various health foods were reputed to be cures.

## World War II

World War II found us with widespread rationing which limited travel and food choices. Blackouts with blackout curtains, air-raid practice, volunteer air raid wardens, and aircraft spotters were ever on the alert. These were anxious times with always the threat of sabotage being present.

When Pearl Harbor was attacked, my father was in the midst of an every member solicitation for our church, the remainder of our family at home. All reacted with varying degrees of uncertainty and fear followed by the period of great leadership by President Roosevelt and others. I remember massive patriotism via enlistment in the services and civilian volunteerism.

## Community Philanthropy

Education was always important. Some parents in the city have impressed upon their children, "You're not going to get anywhere without an education." Private industry took the initiative in education. Bradford Durfee Tech trained workers to be in supervisory positions, to be creative, to invent, and so forth. New Bedford did the same with New Bedford Tech.

Private interests formed the Deaconess Home and the Ninth Street Day Nursery to assist young women. The Women's Union was formed to provide single ladies a place to live. These came about because of a social consciousness that mill owners and banks should be applauded for. Then, it became the responsibility of the government.

Bradford Durfee Textile School, 64 Durfee Street

The Sagamore was the first good example of benevolence to its employees. Mr. Burke was the Superintendent there. The Braytons were the president and treasurer of the mill. Burke's son-in-law was Dr. Shea, who built a clinic in one of the Sagamores in back of the mill on Cove Street. All of their employees got medical care there. Dr. Shea ran it all. The Braytons started the B.M.C. Durfee Trust Company. Brayton family members provided major gifts to the city. Mrs. Young not only gave the B.M.C. Durfee High School building but also endowed it with scholarships so graduates could attend college. The city has a tremendous tradition of benevolence.

My grandfather, N.B. Borden Jr., and others, gave Alumni Field to the B.M.C. Durfee High School via the Durfee Athletic Association in 1902. The Association was created to run and operate Alumni Field. Peter Collias was the president of it. When it was sold, an endowment was created to purchase necessary items for sports at Durfee. Mr. Corbett was the architect who designed the field and did a great job; the field had remarkable draining capabilities.

The donors never wanted publicity for what they gave or did. E.P. Charlton endowed the business school at UMass Dartmouth. It now boasts many graduates and accounts for over twenty-five percent of the University's present enrollment.

The Truesdale Clinic was the third-oldest clinic in the United States, after the Mayo and Lahey Clinics. Dr. Truesdale became famous with his upside-down stomach procedure that he performed at St. Anne's Hospital around 1910 or 1912. His sons went on to become successful. His only surviving child is Eleanor Marvel.

Betty Welch was the executive director of the Truesdale Clinic for many years. She also worked for Albert Pierce, who was head of the board of directors of the Fall River Trust Company. He and Joseph Faria built it into a major bank. He also did a great deal for the Truesdale Clinic.

# Genevieve (Haggerty) Whitty

*Born on September 13, 1915*

**Family Background**

I was born at 43 Tecumseh Street.

My parents were Patrick Haggerty, born in Fall River, and Elizabeth (Munro) Haggerty, born in Scotland and arrived in the United States when she was ten years old.

I was the fourth oldest child in a family of eleven: Charles, Dorothy, Francis, Mary, John, Betty, Raymond, and Paul.

My husband was Edward P. Whitty.

**Family Life**

When I was born, my parents lived on Dover Street. From 1919 through 1929, the family moved a few times within the city, but we stayed predominately in the area of the SS. Peter and Paul Parish. In 1929, my parents relocated to Tecumseh Street, which was our family home right into the mid-1960s.

We did not have hot water growing up; we heated the water in a pan on our stove. When I was very young, we did not have a bathtub; we had a big round galvanized tub which we washed in. When I was about nine years old, my family got a bathtub. That was a big deal. I remember going out and telling my friends, "We got a bathtub, we got a bathtub!"

We had iceboxes then, not refrigerators. Ice was delivered by horse and wagon. We would refer to the delivery man as "the iceman". When you wanted an ice delivery, you would put a card in your front window, which stated "ICE" on it. The cards were colored—white or blue—which designated the size of the ice block you wanted delivered. I believe the ice cost about fifteen cents a block. I remember we had to be careful about the ice pan under the icebox. As the ice melted, the pan would fill up with water so it had to be emptied on a regular basis, otherwise it would spill over the tray and you would get the water on your floor.

We didn't have a telephone until I was about eleven years old. We never missed not having a phone. Communication, prior to the telephone, often took place across the yard and/or window from neighbor to neighbor or often my mother would send me to someone's home with a note.

There were neighborhood grocery stores. Our grocery store was Romeo's Grocery Store; it was next to our house on Tecumseh Street. I remember it used to be fun to go to the grocery store with my mother.

Everyone had clotheslines hanging from their windows with pulley lines that were connected from one house to another. Small items would be washed by hand and hung out to dry on the clothesline. Big, heavy items like sheets, towels, and men's work clothes were sent to the laundry to be washed. The laundry would be returned wet—hence it was called the "wet wash"—and we would hang it out on the clothesline to dry.

My mother was a great sewer. She made all of our clothes, including our coats. I remember our

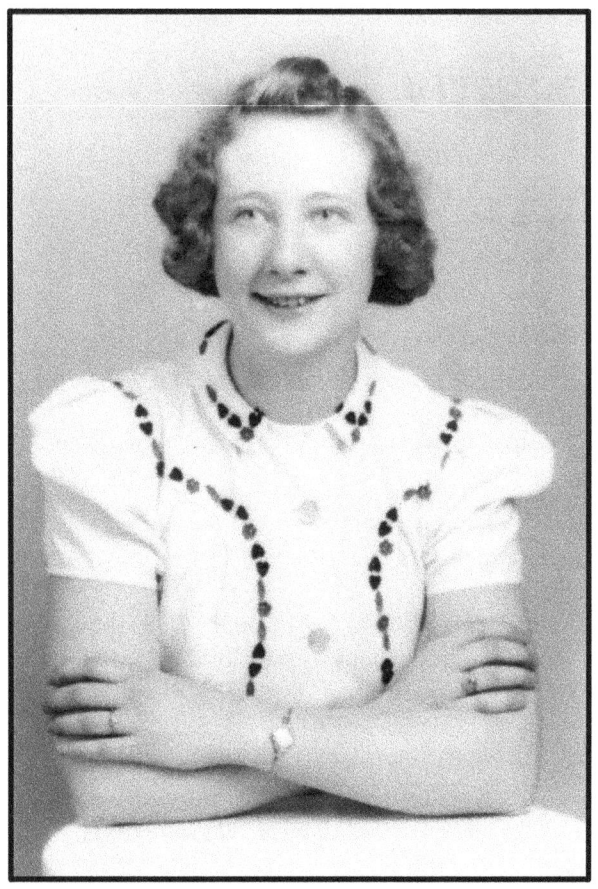

1937 engagement picture of Genevieve Rita Haggerty, married Edward Patrick Whitty

dresses were very pretty with ribbons on them. We always dressed up for Sunday Mass at SS. Peter and Paul Church.

Gas lights were used in the streets and at home. A lamplighter lit the street lights. He was usually about fifteen years old. At night, he would shimmy up the lamp post and light the street light.

There were few cars on the road as I recall.

I recall at the Capital Theatre, they would have a "dish night". One night, each week, upon admission, they would feature a different dish. You would collect the dishes until you had a complete set.

Every so often a man would come through the neighborhood with a pony and kids could take their picture on the pony. This was a real treat and many children would have their picture taken on the pony.

**School Life**

I went to SS. Peter and Paul School. The morning school session was from 8:00 to 11:30 am; the afternoon session was from 1:30 pm to 4:00 or 4:30 pm. I was in the first class that graduated from SS. Peter and Paul School. When the school first opened, the first classes were held in the church hall while the school was being built. We moved into the new school building in the fifth grade. Every summer thereafter, a new classroom would be added, and we would move into it until we reached the eight grade. The first graduation in 1928 was a big event.

During the two hour lunch break from school, I would return to my home and pick up four dinner pails which held lunch for my father and three of my siblings that worked in the Stevens Mill. Each work day, my mother would prepare hot meals for the four of them and have them ready for me to pick up and carry over to the mills for their lunch break. The dinner pails were unique to that era. It had three components to it; the bottom section of the pail would hold hot tea, which would help to keep the food warm. The center section held the dinner; my mother usually prepared meat, potatoes, and a vegetable. The top section held the dessert, usually a donut or a piece of cake. My mother would tie to the handle of the pail a brown paper bag which contained two slices of buttered bread.

I would walk from Tecumseh Street to the Stevens Mill and deliver the dinner pails. Then I would walk back home, have my lunch, and return to school. Many of my friends delivered dinner pails as well. We thought nothing of it; it was just something that you did at that time.

We girls played basketball at the Susan Wixon School two or three nights a week. We won a championship in 1928.

On the evening of February 2, 1928, after playing basketball, upon leaving the Wixon School, on Hamlet Street, we noted that the sky was all red and the air was thick with smoke. We were frightened; it seemed so unreal and scary. I thought it was the end of the world. We didn't realize it at the time but it was the "GREAT" fire in Fall River; all downtown was burning.

After I graduated from SS. Peter and Paul School, I attended Henry Lord Junior High School for one year and graduated from there in the ninth grade. Then I went to work.

**Recreation and Entertainment**

We played outside constantly. We played many games and usually in the road as few people had cars back then and there was no traffic. Popular games were jumping rope, rolling skating, hopscotch, and hide and seek. Often the girls would play a game of jacks and the boys played marbles. Another popular game was May I? The object of the game was to get permission from the captain—hence May I?—to progress from a designated start line to a designated finish line, without having the captain catch you in your movement.

During the winter, when it snowed, we would sled down the hilly streets in our neighborhood in a toboggan. Often we would get on at the top of Plymouth Avenue and slide right down to the bottom of Rodman Street. We had just as much fun walking back up the hill as sliding down as we would joke with each other as we walked back up the avenue.

We walked everywhere—to school, church, the movies, downtown shopping and to work—it was healthy for us.

Sandy Beach was a popular recreational spot in the city. Our families would get together and rent a truck to take us to Sandy Beach for the day on Sunday. The truck was an open-back truck with benches on either side. The adults would sit on the benches and we kids would sit on the floor of the truck. We would spend the day at Sandy Beach and inform the driver of a time to come back to pick us up.

That was always a fun, relaxing day for the family.

**Neighborhood Experiences**

There was a great sense of community at that time. People were very neighborly and helped one another out when sickness or hardship occurred. My mother was a good neighbor and active within the community. She would send a home-made meal to anyone sick in the neighborhood. It was not uncommon, when a neighbor had a family member who was sick and/or dying, for other neighbors to keep vigil with the family through the night.

People were waked in their homes for three nights. Relatives came and stayed with the family all night so they weren't alone with the deceased. The front door had a large wreath draped on it indicating that someone in the house had died. If the deceased was an adult, the wreath had a purple ribbon on it; for a child, the ribbon would be white.

Regardless of whether you knew the person or not, you would stop by the house and pay your respects to the family and say a prayer for the deceased. That was another example of the strong sense of community within the neighborhood.

## Downtown

Downtown was crowded when I was growing up. Everyone walked downtown. I liked the Cherry & Webb and McWhirr's stores—they had everything; also the 5 & 10 cent stores—Woolworth's, Grant's, and Kresge's. I recall that on Fridays, the stores would remain open later into the evening.

## Food and Meals

The Sunday dinner was a family dinner because work schedules during the week often did not allow the family to dine together. Our typical Sunday dinner was roast beef, mashed potatoes, and carrots and turnips as the vegetable. We had dessert only on Sundays and that was usually homemade pie or cake, always made from scratch.

Week day meals often were stews, spaghetti, and/or hamburger dishes. It was typical during that era for the Saturday night meal to be baked beans and franks (hot dogs) with homemade biscuits.

Our breakfast consisted or oatmeal and toast before we left for school.

My mother was a great cook and baker. She would bake bread three times a week.

Genevieve Whitty and the author, Al Lima

She had a large black coal stove. The house always had the pleasant smell of fresh baked bread. When we came home from school, our snack would be a piece of the baked bread with some molasses on it!

## Work Life

When it was time for me to go to work, the employment options at the time were to work in the cotton mills or as a domestic in the homes at the Highlands, which used to be called The Hill. My mother encouraged me to work as a domestic on The Hill.

Many of the families in the Highlands had two maids—a cook and a second girl; or three maids—a cook, second girl and the nursemaid (sometimes a registered nurse.) The cook was responsible for all the cooking; the second girl made the beds, cleaned the house and served the meals; the nursemaid took care of the children.

I was fortunate to be employed in this field for about eight years and during this period worked for four very nice families. Initially, I was employed as a second girl and then, after a couple of years, worked my way to the position of a cook.

While working as a second girl, you wore a uniform (provided by the family). I recall during the workday I wore a powder blue dress; when there was a dinner party in the evening, I would wear a black uniform with a white apron over it. In the 1930s, the female guests would wear lovely evening gowns when there was a dinner party.

When I first started employment, my wages were seven dollars a week, plus room and board. After eight years in this field, my weekly wage increased to twelve dollars a week, plus room and board. It was typical at that time to give your weekly wages to your parents to help support the family and the household expenses.

**Courtship and Marriage**

I was introduced to my husband, Edward, through a group of friends. Dating often took place in groups in those days—typical activities would be the movies, dancing, or ice skating (in the winter).

Walking was the mode of transportation at that time, so whenever we went out, we would walk to wherever we were going.

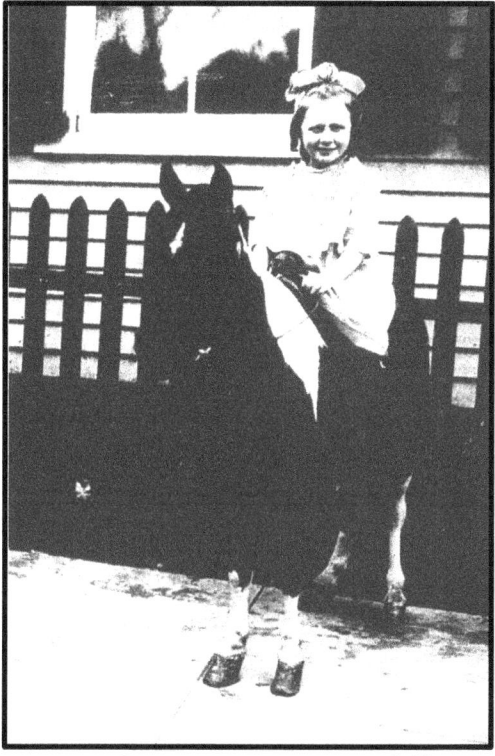

Genevieve Rita Haggerty as a child

**Health and Illness**

When we had colds, we were given Father John's Medicine. Doctors made house calls back then—a visit to the doctor's office was infrequent. I recall the black bag that the doctor carried when he would come to the house.

I remember when houses were tagged with different-colored cards for communicable diseases. A card was tagged on the outside door to say that the house was quarantined so that you would not enter and be exposed. A yellow card was for measles, red for scarlet fever, and blue for diphtheria.

There was a contagious hospital located off of President Avenue. The sick would be removed from the family and they would go to that hospital to avoid other contagion within their family. You were not allowed to enter the hospital to visit them, so, when you wanted to visit, you would stand outside the building and wave to them.

# Mary Ann Wordell & William Francis Wordell

*Mary Ann was born in 1939*
*William was born in 1941*

*Present at the interview were both Mary Ann Wordell and her brother William Francis Wordell. Unless indicated, all content is to be considered the words of William Wordell.*

**Family Background**

Our parents were Clyde A. (laborer) and Alice M. (Boulay) Wordell (French and Portuguese ancestry; presser in curtain factory).

Our father's parents were William Frank and Catherine (Flaherty) Wordell. Our mother's parents were Louis and Marianne (Ramos) Boulay.

Grandfather Wordell was of English ancestry. His ancestors came into Boston and were established in Massachusetts by 1630. Grandmother Wordell was born in Tuam, Ireland. William was a landscaper and Catherine a maid.

Grandfather Wordell died before I was born. He was a bird fancier and had sulky racing horses. He also had beagle dogs and lots of animals.

Paternal Grandmother Wordell took care of us when we were small; funny, but I can't remember a whole lot about her. She liked tea. She was religious and prayed a lot. I don't ever remember being hugged by her or sharing a good laugh. I do remember that, when visiting her when she was a lot older and living with my aunt, she would always put a dollar in my hand when I was leaving. She had handkerchiefs with perfume, lily of the valley. When she went out, she always wore a hat and gloves.

Our maternal grandfather, Louis Boulay, lived with us when I was a teenager in the 1950s. Prior to that, he lived with my uncle Tony on Monte Street. Mother always said that he was a very hard worker. He came from Canada and started working in the mills here in Fall River when he was eight years old. He always had a job, even in the Depression. I remember him as being good-natured, also religious, getting down on his knees to say prayers every night in French even into his eighties. He liked to drink beer. He once carved a whistle for us out of a cherry branch. He enjoyed pigeons and raced them. He had a pigeon coop at the current site of the Holmes Apartments on Essex Street.

Our maternal grandmother, Maryanne (Ramos) Boulay, died when I was very young; my only recollection of her is at her home on North Underwood Street. She would hold me on her lap and send me to the pantry area for candy. She had a canary in a cage that she covered with a big cloth at bedtime. She also came to our house on Brookside Street; we have pictures of her in our yard, probably about 1942 or 1943.

Mary Ann's husband was Robert M. Dias and their children are Jennifer Dias-Rezendes and Kristin Dias Martin.

## Family Life

There were lots of animals, flowers, fun, and running around. We played with friends and watched and helped my dad plant vegetables. We had a wood stove, and that required Dad to chop wood and throw it down the cellar. There was no heat upstairs in our bedrooms except what rose up through the stairwell.

Barbara and Bub were our two workhorses. Dad used a drag to haul stones and clear fields. He also had a V-shaped plow to clear Brookside Street of snow, and it seemed to me that there was a tremendous amount of snow during the winters. I remember Dad carrying us on his shoulders from the house to the barn and around outside. We also swung on swings in Carol Ann Leonard's yard. She was my cousin.

Dad had one or two milking cows. There was a large barn that he kept them in. At milking time, several cats would gather around, waiting for dad to squirt milk from the cow's teat so they could get a little milk. We laughed a lot watching those cats.

Dad was very tender-hearted. I had a little Beagle that died from distemper. When it got sick, I took my piggy bank, got on a bus, and took the Beagle pup to the vet, all by myself. The vet put the pup to sleep, and when I came home crying, my dad cried right along with me. He didn't like to see me so unhappy and sad.

Dad loved piano music, especially that played by his sister Eleanor that he begged her to play for him by the hour.

Mom was playful. When someone took a picture of her, it was unique. One of those unique photos was of her posing in a baby carriage, posing as a little girl.

Our cousins on Brookside Street included our paternal cousins Carol Ann Leonard, Richard Barry Wordell, and Eleanor (Penny) Kaylor Phillips, who didn't live on Brookside Street but visited often. Our maternal cousins included Louis and Anne Boulay, Eva and George Bettencourt, Mary Lou Cabral, Alice Charlie, and Robert and Elizabeth Boulay. There was also Joseph, George, Rita, and Lena Boulay.

Our mother's brother Frank came to visit often, other brothers less often. Mother's sister Laura lived in Maine and always visited once or twice a year. Our cousins Eva Bettencourt and Anne Boulay visited a lot, especially as teenagers.

*Maryann Wordell:* During the war, our father worked at Quonset Point. Mom stayed alone on Brookside Street with the kids and no lock on the door. All she had was a dog. One day, I stepped on the dog's tail and he bit the top of Bill's head. The dog's name was Pekoe and he belonged to Grandmother Wordell or to my aunt and uncle who lived across the street at 122 Brookside.

## School Life

Uncle Tommy Leonard would drive us to school and let us off at the top of Hood or Weetamoe Streets to walk down the hill to St. Joseph's School. We had beautiful nuns in first and second grade at St. Joseph's School, including Sister Mary Joel, Sister Mary Proteus, and Sister Mary Constance. Playing marbles in the schoolyard; maypoles and crowning the Virgin Mother in May.

After school, we took the bus home. We would get off at Wilson Road and walk up Wilson Road to Driftwood Street, then to Highland Avenue and Driftwood Street. Ernest Desmarais and his sister walked ahead of us. He was a quick walker and walked up the hill way ahead of us.

## Recreation and Entertainment

Mom did all kinds of fun activities with us, from making tepees out of blankets and draping them over clothes lines, to flying kites with long tails made from ripped sheets to sledding on Highland Avenue.

Family activities included playing cards, including war, 500 rummy, old maid. We visited Pee Wee Desmarais and family and had visits from Uncle Frank or Auntie Irene. We had clamboils with mom's family members.

*Mary Ann:* My friends included Nancy Moniz, Nancy Desmaris, Evelyn Castanho, all of the Moniz clan, and Jerry Rego, Arthur Gladu, and Linda Ward. I would go driving in cut-off hot rods with Nancy Desmarais, Lydia Gomes, and Nancy Reed. Sunny Reed and Junie Brightman drove all through fire lanes with the girls hanging on for dear life. Those hot rods had no windshields and no doors. I remember going out with a yellow blouse and returning with a brown one due to the mud. One of those hot rods flipped, and Nancy sustained a leg fracture. Junie carried her home.

*William Wordell:* The big thing in winter was ice skating on the Mill Pond. We would build a bonfire with the Moniz kids. Their father bought wood slabs off of Pee Wee Demaris.

We played games. Whip involved kids skating front to back. The biggest or strongest skater was in front. The one in front would skate fast and then stop quickly; then the others would whip around and some would stay connected and others broke off.

In the summer, we practically lived at Bliffins Beach. Our aunt and uncle, Bill and Eleanor Kaylor, ran it. There were three rafts and a diving board and a tower and a handball court there. My aunt made hot dogs and hamburgers at the concession stand. Our uncle's friend, Eddie Massey, was a good swimmer. Rudy Cummings hung around the beach. Al Lima from Border City, who was also in the Merchant Marine, also came to the beach. Jordan, Paul and Arthur DeCoste also.

The guys and Mary Ann played a lot of handball. Mary Ann played softball in the summer, including in the summer leagues at North Park. We had great fun playing softball, volleyball, and water skiing. Families didn't go away for extended vacations; my father didn't own a car until his sixties.

*Mary Ann:* I spent a lot of time at Bessie's Beach as a teenager. Eva Davis owned a camp there. The Tempesta and Giovanni families from Revere came to visit there, and I am still friends with them. They were Eva Davis' sister's families. They eventually had their own camp at Bessie's.

*William Wordell:* Many kids from around the area were caddies at the Fall River Country Club. The Read kids were caddies; their father was a bus driver for the Eastern Mass Street Railway Company. They lived on the west side of Wilson Road. "Boom Bah" was the nickname of one of the Read boys.

We played a lot. There were paths through the woods where we played cowboys and Indians. We rode our bikes, climbed trees, and swung from a grapevine. We picked flowers and caught frogs.

Dad talked about the clay pits. When we were kids, they were there and filled with water. Kids would fish there for hornpout and snakes.

In the wintertime, in the 1940s, we would go sledding down Highland Avenue. We would lay on top of Mom and slide down the hill to the bottom of Highland Avenue. When kids went sliding down Wilson Road, someone at the bottom of Wilson at North Main Street would stop traffic to let the kids slide by to the railroad tracks below.

Once, I was riding my bike down Wilson Road and lost control and crashed into the Read house. We would roller skate in the front driveway of the Catholic Memorial Home.

**Food and Meals**

We had loads of vegetables. Dad had a good-sized garden that included corn, tomatoes, beans, beets, carrots, turnips, and potatoes. We had chicken, steak, spaghetti and meatballs, pork chops and, on Sunday, usually a roast. Dad also raised Black Angus beef and we had a large freezer filled with beef and also meat from pigs he had raised. Breakfast included cereal, eggs, toast, bananas, and often French toast. Dad often went blueberrying with Pee Wee over at Pond Swamp and brought home a huge stainless steel milk bucket filled with blueberries. Pee Wee sold the blueberries to bakeries. Mom and I picked grapes and rhubarb and we harvested plenty of peaches from Uncle Dick's. Food was preserved in an icebox when we were very little; then we had a refrigerator.

Mother canned a lot: tomatoes, beets, beans, and tomato juice. Uncle Dick Wordell brought over lots of fruit, especially apples from his orchard at the end of Brookside Street and mom made great apple pies from them. We had pear trees in our yard. Father enjoyed cutting wood, hoeing, and cutting brush. We had the best clamboils, and lots of them.

**Neighborhood Experiences**

*Mary Ann:* My earliest memories were of baby ducks, chickens, a pig named Oinky, and my brother Billy carrying food in a sack down the lane to feed it. Mom made us tents out of blankets. I remember picking violets and wildflowers, watching dad milk cows, watching dad and Uncle Dick cut hay, pile it on a hay wagon, and lift it into the hayloft with a big forklift. I remember the sweet smell of newly-mowed hay. My best memory was climbing on the hay wagon and sliding down the hay. I would climb into the hay loft and watch barn swallows fly in and out making their mud nests.

*William Wordell:* Dad was always talking about Steep Brook and the families who lived in the area, including Clark Shaw, Ray Lewin, and Clint Davis. Clint Davis had a horse and wagon and delivered wood with it. Carl Foster was the best ice skater, he said. Roger Heyworth raced his horse at full speed up North Main Street, zig-zag between electric poles. Dad talked about the Steep Brook School, Lannigan's Beach, the bowling alley somewhere near Lannigan's Beach, and the fun he had skating at the Mill Pond and Aaron's Pond and the fun running across the fields.

He often talked about St. Vincent's Orphanage and all of the kids there that became good friends with him. He boxed in the gym there with Anthony Rogers. One memory he talked about was the big fire in downtown Fall River that razed the Granite Block. He often mentioned Joe Ouellette and the Stump Pond and the icehouse there. He said that when Joe Ouellette had to sell the land that included the Stump Pond, he offered it to Dad first, but dad couldn't afford it and the Catholic Diocese bought it. Dad mentioned more than once that my bedroom was originally a room for pigeons that his father had kept. Our house was converted from a small barn or shed.

Tom Flemming lived where Bisson Oil is now on Wilson Road; dad told me that he was a performer and did acts at the Academy Building.

I remember when Dad cut the hay and my mother trying to get up on the hay wagon and having a hard time getting up.

We would go down Ashley Lane, where Benoit had chickens. Our father would go down there with a horse and wagon and cleaned out the coops. He would load up the chicken manure

Old Mill at Mill Pond at Driftwood Street on Steep Brook, Fall River

and spread the chicken manure on the hay field. I was five or six at the time. His horse was named Barbara.

When I was about eleven years old, I stayed a lot at the St. Vincent's Farm. Joe Viveiros worked at the farm. He milked the cows and took care of the milk house. They pasteurized the milk there. I picked up the garbage from St. Vincent's and Rose Hawthorne with Mr. Viveiros.

Our grandfather picked up garbage at Truesdale Hospital early in the century. He had pigs in the barn cellar and fed the hospital's garbage to them.

Frank Bly lived on Wilson Road and rented out a barn to a man named Hartley. The '38 hurricane blew the barn down. His horse, named "Ace of Hearts," ran up to Cody's. I would climb up in the barn and look at the horse. The horse had a goat for a companion. Mr. Bly also owned a monkey. Dot Bly is still living.

Our father took the train from the Steep Brook station at the bottom of Wilson Road to go to

St. Vincent Orphans' Home, 2860 North Main Street

Bristol Aggie, which had a station at the school. At that time, the railroad still crossed the Taunton River from Steep Brook into Somerset. Our grandfather's brother died on the railroad causeway in 1945. He was eighty-four years old and was picking up railroad ties; he died of a heart attack.

Some of the knick-names for the men and guys at Bliffins Beach were "Coke" (Henry Kosier), "Sniffer," "Manah" (Manuel), and "Tubba" (Ray Silva).

Mary Ann has a picture of eeling on the Taunton River. They would pack them in barrels, salt them, and ship them to New York City.

Our father spent time at St. Vincent's and boxed at the gym. He stayed friends with the kids there. Father Gorman was the priest there.

Our grandfather, William Wordell, had a horse named "Jesse Derrill." The sulky was still in the carriage shed when we were kids. He was also a breeder of fancy pigeons, Cocker Spaniel dogs, and Rhode Island Red hens.

Foxes Farm was were the Industrial Park is now. Our grandfather would go hunting with his Beagles with John Driscoll in that area. Sometimes, they would go digging for pirates gold there. You could still see holes and mounds of dirt where they dug. The Pacheco's had a house there, and it is still in the park, but you can't see it from the road. They had a big cow farm there.

The Pest House was at the northeast corner of Brookside Street and Highland Avenue at 2647 Highland Avenue. It was a cape with a central fireplace. There was a fireplace in every room. Manuel and Emily Rego lived there. They had a son, Jerry, who was our age. It was owned by the Diocese, who fixed it up for a priest to live there. Then one day, it was gone; they tore it down. It was an old house. When the wreckers came to tear it down, they first came to our uncle's house to tear it down, but our mother told them, "Not that house, the one on Highland Avenue." If my mother wasn't home, my uncle would have come home to find his house gone. Our grandfather Wordell's second child, Carrie Wordell, died in the Pest House of an infectious disease.

When Grandfather and Grandmother moved into the house, its address was a rear address of Highland Avenue. Before that, it was called Pierce's Lane, then Highland Avenue, then Brookside Street. There is an old family cemetery at the end of Brookside Street. The Lewins, the Reads, and the Brightmans are buried there. The only stone still standing is of Prudence Brightman; the other stones are broken on the ground. There were beautiful stone walls surrounding the cemetery. It is all grown over. Our grandfather bought the Brookside farm in 1909. It could have been the Pierce's that owned it before that.

Some of the stores in the area were Manny's Market on the northwest corner of North Main Street and Wilson Road. Prior to that, it was a market for a long time, called Blake's and Reed's. A little bit further north on the west side of North Main Street was a barber shop. Behind Blake's store, he kept horses. He rented them out. Joe Read played cards and lost money. Once, his wife came after him with a broom because he was losing too much money. His kids were suffering from it.

*Mary Ann:* Emily Reed, his wife, would come to buy strawberries from Jack Driscoll, who lived in the house that I now own (2851 Highland Avenue). The Beaulieu family next door had a chow dog. Two houses on Wilson Road were moved by oxen to Meridian Street when the highway [Route 24] came through. My father told me that the old house owned by the Higgins family and now by Carol Sullivan located to the south of the power lines was moved to Highland Avenue from Brookside Street. Ike Cleveland owned a farm at the end of Driftwood; Driftwood Street was once called Cleveland's Lane.

*William Wordell:* Ed Stebbens had a Collie dog; he would walk with the dog every day down to Codega's to get the paper. He would put the paper in the Collie's mouth and they would walk back up the hill. Ed's house was three houses down from Highland Avenue on Wilson Road. Ray and Rita Dougherty and Alberta Yates were the other two houses on Wilson.

*Mary Ann:* I remember the horse chestnut trees, one at the corner of Wilson Road and North Main Street and one at the corner of Lewin Street and Wilson Road. There was also one at Bob Hayward's on Wilson Road.

*William Wordell:* There were open fields on Meridian Street, part of a CCC [Civilian Conservation Corps] camp located there. The Pearsons had a big cow farm at Meridian Street near the corner of Wilson Road. Dick Pearson lives in California now; he was good friends with Joe Viveiros and was part of the family that owned the cow farm.

There was an apple orchard on Pond Hill. The sisters from St. Vincent's Home would go there to pick apples. It was on the south side of Pond Hill. Pond Hill is the hill that goes down Wilson Road to the causeway. Bob told me about the apple orchard; I never saw it.

Our father worked for a farmer in Somerset and would ride his bike there.

Where Rolling Green apartments is now was once Allen's Orchard and dairy farm of sixty cows. The farmhouse is still there. The orchard was on both sides of North Main Street. At the bottom of Wilson Road was Wilson's Coal Yard. The son of the owner lived nearby on North Main Street. There was a gas station with one pump at the corner of Clark Street and North Main Street, where the vet is now. The bus turned around across the street where Dewey Street starts.

Bob Vernon would come by; he was a real talker. He would come over the house, the kids would go to bed, my father would fall asleep and he would still be talking. We called him Bob Cat because he had lots of cats. Sam Lewin was a savant. If you told him your birthday, he could tell you the day of the year that it would fall on years later. He knew the time of day without looking at his watch.

We were a little leery of going through Driftwood Street because three sons [who lived on that street] were big drinkers. One got hit on Wilson Road and lost a leg. Our mom worked the second shift at the Sagamore Mill and walked through Driftwood to get home. She ran into one of them, who was drunk. It was pitch black. She said that she wasn't afraid because a little push would have made him fall.

# James Henry Wray

*Born on December 8, 1914*

**Family Background**

My parents were Levi Wray and Alice (Lord) Wray.

My father was one of thirteen children. Only seven survived. He came here when he was thirteen years old from Clayton Le Moors, near Manchester, England. His father was in textiles in Manchester. My mother came here from Preston, England, as a baby. They met at a Christian Temperance Society get-together on South Main Street, just before you get to South Park [now Kennedy Park]. It is now a Portuguese Hall. Then, it was a dance hall.

My mother's sisters were Mary Arnold and Amelia (Aunt Millie) Wray.

I was an only child.

My wife was Ruth (Towers) Wray. We were married on February 25, 1938. We had four children, two are now deceased: Ruth (died in the early sixties), James Jr. (died in his fifties), Billy, and Marilyn.

**Family Life**

I grew up at 248 Mt. Pleasant Street, a single-family home. Both my parents lived there until they died. The house was left to me, and I sold it to a Bigelow family.

My aunt took care of me when my mother worked until I was of school age. My mother was a loom weaver until I was five years and of school age and quit working when I was six. My aunt's house was at 340 Hood Street, near the Adams Street. My father would pick me up on Friday night and bring me back on Sunday night. My aunt's name was Amelia Wray; she was married to James Wray, my father's brother. They didn't have children. My father and his brother married two sisters, so my mother and aunt Amelia were sisters.

Henry Langley lived on the northwest corner of Highland Avenue and Hood Street. The next house down on Hood Street from Aunt Amelia's was the Arnold's, my mother's oldest sister Mary Arnold. Dr. McCarty lived in the first house going north on Highland Avenue.

My father's father worked in a Pawtucket textile mill. One day, he fell down an elevator shaft and got killed. He is buried in Pawtucket. I never met my mother's father. My mother's mother is buried in Oak Grove Cemetery in a twelve-lot grave. My mother and father are buried there also. It is located at the back gate; take a right and it is the fourth stone on the right. The plot is now filled. Although my mother is a Lord, she was not related to the Lords of Lord Monuments. They are all from England.

My father had hard time waking up. He has a Big Ben alarm clock but, when it went off, he couldn't hear it. So he put it in a metal wash basin to make more noise to wake him up. My father belonged to the loom fixers organization. Their symbol was a crossed screwdriver and the wrench. My father made the symbol of the screwdriver and wrench from wood. He was a leader in the union, and his father was a union leader in Manchester, England.

I was named after my uncle Jim Wray, who worked in the post office all his life. I would get his mail a lot. He lived at 340 Hood Street and I lived at 34 Hood Street. He was more of a scholar than I was. There were two unions in the post office, and he was head of one of them. He traveled all over the country for the union.

We had gas and electricity on Mt. Pleasant Street. We had to light the gas with a match. I remember using kerosene lamps for light. Kerosene containers were used to fill the lamps. If the wicks were too high, the lamp would smoke. Kerosene was thirteen cents a gallon. At my Socony gas station, I sold ten gallons for a dollar.

**School Life**

When they were building Morton Junior High School, I was in the sixth grade in Wiley. They couldn't take us at Morton, so they put us at the Lincoln School for six months. We went to Morton at grade six and one-half. I was secretary of my class every year. It was a popularity contest. I was at Morton for four years, graduating in 1930.

I then went to Durfee [B.M.C. Durfee High School]. I stayed there only two years and quit. We skipped school all the time and went to the Academy theatre instead. The principal of Durfee used to come into the theatre and make us come back to school. My father came to me with a handful of envelopes from the school saying I was skipping school and said, "I'm sick of this; either go to school or go to work."

**Recreation and Entertainment**

We kids would mingle at the Lord Monument Works at the intersection of Highland Avenue and Robeson Street. It was our hangout. Highland Avenue ended at Wilson Road then; there was a big ledge there at the end of the avenue.

We would play handball and games like that. We would go steal grapes and apples at Allen's Orchard. We would go swimming at Bliffins and Lannigan's beaches. At night, we would go skinny-dipping. People would use Lannigan's Beach house, but Lannigan's beach was stony; the sand at Bliffins beach was better. To prevent people from using Lannigan's beach house and then going to Bliffins Beach, Bliffins put a fence up. Arthur Gladeau ran the concession at Bliffins.

We would play hide and go seek, peggy ball, and baseball. I played football for the Economy Radiator Works, who sponsored the team. I also played baseball for the Lord Monuments team For peggy ball, you hit the front end of the stick with a broom stick. Then you swung at the ball when it went flying. The stick on the ground was flat, with a small hole in it to hold the ball. The end of the stick that you hit was pointed and the stick was balanced on a stick placed on the ground.

In the winter, we would go sledding down Mt. Pleasant or Herman Streets. Sometimes we would sled down Highland Avenue toward Wilson Road or go to President Avenue or North Park. We would also skate on the Mill Pond on Steep Brook.

In the summertime, Mary brought us to their property in Somerset [Massachusetts] and had clamboils at the end of the street. Mary Arnold had a summer house in Ocean Grove in Swansea [Massachusetts]. We had a sailboat anchored off of the Oyster House. When I was really young, my cousins brought me to the Oyster House, cut the top of a sailor hat out, and tied a rope to it and put me through the hat. They then lowered me down in the water from the pier, with my other cousins swimming around me. Once, a blue crab bit me on the toe, and I screamed!

I was sixteen years old when I got my first car. I paid fifteen dollars for it, a '28 Chevy Roadster. It cost me thirty-five dollars to put it on the road. I wanted to get it on a Saturday, but it wouldn't start; it had no battery. I went to Dick LeBrie, who lived on Hathaway Street, and he said that the battery didn't come with the car. So, I bought a new battery from Dick for three dollars. I drove it home without a plate and drove it around the lot and fun with it.

Basically, what men did after work was to drop by the barroom every night of the week before you went home. There were bars on every corner back then.

One of the stunts that we did was to jack up the car of the guy who lived on the corner. When he came out, the wheels just turned and the car wouldn't go.

**Courtship and Marriage**

I went with a girl, Lois, from the First Baptist Church. She had a boyfriend, Stanley Morse, who lived in Tiverton [Rhode Island]. I met Ruth Towers in North Tiverton when she was sliding down the Welsh Hilton Street hill. I was about nineteen years old at the time. Stanley lived on the corner. We would talk and congregate. Sometimes, she was in a group. Stanley and I would pick up extra girls and go on beach parties together. We went steady and then broke up for a while. She told Stanley's friend, "Tell Jim Wray I want to see him;" and we got together again. We were married on February 25, 1938. We were married in her house in Tiverton. I was going to the First Baptist Church in Fall River and she was going to the Methodist Church and the Baptist Church. I had just gotten laid off, but I got another job soon after.

We moved to a tenement at 34 Hood Street, on the third floor, west of North Main Street. It cost three dollars a week and another fifty cents for the garage rental.

I built this house [Ellenwood Avenue, Somerset, Massachusetts] with others. I drew up the plans and went to Allen's Lumber Yard on Rodman Street for lumber. I was in the carpenter's union in Newport and took mechanical drawing in school. I was always mechanically-inclined. I fixed everyone's bicycles when I was young.

**Work Life**

As a kid, I trapped skunks in the area around St. Patrick's Cemetery. I woke up early in the morning to go tend the traps and skunk holes, bring them back, and sell them to Butch's Rendering, off of Plymouth Avenue. I got fifteen cents a skunk, sometimes more. But if I caught an all-black one, I got a dollar. They sold the dead skunks to people who made perfume and the skins to others to make into coats. Never—not once—did I get smelly from a skunk. They were either dead in the trap or I got a stick and whacked him over the head.

When I bought my paper route, it had forty-six customers; then I expanded it to eighty-five. I paid fifteen dollars for the route and got paid six cents per paper. However, I had to give the company nine cents per paper, so I had to collect fifteen cents. I delivered three papers: The *Fall River News*, the *Fall River Globe* and the *Fall River Herald*. Then the *Fall River Herald News* bought the route off me. They wanted to break up the route. They gave me back the forty-eight. Then they owned the route after that. I delivered the paper six days a week; I didn't have a Sunday paper.

I got my papers at the bottom of the hill. My route covered from Truesdale Hospital to Calvin Street. Sometimes, I would bring my tennis racket to Truesdale and played tennis with the girls who lived there and were training to be nurses. They had a doubles tennis court just west of the nurses' building.

When I was twelve years old, I sold magazines for Curtis Publishing Company. The magazines included the *Ladies Home Journal*, the *Saturday Evening Post*, and the *Pathfinder*.

As a kid, I would work for Captain O'Connell in his boat yard. When he first put up the wooden sheds at the marina, we got the lumber from cotton mills. He brought barges in and sank them to use as piers. The remains of the barges are still there. He came down from Taunton with boats and gave boat rides. His boats were *Crest*, *Ripple*, and *Crystal Wave*. He also had a steamboat named *White Cap*. He would organize sewing shop excursions to Rocky Point. He would get the boat going and I would drive the boat to Rocky Point. In the 1938 hurricane, one of his big excursion boats broke loose and landed up on the shore past Montaup in Somerset. During the hurricane, a big schooner owned by the Hancocks came up on the O'Connell dock. I worked for him mostly in the summertime, until I got a car at seventeen years old. I got a dollar a day.

I started full-time work at the American Print Works at seventeen years of age. I opened bales of cloth. Steel straps were wrapped around the bales. We would take the cloth and put it up through the floor and they would singe the face of the cloth to burn off any loose cotton so that it wouldn't interfere with the printing that they put on. It was hard work: ten-hour days, four days a week. I had to get from Mt. Pleasant Street to the bottom of Pocasset Street. A father of a friend of mine got me a job at the Swansea Print Works, where I worked behind a printing machine putting rolls of cloth on. If you worked Fridays, you got overtime. So, I worked Fridays for the extra money. I got five dollars and fifty cents a week at my first job. Back then, you had to know someone to get a job. You had to be an Irishman to be a cop or to work at a street job for the city.

One day, Bob Ramsspot asked me if I wanted to work in the machine shop. I did, and I did everything there: electrical work, digging holes, fixing dryers, everything. I worked there for three and one-half years. One day, they came in and laid four of us off. I then got a job in Warren at a zipper factory. At first, I was an inspector, then became a mechanic there. I got thirteen dollars a week. I had my own car (1937) to get to work. About a month before I was getting married, I got laid off from the Swansea Print Works. I then went to Warren [Rhode Island] for a year.

Then, I got a job with Dave Atwater in Fall River as an oil burner service man. I went up to seventeen dollars a week. We did monthly inspections for all our customers. There were three inspectors and every third week we were on-call for night duty, at no extra pay. If we were on a night call and it was time to go on the regular shift, we had to go right on working.

When the war came, I heard that they were paying laborers in Newport [Rhode Island] a dollar an hour. I joined the laborers union in Newport. When I saw that the carpenters were hiring, I went to work on Aquidneck Island for the Navy. I had a car full of passengers all the time.

Meanwhile, I opened a Socony gas station that had closed at the southeast corner of Madison and Stanley Streets. Years before the gas station was there, a large horse barn was located at the corner of Stanley and Madison Streets. They got a permit to store gasoline and cars there and had their own private gas pump. The owner owned a hat shop in Fall River.

I opened it up in July, 1944. I was still working down in Newport and had two fellas working for me. I opened the gas station and stayed until noon; they came in at noon and stayed until 5:00 pm. At noon, I would leave for Newport. I had two other cars going to Newport bringing passengers in addition to my own car. Johnny Morris said, "I can fill up a car, if you have one. Another fella said the same. I ran sort of a taxi business. The cars were running three shifts to Newport. When one of the fellas who worked at the gas station was drafted, I quit Newport to run the gas station.

When I quit Newport to run the gas station, the draft board called me in. They asked if my wife could work, and I said yes. They never called me; I guess I was too old at twenty-eight and had three kids. When I had the gas station, I wanted a thousand dollars to renew the lease for the third year. They wanted fifteen-hundred dollars. I went to Niagara Falls for a holiday and they didn't renew the lease.

On the Somerset side of the river, there was a Socony gas station. Shell Oil grabbed the lease when it came up. They gave the operator the choice of gas stations. Since my gas station did better because it was the only gas station in the area, Pete chose my station.

I next opened a Richfield gas station at 1117 North Main Street at President Avenue. I later sold it to Joe Torres, who put in a Gulf Station about 1950.

My Richfield station had two pumps. When Shell bought the property at the northwest corner of President Avenue and North Main Street, they tore down the house and the market. They were open twenty-four hours a day and gave away Libby glasses and other things. I couldn't compete with them. I took the pumps out and called the place President Motors. I got a used car license and sold cars there. I sold and repaired cars and had a body shop. I sold it to Joe Torres and moved down to the water, south of Slade's Ferry Bridge, behind Coca Cola. I did body and fender work and sold cars. It was also called President Motors. After a while, I had to have a knee put in and couldn't work. I sold it to Antone (Tony) DeCosta. It is still there. In the meantime, the new highway cut off Brownell Street from the river. Then, the Slade's Ferry Bridge was taken out and he was really cut off. He sold it.

I bought a plane at Mendon, Massachusetts, and eventually owned Yankee Air Ways. I bought a Lord Monuments truck and went to get a seaplane at Hackensack, New Jersey. We put new canvas on it and refurbished the engine. I got the Swansea Boat Yard designated as a seaplane base and put the plane there. Then, the '38 hurricane came and blew the sheds down. The hurricane didn't hurt the planes but, because the sheds were destroyed, they didn't have time to work on the plane and had to fix damaged boats. We then put the two seaplanes at the southeast corner of South Watuppa Pond. I bought out the others in Yankee Air Ways, Inc. and became the sole owner. Phil Desmaris owned the sea planes on the South Watuppa.

We put our Piper Cub up at Everett King's Airport in East Taunton and had it repaired there. We belonged to the Civilian Air Patrol in East Providence, where the Providence wing was based at Stimson Airport. We flew to Maine. The CAP took care of Rhode Island's biplane. We would be brought in on anything to do with aviation. The Stimson Airport was eventually bought out by the State of Rhode Island.

**Neighborhood Experiences**

There was a Hudner's Market on the northwest corner of President Avenue and North Main Street, where the Shell gas station is now. Mulveney's Drug Store was on the southwest corner of President Avenue and North Main Street. Next to it on North Main was an excellent bakery, with a good reputation. Johnny Marques' fruit stand was on the southeast corner of President Avenue and North Main Street. Next to the corner house was Johnny Marques' Open Air Market. I lived in the second house going west. Dumas had a bicycle shop in the basement of the Lima houses at the northeast corner of President Avenue and North Main Street. My gas station was one lot from the Lima houses. Sunnyside Bakery was next to me. Next to Sunnyside was a vacant lot on the corner of Brownell.

The Lima houses had a three-family in front and a two-family in back. The Lima house on the corner was an outstanding house, with a big piazza around it. There was the Lima houses on the corner, another three-family house, my Richfield gas station, and then Sunnyside Bakery. Goodfellows Drug Store was on the southwest corner of North Main and Brownell Streets. On the northwest corner was a doctor's office. Summerfield Methodist Church was on the corner of North Main and Hood Streets.

The Mohegan Bar was just south of the old rail station. I would stop by there to get a coffee malted and a hamburger. I never drank in my life.

There was a Border City School on Crescent and North Main Streets, north of the mills. There was also a Steep Brook School, south of Steep Brook at North Main Street. There was another school just south of Brightman Street on the west side of North Main Street. There was a drug store on the northwest corner of Brightman and North Main Street. Going north, there was a sewing shop, a hot dog place, a hardware store, then a school. Going west on Brightman Street from the drug store on the corner was Moy Lee's Chinese Restaurant, then a gas station. On the other corner of Garside Street was a chourico place. On Brightman Street, just west of the railroad tracks, was the Pastime theatre, later called the Royal. It cost five cents to go there on a Saturday morning. We would see cowboys like Hoot Gibson.

St. James Episcopal Church was located on the corner of North Main and St. James Streets. St. James had a permanent baseball team. I played in the league. The building is a Portuguese club today. There was a Baptist Church on Brownell Street, west of North Main Street. There was a Brownell Chapel and, next to that, the Brownell Hall. Beyond that was the railroad tracks. St. James and than the Brownell Chapel merged with the Summerfield Methodist Church. All of these small churches eventually joined the Methodist Church on Highland Avenue.

Wilson's Coal Yard was on the water. It was at the end of Cove Street, behind the Sagamore Mills. At the bend in the street was the coal yard. James Wilson lived on the southeast corner of Wilson Road and North Main Street. Across the street from Wilson was the Hartford four-tenement house. Jim Blake had the northwest corner of North Main and Wilson Road. He had a big store there. Blake kept a big catboat on the water and sold food to the tankers going to the New England Oil Co. refinery. One time, the NE Oil Co. refinery had an oil spill that caused chunks of oil to come up on Bliffins Beach. You had to clean up the beach before swimming there.

Danny O'Connell is similar to Joe, his dad. Joe O'Connell was an excellent swimmer. When Joe was about to lose the *Crystal Wane* in the '38 hurricane, he threw off the rope, but the rope got caught around his leg and pulled him down. However, he was able to release himself underwater.

**Christmas, Holidays, and Special Occasions**
At Christmas, the family got together at Aunt Mary's house. We always had a tree at Christmas. My uncle would go out and cut down a tree by St. Patrick's Cemetery and bring it home. Later, Lord's Monuments sold trees on their lot.

**World War II**
I sold gas when it was rationed. You had to have stamps and had to save them and turn them in when you got more gas. You had to apply for gas stamps. I had cars running to Newport and got enough ration stamps (a ration book) for the cars. They gave you only enough stamps to cover the essential mileage that you needed.

# Anna (Horvitz) Zalkind

*Born on October 26, 1908*
*Died on November 3, 2010*

**Family Background**

My parents were Solomon and Clara (Katz) Horvitz.

My grandfather came from Europe in 1890 or so. My father was about sixteen years old when they came. They were walking up Columbia Street when a Mr. Yamins saw them and asked where they were going to stay. Mr. Yamins told them where to go to find a place to stay. Mr. Yamins' brother owned all the theatres in town.

My mother was age fifteen when she arrived. My father met her here. He wanted to marry her and wrote a letter to her father in Russia asking for his permission. My mother's father wrote to my mother and said that if he indeed wrote that letter, she should marry him. I guess my father was a good writer.

My father was supposed to be a rabbi but decided not to and went into business instead. He was a very charitable man; his hands were always in his pockets all the time giving to anyone who asked. When my daughter was little, he would get on the floor to play with her. My father was very proud of Isidore when he came back from the war.

My father died in 1946. When my mother got sick, I took care of her for ten years so she wouldn't go into a nursing home.

My brothers are Isidore and Louis Horvitz.

My husband was Joseph Zalkind and we have one daughter, Barbara Eisen.

**Family Life**

My father owned Modern Furniture. I was an interior decorator. I got into interior decorating through my father's store when we would go to the Interior Decorating Center in Boston for clients.

My parents were married on Pleasant Street, above a bakery, in January, 1908. I was born nine months and a few days later. I was born at home; Dr. Schwartz delivered me. His son, Eddie Schwartz, became a dentist.

We lived at 161 Quequechan Street, I believe. A store is still there. That is where my father had his first furniture store. My father owned the property and, when I was ten or eleven years old, I would collect the rents each week. I got all the complaints from tenants who wanted this or that. My father got sick of owning it and gave the property to his nephew.

I remember when I was three watching a fire when we lived on Quequechan Street. The fire was on Pleasant Street and the fire equipment came by. They were the old horse and wagon fire equipment. I remember the horses hooves making sparks on the cobblestones as they ran past.

My brother Isidore and our cousin Isadore "Red" Bogus (Boguslavski) didn't like the way our aunt, Mannie Chessler, was always trying to kiss them all the time. So, one day they locked her in the basement and roller-skated on the wooden first floor so my mother couldn't hear her calling. This was at 41 Chesworth Street. My mother asked the teacher to reprimand Isidore, but the teacher said, "How can I? He gets excellent marks in deportment."

I went to the Davol and Davis Schools when we lived on Quequechan Street, then on to [B.M.C.] Durfee High School, where I graduated in 1925. At the Davol School, I helped teachers a lot. The second grade teacher used me as a model. My mother made me a cape that looked like Little Red Riding Hood and the kids would have to draw me as I stood on a chair. When I was at the Davis School, Mr. Easton was the principal there. He owned the house in the rear of the Historical Society, which is known as the Easton House. We had good teachers at the Davol School. Miss Dodge was great. Miss Hurley was the principal.

On Armistice Day, after World War I, I remember going downtown with my father to watch the parade. When the war ended, church bells were ringing everywhere.

In 1918, during the Influenza outbreak, we were all sick. We almost died. My parents hired a nurse to take care of us.

In 1929, I married Joseph Zalkind. We met when his family lived on Covel Street and were friends of my cousins. My husband had four brothers and a sister: Alex (lived in Providence with his wife Frances); Rebecca (married to Joe Kessler and had five children); Jake (a lawyer who lived in Chicago and also lived in Paris and Madrid; he returned here and died here); and Sam (his sons are Norman, Charles, and Philip).

We had one daughter, Barbara, who went to school at Vassar in 1951 and graduated there in 1955. She now lives in New Jersey with her family. She was married in 1956, and my husband passed away six months later.

My father had eleven brothers and three sisters. My grandfather had two wives; his first wife died and he married her sister. On Sundays, we would visit different aunts and uncles. We kids would put on plays, and they always had me as the leading lady. I was always smiling. On Jewish holidays, we would go to temple. The original temple was on Quarry Street, where the new supermarket is now. Then, in 1929, they built the beautiful temple on High Street.

We moved to 354 County Street and then my father had built the house [across the street] at 41 Chesworth Street, where we lived on the second floor. My uncle built his house at 57 Chesworth Street next to this house [41 Chesworth]. When my husband and I married, we lived next door at 60 Chesworth Street. Our uncle, the father of our cousin Red Bogus, built 60 Chesworth Street; he was also the owner of Stafford Furniture. Our uncle was married to my mother's sister.

**Food and Meals**

My mom was a good cook. We had cereal for breakfast and had hearty meals. I had two brothers, one Isidore and the other Louis. We had five generations of Louis. My great-grandfather was a Louis. The Horvitz and Horvitz law firm are cousins. Their father and my father were brothers. My grandfather's family was big, with fifteen sons and daughters. I was about fifteen years old before I knew there were other people other than the Horvitzes.

**Recreation and Entertainment**

We would play various games like jump rope. When the circus came to the city every year, we would watch the circus parade. When I was seven years old, I would wheel around my new brother Isidore in a carriage. That was the year that my father got a Studebaker and we would go to Lincoln Park [North Dartmouth, Massachusetts].

I would go downtown every day to the store. I remember that there were three 5 & 10s and McWhirr's, Cherry and Webb, and all the other stores.

**World War II**

During World War II, I was chairman of the Red Cross Canteen and Red Cross Blood Bank. We had a committee that made 300 cups of coffee a day. I would go downtown at 3:00 am to begin making coffee for the servicemen; in those days, we weren't afraid to go downtown at that hour. The *Fall River Herald News* trucks brought the coffee to the old railroad station on North Main Street and we would give it out to the servicemen who were going off to war and their families. We had to make enough food for 300 people. It was sad to see the kids go off. I never wanted to see another coffee or donut again. We also made many, many bandages for the servicemen.

I would also go to Newport [Rhode Island] to put on dances for the servicemen. We would also go to Camp Edwards on the Cape to serve coffee there, and my husband and daughter would come to help me. We did it all during the war. Mr. Conroy was head of the Red Cross and had a book with my name in it. Next to my name he had written "Tops." I always did what he asked. People like Tom Hudner gave me anything that I needed. He had the Hudner Store in the Hudner Building, where the Dunkin' Donuts is on South Main Street downtown. His son was given an award for his service in the Korean War.

On our tenth anniversary in 1939, my husband and I went to Havana, Cuba. We went to an open air restaurant for dinner. Some German ships were in the harbor, and the Germans were already misbehaving in 1939. A German officer came up to me and asked to dance and I said that I wouldn't. I made the excuse that I didn't dance. And that was before we knew how bad it was.

**The Fall River Line**

When I was about seven years old, about 1925, I went on the Fall River Line with my father to go to his youngest brother's wedding in Brooklyn, New York. I was going to be the flower girl in the wedding. My mother made me a plum-colored dress to wear on the trip and a white dress for the wedding. The family owned two tenements in Brooklyn and the wedding was in one. The boat had a beautiful dining room. The state room was only one dollar. There was music and dancing. The boat stopped at Newport to take on passengers.

The Fall River Line boats came in at the harbor in Fall River to meet the train. The train would come in at 7:30 pm and the boats would leave at 8:00 pm. On the way back, they would arrive in the morning at 6:30 am, and the train would be waiting for them to go to Boston.

**Work Life**

As an interior decorator, I traveled all over. My clients were in Phoenix, Arizona, California, Florida, and Maine. Relatives of Dr. Resnick had three homes in the United States and one in England, a five-story townhouse painted white, and a place at Third Avenue at 80th Street. They also had a country place that had ten acres and a place in Maine on the ocean. I furnished all of those places.

# AFTERWORD

An oral history of this length and comprehensive nature, about a storied city and its esteemed population, rich in neighborhood character and diversity, may contain some inadvertent errors and, in some cases, an unintentional misstatement or blunder. This book has been an astounding ten years in the making. And while the transcriptions presented here are faithful to the interviews conducted by the author, the impressions of events, people, or places may have been unintentionally altered or expanded since, in most cases, participants were obliged to recall occurrences and incidents that took place as long as seventy-five years in the past. For any such inaccuracies we extend our heartfelt apologies.

If contributors to his volume believe that they have been misquoted, feel free to contact the publisher of this book and your concerns will be earnestly addressed, as we strive to update newer editions with amendments which will reflect the necessary changes. It is with care and great interest that we at PearTree Press, and the author of this work, have compiled and published these captivating, diverse, and most charming narratives. We are happy and thankful to have undertaken this mission and hope all concerned will feel the same.

You may contact us at:
peartreepress@mac.com

PearTree Press
P.O. Box 9585
Fall River, MA 02720

www.ingramcontent.com/pod-product-compliance
Lightning Source LLC
Chambersburg PA
CBHW080436170426
43195CB00017B/2799